Republic CONFIDENTIAL

VOLUME 2
THE PLAYERS

BY JACK MATHIS

FIRST EDITION

July 14, 1992

Published by

JACK MATHIS ADVERTISING

BOX 3580—BARRINGTON, ILLINOIS 60011-3580

Copyright © 1992 by Jack Mathis.

All rights reserved. No part of this book may be reproduced or transmitted in any form by any means, electronic, mechanical, photocopying, recording, or by any information source and retrieval system now known or to be invented, without prior written permission of the publisher, except for the quoting of brief passages in connection with a review of this book.

Many of the still photographs copyright © 1935-59 by Republic Productions, Inc. or by Republic Pictures Corporation, used herein with permission from Republic Pictures Corporation.

Library of Congress Catalog Card Number: 92-90769.

ISBN 0-9632878-0-X [Volume 2].

Manufactured in the United States of America.

THE PLAYERS

FOREWORD

Republic Pictures—with their expert force of managerial, production, and technical personnel—was a studio of many faces, but the ones most recognized and revered by audiences belonged to the players. From the prized marquee countenances of John Wayne, Roy Rogers, and Gene Autry among numerous others to the amorphous extras pervading the background ranks, performers by the thousands brought form and substance to the studio's prodigious number of screenplays.

Selecting the right personalities for a Republic film ultimately rested with the producer whose personal preferences were weighed with those of the director and a Casting Department representative. Budgets were always a cardinal consideration during these tripartite meetings to nominate at least several candidates for each featured role.

Big stars who were able to command commensurate salaries on A pictures required advance approval from the front office while others beyond Republic's normal pay scale were tentatively penciled in pending negotiations with agents, a nod that some celebrities would make wage concessions for the extra exposure and love of practicing their craft in film.

Newcomers also comprised an affordable wellspring of talented fresh faces that alert producers opportunely tapped after conducting interviews and viewing screen tests or film of previous appearances. Another economic imperative in the selection process involved assigning roles to the at-liberty constituents of Republic's stock company who collected weekly stipends regardless of whether or not the studio had parts for them to play.

Pursuant to exploratory discussions with the producer and director, an assistant casting director contacted agents or unrepresented talent to establish firm salaries and availability for the assignments. Sometimes photographs of the finalists were assembled for an executive review, usually presided over by president Herbert J. Yates, before making the conclusive determinations. Those chosen in the final cut were awarded contracts and notified when to appear for wardrobe fittings, in-costume approval by the producer, any special camera, color, or make-up tests, and the start of principal photography. Contracts were traditionally signed from one to several weeks in advance of production, though occasionally the legal formality was not attended to until filming was underway.

Performers employed at Republic were grouped in one of five separate and distinct contract categories:

1. Term contracts running up to seven years duration applied to the stock-company members who exchanged exclusive use of their services for a regular paycheck.

2. Term-picture contracts, which Republic also called multiple-picture contracts when an artist was hired for more than a single film, governed players engaged for one or more pictures that were to commence within a specified period of time.

3. Picture-commitment contracts, similar to term-picture contracts, were generally reserved for the bigger stars who were pledged well in advance of production to accommodate their busy schedules.

4. Contracts for loan-outs were executed between Republic and other producers whose idle term contractees were farmed out to continue earning their keep and turn a handsome profit for their home studio in the bargain.

5. Contracts for both free-lance and day players were the most ubiquitous since they covered not only the all-important character actors and actresses who carried many films but the extras representing the non-speaking—yet necessary—faces in the everpresent crowd.

Each of these contract formats is detailed in the following sections along with the western stars whose hybrid films comprised nearly 40% of Republic's output. Although it would be impossible to place every face that appeared on-camera, the vast majority from the famous to the fleeting are treated in text, well over 2000 photographs, and the Super-Index reference listings. This exhaustive compilation of a unique film-family tree puts into perspective a finite heritage while offering a fond look back at the parade of Republic players who for more than two decades touched the hearts and minds of theatergoers with their memorable interpretations in a wide range of demanding roles.

TABLE OF CONTENTS

	Page
Term-Contract Players	2
Term-Picture Players	70
Picture-Commitment Players	88
Loan-Out Players	112
Free-Lance and Day Players	128
Western Players	140
Super-Index	168

TERM-CONTRACT PLAYERS

The backbone of Republic's on-camera talent was their stock company of performers — officially called term-contract players — who fleshed out the casts on every picture. From 7-year-old hopeful Twinkle Watts to the seasoned septuagenarian Alison Skipworth, the studio assembled 146 individuals into an all-time roster comprised of 127 actors and actresses, 12 dancing girls, the Republic Rhythm Riders musical quintet, and the comedy duo of Oscar [Ed Platt] and Elmer [Lou Fulton].

Scattered among this group were several oddities including three performers who never graced a Republic release. During 1940 Charles Andre, in the United States on a six-month work permit, and silent-film star Greta Nissen received short-term, no-option contracts but suitable vehicles for them were never found. Then in late 1942 John Wayne scouted Mexican actress Esperanza Baur and convinced Republic to put her on the payroll. Arranging for a visa and subsequent legal residence, the studio started Baur at $150 per week in January of 1943 and doled out nearly $80,000 over the course of 10 years without ever casting her in a part.

Erroneously carried on internal lists of term-contractees between 1940-43 were stuntwoman Nellie Walker and actor Howard Hughes; in reality, both were called only as-needed at respective weekly salaries of $60 and $50. Distinct from Walker and companion stunt personnel, Tom Steele was the only regular Republic stuntman ever covered by a term contract; the base rate of his 1943-44 pact was established at $150 weekly for features and $350 for serials plus daily upward adjustments for certain feats.

Becoming a stock player was tantamount to cinematic servitude, the contractees exchanging term commitments of steady employment for exclusive use of their services and domination of their professional lives. Beyond Republic's perpetual right to exploit and advertise them in photoplays with which they were associated, term-contract players agreed to accept all assigned roles, to be visually doubled and have

their voices dubbed in any language, to be loaned out to other studios, to make promotional junkets and appearances in stage, radio, and television productions, and to lend their names for advertising, commercial, and publicity purposes. Even after expiration of their employment they were required at the producer's behest to return for retakes, added scenes, soundtrack replacements, or any other changes deemed necessary on their films. The extent of Republic's considerable rights extended to changing the names of certain personalities as they saw fit. As a result, Charles Hogg became Buddy Baker, Lorna Gray switched to Adrian Booth, Orville O'Donnell progressed from Gene Morgan to James Joyce to Michael Kent, Jean Carmean to Jean Carmen to Julia Thayer, and Lynn Roberts to Mary Hart back to Lynn, then Lynne, Roberts.

Security — the primary personal inducement in these alliances — was fleeting for most players, with nearly 60% contracted for one year or less before they were terminated while only 26 endured for more than three years. Of the top 11 whose options were repeatedly renewed, Roy Rogers was extended for over 11 years, Grant Withers for over 10 years, Roy Barcroft and Esperanza Baur for 10 years, Allan Lane for over nine years, Don Barry and Smiley Burnette for eight years, Vera Ralston and Adele Mara for over seven years, and Monte Hale and Adrian Booth for over six years. Termination did not necessarily spell an end to Republic appearances, however, since many of the 146 either converted to multiple-picture arrangements as did Rogers and Gene Autry or returned in single films as free-lancers.

Early contract terminations were rare but did affect four members of the stock company. Barely two months into their initial 1936 three-month contracts, Mary Bovard and Republic acting-school alumni Marc Kramer and DeWolfe Hopper were dropped from the roster. In June of 1943 Eddie Dew signed a one-year term contract at $100 weekly to star in the new John Paul Revere western

series. Upon completion of the first two films Republic decided Dew was not adaptable to the part and, after paying $1000 in August to settle his contract, replaced him with Robert Livingston in two follow-up titles that concluded the evanescent and ill-fated venture.

In the event Republic elected not to exercise a term player's option that expired during production thereby terminating the contract, protective language authorized extending the agreement until the current film role was completed. Extensions also governed other circumstances including labor strife. When a 1945 industry crafts strike inhibited production, Republic suspended contracts on a number of their stock players and added the lost time onto the end of the agreements. During World War II suspensions were put into effect for Bill Henry and Bruce Langley while they served respective tours of duty in the Army and Navy.

Virtually all contracts contained interval options exercisable at Republic's discretion over a term of seven years, though Doris Day [a dramatic actress, not the popular singer-actress] was inked for a finite four months, Arlyn Roberts for six, and Wela Davies for one year. Longevity was not everyone's cup of stability as June Johnson, a singular hold-out against lengthy obligations, demonstrated. A free agent after her three-month contract as a juvenile at Republic lapsed in 1937, Johnson later declined their 1940 term-contract offer, reasoning she did not want to be tied to one studio for seven years.

Johnson's scratching of the seven-year hitch conflicted with Republic's intent of inserting option clauses for term contracts in single-picture deals. This practice particularly applied when testing the appeal of starlets in B westerns and serials, thus protecting the studio's best interests should a newcomer warrant repeat exposure. Following principal photography on *The Tiger Woman* [1944], Republic within the designated 45 days exercised their term option on co-star Linda Stirling whose successful serial debut and

subsequent popularity kept her working on the lot for almost three years. Equally charmed was Mary Ellen Kay when Republic picked up her 60-day option for one year following completion of *Silver City Bonanza* [1950]. Less fortunate, Peggy Drake was hopefully perceived as another Ann Rutherford when she segued from *Tuttles of Tahiti* at RKO into Republic's serial *King of the Mounties* [1942]. Assessing Drake a capable actress, studio executives nonetheless doubted she would ever evolve from ingenue to leading lady and consequently did not exercise her 30-day option, a fate that also befell Kay Christopher and potential lead actors Lee Powell, Jack Ingram, and Kermit Maynard, among others.

Contracts for stock players in the mid-1930s were generally drawn for a length of three months but soon became fairly standardized at either a semi-annual 20 weeks of guaranteed employment out of 26 weeks or an annual 40 weeks out of 52 weeks. Throughout the active periods it behooved Republic to extract the maximum amount of emoting by shuttling players from picture to picture, often at a heady pace, or corralling the availables into one film. Answering the role call on *Canyon City* [1943], term contractees Don "Red" Barry, Wally Vernon, Helen Talbot, Twinkle Watts, Roy Barcroft, LeRoy Mason, Tom London, Kenne Duncan, Jack Kirk, Bud Geary, and Tom Steele assumed 11 of the 21 principal parts with the first six meriting screen credit.

During the inherent lay-off phases some performers were permitted to pursue outside career activities. By prior consent, Gus Schilling was allowed to make stage appearances during his breaks while Dale Evans was granted eight weeks continuous leave each year to do an outside picture. Claire Carleton's sabbaticals to act in Broadway plays were approved with the provision Republic could suspend and extend her contract for the duration if they desired. Personal appearances were usually condoned and even encouraged so long as they did not conflict with filming schedules. Such engagements proved profitable for both the artists and the studio which in early 1950 mandated a 25% payback of the gate earned by Bill Shirley, Eileen Christy, and the Republic Rhythm Riders. The studio also collected royalties on Rex Allen's published compositions.

One restriction on personal appearances that was diligently enforced concerned exploitation of copyrighted fictional character names Republic had created or to which they had secured motion-picture rights from outside sources. An early 1950s example involved the Rough-Ridin' Kids western series in which Michael Chapin played Red White and Eileen Janssen essayed Judy Dawson, studio-originated roles the juvenile leads could not portray away from the lot without Republic's sanction. Further, as star of *The Lone Ranger Rides Again* [1939], Robert Livingston was expressly prohibited by Republic's contract with rights owner George W. Trendle from identifying himself in-person as the Masked Man. This embargo stemmed from an earlier incident following release of *The Lone Ranger* [1938] when Trendle enjoined Lee Powell from touring in the guise of his serial character.

Players' rights, few that there were in contractual matters, were negotiated individually. With Lester "Smiley" Burnette, Republic had exclusive motion-picture claim to all his music, songs, compositions, orchestrations, and arrangements, though he retained publication rights. Dorothy Patrick and Robert Rockwell were exempted from serials and westerns while Ruth Terry was excluded from serials but could be placed in bigger-budget westerns such as those of Roy Rogers and fellow megastar Gene Autry.

Precious few provisions for screen credit were spelled out but Vera Ralston and Constance Moore were guaranteed star or co-star billing and Dale Evans had to be acknowledged as a featured player with not more than one other featured female player ranked above her name. Ralph Byrd's contract stipulated he was only to star or co-star and could not be cast in bit parts. Hired in November of 1936 at $125 per week, he immediately starred as *Dick Tracy* [1937] which led to a modified contract nine months later calling for a base salary of $150 plus a $100 weekly bonus when he reprised the intrepid sleuth in the serial sequel *Dick Tracy Returns* [1938].

Wardrobe concessions were an occasional aspect of the bargaining process. Typically, Republic supplied

DATES THAT PLAYERS WERE UNDER TERM CONTRACTS

Player	From	To
Adams, Carol	10-15-40	10-14-41
Allan, Edgar	10- 5-36	4- 4-37
Allen, Rex	3- 1-49	10- 6-53
Andre, Charles	2-26-40	8-25-40
Ashley, Edward	4-27-45	4-26-46
Autry, Gene	7- 1-35	6-30-38
Bachelor, Stephanie	12-11-44	5-25-48
Baker, Buddy	10- 7-38	4- 6-39
Baldwin, Ann	7-10-39	4- 9-40
Barcroft, Roy	7-12-43	7-11-53
Barry, Donald	2-11-40	2-10-48
Baur, Esperanza	1-15-43	1-14-53
Beach, Richard	9-29-36	6-28-37
Beers, Bobby	10- 6-41	10- 5-42
Benton, Dean	11-23-36	2-22-37
Booth, Adrian	2-19-45	6-23-51
Bovard, Mary	10- 5-36	11-30-36
Brennan, Ruth	9-10-45	3- 9-46
Burnette, Smiley	7- 1-36	6-30-44
Byrd, Ralph	11-27-36	8-11-39
Byron, George	9- 4-42	3- 3-44
Carleton, Claire	2-12-40	2-11-41
Carson, Sunset	3-18-44	7-15-46
Carter, William	11-24-45	11-23-46
Chapin, Michael	1- 3-51	1- 2-52
Ching, William	3- 6-50	3- 5-52
Christy, Eileen	12- 1-51	11-30-53
Clark, Judy	8-25-41	8-24-43
Cooper, Ben	3- 1-53	12-28-56
Corrigan, Ray	5-25-36	5-24-38
Cravens, Mozelle	3- 1-43	8-31-43
Davies, Wela	3- 4-40	3- 3-41
Day, Doris	9-29-39	1-28-40
Dew, Eddie	6-25-43	8-21-43
Dorree, Bobbie	8-26-44	9-12-47
Doyle, Maxine	6-21-43	6-20-44
Duncan, Kenne	7-12-43	7-11-46
Durkin, Grace	9-28-36	12-27-36
Edwards, Penny	5- 1-50	10-15-51
Evans, Dale	4- 1-43	12-18-47
Frazee, Jane	1- 9-47	1- 8-48
Fuller, Barbra	5- 3-49	5- 2-50
Geary, Bud	7-22-43	7-21-45
Hale, Monte	7-31-44	9-13-50
Hamilton, Fred	10-29-36	1-28-37
Hare, Marilyn	3-11-40	9-10-42
Henry, Bill	1- 2-44	10-13-46
Holland, John	11- 1-36	5-31-37
Hopper, DeWolfe	10-20-36	12-16-36
Hughes, Kay	6- 1-36	12- 1-36
Janssen, Eileen	1- 3-51	1- 2-52
Jeffreys, Anne	2-13-42	1-25-44
Johnson, June	1- 5-37	4- 4-37
Kay, Mary Ellen	1-13-51	1-12-52
Kaye, Lucie	2- 8-37	8- 7-37
Kean, Betty	8- 1-41	7-31-42
Kean, Jane	7- 6-43	7- 5-44
Kent, Michael	5- 9-38	11- 8-38
Kenyon, Mary	3- 6-44	9- 5-44
Kirk, Jack	7-12-43	7-11-44
Kramer, Marc	9-28-36	11- 9-36
Lamont, Marten	6-24-37	12-23-37
Lane, Allan	3- 3-44	5- 3-53
Langley, Bruce	9-17-42	7-27-46
Lawrence, Muriel	11-11-50	11-10-52
Lee, Mary	6-27-40	2-21-45
Lee, Pinky	2-12-45	9- 8-46
Livingston, Bob	5-28-36 / 9- 1-43	5-27-41 / 11-30-45
London, Tom	7-19-43	7-18-47
Loyd, Beverly	11- 1-43	3-21-45
Lynn, Leni	1- 2-41	1- 1-42

Player	From	To
MacFarlane, Bruce	5-13-38	11-12-38
Manning, Hope	10- 5-36	4- 4-37
Maple, Christine	9-28-36	12- 4-36
Mara, Adele	4-24-44	6-25-51
Marshall, William	8-20-45	7- 5-47
Martin, Janet	7-31-43	10-28-48
Martin, Jill	8-22-38	2-21-39
Mason, LeRoy	7-12-43	10-13-47
McKenzie, Fay	8-14-41	5-27-43
McKim, Sammy	9-13-37	2-10-38
McLeod, Catherine	10-26-45	10-25-47
Merrick, Lynn	3-31-41	3-30-43
Middleton, Ray	2-25-41	7- 8-42
Moore, Constance	3-12-45	5-12-47
Newell, William	7-20-36	7-19-37
Nissen, Greta	4- 1-40	8-21-40
O'Dell, Doye	1- 2-46	1- 1-47
Oscar and Elmer	3-30-37	6-29-37
Page, Dorothy	8-16-37	2-14-38
Patrick, Dorothy	11- 1-49	10-31-50
Pepper, Barbara	8-16-35	12- 6-35
Perkins, Valentine	4-26-50	4-25-51
Pickens, Slim	9-19-51	9-18-52
Pulido, Jose	3- 5-45	10-12-45
Ralston, Vera	5-31-43	11-30-50
Ranson, Lois	3-15-40	9-14-41
Renaldo, Duncan	10- 2-39	10- 1-40
Republic Rhythm Riders	10- 4-51	10- 3-52
Rich, Gloria	8-30-37	8-31-38
Roberts, Arlyn	7-24-44	1-23-45
Roberts, Lynne	1- 1-38 / 9-27-44	6-22-39 / 3-26-48
Rockwell, Robert	6- 6-49	6- 5-50
Rodriguez, Estelita	2-13-50	2-12-53
Rogers, Roy	10-13-37	12- 3-48
Russell, Mary	9-28-36	12-27-36
Rutherford, Ann	10- 5-35	5-29-36
Ryan, Tommy	9-23-38	10-31-40
Schilling, Gus	3- 1-49	2-28-50
Shirley, Bill	2-24-41 / 7- 1-52	8-23-42 / 12- 6-53
Skipworth, Alison	8-15-37	8-14-38
Steele, Tom	6-25-43	6-24-44
Stewart, Larry	5- 1-43	4-30-44
Stewart, Peggy	4-24-44	3-22-47
Stirling, Linda	4-11-44	3-19-47
Storey, June	4-21-39	10-20-40
Stuart, Sheila	7-24-44	1-23-45
Talbot, Helen	9-10-43	1- 6-46
Taylor, Brad	4-24-44	4-23-45
Terhune, Max	9-25-36	3-24-39
Terry, Ruth	4-15-42	1-25-46
Thayer, Julia	1- 4-37	4- 3-37
Tyler, Tom	7- 8-41	7- 7-43
Vernon, Wally	5-24-43	5-23-44
Watts, Twinkle	6-15-43	12-14-45
Weeks, Ranny	1- 7-37	9- 6-37
Wilde, Adele	8-26-37	11-25-37
Withers, Grant	2-10-44	4-15-54
Young, Carleton	10- 5-36	10- 4-37

DANCING GIRLS

Player	From	To
Anstead, Melva	9-12-44	9-11-45
Bryon, Lucille	9- 5-44	9- 4-45
Carroll, Martha	9-12-44	9-10-45
Farnum, Geraldine	9-12-44	9-11-45
Gladwin, Frances	9-12-44	9-11-45
Haddon, Harriette	9- 5-44	9- 4-45
James, Rosemonde	9-12-44	9-11-45
Kerrigan, Marian	9-12-44	9-11-45
Morel, Rose Marie	9-12-44	3-11-45
Posten, Patti	9-12-44	3-11-45
Reedy, Beverly	9-12-44	9-11-45
Stevens, Dorothy	9- 5-44	9- 4-45

TERM-CONTRACT PLAYERS

"character" and "period" costumes but expected most stock players to furnish their own contemporary apparel. Exceptions were made for some actresses who the studio outfitted completely save for modern shoes, hosiery, and undergarments. For one, Constance Moore had an understanding that all her costumes were to be created by Gilbert Adrian, Howard Greer, or another well-known designer.

When importing fresh faces to Los Angeles from distant locations, Republic sometimes agreed to pay the cost of one-way or round-trip transportation. Gloria Rich, Ray Middleton, and Ben Cooper embarked from New York City to begin their movie contracts using studio-bought train tickets as did 17-year-old nightclub entertainer Judy Clark who also was accorded free travel expenses for her mother and the promise of return fare to Manhattan for them both if her first option was not exercised, which it was. For Wela Davies, Republic booked gratis passage back to England at the end of her firm one-year optionless commitment.

Salaries were disbursed weekly during the 20 or 40 weeks actually worked or, at the player's request, pro-rated across the 26 or 52 weeks of a complete contract cycle. Fully 85% of the contractees started at weekly salaries of $200 or less, a realistic figure considering most were young and acting in low-budget films, factors that justified conservative compensation. As an indicator of how taut the purse strings were drawn, only five performers started at term salaries of over $400 per week: Ruth Terry and Pinky Lee at $425, Alison Skipworth at $500, Jane Frazee at $625, and Constance Moore at $1500 just for openers.

In a class by herself, Moore was far and away the highest paid on a weekly basis. Her superstar term contract, which ensued from

triumphs in *Atlantic City* [1944] and *Earl Carroll Vanities* [1945], covered seven years constituting three consecutive annual options followed by two two-year options. Weekly payments for the first three were fixed at $1500 in 1945, $2000 in 1946, and $2500 in 1947 for annual aggregate sums of $60,000, $80,000, and $100,000. Related amendments specified she would not have to appear in more than three pictures per year with a respite of at least four weeks off in-between each one and that all her films were to have budgets of $500,000 or more. Moore's one-of-a-kind contract proved short-lived, however; after four pictures it was terminated by mutual consent in May of 1947 with Republic paying her a $40,000 consideration.

The closest in approximations to Moore's pay scale were Roy Rogers and Smiley Burnette whose raises over their 10-year tenures gradually elevated them from $75 to $1000 per week. Comparative salary hikes also over a 10-year span upped Grant Withers from $400 to $500 and Roy Barcroft from $125 to $300.

In September of 1943 Barcroft and fellow free-lancers Kenne Duncan, Bud Geary, Jack Kirk, Tom London, and LeRoy Mason — curiously classified as "cowboys" by Republic — were placed under term contracts. The studio regularly assessed the wages of such contract players against the estimated expenditures of hiring outside talent for the same portrayals. Vindication of cost-effectiveness was forthcoming in mid-June of 1944 when the combined $6,839 six-month earnings of Barcroft, Duncan, and Mason compared favorably to the $10,565 projection for three comparable free-lance substitutes, a $3,726 imaginary net savings.

Of the stock company, Mason was the only one to die while under contract. Late in the morning of

October 13, 1947, he suffered chest pains and dizziness on the set of *California Firebrand* [1948] and succumbed from a heart attack in the hospital at 5:30 that afternoon.

Typecasting was a fact of Hollywood life as amply illustrated by the six so-called cowboys and notwithstanding the fact they were utilized in contemporary scenarios as well as westerns. Plucked from the Ice-Capades rink-revue troupe, Bobbie Dorree rendered bit parts but was primarily occupied as a natural stand-in for Vera Ralston, herself a champion ice-skater. Band singers were much coveted to make the horizontal vocational move into pictures while broadening their horizons in the acting realm. Dale Evans, Ruth Terry, Mary Lee, Adele Mara, and others made the transition from bandstand to sound stage with ease, though Mara, who fronted with Xavier Cugat for two years, was apprehensive about horses and asked to be excused from her pending part in the Roy Rogers western *San Fernando Valley* [1944]. Lee's situation was unusual in that she was already under contract to orchestra leader Ted Weems in 1940 when her first movie agreement was prepared. Because of this ramification, Republic dealt with Weems for her services rather than the 15-year-old singer directly.

Republic's term contracts represented a two-way street on which studio and players honored each other's covenants and the artists' union trafficked to pave any potholes encountered by their members. During the summer of 1942 the Screen Actors Guild grieved the overly hot conditions under which Ruth Terry, Lynn Merrick, and a line of dancers executed routines for *Youth on Parade* [1942] on July 7 from 8:30 in the morning until 8:15 that evening. Although Republic installed a large fan blowing across ice to reduce the temperature on Stage 10 and had a standard

operating procedure of scheduling regular rest and meal breaks, the union complaint charged that a second meal period due subsequent to the 12:40 lunch recess wasn't called for the sweltering company.

Minor discords aside, harmony between Republic and their stock company reached fever pitch during the throes of World War II as patriotism ran rampant on the Hollywood home front. Doing their share in the effort with Republic's blessing, Dale Evans gave of her time to the Victory Committee and Ray Middleton served with the Hollywood Victory Caravan, Don Barry, Gabby Hayes, and Ruth Terry performed at USO camp shows, Bill Elliott traveled on War Bond tours, Smiley Burnette and Peggy Stewart boosted morale via personal appearances, and Helen Talbot accompanied the Victory Committee on a three-and-a-half month tour of the South Seas which resulted in a B-24 bomber being named in her honor. Budding starlet Janet Martin, just 14 years old when she signed a term contract in 1943, requested that 10% of her weekly wages be deposited into War Bonds. Meantime, Republic altruistically assisted some of their own, productively employing actress Maxine Doyle in 1943-44 while her staff-director husband William Witney was away in military service.

In the multi-layered scheme of populating a film production, the stock company personified a ready human canvas upon which other artists added their own distinctive touches to complete the overall motion picture. Toward this end, Republic artistically mixed and matched from a living palette of term-picture players, performers signed to individual picture commitments, loan-outs from other studios, free-lance and day players, and western stars to augment the complementary strokes applied by their capable term-contractees.

4

CAROL ADAMS

EDGAR ALLAN **REX ALLEN** **CHARLES ANDRE**

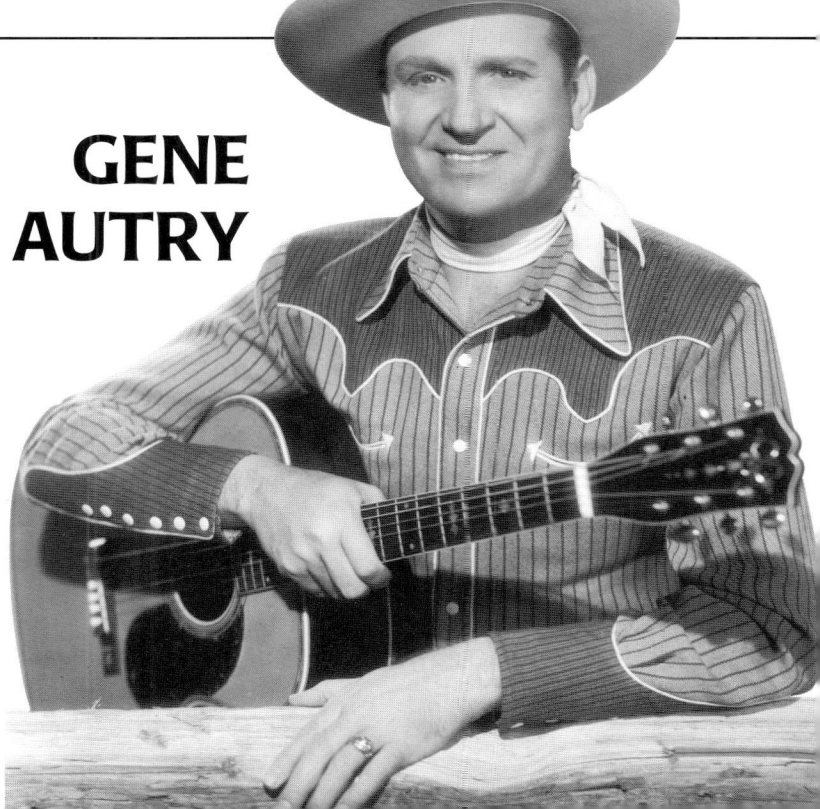

EDWARD ASHLEY **GENE AUTRY**

STEPHANIE

BACHELOR

ROY

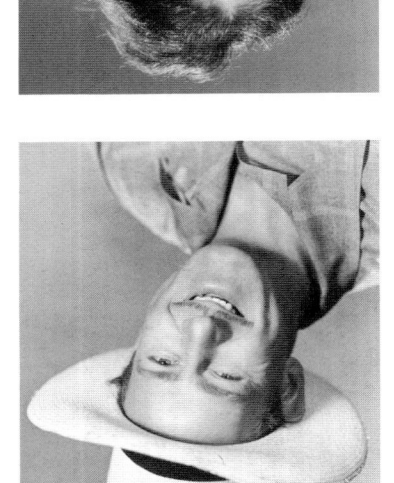

BUDDY BAKER   ANN BALDWIN

BARCROFT

DONALD

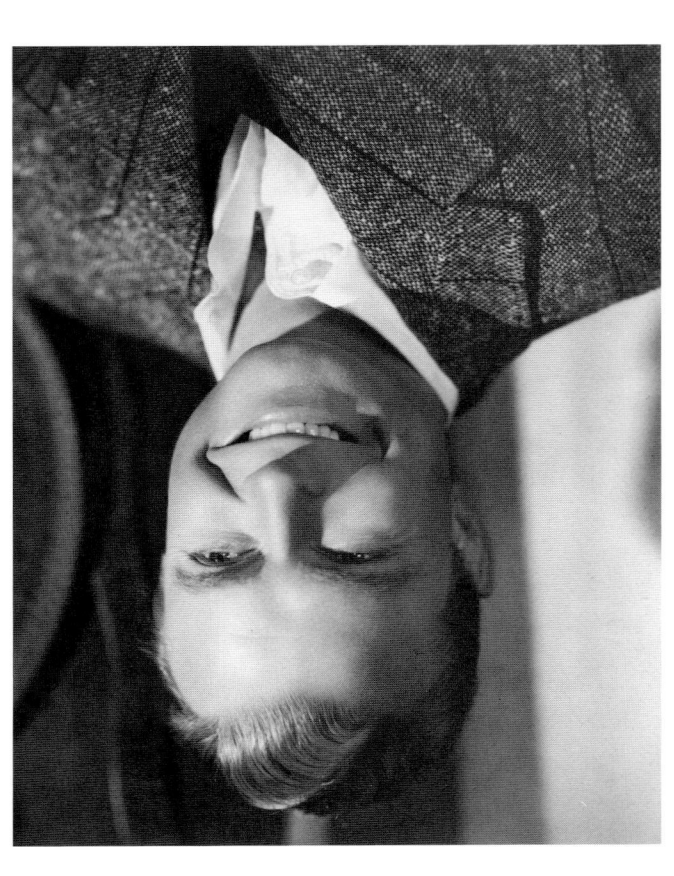

ESPERANZA BAUR

RICHARD BEACH

BARRY

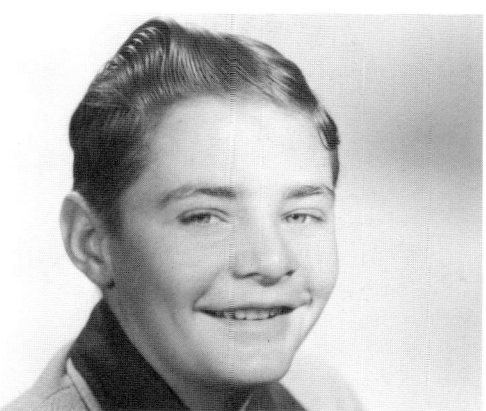

BOBBY BEERS

DEAN BENTON

ADRIAN

[as Lorna Gray]

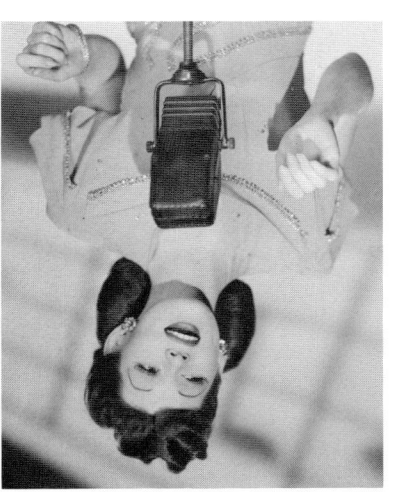

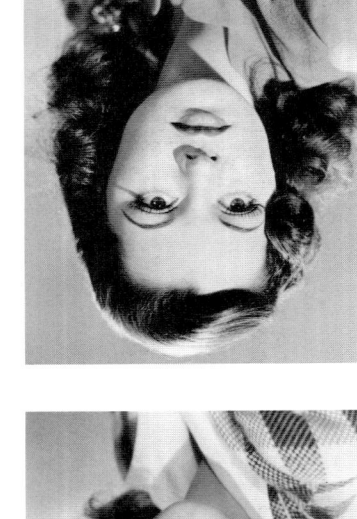

BOOTH

SMILEY BURNETTE

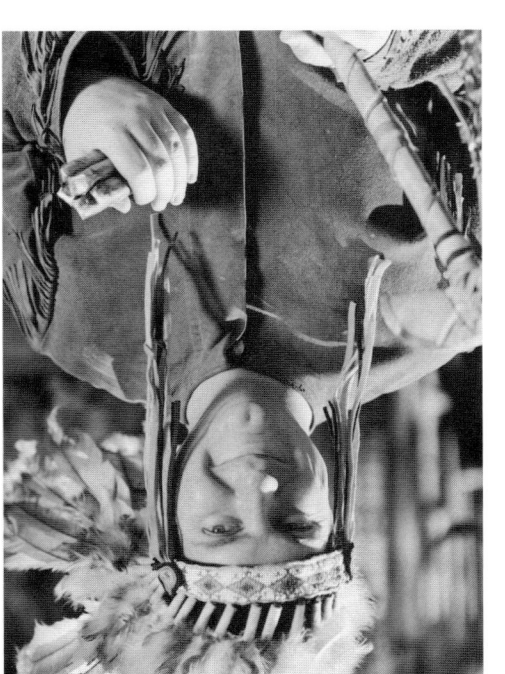

MARY BOVARD

RUTH BRENNAN

RALPH BYRD

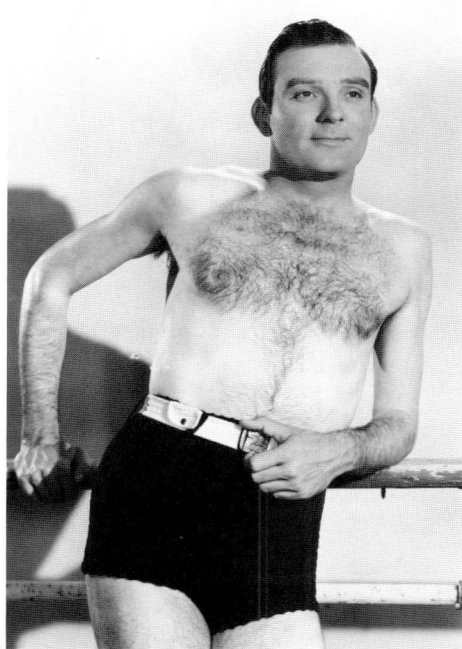

SUNSET CARSON

WILLIAM CARTER

MICHAEL CHAPIN

GEORGE BYRON

CLAIRE CARLETON

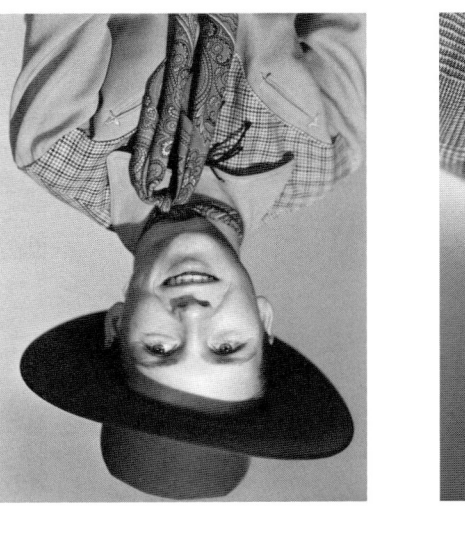

WILLIAM CHING

EILEEN CHRISTY

BEN COOPER

JUDY CLARK

RAY CORRIGAN

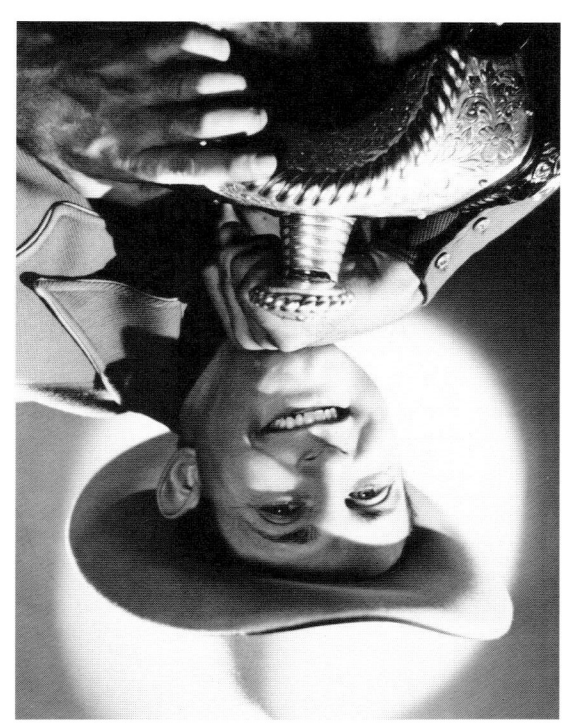

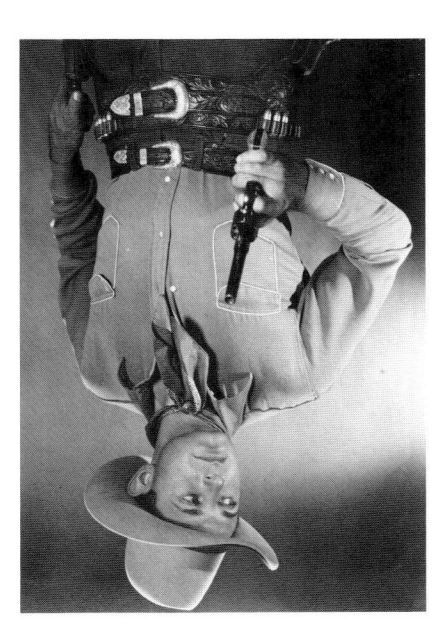

MOZELLE CRAVENS

WELA DAVIES

DORIS DAY

EDDIE DEW **BOBBIE DORREE**

MAXINE DOYLE

KENNE DUNCAN   GRACE DURKIN

PENNY EDWARDS

DALE

JANE FRAZEE

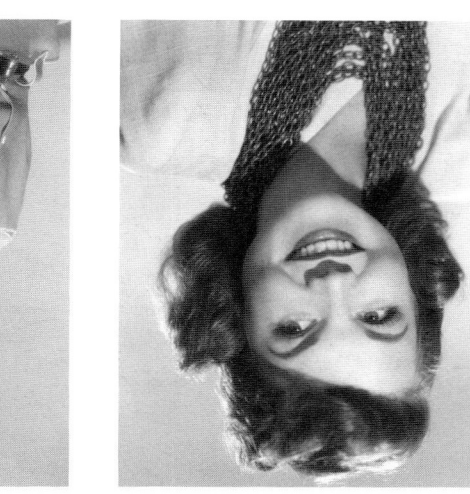

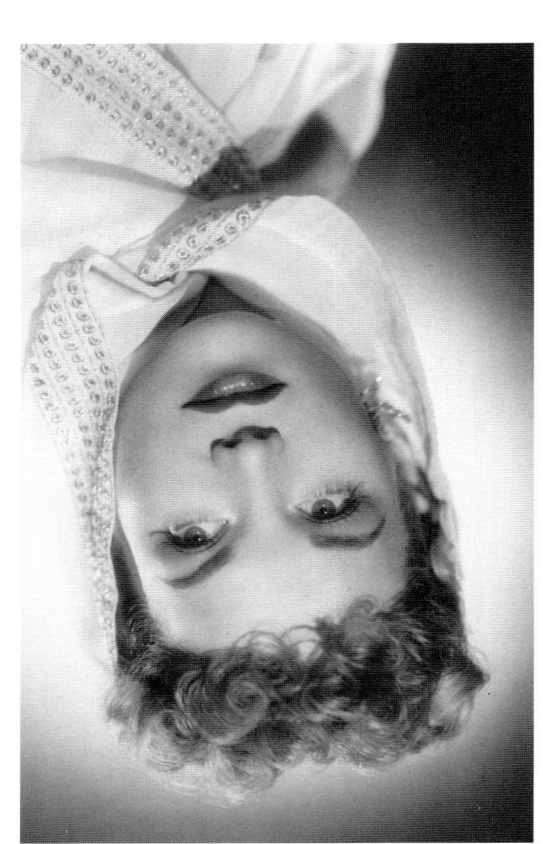
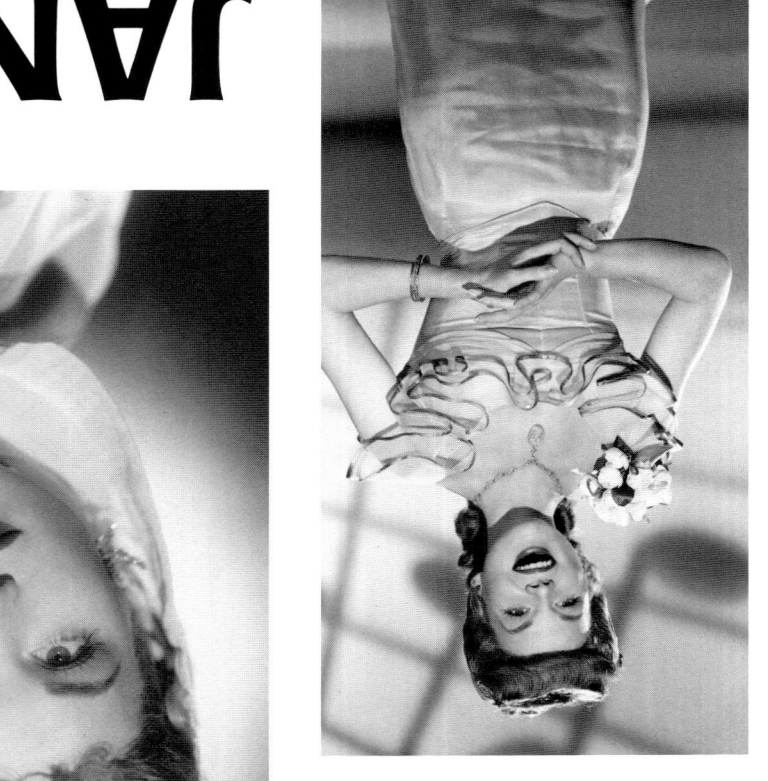

BUD GEARY

MONTE HALE

FRED HAMILTON

BARBRA FULLER

MARILYN HARE

BILL HENRY

KAY HUGHES

JOHN HOLLAND

DeWOLFE HOPPER

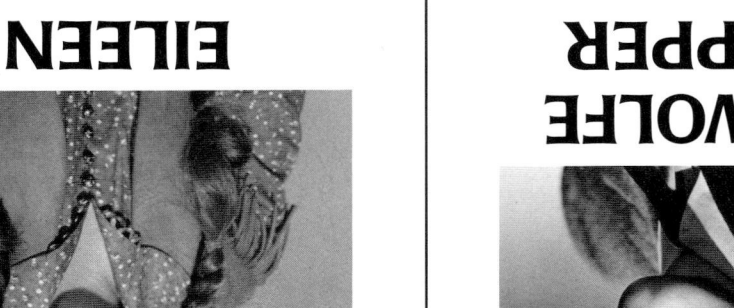
EILEEN JANSSEN

ANNE JEFFREYS

MARY KENYON

JACK KIRK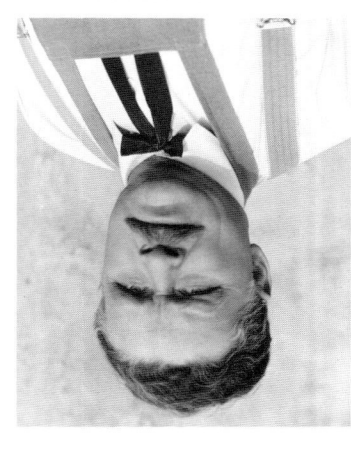

MARC KRAMER

MARTEN LAMONT

MICHAEL KENT

JANE KEAN

BETTY KEAN

LUCIE KAYE

MARY ELLEN KAY

JUNE JOHNSON

ALLAN LANE

BRUCE LANGLEY

MURIEL LAWRENCE

PINKY LEE

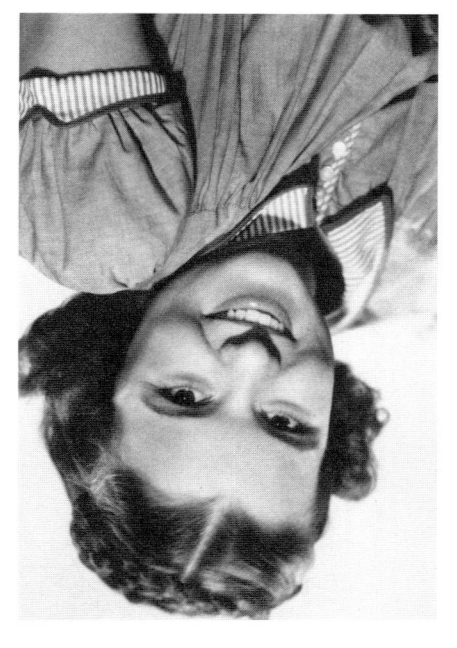

MARY LEE

ROBERT LIVINGSTON

BEVERLY LOYD

TOM LONDON

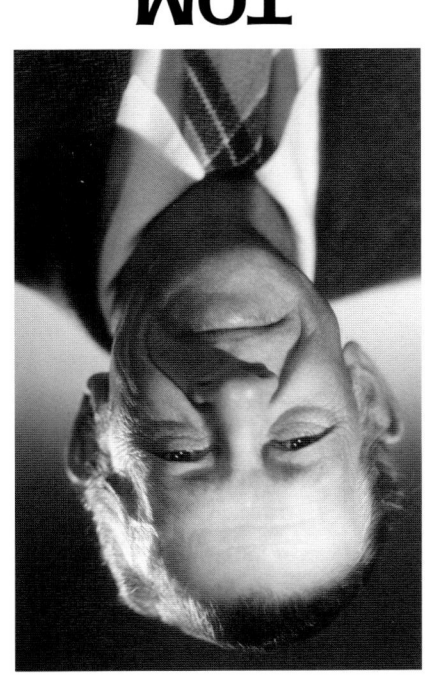

LENI LYNN

BRUCE MacFARLANE

HOPE MANNING

CHRISTINE MAPLE

ADELE

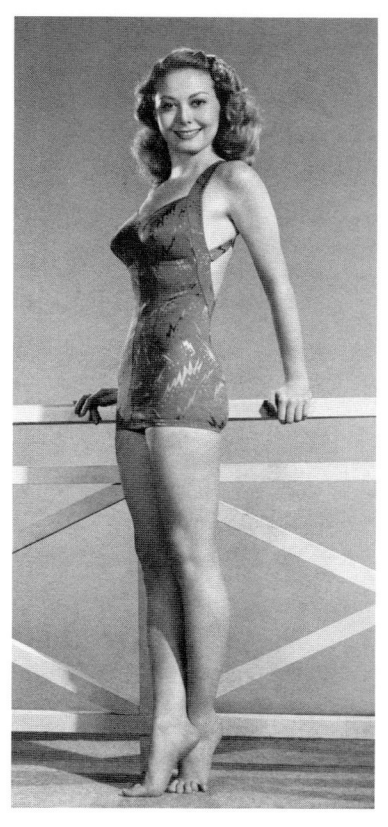

MARA

WILLIAM MARSHALL

JANET MARTIN

SAMMY McKIM

FAY McKENZIE

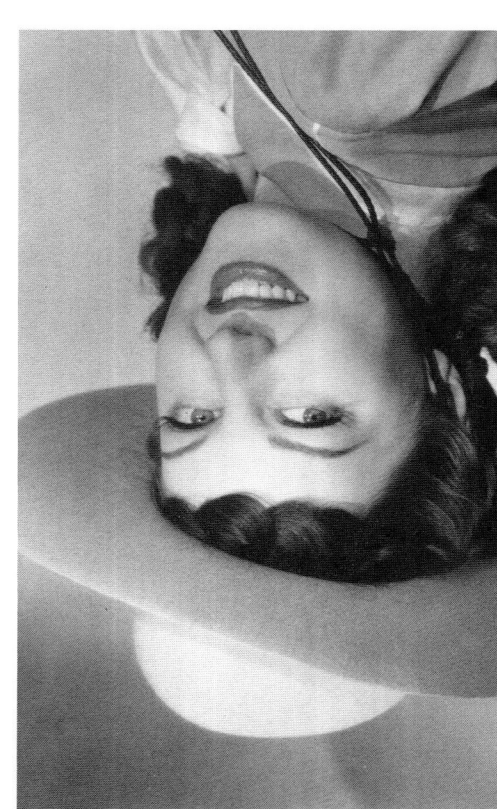

JILL MARTIN

LEROY MASON

CATHERINE McLEOD

RAY MIDDLETON

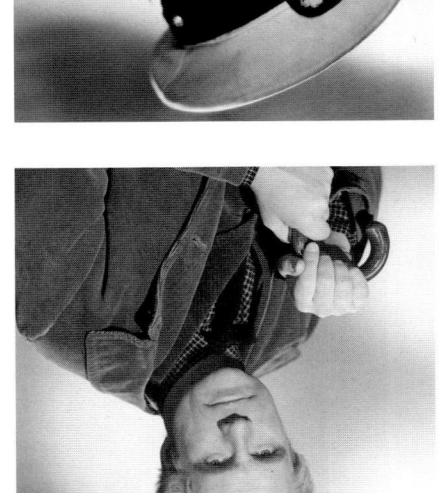

LYNN MERRICK

CONSTANCE MOORE

DOROTHY PAGE

WILLIAM NEWELL

DOROTHY PATRICK

OSCAR AND ELMER

DOYE O'DELL

GRETA NISSEN

BARBARA PEPPER

SLIM PICKENS

JOSE PULIDO

VALENTINE PERKINS

VERA

[as Vera Hruba]

RALSTON

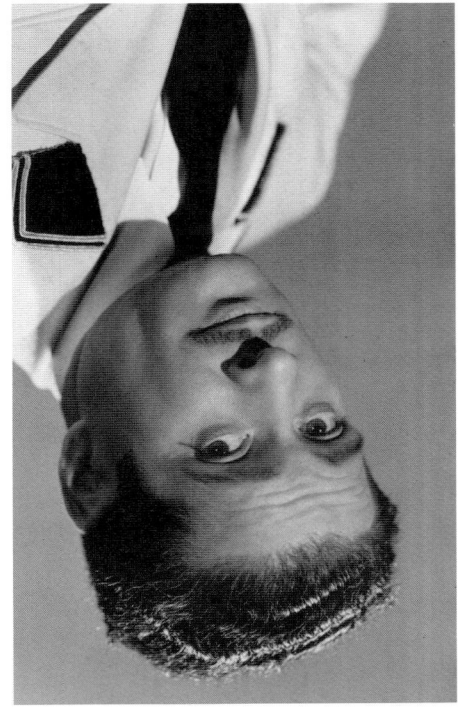

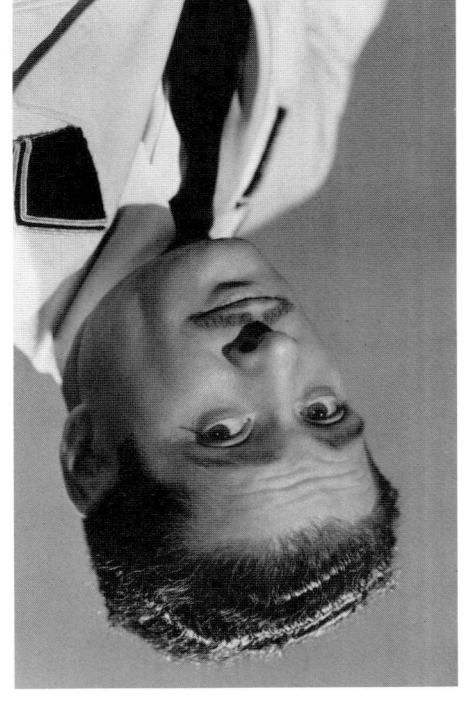

DUNCAN RENALDO

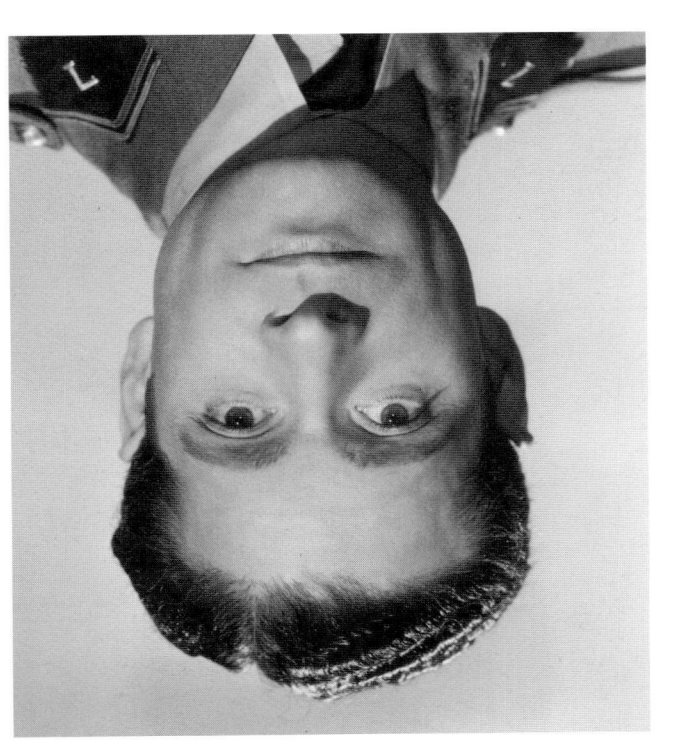

LOIS RANSON

REPUBLIC RHYTHM RIDERS

ARLYN ROBERTS

GLORIA RICH

ROBERT ROCKWELL

LYNNE

[as Mary Hart]

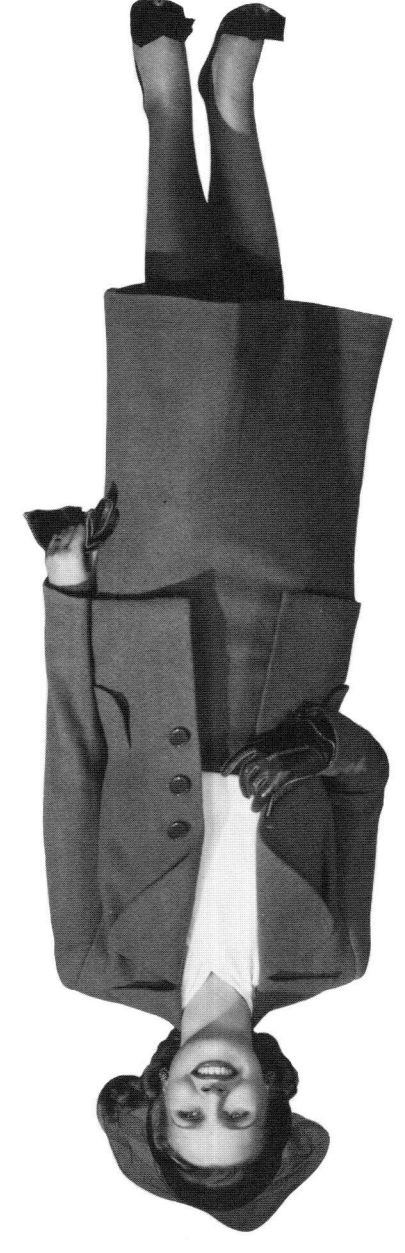

ROBERTS

ESTELITA

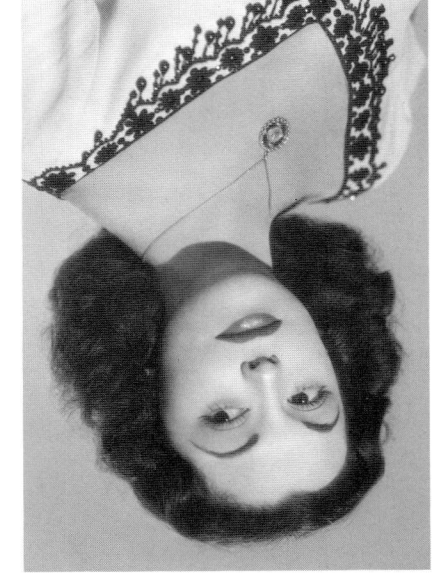

RODRIGUEZ

ANN RUTHERFORD

ROY ROGERS

MARY RUSSELL

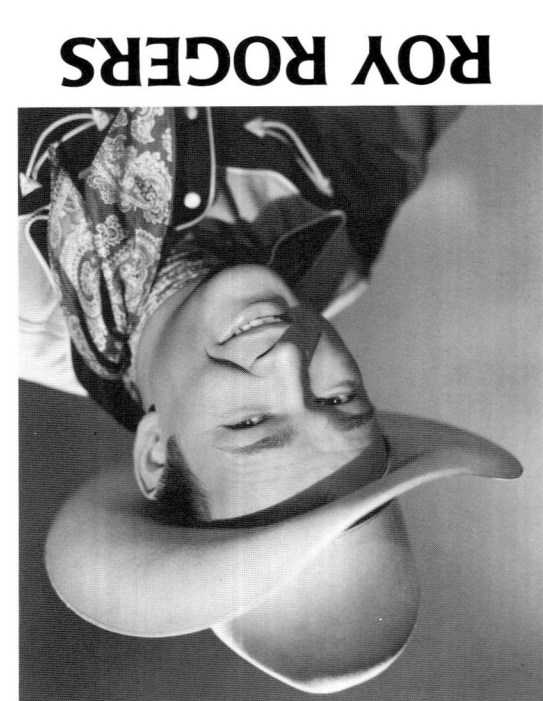

TOMMY RYAN

GUS SCHILLING

BILL SHIRLEY

ALISON SKIPWORTH

TOM STEELE

LARRY STEWART

PEGGY

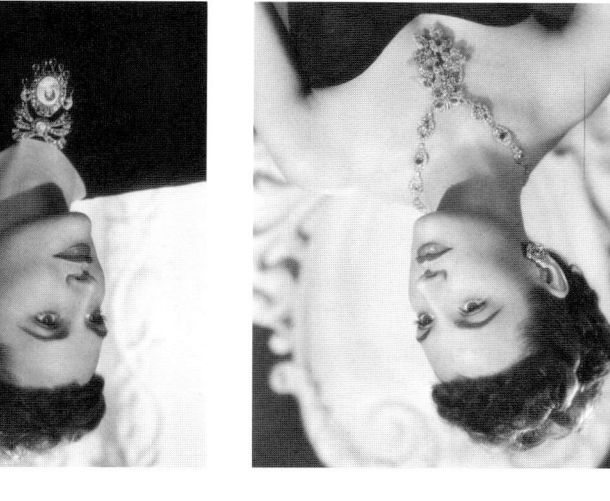

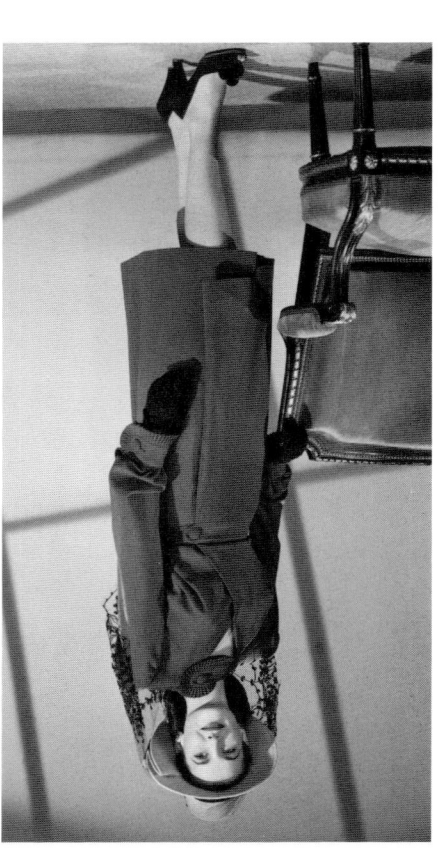

LINDA

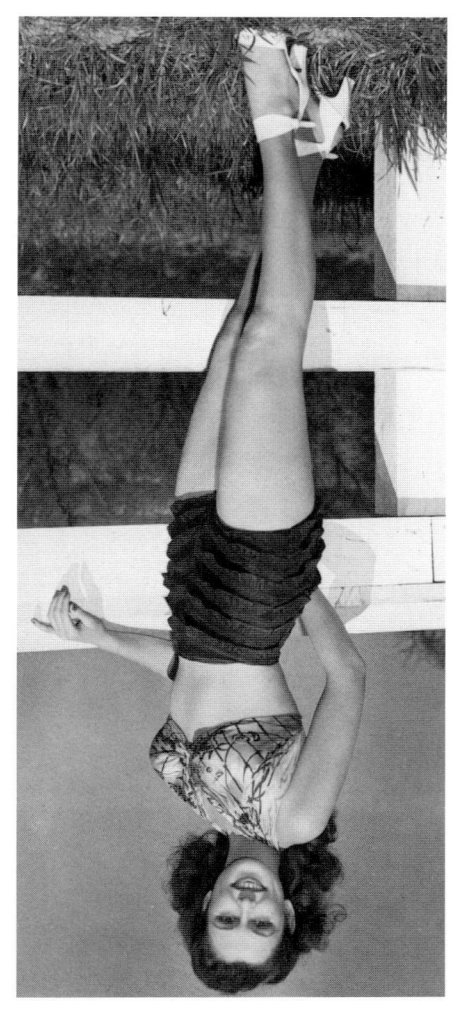

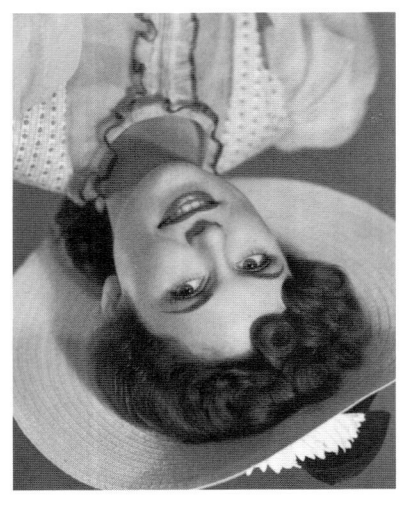

STIRLING

JUNE

STOREY

SHEILA STUART

HELEN

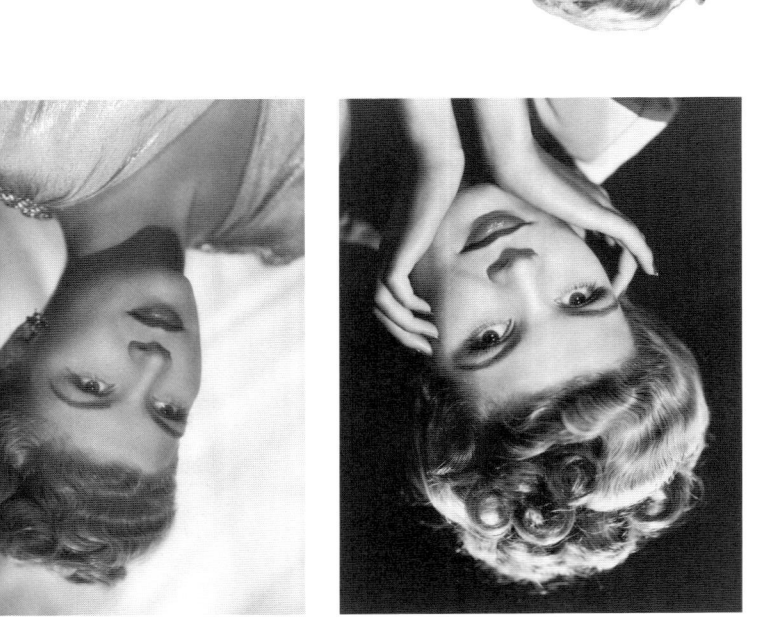

TALBOT

RUTH

MAX TERHUNE
BRAD TAYLOR

TERRY

RANNY WEEKS

ADELE WILDE

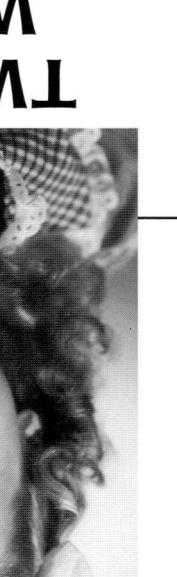

TWINKLE WATTS

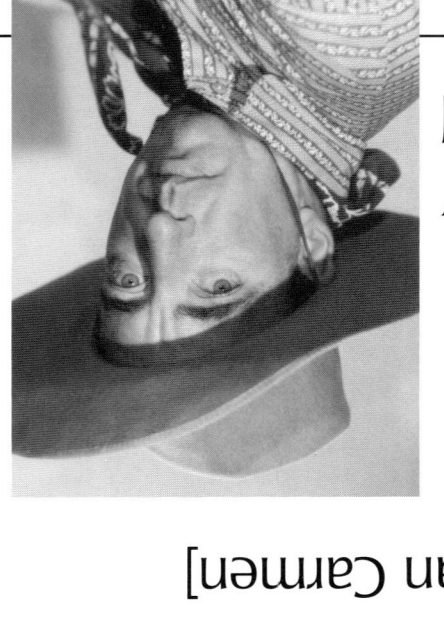

WALLY VERNON

TOM TYLER

JULIA THAYER
[Jean Carmen]

GRANT WITHERS

CARLETON YOUNG

Haddon, Bryon, Farnum, Kerrigan, Stevens, James, Morel, Reedy, Posten.

DANCING

LUCILLE BRYON

MELVA ANSTEAD

MARTHA CARROLL

GERALDINE FARNUM

FRANCES GLADWIN

HARRIETTE HADDON

ROSEMONDE JAMES

MARIAN KERRIGAN

GIRLS

ROSE MARIE MOREL

PATTI POSTEN

BEVERLY REEDY

DOROTHY STEVENS

TERM-PICTURE PLAYERS

Whereas term-contract players could be beholden to Republic for seven years of unlimited assignments, term-picture players rendered exclusive use of their services for a specified number of films during a much shorter period. Over the years, 161 term-picture or multiple-picture contracts covered 115 actors and actresses, comedians Olsen and Johnson, the Weaver brothers and Elviry rustic threesome, the Ice-Capades skating troupe, and seven musical groups: the Cass County Boys, the Kidoodlers, Lulubelle and Scotty, the Riders of the Purple Sage, the Roy Rogers Riders, the Sons of the Pioneers, and the trio of singing-dancing Tic Toc Girls.

The 161 contracts executed — but not always consummated — ranged from one to four pictures within six months to five pictures spread over five years with numerous intermediate variations. Most common at 57% of the total were three categories of one-year deals that involved 26 players committing for a single picture in one year, 38 for two per year, and 28 for three per year. Top honors for the shortest term went to Ole Olsen and Chic Johnson whose June 1 through July 30, 1937, pact paid them $6250 for *All Over Town* [1937]. George Brent's 1948 contract for five pictures in five years was theoretically the longest term, though it was canceled following *Angel on the Amazon* [1948] and *The Kid from Cleveland* [1949]. At that, Brent remained the highest paid, receiving $100,000 for each of his two completed films plus a $150,000 settlement to annul the remaining three. Kay Aldridge, the sole term-picture serial performer, satisfied her accord for two chapterplays in two years with *Daredevils of the West* [1943] and *Haunted Harbor* [1944] at respective four-week-guaranteed weekly minimums of $250 and $350 plus overtime.

Although the preponderance of term-picture participants were hired from outside, eight made the internal transition from Republic's term-contract ranks: Gene Autry, Stephanie Bachelor, Don Barry, Ray Corrigan, Jane Frazee, Ray Middleton, Vera Ralston, and Roy Rogers. Converting to a term-picture agreement in 1948 after 11 years as a stock player, Rogers agreed not to make any television appearances as well as to furnish his own western apparel for which Republic reimbursed him $500 per picture.

Most conventions pertaining to term-contract players also governed their term-picture counterparts save that Republic could not enter into commercial tie-ins without the artist's permission. Nelson Eddy's contract prohibited endorsement of any commercial product except his Republic films while George Brent and Rod Cameron among others consented to one personal appearance and one radio broadcast — sometimes at no additional compensation — in connection with each of their photoplays. Approval for outside engagements remained in Republic's province subject to such pre-emptive services claims as those Bob Hope could exert on Jerry Colonna and Barbara Jo Allen, who was either parenthetically or solely billed by her radio-character name Vera Vague in 11 Republic films. Likewise, songstress Frances Langford was exempted from Wednesday shooting schedules while making *The Hit Parade* [1937] and *Hit Parade of 1941* [1940] to participate in Hope's network radio show. And Chill Wills' prior contract with Universal took precedence over his Republic commitments of 1954-55.

In the higher-stakes game of term-picture negotiations where bigger names and established reputations translated into powerful drawing cards at the box office, players dealt closer to the top of the deck in getting Republic to ante up commensurate wages as well as billing and personal concessions. Appropriate screen credit was a key consideration for the majority of performers who had it stipulated they would be listed as star or co-star in their pictures. In general, lead actors would take second billing only to a leading actress and then only if both their names were set in the same-size type. John Wayne's star or co-star status dated to his early roles in the Three Mesquiteers series when he was designated to be top-ranked in a larger type size than any other cast member. As of 1948, Roy Rogers and his horse Trigger were awarded top and first-star billing.

Script approval — granted Eddie Albert, George Brent, Wendell Corey, Richard Dix, Brian Donlevy, and Nelson Eddy to name a few — usually entailed submitting no more than three scripts on one title to the pertinent individuals; if all scripts were rejected, Republic reserved the right to then terminate the picture. John Carroll's aspiration of becoming an associate producer was delineated in his 1947 contract which indicated he was to be given the eventual supervised opportunity of producing, though he never received on-screen credit in this behind-the-scenes capacity.

Miscellaneous demands ran the gamut from the mundane to the sublime. For location work it was customary for Republic to secure first-class transportation and, when available, drawing rooms on railroad accommodations and first-class lodgings at the site. In addition, the studio footed the round-trip fares between New York and Los Angeles for such bi-coastal talent as Ella Raines and Estelita Rodriguez when they were between pictures. Clauses in Nelson Eddy's contract took into account his unavailability in the months of March and April and a restriction that only the Technicolor process could be used if any of his films were photographed in color. Bill Elliott was excluded from appearing in serials and allowed to furnish the horses he rode, on some pictures providing his own mounts Sonny, Penny, and Red Man for which Republic paid him the going rate charged by rental stables for stock steeds.

Top-seeded talent had to be booked well in advance of need even when definite roles had not yet been established, a hedging of bets that occasionally proved fruitless. As a result of this and other mitigating circumstances, a few of the 161 contracts including George Brent's went partially or completely unfulfilled, benefitting the affected players financially in the form of buy-outs. Edward Ellis in 1940 signed for a six-month term at $8000 to appear in one picture which was not made, netting him a $2000 settlement. Gloria Dickson, who did not make any of the three films contracted for during 1942-43, settled in the amount of $3825, or half her originally negotiated fee.

A horse opera of a different color nagged Republic when attempting to implement Ann Dvorak's one-year, two-picture pact slated to be in effect from February 12, 1945, through February 11, 1946, at salaries of $15,000 for the first film and $18,000 for the second. Informed in September of 1945 that the studio wished to place her opposite Bill Elliott in *In Old Sacramento* [1946] as her first commitment, Dvorak replied that her co-star should be a bigger name than herself and she suggested John Wayne, Randolph Scott, or George Raft as suitable alternatives. Instead, Republic substituted Constance Moore and, by mutual agreement, extended Dvorak's contract to August 11, 1946. Then on March 11, 1946, Dvorak's agent asked Republic's permission for his client to accept seven weeks employment in United Artists' *The Affairs of Bel Ami* [1947] starting in late April. When Republic responded with a pre-emption stating they would need the actress' services at about the same time, brisk negotiations culminated on March 14 with Dvorak paying Republic $25,000 to be released from her contract, expressing pleasure by drawing a smiling face inside the A of her first name on signing the release form.

Coincident with the impending resolution of Dvorak's dilemma, Joseph Schildkraut was agonizing over his own casting problems at the studio. Under contract for three pictures in one year during March of 1946, Schildkraut expressed personal reservations about playing Peter Marquette in *Plainsman and the Lady* [1946] and asked to be withdrawn. Republic was vindicated after refusing the request, however, when Schildkraut gave his usual professional performance and earned high marks in trade reviews for his portrayal of the villain.

70

ROY ACUFF

EDDIE ALBERT

KAY ALDRIDGE

LONA ANDRE

RICHARD ARLEN

GENE AUTRY

LEW AYRES

BOBBY BLAKE

CHARLES BICKFORD

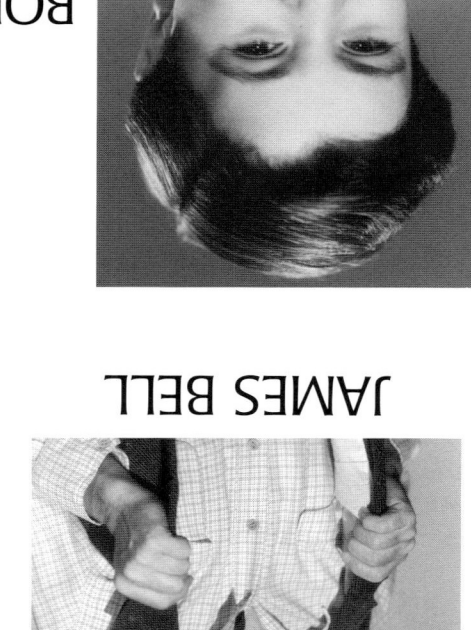

JAMES BELL

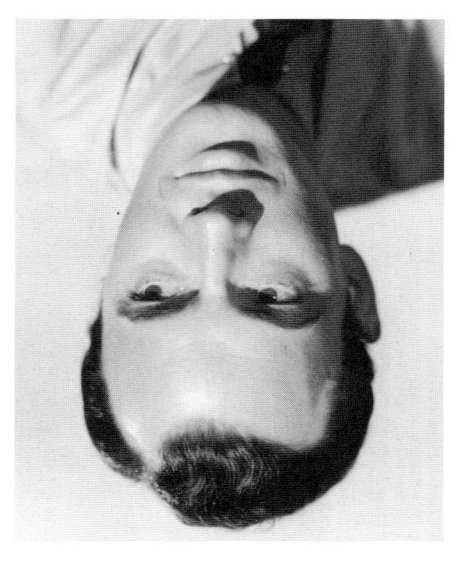

JOHN BEAL

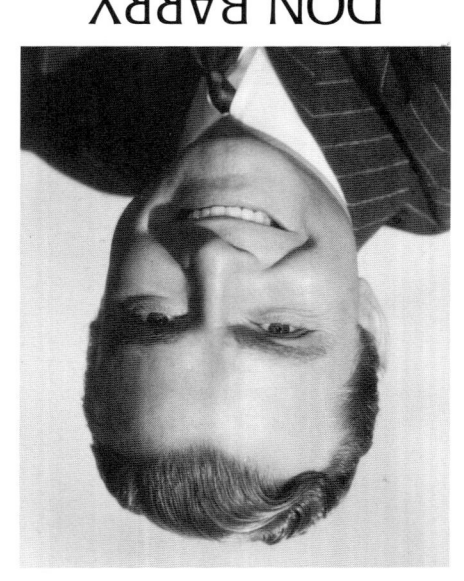

DON BARRY

BINNIE BARNES

ROBERT BALDWIN

STEPHANIE BACHELOR

 PAT BRADY
 GEORGE BRENT
 JOE E. BROWN

 ROD CAMERON
 JUDY CANOVA

 JOHN CARRADINE
 JOHN CARROLL

JERRY COLONNA

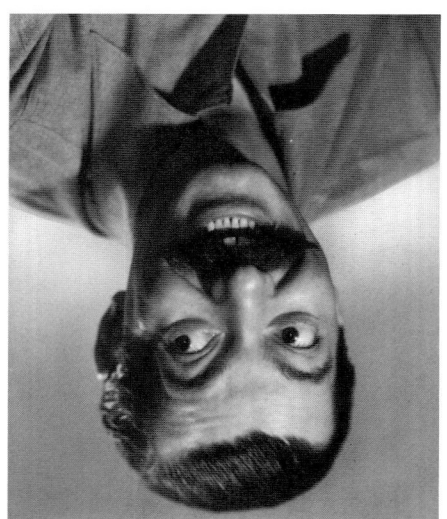

BILLY CONN

HARRY V. CHESHIRE

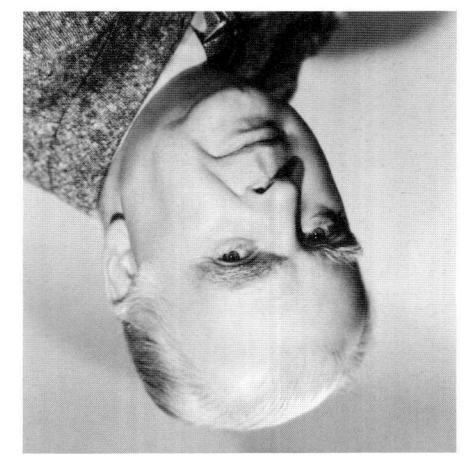

MAE CLARKE

CASS COUNTY BOYS

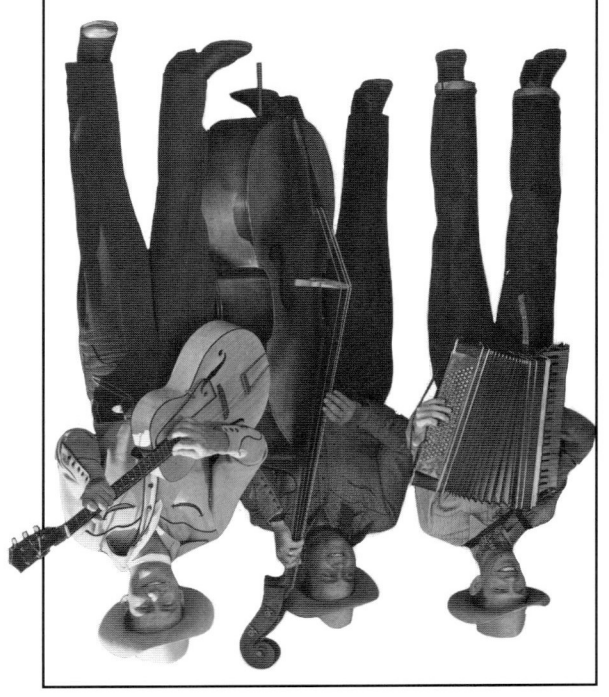

WALTER CATLETT

SPENCER CHARTERS

DONALD COOK

WENDELL COREY

RAY CORRIGAN

JIM DAVIS

RICHARD CROMWELL

HARRY DAVENPORT

RUFE DAVIS

ANDY DEVINE

ANN DVORAK

NELSON EDDY

BRIAN DONLEVY

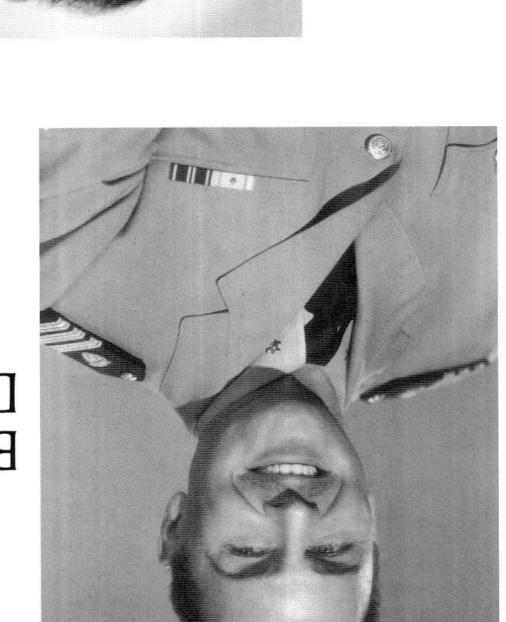

RUTH DONNELLY

GLORIA DICKSON

RICHARD DIX

JIMMIE DODD

JOAN EDWARDS

BILL ELLIOTT

EDWARD ELLIS

JAMES ELLISON

GEORGE ERNEST

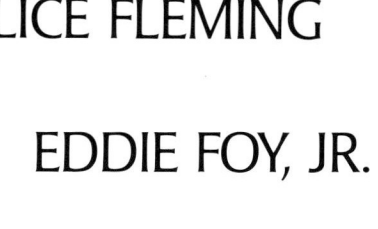
ALICE FLEMING

EDDIE FOY, JR.

JANE FRAZEE

NEIL HAMILTON

STUART HAMBLEN

TITO GUIZAR

CHARLOTTE GREENWOOD

RUSSELL GLEASON

LUCILE GLEASON

JAMES GLEASON

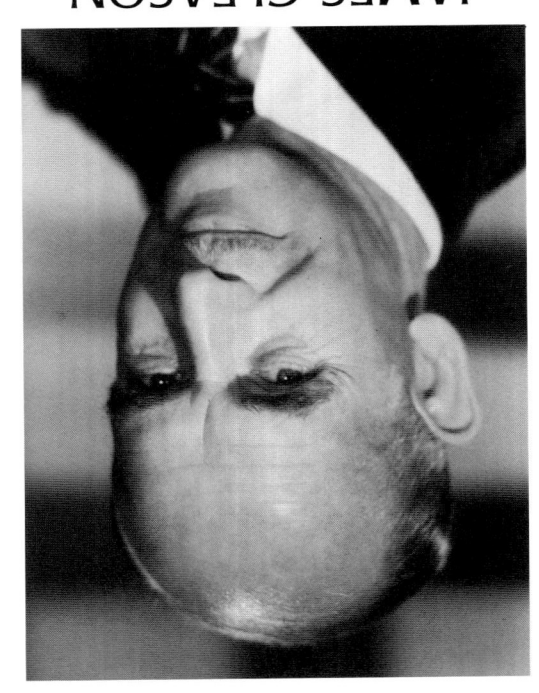

RAYMOND HATTON

STERLING HAYDEN

GABBY HAYES

CHARLOTTE HENRY

STERLING HOLLOWAY

JOHN HUBBARD

MARY BETH HUGHES

JOAN LESLIE

FRANCES LANGFORD

THE KIDOODLERS

ROSCOE KARNS

JIL JARMYN

 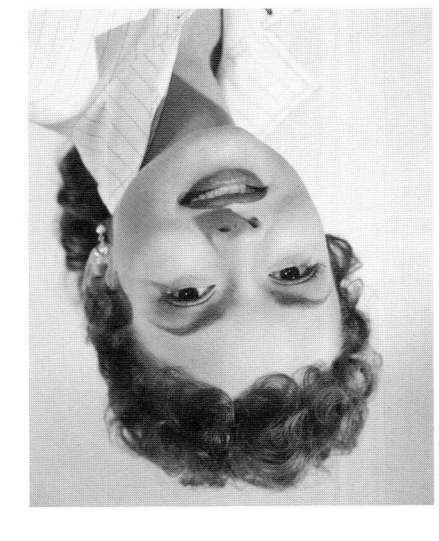

FRIEDA INESCORT

ICE-CAPADES TROUPE

DOROTHY LEWIS

LULUBELLE AND SCOTTY

JIMMY LYDON

DONALD MacBRIDE

MARIAN MARSH

ILONA MASSEY

VICTOR McLAGLEN

EDWARD NORRIS

LUCILLE NORMAN

MARY MURPHY

ONA MUNSON

POLLY MORAN

RAY MILLAND

RAY MIDDLETON

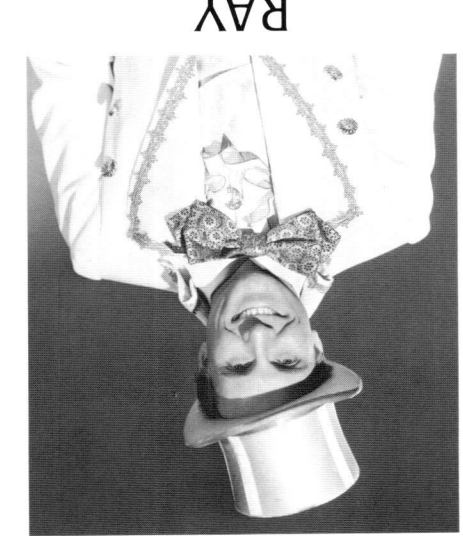

RAMON NOVARRO

EDDIE NUGENT

OLSEN AND JOHNSON

DENNIS O'KEEFE

EUGENE PALLETTE

SALLY PAYNE

AL PEARCE

BARBARA PEPPER

LYNNE ROBERTS

BEATRICE ROBERTS

RIDERS OF THE PURPLE SAGE

PHIL REGAN

ELLA RAINES

VERA RALSTON

ROGER PRYOR

ESTELITA RODRIGUEZ

ROY ROGERS

ROY ROGERS RIDERS

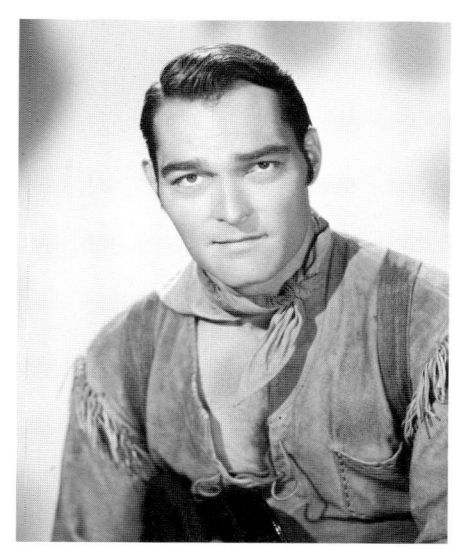
JOHN RUSSELL

SYD SAYLOR

JOSEPH SCHILDKRAUT

SONS OF THE PIONEERS

BOB STEELE

VERA VAGUE

EVELYN VENABLE

ERNO VEREBES

FORREST TUCKER

COLONEL ROSCOE TURNER

MARION TALLEY

JOE STRAUCH, JR.

TIC TOC GIRLS

EDDY WALLER

JOHN WAYNE

WEAVER BROTHERS AND ELVIRY

MARTHA WENTWORTH

HENRY WILCOXON

CHILL WILLS

JANE WITHERS

PICTURE-COMMITMENT PLAYERS

Picture commitments represented single contracts for individual films signed by a galaxy of the brightest stars in the Hollywood heaven, some of whom were just beginning their ascendancy when apprenticing at Republic. Still on the cusp of attaining celebrity status as Rita Hayworth, Rita Cansino was paid $125 for her part in the Three Mesquiteers western *Hit the Saddle* [1937]. The daughter of a southwestern regional Republic exhibitor, Phylis Isley appeared in the Three Mesquiteers entry *New Frontier* [1939] and the serial *Dick Tracy's G-Men* [1939] at salaries of $75 each before David O. Selznick took an interest in her career and changed her name to Jennifer Jones. Alan Ladd during his journeyman phase at different studios made six Republic pictures, the last being *Petticoat Politics* [1941] for $125 immediately preceding his meteoric rise at Paramount. Peter Lawford also began burnishing his silver-screen persona at Republic with four films produced and released during 1943: *London Blackout Murders, The Purple V, Someone to Remember,* and *The West Side Kid.*

But the majority of Republic's picture commitments involved already well-established names whose marquee value gave them commensurable bargaining power for salaries and perquisites. Co-starring in *Lady for a Night* [1942], Joan Blondell negotiated a $35,000 salary plus the right to choose Dorothy Pondell as her personal make-up artist, Ruth Pursely as her personal hairdresser, Irene Martin as her stand-in, and Walter Plunkett as her wardrobe designer. Maureen O'Hara was guaranteed a minimum of 10 weeks employment at $6500 weekly for *The Quiet Man* [1952] and selected her own make-up artist, hairdresser, stand-in, and publicist.

Paid $80,000 to play pugilist George Wilson in the prizefight picture *Champ for a Day* [1953], Alex Nicol garnered an extra $1000 for boxing training during the week prior to filming. Co-starring in *Come Next Spring* [1956] at a sum of $50,000, Ann Sheridan appointed her own hairdresser and stand-in. And on *Magic Fire* [1956], Yvonne DeCarlo had approval of costume sketches and augmented her $50,000 salary with $500 weekly living expenses while on location in Munich, Germany.

Some performers were able to command percentages of net profits over and above their regular salaries. Judith Anderson worked for only $5000 on *Specter of the Rose* [1946] but acquired 3% of the net profits in supplemental compensation. For her seven days on *Moonrise* [1948], Ethel Barrymore was paid $25,000 plus 5% of the net profits, the same percentage given Louis Hayward on top of his $75,000 payment for *House by the River* [1950]. Hayward was also designated to receive star or co-star billing, the name of no artist to precede his except that of a female star of greater importance based upon the Audience Research Institute "Continuing Audit of Marquee Values," a periodic popularity poll used by studios and talent as the final arbiter in determining credit positions. Singer-actor Vaughn Monroe, who retained approval of the songs he sang in his westerns, starred in *Singing Guns* [1950] at a flat $87,500, then offset his lowered fee of $5000 for *Toughest Man in Arizona* [1952] with a whopping 25% of the net profits.

Sacrificing percentages in favor of substantial straight salaries were Errol Flynn in *Adventures of Captain Fabian* [1951], Fred MacMurray in *Fair Wind to Java* [1953], and Barbara Stanwyck in *The Maverick Queen* [1956], each of whom was paid $100,000. In addition, MacMurray was accorded first billing above the title and a limitation on his work day of not more than eight hours unless night scenes were scheduled. Upscale from this trio, Don Ameche was remunerated $125,000 for his role in *That's My Man* [1947]. Reservations in his contract stipulated he could pre-empt the Republic agreement if a part in a Technicolor picture was secured, and that his services could not be required on Saturdays and Sundays owing to his weekly appearance as a regular on the Edgar Bergen and Charlie McCarthy Show network radio broadcasts.

By far the highest-paid players in any Republic film at a guaranteed minimum of $200,000 each were two actresses: Myrna Loy in *The Red Pony* [1949] and Joan Crawford in *Johnny Guitar* [1954]. Among Loy's contractual conditions were a portable star dressing room placed at her disposal on the stage set where she was working, call times of not earlier than 9 a.m. and daily dismissals no later than 6 p.m. except for night scenes, and a minimum of 12 hours off between calls.

Unlike Loy's relatively minimal list of adjuncts, Joan Crawford's agreement comprised one of the most comprehensive individual contracts Republic ever entered into, a 39-page document filled with approval qualifications that offered insight into the complexities of hiring a stellar light. Doing so launched a chain of events initiated during the late spring and early summer when each year's program of releases was being planned and the need for star-caliber talent determined. At this juncture Republic began contacting prospects for picture commitments well in advance in order to determine general availability times and thus efficiently line up not only filming dates for their entire annual slate but associated personnel and facilities as well. Achieving this delicate balance demanded a certain flexibility and adaptation to changing circumstances since players had to honor their commitment at one studio before going to the next.

Delays encountered in starting or completing a film or both were a common disruption to the smooth flow of talent from one job to another, though fortuitously the reverse was true of Crawford's immediate situation. Scheduling *Johnny Guitar* for production was contingent upon her first fulfilling an obligation to Paramount for *Lisbon,* a feature she was contracted to start in 1953 between May 18 and June 29 for 12 weeks. But when Paramount terminated the project, their misfortune twice blessed Republic since they obtained Crawford in timely fashion and picked up the abandoned title for an original photoplay of their own starring Ray Milland which was subsequently released in 1956.

Free to proceed with *Johnny Guitar,* Crawford began focusing on the numerous contract details over which she had been granted authority. In August she accepted Philip Yordan's screenplay, then in September approved wardrobe designer Sheila O'Brien, cameraman Harry Stradling after reviewing other photographic tests, and even the three-strip Trucolor process in which the film was to be shot.

Ground rules for casting the title role of Johnny Guitar were predicated on the actor earning not more than $50,000 and a game plan that kicked off with Republic submitting the names of three candidates to Crawford. Rejection placed the ball back in Crawford's court, requiring her to offer three names for Republic's consideration. In the event her nominations were unacceptable or unavailable to the studio she had 48 hours to reconsider Republic's original choices. Although never reached, an impasse following several more return volleys gave Republic the right to cancel her contract. In the final analysis term-picture player Sterling Hayden at a salary of $30,000 was mutually agreed upon as the leading man on September 30. For her part, Crawford had to be billed on a separate card ahead of the main title and in type the same size as the title of the picture.

Other of Crawford's contractual stipulations included approval of all still photographs in which she appeared and the right to designate make-up artist Eddie Allen, hairdresser Jane Gorton, wardrobe woman Elva Hill, and stand-in Sylvia Lamarr. Previously confirmed, Nicholas Ray had been slated to direct the ill-fated *Lisbon* and was thus ready for his Republic assignment when principal photography commenced on October 19. Crawford's final bonus extended beyond conclusion of production with Republic consenting to furnish a free 35mm composite print of the photoplay for her personal use.

WALTER ABEL NICK ADAMS

LUTHER ADLER

BRIAN AHERNE

JUDITH ALLEN DON AMECHE

ANNA MARIA ALBERGHETTI

06

ETHEL BARRYMORE

LYNN BARI

KENNY BAKER

EDWARD ARNOLD

EVE ARDEN

HEATHER ANGEL

JUDITH ANDERSON

CONSTANCE BENNETT

SIDNEY BLACKMER

MARI BLANCHARD

JOAN BLONDELL

WARD BOND

ERNEST BORGNINE

LEE BOWMAN

LLOYD BRIDGES

BARBARA BRITTON

VIRGINIA BRUCE

DAVID BRIAN

WALTER BRENNAN

ALICE BRADY

SCOTT BRADY

BILLIE BURKE

RAYMOND BURR

SPRING BYINGTON

BRUCE CABOT

LOUIS CALHERN

RITA CANSINO
[Rita Hayworth]

HARRY CAREY, SR.

JACKIE COOGAN

TOUCH CONNORS

STEVE COCHRANE

CHARLES COBURN

LEE J. COBB

RICHARD CARLSON

MACDONALD CAREY

BRODERICK CRAWFORD

JOAN CRAWFORD

YVONNE DeCARLO

ROBERT CUMMINGS

LINDA DARNELL

FRANCES DEE

WILLIAM DEMAREST

JAMES DUNN

JIMMY DURANTE

DAN DURYEA

ROBERT DOUGLAS

HOWARD DUFF

ANGIE DICKINSON

FAITH DOMERGUE

BUDDY EBSEN BARBARA EDEN JOAN EVANS

MADGE EVANS BARRY FITZGERALD

ERROL FLYNN JOAN FONTAINE

OLIVER HARDY

PHIL HARRIS

JUNE HAVOC

JON HALL

MARGARET HAMILTON

THOMAS GOMEZ

WILLIAM GARGAN

PRESTON FOSTER

LOUIS HAYWARD

PAUL HENREID

HEDDA HOPPER

EDWARD EVERETT HORTON

HENRY HULL

WARREN HULL

ARTHUR HUNNICUTT

DEAN JAGGER

ELSIE JANIS

BUCK JONES

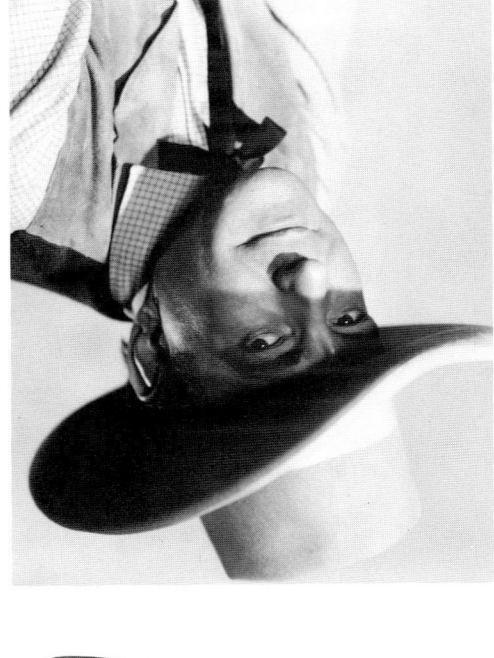

JOHN IRELAND

PHYLIS ISLEY
[Jennifer Jones]

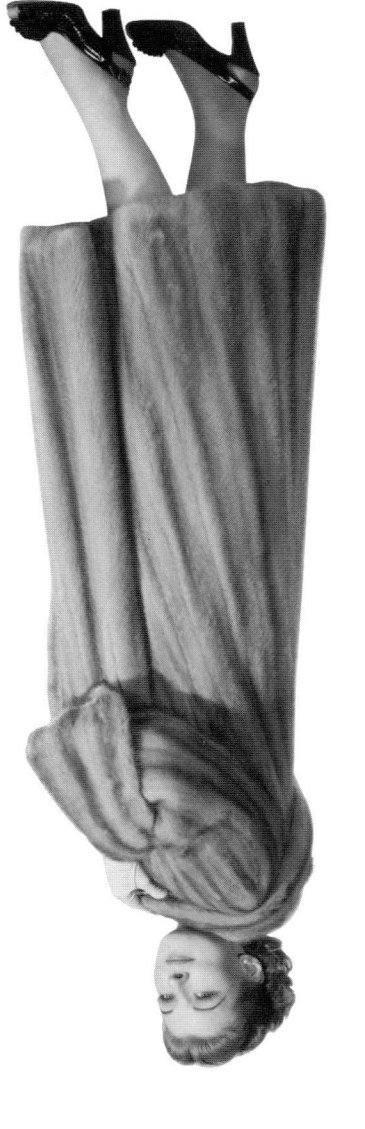

RUTH HUSSEY

MARSHA HUNT

VICTOR JORY

ALLYN JOSLYN

KATY JURADO

NANCY KELLY

PAUL KELLY

EVELYN KEYES

GUY KIBBEE

PETER LORRE

MYRNA LOY

CAROLE LANDIS

PETER LAWFORD

FERNANDO LAMAS

PATRIC KNOWLES

ALAN LADD

JOHN LUND

BEN LYON

FRED MacMURRAY

JAMES MASON

MERCEDES McCAMBRIDGE

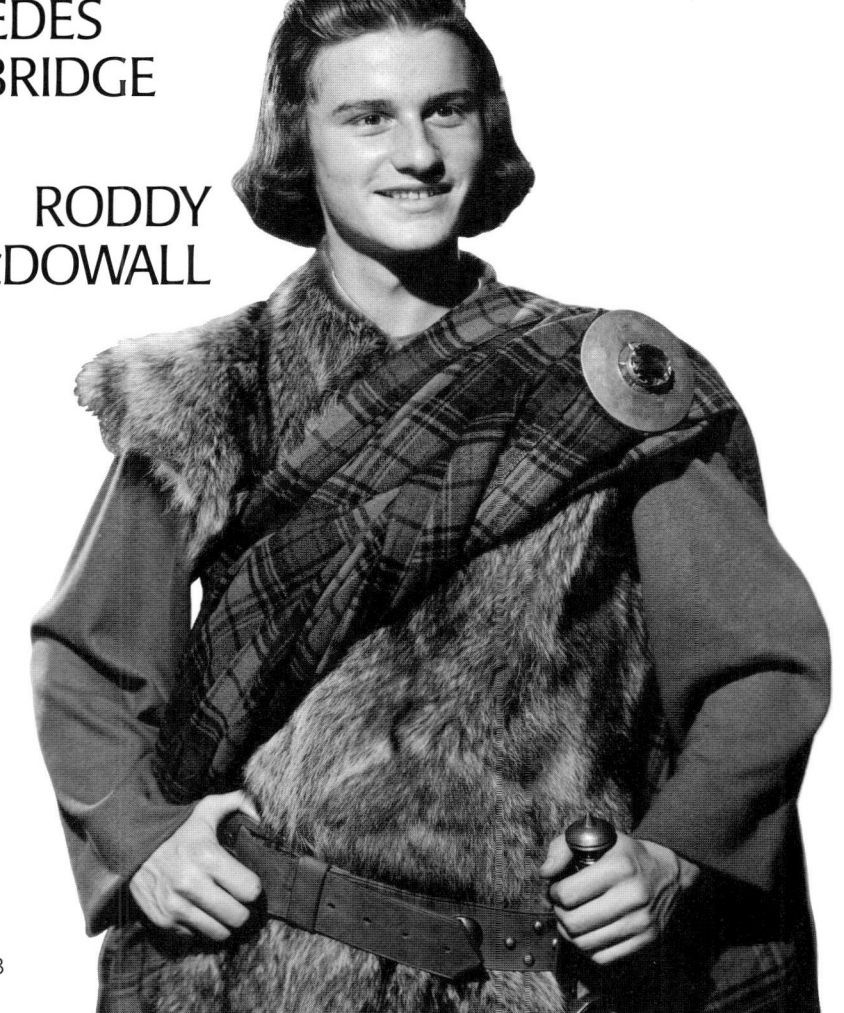
RODDY McDOWALL

HATTIE McDANIEL

ROBERT MIDDLETON

ADOLPHE MENJOU

RALPH MEEKER

PATRICIA MEDINA

BUTTERFLY McQUEEN

DOROTHY McGUIRE

STEPHEN McNALLY

ANN MILLER

VAUGHN MONROE

GEORGE MONTGOMERY

AGNES MOOREHEAD

RITA MORENO

CHESTER MORRIS

J. CARROL NAISH

JOHN PAYNE

JEAN PARKER

MME. MARIA OUSPENSKAYA

PAT O'BRIEN

EDMOND O'BRIEN

LLOYD NOLAN

ALEX NICOL

MICHELINE PRELLE | VINCENT PRICE | EDDIE QUILLAN

CLAUDE RAINS | MARJORIE RAMBEAU

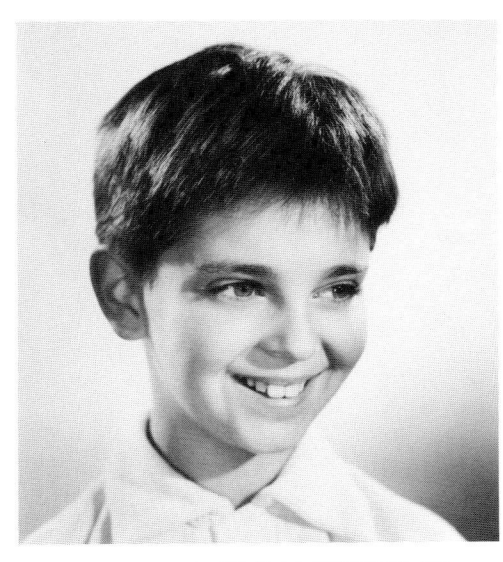 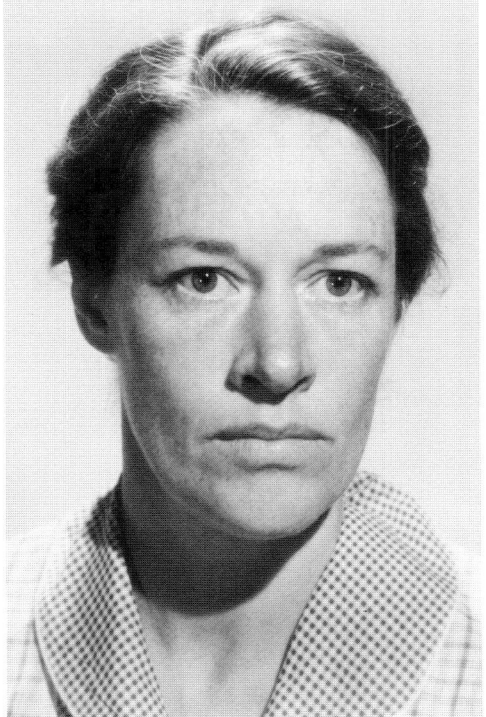

TOMMY RETTIG | ANNE REVERE | BEVERLY ROBERTS

JANICE RULE

SABU

LIZABETH SCOTT

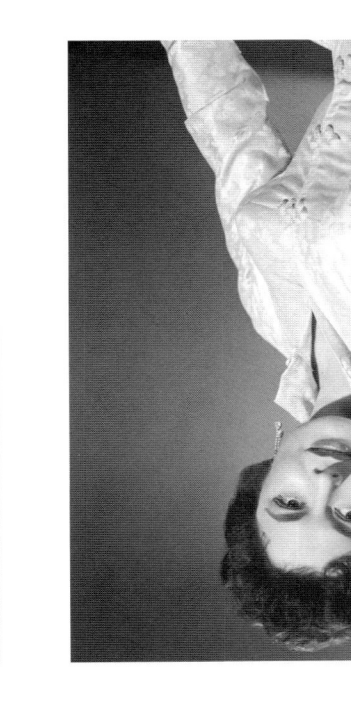

RUTH ROMAN

MICKEY ROONEY

DALE ROBERTSON

GILBERT ROLAND

MARTHA SCOTT

ZACHARY SCOTT

ANN SHERIDAN

ANNE SHIRLEY

ROBERT STACK

ALEXIS SMITH

SIR C. AUBREY SMITH

BARBARA STANWYCK

ERICH VON STROHEIM

ROBERT VAUGHN

HELEN TWELVETREES

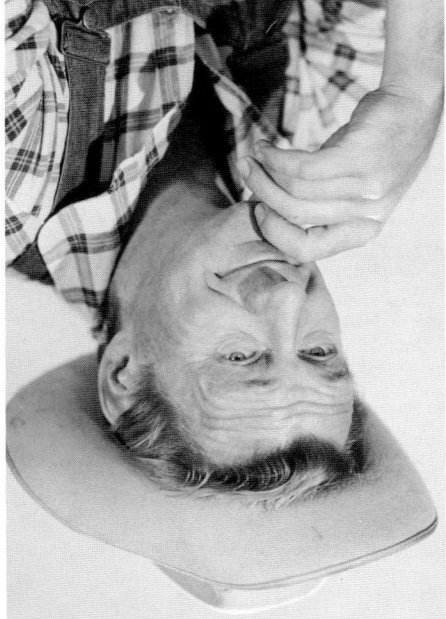

SONNY TUFTS

CLAIRE TREVOR

BARRY SULLIVAN

SHEPPERD STRUDWICK

GALE STORM

HELEN WALKER

RUTH WARRICK

ORSON WELLES

BILL WILLIAMS

RICHARD WEBB

CHARLES WINNINGER

JANE WYATT

LOAN-OUT PLAYERS

Considering it good business to counter the proverb of neither a borrower nor a lender be, studios supporting a stable of stock players defrayed the costs of inactive contractees collecting steady paychecks by loaning them out to competitors at inflated prices, then reciprocally borrowing from same in time of need. Despite the superficial earmarks of a chattel call, this balance of human trade benefited both parties since studios turned a cash profit in the bargain while those farmed out from their home turf gained valuable experience and wider recognition through further on-screen exposure. A prime example of the common good was Republic's loan-out of John Wayne to Walter Wanger during November and December of 1938 at $600 per week. Although Wayne received only a portion of the sum while Republic reaped the remainder, his role in *Stagecoach* [1939], released by United Artists, catapulted him to virtual overnight stardom.

Republic began using loan-outs in 1936 and eventually borrowed 108 players covered by 132 contracts, a disparity reconciled by performers who were loaned more than once. Forrest Tucker held the record, migrating to Republic on four occasions from as many studios. Runners-up at three times each were June Travis from Warner Bros. and Albert Dekker, Susan Hayward, and Gail Russell from Paramount. The greatest number borrowed by Republic in a single year was 20 in 1943 when wartime shortages created a demand for leading men, though in this instance the ranks were evenly divided at 10 actors and 10 actresses.

Paramount proved to be Republic's biggest talent subsidizer, supplying 35 loan-outs over the years compared to 18 from Warner Bros., 13 from 20th Century-Fox, and 12 from RKO of the double-digit contributors. Included among Paramount's loan-outs were players who essayed leads in four serials: Ella Neal in *Mysterious Doctor Satan* [1940], Frances Gifford in *Jungle Girl* [1941], and Rod Cameron in *G-Men Vs. The Black Dragon* [1943] and *Secret Service in Darkest Africa* [1943]. Still another loan-out serial lead was Constance Worth, borrowed from Columbia to co-star as British secret agent Vivian Marsh in *G-Men Vs. The Black Dragon*.

The price structure for players made available to other studios instead of languishing between assignments on their home lot was computed at their regular salary plus an arbitrary premium pocketed by the lender. Aware of this practice while under contract to Republic in 1937, veteran actress Alison Skipworth demanded 50% of the overage if she was loaned to another studio. Variations on the basic arrangement called for a supplemental signing bonus also retained by the lending studio or a bonus paid to the loan-out player either in advance or at the end of a mission as a good-will gesture. Borrowing dancer Johnny Coy from Paramount for $1200, or twice his usual $600 weekly rate, Republic at the end of filming on *Earl Carroll Sketchbook* [1946] awarded Coy a $2000 completion bonus. Sums agreed upon were always disbursed by the borrower to the lender who continued to payroll their own talent. A case in point, Republic paid RKO $2125 per week for the services of William Talman for *City that Never Sleeps* [1953] while RKO continued to cut Talman his standard $850 paycheck.

Highest paid of the loan-outs to Republic was Robert Mitchum, borrowed from David O. Selznick's Vanguard Films for *The Red Pony* [1949] at $10,000 per week on a 10-week guarantee, or a minimum total of $100,000. Vanguard's contract for Mitchum contained free-time provisions in the event production took longer than anticipated, a customary clause in such big-ticket agreements. Accordingly, Mitchum's 11th and 12th week were to cost Republic nothing with a reversion to $10,000 weekly for the 13th and 14th week if needed and extensions beyond that time at Vanguard's discretion. In lending John Agar for *Sands of Iwo Jima* [1950], Vanguard retained approval of all stills featuring Agar, obligating Republic to submit unapproved negatives to Vanguard

for their personal destruction.

Other top-money loan-outs included Maureen O'Hara at $50,000 for *Rio Grande* [1950], Michael O'Shea at $40,000 for *Man from Frisco* [1944], John Carroll at $35,000 each for *Flying Tigers* [1942] and *Hit Parade of 1943* [1943], Gail Russell at $30,000 for *Angel and the Badman* [1947], and Gig Young at $25,000 for *City that Never Sleeps* [1953]. As with most contracts, the question arose about the right to dub Young's voice for foreign-language versions. Approval was granted by MGM production chief Dore Schary once Republic offered to have Young's dialogue translated into French, German, Italian, and Spanish by the same overseas firms that did MGM's dubbing. Another MGM loan-out, John Carroll was the subject of an unusual reciprocal arrangement whereby Republic not only paid $35,000 for his services but granted an option at the same figure for MGM to borrow John Wayne within one year from the completion of *Flying Tigers*. MGM exercised the option and paired Wayne with Joan Crawford in their melodrama *Reunion in France* [1942].

Some loan-out negotiations failed to materialize. In August of 1938 Republic offered Samuel Goldwyn $75,000 for Randolph Scott to play Sam Houston in *Man of Conquest* [1939] but Scott instead was signed by Cecil B. DeMille for *Union Pacific*. Learning one year later that the Ritz brothers owed 20th Century-Fox one more picture at $60,000 under terms of their contract, Republic attempted to buy the picture commitment to place them in *Hit Parade of 1941* [1940]. Unwilling to be loaned, the brothers requested and received a release from their Fox contract.

On loan from Paramount in 1941, Patricia Morison objected to both script and wardrobe and balked at participating in Gene Autry's *The Singing Hill* [1941] whereupon Paramount suspended her and substituted Virginia Dale. Craig Stevens from Warner Bros. was originally set at $1200 to star as John Bennett, Jr. in *Moonlight*

Masquerade [1942] but re-casting the role with Dennis O'Keefe upped Republic's cost to $7500. Conversely, when Peter Lorre who was on loan from Lorre, Inc. at $30,000 bowed out of *The Flame* [1947], Broderick Crawford stepped into the part of Ernie Hicks at a cost-effective $20,000. On a more even keel, George Macready from Columbia was the tentative choice to play Mayrant Sidneye in *Wake of the Red Witch* [1949] for $10,667 but he was replaced before principal photography commenced by Luther Adler at a flat $10,000.

A convoluted deal by usual standards was transacted in 1948 when Howard Welsch of Fidelity Pictures acquired Jane Russell on loan-out from Howard Hughes for *Montana Belle*. Providing partial financing and intending to release the independent production, Republic also furnished their facilities, a number of acting regulars, the majority of technical personnel, and loaned to Welsch actor Roy Barcroft and cameraman Jack Marta. Subsequent to its completion, however, Hughes bought out all interests in the film and eventually released the western through RKO in 1952.

Compared to their number of imports, Republic's export quota was minimal. Apart from John Wayne's outside ventures, William Newell was loaned to MGM for *Libeled Lady* [1936] and Donald Barry went to 20th Century-Fox for *The Purple Heart* [1943]. During 1944 when he was earning $600 per week as a term-contract player, Roy Rogers trooped with Trigger to *Hollywood Canteen* at Warner Bros. who Republic charged $2000 weekly for their combined performance. Also in 1944 Dale Evans was loaned to Sydney Williams for *The Big Show-Off* and Adele Mara to James A. Fitzpatrick for *Song of Mexico*, both independent productions released by Republic. The most frequent loan-out, Grant Withers traveled to MGM for *Dangerous Partners* [1945], to 20th Century-Fox for *My Darling Clementine* [1946], and with Estelita Rodriguez to Pine-Thomas Productions for *Tropic Zone* [1951], released by Paramount.

JOHN AGAR
[Vanguard] *Sands of Iwo Jima*

ROBERT ALLEN
[20th Century-Fox] *Fighting Thoroughbreds*

JOHN ARCHER
[20th Century-Fox]
The Purple V
Shantytown

JAMES ARNESS
[Batjac] *Flame of the Islands*

NILS ASTHER
[Paramount] *Mystery Broadcast*

DOROTHY BABB
[Paramount] *Earl Carroll Sketchbook*

WENDY BARRIE
[RKO] *Public Enemies*

CHICK CHANDLER
[20th Century-Fox] *The Mysterious Miss X*

JOHN CARROLL
[MGM] *Flying Tigers, Hit Parade of 1943*

DANE CLARK
[20th Century-Fox] *Moonrise*

ROD CAMERON
[Paramount] *G-Men Vs. The Black Dragon, Secret Service in Darkest Africa*

JOHN BARRYMORE, JR.
[RKO] *Thunderbirds*

HARRY CAREY, JR.
[Argosy] *Rio Grande*

WALTER BRENNAN
[Goldwyn] *Affairs of Cappy Ricks*

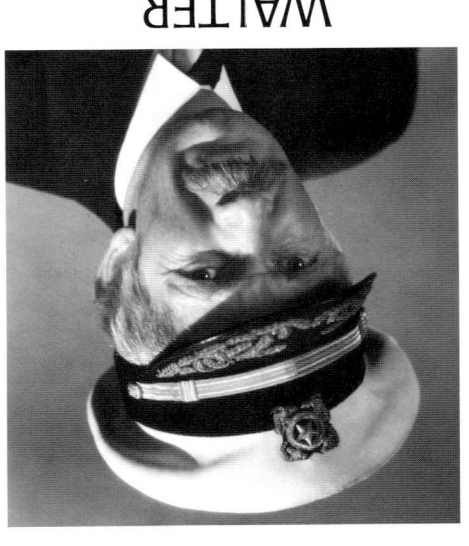

MAMO CLARK
[MGM] *Robinson Crusoe of Clipper Island*

MILDRED COLES
[Warner Bros.] *Sleepytime Gal*

JOHNNY COY
[Paramount] *Earl Carroll Sketchbook*

JOHN CRAVEN
[MGM] *Someone to Remember*

WENDELL COREY
[Imperadio] *Laughing Anne*

VIRGINIA DALE
[Paramount] *The Singing Hill*

HENRY DANIELS
[MGM] *The Chicago Kid*

ELLEN DREW
[Paramount] *Ice-Capades Revue*

SALLY EILERS
[RKO] *Lady, Behave!*

JOHN DEREK
[Columbia] *Thunderbirds, Sea of Lost Ships*

PHILIP DORN
[MGM] *I've Always Loved You*

CLAIRE DODD
[Warner Bros.] *Navy Born*

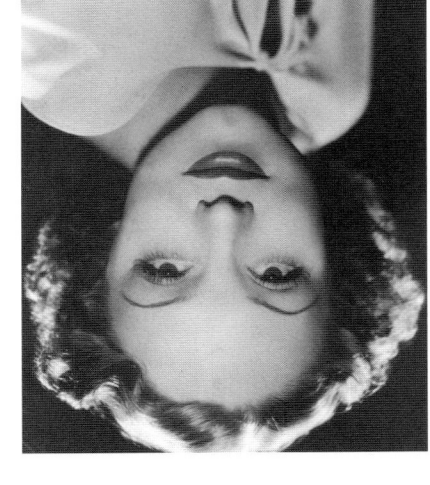

DORIS DAVENPORT
[Goldwyn] *Behind the News*

ALBERT DEKKER
[Paramount] *Yokel Boy, In Old California, In Old Oklahoma*

RICHARD DENNING
[Paramount] *Ice-Capades Revue*

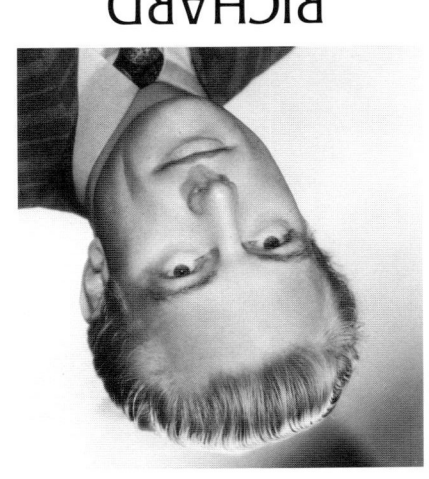

PATRICIA ELLIS
[Warner Bros.] *Rhythm in the Clouds*

PATRICIA FARR
[Columbia] *Lady, Behave!*

MONA FREEMAN
[Paramount] *That Brennan Girl*

YVONNE FURNEAUX
[Associated British] *Lisbon*

RICHARD FRASER
[Warner Bros.] *Thumbs Up*

BETTY FURNESS
[MGM] *The President's Mystery*

FRANCES GIFFORD
[Paramount] *Jungle Girl*

DICK HOGAN
[RKO] *Rancho Grande*

WILLIAM HENRY
[MGM] *Mama Runs Wild*

SUSAN HAYWARD
[Paramount]
Sis Hopkins, Hit Parade of 1943, The Fighting Seabees

WILLIAM HALL
[MGM] *Escape by Night*

VIRGINIA GREY
[MGM] *Ladies in Distress*

MIRIAM GOLDEN
[MGM] *Specter of the Rose*

VIRGINIA GILMORE
[Goldwyn] *Mr. District Attorney in the Carter Case*

BILLY GILBERT
[RKO] *Army Girl*

JOHN HUBBARD
[Roach] *Who Killed Aunt Maggie?*

CAROL HUGHES
[Warner Bros.] *Meet the Boy Friend*

BEN JOHNSON
[Argosy] *Rio Grande*

BRENDA JOYCE
[20th Century-Fox] *Thumbs Up*

ANDREA LEEDS
[Warner Bros.] *It Could Happen to You*

MARJORIE LORD
[Universal] *Shantytown*

WILLIAM LUNDIGAN
[MGM] *Head.n' for God's Country*

MARY McLEOD
[MGM] *London Blackout Murders*
The Purple V

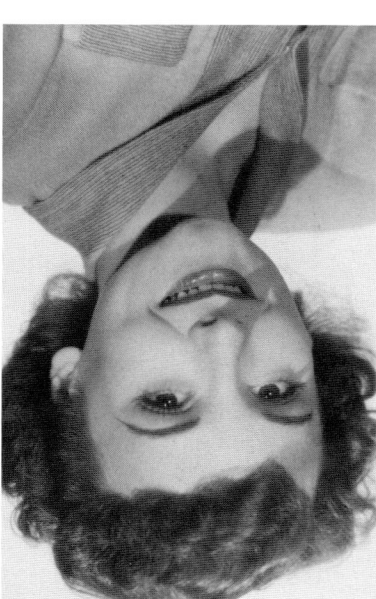

PETER MILES
[Roach] *The Red Pony*

MARIE McDONALD
[Paramount] *A Scream in the Dark*

VICTOR McLAGLEN
[Everest] *Trouble in the Glen*

JIMMY LYDON
[RKO] *Bowery Boy*
[Paramount] *My Best Gal*

FAYE MARLOWE
[20th Century-Fox] *Rendezvous With Annie*

MAE MARSH
[20th Century-Fox] *The Quiet Man*

ROBERT MITCHUM
[Vanguard] *The Red Pony*

JACKIE MORAN
[Selznick] *Michael O'Halloran*

DOROTHY MORRIS
[MGM] *Someone to Remember*

AL MURPHY
[RKO] *Angel and the Badman*

MARY MURPHY
[Paramount] *Make Haste to Live, A Man Alone*

ANNE NAGEL
[Warner Bros.] *Escape by Night*

CONRAD NAGEL
[Hirliman] *The Girl from Mandalay*

MICHAEL O'SHEA
[Stromberg] *Man from Frisco*

GORDON OLIVER
[Warner Bros.] *Youth on Parole*

MABEL PAIGE
[Paramount] *Someone to Remember*

DENNIS O'KEEFE
[RKO] *Affairs of Jimmy Valentine*

MAUREEN O'HARA
[20th Century-Fox] *Rio Grande*

MARTHA O'DRISCOLL
[Paramount] *Youth on Parade*

ELLA NEAL
[Paramount] *Mysterious Doctor Satan*

GAIL PATRICK
[Paramount] *Man of Conquest*

LEONARD PENN
[MGM] *Ladies in Distress*

BARBARA PEPPER
[RKO] *Portia on Trial*

WALTER PIDGEON
[MGM] *Dark Command*

JEAN PORTER
[MGM] *San Fernando Valley*

MALA POWERS
[RKO] *City That Never Sleeps, Geraldine*

PURNELL PRATT
[Paramount] *Join the Marines*

DICK PURCELL
[Warner Bros.] *Navy Blues*

JOHNNY SANDS
[Vanguard] *Affairs of Geraldine, The Fabulous Texan*

FRANK SHIELDS
[Goldwyn] *Affairs of Cappy Ricks*

GAIL RUSSELL
[Paramount] *Angel and the Badman, Moonrise, Wake of the Red Witch*

SHEILA RYAN
[20th Century-Fox] *Pardon My Stripes, Song of Texas*

ALBERT RUIZ
[Paramount] *Hit Parade of 1947*

ANN RUTHERFORD
[MGM] *Public Cowboy No. 1*

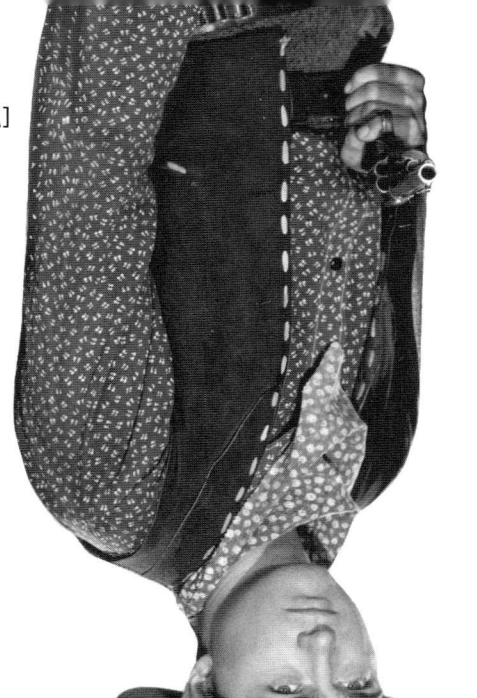

MIKHAIL RASUMNY
[Paramount] *Yokel Boy*

PHIL SILVERS
[MGM] Hit Parade of 1941

CHARLES SMITH
[Paramount] Youth on Parade

JAMES STEPHENSON
[Warner Bros.] Wolf of New York

JUNE STOREY
[20th Century-Fox]
Orphans of the Street, Down in "Arkansaw"

WILLIAM TALMAN
[RKO] City that Never Sleeps

PHILLIP TERRY
[Paramount] Public Enemies

MARGARET TALLICHET
[Selznick] A Desperate Adventure

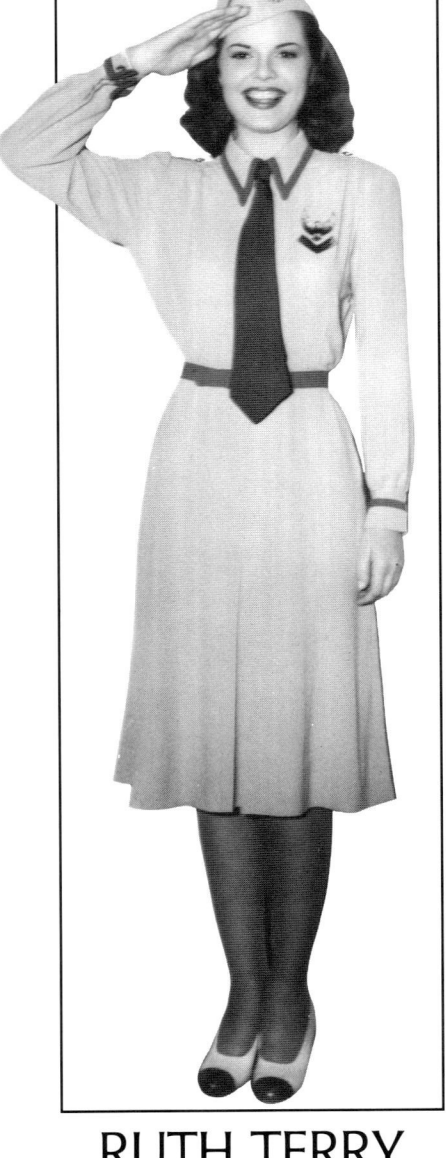

RUTH TERRY

[Hughes] *Rookies on Parade*

AUDREY TOTTER

[Columbia] *Woman They Almost Lynched, Champ for a Day*

JUNE TRAVIS

[Warner Bros.]
Circus Girl, Exiled to Shanghai, Join the Marines

FORREST TUCKER

[Realist] *Brimstone*
[Elliott-McGowan] *Hellfire*
[Everest] *Trouble in the Glen*
[Imperadio] *Laughing Anne*

LUANA WALTERS

[Paramount] *Mexicali Rose*

JACQUELINE WELLS

[Warner Bros.] *Back in the Saddle*

ARLEEN WHELAN

[20th Century-Fox] *Sabotage*

MARIE WILSON
[Warner Bros.] *Should Husbands Work?*

NATALIE WOOD
[Universal] *Driftwood*

WILLIAM WRIGHT
[Paramount] *The Devil Pays Off*

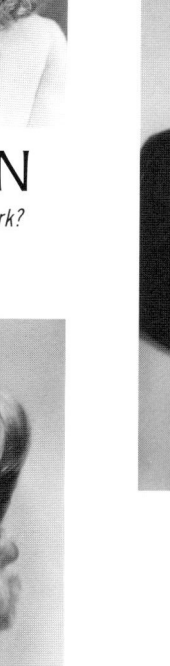

MARIS WRIXON
[Warner Bros.] *Jeepers Creepers*

CONSTANCE WORTH
[Columbia] *G-Men Vs. The Black Dragon*

CHARLENE WYATT
[Paramount] *Michael O'Halloran*

GIG YOUNG
[MGM] *City that Never Sleeps*

FREE-LANCE AND DAY PLAYERS

Most ubiquitous in the studio system's performer census were the free-lance and day players. Hollywood's hard-working middle class whose familiar faces and personalities in support of the leads were crucial to the proper casting mix. While sharing the limelight and audiences' affections with their star contemporaries, they were equally respected by directors and crews as the essence of dependability for the solid performances and dedicated professionalism brought to every picture. Although the distinction between the two categories tended to blur somewhat since all day players worked free-lance, true free-lancers were not considered day players because they signed lengthier commitments by the week instead of the day at customarily higher fees to enact the more important characterizations. Like the day players, free-lancers were sometimes represented by talent agents but occasionally contracted directly with studio casting offices for their services. Accepting a wide range of acting opportunities from unbilled bit parts through featured and starring roles as circumstances dictated, they were dignified under terms of the Screen Actors Guild Minimum Contract for Free-Lance Players which stipulated at least one week's salary per week regardless of the fractional number of days needed to complete a performance. As of 1943, a week at Republic was deemed to start at 12:01 a.m. Sunday and end at midnight the next Saturday, with Wednesday designated as payday. Salaries and commitments were generally limited at Republic but could fluctuate with the prevailing trade winds. After portraying the title role in Republic's first three Dick Tracy serials as a term-contract player, Ralph Byrd reached one of the higher notes on the pay scale when he returned as a free-lancer for *Dick Tracy Vs. Crime, Inc.* [1941] at $1000 per week on a five-week guarantee. On the more affluent distaff side, Jean Rogers in what would be her only Republic appearance signed for the Allan Lane hockey picture *Gay Blades* [1946] at $1000 per week on a three-week guarantee plus options

involved, invariably at least a minor support and walk-ons that contributing essential structure, the cast maintained a lower yet no less visible profile in the day players over Republic, Universal, RKO, Goldwyn, and Columbia at salaries of from $75 to $250.

A rung below free-lancers, day players and wage record that showed eight jobs spread over Republic, Universal, RKO, Goldwyn, and Columbia at salaries of from $75 to $250.

A rung below free-lancers, day players compiled his entire 1942 employment and wage record that showed eight jobs spread over Republic, Universal, to qualify. Republic obligingly and dress — the dress extras realized for Lewis' higher rate on the western when wages were frozen. In order to qualify, Republic obligingly and dress — the dress extras realized approximately 50% more each day for furnishing their own tuxedos, evening gowns, and other gala apparel or specialty costumes. Cast essentially as human background set decoration, extras constituted an extensive Hollywood work force, eking out a living by traveling from lot to lot wherever work became available and partially subsisting on free studio lunches. The extent of

demand for extras was such during 1941 that Republic doled out $253,541 for their services, placing them fourth in disbursements behind MGM, Paramount, and 20th Century-Fox of 11 studios.

Intertwined with the history of the movie colony were its performer unions and the industry-sponsored Central Casting Corporation. Under the auspices of the Association of Motion Picture Producers alliance founded by the major film companies, Central Casting was established in 1925 and funded by signatories as a clearing house where extras registered their names and checked for job assignments. At first casting their extras through Vance Carroll, the Los Angeles representative for the Chicago-based WLS Artists Bureau, Republic switched to Central Casting in 1941 upon joining AMPP. By this time the Screen Actors Guild had become firmly entrenched as the ecumenical representational union voice for their members. Organized from Depression-era desperation after studios in 1933 mandated 50% salary cuts for contract players and 20% reductions for independent performers who had no unified recourse but to accept the decreases, SAG also spoke for the extras until 1945 when this contingent was spun off into the Screen Extras Guild which then negotiated pay scales and working conditions with producers.

One of the greatest financial impacts felt by Republic in honoring their SEG contract occurred on *Sands of Iwo Jima* [1950]. Production of this John Wayne World War II epic called for extensive beachhead location shooting at Southern California's Camp Pendleton Marine Corps base where security and other restrictions limited the number of Republic personnel who could be brought on-site. SEG contended, however, that the military training grounds fell within their 300-mile zone of jurisdiction and that they could provide a substantial number of ex-Marine extras for battle scenes. Caught in the crossfire of red tape, Republic preserved the peace by using non-union Marines from the base and paying SEG $12,000 in non-compliance damages.

When work weeks consisted of six days as they did throughout most of the Republic era, weekly rates were usually quoted at five times the daily rate. This amounted to a 1/5 savings to studios on the long-term differential as opposed to paying six times the daily figure in the event a day player's presence was required for a longer than anticipated interval. Before attaining screen prominence as Rhonda Fleming, Marilyn Lane under her original stage-name spelling of Ronda Fleming hired on at Republic as a dance-hall girl for her first film *In Old Oklahoma* [1943] at $25 per day or $125 per week, representing a potential gross reduction of $25 if her services were needed beyond the second or third day when the conversion was normally applied.

A subculture of the day players, extras comprised the non-speaking sector of a picture's populace whose ranks were further compartmentalized as atmosphere, character, specialized, and dress — the dress extras realized approximately 50% more each day for furnishing their own tuxedos, evening gowns, and other gala apparel or specialty costumes. Cast essentially as human background set decoration, extras constituted an extensive Hollywood work force, eking out a living by traveling from lot to lot wherever work became available and partially subsisting on free studio lunches. The extent of

More characteristic of the average free-lance situation was George J. Lewis whose numerous appearances in Republic features, westerns, and serials ran the gamut from co-star to character cameos. Typical was his participation in the Three Mesquiteers series entry *The Blocked Trail* [1943] as fourth leading man credited fifth behind stars Tom Tyler, Bob Steele, Jimmie Dodd, and leading lady Helen Deverell. For his one week of work on this title during December of 1942 Lewis received $150 once the figure was ruled appropriate according to guidelines set by the Salary Stabilization Unit, a U. S. government agency empowered to freeze wages for the duration of World War II. Pending a review determination, Republic at first held $25 of the $150 in abeyance since Lewis was earning only $125 per week for the serial *G-Men Vs. The Black Dragon* [1942] on October 3 when wages were frozen. In order to qualify, Republic obligingly compiled his entire 1942 employment and wage record that showed eight jobs spread over Republic, Universal, RKO, Goldwyn, and Columbia at salaries of from $75 to $250.

A rung below free-lancers, day players maintained a lower yet no less visible profile in the cast structure, contributing essential minor support and walk-ons that invariably involved at least a

modicum of dialogue. Their mantle was self-descriptive if somewhat misleading since many times they were engaged for more than one day on a picture. In the early days, Republic commonly signed day players to an Artists Contract at an agreed-upon fixed price for the few specified days projected to complete a minor part. During the late 1930s the Artists Contract was superseded by the now-standard Day Player Agreement which carried both daily and weekly salary scales, a variable form that protected the players' financial interests on a day-to-day basis while enabling studios to pay the lesser amount depending on the length of employment.

for additional commitments that were never exercised.

An added incentive for some free-lancers including Rogers was extended in the form of options exercisable at Republic's discretion to place them under term-picture contracts following their immediate assignment. In June of 1947 executive in charge of talent Jack Grant surveyed the affected performers for the two-year period from July 1, 1945, to date and reported that options on William Carter, Sterling Holloway, and the Riders of the Purple Sage had been exercised, 12 others had not been exercised, and those on Virginia Lindley, Eddy Waller, and Max Terhune were still pending final decisions.

TREVOR BARDETTE WILLIAM BENEDICT

HOOPER
ATCHLEY

WADE
BOTELER

LYNTON BRENT

VIRGINIA
CARROLL

EDWARD
CASSIDY

WHEATON
CHAMBERS

JEROME COWAN

TRISTRAM COFFIN

LLOYD CORRIGAN

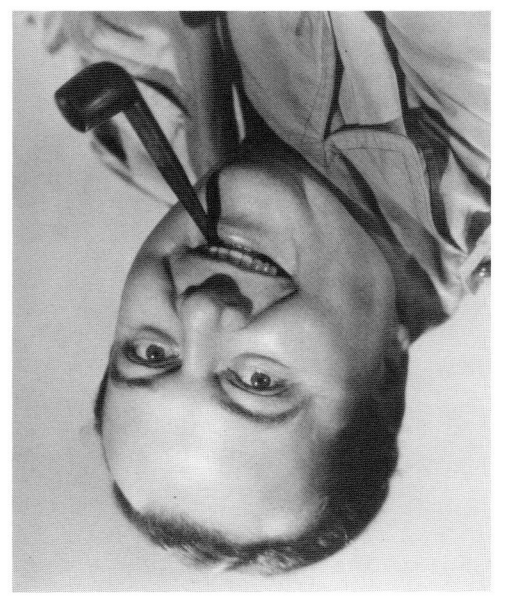

CHESTER CLUTE

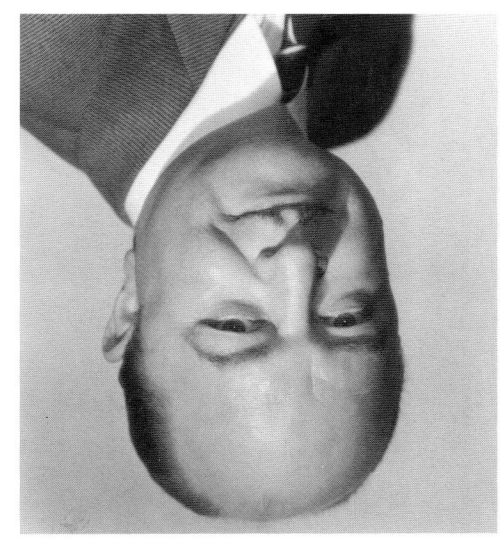

GEORGE CLEVELAND

TOM CHATTERTON

LANE CHANDLER

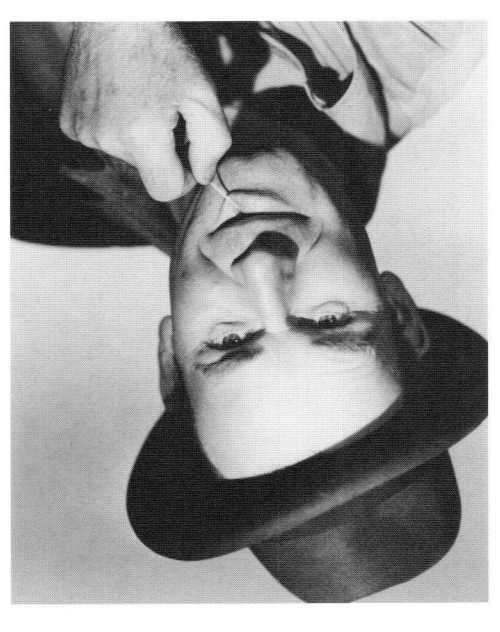

GEORGE CHANDLER

JOSEPH CREHAN

JOHN DAVIDSON

JOHN DILSON

MAUDE EBURNE

JOHN ELDREDGE

DICK ELLIOTT

FERN EMMETT

VIRGINIA FARMER

HARRISON GREENE

JODY GILBERT

WILLIAM FORREST

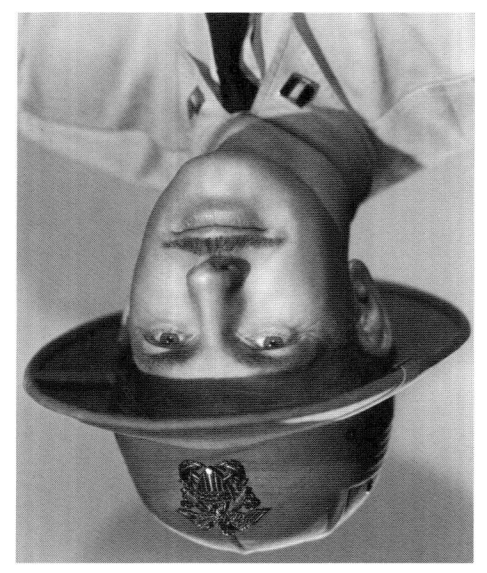

MARTIN GARRALAGA

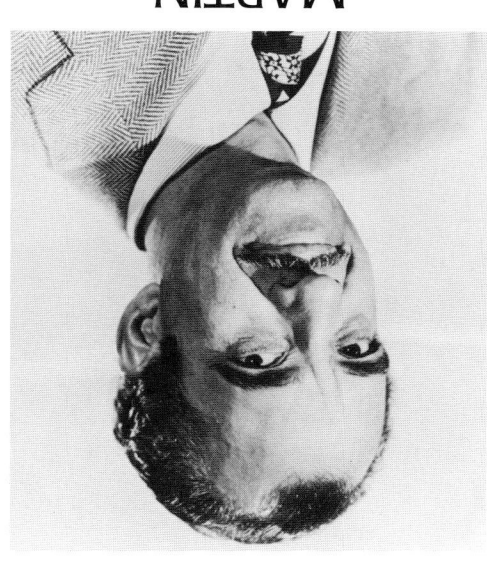

BYRON FOULGER

SAM FLINT

PAUL FIX

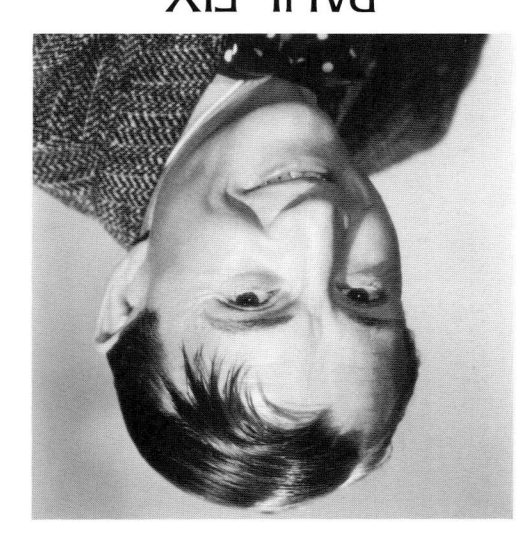

GEORGE FISHER

WILLIAM HAADE

JOHN HAMILTON

HARRY HARVEY

PAUL HARVEY

HOWARD HICKMAN

RUSSELL HICKS

EARLE HODGINS

ROBERT HOMANS

CY KENDALL

EDDIE KANE

FRANK JAQUET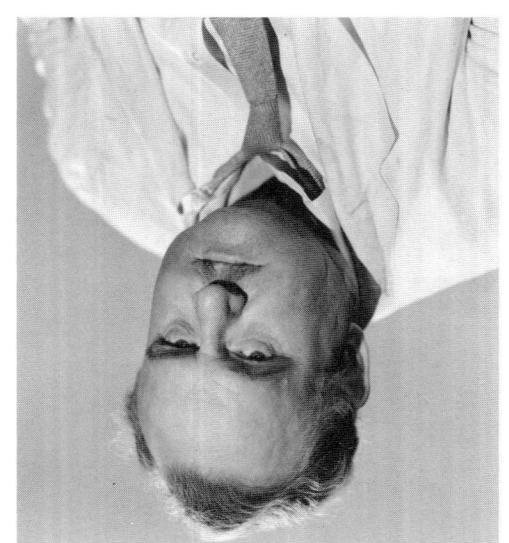

SELMER JACKSON

JACK INGRAM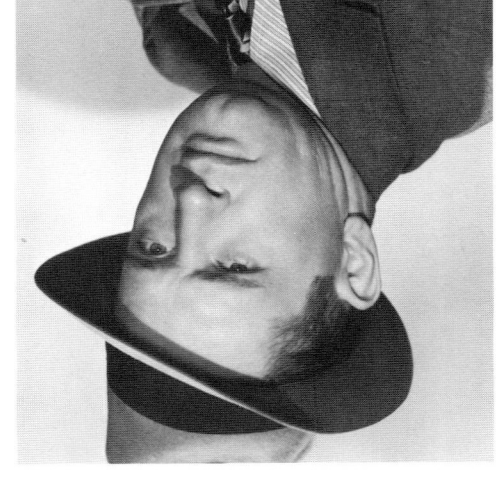

LLOYD INGRAHAM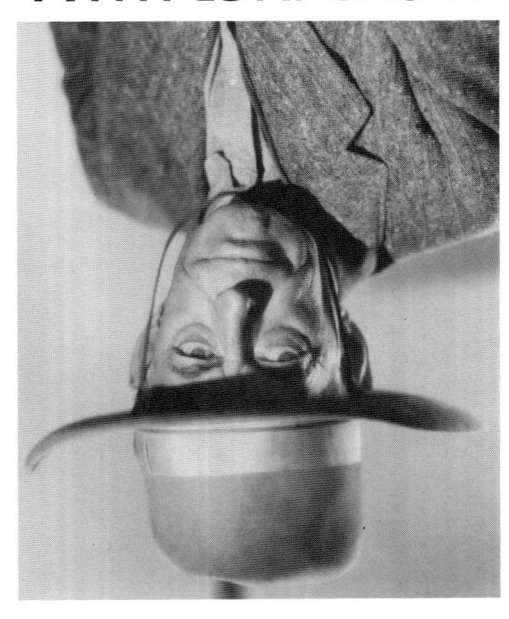

PAUL HURST

OLIN HOWLIN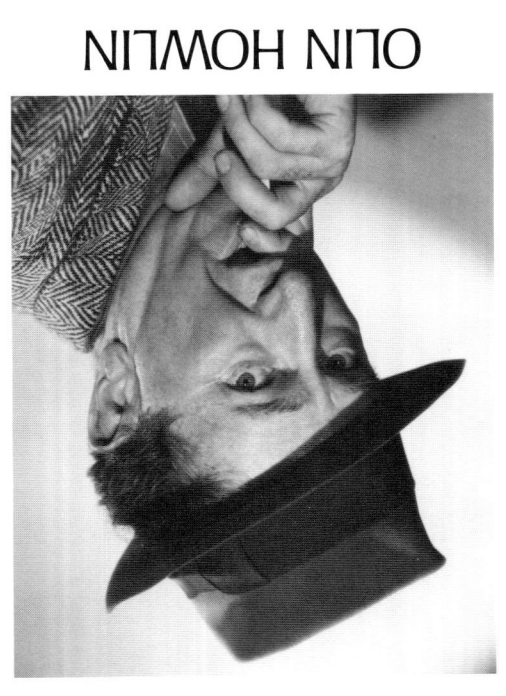

JACK LaRUE

NOLAN LEARY

GEORGE J. LEWIS

GEORGE LLOYD

ARTHUR LOFT

J. FARRELL MacDONALD

MARY MacLAREN

MARIAN MARTIN

EMORY PARNELL

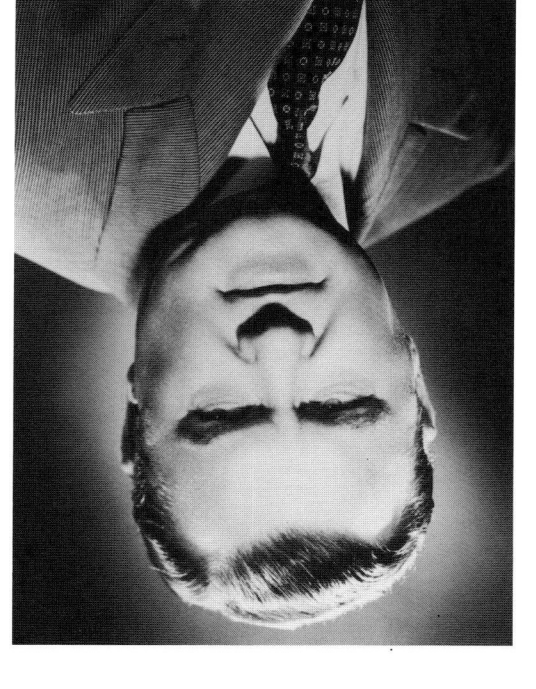

JACK O'SHEA

FRANKLIN PANGBORN

FRANK O'CONNOR

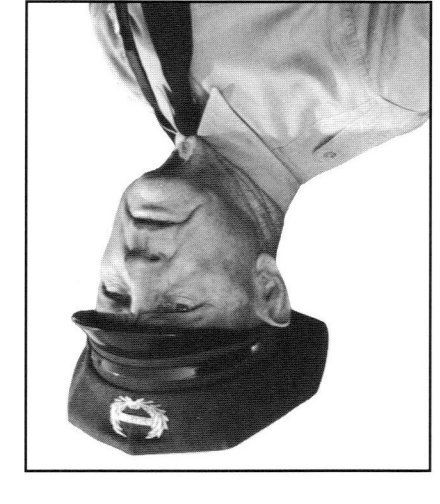

GEORGE MEEKER

JAY NOVELLO

CHARLES MIDDLETON

FRANCIS PIERLOT

HAL PRICE

HERBERT RAWLINSON

ADDISON RICHARDS

EDWIN STANLEY

CHARLES SULLIVAN

GRADY SUTTON

FERRIS TAYLOR

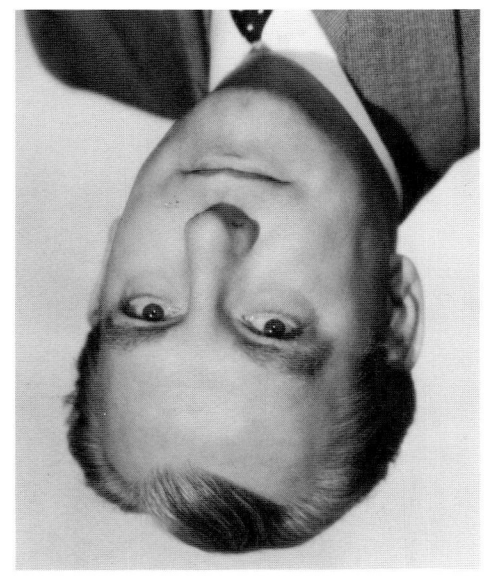
EMMETT VOGAN

MINERVA URECAL

HARRY TYLER

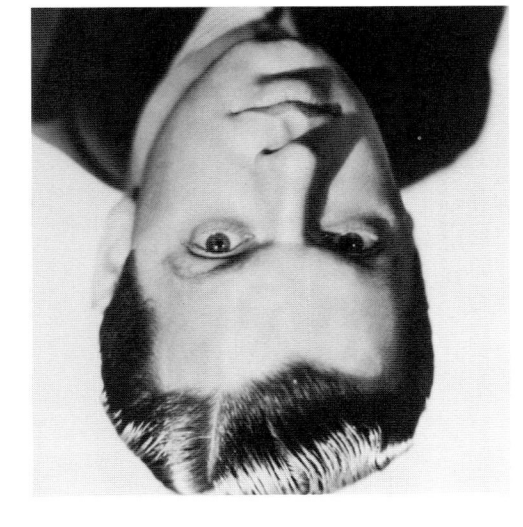
ARCHIE TWITCHELL

CHARLES TROWBRIDGE

MARY TREEN

ANDREW TOMBES

FORREST TAYLOR

RAY WALKER

PIERRE WATKIN

CRANE WHITLEY

BOB WILKE

CHARLES WILLIAMS

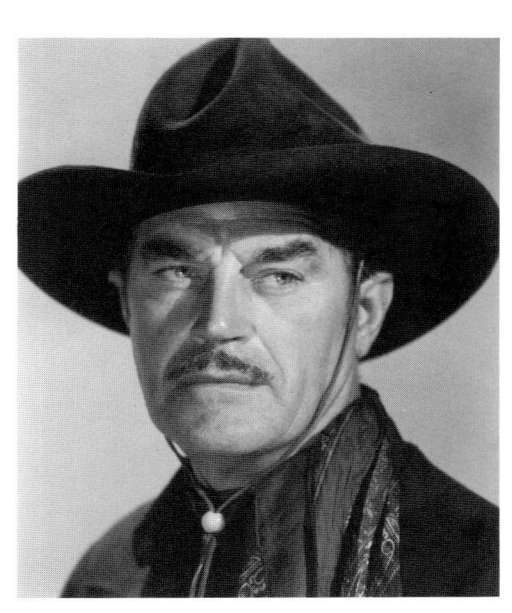

HARRY WOODS

HANK WORDEN

WILL WRIGHT

WESTERN PLAYERS

Right at home on the Hollywood range tending a blue-ribbon herd of B westerns and the stars who made them prime box-office, Republic stamped their unmistakable brand on 386 of these releases which excluded serials and such A westerns as *Johnny Guitar* [1954] and *The Road to Denver* [1955] among many others. Budgets were one bench mark distinguishing the two classifications with the majority of B westerns allocated a modest $20,000 to $100,000, though some of the later Roy Rogers entries in Trucolor bucked the limits at over $300,000. Format was another criteria since B westerns could be strictly or loosely defined as series having the common denominator of continuing characters played by the same or different stars or stars appearing essentially as themselves in a succession of otherwise individualistic pictures.

Analogous to the plot line in a number of their B westerns, Republic represented eastern money interests investing in western properties. This scenario found Herbert J. Yates during the mid-1930s logically expanding his film-laboratory holdings to include production by consolidating the Liberty, Monogram, and Mascot studios under a unified corporate banner. Among the human resources retained in these acquisitions, John Wayne started the tumbleweeds rolling at Republic and went on to become their foremost asset.

Starring in Republic's first film, aptly titled *Westward Ho* [1935], Wayne at the time was under contract to Trem Carr Pictures and appeared by arrangement with Carr who had joined Republic from the Monogram segment of the merger. Under terms of the initial contract for eight pictures, Carr charged Republic $1750 per film for Wayne's services, named Paul Malvern as producer, and retained script, director, and cast approval. In addition, Republic paid the premiums on Wayne's life, health, and accident insurance even though they retained no interest in the policies or proceeds which belonged solely to Carr.

Riding onto the Republic spread directly behind Wayne and under similar circumstances, Gene Autry

on May 17, 1935, had signed a Mascot contract which was transferred to Republic soon after Nat Levine's company joined the combine. Autry's original three-year pact with six-month options started at $100 per week for Republic's second production *Tumbling Tumbleweeds* [1935] and rose to $350 by midyear of 1938. From then on he was signed to yearly contracts, the first covering the 1938-39 period calling for $6000 each for the first two pictures and $10,000 each for the remainder. Payments thereafter escalated to $11,000 per picture in 1940-41, $12,000 in 1941-42, and $13,000 in 1942-43, though only three pictures were made under the last term.

On July 26, 1942, two days after *Bells of Capistrano* [1942] wound principal photography, Autry enlisted in the service and by the end of the year had attained the rank of technical sergeant in the Air Transport Command. He returned after the war to complete five more westerns for Republic.

Third in the chronology to implement Republic's western stars was the studio's first true sagebrush series: the Three Mesquiteers. Based upon characters from the popular novels by William Colt MacDonald who also wrote some of the screen treatments, the long-lived film series randomly set in either the old or contemporary west featured the exploits of Stony Brooke, Tucson Smith, Lullaby Joslin, and others played by a succession of 12 actors throughout a 51-title run.

Most recurrent in the lead role and the entire series as well, term contractee Bob Livingston portrayed Stony Brooke 29 times from 1936-38 and again from 1939-41 at salaries ranging from $125 to $350 per week. When Livingston briefly went on the disabled list in the midst of his first cycle, fellow stock player Ralph Byrd stepped in to pinch hit on *The Trigger Trio* [1937] at $150 per week. Subsequently taking up the Brooke part for eight films in 1938-39 at $3000 each under a term-picture contract, John Wayne stepped out briefly after completing the first four westerns to perform

his breakthrough role in United Artists' *Stagecoach* [1939], then came back for the remaining four titles. Following Livingston's interim return for 14 more oaters, Tom Tyler appeared in the final 13 and concluded the series on a two-year term contract starting at $150 and ending at $200 weekly.

The first and most frequent portrayer of Tucson Smith at 24 consecutive titles, Ray Corrigan started on a term contract at $75 per week with six-month escalations to $225 per week through 1938; thereafter he converted to a term-picture agreement that paid him $1000 each for his last six Mesquiteer appearances. Next in line to replace Corrigan, Duncan Renaldo earned $150 weekly on a 52-week basis during his seven outings. Wrapping up the final 20 titles, Bob Steele came under a term-picture deal compensating him $1250 each for the first four, then $1500 for each of the remaining 16.

Participating only in the lead-off *The Three Mesquiteers* [1936] as comedy relief Lullaby Joslin, Syd Saylor was paid $250 for satisfying one of his four term-picture commitments that year. A regular over the ensuing 21 titles, Max Terhune began his 36-month term contract at $75 per week and finished at $200 per week. His three successors, all under term-picture contracts, were Raymond Hatton at $600 per film for nine entries, Rufe Davis at $500 each for his first six titles and $650 apiece for the remaining eight, and Jimmie Dodd at $250 for each of his six appearances that concluded the action-packed series.

Paralleling the start of the Three Mesquiteers series in 1936, Republic added to their already prodigious annual number of B westerns in a contract with independent producer A. W. Hackel through his Supreme Pictures. Hackel delivered 16 westerns starring Bob Steele and eight starring Johnny Mack Brown.

Promoted as the King of the Cowboys and reigning the longest of his Republic saddle pals with 81 starring westerns under his belt, Roy Rogers started in 1938 as a

stock player at $75 per week. After 10 years and incremental salary raises to $1000 weekly, he converted in March of 1948 to a term-picture contract paying $21,000 each for 11 films over two years plus a one-time signing bonus of $10,000 for executing the deal and a $500 specialty clothing allowance per picture. When this two-year contract ended in February of 1950, Republic exercised their option for an additional six films in one year at $21,667 each, then by mutual consent extended the option for three more months through May of 1951 that paid Rogers $25,000 apiece for his last two westerns on the lot.

Chosen from a flock of applicants in a talent search to select Republic's next white hat, Don "Red" Barry was signed to a term contract in February of 1940 at a salary escalating from $150 to $225 weekly during the course of 29 low-budget westerns released between 1940 and 1944. Along with other of his peers who were also cast in non-western parts, Barry was credited under two different names which Republic felt would differentiate their screen images. Thus he was billed as Don "Red" Barry in Republic's westerns but otherwise as Donald Barry just as Bob Livingston went by his informal first name in westerns and Robert Livingston in features.

Wild Bill Elliott was the ordained split-personality moniker given William Elliott when he entered into a one-year term-picture contract for eight westerns at $2750 each with the contractual stipulation that he receive top billing. Apart from this commitment and not counted against any of his eight starring films, Elliott was paid $2000 for a cameo appearance in Roy Rogers' *Bells of Rosarita* [1945] and waived his top-billing clause on the condition of being credited first of the other cowboy guest stars.

With Elliott going great guns during 1943 while the Three Mesquiteers headed into the sunset, Republic saddled up a replacement series centering around an original character called John Paul Revere. Screen tests conducted on April 27 at the back-lot Melody Ranch resulted in Eddie Dew being designated for the lead at $100 per week on a

COWBOY	Films	1935	1936	1937	1938	1939	1940	1941	1942	1943	1944	1945	1946	1947	1948	1949	1950	1951	1952	1953	1954
John Wayne	8	3	5																		
Gene Autry	56	3	9	7	6	8	5	7	6				1	4							
The Three Mesquiteers	51		3	8	9	6	8	7	6	4											
Johnny Mack Brown	8		2	6																	
Bob Steele	16		3	8	5																
Roy Rogers	81				4	8	6	7	8	6	5	6	7	4	6	3	6	5			
Don Barry	29						5	8	7	8	1										
Bill Elliott	8									6	2										
John Paul Revere	4									2	2										
Johnny Rapidan	1										1										
Red Ryder	23										6	6	6	5							
Sunset Carson	15										4	6	5								
Allan Lane	44										3	3		2	8	7	7	5	5	4	
Monte Hale	19												4	2	3	7	3				
Rex Allen	19																4	4	5	5	1
Rough-Ridin' Kids	4																3	1			
TOTAL	386	6	22	29	24	22	24	29	27	26	24	21	23	17	17	17	20	17	11	9	1

40-week guarantee. Production began immediately on the first two titles, but even before they were released Republic bought out the remaining 33 weeks of Dew's contract for a $1000 settlement and recast the Revere role with Bob Livingston who was earning $16,000 annually on his current pact. Despite Livingston's presence in the next two entries, the star-crossed series was terminated after four films.

A lone stranger amid Republic's spate of B westerns was the one-shot sagebrush whodunit *The Laramie Trail* [1944] based upon Jackson Gregory's novel "Mystery at Spanish Hacienda." Seguing from his John Paul Revere duties at the same salary terms, Bob Livingston as hero Johnny Rapidan followed a convoluted trail of clues to ferret out the murderer from a number of red-herring prospects.

Aiming for a sure-fire success after John Paul Revere bit the dust, Republic — having scored earlier with their serial *Adventures of Red Ryder* [1940] — again hit home by adapting cartoonist Fred Harman's famous fighting redhead into 23 live-action features. Fresh from his own series, Bill Elliott took on the title role in the first 16 entries under two successive term-picture contracts calling for eight pictures in the first year at $3750 each, then eight more the second year at $4750 each. Cast as Red Ryder's juvenile sidekick Little Beaver, Bobby Blake was governed by a term-picture contract for four pictures in one year plus options that were exercised for four more at $300 each for the first eight films and $350 each for the second eight. Also under the four-plus-four annual arrangement, Alice Fleming as the Duchess was paid $350 for each of the first eight and $400 for each of the second eight in the series.

When Elliott departed the series, Republic filled Red Ryder's boots with Allan Lane under his term contract that specified pay escalations from $350 to $450 per week over the duration of the remaining seven titles. Concurrently, Alice Fleming was replaced by Martha Wentworth whose term-picture contract earned her $500 per film. Reprising Little Beaver throughout the entire series, Bobby Blake was raised to $400 for each of the last seven installments.

Republic intended to continue production on the popular Red Ryder westerns, but an option-renewal date with copyright owner Stephen Slesinger was overlooked in 1947 due to a clerical error. Contacted several days past the due date once the oversight was discovered, Slesinger agreed to a continuing relationship but suggested higher royalty payments. Feeling an increase would render their profit margin too tight, studio executives declined and the series lapsed into oblivion.

Republic passed a milestone in 1944 when they had eight different western series in release, the most ever in a single year. But the record for total westerns actually released to theaters was 29 in both 1937 and 1941. The debut of the Red Ryder series in 1944 also coincided with the studio's introduction of two more Saturday matinee idols. Slapping leather in 15 starring vehicles on a three-year term contract guaranteeing 40 weeks annual employment, Sunset Carson was compensated $150 per week the first year, $200 the second, and $250 the third. Allan Lane's longer stride was measured in three steps, the first consisting of six westerns produced and released in 1944-45 under a term contract at $250 per week. Following a one-year break to leave his imprint on the Red Ryder series, he returned to star as Allan "Rocky" Lane in 38 more films under the same contract terms but at salaries gradually increasing from $450 to $700 weekly through the end of the series in 1953.

During Lane's Red Ryder hiatus, Republic added to their roster by elevating Monte Hale from bit-player to starring status in his own singing-cowboy series which had the distinction of introducing both Magnacolor and its two-color Trucolor successor to the studio's B westerns. Working under six-month contracts, Hale started at $150 per week and finished at $300 in 1950.

Republic's twilight western star, singing cowboy Rex Allen shone in 19 films beginning in 1950 at $300 per week. The price of fame was reflected soon thereafter when he negotiated a contract extension with a raise to $1050 weekly that kicked in down the road. On top of the salary hike, Republic paid a supplementary $500 per picture to Allen for furnishing for himself and his stunt and riding double all modern wardrobe and all western wardrobe except the double's boots which the studio supplied. The allowance also covered rental of Allen's horse Koko and any other of his own horses made available on an as-needed basis, plus attendant gear and equipment including saddles and horse-transportation vans.

Adult western stars appealed to all age groups, but for their final series Republic targeted the youthful audience directly by casting juveniles as leads in the four Rough-Ridin' Kids installments. Pre-teens Michael Chapin as Red White and Eileen Janssen as Judy Dawson were hired under identical agreements, starting as free-lancers at $350 per week, then converting to one-year term contracts at $125 per week.

REX ALLEN

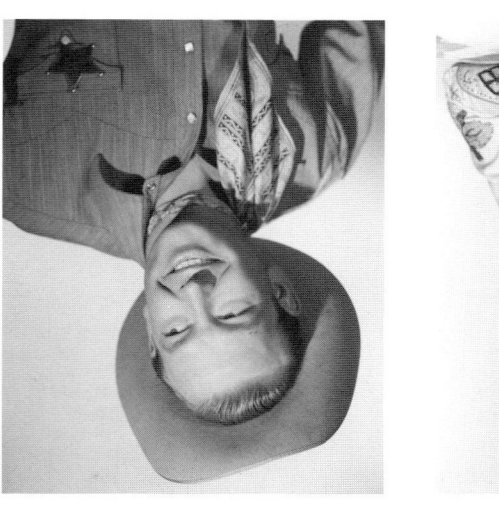
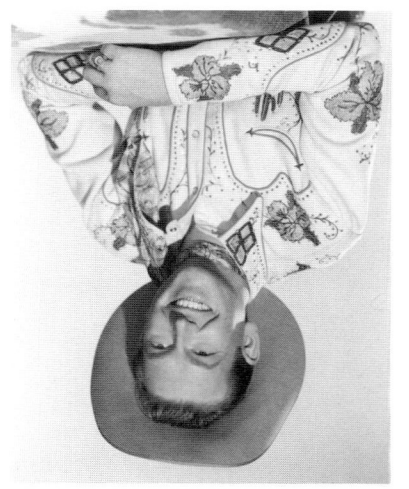
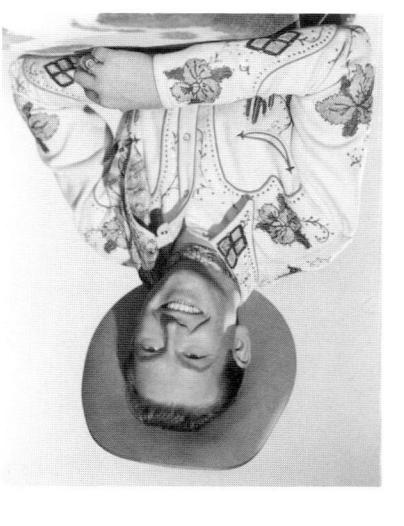

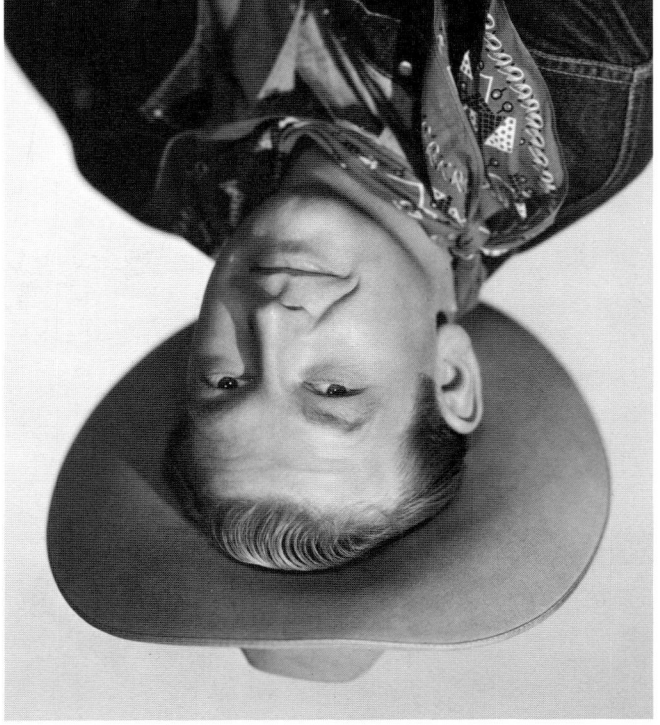

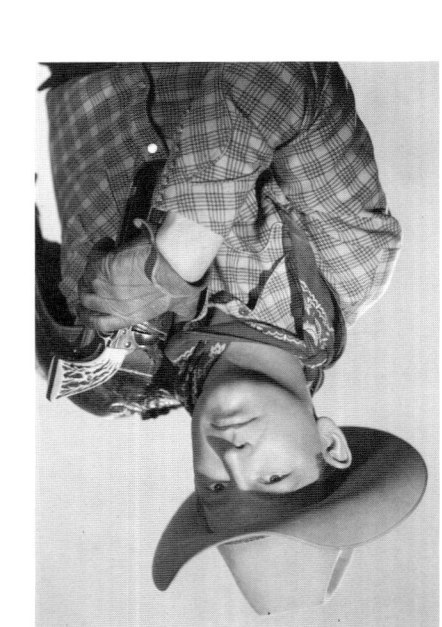

GENE

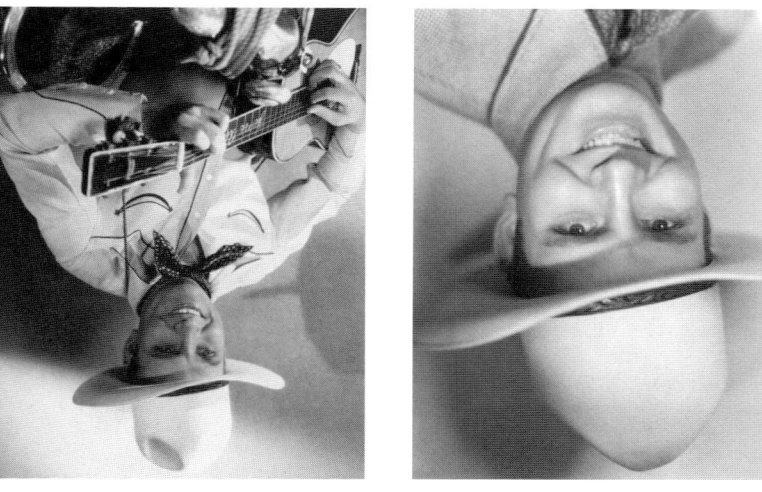
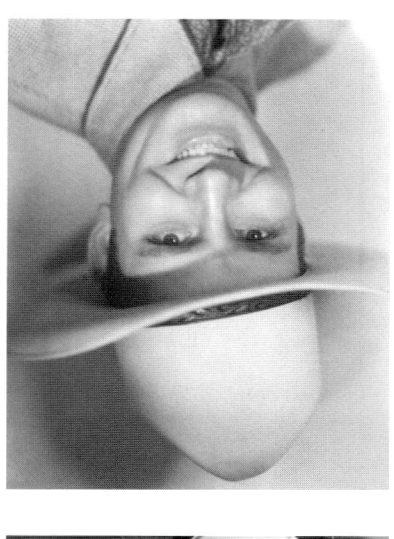
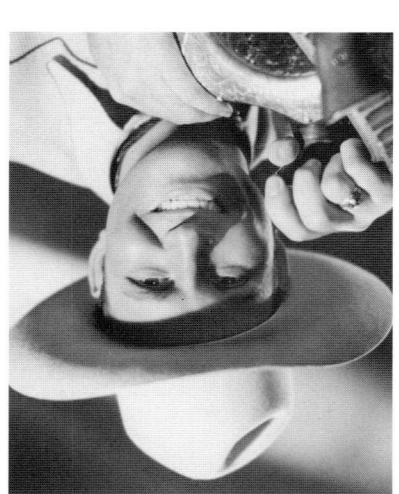
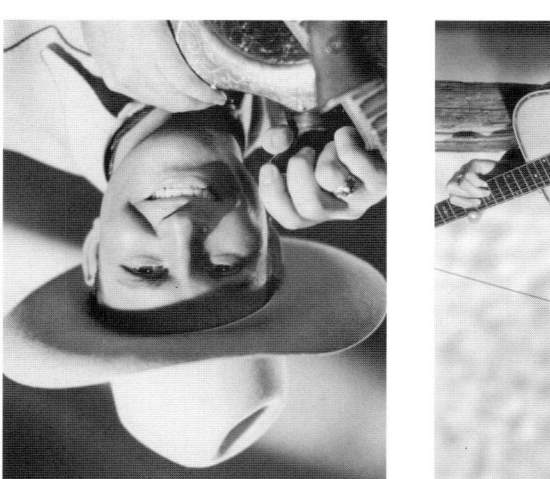

AUTRY

DON "RED"

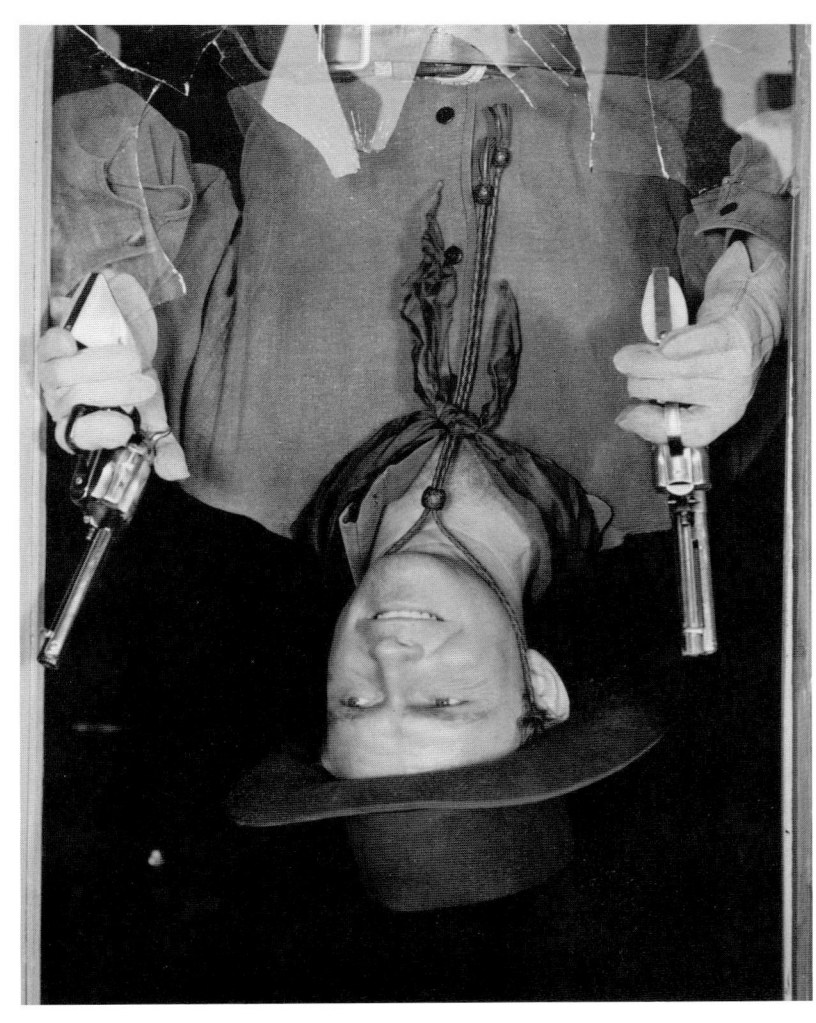

JOHNNY MACK BROWN

BARRY

SUNSET

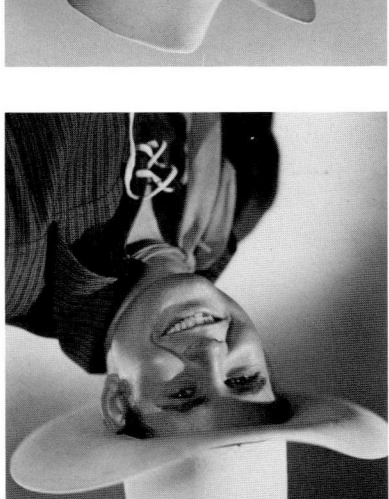
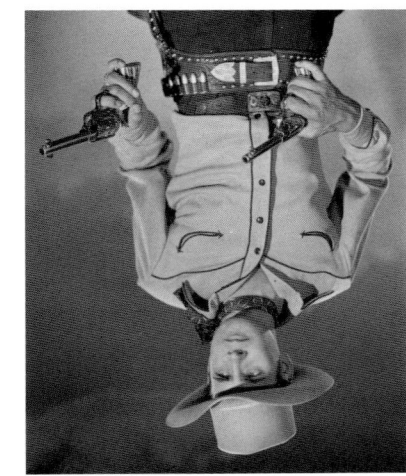

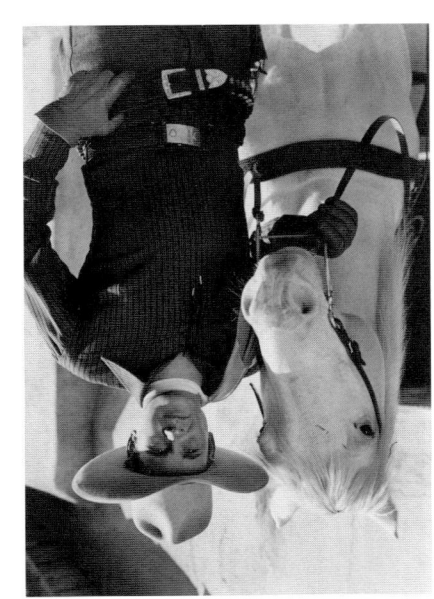

CARSON

WILD BILL

ELLIOTT

151

MONTE

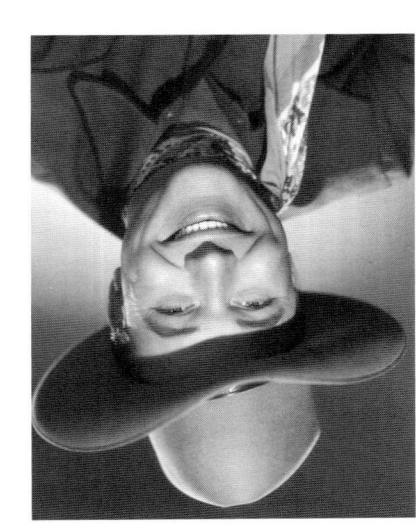

HALE

ALLAN LANE

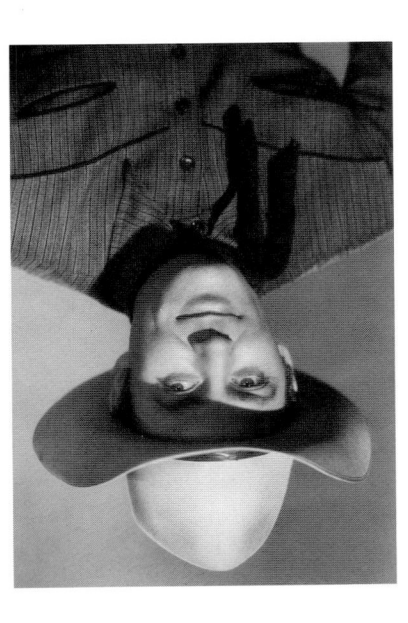

JOHN PAUL REVERE

BOB LIVINGSTON

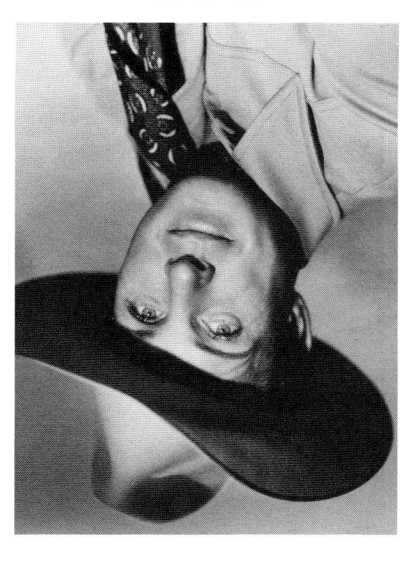

EDDIE DEW

BOB LIVINGSTON
JOHNNY RAPIDAN

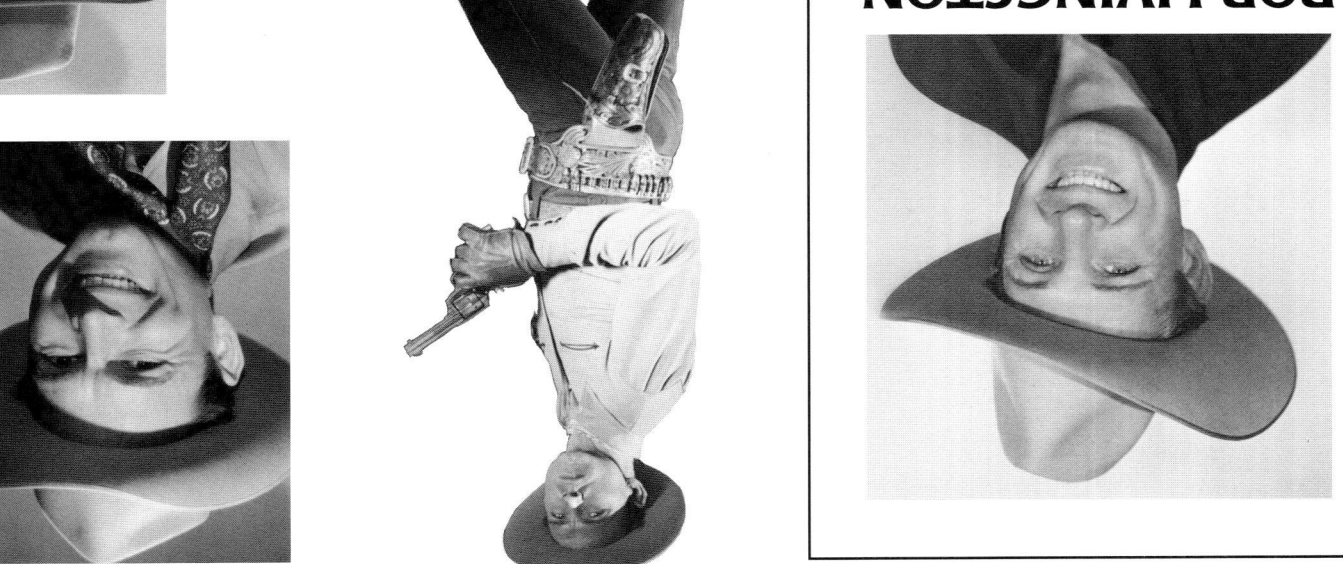

MICHAEL CHAPIN

EILEEN JANSSEN

ROUGH-RIDIN' KIDS

ROY

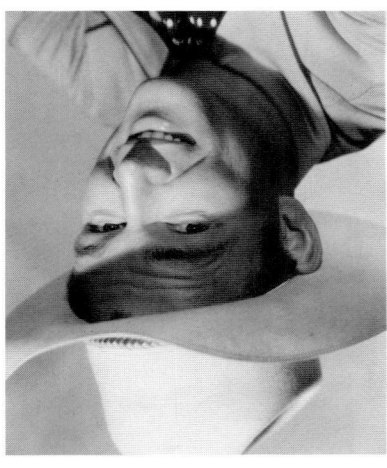

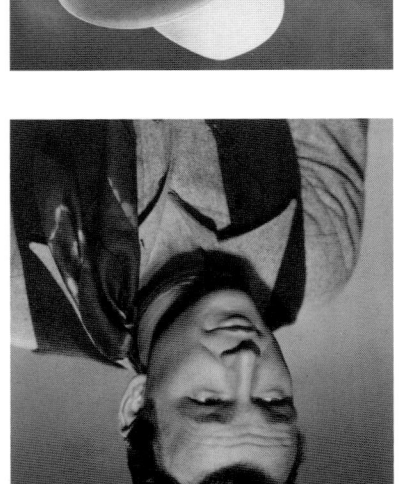
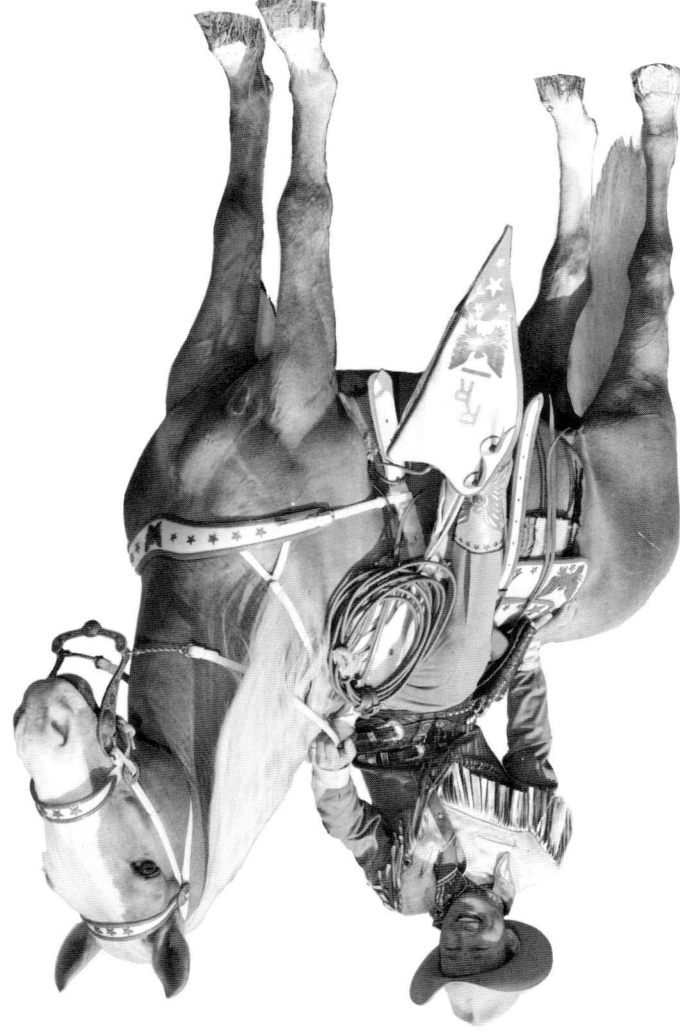

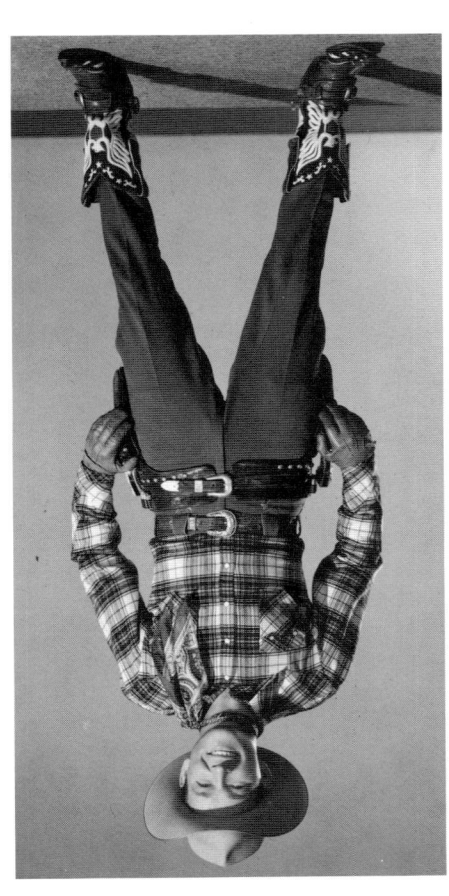

ROGERS

ALICE FLEMING

BOBBY BLAKE

RED

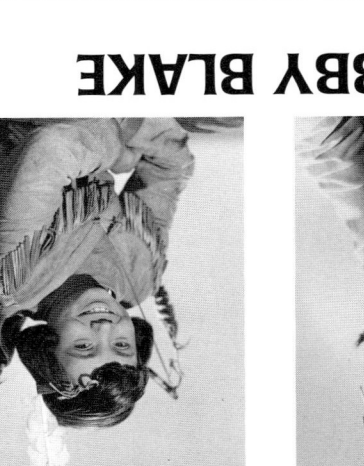

WILD BILL ELLIOTT

ALLAN LANE

RYDER

BOBBY BLAKE

MARTHA WENTWORTH

THE THREE

BOB STEELE

DUNCAN RENALDO

BOB STEELE

SYD SAYLOR

RALPH BYRD

RAY CORRIGAN

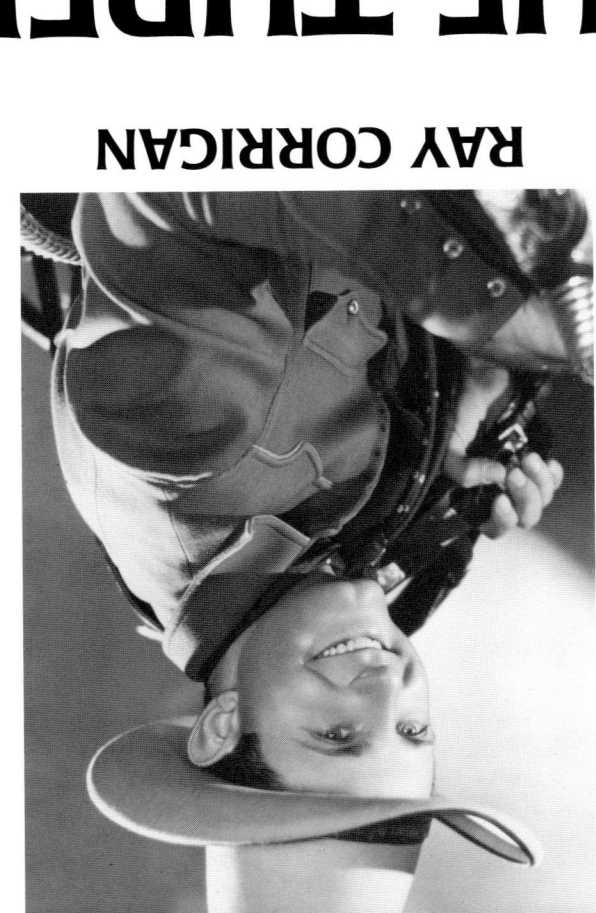

BOB STEELE

RUFE DAVIS

JIMMIE DODD

RAYMOND HATTON

BOB LIVINGSTON

MESQUITEERS PLAYERS

MAX TERHUNE

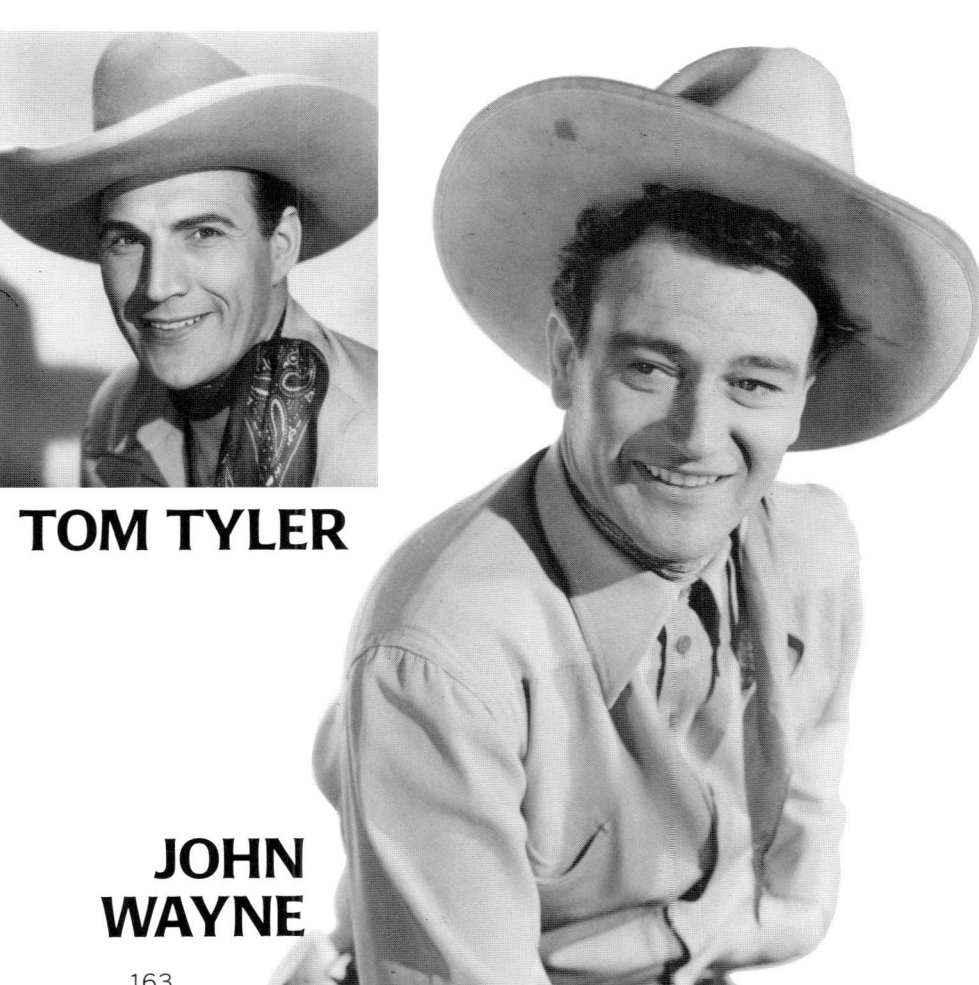
TOM TYLER

JOHN WAYNE

1. Saylor, Corrigan, Livingston [1].

3. Byrd, Corrigan, Terhune [1].

2. Terhune, Livingston, Corrigan [14].

THE THREI

4. Terhune, Wayne, Corrigan [6].

5. Hatton, Wayne, Corrigan [2].

6. Renaldo, Livingston, Hatton [7].

7. Steele, Livingston, Davis [7].

MESQUITEERS TRIOS

8. Davis, Tyler, Steele [7].

9. Tyler, Dodd, Steele [6].

JOHN

WAYNE

THE PLAYERS SUPER-INDEX

Thousands of faces graced the frames of Republic's pictures, and this Super-Index quantifies the appearances of every player who received screen credit in all films released by the studio including independent productions and foreign imports. The term-contract players receive comprehensive recognition here since they were the heart of Republic and their body of work ranged from major to minor parts, both credited and uncredited on-screen; these performers made many appearances — some fleeting — and their inclusion is an exhaustive representation of their contributions.

The principal source material for credited performances was the original-release versions of the films, an important factor. Republic edited a number of their longer first-run features down to approximately 60 minutes to satisfy the requirements of theatrical double features, and they cut many westerns to approximately 54 minutes to cater to television time slots. Many of these abridgments were not only re-titled but deleted the names of cast members whose characterizations were removed in the condensing process. In the instances where only theatrical re-releases or television prints survive, archival footage of the original credits or cutting continuities became the basis for researching on-screen credits.

Scrupulous attention to original film does not deny that some players credited on-screen were not actually seen in the films. Such anomalies are attributable to the fact that artwork for the cast cards was usually prepared before editing had been completed, resulting in the credited players' scenes ending up on the cutting-room floor. The most flagrant example of faceless names occurred on *No Place to Land* [1958] in which Whitey Hughes, Bill Blatty, John Carpenter, and Bill Coontz were credited on-screen but did not appear in the feature.

When stock footage was picked up for subsequent use, recognizable players are listed for the later excerpts as well as the original pictures. But players are not listed for feature versions of serials except when new footage was added such

as the Raymond Hatton-Dickie Jones wraparounds to tie up loose continuity threads in *Hi-Yo-Silver* [1940], the feature version of the serial *The Lone Ranger* [1938].

Players' names are listed exactly as they were most frequently displayed on-screen save for the occasional typographical or personal-preference spelling variation. As examples, Eduardo Ciannelli participated in four Republic productions and his first name is so spelled even though he requested on-screen credit as Edward Ciannelli in the serial *Mysterious Doctor Satan* [1940]. Likewise, Theodor Von Eltz is carried accordingly despite his first name appearing on-screen as Theodore in *A Man Betrayed* [1936] and *Trial Without Jury* [1950].

Some performers underwent spelling or name changes during their careers. Douglass Dumbrille is listed only once by his most common first-name spelling, though he did spell it with just one "s" early on. In checking Vera Hruba, referral is made to Vera Ralston; then for Vera Ralston a finding line in brackets identifies the films she made first under the name Vera Hruba, then changed to Vera Hruba Ralston, and finally as Vera Ralston — the name she is most closely identified with.

After compiling all the personalities credited on-screen, the day-by-day schedules of term-contract players were checked to determine every film on which they worked while they were under term contract. On many films they were credited on-screen; in others they were not. While increasing the total number of appearances for many of the performers, this analysis tacked on films that no other source will show for these players. Most prominently, Monte Hale is shown to have worked on *Sundown in Sante Fe* [1948]; in fact, he fractured his arm during the first day of principal photography whereupon the title was transferred to the Allan "Rocky" Lane series of westerns. But the film is listed for Hale because he worked on it despite not being glimpsed in the final product; it was counted against the days for

which he was paid. Similarly, Helen Talbot was given Technicolor tests for *I've Always Loved You* [1946]; though she did nothing further on the film, it is shown under her listing because while a term contractee she did something in connection with the production. In some instances there were peripheral assignments for wardrobe fittings, screen tests, voice-over narrations, or looping sessions to replace the dialogue of other performers; all these films are included in listings for term-contract players because they actually worked on the production. Excluded are cases where term-contract players were represented only in photographs or framed portraits that were seen in various places on-screen.

Finally, the contract packages and billings jackets on every film plus files on the free-lance and day players were reviewed to ascertain any additional uncredited roles portrayed by term-contract players outside their contract periods. At the same time extraordinary selected roles of notable players were extracted including appearances by Don Barry, Kane Richmond, and others in training films made by Republic for the armed services during World War II. In addition, screenings of numerous Republic product unearthed early uncredited sightings for later popular name personalities such as Barrie Chase and Gavin MacLeod, to name just two of the many.

This study repeatedly turned up a host of familiar yet usually uncredited players whose sheer number of appearances in bit and background parts demanded at least a pictorial salute, among them brothers Bob and Fred Burns and brothers Ralph and Roy Bucko [Bouckou]. Cactus Mack [Taylor McPeters] and Jack O'Shea appeared in literally hundreds of films, but no attempt has been made to document all their appearances. Nor could listings be complete for stunt personnel; they are treated as best possible considering their contracts for individual films were sometimes kept in incomplete outside files and it was difficult to

identify them visually in fast-paced action sequences.

Rounding out the Super-Index are cross-reference listings for certain series pictures including the Three Mesquiteers, Red Ryder, John Paul Revere, the Rough-Ridin' Kids, the Higgins family, Ellery Queen, Mr. District Attorney, Cappy Ricks, the Earl Carroll and Hit Parade musicals, and those featuring the Ice-Capades troupe. Separately cataloging these character or title series — as opposed to the self-referenced star series of Gene Autry, Roy Rogers, and others — includes in some cases identification of the various cast members who migrated through them. Also showcased are selected short-subjects series such as Commando Cody — Sky Marshal of the Universe, Land of Opportunity, and Harriet Parsons' Meet the Stars one-reelers that offered glances of many of Hollywood's biggest celebrities. The training films made during World War II are enumerated as are groups of films dealing with fictional properties such as Jimmy Valentine and Zorro which are listed under the character names.

The scope of this directory thus combines all credited players in Republic's releases with an extensive — though by no means all-inclusive — treatment of uncredited performances by term contractees, key players, stunt aces, newcomers, and ranking bit players listed in order of release dates.

LEGEND

Albertson, Frank[169]
Superscript number after name indicates page number on which a picture of that player can be found.

I've Always Loved You*
Asterisk after a film title indicates the player worked on the film but was not credited on-screen.

A

Abbas, Abdullah
1944—The Fighting Seabees*
1948—Sons of Adventure*
Angel in Exile*
1952—Gobs and Gals*
1956—Jaguar*

Abbott, Bud
1941—Los Angeles Examiner Benefit*

Abbott, John[169]
1943—London Blackout Murders
1944—Secrets of Scotland Yard
End of the Road
1945—The Vampire's Ghost

Abel, Walter[89]
1937—Portia on Trial
1940—Who Killed Aunt Maggie?
1941—Stars Past and Present*

Ace
1938—Orphans of the Street

Tommye Adams

Iris Adrian

Philip Ahn

Mary Ainslee

Ackland, Rodney
1943—Alibi

Acosta, Rodolfo[169]
1951—Bullfighter and the Lady
1953—San Antone

Acuff, Eddie[169]
1938—Gangs of New York*
Ladies in Distress
I Stand Accused*
Rhythm of the Saddle
1939—Fighting Thoroughbreds*
The Mysterious Miss X
Rough Riders' Round-Up
Flight at Midnight*
Days of Jesse James*
1940—The Border Legion*
1941—Robin Hood of the Pecos
Arkansas Judge*
The Great Train Robbery*
Mr. District Attorney*
Jungle Girl
Rags to Riches
Bad Man of Deadwood*
Mr. District Atty. in the Carter Case
1942—Sleepytime Gal*
The Old Homestead*
Bells of Capistrano*
Youth on Parade*
The Traitor Within
1943—Daredevils of the West
Headin' for God's Country
1944—Silent Partner*
1945—Flame of Barbary Coast*
1946—Heldorado
1947—Bells of San Angelo
Wyoming*
Exposed*
The Fabulous Texan*
Bandits of Dark Canyon
1948—Slippy McGee
G-Men Never Forget
The Timber Trail
Out of the Storm*

Acuff, Roy[71]—**and his Smoky Mountain Boys**
1940—Grand Ole Opry
1942—Hi, Neighbor
1943—O, My Darling Clementine
1944—Sing Neighbor Sing
1946—Night Train to Memphis
1949—The Fighting Kentuckian*

Adair, Phyliss
1946—The Glass Alibi

Adams, Carol[5]
1940—Behind the News*
Bowery Boys*
1941—Ridin' on a Rainbow
Sis Hopkins
The Gay Vagabond
Ice-Capades*
Bad Man of Deadwood
Dick Tracy Vs. Crime, Inc.*

Adams, Dorothy[169]
1939—Mickey, the Kid*
1946—The Inner Circle
1947—That's My Man

Adams, Ernie[169]
1936—The Return of Jimmy Valentine*
Bulldog Edition*
The Gun Ranger
1937—Bar-Z Bad Men
The Trusted Outlaw*
"Lightnin'" Crandall
Gun Lords of Stirrup Basin
Come on, Cowboys!*
Doomed at Sundown*
Range Defenders*
The Arizona Gunfighter
Ridin' the Lone Trail
The Colorado Kid
1938—The Purple Vigilantes
Hollywood Stadium Mystery!*
Thunder in the Desert
Durango Valley Raiders*
1939—The Lone Ranger Rides Again*
Frontier Pony Express*
Man of Conquest*
1940—Dark Command*
Bowery Boy*
1941—Bad Man of Deadwood*
1943—Headin' for God's Country
Beyond the Last Frontier
The Masked Marvel*
Mystery Broadcast*
1944—Outlaws of Santa Fe*
Lake Placid Serenade*
1945—Federal Operator 99*
1946—A Guy Could Change*
King of the Forest Rangers
One Exciting Week*
Traffic in Crime*
The Mysterious Mr. Valentine
That Brennan Girl*
1947—Son of Zorro
Yankee Fakir
The Pretender
The Black Widow

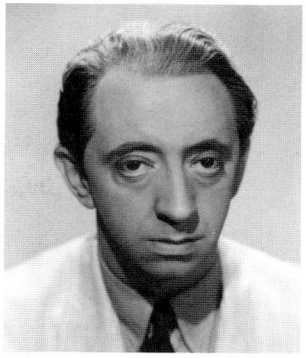
John Abbott

Dorothy Adams

Adams, Jane
1951—Street Bandits

Adams, Jill
1956—Doctor at Sea

Adams, Lee
1944—The Fighting Seabees*

Adams, Nick[89]
1956—A Strange Adventure

Adams, Stanley
1954—The Atomic Kid
1958—Hell Ship Mutiny

Adams, Ted[169]
1936—Under Cover Man
Lawless Land
1937—The Gambling Terror
Guns in the Dark
The Arizona Gunfighter
The Colorado Kid
1938—The Lone Ranger*
Desert Patrol
Pals of the Saddle
Durango Valley Raiders
1939—Three Texas Steers
1940—Gaucho Serenade
1942—The Sundown Kid
1943—Daredevils of the West
1945—Bells of Rosarita*
1946—Red River Renegades
Stagecoach to Denver
1947—Son of Zorro
Vigilantes of Boomtown
Under Colorado Skies
1948—Dangers of the Canadian Mounted
1949—King of the Rocket Men
San Antone Ambush*
Navajo Trail Raiders
1950—Hills of Oklahoma
Frisco Tornado*
1951—Night Riders of Montana
Heart of the Rockies*

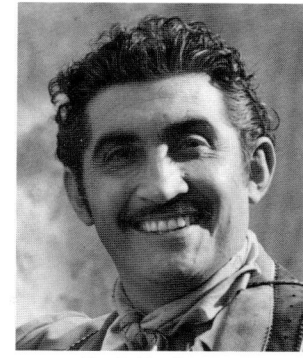
Rodolfo Acosta

Ernie Adams

Adams, Tommye[169]
1942—Moonlight Masquerade
Hi, Neighbor*
1943—Tahiti Honey

Adams, Victor
1937—The Duke Comes Back

Adler, Luther[89]
1949—Wake of the Red Witch
1952—Hoodlum Empire

Adreon, Franklin
1936—The Leathernecks Have Landed*
Hearts in Bondage*
1937—Join the Marines*

Adrian, Iris[169]
1942—Moonlight Masquerade*
1945—Steppin' in Society
Road to Alcatraz
1948—Out of the Storm

Agar, John[113]
1950—Sands of Iwo Jima
1952—Woman of the North Country

Agay, Iren
1946—The Fabulous Suzanne

Aguglia, Mimi
1951—Cuban Fireball

Ahern, Will and Gladys
1937—Git Along Little Dogies

Aherne, Brian[89]
1948—Angel on the Amazon

Ahn, Philip[169]
1940—Drums of Fu Manchu*
1951—Secrets of Monte Carlo
1953—Fair Wind to Java
1954—Hell's Half Acre
The Shanghai Story

Ainley, Joe
1956—Daniel Boone, Trail Blazer

Frank Albertson

Eddie Acuff

Ted Adams

Ainslee, Mary[169]
1940—Earl of Puddlestone
1941—Sis Hopkins
Sailors on Leave

Ainsworth, Cupid
1938—Gold Mine in the Sky

Airaldi, Roberto
1950—The Avengers

Alberghetti, Anna Maria[89]
1955—The Last Command
1957—Duel at Apache Wells

Alberni, Luis
1936—Ticket to Paradise
Follow Your Heart
1937—Two Wise Maids
Manhattan Merry-Go-Round
1940—Scatterbrain
1943—Here Comes Elmer

Albert, Eddie[71]
1946—Rendezvous with Annie
1947—Hit Parade of 1947

Albertson, Frank
1940—Behind the News
1941—Citadel of Crime
1942—Shepherd of the Ozarks
1943—Here Comes Elmer
Mystery Broadcast
O, My Darling Clementine
1944—Rosie, the Riveter
1946—Gay Blades

Albright, Hardie[169]
1940—Carolina Moon
1941—Sis Hopkins*
1945—Sunset in El Dorado
Captain Tugboat Annie

Albright, John
1948—King of the Gamblers
I, Jane Doe

Albright, Lola[169]
1957—Pawnee

Hardie Albright

Lola Albright

Albright, Wally
1939 — Mexicali Rose

Alderson, John
1957 — Spoilers of the Forest
Last Stagecoach West

Aldridge, Kay[71]
1940 — Chinese Garden Festival*
1942 — Perils of Nyoka
1943 — Daredevils of the West
1944 — Haunted Harbor

Alexander, Ben
1936 — Hearts in Bondage

Alexander, Betty
1947 — The Trespasser

Alexander, Dick[170]
1937 — S O S Coast Guard
Zorro Rides Again
1938 — Santa Fe Stampede*
1939 — The Kansas Terrors
1940 — Dark Command*
Covered Wagon Days*
1942 — Code of the Outlaw*
Raiders of the Range*
Romance on the Range*
In Old California*
1943 — King of the Cowboys*
1944 — Man from Frisco*
Call of the South Seas
Three Little Sisters*
Storm Over Lisbon*
1947 — Northwest Outpost*
Jesse James Rides Again*
The Wild Frontier*
1949 — Hellfire*
The Fighting Kentuckian*
1950 — Rock Island Trail*
1952 — I Dream of Jeanie
Woman of the North Country*
1953 — Woman They Almost Lynched*
A Perilous Journey*
1954 — Trader Tom of the China Seas*
1955 — Timberjack*
The Road to Denver*
King of the Carnival*

Alexander, Jimmy[170]
1941 — Rookies on Parade
1945 — Earl Carroll Vanities

Alexander, Katharine[170]
1941 — Sis Hopkins
Angels with Broken Wings

Alexander, Suzanne
1954 — Flight Nurse*

Allan, Edgar[5]
1936 — The Mandarin Mystery
Beware of Ladies*
1937 — Join the Marines*
Dick Tracy*
Michael O'Halloran*

Allan, Victor
1937 — Come on, Cowboys!

Alland, William
1950 — Macbeth

Allen, Barbara Jo
See Vera Vague.

Allen, Cliff
1945 — An Angel Comes to Brooklyn

Allen, Corey
1958 — Juvenile Jungle

Allen, Drew[170]
1948 — G-Men Never Forget
1950 — Unmasked*

Allen, Gracie
1941 — Variety Reel*

Allen, Harry
1936 — The Girl from Mandalay
1938 — Outside of Paradise

Allen, Jack
1957 — Thunder Over Tangier

Allen, Jr., Joseph[170]
1943 — Mountain Rhythm
The Mantrap

Dick Alexander

Jimmy Alexander

Katharine Alexander

Allen, Judith[89]
1935 — Burning Gold
1936 — Beware of Ladies
1937 — Bill Cracks Down
Git Along Little Dogies
Boots and Saddles

Allen, Lester
1945 — The Great Flamarion

Allen, Maude Pierce
1940 — Adventures of Red Ryder

Allen, Patrick
1955 — Cross Channel

Allen, Rex[142]
1950 — The Arizona Cowboy
Hills of Oklahoma
Redwood Forest Trail
Under Mexicali Stars
Trail of Robin Hood
1951 — Silver City Bonanza
Thunder in God's Country
Rodeo King and the Senorita
Utah Wagon Train
1952 — Colorado Sundown
The Last Musketeer
Border Saddlemates
I Dream of Jeanie
Old Oklahoma Plains
South Pacific Trail
1953 — Old Overland Trail
Iron Mountain Trail
Sweethearts on Parade*
Down Laredo Way
Shadows of Tombstone
Red River Shore
1954 — Phantom Stallion

Allen, Ricky
1959 — Plunderers of Painted Flats

Allen, Robert
1939 — Fighting Thoroughbreds

Allister, Claude[170]
1937 — Bulldog Drummond at Bay
1938 — Storm Over Bengal

Allman, Elvia[170]
1941 — Sis Hopkins

Allwyn, Astrid[170]
1937 — It Could Happen to You
1940 — Gangs of Chicago
Meet the Missus
1941 — Puddin' Head
1943 — Hit Parade of 1943

Drew Allen

Joseph Allen, Jr.

Alper, Murray
1937 — Escape by Night
1941 — Down Mexico Way
1948 — Slippy McGee

Alsace, Gene
1940 — Adventures of Red Ryder

Alten, Frank
1945 — Manhunt of Mystery Island

Alvarado, Don
1936 — Federal Agent

Alvin, John[170]
1947 — Under Colorado Skies
1948 — The Bold Frontiersman
Train to Alcatraz
1951 — Missing Women
1954 — The Shanghai Story

Alyn, Kirk[170]
1943 — The Man from the Rio Grande
Overland Mail Robbery
Mystery Broadcast*
Pistol Packin' Mama
1944 — Cowboy and the Senorita*
Goodnight Sweetheart*
Call of the Rockies
The Girl Who Dared
Storm Over Lisbon*
1946 — Daughter of Don Q
1949 — Federal Agents Vs. Underworld, Inc.
Radar Patrol Vs. Spy King
1957 — Beginning of the End*

Ambrogi, Adriano
1951 — Fugitive Lady

Ameche, Don[89]
1947 — That's My Man

American G.I. Chorus, The
1947 — Northwest Outpost

Ames, Adrianne[170]
1939 — The Zero Hour

Ames, Jimmy
1942 — Sleepytime Gal
1946 — Daughter of Don Q
1947 — Hit Parade of 1947*
1952 — Tropical Heat Wave*

Ames, Leon[170]
1938 — Come on, Leathernecks
1939 — I Was a Convict
Man of Conquest
Calling All Marines

Ames, Ramsay[171]
1947 — The Black Widow
1948 — G-Men Never Forget

Andelin, James
1953 — City that Never Sleeps

Claude Allister

Elvia Allman

Astrid Allwyn

Kirk Alyn

Adrianne Ames

Leon Ames

Richard Jaeckel, Frances Rafferty, Edmond O'Brien, Victor Sun Yung, James Griffith, John Alvin, Barry Kelley

SCENE FROM "THE SHANGHAI STORY"

170

Ramsay Ames

Luana Anders

Lloyd "Slim" Andrews, Alex Callam

Eddie Anderson

Anders, Luana[171]
1958—The Notorious Mr. Monks
The Man Who Died Twice

Anderson, Bernie
1937—Round-Up Time in Texas

Anderson, Bob
1958—The Man Who Died Twice

Anderson, Dave
1947—Jesse James Rides Again
The Black Widow*
1948—I, Jane Doe*
Train to Alcatraz*
1949—Federal Agents Vs. Underworld, Inc.
The Fighting Kentuckian*

Anderson, Eddie [Rochester][171]
1937—Bill Cracks Down

Anderson, Erville
1936—Hearts in Bondage
1944—Man from Frisco

Anderson, George
1938—Born to be Wild
1948—King of the Gamblers

Anderson, Ivie
1937—The Hit Parade

Anderson, James
1952—The Last Musketeer

Anderson, Judith[90]
1946—Specter of the Rose

Anderson, Richard
1950—The Vanishing Westerner

Andre, Charles[5]
No films.

Andre, Dorothy[171]
Many films.
1943—Chatterbox*
Raiders of Sunset Pass*
1944—San Fernando Valley*
1955—Santa Fe Passage*
King of the Carnival*
The Vanishing American*

Andre, Gwili[171]
1937—Meet the Boy Friend

Andre, Joyce
1957—Eighteen and Anxious

Andre, Lona[71]
1940—Ghost Valley Raiders

Andren, Jean
1947—That's My Man*
1950—Belle of Old Mexico*

Andres, Rudolph
See Robert O. Davis.

Andrews, Lloyd "Slim"[171]
1942—Cowboy Serenade
The Cyclone Kid
The Sombrero Kid

Andrews Sisters
1941—Los Angeles Examiner Benefit*

Andrews, Stanley[171]
1936—Happy Go Lucky
1938—The Lone Ranger
The Higgins Family*
Prairie Moon
Shine on Harvest Moon
1940—Colorado*
King of the Royal Mounted
1943—Daredevils of the West
Canyon City
In Old Oklahoma*
1944—Rosie, the Riveter*
Tucson Raiders
Man from Frisco
Atlantic City
Vigilantes of Dodge City*
Faces in the Fog*
Lake Placid Serenade*
1945—Steppin' in Society*
1947—Robin Hood of Texas
The Fabulous Texan*
1948—Adv. of Frank and Jesse James
1949—The Last Bandit
Brimstone
1950—The Arizona Cowboy
Salt Lake Raiders
Rock Island Trail*
Trigger, Jr.
Under Mexicali Stars
1951—Utah Wagon Train
1952—Thundering Caravans
Woman of the North Country*
1953—Ride the Man Down*
Can. Mounties Vs. Atomic Invaders
El Paso Stampede
1955—The Twinkle in God's Eye*

Angel, Heather[90]
1937—The Bold Caballero
Portia on Trial
The Duke Comes Back
1938—Army Girl

Angold, Edit
1952—Woman in the Dark

Ankers, Evelyn[171]
1945—The Fatal Witness
1946—The French Key
1947—Spoilers of the North

Ankrum, Morris[171]
1951—Fighting Coast Guard
1954—Flight Nurse*
1955—The Eternal Sea
The Last Command*
No Man's Woman
1956—When Gangland Strikes
1957—Hell's Crossroads
Beginning of the End
1958—Young and Wild

Annabella
1941—Stars at Play*

Anstead, Melva[68]
1944—San Fernando Valley*
Lake Placid Serenade*
1945—Utah*
Earl Carroll Vanities*
The Phantom Speaks*
Three's a Crowd*
Flame of Barbary Coast*
Bells of Rosarita*
The Cheaters*
Hitchhike to Happiness*
Man from Oklahoma*
Tell It to a Star*
Behind City Lights*
Bandits of the Badlands*
Love, Honor and Goodbye*
Sunset in El Dorado*
The Purple Monster Strikes*
Marshal of Laredo*
Don't Fence Me In*
Girls of the Big House*
An Angel Comes to Brooklyn*
Mexicana*
The Tiger Woman*
Along the Navajo Trail*
Dakota*
1946—A Guy Could Change*
Sheriff of Redwood Valley*

Apfel, Oscar[171]
1935—Cappy Ricks Returns
1936—Hearts in Bondage
Bulldog Edition
1937—Jim Hanvey - Detective

Appleby, Dorothy
1937—Paradise Express

Appleton, Elinor
1947—Yankee Fakir

Archer, John[113]
[as Ralph Bowman]
1938—Dick Tracy Returns*
Overland Stage Raiders
1940—Barnyard Follies
[as John Archer]
1941—Mountain Moonlight
1942—Hi, Neighbor
1943—The Purple V
Shantytown
1955—No Man's Woman
1957—Affair in Reno

Arden, Eve[90]
1943—Hit Parade of 1943
1945—Earl Carroll Vanities
1953—The Lady Wants Mink

Arden, Mary
1946—California Gold Rush

Argyle, Jean
1945—Gangs of the Waterfront*
Girls of the Big House*

Arledge, John
1938—Prison Nurse

Arlen, Richard[71]
1938—Call of the Yukon
1944—The Lady and the Monster
That's My Baby
Storm Over Lisbon
The Big Bonanza
1945—Identity Unknown
The Phantom Speaks
1956—Hidden Guns

Armetta, Henry
1937—Manhattan Merry-Go-Round

Armida
1937—Rootin' Tootin' Rhythm

Armontel, Roland
1955—Don Juan's Night of Love

Arms, Russell
1948—Daredevils of the Clouds

Armstrong, Henry
1941—The Pittsburgh Kid

Armstrong, Louis—and orchestra
1944—Atlantic City

Armstrong, Margaret
1938—Western Jamboree

Armstrong, Mary
1943—Chatterbox*

Armstrong, Robert[171]
1938—The Night Hawk
1939—Man of Conquest
Fight at Midnight
1940—Forgotten Girls
Behind the News
1941—Citadel of Crime
1945—Gangs of the Waterfront
1946—Gay Blades
G.I. War Brides
1947—Exposed
1949—Streets of San Francisco
1950—Destination Big House
1955—Double Jeopardy
1957—The Crooked Circle

Arnac, Beatrice
1959—C.S.S. 117 is Not Dead

Arnall, Julia[171]
1957—Tears for Simon

Arnaud, Yvonne
1943—At Dawn We Die

Arnaz, Desi
1941—Stars at Play*

Arness, James[113]
1951—Belle LeGrand*
1955—Flame of the Islands

Arnheim, Gus—and orchestra
1944—Trocadero

Arnold, Edward[90]
1941—Variety Reel*
1953—City that Never Sleeps

Arnold, Melvyn
1954—Crazylegs

Arnold, Phil
1943—The Main Street Kid

Arnova, Alba
1951—Fugitive Lady

Dorothy Andre

Gwili Andre

Stanley Andrews

Evelyn Ankers

Morris Ankrum

Oscar Apfel

Robert Armstrong

Julia Arnall

Arnt, Charles[172]
1940—Grandpa Goes to Town*
1941—Mr. District Attorney
1943—In Old Oklahoma*
1944—Three Little Sisters
1946—That Brennan Girl
1947—Calendar Girl
Saddle Pals

Charles Arnt

Johnny Arthur

Robert Arthur

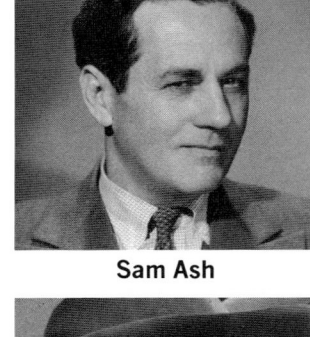

Sam Ash

Warren Ashe

Earl Askam

Roscoe Ates

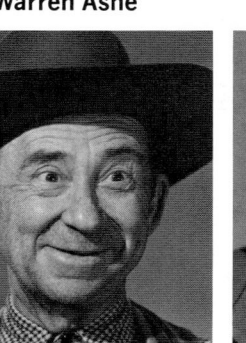

Lionel Atwill

Arslan, Sylvia
1945—Great Stagecoach Robbery
Sheriff of Cimarron

Arthur, Henry
1939—My Wife's Relatives

Arthur, Johnny[172]
1937—The Hit Parade*
Exiled to Shanghai
1939—Jeepers Creepers
1940—Scatterbrain*
1941—Mountain Moonlight
1942—Shepherd of the Ozarks
Moonlight Masquerade*
1943—The Masked Marvel

Arthur, Louise
1958—Juvenile Jungle

Arthur, Robert[172]
1958—Young and Wild

Arundell, Dennis
1943—The Saint Meets the Tiger

Arvan, Jan
1954—Trader Tom of the China Seas

Ash, Sam[172]
Many films.
1936—A Man Betrayed*
1943—The Masked Marvel*
O, My Darling Clementine*
1944—Captain America*
1945—Man from Oklahoma*
1946—King of the Forest Rangers*

Ashdown, Nadene
1952—Toughest Man in Arizona

Ashe, Warren[172]
1943—Deerslayer

Asherson, Renee
1957—Time is My Enemy

Ashley, Edward[5]
1945—Love, Honor and Goodbye
1946—Gay Blades
The Madonna's Secret

Askam, Earl[172]
1937—The Wrong Road*
1938—Dick Tracy Returns*
Down in "Arkansaw"*
Hawk of the Wilderness*
Red River Range
1939—Mexicali Rose*
Frontier Pony Express*
Man of Conquest*
Daredevils of the Red Circle*
1940—Pioneers of the West
Dark Command*

Askin, Leon[172]
1955—Carolina Cannonball

Asther, Nils[113]
1943—Mystery Broadcast
1945—Jealousy
Love Honor and Goodbye

Astor, Gertrude
1937—All Over Town

Astor, Mary
1941—Variety Reel*

Atchley, Hooper[129]
1935—The New Frontier*
Sagebrush Troubadour
1936—The Return of Jimmy Valentine
Navy Born
Hearts in Bondage*
Roarin' Lead
1937—Navy Blues*
Portia on Trial*
1938—The Old Barn Dance
Orphans of the Street*
1939—S.O.S. Tidal Wave*
Mountain Rhythm
Saga of Death Valley*
1940—Wolf of New York*
Adventures of Red Ryder
1941—Rags to Riches*
King of the Texas Rangers*
Dick Tracy Vs. Crime, Inc.
1942—Arizona Terrors*
In Old California*
1943—G-Men Vs. The Black Dragon
Idaho*
Hit Parade of 1943*
The Black Hills Express
The West Side Kid*
In Old Oklahoma*

Ates, Roscoe[172]
1938—Riders of the Black Hills
1939—Three Texas Steers
1940—Rancho Grande
1941—Robin Hood of the Pecos
Meet Roy Rogers*
Mountain Moonlight
1942—Affairs of Jimmy Valentine
1950—Hills of Oklahoma
1951—Honeychile
1956—Come Next Spring

Atterbury, Malcolm
1956—Stranger at My Door
Dakota Incident

Atwell, Roy
1936—The Harvester

Atwill, Lionel[172]
1937—The Wrong Road
1944—Captain America
Secrets of Scotland Yard

Atwood, Donna
1942—Ice-Capades Revue

Aubert, Lenore[173]
1946—The Catman of Paris

Aubrey, Jimmy
1936—Go-Get-'Em, Haines
1945—The Vampire's Ghost

Auer, Mischa[172]
1936—The House of a Thousand Candles

Auerbach, Artie
1943—Here Comes Elmer

Aumont, Geneviv
1957—Journey to Freedom

Austin, Charlotte
1957—Pawnee

Austin, Frank
1936—Roarin' Lead
1937—Git Along Little Dogies*
1943—Sleepy Lagoon*
1944—That's My Baby
1947—The Fabulous Texan*

Austin, Lois
1946—G.I. War Brides
1947—The Pilgrim Lady*
That's My Gal*
That's My Man*
1950—Lonely Heart Bandits*
1953—Sweethearts on Parade*

Austin, William
1935—$1000 a Minute
1947—The Ghost Goes Wild

Autry, Gene[144]
1935—Tumbling Tumbleweeds
Melody Trail
Sagebrush Troubadour
1936—The Singing Vagabond
Red River Valley
Comin' 'Round the Mountain
The Singing Cowboy
Guns and Guitars
Oh, Susanna!
Ride Ranger Ride
The Big Show
The Old Corral
1937—Round-Up Time in Texas
Git Along Little Dogies
Rootin' Tootin' Rhythm
Yodelin' Kid from Pine Ridge
Public Cowboy No. 1
Boots and Saddles
Manhattan Merry-Go-Round
Springtime in the Rockies
1938—The Old Barn Dance
Gold Mine in the Sky
Man from Music Mountain
Prairie Moon
Rhythm of the Saddle
Western Jamboree
1939—Home on the Prairie
Mexicali Rose
Blue Montana Skies
Mountain Rhythm
Colorado Sunset
In Old Monterey
Rovin' Tumbleweeds
South of the Border
1940—Rancho Grande
Gaucho Serenade
Carolina Moon
Ride, Tenderfoot, Ride
Melody Ranch
1941—Ridin' on a Rainbow
Variety Reel*
Back in the Saddle
The Singing Hill
Stars at Play*
Meet Roy Rogers*
Sunset in Wyoming
Stars Past and Present*
Under Fiesta Stars
Down Mexico Way
Sierra Sue
1942—Cowboy Serenade
Heart of the Rio Grande
Home in Wyomin'
Stardust on the Sage
Call of the Canyon
Bells of Capistrano
1946—Sioux City Sue
1947—Trail to San Antone
Twilight on the Rio Grande
Saddle Pals
Robin Hood of Texas

Avery, Tol[172]
1955—Headline Hunters*

Avonde, Richard
1951—The Wild Blue Yonder*
1952—Wild Horse Ambush
1953—Savage Frontier
Shadows of Tombstone

Axman, Hanne[172]
1949—The Red Menace

Aylesworth, Doug
1948—G-Men Never Forget

Aylmer, Felix
1937—Glamorous Night

Mischa Auer

Tol Avery

Hanne Axman

Arthur Aylsworth

Leon Askin, Sig Ruman, Jack Kruschen

Jim Backus

David Bacon

Irving Bacon

Rod Bacon

Buddy Baer

John Baer

John Bagni

Richard Bailey

Aylsworth, Arthur[172]
1935 — The Spanish Cape Mystery*
Forced Landing
1936 — King of the Pecos
The President's Mystery
1937 — Escape by Night
1939 — Man of Conquest*

Ayres, Lew[71]
1936 — The Leathernecks Have Landed
1938 — King of the Newsboys

B

Babb, Dorothy
1946 — Earl Carroll Sketchbook

Baby Dumpling
1941 — Los Angeles Examiner Benefit*

Backus, Georgia
1941 — Mr. District Atty. in the Carter Case*

Backus, Jim[173]
1954 — Geraldine
1957 — Eighteen and Anxious

Bacon, David[173]
1943 — Someone to Remember
The Masked Marvel

Bacon, Irving[173]
1935 — Hitch Hike Lady
1943 — King of the Cowboys
In Old Oklahoma
1945 — Hitchhike to Happiness
1946 — Night Train to Memphis
1947 — Saddle Pals
1948 — Moonrise
1951 — Honeychile
Desert of Lost Men
1953 — Sweethearts on Parade
1956 — Hidden Guns
Dakota Incident

Bacon, Rod[173]
1936 — The Harvester*
1941 — Sis Hopkins*
Rookies on Parade*
The Gay Vagabond
Hurricane Smith*
Ice-Capades*
Public Enemies*
1942 — Cowboy Serenade*
A Tragedy at Midnight*
Yokel Boy*
1943 — The Masked Marvel
1946 — Gay Blades*
The Crimson Ghost*
Out California Way*

Bacon, Ruth
1937 — Springtime in the Rockies

Bacon, Shelby
1945 — Corpus Christi Bandits

Badel, Alan
1956 — Magic Fire

Baer, Buddy[173]
1953 — Fair Wind to Java
1954 — Jubilee Trail
1957 — Hell Canyon Outlaws

Baer, John[173]
1951 — Arizona Manhunt
1955 — City of Shadows

Bagni, John[173]
1939 — Calling All Marines*
1940 — Drums of Fu Manchu*
King of the Royal Mounted*
Mysterious Doctor Satan*
Bowery Boy*
1941 — Adventures of Captain Marvel
Citadel of Crime*
King of the Texas Rangers*
Dick Tracy Vs. Crime, Inc.*
1942 — Perils of Nyoka
1944 — Captain America
My Buddy*
1946 — Heldorado
1947 — The Pretender
1948 — The Far Frontier

Bagues, Salvador
1958 — Hell Ship Mutiny

Bailer, Dorothy
1943 — Hit Parade of 1943*
Swing Your Partner*
1944 — The Yellow Rose of Texas*
Song of Nevada*
San Fernando Valley*
1945 — Mexicana*

Bailey, Claude
1943 — The Saint Meets the Tiger

Bailey, Raymond
1939 — Woman Doctor*
S.O.S. Tidal Wave
Daredevils of the Red Circle
Flight at Midnight
Sabotage*
1940 — Forgotten Girls*
Gangs of Chicago*
1941 — A Man Betrayed*

Bailey, Richard[173]
1944 — That's My Baby
1945 — Manhunt of Mystery Island
1947 — Yankee Fakir*

Bainter, Fay
1941 — Variety Reel*

Baird, Antony
1957 — Operation Conspiracy

Bakalyan, Richard[173]
1958 — Juvenile Jungle

Baker, Belle
1944 — Atlantic City

Baker, Benny
1939 — She Married a Cop
1948 — Homicide for Three
1949 — Rose of the Yukon
1952 — Thunderbirds

Baker, Bob
1941 — Meet Roy Rogers*

Baker, Buddy[8]
1938 — Orphans of the Street*

Baker, Eddie
1945 — Identity Unknown

Baker, Kenny[90]
1940 — Hit Parade of 1941
1947 — Calendar Girl

Baker, Tommy
1939 — Saga of Death Valley

Bakewell, William[173]
1937 — Dangerous Holiday
Exiled to Shanghai
1938 — The Higgins Family
1940 — Chinese Garden Festival*
1942 — King of the Mounties
1947 — The Trespasser
1951 — Oh! Susanna*
Wells Fargo Gunmaster
1952 — Radar Men from the Moon

Baldra, Chuck
1936 — The Lawless Nineties

Baldwin, Ann[8]
1939 — Wall Street Cowboy
The Kansas Terrors*
1940 — Wolf of New York
Village Barn Dance*
Forgotten Girls*
Drums of Fu Manchu*
Fancho Grande
The Crooked Road*

Baldwin, Bill
1950 — Trial Without Jury

Baldwin, Robert[72]
1939 — Main Street Lawyer
1940 — Village Barn Dance

Baldwin, Walter[173]
1941 — Faces in the Fog*
1951 — Rough Riders of Durango

Balenda, Carla[173]
1954 — Phantom Stallion

Balfour, Michael
1955 — Secret Venture
1957 — Thunder Over Tangier

Ball, Betty
1951 — Street Bandits*
1952 — Hoodlum Empire*

Carl Esmond, Lenore Aubert, Bob Wilke [the Catman]

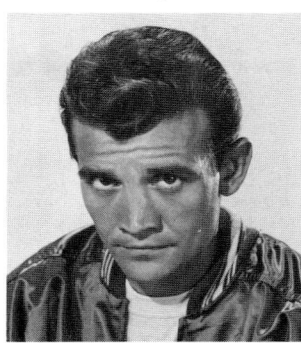
Richard Bakalyan

William Bakewell

Walter Baldwin

Carla Balenda

Ball, Frank[174]
1935—The New Frontier
1936—The Gun Ranger
Lawless Land
Border Phantom
1937—The Trusted Outlaw
The Gambling Terror
Trail of Vengeance
Gun Lords of Stirrup Basin
The Red Rope
Boothill Brigade
The Arizona Gunfighter
Ridin' the Lone Trail
The Colorado Kid
1938—Paroled—to Die
The Feud Maker

Frank Ball

Smith Ballew

George Barbier

Stephen Barclay

Vince Barnett

Ball, Lucille
1941—Stars at Play*

Ballew, Smith[174]
1940—Gaucho Serenade

Ballou, Marion
1937—Portia on Trial

Balter, Sam
1941—The Pittsburgh Kid

Bane, Holly
See Mike Ragan.

Banning, Leslye[174]
1952—Black Hills Ambush

Bannon, Jim[174]
1948—Dangers of the Canadian Mounted
1949—Daughter of the Jungle

Barber, Bobby
1947—Vigilantes of Boomtown

Barbier, George[174]
1939—S.O.S. Tidal Wave
Smuggled Cargo
1940—Village Barn Dance

Barclay, Don
1936—Border Phantom
1938—Thunder in the Desert

Barclay, Joan[174]
1936—Follow Your Heart*
1937—The Trusted Outlaw
1938—The Purple Vigilantes

Jim Bannon

Joan Barclay

Brigitte Bardot

Barclay, Stephen[174]
1944—Pride of the Plains
Vigilantes of Dodge City
1945—Utah*
The Great Flamarion
A Sporting Chance
Don't Fence Me In
Girls of the Big House
1946—G.I. War Brides*

Barcroft, Roy[8]
See page 175.

Bardette, Trevor[129]
1940—Young Buffalo Bill
Dark Command
Wagons Westward
Three Faces West
Girl from Havana
1941—Jungle Girl
Red River Valley
1943—Deerslayer
1944—Faces in the Fog*
1947—Wyoming
Marshal of Cripple Creek
1948—Secret Service Investigator
The Gallant Legion*
Marshal of Amarillo
Sundown in Santa Fe
1949—Sheriff of Wichita
Hellfire
The Wyoming Bandit
San Antone Ambush
1950—Hills of Oklahoma
1951—Fort Dodge Stampede
Honeychile*
1953—A Perilous Journey*
The Sun Shines Bright
Bandits of the West
Red River Shore
1954—Johnny Guitar*

Bardot, Brigitte[174]
1956—Doctor at Sea

Bari, Lynn[90]
1949—The Kid from Cleveland
1952—I Dream of Jeanie

Barker, Abe
1956—Doctor at Sea

Barker, Lex
1955—Mystery of the Black Jungle

Barkley, Lucille
1951—Arizona Manhunt

Barlow, Reginald
1936—The Girl from Mandalay
1939—New Frontier
Wall Street Cowboy
Rovin' Tumbleweeds

Barlowe, Joy[174]
1942—Call of the Canyon*
1945—Earl Carroll Vanities*
Don't Fence Me In*
1947—The Trespasser
Blackmail*
1950—Macbeth*

Joy Barlowe

Byron Barr

Robert H. Barrat

Barnes, Binnie[72]
1941—Variety Reel*
Stars at Play
Angels with Broken Wings
Stars Past and Present*
1942—In Old California
1951—Fugitive Lady

Barnes, Rayford
1957—Beginning of the End

Barnett, Vince[174]
1936—Dancing Feet
Down to the Sea
1940—Heroes of the Saddle
1941—Mr. District Attorney*
Puddin' Head
Sierra Sue*
1942—Stardust on the Sage
The Phantom Plainsmen*
X Marks the Spot
1943—Thundering Trails*
1947—The Trespasser
The Flame*

Barnette, Griff
1940—Frontier Vengeance
1942—Shadows on the Sage

Baron, Steven
1948—Train to Alcatraz

Barr, Byron[174]
1948—The Main Street Kid
1949—Down Dakota Way
1950—Tarnished
Covered Wagon Raid

Barr, Patrick
1957—Time is My Enemy

Barrat, Robert H.[174]
1939—Man of Conquest
Colorado Sunset
1942—The Girl from Alaska
1945—Grissly's Millions
Dakota
1947—The Fabulous Texan
1951—Pride of Maryland

Barrett, Claudia[175]
1950—The Old Frontier
Rustlers on Horseback
1951—Night Riders of Montana
1952—Desperadoes' Outpost

Barrett, Edith
1942—Lady for a Night
1944—Strangers in the Night

Barrett, Judith
1941—Stars at Play*

Barrett, Katharine
1957—The Wayward Girl
Eighteen and Anxious

Barrett, Michael
1958—Hell Ship Mutiny

Barrett, Tony[175]
1949—Flame of Youth
1950—Prisoners in Petticoats

Barrie, Mona[175]
1940—Who Killed Aunt Maggie?
1942—A Tragedy at Midnight
1944—Storm Over Lisbon

Leslye Banning, Michael Hall

Barrie, Wendy[113]
1936—Ticket to Paradise
1940—Women in War
Who Killed Aunt Maggie?
1941—Public Enemies

Barrier, Edgar[175]
1944—Secrets of Scotland Yard
1945—Song of Mexico
1950—Macbeth

Barris, Harry
1945—Steppin' in Society

Barron, Baynes
1952—Radar Men from the Moon

Barron, Robert[175]
1941—Back in the Saddle
Jungle Girl
The Pittsburgh Kid
King of the Texas Rangers
1942—Perils of Nyoka*
1943—The Man from Thunder River*
1947—The Black Widow*
1948—G-Men Never Forget*

Barry, Don[146]
1939—S.O.S. Tidal Wave
Wyoming Outlaw
Calling All Marines
Saga of Death Valley
Days of Jesse James
1940—Ghost Valley Raiders
Adventures of Red Ryder
One Man's Law
The Tulsa Kid
Frontier Vengeance
Texas Terrors
1941—Wyoming Wildcat
The Phantom Cowboy
Two Gun Sheriff
Desert Bandit
Kansas Cyclone
The Apache Kid
Death Valley Outlaws
A Missouri Outlaw
1942—Arizona Terrors
Stagecoach Express
Jesse James, Jr.
Remember Pearl Harbor!
The Cyclone Kid
The Sombrero Kid
Outlaws of Pine Ridge
The Traitor Within
The Sundown Kid
Army 681—Keep It Clean*
1943—Dead Man's Gulch
Carson City Cyclone
Days of Old Cheyenne
Fugitive from Sonora
The Black Hills Express
The West Side Kid
The Man from the Rio Grande
Canyon City
California Joe
1944—Outlaws of Santa Fe
My Buddy
1945—Bells of Rosarita
The Chicago Kid
1946—The Last Crooked Mile
Plainsman and the Lady
Out California Way
1947—That's My Gal
1948—Slippy McGee
Madonna of the Desert
Lightnin' in the Forest
Dangers of the Canadian Mounted
Train to Alcatraz
1954—The Untamed Heiress
1955—The Twinkle in God's Eye

Barry, Phyllis[175]
1935—Forbidden Heaven
1937—Affairs of Cappy Ricks

Barrymore, Ethel[90]
1948—Moonrise

Barrymore, Jr., John[114]
1952—Thunderbirds

Bartell, Eddie
1944—Trocadero

Bartell, Harry
1957—Affair in Reno

Barthelmess, Richard
1941—Hollywood Visits the Navy*

Bartlett, Bennie
1939—Mickey, the Kid
1942—Code of the Outlaw
1943—Nobody's Darling
1948—Heart of Virginia

Bartlett, Hall
1951—The Wild Blue Yonder

Bartlett, Michael[175]
1936—Follow Your Heart

Bartlett, Richard
1951—Street Bandits

Barton, Ann
1957—Pawnee

Barton, Gregg
1942—Flying Tigers
1951—Silver City Bonanza

Barton, Joan[175]
1947—Angel and the Badman

Barton, Michael
1952—Black Hills Ambush

Basie, Count[175]—and orchestra
1943—Hit Parade of 1943

Bass, Alfie
1955—The Square Ring
1957—Time is My Enemy

Batanides, Arthur
1957—The Unearthly

Bates, Florence[175]
1948—The Inside Story
1950—Belle of Old Mexico
1951—Havana Rose

Bates, Granville
1937—Larceny on the Air
1938—Romance on the Run
1939—Thou Shalt Not Kill

Bat Men
1936—Darkest Africa

Claudia Barrett

Count Basie, Dorothy Dandridge

Marion Talley, Michael Bartlett

Tony Barrett

Mona Barrie

Roy Barcroft[8]

1937—Join the Marines*
　Dick Tracy*
　S O S Coast Guard*
1938—Heroes of the Hills
1939—Mexicali Rose
　Daredevils of the Red Circle*
1940—Rancho Grande*
1941—Pals of the Pecos
　Sheriff of Tombstone*
　Outlaws of Cherokee Trail
　King of the Texas Rangers
　Jesse James at Bay
　West of Cimarron
1942—Sunset on the Desert
　Romance on the Range
　Stardust on the Sage
　Sunset Serenade
　Ridin' Down the Canyon
1943—Idaho*
　Carson City Cyclone
　Chatterbox*
　Calling Wild Bill Elliott
　Riders of the Rio Grande
　Bordertown Gun Fighters
　Wagon Tracks West
　The Man from the Rio Grande
　Man from Music Mountain*
　The Masked Marvel*
　Overland Mail Robbery
　Canyon City
　In Old Oklahoma*
　Raiders of Sunset Pass
　Hands Across the Border*
1944—The Fighting Seabees*
　Hidden Valley Outlaws
　The Laramie Trail
　Rosie, the Riveter*
　Tucson Raiders*
　Man from Frisco*
　Marshal of Reno*
　Call of the South Seas
　The Girl Who Dared
　Bordertown Trail*
　The Port of Forty Thieves*
　Haunted Harbor
　Stagecoach to Monterey
　Cheyenne Wildcat
　Code of the Prairie
　Storm Over Lisbon*
　Lights of Old Santa Fe
　Sheriff of Sundown
　Firebrands of Arizona
　The Big Bonanza
1945—The Topeka Terror
　Manhunt of Mystery Island
　Corpus Christi Bandits
　The Phantom Speaks*
　Lone Texas Ranger
　The Vampire's Ghost
　Santa Fe Saddlemates
　Bells of Rosarita
　Federal Operator 99*
　Trail of Kit Carson
　Love, Honor and Goodbye*
　Sunset in El Dorado
　The Purple Monster Strikes
　Marshal of Laredo
　Girls of the Big House*
　An Angel Comes to Brooklyn*
　Colorado Pioneers
　The Cherokee Flash
　Along the Navajo Trail
　Wagon Wheels Westward
　Dakota
　Song of Mexico*
1946—Gay Blades*
　The Phantom Rider
　The Madonna's Secret*
　Strange Impersonation*
　Sheriff of Redwood Valley*
　Murder in the Music Hall*
　Alias Billy the Kid
　Home on the Range
　Sun Valley Cyclone
　Passkey to Danger*
　In Old Sacramento*
　Traffic in Crime
　My Pal Trigger
　Night Train to Memphis
　Red River Renegades*
　Daughter of Don Q
　G.I. War Brides*
　Earl Carroll Sketchbook*
　The Mysterious Mr. Valentine*
　Plainsman and the Lady*
　Affairs of Geraldine*
　Sioux City Sue*
　Stagecoach to Denver
1947—Son of Zorro
　Last Frontier Uprising
　Vigilantes of Boomtown
　Spoilers of the North
　Oregon Trail Scouts
　That's My Man*
　Web of Danger
　Saddle Pals*
　Northwest Outpost*
　Rustlers of Devil's Canyon
　Robin Hood of Texas*
　Springtime in the Sierras
　Blackmail
　Wyoming
　Jesse James Rides Again
　Marshal of Cripple Creek
　Along the Oregon Trail
　The Wild Frontier
　The Fabulous Texan
　Bandits of Dark Canyon
　Under Colorado Skies*
1948—The Main Street Kid
　G-Men Never Forget
　Campus Honeymoon*
　Oklahoma Badlands
　Madonna of the Desert
　Lightnin' in the Forest
　California Firebrand*
　The Bold Frontiersman
　Dangers of the Canadian Mounted*
　Old Los Angeles
　I, Jane Doe*
　Secret Service Investigator
　The Timber Trail
　Train to Alcatraz
　Eyes of Texas
　Marshal of Amarillo
　Daredevils of the Clouds*
　Out of the Storm
　Sons of Adventure
　Angel in Exile*
　Desperadoes of Dodge City
　Grand Canyon Trail
　Adv. of Frank and Jesse James*
　Sundown in Santa Fe
　Renegades of Sonora
　The Far Frontier
1949—Rose of the Yukon*
　Sheriff of Wichita
　Federal Agents Vs. Underworld, Inc.
　Wake of the Red Witch*
　Ghost of Zorro
　The Red Pony*
　Prince of the Plains
　Frontier Investigator
　Law of the Golden West
　Outcasts of the Trail
　South of Rio
　Bandit King of Texas*
　The James Brothers of Missouri
　Down Dakota Way
　San Antone Ambush
　Ranger of Cherokee Strip
　Radar Patrol Vs. Spy King*
　Powder River Rustlers
　Pioneer Marshal
1950—Gunmen of Abilene
　Singing Guns*
　Sands of Iwo Jima*
　Federal Agent at Large
　Code of the Silver Sage
　The Vanishing Westerner
　The Arizona Cowboy
　Salt Lake Raiders
　Women from Headquarters*
　Rock Island Trail
　The Savage Horde
　Desperadoes of the West
　Vigilante Hideout
　Lonely Heart Bandits*
　Surrender
　Prisoners in Petticoats*
　Rustlers on Horseback
　North of the Great Divide
　Under Mexicali Stars
　The Missourians
1951—Missing Women*
　Night Riders of Montana
　Insurance Investigator
　Don Daredevil Rides Again
　In Old Amarillo
　Wells Fargo Gunmaster
　The Dakota Kid
　Govt. Agents Vs. Phantom Legion*
　Rodeo King and the Senorita
　Fort Dodge Stampede
　Arizona Manhunt
　Utah Wagon Train
　Honeychile
　Street Bandits
　Desert of Lost Men
　The Wild Blue Yonder*
　Pals of the Golden West
1952—Radar Men from the Moon
　Captive of Billy the Kid
　Leadville Gunslinger
　Oklahoma Annie
　Border Saddlemates
　Hoodlum Empire
　Wild Horse Ambush
　Black Hills Ambush
　Bal Tabarin*
　Zombies of the Stratosphere*
　Thundering Caravans
　Old Oklahoma Plains
　Tropical Heat Wave*
　Desperadoes' Outpost
　The Wac from Walla Walla
　South Pacific Trail
　Thunderbirds*
1953—Ride the Man Down
　Marshal of Cedar Rock
　Old Overland Trail
　The Lady Wants Mink*
　A Perilous Journey*
　Cosmic Vengeance*
　Iron Mountain Trail
　Savage Frontier
　Nightmare Typhoon*
　Destroyers of the Sun*
　Down Laredo Way
　Bandits of the West
　El Paso Stampede
　Shadows of Tombstone
1954—Man with the Steel Whip
1957—Last Stagecoach West

Edgar Barrier

Robert Barron

Phyllis Barry　　**Joan Barton**

Florence Bates

175

"Slingin' Sammy" Baugh

Alan Baxter

John Beach

Scotty Beckett

Baugh, "Slingin' Sammy"[176]
1941—King of the Texas Rangers

Baur, Esperanza[11]
No films.

Baxter, Alan[176]
1937—It Could Happen to You
1938—Gangs of New York
1941—Rags to Riches
       The Pittsburgh Kid
1942—Army 156—Horsemanship*

Baxter, George
1935—The Spanish Cape Mystery

Bayless, Mary
1939—Days of Jesse James*
1940—In Old Missouri*
1941—Petticoat Politics*
1943—G-Men Vs. The Black Dragon*
1944—Storm Over Lisbon*
1947—The Magnificent Rogue*
       That's My Gal*
       Blackmail*

Baylor, Hal[176]
       [As Hal Fieberling]
1950—Sands of Iwo Jima
       Destination Big House*
       [As Hal Baylor]
1951—The Wild Blue Yonder
1953—Woman They Almost Lynched*
       The Sun Shines Bright
       Champ for a Day
1954—Flight Nurse
       Tobor the Great

Bayne, Al
1938—Hollywood Stadium Mystery!

Beach, Brandon
1937—The Wrong Road*
1938—The Purple Vigilantes*
       Under Western Stars
1939—Street of Missing Men*
       Southward, Ho!*
1940—Rocky Mountain Rangers*
       The Trail Blazers*
1944—Call of the Rockies*
1949—Rose of the Yukon*
       Alias the Champ*
1950—Lonely Heart Bandits*
1953—A Perilous Journey*

Beach, John[176]
1937—Circus Girl*
1938—Gold Mine in the Sky*
       Heroes of the Hills
       Overland Stage Raiders*
       Rhythm of the Saddle*
       Come on, Rangers*
       Red River Range*
1939—Fighting Thoroughbreds
       Home on the Prairie
       The Lone Ranger Rides Again
       Mexicali Rose
       The Night Riders*
       Blue Montana Skies
       Three Texas Steers*
       Mountain Rhythm*
       Wyoming Outlaw*
       Colorado Sunset*
       New Frontier*
1940—Ghost Valley Raiders*
       The Tulsa Kid*
       Under Texas Skies*
       Texas Terrors*
       Lone Star Raiders*
       Bowery Boy*

Beach, Richard[11]
1936—Laughing Irish Eyes*
       The Big Show*
       The Mandarin Mystery
       Beware of Ladies*
       A Man Betrayed*
1937—Join the Marines
       Dick Tracy
       Jim Hanvey - Detective*
       Navy Blues*
       The Hit Parade*
       Gunsmoke Ranch*
       Michael O'Halloran*
       Rhythm in the Clouds*
       It Could Happen to You*
       S O S Coast Guard*

Beal, John[72]
1941—Doctors Don't Tell

Bear, Mary
1950—Singing Guns

Bearden, Gene
1949—The Kid from Cleveland

Beaton, Betzi
1945—An Angel Comes to Brooklyn

Beatty, Bob
1942—Suicide Squadron

Beatty, Clyde
1936—Darkest Africa

Beatty, Robert
1955—The Square Ring

Beaumont, Victor
1943—At Dawn We Die

Beavers, Louise
1952—Colorado Sundown
       I Dream of Jeanie

Beban, Bob
1951—The Wild Blue Yonder

Beban, George
1947—The Fabulous Texan
1949—Duke of Chicago

Beck, John
1936—King of the Pecos

Beck, Thomas
1938—I Stand Accused

Beckett, Scotty[176]
1939—Mickey, the Kid
       Days of Jesse James

Beddoe, Don[176]
1949—Hideout
       Flame of Youth
1950—Tarnished
1951—Belle LeGrand*
       Million Dollar Pursuit
       Rodeo King and the Senorita
1952—Hoodlum Empire
1954—Jubilee Trail*

Bedford, Barbara
1935—The Spanish Cape Mystery
       Forced Landing

Bedoya, Alfonso[176]
1948—Angel in Exile
       Angel on the Amazon

Beebe, Jane
1944—Cowboy and the Senorita

Beeby, Bruce
1957—The Man in the Road

Beecher, Janet[176]
1939—I Was a Convict
       Man of Conquest
1942—A Tragedy at Midnight*
       Hi, Neighbor

Beers, Bobby[11]
1942—South of Santa Fe*

Beery, Jr., Noah[176]
1939—Flight at Midnight
1940—The Carson City Kid
1950—The Savage Horde

Beery, Sr., Noah[176]
1937—Zorro Rides Again
1939—Mexicali Rose
1940—Pioneers of the West
       Grandpa Goes to Town
       Adventures of Red Ryder
       The Tulsa Kid
1941—A Missouri Outlaw
1942—Outlaws of Pine Ridge
1943—Carson City Cyclone

Beirute, Yerye
1956—A Woman's Devotion

Bekassy, Stephen[176]
1951—Secrets of Monte Carlo
1952—Woman of the North Country
1953—Fair Wind to Java

Belasco, Leon[176]
1940—Melody and Moonlight*
1941—The Singing Hill*
       Mountain Moonlight*
1944—Storm Over Lisbon
1945—Earl Carroll Vanities
1948—I, Jane Doe
1951—Cuban Fireball
       Havana Rose
1952—The Fabulous Senorita
       Gobs and Gals
1954—Geraldine

Belita
1941—Ice-Capades

Bell, Hank[176]
1935—Westward Ho
1936—Red River Valley*
       Comin' 'Round the Mountain*
1938—The Lone Ranger*
1939—Rough Riders' Round-Up*
       Frontier Pony Express*
1940—Rancho Grande*
       Young Buffalo Bill*
       Rocky Mountain Rangers*
       The Carson City Kid*
       Oklahoma Renegades*
       Young Bill Hickok*
1941—The Phantom Cowboy*
       Nevada City*
       Down Mexico Way*
       Jesse James at Bay*
1942—South of Santa Fe*
       The Sombrero Kid*
       Heart of the Golden West*
1943—Thundering Trails*
       Calling Wild Bill Elliott*
       Song of Texas*
       Wagon Tracks West*
       Man from Music Mountain
       Overland Mail Robbery*
       Raiders of Sunset Pass*
1944—San Fernando Valley*
       Code of the Prairie*
       Firebrands of Arizona*
1945—The Topeka Terror*
       Great Stagecoach Robbery*
       Flame of Barbary Coast*
       Bells of Rosarita*
       Sunset in El Dorado*
       Rough Riders of Cheyenne*
       The Cherokee Flash*
       Along the Navajo Trail*
1946—Plainsman and the Lady*
1948—California Firebrand*
       Old Los Angeles*
       The Gallant Legion*
       The Plunderers*
1949—The Last Bandit*
       Frontier Investigator*
       Outcasts of the Trail*
       Brimstone*

Don Beddoe

Alfonso Bedoya

Janet Beecher

Noah Beery, Jr.

Noah Beery, Sr.

Stephen Bekassy

Leon Belasco

Hank Bell

Judy Sochor, Joy Windsor, Hal Baylor, Carole Gallagher

Bell, James[72]
1947 — Driftwood
1948 — I, Jane Doe
1951 — Buckaroo Sheriff of Texas
 The Dakota Kid
 Arizona Manhunt
1952 — Wild Horse Ambush
1953 — Ride the Man Down
1955 — Lay that Rifle Down

Bell, Mostyn
1955 — In Old Vienna

Bell, Rodney
1945 — An Angel Comes to Brooklyn

Bellis, Guy
1951 — Pride of Maryland

Belmont, Virginia[177]
1948 — Dangers of the Canadian Mounted

Belmore, Daisy
1936 — The Girl from Mandalay

Belmore, Lionel
1935 — Forced Landing
 Hitch Hike Lady

Benaderet, Bea
1959 — Plunderers of Painted Flats

Benard, Ray
See Ray Corrigan.

Bendixen, Holger
1943 — The Purple V*

Benedict, Richard[177]
1949 — Streets of San Francisco
 Post Office Investigator
1950 — Destination Big House
1952 — Woman in the Dark
 Hoodlum Empire
1956 — The Man is Armed
1957 — Beginning of the End

Benedict, William[129]
1937 — Jim Hanvey - Detective*
 Rhythm in the Clouds*
1938 — King of the Newsboys
1939 — Man of Conquest*
1940 — Grand Ole Opry*
 Adventures of Red Ryder*
 Melody Ranch
 Bowery Boy*
1941 — Variety Reel*
 Mr. District Attorney*
 In Old Cheyenne*
 Adventures of Captain Marvel
 Citadel of Crime
 Bad Man of Deadwood*
 Jesse James at Bay*
 Tuxedo Junction
1942 — A Tragedy at Midnight*
 Affairs of Jimmy Valentine*
 Home in Wyomin'*
 Perils of Nyoka
 Valley of Hunted Men*
 Heart of the Golden West*
1943 — Nobody's Darling*
 Whispering Footsteps
1944 — The Lady and the Monster*
 Goodnight Sweetheart
 That's My Baby
1946 — Gay Blades*
1947 — The Pilgrim Lady*
1948 — Secret Service Investigator

Benge, Wilson[177]
1936 — Dancing Feet
 Happy Go Lucky*
1940 — Women in War*
 Melody and Moonlight
 Bowery Boy*
1941 — Adventures of Captain Marvel*
 Country Fair*
1942 — Moonlight Masquerade*
1944 — Captain America*
 Casanova in Burlesque*

Bennett, Anne
1937 — Come on, Cowboys!

Bennett, Bruce[177]
 [as Herman Brix]
1938 — The Lone Ranger
 The Fighting Devil Dogs
 Hawk of the Wilderness
1939 — Daredevils of the Red Circle
 [as Bruce Bennett]
1956 — Hidden Guns
 Daniel Boone, Trail Blazer

Bennett, Constance[91]
1948 — Angel on the Amazon

Bennett, Fran[177]
1955 — King of the Carnival

Bennett, Lee
1951 — The Dakota Kid

Bennett, Mickey
1936 — The Gentleman from Louisiana

Bennett, Raphael[177]
1937 — Public Cowboy No. 1*
1938 — The Old Barn Dance
 The Lone Ranger
 Dick Tracy Returns
 Prairie Moon
1940 — Dark Command
1941 — Gauchos of Eldorado
 A Missouri Outlaw*
 Dick Tracy Vs. Crime, Inc.*
1942 — Call of the Canyon*
1943 — King of the Cowboys*
1951 — Heart of the Rockies*
1952 — Woman of the North Country*
1955 — African Manhunt

Bennett, Rex—series
1943 — G-Men Vs. The Black Dragon
 Secret Service in Darkest Africa

Bennett, Richard
1941 — Stars Past and Present*

Bennett, Tony
1956 — Come Next Spring*

Benny, Joan
1941 — Variety Reel*

Virginia Belmont

Richard Benedict

Wilson Benge

Benoits, The
1941 — Ice-Capades
1942 — Ice-Capades Revue

Benson, George
1955 — Doctor in the House

Benson, Martin[177]
1957 — Thunder Over Tangier

Benton, Dean[11]
1935 — Forced Landing
1937 — Join the Marines*
 Jim Hanvey - Detective*

Berarcino, John
1949 — The Kid from Cleveland
1955 — I Cover the Underworld*

Berela, Armanda
1940 — Chinese Garden Festival*

Berens, Harold
1957 — Thunder Over Tangier

Berg, Kid
1955 — The Square Ring

Berkes, Johnnie
1942 — Cowboy Serenade

Berkova, Saundra[177]
1945 — Captain Tugboat Annie

Berle, Milton
1941 — Los Angeles Examiner Benefit*

Berlin, Patsy
1935 — The Crime of Doctor Crespi

Berliner, Martin
1955 — In Old Vienna

Bernard, Barry
1945 — The Fatal Witness

Bernard, Bert[177]
1952 — Gobs and Gals

Bernard, George[177]
1952 — Gobs and Gals

Bernard, Joelle
1959 — O.S.S. 117 is Not Dead

Bernard, Sam
1942 — Ice-Capades Revue
1944 — Thoroughbreds

Bernard, Tommy
1947 — Yankee Fakir

Bertrand, Rosemary[177]
1947 — Angel and the Badman*
1950 — The Arizona Cowboy*

Besbas, Peter E.
1957 — Journey to Freedom

Besser, Joe
1955 — Headline Hunters
1959 — Plunderers of Painted Flats

Best, James
1955 — The Eternal Sea*
1956 — Come Next Spring
 When Gangland Strikes*

Best, Willie[177]
1939 — The Covered Trailer
1940 — Who Killed Aunt Maggie?
1944 — The Girl Who Dared
1951 — South of Caliente

Bestar, Barbara[177]
1949 — Navajo Trail Raiders
1954 — Man with the Steel Whip

Bevan, Billy[177]
1937 — The Sheik Steps Out
 The Wrong Road
1943 — London Blackout Murders

Bruce Bennett    **Fran Bennett**   **Raphael Bennett**   **Martin Benson**

Saundra Berkova   **Rosemary Bertrand**

George Bernard, Bert Bernard

Willie Best   **Barbara Bestar**   **Billy Bevan**

Clem Bevans, Clara Blandick

Bevans, Clem[178]
1936 — The President's Mystery*
1939 — Main Street Lawyer
1940 — Girl from God's Country
    Who Killed Aunt Maggie?*
1945 — Grissly's Millions
1947 — Yankee Fakir
1948 — Moonrise
1951 — Silver City Bonanza
1952 — Captive of Billy the Kid
1955 — The Twinkle in God's Eye*

Beverly Hill Billies
1936 — The Big Show
1937 — Meet the Boy Friend

Biberman, Abner[178]
1940 — Girl from Havana
1941 — The Gay Vagabond
    The Devil Pays Off
1942 — King of the Mounties

Bice, Robert[178]
1946 — G.I. War Brides*
    The Mysterious Mr. Valentine
1949 — Susanna Pass
    Flaming Fury*
    Bandit King of Texas
    The James Brothers of Missouri
1950 — Bells of Coronado
    Prisoners in Petticoats*
    Hit Parade of 1951*
    Under Mexicali Stars
1953 — Bandits of the West
1954 — Trader Tom of the China Seas*

Bickford, Charles[72]
1938 — Gangs of New York
1939 — Street of Missing Men
    Thou Shalt Not Kill
1940 — Girl from God's Country

Bikel, Theodore
1955 — A Day to Remember
    The Divided Heart
1956 — Above Us the Waves

Bilbrook, Lydia
1943 — Pistol Packin' Mama

Bildt, Paul
1958 — International Counterfeiters

Billie, Jose
1955 — Yellowneck

Billingsley, Barbara[178]
1950 — Trial Without Jury
1951 — Oh! Susanna*
1952 — Woman in the Dark
1953 — The Lady Wants Mink*

Bing, Herman[178]
1935 — $1000 a Minute
1936 — Laughing Irish Eyes

Birch, Paul
1955 — The Fighting Chance
1956 — When Gangland Strikes

Bird, Billie
1957 — Panama Sal

Bird, Richard
1937 — Bulldog Drummond at Bay

Birell, Tala[178]
1938 — Invisible Enemy
1945 — Girls of the Big House
1948 — Homicide for Three

Birgel, Willy
1956 — Circus Girl

Bishop, Julie[178]
    [as Jacqueline Wells]
1939 — The Kansas Terrors
1940 — The Ranger and the Lady
    Young Bill Hickok
1941 — Wampas Baby Stars*
    Back in the Saddle
    [as Julie Bishop]
1946 — Murder in the Music Hall
1950 — Sands of Iwo Jima
1955 — Headline Hunters

Bissell, Whit[178]
1952 — Hoodlum Empire*
1954 — The Shanghai Story
    The Atomic Kid
1956 — Dakota Incident
1957 — The Wayward Girl

Black Jack
Horse. Credited on-screen in all 38
Allan "Rocky" Lane westerns and one
Land of Opportunity short subject.

Black, Maurice
1936 — Laughing Irish Eyes

Blackman, Don
1953 — Jungle Drums of Africa

Blackmer, Sidney[91]
1935 — Forced Landing
1936 — The President's Mystery
1937 — Michael O'Halloran
1938 — Orphans of the Street
1941 — Rookies on Parade
    Angels with Broken Wings
    Down Mexico Way
1943 — In Old Oklahoma
1944 — The Lady and the Monster
1956 — Accused of Murder

Blackwell, Jr., Carlyle
1947 — The Pilgrim Lady

Blair, Joan[178]
1941 — Mr. District Attorney
    Rags to Riches
1943 — Whispering Footsteps
1944 — Silent Partner
1945 — Grissly's Millions
    Earl Carroll Vanities*
1946 — A Guy Could Change*
    That Brennan Girl*
1948 — Sons of Adventure

Blair, Robert
1940 — Rocky Mountain Rangers
    The Trail Blazers
1947 — Last Frontier Uprising

Blake, Bobby[160]
1944 — Tucson Raiders
    Marshal of Reno
    The San Antonio Kid
    Cheyenne Wildcat
    Vigilantes of Dodge City
    Sheriff of Las Vegas
1945 — Great Stagecoach Robbery
    Lone Texas Ranger
    Phantom of the Plains
    Marshal of Laredo
    Colorado Pioneers
    Wagon Wheels Westward
    Dakota
1946 — A Guy Could Change
    California Gold Rush
    Sheriff of Redwood Valley
    Home on the Range
    Sun Valley Cyclone
    In Old Sacramento
    Conquest of Cheyenne
    Santa Fe Uprising
    Out California Way
    Stagecoach to Denver
1947 — Vigilantes of Boomtown
    Homesteaders of Paradise Valley
    Oregon Trail Scouts
    Rustlers of Devil's Canyon
    Marshal of Cripple Creek

Blake, Gladys
1939 — Money to Burn

Blake, Larry J.[179]
1946 — The Undercover Woman
1949 — The Blonde Bandit
1950 — Destination Big House
1951 — In Old Amarillo*
1953 — Champ for a Day*
1955 — The Twinkle in God's Eye*
1956 — The Man is Armed
1957 — Beginning of the End
1958 — Outcasts of the City

Blake, Marie
1943 — Whispering Footsteps

Blake, Oliver
1954 — Hell's Outpost

Blake, Pamela[179]
    [as Adele Pearce]
1939 — Wyoming Outlaw
    [as Pamela Blake]
1945 — Three's a Crowd
    Captain Tugboat Annie
1948 — Son of God's Country
1949 — Ghost of Zorro

Blakeney, Olive
1944 — The Port of Forty Thieves
1945 — Dakota
1954 — Roogie's Bump

Blanchard, Mari[91]
1958 — No Place to Land

Blandick, Clara[178]
1939 — I Was a Convict
    Main Street Lawyer*

Blane, Sally
1941 — Wampas Baby Stars*

Blatty, Bill
1958 — No Place to Land

Bleifer, John
1940 — Girl from God's Country
1943 — Headin' for God's Country

Bletcher, Billy[179]
1938 — The Purple Vigilantes*
    The Lone Ranger*
    The Higgins Family*
    Orphans of the Street*
1939 — The Lone Ranger Rides Again*
    Should Husbands Work?*
    The Covered Trailer*
    Zorro's Fighting Legion*
    Money to Burn*
1940 — Grandpa Goes to Town*
    Scatterbrain*
    Hit Parade of 1941*
    Melody Ranch*
1941 — Angels with Broken Wings*
    Chatterbox
1943 — In Old Oklahoma*
1946 — Gay Blades*

Blin, Roger
1951 — Adventures of Captain Fabian

Blomfield, Derek
1943 — Alibi

Blondell, Joan[91]
1941 — Wampas Baby Stars*
1942 — Lady for a Night

Bloom, Joe
1955 — The Square Ring

Blore, Eric[179]
1938 — A Desperate Adventure
1940 — Earl of Puddlestone
1947 — Winter Wonderland

Blue, Ben
1936 — Follow Your Heart

Blue, Monte[179]
1936 — Undersea Kingdom
    Ride Ranger Ride
1937 — Rootin' Tootin' Rhythm
1938 — Hawk of the Wilderness
1939 — Frontier Pony Express
    Days of Jesse James
1940 — Young Bill Hickok
1941 — Arkansas Judge
    The Great Train Robbery
    Sunset in Wyoming
    Citadel of Crime*
    Bad Man of Deadwood
    King of the Texas Rangers
1949 — Ranger of Cherokee Strip
    The Blonde Bandit
1951 — The Sea Hornet

Robert Bice

Barbara Billingsley

Herman Bing

Tala Birell

Julie Bishop

Abner Biberman, Steffi Duna

Whit Bissell

Joan Blair

 **Larry J. Blake**
 **Pamela Blake**
 **Billy Bletcher**
 **Shirley Eaton, Dirk Bogarde**
 **Eric Blore**
 **Monte Blue**
 **Stanley Blystone**

 **Betty Blythe**
 **Mary Boland**
 **Hannelore Bollmann**

 **Roman Bohnen**
 **Anita Bolster**
Fortunio Bonanova
 **Karin Booth**
 **Veda Ann Borg**

Blystone, Stanley[179]
1936 – The Vigilantes Are Coming*
  The Three Mesquiteers*
1937 – Two Wise Maids
  Youth on Parole*
  Boots and Saddles
  Manhattan Merry-Go-Round*
1938 – Born to be Wild*
  Red River Range
1939 – The Lone Ranger Rides Again
  Three Texas Steers
  Man of Conquest*
  Southward, Ho!*
1940 – Dark Command
  Grandpa Goes to Town*
  The Tulsa Kid
1941 – Back in the Saddle*
  Lady from Louisiana*
  Country Fair*
  Sunset in Wyoming
  King of the Texas Rangers
  West of Cimarron*
1942 – Arizona Terrors*
  Pardon My Stripes*
  Jesse James, Jr.
  In Old California*
  The Old Homestead*
  Ice-Capades Revue*
  The Traitor Within*
1946 – King of the Forest Rangers
  That Brennan Girl*
1947 – Hit Parade of 1947*
  Yankee Fakir*
  That's My Gal*
  The Wild Frontier*
  Under Colorado Skies*
1948 – I, Jane Doe*
  Eyes of Texas
  Out of the Storm*
  The Denver Kid*
  The Far Frontier*
1949 – Rose of the Yukon*
  Ghost of Zorro*
  Navajo Trail Raiders*
  Powder River Rustlers
1950 – Singing Guns*
  Covered Wagon Raid*
  Desperadoes of the West
  Lonely Heart Bandits*
  Sunset in the West*
  Trail of Robin Hood*
1951 – Havana Rose*
  Honeychile*
1952 – Colorado Sundown*
1953 – A Perilous Journey*
1955 – I Cover the Underworld*
  Headline Hunters

Blythe, Betty[179]
1935 – The Spanish Cape Mystery
1940 – Earl of Puddlestone
1941 – Tuxedo Junction
1946 – The Undercover Woman
1948 – Madonna of the Desert

Boardman, Eleanor
1941 – Wampas Baby Stars*

Boddey, Martin
1955 – Doctor in the House
  Secret Venture

Boddy, Philip L.
1953 – City that Never Sleeps

Bogarde, Dirk[179]
1955 – Doctor in the House
1956 – Doctor at Sea

Bohn, John
1935 – The Crime of Doctor Crespi

Bohnen, Roman[179]
1942 – Affairs of Jimmy Valentine
1947 – Winter Wonderland

Boland, Ed
1937 – Hit the Saddle

Boland, Mary[179]
1938 – Mama Runs Wild
1940 – Hit Parade of 1941

Bollmann, Hannelore[179]
1957 – The Congress Dances

Bolster, Anita[179]
1943 – London Blackout Murders

Bomber Kulkovich [Henry Kulky]
1949 – Alias the Champ
1952 – Gobs and Gals
1954 – Tobor the Great

Bonanova, Fortunio[179]
1944 – My Best Gal
  Brazil
1948 – Angel on the Amazon
1951 – Havana Rose
1956 – Jaguar

Bond, Derek
1955 – Trouble in Store

Bond, Lilian
1942 – A Tragedy at Midnight

Bond, Richard
1942 – Spy Smasher

Bond, Tommy
1944 – Man from Frisco

Bond, Ward[91]
1935 – Hitch Hike Lady
1936 – The Leathernecks Have Landed
1937 – Escape by Night
1938 – Born to be Wild
1941 – A Man Betrayed
  Doctors Don't Tell
1945 – Dakota
1950 – Singing Guns
1952 – The Quiet Man
  Thunderbirds
1954 – Johnny Guitar
1955 – A Man Alone
1956 – Dakota Incident

Bondi, Beulah
1940 – Chinese Garden Festival*
1941 – Variety Reel*

Bonga
1936 – Darkest Africa

Boone, Ray
1949 – The Kid from Cleveland

Booth, Adrian[12]
  [as Lorna Gray]
1938 – Red River Range
1941 – Tuxedo Junction
1942 – Perils of Nyoka
  Ridin' Down the Canyon
1943 – O, My Darling Clementine
1944 – Captain America
  The Girl Who Dared
1945 – Federal Operator 99
  [as Adrian Booth]
  Tell It to a Star
  The Tiger Woman*
  Dakota*
1946 – Home on the Range
  Valley of the Zombies
  Man from Rainbow Valley
  Daughter of Don Q
  The Invisible Informer*
  I've Always Loved You*
  Out California Way
1947 – Last Frontier Uprising
  Spoilers of the North
  Along the Oregon Trail
  Exposed
  Under Colorado Skies
1948 – Lightnin' in the Forest
  California Firebrand
  I, Jane Doe*
  The Gallant Legion
  The Plunderers
1949 – Hideout
  The Last Bandit
  Brimstone
1950 – Rock Island Trail
  The Savage Horde
1951 – Oh! Susanna
  The Sea Hornet

Booth, Karin[179]
1954 – Tobor the Great
1955 – African Manhunt

Borchers, Cornell
1955 – The Divided Heart

Borell, Louis
1943 – London Blackout Murders

Borg, Sven Hugo
1944 – Secrets of Scotland Yard*
  My Buddy*

Borg, Veda Ann[179]
1940 – Hit Parade of 1941*
  Melody Ranch*
  Behind the News
1941 – Arkansas Judge
  The Pittsburgh Kid
1943 – False Faces
1944 – The Girl Who Dared
1945 – Love, Honor and Goodbye
1946 – The Fabulous Suzanne
1947 – The Pilgrim Lady
1953 – A Perilous Journey

Borgnine, Ernest[91]
1954 – Johnny Guitar
1955 – The Last Command

Boros, Ferike
1940 – Girl from God's Country
1946 – Specter of the Rose

Bosworth, Hobart
1937 – Portia on Trial

Boteler, Wade[129]
1935 – Melody Trail
1936 – The Return of Jimmy Valentine
  The President's Mystery
  Country Gentlemen
  The Mandarin Mystery
1937 – Jim Hanvey - Detective
  Dangerous Holiday
  Youth on Parole
1938 – Billy the Kid Returns
1939 – The Mysterious Miss X
  Southward, Ho!
  Sabotage
  Days of Jesse James
1940 – Young Buffalo Bill
  Gaucho Serenade
  Three Faces West
  Under Texas Skies
1941 – Robin Hood of the Pecos*
  The Singing Hill
  Hurricane Smith*
1942 – Affairs of Jimmy Valentine*

Botiller, Dick[180]
1936—Comin' 'Round the Mountain*
1939—Mexicali Rose
    Man of Conquest*
    The Kansas Terrors*
    South of the Border
1940—Young Buffalo Bill*
1941—Wyoming Wildcat
1943—In Old Oklahoma*
1944—The Yellow Rose of Texas
    Haunted Harbor*

Dick Botiller

William "Bill" Boyd, Sheila Terry

Bouchey, Willis[180]
1955—The Eternal Sea*
    I Cover the Underworld
1957—Last Stagecoach West

Boudreau, Lou
1949—The Kid from Cleveland

Boulton, Matthew
1944—Secrets of Scotland Yard

Bovard, Mary[14]
1936—The Mandarin Mystery
    A Man Betrayed
1939—Forged Passport*
1941—A Man Betrayed*

Bowden, Doris
1940—Chinese Garden Festival*

Bowen, Harry
1936—The Harvester
    The Gentleman from Louisiana

Bower, Aubrey
1951—Adventures of Captain Fabian

Bowman, Empsie
1941—Poison Pen

Bowman, Lee[91]
1950—House by the River

Bowman, Ralph
See John Archer.

Boxer, John
1955—Secret Venture

Boyd, Beverly
1943—Nobody's Darling

Boyd, William "Bill"[180]
1935—Racing Luck
    Burning Gold
1936—Federal Agent
    Go-Get-'Em, Haines

Boyle, Jack
1944—My Best Gal

Boyle, Ray
1952—Zombies of the Stratosphere

Boys' Choir—of St. Joseph's School
1940—Rancho Grande

Bradford, John
1936—Undersea Kingdom
    The Old Corral
1937—Dick Tracy*

Bradford, Lane[180]
1943—Thundering Trails*
    Riders of the Rio Grande*
1945—Marshal of Laredo*
1948—Adv. of Frank and Jesse James
    Sundown in Santa Fe
    The Far Frontier
1949—Sheriff of Wichita*
    Death Valley Gunfighter
    Prince of the Plains
    Law of the Golden West
    The Wyoming Bandit
    South of Rio
    Bandit King of Texas
    The James Brothers of Missouri
    San Antone Ambush
    Ranger of Cherokee Strip*
1950—Bells of Coronado
    Code of the Silver Sage
    The Arizona Cowboy
    Hills of Oklahoma
    The Invisible Monster
    The Old Frontier
    Frisco Tornado
    The Missourians
    Trail of Robin Hood*
1951—Don Daredevil Rides Again
    Wells Fargo Gunmaster*
1952—Zombies of the Stratosphere
    Desperadoes' Outpost
1953—Solar Sky Raiders
    Bandits of the West*
1954—Man with the Steel Whip

Bradford, Marshall
1951—Night Riders of Montana

Bradley, Betty
1944—Trocadero

Bradley, Grace[180]
1936—Sitting on the Moon
1937—Larceny on the Air
1938—Romance on the Run

Bradley, Harry
1935—$1000 a Minute
1936—Dancing Feet
1939—Should Husbands Work?

Bradley, John H.
1950—Sands of Iwo Jima

Bradna, Olympe
1941—Hollywood Visits the Navy*

Brady, Alice[92]
1936—The Harvester

Brady, Buff
1951—Rodeo King and the Senorita

Brady, Ed
1938—Thunder in the Desert
1939—Southward, Ho!
1941—Wyoming Wildcat

Brady, Pat[73]
1941—Red River Valley*
1942—Man from Cheyenne*
    South of Santa Fe*
    Sunset on the Desert*
    Romance on the Range*
    Sons of the Pioneers*
    Call of the Canyon*
    Sunset Serenade*
    Heart of the Golden West*
    Ridin' Down the Canyon*
1943—Idaho*
    King of the Cowboys*
    Song of Texas
    Silver Spurs*
    Man from Music Mountain
    Hands Across the Border*
1946—Under Nevada Skies*
    Roll on Texas Moon*
    Home in Oklahoma*
    Heldorado*
1947—Apache Rose*
    Hit Parade of 1947*
    Bells of San Angelo*
    Springtime in the Sierras*
    On the Old Spanish Trail*
1948—The Gay Ranchero*
    Under California Stars*
    Eyes of Texas*
    Night Time in Nevada*
1949—Down Dakota Way*
    The Golden Stallion
1950—Bells of Coronado
    Twilight in the Sierras*
    Trigger, Jr.
1951—In Old Amarillo*
    South of Caliente
    Pals of the Golden West*

Brady, Scott[92]
1953—A Perilous Journey
1954—Johnny Guitar
1955—The Vanishing American
1956—Terror at Midnight
    The Maverick Queen

Brady, William
1940—Earl of Puddlestone

Braham, Lionel
1950—Macbeth

Brand, George
1951—Million Dollar Pursuit

Branden, Michael
    [as Archie Twitchell]
1939—Street of Missing Men*
    Mickey, the Kid
    Smuggled Cargo*
    Flight at Midnight*
    Calling All Marines*
    The Arizona Kid*
1940—Wolf of New York
    Young Bill Hickok
    Barnyard Follies*
    Mysterious Doctor Satan
    Behind the News
1941—Petticoat Politics*
    Mr. District Attorney*
    Sis Hopkins*
    Rags to Riches*
    Bad Man of Deadwood*
    Dick Tracy Vs. Crime, Inc.*
1942—A Tragedy at Midnight
1945—Swingin' on a Rainbow*
    Behind City Lights*
    [as Michael Branden]
    Don't Fence Me In*
1946—The French Key
    Affairs of Geraldine
    That Brennan Girl*
1947—That's My Man*
    Web of Danger
    Robin Hood of Texas
1948—Moonrise*
1951—In Old Amarillo*

Brandon, Henry[180]
1940—Drums of Fu Manchu
    The Ranger and the Lady
    Under Texas Skies
1941—Hurricane Smith
    Bad Man of Deadwood
1947—Northwest Outpost*
1948—Old Los Angeles
1949—Wake of the Red Witch*
1957—Hell's Crossroads

Walter Brennan, Jr.

Evelyn Brent

Brannan, Carol[180]
1949—Flame of Youth

Brasselle, Keefe
1944—Three Little Sisters*
    Navy MN 3387—Your Weapons*
1947—Bells of San Angelo*
1957—The Fighting Wildcats

Breakston, George
1950—Jungle Stampede

Brecher, Egon
1938—Invisible Enemy
1943—The Purple V*

Breen, Bobby[180]
1942—Johnny Doughboy

Bremen, Lennie
1952—Tropical Heat Wave

Brennan, Michael
1955—Trouble in Store

Brennan, Ruth[14]
1946—Gay Blades*
    The Last Crooked Mile*
    Affairs of Geraldine*
1950—California Passage
1951—Oh! Susanna
1954—Sea of Lost Ships*
    Hell's Outpost*

Brennan, Jr., Walter [Andy][180]
1951—The Wild Blue Yonder*
1952—Hoodlum Empire*
    Woman of the North Country*
    Toughest Man in Arizona*
1953—Ride the Man Down*
    San Antone
    Woman They Almost Lynched*
1954—Sea of Lost Ships*
    Jubilee Trail*

Brennan, Sr., Walter[92]
1937—Affairs of Cappy Ricks
1945—Dakota
1947—Driftwood
1949—Brimstone
1950—Singing Guns
    The Showdown
    Surrender
1951—The Wild Blue Yonder
1954—Sea of Lost Ships
1956—Come Next Spring

Brent, Evelyn[180]
1936—The President's Mystery
1941—Wampas Baby Stars*
1942—Westward Ho

Brent, George[73]
1948—Angel on the Amazon
1949—The Kid from Cleveland

Brent, Linda[181]
1942—Affairs of Jimmy Valentine*
    The Old Homestead
    Flying Tigers*
1943—A Scream in the Dark
    In Old Oklahoma*
1944—The Laramie Trail

Willis Bouchey

Lane Bradford

Grace Bradley

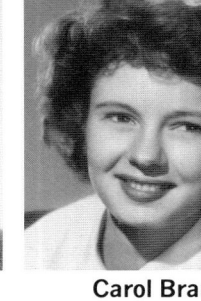

Henry Brandon

Carol Brannan

Bobby Breen

 Linda Brent
 Roy Brent
 Felix Bressart
 Mary Brian
 Alan Bridge

 Virginia Brissac
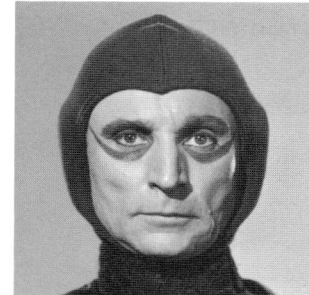 Peter Brocco

Helen Broderick

Steve Brodie

 J. Edward Bromberg

Brent, Lynton[129]
1936 — Dancing Feet
Federal Agent*
The Old Corral
1937 — Git Along Little Dogies*
Affairs of Cappy Ricks*
Boots and Saddles*
Portia on Trial*
1938 — Romance on the Run*
Army Girl*
Dick Tracy Returns*
I Stand Accused*
1939 — Street of Missing Men*
S.O.S. Tidal Wave*
Flight at Midnight*
Wall Street Cowboy*
Calling All Marines*
Days of Jesse James*
1940 — Village Barn Dance*
Young Buffalo Bill*
Wagons Westward*
Adventures of Red Ryder
Hit Parade of 1941*
Mysterious Doctor Satan
Bowery Boy*
1941 — A Man Betrayed*
Adventures of Captain Marvel*
Country Fair*
Bad Man of Deadwood*
Red River Valley
Dick Tracy Vs. Crime, Inc.*
1942 — Man from Cheyenne*
South of Santa Fe*
Shepherd of the Ozarks*
Sunset Serenade*
The Traitor Within*
1943 — Idaho*
King of the Cowboys*
Calling Wild Bill Elliott
Man from Music Mountain*
The Masked Marvel*
Here Comes Elmer*
In Old Oklahoma*
1944 — Captain America*
Rosie, the Riveter*
Jamboree*
Cowboy and the Senorita*
Goodnight Sweetheart*
My Buddy*

Brent, Roy[181]
1939 — Pride of the Navy*
Mexicali Rose*
Daredevils of the Red Circle*
Calling All Marines*
1940 — Adventures of Red Ryder*
One Man's Law*
1941 — Angels with Broken Wings*
1942 — Spy Smasher*
Outlaws of Pine Ridge*
1943 — Carson City Cyclone*
The Man from Thunder River*
1944 — Captain America*
The Fighting Seabees*
Man from Frisco*
Song of Nevada*
Zorro's Black Whip*
1945 — Hitchhike to Happiness*

Bressart, Felix[181]
1946 — I've Always Loved You

Brewster, Barbara
1940 — Chinese Garden Festival*

Brewster, Carol
1956 — The Maverick Queen*

Brewster, Gloria
1940 — Chinese Garden Festival*

Brian, David[92]
1953 — A Perilous Journey
1955 — Timberjack
1956 — Accused of Murder

Brian, Eddie
1939 — Fighting Thoroughbreds

Brian, Mary[181]
1937 — Navy Blues
Affairs of Cappy Ricks

Bridge, Alan[181]
1935 — The New Frontier
Melody Trail
1936 — The Lawless Nineties
The Three Mesquiteers
1937 — Springtime in the Rockies
1938 — Born to be Wild*
Down in "Arkansaw"
1939 — Blue Montana Skies
1940 — Dark Command*
Meet the Missus*
1941 — Lady from Louisiana*
Country Fair*
The Gay Vagabond*
Rags to Riches*
Tuxedo Junction*
1942 — Pardon My Stripes*
Affairs of Jimmy Valentine*
Bells of Capistrano*
The Traitor Within*
1943 — Idaho*
The Man from Thunder River*
Nobody's Darling*
1944 — Lights of Old Santa Fe*
1946 — My Pal Trigger*
1947 — Robin Hood of Texas
1950 — North of the Great Divide*
California Passage
1951 — Oh! Susanna
In Old Amarillo*
Utah Wagon Train*
1952 — The Last Musketeer
1953 — Iron Mountain Trail
1954 — Jubilee Trail*
Hell's Outpost*

Bridge, Loie
1943 — O, My Darling Clementine

Bridges, Beau
1949 — The Red Pony

Bridges, Lloyd[92]
1936 — Dancing Feet*
1948 — Secret Service Investigator
Moonrise
1949 — Hideout

Brier, Barbara
1951 — Fighting Coast Guard*

Briggs, Harlan
1936 — Happy Go Lucky
1939 — The Mysterious Miss X
Flight at Midnight
1946 — My Pal Trigger
1947 — Spoilers of the North

Brilliant
1943 — The Blocked Trail

Brinckman, Nancy
1943 — Sleepy Lagoon*
Hoosier Holiday*
1945 — An Angel Comes to Brooklyn*

Brink, Larry
1954 — Crazylegs

Brisbane, William
1939 — Should Husbands Work?

Brissac, Virginia[181]
1939 — Woman Doctor
1940 — Wagons Westward
1943 — Someone to Remember*
1944 — Sing Neighbor Sing
Faces in the Fog*
1945 — Three's a Crowd
1946 — The Mysterious Mr. Valentine
1948 — Old Los Angeles
1949 — The Last Bandit
1952 — Woman of the North Country
1953 — Fair Wind to Java*

Brister, Robert
1937 — Sea Racketeers*
1939 — Flight at Midnight*
Dick Tracy's G-Men*
Main Street Lawyer*

Britt, May
1954 — The She Wolf

Britton, Barbara[92]
1946 — The Fabulous Suzanne
1953 — Ride the Man Down

Brix, Herman
See Bruce Bennett.

Brocco, Peter[181]
1949 — Susanna Pass*
Flaming Fury
Post Office Investigator
1950 — Gunmen of Abilene
House by the River
1951 — Belle LeGrand*
1952 — Radar Men from the Moon
Woman in the Dark
1953 — Enemies of the Universe
Atomic Peril
1954 — Tobor the Great*
The Atomic Kid*
1956 — Stranger at My Door*

Broderick, Helen[181]
1945 — Love, Honor and Goodbye

Brodie, Steve[181]
1949 — Rose of the Yukon
1951 — Fighting Coast Guard
1952 — Bal Tabarin
1954 — Sea of Lost Ships
1957 — The Crooked Circle

Bromberg, J. Edward[181]
1941 — Hurricane Smith
The Devil Pays Off

Bromley, Sheila[181]
1938 — King of the Newsboys
1939 — Thou Shalt Not Kill
1957 — Spoilers of the Forest
The Lawless Eighties

Bronson, Betty
1937 — Yodelin' Kid from Pine Ridge

Bronson, Bunny
1936 — Roarin' Lead*
1940 — Sing, Dance, Plenty Hot*
1942 — Lady for a Night*

Bronson, Lillian
1945 — Road to Alcatraz

Brook, Claude
1956 — Daniel Boone, Trail Blazer

Brook, Lyndon
1956 — Above Us the Waves

Brook, Patrick[181]
1942 — Johnny Doughboy

Brooke, Clifford
1946 — The Madonna's Secret

Brooke, Hillary[181]
1941 — Country Fair*
1942 — Sleepytime Gal*
1946 — Strange Impersonation
Earl Carroll Sketchbook
1950 — Unmasked
1951 — Insurance Investigator
1953 — The Lady Wants Mink
1957 — Spoilers of the Forest

Brooklyn Dodgers, The
1954 — Roogie's Bump

Brooks, Barry
1948 — G-Men Never Forget

Brooks, Howard
1937 — Affairs of Cappy Ricks*

Brooks, Louise[181]
1938 — Overland Stage Raiders

 Sheila Bromley
 Patrick Brook
 Hilliary Brooke
 Louise Brooks

Phyllis Brooks

Edward Brophy

Charles D. Brown

James Brown

Brown, Helen
1941—Mr. District Attorney

Brown, James[182]
1947—The Fabulous Texan
1948—The Gallant Legion
1949—Brimstone
1950—Sands of Iwo Jima
1951—Missing Women
  The Sea Hornet
  The Wild Blue Yonder
1953—Woman They Almost Lynched
1954—Sea of Lost Ships
  Crazylegs
  Flight Nurse

Brown, Jr., Joe
1951—The Wild Blue Yonder

Brown, Joe E.[73]
1941—Stars at Play*
1942—Joan of Ozark
1943—Chatterbox
1944—Casanova in Burlesque

Brown, John
1954—Crazylegs

Brown, Johnny Mack[147]
1936—Under Cover Man
  Lawless Land
1937—Bar-Z Bad Men
  The Gambling Terror
  Trail of Vengeance
  Guns in the Dark
  A Lawman is Born
  Boothill Brigade

Brown, Kenneth
See Butch and Buddy.

Brown, Lowell
1957—Eighteen and Anxious

Brown, Naaman
1955—Panther Girl of the Kongo

Brown, Phil
1948—Moonrise

Brown, Raymond
1936—Comin' 'Round the Mountain
1937—Two Wise Maids

Brown, Slavina
1940—Chinese Garden Festival*

Brown, Tom[182]
1937—Jim Hanvey - Detective
1942—Sleepytime Gal
  Youth on Parade
1948—Slippy McGee
1949—Duke of Chicago
1958—The Notorious Mr. Monks

Brown, Vanessa[182]
1946—I've Always Loved You

Browne, Lucile[182]
1935—Tumbling Tumbleweeds
1940—Ride, Tenderfoot, Ride*
  Who Killed Aunt Maggie?*
1941—Mr. District Attorney*
  Doctors Don't Tell*
1942—A Tragedy at Midnight*

Browne, Michael[182]
1946—Crime of the Century

Browning, Jill
1945—Utah

Browning, Lynne
1937—Navy Blues*
  Michael O'Halloran*
1938—Gangs of New York*

Brownlee, Frank[182]
1935—Tumbling Tumbleweeds*
1940—Three Faces West*
  Mysterious Doctor Satan*
1941—Country Fair*
  Puddin' Head*
  Gangs of Sonora*
  Citadel of Crime*
  The Apache Kid*
  A Missouri Outlaw
1942—Arizona Terrors
  Man from Cheyenne*
  South of Santa Fe*
  Jesse James, Jr.*
  Romance on the Range*
  In Old California*
  Sons of the Pioneers*
  The Sombrero Kid*
  Shadows on the Sage*
  Ice-Capades Revue*
1943—Mountain Rhythm*
  Dead Man's Gulch*

Bruce, David
1942—Flying Tigers

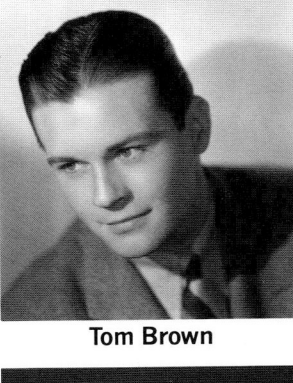

Tom Brown

Vanessa Brown

Lucile Browne

Michael Browne

Frank Brownlee

Nigel Bruce

George "Gabby" Hayes, Lynne Carver, James Seay, Fred Burns, Jack Kirk, Bob Burns

Bruce, Gary
1943—Fugitive from Sonora

Bruce, Lorraine
1959—O.S.S. 117 is Not Dead

Bruce, Nigel[182]
1936—Follow Your Heart

Bruce, Virginia[92]
1944—Brazil
1945—Love, Honor and Goodbye

Brundige, Bill
1954—Crazylegs

Brune, Gabrielle
1943—At Dawn We Die

Brunetti, Argentina[183]
1949—The Blonde Bandit
1952—Woman in the Dark
  Bal Tabarin*
1953—San Antone
1954—Make Haste to Live*
1955—The Last Command*
1957—Duel at Apache Wells

Brunn, Frederic[183]
1943—The Purple V*
  Secret Service in Darkest Africa
1948—I, Jane Doe*

Bruno, Frank
1941—King of the Texas Rangers

Bruno, Leo
1958—Invisible Avenger

Bryan, Arthur Q.
1954—Hell's Outpost

Bryan, Ella
1941—Wampas Baby Stars*

Bryant, Nana[183]
1939—Street of Missing Men
1941—Public Enemies
1942—Youth on Parade
1943—The West Side Kid
1948—Eyes of Texas
1949—Hideout
  The Blonde Bandit
1954—Geraldine
  The Outcast

Bryar, Paul[183]
1938—Tenth Avenue Kid
1942—Spy Smasher
1947—Robin Hood of Texas
1955—No Man's Woman*

Bryde, June
1941—Doctors Don't Tell*
1945—Man from Oklahoma
1946—Affairs of Geraldine*

Bryon, Lucille[68]
1944—Lake Placid Serenade*
  The Big Bonanza*
1945—Great Stagecoach Robbery*
  Utah*
  Earl Carroll Vanities*
  Bells of Rosarita*
  Federal Operator 99*
  The Cheaters*
  Hitchhike to Happiness*
  Man from Oklahoma*
  Tell It to a Star*
  Behind City Lights*
  Love, Honor and Goodbye*
  Sunset in El Dorado*
  The Purple Monster Strikes*
  Don't Fence Me In*
  Girls of the Big House*
  An Angel Comes to Brooklyn*
  Mexicana*
  The Tiger Woman*
  Wagon Wheels Westward*
  Dakota*
  Song of Mexico*
1946—Murder in the Music Hall*

Buchanan, Edgar[183]
1952—Toughest Man in Arizona
1954—Make Haste to Live
1956—Come Next Spring
1957—Spoilers of the Forest

Buchanan, Elsa
1938—Invisible Enemy

Buchanan, Morris
1955—Panther Girl of the Kongo

Brooks, Phyllis[182]
1943—Silver Spurs

Brooks, Rand
1942—Cowboy Serenade
  Affairs of Jimmy Valentine*
  The Sombrero Kid
  Valley of Hunted Men*
1948—Sundown in Santa Fe
1949—The Wyoming Bandit
1950—The Vanishing Westerner
1951—Heart of the Rockies

Brophy, Edward[182]
1935—$1000 a Minute
1937—Jim Hanvey - Detective
  The Hit Parade
1938—Romance on the Run
  Come on, Leathernecks
1943—A Scream in the Dark

Brower, Tom
1936—The Lawless Nineties

Brown, Charles D.[182]
1940—Wolf of New York
  Forgotten Girls
1941—The Devil Pays Off
1946—The Last Crooked Mile

Argentina Brunetti

Frederic Brunn

Nana Bryant

Paul Bryar

Edgar Buchanan

Buck

Norman Budd

James Burke

Buchel, Brian
1937 – Bulldog Drummond at Bay

Buck[183]
1935 – Melody Trail
1936 – The Harvester
Robinson Crusoe of Clipper Island
1937 – The Trigger Trio
1938 – Call of the Yukon

Buck and Bubbles
1944 – Atlantic City

Buckley, Buz
1939 – Saga of Death Valley

Bucko [Bouckou], Ralph[183]
Many films, mostly westerns.

Bucko [Bouckou], Roy[183]
Many films, mostly westerns.

Budd, Norman[183]
1949 – The Red Menace
The Blonde Bandit
1950 – Unmasked
Women from Headquarters
Surrender
1951 – Million Dollar Pursuit
1952 – Tropical Heat Wave*
Thunderbirds
1954 – Geraldine*

Buetel, Jack
1941 – Stars Past and Present*

Buferd, Marylyn
1957 – The Unearthly

Bullet[183]
1948 – Eyes of Texas*
1949 – Susanna Pass*
1950 – North of the Great Divide*
Trail of Robin Hood*
1951 – Spoilers of the Plains*
Heart of the Rockies*
In Old Amarillo*
South of Caliente*
Pals of the Golden West*

Bunn, Earl
Many films.
1937 – S.O.S. Coast Guard*
1938 – Dick Tracy Returns*
1939 – Daredevils of the Red Circle*
Dick Tracy's G-Men*
1940 – King of the Royal Mounted*
1941 – Adventures of Captain Marvel*
King of the Texas Rangers*
1942 – King of the Mounties*
1943 – Daredevils of the West*
1953 – Can. Mounties Vs. Atomic Invaders*

Bupp, Sonny
1940 – Three Faces West

Bupp, Tommy
1936 – Roarin' Lead

Burgess, Dorothy
1942 – Lady for a Night

Burke, Barbara
1957 – Operation Conspiracy

Burke, Billie[93]
1945 – The Cheaters

Burke, James[183]
1935 – Frisco Waterfront
1936 – Dancing Feet
The Leathernecks Have Landed
1938 – Orphans of the Street
1948 – The Timber Trail

Burke, Kathleen
1937 – The Sheik Steps Out

Burnette, Smiley [Lester][14]
1935 – Tumbling Tumbleweeds
Melody Trail
$1000 a Minute*
Sagebrush Troubadour
1936 – The Singing Vagabond
Red River Valley
Comin' 'Round the Mountain
The Singing Cowboy
Undersea Kingdom
Guns and Guitars
Hearts in Bondage*
Oh, Susanna!
Ride Ranger Ride
The Big Show
The Old Corral
A Man Betrayed
1937 – Larceny on the Air
Round-Up Time in Texas
Dick Tracy
Git Along Little Dogies
Rootin' Tootin' Rhythm
Yodelin' Kid from Pine Ridge
Meet the Boy Friend
Public Cowboy No. 1
Boots and Saddles
Manhattan Merry-Go-Round
Springtime in the Rockies
1938 – The Old Barn Dance
Hollywood Stadium Mystery!
Under Western Stars
Gold Mine in the Sky
Man from Music Mountain
Billy the Kid Returns
Prairie Moon
Rhythm of the Saddle
Western Jamboree
1939 – Home on the Prairie
Mexicali Rose
Blue Montana Skies
Mountain Rhythm
Colorado Sunset
In Old Monterey
Rovin' Tumbleweeds
South of the Border
1940 – Rancho Grande
Gaucho Serenade
Carolina Moon
Ride, Tenderfoot, Ride
1941 – Ridin' on a Rainbow
Back in the Saddle
The Singing Hill
Sunset in Wyoming
Stars Past and Present*
Under Fiesta Stars
Down Mexico Way
Sierra Sue
1942 – Cowboy Serenade
Heart of the Rio Grande
Home in Wyomin'
Stardust on the Sage
Call of the Canyon
Bells of Capistrano
Heart of the Golden West
1943 – Idaho
King of the Cowboys
Silver Spurs
Beyond the Last Frontier
Raiders of Sunset Pass
1944 – Pride of the Plains
Beneath Western Skies
The Laramie Trail
Call of the Rockies
Bordertown Trail
Code of the Prairie
Firebrands of Arizona

Burns, Bob[182]
Many films, mostly westerns.
1936 – The Lonely Trail
1950 – Redwood Forest Trail

Burns, Forest
Many films.
1950 – The Invisible Monster

Burns, Fred[182]
Many films, mostly westerns.
1937 – Springtime in the Rockies
1939 – The Arizona Kid
Days of Jesse James
1940 – Colorado
1942 – Sunset on the Desert
Sons of the Pioneers

Burns, George
1941 – Variety Reel*

Burns, Harry
1937 – Two Wise Maids
1943 – G-Men Vs. The Black Dragon

Burns, Paul E.[183]
1945 – Dakota*
1946 – My Pal Trigger*
1947 – The Pilgrim Lady
Saddle Pals*
Exposed
1948 – Madonna of the Desert
1949 – Hideout
1950 – Tarnished
Sunset in the West
1952 – Oklahoma Annie*
Toughest Man in Arizona*
1955 – Lay that Rifle Down*
1956 – Stranger at My Door*

Burns, Sandra
1941 – Variety Reel*

Burr, Raymond[93]
1940 – Earl of Puddlestone*
1950 – Unmasked
1955 – A Man Alone

Burrud, Billy
1938 – The Night Hawk

Burson, Polly
Many films.
1945 – The Purple Monster Strikes*
1946 – The Crimson Ghost*

Burson, Wayne
1952 – Wild Horse Ambush

Burt, Benny
1937 – Sea Racketeers

Burtis, James[183]
1935 – $1000 a Minute
Frisco Waterfront
1936 – Dancing Feet
The Return of Jimmy Valentine

Burton, Frederick
1937 – The Duke Comes Back
1940 – Bowery Boy

Burton, George
1937 – Come on, Cowboys!
1943 – Bill and Coo

Ray Corrigan, Ralph Bucko, Roy Bucko, John Merton, George Plues

Bullet, Roy Rogers

Paul E. Burns

James Burtis

John Burton

Robert Burton

Donia Bussey

Budd Buster

Burton, John[184]
1938—Storm Over Bengal

Burton, Julian
1958—Man or Gun

Burton, Robert[184]
1955—The Road to Denver
Lay that Rifle Down
1958—Man or Gun

Burton, Sam
1944—Cheyenne Wildcat

Busch, Mae
1941—Stars Past and Present*

Busch, Jr., Paul
1956—Circus Girl

Bush, James
1938—Come on, Leathernecks
1941—West of Cimarron
1943—King of the Cowboys

Bushman, Francis X.
1937—Dick Tracy

Bushman, Lenore
1938—Red River Range

Bussey, Donia[184]
1945—The Tiger Woman
1946—A Guy Could Change*
Passkey to Danger
The Invisible Informer*
Affairs of Geraldine
1947—The Magnificent Rogue
Along the Oregon Trail*
1948—Slippy McGee*
1949—The Blonde Bandit*
1951—Honeychile*

Buster, Budd[184]
1936—Cavalry
The Gun Ranger
1937—Bar-Z Bad Men*
The Trusted Outlaw
The Gambling Terror
Hit the Saddle*
Trail of Vengeance*
Guns in the Dark*
Gun Lords of Stirrup Basin*
Doomed at Sundown*
A Lawman is Born*
The Arizona Gunfighter*
The Colorado Kid
1938—Paroled—to Die
Thunder in the Desert
The Feud Maker
Desert Patrol
Dick Tracy Returns*
Durango Valley Raiders*
1939—Wyoming Outlaw*
Colorado Sunset*
Dick Tracy's G-Men*
Zorro's Fighting Legion
1940—Drums of Fu Manchu*
Dark Command*
Grandpa Goes to Town*
Rocky Mountain Rangers*
Adventures of Red Ryder*
King of the Royal Mounted
1941—Gangs of Sonora
Jesse James at Bay*
Sierra Sue
West of Cimarron
1942—Heart of the Rio Grande*
Westward Ho
The Cyclone Kid*
Call of the Canyon*
Sunset Serenade*
Valley of Hunted Men*
1943—Thundering Trails*
The Blocked Trail
Santa Fe Scouts
Daredevils of the West
Riders of the Rio Grande*
Raiders of Sunset Pass*
1944—Pride of the Plains*
Beneath Western Skies*
My Best Gal*
Hidden Valley Outlaws
Call of the South Seas
Firebrands of Arizona*
1945—Lone Texas Ranger
Along the Navajo Trail*
1946—California Gold Rush*
Sheriff of Redwood Valley
Home on the Range
Rainbow Over Texas*
Traffic in Crime*
Stagecoach to Denver*
1947—Vigilantes of Boomtown*
Marshal of Cripple Creek*
The Wild Frontier
1948—Oklahoma Badlands*
Desperadoes of Dodge City*
1954—Trader Tom of the China Seas*

Charles Butterworth

Butch and Buddy
[Billy Lenhart and Kenneth Brown]
1941—Los Angeles Examiner Benefit*
1942—Johnny Doughboy

Butler, John
1950—Code of the Silver Sage

Butterworth, Charles[184]
1941—Sis Hopkins
Hollywood Visits the Navy*

Byington, Spring[93]
1941—Arkansas Judge

Byrd, Ralph[15]
1937—Dick Tracy
S O S Coast Guard
The Trigger Trio
1938—Born to be Wild
Army Girl
Dick Tracy Returns
Down in "Arkansaw"
1939—Fighting Thoroughbreds
S.O.S. Tidal Wave
Mickey, the Kid
Dick Tracy's G-Men
1941—Dick Tracy Vs. Crime, Inc.

Byrne, Eddie
1954—Trouble in the Glen
1955—The Square Ring
The Divided Heart

Byron, George[16]
1942—Ice-Capades Revue
1943—Chatterbox
Thumbs Up
Hoosier Holiday
Mystery Broadcast*
Raiders of Sunset Pass*
1944—Captain America*
Jamboree

Byron, Kathleen
1955—Secret Venture

Byron, Richard
1944—Faces in the Fog

C

Cabin Kids
1937—Round-Up Time in Texas
Git Along Little Dogies

The Cackle Sisters

Cabot, Bruce[93]
1938—Tenth Avenue Kid
1939—Mickey, the Kid
1947—Angel and the Badman
1948—The Gallant Legion
1950—Rock Island Trail

Cackle Sisters, The[184]
1940—Barnyard Follies

Caine, Georgia
1936—Navy Born
1937—Bill Cracks Down
Affairs of Cappy Ricks
1941—Ridin' on a Rainbow

Cairns, Sally
1941—Sis Hopkins*
Ice-Capades*
1942—Hi, Neighbor*
Joan of Ozark*
Johnny Doughboy*
1943—Hit Parade of 1943*

Caits, Joe
1937—Youth on Parole
1940—Grandpa Goes to Town

Calhern, Louis
1943—Nobody's Darling
1949—The Red Pony

Calkins, Johnny
1946—Song of Arizona

Callam, Alex[171]
1942—The Cyclone Kid
The Phantom Plainsmen
1944—That's My Baby

Callard, Kay
1957—The Fighting Wildcats
1958—Scotland Yard Dragnet

**Calloway, Cab—and his
Cotton Club Orchestra**
1937—Manhattan Merry-Go-Round

Calvert, E. H.
1936—Oregon Trail

Calvet, Corinne[185]
1959—Plunderers of Painted Flats

Camargo, Ana
1936—Lawless Land

Camax, Valentine
1951—Adventures of Captain Fabian

Cameron, Rod[73]
1943—G-Men Vs. The Black Dragon
Secret Service in Darkest Africa
1948—The Plunderers
1949—Brimstone
1951—Oh! Susanna
The Sea Hornet
1952—Woman of the North Country
1953—Ride the Man Down
San Antone
1954—Hell's Outpost
1955—Santa Fe Passage
Double Jeopardy
Headline Hunters
The Fighting Chance
1957—Spoilers of the Forest
1958—The Man Who Died Twice

Campan, Zanie
1951—Adventures of Captain Fabian

Campana, Nina[185]
1937—Rootin' Tootin' Rhythm
It Could Happen to You
1938—Call of the Yukon*
1940—Behind the News*
Bowery Boy*
1941—Two Gun Sheriff*
1944—Call of the South Seas
1947—Twilight on the Rio Grande*

Campanella, Roy
1954—Roogie's Bump

Campbell, Colin
1945—The Fatal Witness
Scotland Yard Investigator
1947—Exposed

Campbell, Louise[185]
1940—Bowery Boy

Campbell, Muriel
1939—She Married a Cop

Campbell, Paul
1950—Vigilante Hideout

Campbell, Sterling
1935—Forced Landing

Campbell, William
1957—Eighteen and Anxious

Guy Teague, Nacho Galindo, Yakima Canutt, William Steele, Jim Davis, Rhys Williams, Charles Stevens

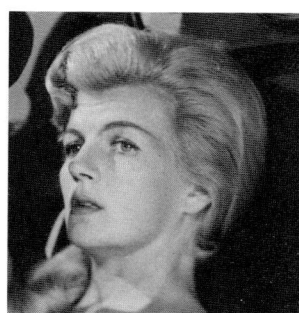
Corinne Calvet

Nina Campana

Candido, Candy
1959—Plunderers of Painted Flats

Cane, Charles[185]
1942—Bells of Capistrano
1943—Shantytown*
1944—The Lady and the Monster
1946—Crime of the Century
   Valley of the Zombies
1949—Streets of San Francisco
   Brimstone*
   The Fighting Kentuckian*
   The Blonde Bandit
1951—Belle LeGrand
1953—San Antone*

Cannon, Tony
See Danny Morton.

Canova, Judy
1940—Scatterbrain
1941—Variety Reel*
   Sis Hopkins
   Meet Roy Rogers*
   Puddin' Head
   Stars Past and Present*
1942—Sleepytime Gal
   Joan of Ozark
1943—Chatterbox
   Sleepy Lagoon
1951—Honeychile
1952—Oklahoma Annie
   The Wac from Walla Walla
1954—The Untamed Heiress
1955—Carolina Cannonball
   Lay that Rifle Down

Louise Campbell

Charles Cane

Canova, Tweeny
1954—The Untamed Heiress*
1955—Lay that Rifle Down

Canova, Zeke
1942—In Old California*

Cansino, Rita
See Rita Hayworth.

Cansino, Vernon
1948—Madonna of the Desert

Canty, Marietta
1951—Belle LeGrand

Canutt, Yakima[184]
1935—Westward Ho
   Lawless Range
1936—Oregon Trail
   King of the Pecos
   The Lonely Trail
   Winds of the Wasteland*
   The Vigilantes are Coming
   Ghost-Town Gold
   Roarin' Lead
1937—The Riders of the Whistling Skull
   The Bold Caballero*
   Hit the Saddle
   Gunsmoke Ranch
   Come on, Cowboys!
   The Painted Stallion
   It Could Happen to You*
   Range Defenders
   S O S Coast Guard*
   Heart of the Rockies
   Boots and Saddles*
   The Trigger Trio*
   Zorro Rides Again*
1938—The Lone Ranger*
   Hollywood Stadium Mystery*
   Call the Mesquiteers*
   Riders of the Black Hills
   Army Girl*
   Pals of the Saddle
   Dick Tracy Returns*
   Overland Stage Raiders*
   Storm Over Bengal*
   Santa Fe Stampede*
1939—The Night Riders*
   Three Texas Steers*
   Man of Conquest*
   Daredevils of the Red Circle*
   Wyoming Outlaw
   The Kansas Terrors
   Cowboys from Texas
   Zorro's Fighting Legion*
1940—Pioneers of the West
   Ghost Valley Raiders
   Dark Command*
   Covered Wagon Days*
   The Carson City Kid*
   The Ranger and the Lady
   Oklahoma Renegades*
   Under Texas Skies
   Frontier Vengeance
   The Trail Blazers*
   Melody Ranch*
   The Border Legion*
   Mysterious Doctor Satan*
   Lone Star Raiders*
1941—Prairie Pioneers
   The Great Train Robbery*
   Pals of the Pecos*
   Country Fair*
   Saddlemates*
   Nevada City*
   Jungle Girl*
   Kansas Cyclone*
   Gangs of Sonora*
   Citadel of Crime*
   Rags to Riches*
   Bad Man of Deadwood*
   Outlaws of Cherokee Trail*
   Gauchos of Eldorado
   West of Cimarron*
1942—Code of the Outlaw*
   Raiders of the Range*
   Spy Smasher*
   Westward Ho*
   The Phantom Plainsmen*
   Perils of Nyoka*
   Shadows on the Sage
   Valley of Hunted Men*
1943—Thundering Trails*
   The Blocked Trail*
   King of the Cowboys*
   Santa Fe Scouts*
   Calling Wild Bill Elliott*
   Riders of the Rio Grande*
   Song of Texas*
   Bordertown Gun Fighters*
   Silver Spurs*
   In Old Oklahoma*
1944—The Fighting Seabees*
   Pride of the Plains
   Hidden Valley Outlaws
   Cowboy and the Senorita*
1945—Dakota*
1950—The Showdown

Cappella and Patricia
1944—Cowboy and the Senorita

Cappo, Joe
1945—An Angel Comes to Brooklyn

Carbajal, Tony
1956—A Woman's Devotion

Cardwell, James[185]
1947—Robin Hood of Texas
1948—King of the Gamblers
   Daredevils of the Clouds
1949—Daughter of the Jungle
   Down Dakota Way
   San Antone Ambush
1950—The Arizona Cowboy

Carey, Jr., Harry[114]
1948—Moonrise
1950—Rio Grande
1951—The Wild Blue Yonder
1953—San Antone
   Sweethearts on Parade
1954—The Outcast

Carey, Sr., Harry[93]
1939—Street of Missing Men
1947—Angel and the Badman

Carey, Leonard[185]
1939—The Zero Hour
1940—In Old Missouri
   Sing, Dance, Plenty Hot
1941—Mountain Moonlight
   Tuxedo Junction

James Cardwell

George Carleton

Hoagy Carmichael

Carey, Macdonald[94]
1956—Stranger at My Door
1958—Man or Gun

Carle, Richard
1937—Rhythm in the Clouds

Carleton, Claire[16]
1940—The Crooked Road
   Grand Ole Opry
   Sing, Dance, Plenty Hot
   Girl from Havana
   Melody and Moonlight
1941—Petticoat Politics
   The Great Train Robbery
1951—Honeychile
1952—Bal Tabarin
1953—Ride the Man Down
1954—Jubilee Trail*
1956—Accused of Murder*

Carleton, George[185]
1944—The Big Bonanza*
1945—The Vampire's Ghost*
   A Sporting Chance*
   Behind City Lights
   The Purple Monster Strikes
   Marshal of Laredo
   An Angel Comes to Brooklyn*
1946—The Phantom Rider*
   Song of Arizona*
   Home in Oklahoma
   Affairs of Geraldine
   Sioux City Sue*
1947—That's My Gal
1948—Night Time in Nevada
1949—Daughter of the Jungle
   Prince of the Plains

Leonard Carey

Mary Carlisle

John Carpenter

Carleton, William P.
1935—Two Sinners
1936—The Return of Jimmy Valentine

Carlisle, Mary[185]
1935—Fighting Thoroughbreds
   Rovin' Tumbleweeds
1941—Rags to Riches

Carlson, Richard[94]
1955—The Last Command

Carlyle, David
See Robert Paige.

Carmen, Jean[66]
   [as Julia Thayer]
1937—Bill Cracks Down*
   Gunsmoke Ranch
   The Painted Stallion
   [as Jean Carmen]
   The Arizona Gunfighter

Carmichael, Hoagy[185]
1955—Timberjack

Carmichael, Patsy
1940—Heroes of the Saddle

Carnahan, Suzanne
1940—Chinese Garden Festival*

Carney, Alan
1947—The Pretender
1949—Hideout

Carol, Sue
1941—Wampas Baby Stars*

Carpenter, Horace
Many films, mostly westerns.
1937—Gunsmoke Ranch
   Doomed at Sundown
   Range Defenders

Carpenter, John [Josh][185]
1945—Santa Fe Saddlemates
1946—The El Paso Kid
1958—No Place to Land

Carpenter, Ken
1943—Mystery Broadcast
1947—Winter Wonderland*

Carpenter, Paul
1958—Scotland Yard Dragnet

Carr, Harry
1947—Rustlers of Devil's Canyon

Carr, Jack[185]
1938—Ladies in Distress
1940—Bowery Boy
1941—A Man Betrayed*
   Rookies on Parade*
   Mountain Moonlight*
   Hurricane Smith*

Carr, Jane
1943—Alibi

Carr, Marian[185]
1956—When Gangland Strikes

Carr, Mary
1945—Oregon Trail

Carr, Michael[185]
1948—Sippy McGee
   Train to Alcatraz
1949—Fame of Youth
1950—Hills of Oklahoma
   Prisoners in Petticoats
   Flying Disc Man from Mars

Jack Carr

Michael Carr

Marian Carr

Carr, Thomas
1937—Range Defenders
　　　S O S Coast Guard
1938—The Fighting Devil Dogs*
1939—The Zero Hour*
　　　S.O.S. Tidal Wave*
　　　Wall Street Cowboy*
　　　Calling All Marines*

Carradine, John[73]
1943—Silver Spurs
1954—Johnny Guitar
1956—Hidden Guns
1957—The Unearthly
1958—Hell Ship Mutiny

Carrell, Anita[186]
1949—Flame of Youth

Carrere, Anne
1959—O. S. S. 117 is Not Dead

Carrier, Albert
1957—Panama Sal

Carrillo, Leo[186]
1937—Manhattan Merry-Go-Round
1945—Mexicana

Carroll, Anne
1955—The Road to Denver

Carroll, Earl—series
1945—Earl Carroll Vanities
1946—Earl Carroll Sketchbook

Carroll, Georgia
1940—Chinese Garden Festival*

Carroll, John[73]
1937—Zorro Rides Again
1942—Flying Tigers
1943—Hit Parade of 1943
1947—Wyoming
　　　The Fabulous Texan
　　　The Flame
1948—Old Los Angeles
　　　I, Jane Doe
　　　Angel in Exile
1950—The Avengers
　　　Surrender
　　　Hit Parade of 1951
1951—Belle LeGrand
1954—Geraldine
1959—Plunderers of Painted Flats

Carroll, June
1945—An Angel Comes to Brooklyn

Carroll, Lucia
1941—Wampas Baby Stars*

Carroll, Martha[68]
1943—Swing Your Partner*
　　　Hands Across the Border*
1944—The Yellow Rose of Texas*
　　　Lake Placid Serenade*
　　　The Big Bonanza*
1945—Earl Carroll Vanities*
　　　Bells of Rosarita*
　　　Oregon Trail*
　　　Hitchhike to Happiness*
　　　Man from Oklahoma*
　　　Behind City Lights*
　　　The Purple Monster Strikes*
　　　Don't Fence Me In*
　　　The Tiger Woman*
　　　Along the Navajo Trail*
　　　Dakota*
　　　Song of Mexico*
1946—Murder in the Music Hall*

Carroll, Virginia[129]
1938—Dick Tracy Returns*
1940—Mysterious Doctor Satan*
1941—The Phantom Cowboy
1943—G-Men Vs. The Black Dragon*
1944—Man from Frisco*
　　　Faces in the Fog*
　　　Lake Placid Serenade*
1945—The Cheaters*
　　　Behind City Lights*
1946—A Guy Could Change*
　　　Murder in the Music Hall*
　　　Daughter of Don Q*
　　　G. I. War Brides
　　　The Crimson Ghost*
　　　Affairs of Geraldine*
　　　Heldorado*
1947—That's My Gal*
　　　The Black Widow
1950—Trail of Robin Hood*
1951—Pals of the Golden West*
1952—The Wac from Walla Walla*
1953—Champ for a Day*
　　　Red River Shore*
1955—Headline Hunters
1956—Stranger at My Door*
1957—Affair in Reno*
　　　Spoilers of the Forest*

Carson, Charles
1937—Glamorous Night

Carson, Jack
1937—It Could Happen to You*

Carson, Kit
1952—I Dream of Jeanie*

Carson, Robert
1939—Dick Tracy's G-Men

Carson, Sunset[148]
1944—Call of the Rockies
　　　Bordertown Trail
　　　Code of the Prairie
　　　Firebrands of Arizona
1945—Sheriff of Cimarron
　　　Santa Fe Saddlemates
　　　Bells of Rosarita
　　　Oregon Trail
　　　Bandits of the Badlands
　　　Rough Riders of Cheyenne
　　　The Cherokee Flash
1946—Days of Buffalo Bill
　　　Alias Billy the Kid
　　　The El Paso Kid
　　　Red River Renegades
　　　Rio Grande Raiders

Carter, Ben
1940—Earl of Puddlestone

Carter, William[16]
1946—I've Always Loved You

Caruso, Anthony[186]
1946—The Catman of Paris
　　　The Last Crooked Mile
1950—Prisoners in Petticoats
1951—Pals of the Golden West
1955—Santa Fa Passage
　　　City of Shadows
1956—When Gangland Strikes
1957—The Lawless Eighties

Caruth, Burr[186]
1936—The Harvester
　　　Ghost-Town Gold
1937—Gunsmoke Ranch
1938—Under Western Stars
　　　Red River Range
1939—New Frontier
1940—Rocky Mountain Rangers
1941—Ridin' on a Rainbow
　　　The Phantom Cowboy
1943—Calling Wild Bill Elliott

Carver, Lynne[186]
1941—Mr. District Atty. in the Carter Case
1942—Man from Cheyenne
　　　Yokel Boy
　　　Sunset on the Desert

Casey, Angel
1953—City that Never Sleeps*

Casey, Sue
1951—Secrets of Monte Carlo

Casey, Taggart
1958—Juvenile Jungle

Caskey, Ted
1935—Racing Luck

Cason, John[186]
1942—Westward Ho*
　　　Shadows on the Sage*
1950—Desperadoes of the West
　　　Prisoners in Petticoats*
　　　Redwood Forest Trail
　　　Rustlers on Horseback
1951—Don Daredevil Rides Again
1952—Black Hills Ambush
1953—Jungle Drums of Africa
　　　Savage Frontier
　　　Red River Shore
1955—King of the Carnival*

Cass County Boys[74]
1946—Sioux City Sue
1947—Trail to San Antone
　　　Twilight on the Rio Grande
　　　Saddle Pals
　　　Robin Hood of Texas

Cass, Maurice[186]
1937—Exiled to Shanghai
1938—Gangs of New York
　　　A Desperate Adventure
1941—Country Fair
1942—Youth on Parade*
1945—Federal Operator 99
1946—The Catman of Paris
　　　I've Always Loved You*
1947—Spoilers of the North
　　　Saddle Pals*

Cassell, Wally[186]
1949—Streets of San Francisco
1950—Sands of Iwo Jima
1951—Oh! Susanna
　　　The Wild Blue Yonder
1952—Thunderbirds
1953—City that Never Sleeps
1955—Timberjack
1956—Accused of Murder*

Cassidy, Edward[129]
1936—Winds of the Wasteland
　　　Under Cover Man
　　　Cavalry
　　　Robinson Crusoe of Clipper Island*
　　　Lawless Land
　　　Border Phantom*
1937—Hit the Saddle
　　　Come on, Cowboys!
　　　The Red Rope
　　　Boothill Brigade
　　　S O S Coast Guard*
1938—The Purple Vigilantes
　　　The Fighting Devil Dogs*
　　　Man from Music Mountain
　　　Red River Range*
　　　Federal Man-Hunt*
1939—Mountain Rhythm
　　　Colorado Sunset*
　　　Dick Tracy's G-Men*
　　　The Arizona Kid*
　　　Rovin' Tumbleweeds*
　　　Cowboys from Texas
1940—Gaucho Serenade*
　　　Adventures of Red Ryder*
　　　Colorado*
　　　Mysterious Doctor Satan*
1941—Wyoming Wildcat
　　　Ridin' on a Rainbow*
　　　Adventures of Captain Marvel*
　　　The Gay Vagabond*
　　　Saddlemates*
　　　Mountain Moonlight*
　　　King of the Texas Rangers*
1942—Sunset on the Desert*
　　　Stardust on the Sage*
　　　In Old California*
　　　The Phantom Plainsmen*
　　　The Sombrero Kid*
　　　The Traitor Within*
　　　Ridin' Down the Canyon*
1943—Thundering Trails
　　　Carson City Cyclone*
　　　King of the Cowboys*
　　　Santa Fe Scouts*
　　　Daredevils of the West*
　　　The Man from Thunder River*
1944—Captain America*
　　　Hidden Valley Outlaws*
　　　Tucson Raiders
　　　Goodnight Sweetheart*
　　　San Fernando Valley*
　　　My Buddy*
1945—Sheriff of Cimarron
　　　Manhunt of Mystery Island
　　　Utah*
　　　Corpus Christi Bandits
　　　The Phantom Speaks*
　　　Bells of Rosarita*
　　　Sunset in El Dorado
　　　Colorado Pioneers*
　　　Along the Navajo Trail*
1946—Days of Buffalo Bill
　　　Alias Billy the Kid
　　　Sun Valley Cyclone
　　　The El Paso Kid
　　　The Mysterious Mr. Valentine*
　　　Roll on Texas Moon
　　　Out California Way*
　　　Stagecoach to Denver
1947—Son of Zorro
　　　Homesteaders of Paradise Valley
　　　Oregon Trail Scouts
　　　Jesse James Rides Again
　　　On the Old Spanish Trail*
　　　The Fabulous Texan*
1948—The Bold Frontiersman
　　　Desperadoes of Dodge City
1950—Singing Guns*
　　　The Savage Horde*
　　　Trail of Robin Hood
1951—Belle LeGrand*
　　　Buckaroo Sheriff of Texas
　　　Million Dollar Pursuit
1952—Colorado Sundown*
　　　Black Hills Ambush
　　　Desperadoes' Outpost
1953—Savage Frontier*

Cassidy, John F.
1938—Santa Fe Stampede

Castaine, Robert B.[187]
1944—Atlantic City

Castel, Colette
1959—O. S. S. 117 is Not Dead

Castello, Willy
1935—Melody Trail

Castelot, Jacques
1955—Don Juan's Night of Love

Maurice Cass

Wally Cassell

Castile, Lynn
1948—Marshal of Amarillo

Castillo, Gloria
1955—The Vanishing American

Castle, Don[187]
1948—Madonna of the Desert

Castle, Mary[187]
1957—Last Stagecoach West

Castle, Peggie[187]
1957—Hell's Crossroads
　　　Beginning of the End

Catlett, Walter[74]
1936—Follow Your Heart
1942—Heart of the Golden West
1943—Hit Parade of 1943
　　　The West Side Kid
1944—Lake Placid Serenade
1951—Honeychile

Caudebec, Al
1953—Ride the Man Down

Cavan, Allan[187]
1935—The New Frontier
1936—Ticket to Paradise*
　　　Hearts in Bondage*
　　　The Gentleman from Louisiana*
　　　Robinson Crusoe of Clipper Island*
1937—Hit the Saddle*
　　　Portia on Trial*
1938—The Purple Vigilantes*
　　　The Lone Ranger*
　　　King of the Newsboys*
　　　Dick Tracy Returns*
　　　Come on, Rangers*
1939—Pride of the Navy*
　　　Rough Riders' Round-Up*
　　　The Night Riders*
　　　Blue Montana Skies*
　　　Wyoming Outlaw*
　　　Dick Tracy's G-Men*

Cavanagh, Paul
1950—Hit Parade of 1951

Cavanaugh, Hobart[187]
1938—Orphans of the Street
1939—The Covered Trailer
1942—A Tragedy at Midnight
1943—A Scream in the Dark
1947—Driftwood
1948—The Inside Story

Cawthorn, Joseph
1940—Scatterbrain

CBS-KMBC Texas Rangers, The
1939—Colorado Sunset

Celano, Guido
1952—The Flying Squadron

Centa, Tony[187]
1951—Fugitive Lady

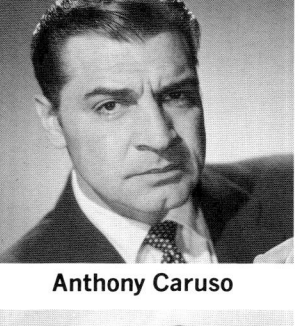

Anita Carrell

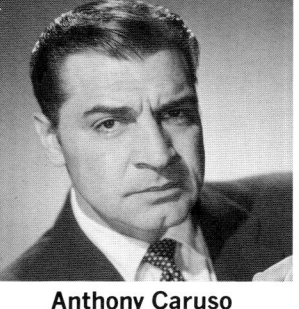

Leo Carrillo

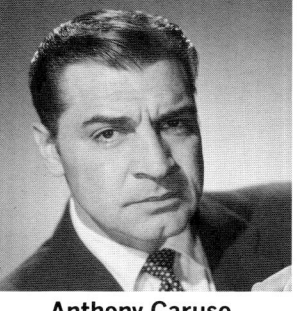

Anthony Caruso

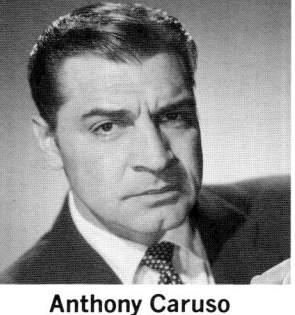

Burr Caruth

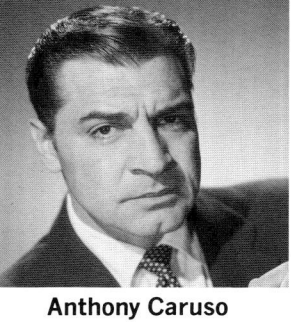

Lynne Carver

John Cason

Robert B. Castaine

Don Castle

Mary Castle

Peggie Castle

Allan Cavan

Hobart Cavanaugh

Chamberlain, Cyril
1941 – Poison Pen
1955 – Trouble in Store
　　　　Doctor in the House
1956 – Doctor at Sea
　　　　Above Us the Waves

Chamberlin, Howland[187]
1947 – Driftwood
1948 – Angel in Exile
1950 – House by the River
　　　　Surrender

Chambers, Wheaton[129]
1935 – Frisco Waterfront*
1936 – Ticket to Paradise*
1938 – The Higgins Family*
1940 – Drums of Fu Manchu
　　　　Adventures of Red Ryder
1941 – Prairie Pioneers*
　　　　Dick Tracy Vs. Crime, Inc.*
1942 – Stagecoach Express*
　　　　Outlaws of Pine Ridge*
1943 – Bordertown Gun Fighters*
　　　　The Black Hills Express*
　　　　Beyond the Last Frontier*
1945 – The Topeka Terror*
　　　　Hitchhike to Happiness*
　　　　Behind City Lights*
　　　　The Purple Monster Strikes
　　　　Marshal of Laredo
1946 – Murder in the Music Hall*
　　　　King of the Forest Rangers*
　　　　The El Paso Kid
　　　　Valley of the Zombies*
　　　　The Last Crooked Mile*
　　　　The Crimson Ghost
　　　　Stagecoach to Denver
1947 – Son of Zorro
　　　　That's My Gal*
　　　　The Wild Frontier
　　　　On the Old Spanish Trail
1948 – The Plunderers*
1958 – The Notorious Mr. Monks*

Champion
Horse. Credited on-screen intermittently in Gene Autry westerns during 1935-37.

Champion, Jr.
Horse. Credited on-screen in last five Gene Autry westerns during 1946-47 as "Wonder Horse of the West."

Chandler, Chick[114]
1937 – Portia on Trial
1939 – The Mysterious Miss X
1941 – Puddin' Head
　　　　Sailors on Leave
1942 – Home in Wyomin'
　　　　Youth on Parade
1943 – The West Side Kid
1945 – The Chicago Kid
1954 – The Untamed Heiress

Chandler, Eddie
1943 – Sleepy Lagoon

Chandler, Fletcher
1949 – Hideout

Chandler, George[130]
1937 – The Duke Comes Back*
1939 – Calling All Marines
　　　　Thou Shalt Not Kill
1940 – Forgotten Girls*
　　　　Melody Ranch*
1941 – The Gay Vagabond*
　　　　Mountain Moonlight
1942 – A Tragedy at Midnight*
　　　　Secrets of the Underground*
1943 – A Scream in the Dark*
　　　　Here Comes Elmer*
　　　　In Old Oklahoma*
1945 – Man from Oklahoma*
　　　　Tell It to a Star
1946 – A Guy Could Change
　　　　Strange Impersonation
　　　　The Glass Alibi
　　　　The French Key*
　　　　Rendezvous with Annie*
　　　　The Last Crooked Mile*
　　　　Heldorado*
1947 – Saddle Pals
1948 – Lightnin' in the Forest
　　　　Sons of Adventure
1950 – Singing Guns
1952 – Woman of the North Country*
　　　　The Wac from Walla Walla

Chandler, Lane[130]
1936 – The Return of Jimmy Valentine*
　　　　The Lawless Nineties
　　　　Undersea Kingdom
　　　　Winds of the Wasteland
　　　　Hearts in Bondage*
1937 – Sea Racketeers
　　　　The Wrong Road*
　　　　Zorro Rides Again*
1938 – The Lone Ranger
　　　　Come on, Rangers
　　　　Hawk of the Wilderness*
1939 – Man of Conquest*
　　　　Southward, Ho!
　　　　Smuggled Cargo*
　　　　Calling All Marines*
　　　　Saga of Death Valley*
1940 – Pioneers of the West
　　　　Dark Command*
　　　　Wagons Westward*
1941 – Lady from Louisiana*
　　　　Hurricane Smith*
1943 – In Old Oklahoma*
1944 – The Lady and the Monster*
　　　　Silent Partner*
　　　　Silver City Kid
　　　　Lights of Old Santa Fe*
　　　　Navy MN 3387 – Your Weapons*
1945 – Manhunt of Mystery Island
1946 – A Guy Could Change*

Chandler, Tanis[187]
1946 – The Madonna's Secret*
　　　　The Catman of Paris
　　　　Affairs of Geraldine

Chaney, Jr., Lon[187]
1936 – The Singing Cowboy
　　　　Undersea Kingdom
　　　　The Old Corral
1956 – Daniel Boone, Trail Blazer

Chapin, Billy[187]
1954 – Tobor the Great

Chapin, Michael[157]
1946 – Song of Arizona
1948 – Under California Stars
1951 – Buckaroo Sheriff of Texas
　　　　Wells Fargo Gunmaster
　　　　The Dakota Kid
　　　　Arizona Manhunt
1952 – Wild Horse Ambush

Chapman, Edward
1955 – A Day to Remember
1956 – Lisbon

Chapman, Freddie
1945 – Great Stagecoach Robbery
　　　　Corpus Christi Bandits
　　　　Trail of Kit Carson
　　　　Colorado Pioneers

Chapman, Marguerite
1942 – Spy Smasher

Chapman, Pattee
1952 – The Wac from Walla Walla

Charles, Frances
1950 – Women from Headquarters

Charlita[187]
1949 – Brimstone
1951 – South of Caliente
1952 – Toughest Man in Arizona

Charlot, Andre
1943 – Thumbs Up

Charney, Kim
1958 – Girl in the Woods

Charters, Spencer[74]
1935 – $1000 a Minute
1936 – The Harvester
1938 – Lady, Behave!
1939 – Woman Doctor
　　　　The Covered Trailer
1940 – Three Faces West
　　　　Girl from God's Country
　　　　Friendly Neighbors
　　　　Meet the Missus
1941 – Petticoat Politics
　　　　The Singing Hill
　　　　Mr. District Atty. in the Carter Case
1942 – Affairs of Jimmy Valentine

Chase, Alden
See Stephen Chase.

Chase, Barrie
1955 – Timberjack*

Chase, Howard
1938 – Man from Music Mountain

Chase, Stephen[187]
　　　　[as Alden Chase]
1938 – Under Western Stars
1941 – Doctors Don't Tell*
　　　　[as Stephen Chase]
1949 – Flame of Youth
　　　　Alias the Champ
1950 – Tarnished
　　　　Frisco Tornado
　　　　Prisoners in Petticoats*
　　　　North of the Great Divide*
1951 – Belle LeGrand
1952 – Old Oklahoma Plains
1953 – El Paso Stampede
1954 – Jubilee Trail*

Chatterton, Tom[130]
1937 – Youth on Parole*
1938 – Under Western Stars
　　　　Hawk of the Wilderness*
1939 – Man of Conquest*
　　　　Calling All Marines*
　　　　Jeepers Creepers*
　　　　Rovin' Tumbleweeds*
1940 – Village Barn Dance*
　　　　Drums of Fu Manchu
　　　　Covered Wagon Days
　　　　The Trail Blazers
1941 – Desert Bandit
　　　　Outlaws of Cherokee Trail
1942 – Raiders of the Range
1943 – Santa Fe Scouts
1944 – Captain America
　　　　Rosie, the Riveter*
　　　　Tucson Raiders
　　　　Man from Frisco*
　　　　Marshal of Reno
　　　　Cheyenne Wildcat
　　　　Code of the Prairie
　　　　Zorro's Black Whip
1945 – The Phantom Speaks*
　　　　Lone Texas Ranger
　　　　Love, Honor and Goodbye*
　　　　Marshal of Laredo
　　　　Colorado Pioneers
　　　　Wagon Wheels Westward*
1946 – Gay Blades*
　　　　Sheriff of Redwood Valley
　　　　Alias Billy the Kid
　　　　Home on the Range
　　　　Conquest of Cheyenne
　　　　Stagecoach to Denver
1947 – Jesse James Rides Again*
　　　　The Fabulous Texan*
1948 – Heart of Virginia
　　　　Carson City Raiders
　　　　Marshal of Amarillo
　　　　The Denver Kid*
1949 – Prince of the Plains*
　　　　The Wyoming Bandit*

Checchi, Andrea
1951 – Stormbound
1952 – The Flying Squadron

Checkerboard Band, The
1939 – South of the Border

Cheke, Jack
1944 – That's My Baby

Chekhov, Michael[187]
1946 – Specter of the Rose

Cherkose, Eddie
1938 – Gold Mine in the Sky

Tony Centa

Howland Chamberlin

Tanis Chandler

Lon Chaney, Jr.

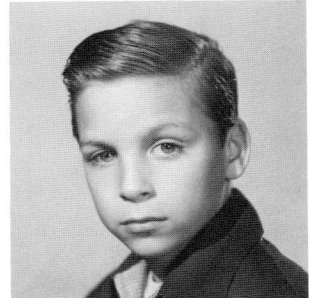
Billy Chapin

Charlita

Stephen Chase

Michael Chekhov

Chesebro, George[188]
1935 – Tumbling Tumbleweeds
1936 – The Return of Jimmy Valentine*
  The Lawless Nineties
  Red River Valley
  Robinson Crusoe of Clipper Island
  The Big Show*
  Roarin' Lead
1937 – S O S Coast Guard
  Springtime in the Rockies
1938 – The Purple Vigilantes
  Prison Nurse*
  Outlaws of Sonora
  Santa Fe Stampede*
1939 – Rough Riders' Round-Up*
  Southward, Ho!*
  Daredevils of the Red Circle
  New Frontier*
  Wall Street Cowboy*
1940 – Pioneers of the West*
  Young Buffalo Bill*
  Colorado*
  Melody Ranch*
1941 – Back in the Saddle*
  Pals of the Pecos*
  Nevada City*
1942 – Jesse James, Jr.*
1945 – Sheriff of Cimarron
  Santa Fe Saddlemates
  Federal Operator 99*
  Trail of Kit Carson
  Sunset in El Dorado*
  The Purple Monster Strikes*
  Marshal of Laredo
  Colorado Pioneers
  The Cherokee Flash*
  Wagon Wheels Westward
1946 – The Phantom Rider*
  Days of Buffalo Bill
  Rainbow Over Texas*
  Sun Valley Cyclone
  In Old Sacramento*
  Daughter of Don Q*
  Santa Fe Uprising*
  Stagecoach to Denver
1947 – Son of Zorro*
  Vigilantes of Boomtown
  Homesteaders of Paradise Valley
  Wyoming
  Jesse James Rides Again*
  The Black Widow*
1948 – The Gallant Legion*
  Adv. of Frank and Jesse James
1949 – Ghost of Zorro*
  Death Valley Gunfighter
  The Last Bandit*
  The Wyoming Bandit*
  Brimstone*
  Ranger of Cherokee Strip*
1950 – Gunmen of Abilene
  The Arizona Cowboy*
  Salt Lake Raiders
  The Savage Horde*
  Desperadoes of the West*
  Frisco Tornado
  Trail of Robin Hood
  California Passage*
1951 – Night Riders of Montana
  Oh! Susanna*
1953 – Woman They Almost Lynched*

Cheshire, Harry V. "Pappy"[74]
1940 – Barnyard Follies
1942 – Hi, Neighbor
1943 – Swing Your Partner
  O, My Darling Clementine
1944 – Sing Neighbor Sing
1946 – Traffic in Crime
  Affairs of Geraldine
  Sioux City Sue*
1947 – The Pilgrim Lady
  Springtime in the Sierras
  The Fabulous Texan*
  The Flame
1948 – Slippy McGee
  Moonrise
1949 – Brimstone
1950 – The Arizona Cowboy
  Lonely Heart Bandits
1951 – Thunder in God's Country
1952 – Woman of the North Country*
1953 – Ride the Man Down*

Chester, Bob—and orchestra
1944 – Trocadero

Ching, William[17]
1950 – The Showdown
  Surrender
1951 – Belle LeGrand
  Oh! Susanna
  Buckaroo Sheriff of Texas*
  The Sea Hornet
  The Wild Blue Yonder
1952 – Woman in the Dark*
  Lady Possessed*
  Bal Tabarin

Chinita
1943 – Hit Parade of 1943

Chiquita[188]
1956 – Jaguar

Chirello, George
1950 – Macbeth

Chissell, Noble "Kid"[188]
1937 – Youth on Parole*
1938 – Hollywood Stadium Mystery!*
  Come on, Leathernecks*
  Federal Man-Hunt*
1939 – Man of Conquest*
1940 – Dark Command*
1941 – Lady from Louisiana*
  Public Enemies*
1943 – Pistol Packin' Mama*
1944 – My Buddy*
1945 – Jealousy*
  Dakota*
1946 – Song of Arizona
1949 – The Fighting Kentuckian*
1952 – The Quiet Man*

Chitty, Erik
1957 – Time is My Enemy

Christian, Diana
1952 – Toughest Man in Arizona

Christian, Helen[188]
1937 – Manhattan Merry-Go-Round*
  Zorro Rides Again

Christine, Virginia[188]
1945 – Phantom of the Plains
  Girls of the Big House
1946 – The Inner Circle
  The Mysterious Mr. Valentine
1953 – Woman They Almost Lynched

Christopher, Kay[188]
1949 – South of Rio
1950 – Code of the Silver Sage
1951 – Fighting Coast Guard*

Christy, Dorothy[189]
1941 – Sailors on Leave*
  Sierra Sue
1944 – Cowboy and the Senorita
1947 – The Pilgrim Lady
  The Magnificent Rogue
  That's My Man*

Christy, Eileen[17]
1952 – I Dream of Jeanie
  Thunderbirds
1953 – A Perilous Journey
  Sweethearts on Parade

Christy, Ken
1942 – Secrets of the Underground

Christy, Whitey
1947 – Springtime in the Sierras

Chrystall, Belle
1941 – Poison Pen

Chuman, Howard
1951 – Secrets of Monte Carlo

Churchill, Berton[188]
1935 – The Spanish Cape Mystery
1938 – Ladies in Distress
  Down in "Arkansaw"
1939 – Should Husbands Work?

Ciannelli, Eduardo[188]
1940 – Forgotten Girls
  Mysterious Doctor Satan
1944 – Storm Over Lisbon
1951 – Fugitive Lady

Claire, Willis
1940 – In Old Missouri

Clarence, O. B.
1942 – Suicide Squadron

Clark, Cliff[188]
1940 – The Crooked Road*
  Gangs of Chicago*
1948 – I, Jane Doe*
1949 – Flaming Fury
  Post Office Investigator
  Powder River Rustlers
1950 – Desperadoes of the West*
  Vigilante Hideout
1951 – Desert of Lost Men
1952 – Toughest Man in Arizona*

Clark, Dane[114]
1948 – Moonrise
1956 – The Man is Armed

Clark, Davison
1938 – Born to be Wild
1941 – Prairie Pioneers
1943 – Death Valley Manhunt
1945 – Gangs of the Waterfront

Clark, Edward
1951 – Million Dollar Pursuit
1952 – Thundering Caravans
1953 – El Paso Stampede

Clark, Ernest
1955 – Doctor in the House

Clark, Harry
1941 – Ice-Capades

Clark, Harvey[188]
1936 – The Singing Cowboy
  Sitting on the Moon
1937 – Dangerous Holiday

Clark, John
1958 – Outcasts of the City

Clark, Judy[17]
1942 – South of Santa Fe*
  Hi, Neighbor*
1943 – King of the Cowboys*
  Chatterbox*
  Swing Your Partner
1947 – That's My Gal
1950 – Desperadoes of the West

Clark, Mamo[115]
1936 – Robinson Crusoe of Clipper Island
1940 – Girl from God's Country

Clark, Petula
1956 – Track the Man Down

Clark, Roger[188]
1943 – Swing Your Partner
1944 – Faces in the Fog
1945 – A Song for Miss Julie

Clark, Roydon
1953 – Ride the Man Down

Clark, Russ
1946 – Valley of the Zombies

Clark, Steve[188]
1935 – Tumbling Tumbleweeds*
1936 – The Lawless Nineties*
  Comin' 'Round the Mountain*
1937 – The Gambling Terror*
  Trail of Vengeance*
  Guns in the Dark
  Gun Lords of Stirrup Basin
  A Lawman is Born
  Boothill Brigade
  The Arizona Gunfighter
  Ridin' the Lone Trail
1938 – Paroled—to Die
  Thunder in the Desert
  The Feud Maker
  Desert Patrol
  Durango Valley Raiders
1942 – Sunset Serenade*
1944 – Cheyenne Wildcat*
1948 – Oklahoma Badlands*
  Under California Stars*
  Adv. of Frank and Jesse James*
  The Plunderers*
1949 – Ghost of Zorro
  The Last Bandit*
  Bandit King of Texas
  Navajo Trail Raiders
1950 – Gunmen of Abilene
  Desperadoes of the West*
1952 – Captive of Billy the Kid*
1953 – El Paso Stampede*

Clark, Wallis
1937 – Escape by Night
1938 – The Higgins Family
1939 – Smuggled Cargo
  Main Street Lawyer

Clarke, David
1949 – The Blonde Bandit

Clarke, Mae[74]
1935 – Hitch Hike Lady
1936 – The House of a Thousand Candles
  Hearts in Bondage
1940 – Women in War
1941 – Sailors on Leave
1942 – Flying Tigers
1948 – Daredevils of the Clouds
1949 – Streets of San Francisco
  King of the Rocket Men
1952 – Thunderbirds
1956 – Come Next Spring

Clarke, Richard[189]
1943 – Beyond the Last Frontier
  The Masked Marvel

Clarke, Robert[189]
1951 – Street Bandits
1952 – The Fabulous Senorita
1955 – King of the Carnival

Clauser, Al—and his Oklahoma Outlaws
1937 – Rootin' Tootin' Rhythm

Clavering, Eric
1943 – The Saint Meets the Tiger

George Chesebro

Chiquita

Noble "Kid" Chissell

Helen Christian

Virginia Christine

Kay Christopher

Berton Churchill

Eduardo Ciannelli

Cliff Clark

Harvey Clark

Roger Clark

Steve Clark

Richard Clarke

Robert Clarke

Patricia Knox, Chick Chandler, Dorothy Christy

Dora Clemant

Clay Clement

Cleary, Leo
1949 – The Red Menace
　　　Brimstone*
1950 – Bells of Coronado
1951 – Desert of Lost Men
1952 – Woman of the North Country*

Clemant, Dora[189]
1938 – Mama Runs Wild*
　　　Under Western Stars
1939 – The Covered Trailer*
1940 – Sing, Dance, Plenty Hot*
1941 – The Gay Vagabond*
　　　Puddin' Head*
1942 – Sleepytime Gal*

Clement, Clay[189]
1935 – Hitch Hike Lady
1936 – The Leavenworth Case
　　　The Leathernecks Have Landed
　　　Hearts in Bondage
1938 – Arson Gang Busters

Clement, Greta
1947 – The Pretender

Clemente, Steve
1936 – The Vigilantes Are Coming

Clements, John
1943 – At Dawn We Die

Clements, Stanley[189]
1951 – Pride of Maryland

Cleveland, George[130]
1935 – The Spanish Cape Mystery
　　　Forced Landing
1936 – The Gentleman from Louisiana*
　　　Robinson Crusoe of Clipper Island
1937 – Paradise Express*
1938 – The Lone Ranger
　　　Born to be Wild*
　　　Outlaws of Sonora*
1939 – Home on the Prairie
　　　Smuggled Cargo*
　　　Dick Tracy's G-Men*
1940 – Pioneers of the West
　　　Drums of Fu Manchu
　　　One Man's Law
1941 – Nevada City
　　　Sunset in Wyoming
1942 – The Traitor Within
1943 – Man from Music Mountain
1944 – My Best Gal
　　　The Yellow Rose of Texas
　　　Man from Frisco*
1945 – Dakota
1948 – The Plunderers
1950 – Trigger, Jr.
1952 – The Wac from Walla Walla
1953 – San Antone
1954 – The Untamed Heiress

Cleveland Indians
1949 – The Kid from Cleveland*

Clifford, Jack
1936 – King of the Pecos
1948 – Dangers of the Canadian Mounted

Clifton, Herbert
1940 – Ride, Tenderfoot, Ride

Clive, E. E.
1936 – Ticket to Paradise

Stanley Clements

Andy Clyde

June Clyde

Phyllis Coates

Close, John
1951 – Belle LeGrand*
　　　Fighting Coast Guard*
1957 – Beginning of the End
1958 – Outcasts of the City
　　　Street of Darkness

Cloutier, Suzanne
1955 – Doctor in the House

Clute, Chester[130]
1937 – Navy Blues
　　　The Wrong Road
1939 – I Was a Convict
　　　Calling All Marines*
　　　Thou Shalt Not Kill*
1940 – Who Killed Aunt Maggie?*
1942 – A Tragedy at Midnight*
　　　Joan of Ozark*
1943 – Chatterbox
　　　False Faces
　　　Someone to Remember
　　　The West Side Kid
　　　Here Comes Elmer
1944 – Lake Placid Serenade*
1945 – Earl Carroll Vanities
　　　Steppin' in Society
1946 – One Exciting Week
　　　That Brennan Girl*
1947 – Hit Parade of 1947
　　　Web of Danger
1948 – Train to Alcatraz
1950 – Hit Parade of 1951*
1951 – Belle LeGrand*
1952 – Colorado Sundown

Tommy Coats

Clyde, Andy[189]
1946 – Plainsman and the Lady
1955 – Carolina Cannonball
　　　The Road to Denver

Clyde, David
1936 – The Girl from Mandalay

Clyde, June[189]
1941 – Country Fair

Coates, Phyllis[189]
1953 – Jungle Drums of Africa
　　　Marshal of Cedar Rock
　　　El Paso Stampede
1955 – Panther Girl of the Kongo

Coats, Tommy[189]
Many films, mostly westerns.
1935 – Tumbling Tumbleweeds*
1936 – The Vigilantes Are Coming*
1938 – Outlaws of Sonora*
　　　Under Western Stars*
　　　Gold Mine in the Sky*
　　　Heroes of the Hills*
　　　Pals of the Saddle*
　　　Overland Stage Raiders*
　　　Prairie Moon*
1939 – The Lone Ranger Rides Again*
　　　Wyoming Outlaw*
1940 – Heroes of the Saddle*
　　　Drums of Fu Manchu
　　　Ghost Valley Raiders*
　　　Rocky Mountain Rangers*
　　　King of the Royal Mounted*
1941 – Wyoming Wildcat*
　　　The Phantom Cowboy*
　　　Two Gun Sheriff*
　　　The Singing Hill*
　　　Desert Bandit*
　　　Sunset in Wyoming*
　　　The Apache Kid*
　　　King of the Texas Rangers*
　　　West of Cimarron*
1942 – Arizona Terrors*
　　　Stagecoach Express*
　　　Jesse James, Jr.*
　　　Spy Smasher*
　　　The Cyclone Kid*
　　　The Phantom Plainsmen*
　　　King of the Mounties*
　　　Heart of the Golden West*
　　　Ridin' Down the Canyon*
1943 – Idaho*
　　　Fugitive from Sonora
　　　Hands Across the Border*
1944 – Tucson Raiders*
　　　Song of Nevada*
　　　Lights of Old Santa Fe*
　　　The Big Bonanza*
1945 – Sheriff of Cimarron*
　　　Oregon Trail*
　　　Bandits of the Badlands*
　　　The Cherokee Flash*
1946 – The Phantom Rider
　　　Roll on Texas Moon*
　　　Sioux City Sue*
1947 – Son of Zorro*
　　　Vigilantes of Boomtown*
　　　Springtime in the Sierras*
　　　Jesse James Rides Again*
　　　The Wild Frontier*
1948 – The Bold Frontiersman*
　　　Under California Stars*
　　　The Timber Trail*
　　　Grand Canyon Trail
1949 – The Wyoming Bandit*
　　　South of Rio*
　　　The James Brothers of Missouri*
　　　San Antone Ambush
　　　Navajo Trail Raiders*
　　　Ranger of Cherokee Strip*
　　　Pioneer Marshal*
1950 – Gunmen of Abilene*
　　　The Arizona Cowboy*
1951 – Buckaroo Sheriff of Texas*

Cobb, Edmund[189]
1936 – The Singing Vagabond*
　　　Darkest Africa
　　　Robinson Crusoe of Clipper Island*
1937 – Springtime in the Rockies
　　　Zorro Rides Again
　　　Wild Horse Rodeo
1938 – The Lone Ranger*
　　　The Fighting Devil Dogs
1939 – Blue Montana Skies
　　　Man of Conquest*
　　　Daredevils of the Red Circle*
　　　Dick Tracy's G-Men*
　　　Zorro's Fighting Legion
1940 – Dark Command*
　　　Wagons Westward*
　　　One Man's Law
　　　Melody Ranch*
　　　Texas Terrors*
1941 – Wyoming Wildcat*
　　　Back in the Saddle
　　　The Pittsburgh Kid*
　　　Gauchos of Eldorado*
　　　Tuxedo Junction*
　　　Dick Tracy Vs. Crime, Inc.*
1942 – Heart of the Rio Grande*
　　　Affairs of Jimmy Valentine*
　　　The Girl from Alaska*
　　　Westward Ho*
　　　Stardust on the Sage*
　　　The Cyclone Kid*
　　　The Old Homestead*
　　　X Marks the Spot*
　　　The Traitor Within*
1943 – G-Men Vs. The Black Dragon*
　　　Santa Fe Scouts*
　　　Daredevils of the West*
　　　The Man from Thunder River*
　　　Headin' for God's Country*
　　　Here Comes Elmer*
　　　Mystery Broadcast*
　　　In Old Oklahoma*
　　　California Joe
1944 – Outlaws of Santa Fe*
　　　Marshal of Reno*
　　　Call of the Rockies*
　　　Three Little Sisters*
　　　Faces in the Fog*
1945 – The Phantom Speaks*
　　　Flame of Barbary Coast*
　　　Santa Fe Saddlemates*
　　　Federal Operator 99*
　　　Man from Oklahoma
　　　Sunset in El Dorado*
　　　The Cherokee Flash
1946 – Days of Buffalo Bill
　　　Song of Arizona
　　　Sun Valley Cyclone
　　　The El Paso Kid
　　　Red River Renegades
　　　Rio Grande Raiders
　　　Santa Fe Uprising
　　　Stagecoach to Denver
1947 – Son of Zorro
　　　Last Frontier Uprising
　　　Yankee Fakir*
　　　Oregon Trail Scouts
　　　Robin Hood of Texas*
　　　Jesse James Rides Again
　　　Under Colorado Skies*
1948 – G-Men Never Forget
　　　The Bold Frontiersman
　　　Heart of Virginia
　　　Carson City Raiders
　　　Out of the Storm*
　　　The Far Frontier
1949 – Sheriff of Wichita
　　　Prince of the Plains*
　　　The Wyoming Bandit
　　　South of Rio*
　　　The James Brothers of Missouri
　　　San Antone Ambush
1950 – Bells of Coronado
　　　The Vanishing Westerner
　　　The Arizona Cowboy
　　　Hills of Oklahoma
　　　Covered Wagon Raid*
　　　Desperadoes of the West
　　　Frisco Tornado
1951 – Silver City Bonanza*
　　　Govt. Agents Vs. Phantom Legion
1952 – Toughest Man in Arizona*
1953 – Can. Mounties Vs. Atomic Invaders
1954 – Crazylegs*
　　　Geraldine*
　　　Man with the Steel Whip
1955 – Lay that Rifle Down*
1956 – Hidden Guns

Edmund Cobb

Cobb, Lee J.[94]
1955 — The Road to Denver

Coburn, Charles[94]
1940 — Three Faces West
        Chinese Garden Festival*

Coby, Fred
1951 — Govt. Agents Vs. Phantom Legion

Cochran, Steve[94]
1956 — Come Next Spring
1957 — The Weapon

Cochrane, Frank
1937 — Bulldog Drummond at Bay

Cochrane, Nick
1943 — Here Comes Elmer

Cody, Iron Eyes[190]
Many films, mostly westerns.
1936 — Ride Ranger Ride*
1937 — The Riders of the Whistling Skull*
        The Bold Caballero*
1938 — The Lone Ranger*
        Hawk of the Wilderness*
1939 — Man of Conquest*
1940 — Young Buffalo Bill*
        Colorado*
        Young Bill Hickok*
1941 — In Old Cheyenne*
        Saddlemates
        Outlaws of Cherokee Trail*
        King of the Texas Rangers*
1942 — The Girl from Alaska*
        Perils of Nyoka*
1946 — Under Nevada Skies*
        Plainsman and the Lady*
1948 — Train to Alcatraz
        The Gallant Legion*
1950 — North of the Great Divide*
        California Passage

Coe, Peter
1950 — Sands of Iwo Jima
1951 — The Wild Blue Yonder
1958 — Hell Ship Mutiny

Coe, Vivian
1940 — Adventures of Red Ryder

Coffin, Tristram[130]
1939 — Dick Tracy's G-Men*
1940 — Melody and Moonlight*
        Mysterious Doctor Satan*
        Bowery Boy*
1941 — A Man Betrayed*
        Sailors on Leave*
        Tuxedo Junction*
1942 — Cowboy Serenade*
        A Tragedy at Midnight*
        Spy Smasher
        Perils of Nyoka
        Bells of Capistrano
1943 — Idaho*
1946 — Rendezvous with Annie*
        G. I. War Brides*
        The Invisible Informer
        Under Nevada Skies
        The Mysterious Mr. Valentine
        Rio Grande Raiders
        Sioux City Sue*
1947 — Trail to San Antone
        Blackmail
        Jesse James Rides Again
        The Fabulous Texan*
1948 — California Firebrand
        Desperadoes of Dodge City
1949 — Federal Agents Vs. Underworld, Inc.
        Duke of Chicago*
        King of the Rocket Men
        Radar Patrol Vs. Spy King
1950 — The Old Frontier
1951 — Buckaroo Sheriff of Texas
        Rodeo King and the Senorita
1956 — The Maverick Queen*
1957 — Last Stagecoach West

Cogan, Dick
1950 — Flying Disc Man from Mars
1951 — Street Bandits
1952 — Radar Men from the Moon

Coghlan, Jr., Frank[190]
1941 — Adventures of Captain Marvel
1942 — Pardon My Stripes*
        Youth on Parade*

Cole, George[190]
1957 — The Weapon

Colebrook, Edward
1937 — It Could Happen to You

Coleman, Charles
1943 — The West Side Kid*
1946 — I've Always Loved You*
1947 — The Pilgrim Lady
        The Magnificent Rogue
1948 — Grand Canyon Trail

Coleman, Claudia
1936 — Navy Born

Iron Eyes Cody

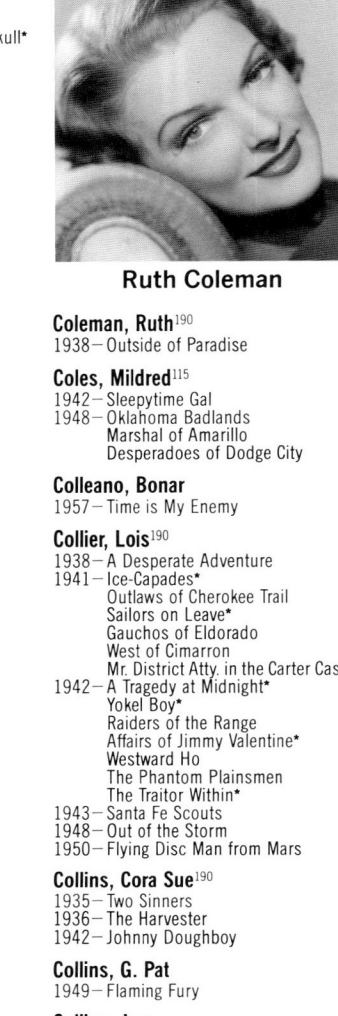
Ruth Coleman

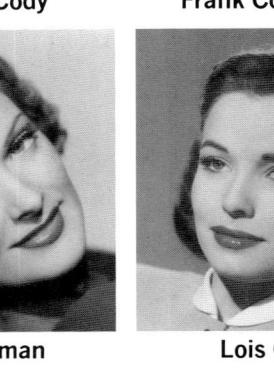
Frank Coghlan, Jr.

Lois Collier

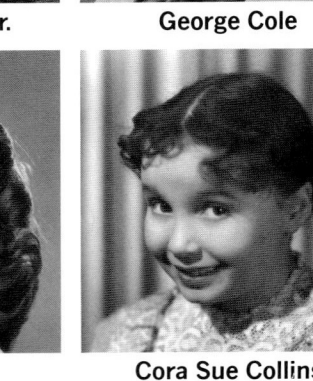
George Cole

Cora Sue Collins

Coleman, Ruth[190]
1938 — Outside of Paradise

Coles, Mildred[115]
1942 — Sleepytime Gal
1948 — Oklahoma Badlands
        Marshal of Amarillo
        Desperadoes of Dodge City

Colleano, Bonar
1957 — Time is My Enemy

Collier, Lois[190]
1938 — A Desperate Adventure
1941 — Ice-Capades*
        Outlaws of Cherokee Trail
        Sailors on Leave*
        Gauchos of Eldorado
        West of Cimarron
        Mr. District Atty. in the Carter Case*
1942 — A Tragedy at Midnight*
        Yokel Boy*
        Raiders of the Range
        Affairs of Jimmy Valentine*
        Westward Ho
        The Phantom Plainsmen
        The Traitor Within*
1943 — Santa Fe Scouts
1948 — Out of the Storm
1950 — Flying Disc Man from Mars

Collins, Cora Sue[190]
1935 — Two Sinners
1936 — The Harvester
1942 — Johnny Doughboy

Collins, G. Pat
1949 — Flaming Fury

Collins, Joan
1955 — The Square Ring

Collins, Ray[190]
1949 — Hideout
1957 — Spoilers of the Forest

Collyer, June
1941 — Wampas Baby Stars*
        Variety Reel*
        Stars at Play*

Colmans, Edward
1955 — Headline Hunters

Colonna, Jerry[74]
1940 — Melody and Moonlight
1941 — Sis Hopkins
        Ice-Capades
1942 — Ice-Capades Revue
1944 — Atlantic City

Commando Cody[190] — series
1953 — Enemies of the Universe
        Atomic Peril
        Cosmic Vengeance
        Nightmare Typhoon
        War of the Space Giants
        Destroyers of the Sun
        Robot Monster from Mars
        The Hydrogen Hurricane
        Solar Sky Raiders
        S. O. S. Ice Age
        Lost in Outer Space
        Captives of the Zero Hour

Compson, Betty[190]
1936 — Laughing Irish Eyes
        Bulldog Edition
1937 — Circus Girl
1939 — Cowboys from Texas
1940 — Texas Terrors*

Compton, Fay
1952 — Lady Possessed

Compton, John[190]
1947 — Jesse James Rides Again
1950 — Rock Island Trail*
        California Passage
1951 — Oh! Susanna
1956 — Thunder Over Arizona
1957 — Spoilers of the Forest

Compton, Joyce[190]
1936 — The Harvester
        Sitting on the Moon
        Country Gentlemen
1937 — Rhythm in the Clouds
        Sea Racketeers
1940 — Who Killed Aunt Maggie?
1943 — A Gentle Gangster
        Silver Spurs
1945 — Hitchhike to Happiness
1946 — Rendezvous with Annie*
1947 — Exposed
1958 — Girl in the Woods

Comstock, William
1943 — Here Comes Elmer

Condon and Bohland
1946 — Murder in the Music Hall

Condos, Nick
1936 — Dancing Feet

Conklin, Chester[190]
1940 — Adventures of Red Ryder*
1941 — Stars Past and Present*
1942 — Sons of the Pioneers
1944 — Goodnight Sweetheart
1947 — Springtime in the Sierras
        Jesse James Rides Again*
1949 — The Golden Stallion

Conklin, Frank
1938 — Federal Man-Hunt

Conley, Joe
1958 — Juvenile Jungle

Conley, Onest
1935 — Racing Luck

Conlin, Jimmy
1941 — Ridin' on a Rainbow
1945 — An Angel Comes to Brooklyn

Conn, Billy[74]
1941 — The Pittsburgh Kid

Connor, Allen[191]
1936 — The Three Mesquiteers
        Robinson Crusoe of Clipper Island
1937 — Gunsmoke Ranch
        S O S Coast Guard

Connor, Frank
1957 — Beginning of the End

Connors, Touch [Mike][94]
1955 — The Twinkle in God's Eye
1956 — Jaguar

Conover, Theresa
1937 — Two Wise Maids

Conrad, Eddy
1939 — In Old Monterey
1940 — Behind the News

Conrad, Jack[191]
1946 — The Glass Alibi

Conrad, Mikel
1951 — Million Dollar Pursuit

Conreid, Hans
1956 — Carnival in Munich

Constantine
1946 — Specter of the Rose

Conway, Bert
1950 — Women from Headquarters
        Prisoners in Petticoats

Conway, Lita
1940 — King of the Royal Mounted
1941 — Puddin' Head*

Conway, Morgan[191]
1942 — Bells of Capistrano
1943 — Canyon City

Conway, Robert
1942 — The Old Homestead

Conway, Russ
1950 — Prisoners in Petticoats
1952 — Colorado Sundown*

Coogan, Jackie[94]
1957 — Eighteen and Anxious
1958 — No Place to Land

Coogan, Robert
1942 — Johnny Doughboy

Cook, Clyde
1938 — Storm Over Bengal
1951 — Pride of Maryland

Cook, Donald[75]
1935 — The Spanish Cape Mystery
1936 — The Leavenworth Case
        The Girl from Mandalay
        Beware of Ladies
1937 — Two Wise Maids
        Circus Girl

Cook, Jr., Elisha[191]
1942 — Sleepytime Gal
1955 — Timberjack
1956 — Accused of Murder

Cook, Tommy[191]
1940 — Adventures of Red Ryder
1941 — Mr. District Attorney*
        Jungle Girl
1946 — Song of Arizona
1949 — The Kid from Cleveland

Ray Collins

Commando Cody

Betty Compson

John Compton

Joyce Compton

Chester Conklin

John Vosper, Clancy Cooper

Allen Connor

Jack Conrad

Morgan Conway

Elisha Cook, Jr.

Tommy Cook

Peter Cookson

Bobby Cooper

George Cooper

Cooke, Victor Ray
1938 – King of the Newsboys

Cookson, Peter[191]
1944 – The Girl Who Dared
1945 – Behind City Lights

Cooley, Clyde "Spade"
1939 – Frontier Pony Express*
        The Arizona Kid*
1940 – Young Bill Hickok*
        The Border Legion*
1941 – Robin Hood of the Pecos*
        Arkansas Judge*
        In Old Cheyenne*
        Sheriff of Tombstone*
        Nevada City*
        Bad Man of Deadwood*
1942 – Man from Cheyenne*
        South of Santa Fe*
        Sunset on the Desert*
        Home in Wyomin'*
        Romance on the Range*
        Heart of the Golden West*
1943 – Chatterbox

Cooley, Marjorie
1942 – The Traitor Within

Coontz, Bill
1956 – Hidden Guns
1957 – Raiders of Old California
1958 – No Place to Land

Cooper, Ben[17]
1952 – Thunderbirds
1953 – Woman They Almost Lynched
        A Perilous Journey
        Shadows of Tombstone*
1954 – Sea of Lost Ships
        Flight Nurse
        Geraldine*
        Johnny Guitar
        The Outcast
        Hell's Outpost
1955 – The Eternal Sea
        Santa Fe Passage*
        The Last Command
        Headline Hunters
        The Fighting Chance
1956 – Come Next Spring*
        A Strange Adventure
1957 – Duel at Apache Wells

Cooper, Bobby[191]
1944 – Secrets of Scotland Yard

Cooper, Clancy[191]
1943 – Dead Man's Gulch
        Deerslayer
1944 – Haunted Harbor
1945 – Steppin' in Society*

Cooper, George
1936 – Federal Agent
        Sitting on the Moon
1937 – Portia on Trial
        The Duke Comes Back

Cooper, George[191]
1949 – Flaming Fury

Cooper, Georgie
1943 – The Man from Thunder River

Cooper, Jeanne[191]
1953 – Shadows of Tombstone

Cooper, Ken
Many films, mostly westerns.
1936 – Red River Valley
        Comin' 'Round the Mountain
        The Singing Cowboy
        Guns and Guitars
        The Vigilantes Are Coming*
1937 – Round-Up Time in Texas
1938 – The Lone Ranger*
        The Fighting Devil Dogs*
1939 – Dick Tracy's G-Men*
1950 – Desperadoes of the West*

Cooper, Melville
1943 – Hit Parade of 1943

Cooper, Ted
1951 – Arizona Manhunt
1952 – Wild Horse Ambush

Coote, Robert
1937 – The Sheik Steps Out

Cope, Annette
1957 – Operation Conspiracy

Coplen, Yorke
1950 – Jungle Stampede

Corbett, Ben[191]
1938 – Gold Mine in the Sky

Corby, Ellen[191]
1946 – In Old Sacramento*
1947 – Driftwood*
1948 – I, Jane Doe*
1951 – The Sea Hornet
1953 – Woman They Almost Lynched
1954 – The Untamed Heiress

Corday, Mara[191]
1952 – Toughest Man in Arizona*
1953 – The Lady Wants Mink
        Sweethearts on Parade

Corday, Sandra[191]
1937 – The Trigger Trio

Cording, Harry[191]
1940 – Dark Command*
        King of the Royal Mounted
1942 – King of the Mounties*
1943 – Fugitive from Sonora
        The Man from the Rio Grande
1945 – The Fatal Witness*
1948 – Dangers of the Canadian Mounted

Cordova, Fred
1944 – Storm Over Lisbon*

Corey, Jeff[191]
1941 – Petticoat Politics
1946 – Rendezvous with Annie*
1947 – The Flame*
1948 – I, Jane Doe*
1949 – Wake of the Red Witch
        Hideout
1950 – Singing Guns
        Rock Island Trail

Corey, Jim
1936 – Guns and Guitars
1937 – Guns in the Dark
1938 – Gold Mine in the Sky

Corey, Wendell[75]
1951 – The Wild Blue Yonder
1954 – Laughing Anne
        Hell's Half Acre

Corrado, Gino
1936 – Oregon Trail

Jeanne Cooper

Ben Corbett

Ellen Corby

Dennis O'Keefe, Mary Field, Mara Corday

Sandra Corday

Harry Cording

Jeff Corey

Correll, Mady[192]
1938 — Invisible Enemy

Corrigan, D'Arcy
1937 — All Over Town

Corrigan, Lloyd[130]
1942 — Secrets of the Underground
1943 — London Blackout Murders
　　　King of the Cowboys
　　　The Mantrap
　　　Nobody's Darling
1944 — Rosie, the Riveter
　　　Goodnight Sweetheart
　　　Song of Nevada
　　　Lights of Old Santa Fe
　　　Lake Placid Serenade
1947 — The Ghost Goes Wild
1948 — Homicide for Three
1956 — Hidden Guns

Corrigan, Ray "Crash"[18]
　　　[as Ray Benard]
1936 — The Singing Vagabond*
　　　Darkest Africa*
　　　The Leathernecks Have Landed*
　　　[as Ray Corrigan]
　　　Undersea Kingdom
　　　The Vigilantes Are Coming*
　　　The Three Mesquiteers
　　　Ghost-Town Gold
　　　Country Gentlemen
　　　Roarin' Lead
1937 — The Riders of the Whistling Skull
　　　Join the Marines
　　　Hit the Saddle
　　　Gunsmoke Ranch
　　　Come on, Cowboys!
　　　The Painted Stallion
　　　Range Defenders
　　　Heart of the Rockies
　　　The Trigger Trio
　　　Wild Horse Rodeo
1938 — The Purple Vigilantes
　　　Call the Mesquiteers
　　　Outlaws of Sonora
　　　Riders of the Black Hills
　　　Heroes of the Hills
　　　Pals of the Saddle
　　　Overland Stage Raiders
　　　Santa Fe Stampede
　　　Red River Range
1939 — The Night Riders
　　　Three Texas Steers
　　　Wyoming Outlaw
　　　New Frontier
1950 — Trail of Robin Hood

Corsaro, Franco
1942 — A Tragedy at Midnight*
　　　Spy Smasher

Corson, William
1939 — Zorro's Fighting Legion

Cortese, Valentina
1956 — Magic Fire

Cortez, Ricardo[192]
1946 — The Inner Circle
1947 — Blackmail

Corthell, Herbert[192]
1936 — Dancing Feet
1943 — Sleepy Lagoon

Corum, Bill
1953 — Marciano Vs. LaStarza

Cosgrove, Douglas
1936 — Winds of the Wasteland

Costa, Robert
1954 — Hell's Half Acre

Costello, Don
1945 — Great Stagecoach Robbery
　　　Marshal of Laredo
1946 — Crime of the Century

Costello, Grace
1942 — Johnny Doughboy

Costello, Lou
1941 — Los Angeles Examiner Benefit*

Costello, Maurice
1941 — A Man Betrayed*
　　　Lady from Louisiana

Coster, Nicolas
1954 — The Outcast
1955 — City of Shadows

Cota, David
1945 — Along the Navajo Trail

Cotton, Carolina
1944 — Sing Neighbor Sing

Cottrell, Beverly
1954 — Flight Nurse*

Coulouris, George
1955 — Doctor in the House
1956 — Doctor at Sea

Court, Emerton
1957 — Thunder Over Tangier

Courtemarsh, Gerald
1949 — The American Rodeo*

Courtleigh, Stephen
1955 — Yellowneck

Courtney, Inez[192]
1937 — The Hit Parade

Cowan, Jerome[130]
1939 — She Married a Cop
1940 — Wolf of New York
　　　Melody Ranch
1941 — Rags to Riches
1942 — The Girl from Alaska
　　　Joan of Ozark
1943 — Silver Spurs
1945 — Hitchhike to Happiness
　　　Behind City Lights
1946 — Murder in the Music Hall
　　　One Exciting Week
1947 — Driftwood

Coy, Johnny[115]
1946 — Earl Carroll Sketchbook

Coy, Walter
1950 — Rio Grande
1958 — Juvenile Jungle

Mady Correll

Inez Courtney

Crabbe, Larry "Buster"[193]
1939 — Colorado Sunset
1957 — The Lawless Eighties

Craig, Alec
1942 — The Old Homestead*

Craig, Catherine
1947 — The Pretender

Craig, James[192]
1958 — Man or Gun

Craig, May
1952 — The Quiet Man

Craig, Yvonne
1957 — Eighteen and Anxious

Cramer, Dick[192]
1935 — The Spanish Cape Mystery*
1937 — The Trusted Outlaw
　　　"Lightnin'" Crandall*
　　　Trail of Vengeance*
　　　Guns in the Dark*
　　　The Red Rope*
　　　The Wrong Road*
1938 — Thunder in the Desert
　　　The Higgins Family*
1939 — The Mysterious Miss X*
　　　S.O.S. Tidal Wave*
　　　Wyoming Outlaw*
1940 — Wagons Westward*
　　　Girl from Havana*

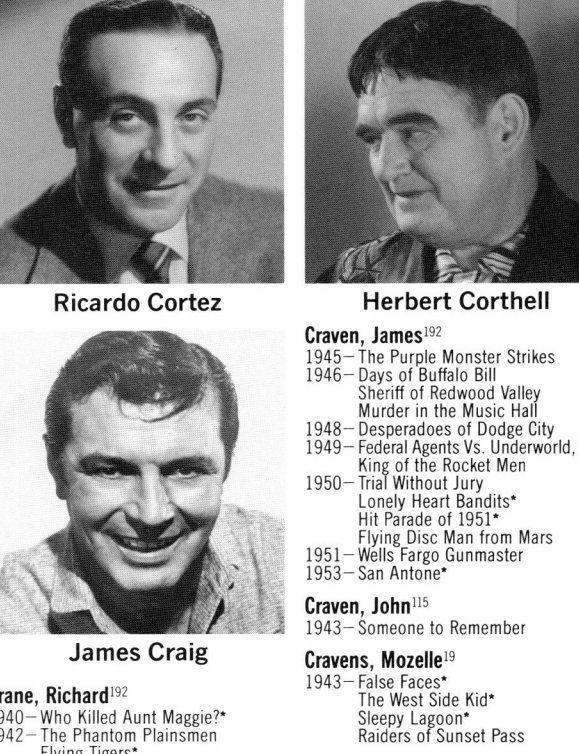

Ricardo Cortez

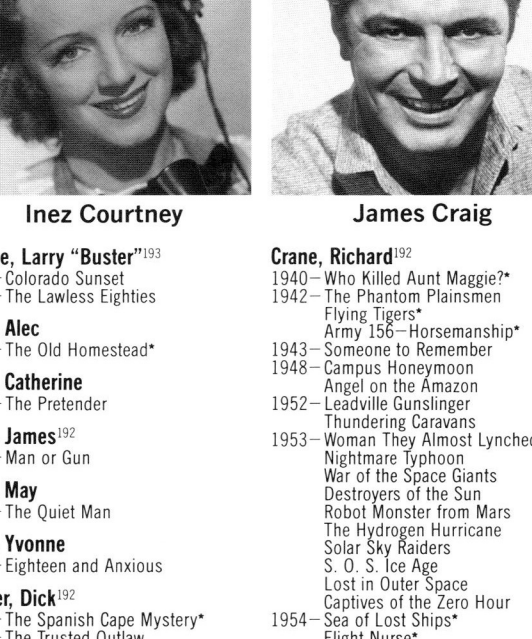

James Craig

Crane, Richard[192]
1940 — Who Killed Aunt Maggie?*
1942 — The Phantom Plainsmen
　　　Flying Tigers*
　　　Army 156 — Horsemanship*
1943 — Someone to Remember
1948 — Campus Honeymoon
　　　Angel on the Amazon
1952 — Leadville Gunslinger
　　　Thundering Caravans
1953 — Woman They Almost Lynched*
　　　Nightmare Typhoon
　　　War of the Space Giants
　　　Destroyers of the Sun
　　　Robot Monster from Mars
　　　The Hydrogen Hurricane
　　　Solar Sky Raiders
　　　S. O. S. Ice Age
　　　Lost in Outer Space
　　　Captives of the Zero Hour
1954 — Sea of Lost Ships*
　　　Flight Nurse*
1955 — The Eternal Sea
　　　No Man's Woman

Cravat, Noel[192]
1943 — G-Men Vs. The Black Dragon
1952 — Radar Men from the Moon

Craven, Frank[192]
1936 — The Harvester
1941 — Variety Reel*
1944 — My Best Gal

Herbert Corthell

Craven, James[192]
1945 — The Purple Monster Strikes
1946 — Days of Buffalo Bill
　　　Sheriff of Redwood Valley
　　　Murder in the Music Hall
1948 — Desperadoes of Dodge City
1949 — Federal Agents Vs. Underworld, Inc.
　　　King of the Rocket Men
1950 — Trial Without Jury
　　　Lonely Heart Bandits*
　　　Hit Parade of 1951*
　　　Flying Disc Man from Mars
1951 — Wells Fargo Gunmaster
1953 — San Antone*

Craven, John[115]
1943 — Someone to Remember

Cravens, Mozelle[19]
1943 — False Faces*
　　　The West Side Kid*
　　　Sleepy Lagoon*
　　　Raiders of Sunset Pass

Crawford, Broderick[95]
1947 — The Flame

Crawford, Joan[95]
1954 — Johnny Guitar

Crawford, John[192]
　　　[as John Royce]
1943 — Secret Service in Darkest Africa*
　　　[as John Crawford]
1944 — Thoroughbreds*
1948 — G-Men Never Forget*
　　　Dangers of the Canadian Mounted
　　　Sons of Adventure
　　　Adv. of Frank and Jesse James
1949 — Ghost of Zorro
　　　The James Brothers of Missouri*
　　　Radar Patrol Vs. Spy King
1950 — Twilight in the Sierras*
　　　The Invisible Monster
　　　Lonely Heart Bandits*
1951 — Cuban Fireball*
　　　Honeychile*
1952 — Zombies of the Stratosphere
　　　Old Oklahoma Plains
1953 — Marshal of Cedar Rock
　　　Nightmare Typhoon
　　　Destroyers of the Sun
　　　Robot Monster from Mars
　　　Lost in Outer Space
　　　Captives of the Zero Hour
1954 — Trader Tom of the China Seas

Crehan, Joseph[131]
1937 — The Wrong Road
　　　The Duke Comes Back
1938 — Mama Runs Wild
　　　Billy the Kid Returns
　　　Shine on Harvest Moon*
1939 — Pride of the Navy
1940 — Gaucho Serenade
　　　Colorado*
1941 — A Man Betrayed*
　　　Nevada City
　　　Doctors Don't Tell
1943 — False Faces
　　　Mystery Broadcast
　　　Hands Across the Border
1945 — The Chicago Kid
　　　Captain Tugboat Annie
1946 — A Guy Could Change
　　　Night Train to Memphis
　　　Plainsman and the Lady*
1947 — The Trespasser
1948 — The Gallant Legion*
　　　Night Time in Nevada
　　　Sundown in Santa Fe
　　　Homicide for Three
1949 — Duke of Chicago
　　　The Last Bandit
　　　Alias the Champ
1950 — The Arizona Cowboy
1951 — Pride of Maryland
1952 — Tropical Heat Wave*
1953 — San Antone*
1954 — Crazylegs
1955 — The Twinkle in God's Eye*

Dick Cramer

Richard Crane

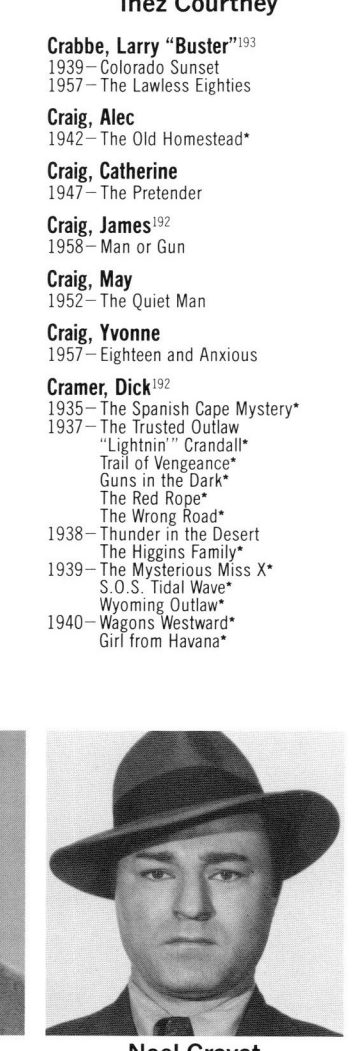

Noel Cravat

Frank Craven

James Craven

John Crawford

Kernan Cripps

Bob Crosby

192

 Wade Crosby
 Kathleen Crowley
 Louise Currie
 Alan Curtis
 Dick Curtis

 Donald Curtis
 Keene Curtis
 Ken Curtis
 Frank Dae   John Daheim

Cripps, Kernans[192]
1937 – Dick Tracy*
Hit the Saddle*
Dangerous Holiday*
1938 – Hollywood Stadium Mystery!*
Prison Nurse*
Dick Tracy Returns*
1939 – I Was a Convict*
Street of Missing Men*
1940 – Wolf of New York*
Gaucho Serenade*
1945 – Federal Operator 99
Captain Tugboat Annie*
1946 – Daughter of Don Q

Crisp, Donald
1941 – Variety Reel*

Crocker, Harry
1945 – A Song for Miss Julie

Crockett, Luther
1952 – Woman in the Dark

Crockett, Richard
1958 – Street of Darkness

Cromwell, Richard[75]
1937 – The Wrong Road
1938 – Come on, Leathernecks
Storm Over Bengal
1940 – Village Barn Dance

Crosby, Bing
1941 – Stars at Play*

Crosby, Bob[192]
1941 – Sis Hopkins
Rookies on Parade

Crosby, Gary
1947 – Hit Parade of 1947*

Crosby, Wade[193]
1941 – Citadel of Crime
1942 – Shepherd of the Ozarks
In Old California*
The Sundown Kid
1943 – Headin' for God's Country
In Old Oklahoma*
1944 – Cheyenne Wildcat
1945 – Bandits of the Badlands
Rough Riders of Cheyenne
1946 – In Old Sacramento*
Traffic in Crime
1947 – Angel and the Badman*
Web of Danger*
Along the Oregon Trail
The Fabulous Texan*
1948 – Under California Stars
The Timber Trail
1949 – Rose of the Yukon
1950 – Hit Parade of 1951
The Missourians*
1952 – Thunderbirds*
1953 – Old Overland Trail
The Lady Wants Mink*
Sweethearts on Parade*
Bandits of the West*

Crosman, Henrietta
1936 – Follow Your Heart

Crosson, Robert
1955 – I Cover the Underworld

Crowe, Eileen
1952 – The Quiet Man

Crowe, Lt. Col. H. P.
1950 – Sands of Iwo Jima

Crowell, William
1936 – Beware of Ladies

Crowley, Kathleen[193]
1955 – City of Shadows

Culver, Roland
1958 – Scotland Yard Dragnet

Cummings, Billy
1945 – Colorado Pioneers
1947 – Oregon Trail Scouts

Cummings, Robert[95]
1938 – I Stand Accused

Cummings, Suzanne
1955 – Headline Hunters*

Cunard, Grace
1944 – Firebrands of Arizona*
1945 – Great Stagecoach Robbery*
Behind City Lights*
Girls of the Big House*

Cunningham, Cecil
1942 – Cowboy Serenade
1943 – In Old Oklahoma

Cunningham, Joe
1936 – Country Gentlemen
1942 – Affairs of Jimmy Valentine

Currie, Finlay
1937 – Glamorous Night

Currie, Louise[193]
1941 – Adventures of Captain Marvel
1942 – Stardust on the Sage
1943 – The Masked Marvel

Currier, Mary
1946 – Crime of the Century
1948 – Angel in Exile

Curtis, Alan[193]
1936 – Undersea Kingdom*
1941 – Variety Reel*
Stars Past and Present*
1942 – Remember Pearl Harbor!

Curtis, Billy
1939 – Three Texas Steers
1948 – Homicide for Three

Curtis, Dick[193]
1935 – Racing Luck
Burning Gold*
1936 – Federal Agent*
1937 – Bar-Z Bad Men
The Gambling Terror
Trail of Vengeance
Guns in the Dark
A Lawman is Born
Boothill Brigade
1945 – Wagon Wheels Westward
1946 – California Gold Rush
Song of Arizona
Traffic in Crime
Santa Fe Uprising
1947 – Wyoming
1949 – Sheriff of Wichita*
Navajo Trail Raiders
1950 – The Vanishing Westerner
Rock Island Trail*
Covered Wagon Raid
1951 – Govt. Agents Vs. Phantom Legion

Curtis, Donald[193]
1942 – Code of the Outlaw
Westward Ho
Joan of Ozark
1954 – The Shanghai Story*
1955 – Flame of the Islands

Curtis, Jack
1935 – Westward Ho
Lawless Range

Curtis, Keene[193]
1950 – Macbeth

Curtis, Ken[193]
1950 – Rio Grande*
1951 – Don Daredevil Rides Again
Fighting Coast Guard*
1952 – The Quiet Man*

Cusack, Cyril
1957 – The Man in the Road

Cushing, Peter
1940 – Women in War*
1956 – Magic Fire

Cuthbertson, Allan
1957 – Operation Conspiracy

Dae, Frank[193]
1937 – Portia on Trial*
1939 – The Covered Trailer
1940 – Carolina Moon
1947 – Springtime in the Sierras*
1948 – Train to Alcatraz*
1949 – The Last Bandit*
Radar Patrol Vs. Spy King
1950 – House by the River*
Trigger, Jr.*
Surrender*
1951 – In Old Amarillo*

Larry "Buster" Crabbe, Marilyn Saris

Daheim, John[193]
[as John Daheim]
1942 – Spy Smasher*
Perils of Nyoka*
1943 – G-Men Vs. The Black Dragon*
Secret Service in Darkest Africa*
The Masked Marvel*
Pistol Packin' Mama*
1944 – Captain America*
The Tiger Woman*
Haunted Harbor*
1945 – The Purple Monster Strikes*
1946 – The Catman of Paris*
Passkey to Danger*
Daughter of Don Q*
The Crimson Ghost*
Home in Oklahoma*
1947 – Son of Zorro*
Saddle Pals*
The Trespasser*
Exposed*
1948 – G-Men Never Forget*
1949 – Federal Agents Vs. Underworld, Inc.*
Ghost of Zorro*
Radar Patrol Vs. Spy King*
1950 – Tarnished*
Trigger, Jr.*
Desperadoes of the West*
Redwood Forest Trail*
Sunset in the West*
Flying Disc Man from Mars*
1951 – South of Caliente*
1952 – Woman in the Dark*
Colorado Sundown
Wild Horse Ambush
Zombies of the Stratosphere*
1953 – Enemies of the Universe*
Cosmic Vengeance*
Destroyers of the Sun
[as John Day]
1955 – Panther Girl of the Kongo*
Headline Hunters*

Dahlen, Armin
1955 – The Divided Heart

Dahms, Tom
1954 – Crazylegs

Dainton, Noel
1943 – The Saint Meets the Tiger

D'Albert, Suzanne
1952 – Thunderbirds

Dale, Arvon[193]
1942 – Shepherd of the Ozarks*
Spy Smasher*
Perils of Nyoka
King of the Mounties
Valley of Hunted Men*
1943 – G-Men Vs. The Black Dragon*
1946 – Daughter of Don Q*
Earl Carroll Sketchbook*
That Brennan Girl*
1947 – Calendar Girl*
The Black Widow*
1948 – Dangers of the Canadian Mounted*
1949 – King of the Rocket Men*
Radar Patrol Vs. Spy King

 Arvon Dale

Dale, Esther[194]
1940 – Village Barn Dance
1943 – Swing Your Partner
1945 – Behind City Lights
1950 – Surrender

Dale, James
1948 – Dangers of the Canadian Mounted
Sons of Adventure
Adv. of Frank and Jesse James
1949 – Federal Agents Vs. Underworld, Inc.

Esther Dale

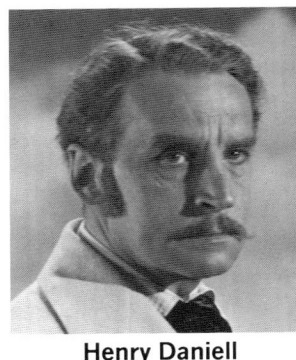

Henry Daniell

Dale, Michael
1958 – Outcasts of the City

Dale, Virginia[115]
1941 – The Singing Hill
1943 – Headin' for God's Country

D'Alvarez, Marguerite
1945 – An Angel Comes to Brooklyn

Dalya, Jacqueline
1941 – Lady from Louisiana
1945 – Song of Mexico

d'Ambricourt, Adrienne
1952 – Bal Tabarin

Damler, John
1955 – The Fighting Chance

Dandridge, Dorothy[175]
1941 – Lady from Louisiana
1943 – Hit Parade of 1943
1944 – Atlantic City

Dandridge, Ruby
1946 – Home in Oklahoma

Danieli, Luciana
1951 – Fugitive Lady

Daniell, Henry[194]
1949 – Wake of the Red Witch

Daniels, Bette[194]
1949 – San Antone Ambush

Daniels, Henry [Hank][115]
1945 – The Chicago Kid
1946 – In Old Sacramento

Daniels, Harold
1937 – Doomed at Sundown
1940 – Oklahoma Renegades

Daniels, Keith
1936 – The House of a Thousand Candles

Daniels, Mark
1958 – Invisible Avenger

Daniely, Lisa
1957 – The Man in the Road

Danko, Betty
Many films.
1942 – In Old California*
1946 – Daughter of Don Q*

Dann, Roger[194]
1948 – I, Jane Doe

Dano, Royal[194]
1954 – Johnny Guitar

Dano, Steve
1958 – Invisible Avenger

Danvers-Walker, Bob
1956 – Zanzabuku

DaPron, Louis
1941 – Rookies on Parade

Darcy, Sheila
1939 – South of the Border
Zorro's Fighting Legion

Dare, Mercedes "Midgie"
1941 – Mr. District Atty. in the Carter Case*
1943 – Hit Parade of 1943*
Nobody's Darling*
1944 – Atlantic City*
1952 – The Wac from Walla Walla*
1956 – A Strange Adventure*

Darien, Frank[194]
1936 – Under Cover Man
1937 – Jim Hanvey - Detective
1938 – The Purple Vigilantes*
The Old Barn Dance*
Born to be Wild*
Western Jamboree
1939 – Sabotage
1941 – Arkansas Judge
Sis Hopkins*
Hurricane Smith
Under Fiesta Stars
King of the Texas Rangers
1943 – Nobody's Darling*
1946 – The Fabulous Suzanne
1947 – That's My Man*

Bette Daniels

Roger Dann

Royal Dano

Frank Darien

Roy Darmour

Steve Darrell

Darmour, Roy[194]
1938 – Dick Tracy Returns*
1939 – S.O.S. Tidal Wave*
Smuggled Cargo*
Calling All Marines*
1941 – A Man Betrayed*
The Devil Pays Off*
1942 – Pardon My Stripes*
1943 – Pistol Packin' Mama*
1944 – The Fighting Seabees*
The Tiger Woman*
Man from Frisco*
Bordertown Trail*
Strangers in the Night*
My Buddy*
Faces in the Fog*
1945 – The Chicago Kid*
Swingin' on a Rainbow*
1948 – I, Jane Doe*

Darnell, Linda[95]
1956 – Dakota Incident

Darrell, Steve[194]
1946 – The Catman of Paris*
Under Nevada Skies*
Roll on Texas Moon
Heldorado
1947 – Angel and the Badman*
On the Old Spanish Trail
Under Colorado Skies
1948 – Carson City Raiders
The Timber Trail
Night Time in Nevada
Son of God's Country
Adv. of Frank and Jesse James
1949 – Ghost of Zorro
Outcasts of the Trail
The Fighting Kentuckian*
1950 – The Arizona Cowboy
Rock Island Trail*
Under Mexicali Stars
1951 – Rough Riders of Durango
1953 – San Antone*
1954 – Sea of Lost Ships*
1955 – The Last Command*

Darrin, Michael
1956 – Hidden Guns

Darrin, Sonia
1948 – I, Jane Doe*
1950 – Federal Agent at Large

Darro, Frankie[194]
1941 – Tuxedo Junction
1947 – That's My Man
1948 – Heart of Virginia
1951 – Pride of Maryland

Darwell, Jane[194]
1939 – The Zero Hour
1945 – Captain Tugboat Annie
1948 – Train to Alcatraz
1950 – Surrender
Redwood Forest Trail
1953 – The Sun Shines Bright

DaSilva, Henry
1944 – Brazil

Daugherty, Dick
1954 – Crazylegs

Davenport, Doris[116]
1940 – Behind the News
1941 – Variety Reel*

Davenport, Harry[75]
1937 – Paradise Express
1938 – The Higgins Family
Orphans of the Street
1939 – My Wife's Relatives
Should Husbands Work?
The Covered Trailer
Money to Burn
1940 – Grandpa Goes to Town
Earl of Puddlestone
1941 – Hurricane Smith
1943 – Shantytown
Headin' for God's Country
1946 – G. I. War Brides
1947 – The Fabulous Texan

Davenport, Havis[194]
1956 – Scandal Incorporated

Davidoff, Alexis
1943 – In Old Oklahoma*

Davidson, John[131]
1938 – The Fighting Devil Dogs
Storm Over Bengal*
1940 – King of the Royal Mounted
1941 – Adventures of Captain Marvel
Dick Tracy Vs. Crime, Inc.
1942 – Perils of Nyoka
1943 – Secret Service in Darkest Africa*
1944 – Captain America
1945 – The Purple Monster Strikes

Davidson, Ronald
1950 – Jungle Stampede

Frankie Darro

Jane Darwell

Havis Davenport

William B. Davidson

Richard Davies

Elaine Davis

Gail Davis

Davidson, William B.[194]
1937 – Affairs of Cappy Ricks
1942 – Affairs of Jimmy Valentine
1945 – Tell It to a Star
1946 – Plainsman and the Lady
1947 – That's My Man

Davies, Emlen
1956 – A Strange Adventure
1958 – Young and Wild

Davies, Lloyd G.
1949 – The Red Menace

Davies, Richard[194]
1945 – Swingin' on a Rainbow

Davies, Wela[19]
1940 – The Crooked Road*
Women in War*
Earl of Puddlestone*
1941 – Lady from Louisiana*

Davis, Audry
1936 – Guns and Guitars

Davis, Bette
1941 – Variety Reel*

Davis, Elaine[194]
1954 – The Atomic Kid

Davis, Gail[194]
1948 – The Far Frontier
1949 – Death Valley Gunfighter
Frontier Investigator
Law of the Golden West

 Joan Davis
 Owen Davis, Jr.
 Robert O. Davis
 Shirley Davis
 Dennis Day

 Richard Deacon
 Nigel de Brulier
 Ted de Corsia
 Babe DeFreest
 John Dehner

 Myrna Dell
 Nita Del Rey

Ted Mapes, Eddie Dean

Davis, George
1946 — The Catman of Paris
1951 — Secrets of Monte Carlo

Davis, Georgia
1943 — Hoosier Holiday

Davis, Jim[75]
1947 — The Fabulous Texan
1949 — Hellfire
    Brimstone
1950 — The Savage Horde
    The Showdown
    California Passage
1951 — Oh! Susanna
    The Sea Hornet
1952 — Woman of the North Country
1953 — Ride the Man Down
    Woman They Almost Lynched
1954 — Jubilee Trail
    The Outcast
    Hell's Outpost
1955 — Timberjack
    The Last Command
    The Vanishing American
1956 — The Maverick Queen
1957 — Duel at Apache Wells
    Last Stagecoach West
    Raiders of Old California

Davis, Joan[195]
1942 — Yokel Boy

Davis, Karl
1955 — Timberjack
    The Road to Denver
1958 — Man or Gun

Davis, Jr., Owen[195]
1937 — It Could Happen to You
1939 — Thou Shalt Not Kill

Davis, Robert
1953 — Jungle Drums of Africa

Davis, Robert O.[195]
    [as Robert O. Davis]
1941 — King of the Texas Rangers
1942 — Spy Smasher
    The Phantom Plainsman
    [as Rudolph Andres]
1946 — Under Nevada Skies

Davis, Rufe[75]
1940 — Under Texas Skies
    The Trail Blazers
    Barnyard Follies
    Lone Star Raiders
1941 — Prairie Pioneers
    Pals of the Pecos
    Saddlemates
    Gangs of Sonora
    Outlaws of Cherokee Trail
    Gauchos of Eldorado
    West of Cimarron
1942 — Code of the Outlaw
    Raiders of the Range
    Westward Ho
    The Phantom Plainsmen
1944 — Jamboree

Davis, Shirley[195]
1949 — Prince of the Plains

Davray, Jo
1959 — O. S. S. 117 is Not Dead

Dawson, Billy
1943 — Nobody's Darling

Dawson, Hal K.
1938 — Mama Runs Wild*
1941 — Angels with Broken Wings*
1947 — The Flame*
1952 — Woman of the North Country*
1955 — City of Shadows*

Day, Dennis[195]
1943 — Sleepy Lagoon

Day, Doris[19]
1939 — Saga of Death Valley
    Thou Shalt Not Kill
1940 — Village Barn Dance

Day, John
See John Daheim.

Dea, Marie
1959 — O. S. S. 117 is Not Dead

Deacon, Richard[195]
1955 — Lay that Rifle Down
1956 — When Gangland Strikes*
1957 — Affair in Reno

de Alva, Racquel
1945 — Song of Mexico

Dean, Eddie[195]
1938 — Western Jamboree*
1939 — The Lone Ranger Rides Again*
1940 — Oklahoma Renegades
1941 — Pals of the Pecos*
    Kansas Cyclone*
    Sunset in Wyoming*
    Outlaws of Cherokee Trail*
    Down Mexico Way*
    Gauchos of Eldorado*
    Sierra Sue
    West of Cimarron*
1942 — Stagecoach Express*
1943 — King of the Cowboys*

Dean, Ivor
1957 — Operation Conspiracy

Dean, Jean
1948 — Sundown in Santa Fe
1949 — Radar Patrol Vs. Spy King

Dean, Marga
1944 — Casanova in Burlesque

Deane, Shirley
1938 — Prairie Moon

Deans, Herbert
1952 — Bal Tabarin

Dearing, Edgar
1945 — Don't Fence Me In
1948 — Out of the Storm

DeBanzie, Brenda
1955 — A Day to Remember
1956 — Doctor at Sea

de Brulier, Nigel[195]
1936 — Down to the Sea
1937 — Zorro Rides Again
1941 — Adventures of Captain Marvel

DeCarlo, Yvonne[95]
1942 — Youth on Parade*
1943 — Deerslayer
1955 — Flame of the Islands
1956 — Magic Fire

Deckers, Eugene
1956 — Doctor at Sea

de Cordoba, Pedro
1938 — Storm Over Bengal
1939 — Man of Conquest
1951 — Cuban Fireball

de Cordova, Leander
1939 — Zorro's Fighting Legion
1944 — The Laramie Trail

de Corsia, Ted[195]
1957 — The Lawless Eighties

Dee, Frances[95]
1941 — A Man Betrayed

DeFreest, Babe [Thelma][195]
1937 — The Painted Stallion*
1942 — Perils of Nyoka*
1943 — Daredevils of the West*
    In Old Oklahoma*
1944 — The Tiger Woman*
    Zorro's Black Whip*
1945 — The Purple Monster Strikes*

Deghy, Guy Stephen
1955 — The Divided Heart

Dehner, John[195]
1944 — Lake Placid Serenade*
1946 — The Undercover Woman
    The Catman of Paris
    The Last Crooked Mile
    Out California Way
1947 — Vigilantes of Boomtown
1956 — Terror at Midnight

Dekker, Albert[116]
1942 — Yokel Boy
    In Old California
1943 — In Old Oklahoma
1946 — The French Key
1947 — Wyoming
    The Pretender
    The Fabulous Texan

Dell, Myrna[195]
1943 — In Old Oklahoma*
1949 — Rose of the Yukon

Delmar, Kenny
1949 — Beyond Civilization to Texas

Del Rey, Nita[195]
1952 — The Fabulous Senorita

Del Rio, Diana
1942 — Remember Pearl Harbor!

Del Rio, Dolores
1940 — Chinese Garden Festival*
1941 — Wampas Baby Stars*

Deltgen, Rene
1956 — Circus Girl

DeMain, Gordon
1937 — The Painted Stallion

Demarest, William[95]
1937 — The Hit Parade
1938 — Romance on the Run
1940 — Wolf of New York
1941 — Rookies on Parade
    Country Fair
    Stars at Play*
1942 — Johnny Doughboy
1953 — The Lady Wants Mink

DeMario, Donna
1947 — Apache Rose

DeMarney, Derrick
1942 — Suicide Squadron

Demetrio, Anna
1940 — Young Buffalo Bill
1944 — Call of the South Seas

DeMille, Katherine[195]
1939 — In Old Caliente

 Katherine DeMille

George DeNormand

Harry Depp

Arthur Hoyt, Reginald Denny, June Travis

de Montez, Rico
1944 – The Tiger Woman
       Haunted Harbor
       Brazil

Demourelie, Vic
1939 – Mexicali Rose

Dench and Stewart
1941 – Ice-Capades
1942 – Ice-Capades Revue

Denham, Maurice
1956 – Doctor at Sea

D'Ennery, Guy
1938 – Storm Over Bengal*
1939 – Zorro's Fighting Legion
1940 – Drums of Fu Manchu
       Covered Wagon Days
1941 – Prairie Pioneers

Denning, Richard[116]
1942 – Ice-Capades Revue
1946 – The Fabulous Suzanne
1950 – Harbor of Missing Men
1951 – Insurance Investigator

Denny, Reginald[196]
1937 – Join the Marines

DeNormand, George[196]
1935 – Melody Trail*
1936 – Undersea Kingdom*
1937 – Dick Tracy
       The Painted Stallion
1938 – Gangs of New York*
       The Fighting Devil Dogs*
       Down in "Arkansaw"*
       Shine on Harvest Moon*
1939 – The Lone Ranger Rides Again*
       Rough Riders' Round-Up*
       Mexicali Rose*
       Daredevils of the Red Circle*
       Wyoming Outlaw*
       Dick Tracy's G-Men*
1940 – King of the Royal Mounted*
1942 – Stardust on the Sage*
       The Sundown Kid*
1943 – G-Men Vs. The Black Dragon*
       Thundering Trails*
       Secret Service in Darkest Africa*
1944 – Captain America*
1953 – Can. Mounties Vs. Atomic Invaders*
1955 – Carolina Cannonball*
       King of the Carnival
1957 – Affair in Reno*

DePalma, Walter
1938 – Rhythm of the Saddle

Depp, Harry[196]
1937 – Bill Cracks Down
1938 – Arson Gang Busters*
       Pals of the Saddle
1941 – Angels with Broken Wings*
       Ice-Capades*
       Sailors on Leave*
       Mr. District Atty. in the Carter Case*
1942 – Heart of the Rio Grande*
1944 – The Lady and the Monster*
       Goodnight Sweetheart*
       The Port of Forty Thieves
1945 – Road to Alcatraz
       Sunset in El Dorado*
       Captain Tugboat Annie*
1946 – Rendezvous with Annie*
       I've Always Loved You*
       That Brennan Girl*

DeRavenne, Charles
1936 – The House of a Thousand Candles

Derek, John[116]
1952 – Thunderbirds
1954 – Sea of Lost Ships
       The Outcast

DeRita, Joe
1946 – The French Key

Derr, Richard
1958 – Invisible Avenger

de Sa, Alfredo
1944 – Brazil

DeSales, Francis
1956 – Terror at Midnight
1957 – The Wayward Girl

DeSimone, Bonnie
1951 – Rodeo King and the Senorita

DeSimone, John
1950 – Women from Headquarters
       Flying Disc Man from Mars
1951 – Million Dollar Pursuit

Desmond, William
1936 – The Vigilantes Are Coming
       Cavalry*
1940 – Young Bill Hickok*
1943 – In Old Oklahoma*

Desmonde, Jerry
1955 – Trouble in Store

Desney, Ivan
1959 – O. S. S. 117 is Not Dead

DeStefani, Joseph
1940 – Rancho Grande

de Valdez, Carlos[196]
1937 – The Bold Caballero

Deverell, Helen[196]
1943 – The Blocked Trail

Devine, Andy[75]
1947 – Bells of San Angelo
       Springtime in the Sierras
       On the Old Spanish Trail
       The Fabulous Texan
1948 – The Gay Ranchero
       Old Los Angeles
       Under California Stars
       Eyes of Texas
       The Gallant Legion
       Night Time in Nevada
       Grand Canyon Trail
       The Far Frontier
1949 – The Last Bandit

Devlin, Joe
1938 – Tenth Avenue Kid*
1939 – Calling All Marines*
1940 – Gangs of Chicago*
       Carolina Moon*
1941 – A Man Betrayed*
       Mr. District Attorney*
       Sis Hopkins*
       Country Fair*
       Hurricane Smith*
1942 – Shepherd of the Ozarks*
       The Old Homestead*
1944 – My Buddy
1951 – Insurance Investigator*

Dew, Eddie[156]
1938 – The Fighting Devil Dogs*
       Army Girl*
       Come on, Leathernecks*
       Dick Tracy Returns*
1940 – Mysterious Doctor Satan*
       Bowery Boy*
1941 – A Man Betrayed*
       Adventures of Captain Marvel*
       Sis Hopkins*
       Sunset in Wyoming*
       King of the Texas Rangers*
1942 – Pardon My Stripes*
       Remember Pearl Harbor!*
       Shadows on the Sage*
       Flying Tigers*
1943 – G-Men Vs. The Black Dragon*
       Beyond the Last Frontier
       Raiders of Sunset Pass
1951 – Govt. Agents Vs. Phantom Legion

Dewey, Earle S.
1940 – In Old Missouri
1943 – Mountain Rhythm

Dewhurst, William
1937 – Bulldog Drummond at Bay

de Wit, Jacqueline[196]
1955 – Lay that Rifle Down

Dexter, Brad
See Barry Mitchell.

Dexter, Maury
1946 – One Exciting Week

Diamond, Anne
1949 – Flaming Fury*

Diamond, Don
1957 – Raiders of Old California

Dibbs, Kem
1955 – The Twinkle in God's Eye
1956 – Terror at Midnight
       Daniel Boone, Trail Blazer

Dickerson, Dudley
1942 – Lady for a Night*
       Spy Smasher*

Dickinson, Angie[96]
1956 – Hidden Guns

Dickson, Gloria[76]
1941 – Mercy Island
1942 – Affairs of Jimmy Valentine

Diebold, Leonard
1953 – City that Never Sleeps

Dierkes, John[196]
1950 – Macbeth
1953 – A Perilous Journey
1954 – Hell's Outpost*
1955 – Timberjack*
       The Road to Denver*
       The Vanishing American
1957 – Duel at Apache Wells

Carlos de Valdez

Helen Deverell

Jacqueline de Wit

John Dierkes

Diggins, Peggy
1941 – Wampas Baby Stars*

Dillard, Art
Many films, mostly westerns.
1937 – Wild Horse Rodeo
1950 – Vigilante Hideout
1952 – Leadville Gunslinger

Dillard, Burt
Many films.
1939 – The Lone Ranger Rides Again*
       Zorro's Fighting Legion*
1940 – Drums of Fu Manchu*

Dillaway, Don
1939 – Frontier Pony Express
1950 – Gunmen of Abilene

Dillon, Dickie
1944 – Sheriff of Las Vegas
1945 – Sheriff of Cimarron
       Corpus Christi Bandits
       Trail of Kit Carson
1946 – California Gold Rush

Dillon, John Webb
1936 – The Leathernecks Have Landed

Dillon, Josephine
1944 – The Lady and the Monster

Dillon, Mary
1943 – Hands Across the Border*

Dilson, Clyde
1937 – The Duke Comes Back

Dilson, John[131]
1936 – The President's Mystery*
       Robinson Crusoe of Clipper Island
1937 – Dick Tracy
       Escape by Night*
1938 – The Night Hawk*
       Down in "Arkansaw"
       Federal Man-Hunt*
1939 – S. O. S. Tidal Wave*
       Sabotage*
       Thou Shalt Not Kill*
1940 – Village Barn Dance*
       Pioneers of the West
       Drums of Fu Manchu
       Dark Command*
       Adventures of Red Ryder
       King of the Royal Mounted
       Meet the Missus*
1941 – Rookies on Parade*
       Sunset in Wyoming
       Doctors Don't Tell*
       Jesse James at Bay*
       Dick Tracy Vs. Crime, Inc.*
1943 – Idaho*
       King of the Cowboys*
       False Faces*
       In Old Oklahoma*
1944 – The Yellow Rose of Texas*

DiMaggio, Joe
1937 – Manhattan Merry-Go-Round

Dingle, Charles[196]
1943 – Someone to Remember

DiReda, Joe
1958 – Juvenile Jungle

Charles Dingle

Mary Eleanor Donahue

Jeff Donnell

Ann Doran

Dix, Billy
1951 — Buckaroo Sheriff of Texas

Dix, Dorothy
1936 — Guns and Guitars

Dix, Richard[76]
1939 — Man of Conquest

Dixon, Lee
1947 — Angel and the Badman

Dobkin, Lawrence
1955 — African Manhunt
1957 — Raiders of Old California

Dobson, James
1952 — I Dream of Jeanie

Doby, Lary
1949 — The Kid from Cleveland

Dodd, Claire[116]
1936 — Navy Born
1939 — Woman Doctor

Dodd, Jimmie[76]
1942 — Shadows on the Sage
        Flying Tigers
        Valley of Hunted Men
1943 — Thundering Trails
        The Blocked Trail
        Santa Fe Scouts
        Riders of the Rio Grande
1948 — Daredevils of the Clouds
1949 — Flaming Fury
        Post Office Investigator
1950 — Singing Guns

Dolin, Anton
1945 — A Song for Miss Julie

Domergue, Faith[96]
1955 — Santa Fe Passage

Don, Jack
1936 — Guns and Guitars

Donahue, Mary Eleanor[196]
1947 — Winter Wonderland
1950 — Singing Guns*
1953 — Sweethearts on Parade*

Donatt, Renee
1948 — Madonna of the Desert

Doner, Jack
1958 — Invisible Avenger

Doner, Maurice
1949 — Flame of Youth

Donlevy, Brian[76]
1951 — Fighting Coast Guard
1952 — Hoodlum Empire
1953 — Ride the Man Down
        Woman They Almost Lynched

Donnell, Jeff[196]
1949 — Outcasts of the Trail
        Post Office Investigator
1950 — Redwood Forest Trail
1954 — Flight Nurse

Donnelly, Ruth[76]
1937 — Portia on Trial
1938 — Army Girl
1940 — Scatterbrain
        Meet the Missus
1941 — Petticoat Politics
        The Gay Vagabond
        Sailors on Leave
1942 — Johnny Doughboy
1943 — Sleepy Lagoon
1946 — In Old Sacramento
1947 — The Ghost Goes Wild
        The Fabulous Texan
1951 — The Wild Blue Yonder

Donnini, Giulio
1955 — Don Juan's Night of Love

Donovan, Arthur
1941 — The Pittsburgh Kid

Donovan, Gloria
1946 — I've Always Loved You

Dooley, Bill
1938 — Call of the Yukon

Doran, Ann[196]
1940 — Forgotten Girls*
1949 — The Kid from Cleveland
1950 — Lonely Heart Bandits

D'Ordan, Cot
1943 — At Dawn We Die

Dorety, Charles
1944 — Beneath Western Skies

Doria, Bianca
1951 — Stormbound

Dorn, Philip[116]
1946 — I've Always Loved You
1949 — The Fighting Kentuckian

Dorr, Lester[197]
Many films.
1936 — Bulldog Edition*
        Country Gentlemen*
        Robinson Crusoe of Clipper Island*
1937 — Join the Marines*
        Dick Tracy*
        Navy Blues*
        Dangerous Holiday*
        Sea Racketeers*
        S O S Coast Guard*
1938 — Prison Nurse*
        Arson Gang Busters*
        Gangs of New York*
        The Fighting Devil Dogs*
        Come on, Leathernecks*
1942 — Pardon My Stripes*
        A Tragedy at Midnight*
        Sleepytime Gal*
1943 — The Masked Marvel
1946 — G. I. War Brides*
        That Brennan Girl*
1947 — Robin Hood of Texas*
1949 — The Blonde Bandit*
1950 — Covered Wagon Raid
        Flying Disc Man from Mars
1951 — Night Riders of Montana

Dorree, Bobbie[19]
1944 — Lake Placid Serenade*
        The Big Bonanza*
1945 — Grissly's Millions*
        The Topeka Terror*
        Utah*
        Earl Carroll Vanities*
        Corpus Christi Bandits*
        The Phantom Speaks*
        Bells of Rosarita*
        The Chicago Kid*
        Steppin' in Society*
        The Cheaters*
        Hitchhike to Happiness*
        Man from Oklahoma*
        Tell It to a Star*
        Swingin' on a Rainbow*
        The Purple Monster Strikes*
        Rough Riders of Cheyenne*
        An Angel Comes to Brooklyn*
        Mexicana*
        Wagon Wheels Westward*
        Dakota*
1946 — Gay Blades*
        California Gold Rush*
        Song of Arizona*
        Murder in the Music Hall*
        Rainbow Over Texas*
        Valley of the Zombies*
        In Old Sacramento*
        One Exciting Week*
        Man from Rainbow Valley*
        Traffic in Crime*
        Rendezvous with Annie*
        The Inner Circle*
        The Last Crooked Mile*
        G. I. War Brides*
        The Invisible Informer*
        Earl Carroll Sketchbook*
        Under Nevada Skies*
        The Mysterious Mr. Valentine*
        Home in Oklahoma*
        Plainsman and the Lady*
        Sioux City Sue*
        I've Always Loved You*
        Heldorado*
        That Brennan Girl*
1947 — Calendar Girl*
        Last Frontier Uprising*
        Apache Rose*
        Hit Parade of 1947*
        Twilight on the Rio Grande*
        Bells of San Angelo*
        Oregon Trail Scouts*
        That's My Gal*
        That's My Man*
        Web of Danger*
        Northwest Outpost*
        Rustlers of Devil's Canyon*
        The Trespasser*
        Blackmail*
        Wyoming*
        On the Old Spanish Trail*
        The Flame*
1948 — The Gay Ranchero*
        Slippy McGee*
        The Inside Story*
1949 — The Red Pony*
1951 — Pride of Maryland*
        Rough Riders of Durango*
        Missing Women*
        Night Riders of Montana*
        Cuban Fireball*
        Insurance Investigator*
        Secrets of Monte Carlo*
        South of Caliente*
1952 — Bal Tabarin*
        I Dream of Jeanie*
        Tropical Heat Wave*
        Thunderbirds*
1953 — Woman They Almost Lynched*
        A Perilous Journey*
        Fair Wind to Java*
        Sweethearts on Parade*
1954 — Geraldine*
        Jubilee Trail*
        The Shanghai Story*
1955 — Timberjack*
        Double Jeopardy*
        The Twinkle in God's Eye*
        The Fighting Chance*
1956 — Jaguar*
        Stranger at My Door*
        The Man is Armed*
        Accused of Murder*

Dors, Diana[197]
1948 — Code of Scotland Yard*

Doucet, Catharine[197]
1937 — Jim Hanvey - Detective

Doucette, John[197]
1948 — Train to Alcatraz
1950 — Singing Guns*
1951 — Thunder in God's Country
1952 — Woman in the Dark
        Toughest Man in Arizona*
1956 — The Maverick Queen
        Dakota Incident
        Thunder Over Arizona
1957 — The Lawless Eighties
        The Crooked Circle
1958 — Gunfire at Indian Gap

Dougherty, Jack
1937 — Yodelin' Kid from Pine Ridge

Douglas, Don[197]
1938 — The Night Hawk*
        Orphans of the Street
1939 — The Mysterious Miss X
        The Zero Hour
        Sabotage
1941 — The Pittsburgh Kid*
        Mercy Island
1945 — Grissly's Millions

Douglas, George[197]
1938 — Pals of the Saddle
1939 — The Night Riders
        Dick Tracy's G-Men
        The Kansas Terrors
1940 — Covered Wagon Days
        The Tulsa Kid
        Lone Star Raiders
1942 — Home in Wyomin'
1947 — The Black Widow*
1948 — G-Men Never Forget*
        Secret Service Investigator*
        Sons of Adventure*
1951 — Street Bandits*

Douglas, Robert[96]
1953 — Fair Wind to Java

Douglas, Warren[197]
1946 — The Inner Circle
1947 — The Pilgrim Lady
        The Magnificent Rogue
        The Trespasser
1948 — Lightnin' in the Forest
        Homicide for Three
1949 — Post Office Investigator
1951 — Cuban Fireball
        Secrets of Monte Carlo

George Douglas

Warren Douglas

Kaye Dowd

Constance Dowling

John Doucette, Jack Elam

Dowd, Kaye[197]
1945 — An Angel Comes to Brooklyn

Dowling, Constance[197]
1947 — The Flame
1951 — Stormbound

Downing, Joseph
1938 — The Night Hawk

Downs, Cathy[197]
1952 — Gobs and Gals
1953 — Bandits of the West

Lester Dorr

Diana Dors

Catharine Doucet

Don Douglas

Cathy Downs

Downs, Johnny[198] [dancer]
1940 – Sing, Dance, Plenty Hot
Melody and Moonlight
1944 – Trocadero

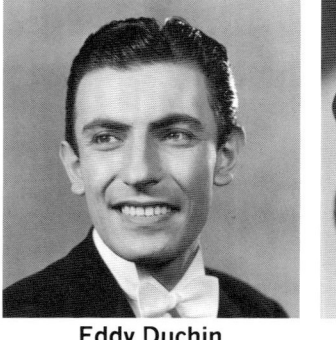

Johnny Downs

Charles Drake

Dona Drake

Bobby Driscoll

Claire DuBrey

Eddy Duchin

Tom Dugan

Downs, Johnny
1950 – Hills of Oklahoma

Doyle, Maxine[20]
1937 – Round-Up Time in Texas
Come on, Cowboys!
S O S Coast Guard
1943 – G-Men Vs. The Black Dragon
Shantytown*
Chatterbox*
Here Comes Elmer*
Overland Mail Robbery*
Mystery Broadcast*
In Old Oklahoma*
Raiders of Sunset Pass
1944 – Beneath Western Skies*
My Best Gal*
Rosie, the Riveter*
The Lady and the Monster*
Jamboree*
Man from Frisco*
Silver City Kid*
Three Little Sisters*
Song of Nevada*
Sing Neighbor Sing*
San Fernando Valley*
End of the Road*
Firebrands of Arizona*
1946 – Daughter of Don Q*
1947 – The Black Widow*

Drake, Charles[198]
1947 – Winter Wonderland
The Pretender
1954 – Tobor the Great

Drake, Dona[198]
1953 – Down Laredo Way

Drake, Pauline
1941 – Arkansas Judge*
Country Fair*
Under Fiesta Stars
1942 – Hi, Neighbor
Secrets of the Underground*
1943 – Here Comes Elmer*
1946 – Affairs of Geraldine*
1956 – When Gangland Strikes*

Drake, Peggy
1942 – King of the Mounties

Drake, Steve
1948 – The Gallant Legion

Dresden, Curley[198]
Many films, mostly westerns.
1936 – The Lawless Nineties*
1937 – Rootin' Tootin' Rhythm*
The Painted Stallion*
Range Defenders*
S O S Coast Guard*
1938 – The Purple Vigilantes*
The Lone Ranger*
Call the Mesquiteers*
Outlaws of Sonora*
Under Western Stars*
Heroes of the Hills*
Pals of the Saddle*
Overland Stage Raiders*
Rhythm of the Saddle*
Santa Fe Stampede*
Red River Range*
1939 – Frontier Pony Express*
Blue Montana Skies*
Southward, Ho!*
Mountain Rhythm*
Daredevils of the Red Circle*
Wyoming Outlaw*
Colorado Sunset*
New Frontier*
In Old Monterey*
Dick Tracy's G-Men*
Wall Street Cowboy*
The Kansas Terrors*
Jeepers Creepers*
South of the Border*
Zorro's Fighting Legion*
1940 – Ghost Valley Raiders
Rocky Mountain Rangers*
Wagons Westward*
Adventures of Red Ryder*
One Man's Law*
The Carson City Kid*
King of the Royal Mounted*
Under Texas Skies
The Trail Blazers*
Melody Ranch*
Texas Terrors*
The Border Legion*
1941 – Wyoming Wildcat*
Prairie Pioneers*
Back in the Saddle*
Adventures of Captain Marvel*
Pals of the Pecos*
Two Gun Sheriff*
Desert Bandit*
Saddlemates*
Kansas Cyclone*
Gangs of Sonora*
Under Fiesta Stars*
Bad Man of Deadwood*
Death Valley Outlaws*
Jesse James at Bay*
A Missouri Outlaw*
1942 – Arizona Terrors*
Westward Ho*
The Cyclone Kid*
The Sombrero Kid*
Sunset Serenade*
Shadows on the Sage*
Valley of Hunted Men*
1943 – Carson City Cyclone*
Santa Fe Scouts*
Riders of the Rio Grande*
The Man from Thunder River*
The Black Hills Express*
Wagon Tracks West*
Beyond the Last Frontier*
Death Valley Manhunt*
In Old Oklahoma*

Drew, Ellen[116]
1942 – Ice-Capades Revue
1944 – That's My Baby

Drew, Lillian
1938 – Man from Music Mountain

Drew, Roland
1944 – Silent Partner

Drew, Winifred
1937 – Youth on Parole*
1939 – Pride of the Navy*
Man of Conquest*
The Zero Hour*
Flight at Midnight*
Sabotage*
Money to Burn*

Driscoll, Bobby[198]
1944 – The Big Bonanza
1945 – Identity Unknown

DuBois, Diane
1956 – Dakota Incident

DuBrey, Claire[198]
1937 – The Wrong Road*
1939 – South of the Border
1942 – Bells of Capistrano
1944 – Lights of Old Santa Fe
1945 – Dakota
1946 – The Catman of Paris*
The Invisible Informer
1948 – Lightnin' in the Forest
Out of the Storm
1949 – Streets of San Francisco
1950 – Destination Big House

Duchin, Eddy[198] —and orchestra
1937 – The Hit Parade

Dudgeon, Elspeth
1945 – Woman Who Came Back*
1947 – Yankee Fakir

Duering, Carl
1955 – The Divided Heart

Duff, Howard[96]
1955 – Flame of the Islands

Duffield, Brainerd
1950 – Macbeth

DuFrane, Frank
1937 – Larceny on the Air

Drew, Winifred
Dugan, Tom[198]
1940 – Who Killed Aunt Maggie?
1942 – Yokel Boy
1945 – Earl Carroll Vanities
Trail of Kit Carson
Tell It to a Star
1947 – The Pilgrim Lady

Dugay, Yvette
1954 – The Shanghai Story

Duggan, Tommy
1942 – Suicide Squadron

Duke, Robert[198]
1945 – An Angel Comes to Brooklyn

Dumbrille, Douglass[198]
1938 – Storm Over Bengal
1939 – Rovin' Tumbleweeds
1942 – King of the Mounties
1946 – The Catman of Paris
Under Nevada Skies
1947 – The Fabulous Texan
1950 – The Savage Horde

Dumke, Ralph
1956 – When Gangland Strikes

Dumont, Margaret[198]
1937 – Youth on Parole
1945 – Sunset in El Dorado

Duna, Steffi[178]
1937 – Escape by Night
1940 – Girl from Havana

Duncan, Archie
1954 – Trouble in the Glen

Duncan, John
1947 – Trail to San Antone

Duncan, Julie[198]
1940 – Texas Terrors
1941 – Wyoming Wildcat

Robert Duke

Douglass Dumbrille

Margaret Dumont

Julie Duncan

Earl Dwire, Warner Richmond

Curley Dresden, Bob Livingston, Merrill McCormick

Duncan, Kenne[20]
1937—The Colorado Kid
1939—Fighting Thoroughbreds
Mickey, the Kid*
1941—Adventures of Captain Marvel
The Apache Kid*
King of the Texas Rangers
A Missouri Outlaw
1942—Code of the Outlaw
Westward Ho*
Perils of Nyoka
The Sombrero Kid*
Valley of Hunted Men*
The Sundown Kid
1943—Santa Fe Scouts*
Daredevils of the West
Days of Old Cheyenne
Fugitive from Sonora
Wagon Tracks West*
The Man from the Rio Grande
Overland Mail Robbery*
Mystery Broadcast*
Canyon City*
In Old Oklahoma*
Pistol Packin' Mama*
Raiders of Sunset Pass
Hands Across the Border
Army 828—First Aid*
1944—Pride of the Plains
Captain America*
Beneath Western Skies
The Fighting Seabees*
Mojave Firebrand
Hidden Valley Outlaws
The Laramie Trail*
Outlaws of Santa Fe
The Lady and the Monster*
Jamboree*
Tucson Raiders*
The Tiger Woman
Silent Partner*
Man from Frisco*
Marshal of Reno
Secrets of Scotland Yard*
The Girl Who Dared*
Song of Nevada*
Bordertown Trail*
Haunted Harbor
San Fernando Valley*
Stagecoach to Monterey
Cheyenne Wildcat
Code of the Prairie*
My Buddy*
Storm Over Lisbon
Sheriff of Sundown
End of the Road
Vigilantes of Dodge City
Brazil*
Firebrands of Arizona*
Lake Placid Serenade*
Thoroughbreds*
Sheriff of Las Vegas
1945—Great Stagecoach Robbery*
Manhunt of Mystery Island
Corpus Christi Bandits
Flame of Barbary Coast*
Santa Fe Saddlemates
A Sporting Chance
Bells of Rosarita*
The Chicago Kid
Road to Alcatraz
Trail of Kit Carson
Oregon Trail
Hitchhike to Happiness*
The Fatal Witness*
Love, Honor and Goodbye*
Sunset in El Dorado*
The Purple Monster Strikes
Marshal of Laredo*
Rough Riders of Cheyenne
Colorado Pioneers*
The Tiger Woman*
The Cherokee Flash*
Dakota*
Wagon Wheels Westward
1946—The Phantom Rider
A Guy Could Change
California Gold Rush
Sheriff of Redwood Valley
Murder in the Music Hall*
Home on the Range
Rainbow Over Texas
Sun Valley Cyclone
Passkey to Danger*
In Old Sacramento
One Exciting Week*
Man from Rainbow Valley
Traffic in Crime*
My Pal Trigger
Night Train to Memphis
Conquest of Cheyenne
Red River Renegades
G. I. War Brides*
The Invisible Informer*
The Mysterious Mr. Valentine
Rio Grande Raiders
Roll on Texas Moon
The Crimson Ghost
Santa Fe Uprising
Sioux City Sue*
1947—Angel and the Badman*
Vigilantes of Boomtown*
Twilight on the Rio Grande*
The Trespasser*
1948—Sundown in Santa Fe*
1950—Code of the Silver Sage
Surrender*

Judy Canova, Stephen Dunne

Duncan, Slim
1952—Desperadoes' Outpost

Duncan, Topsy and Eva
1941—Los Angeles Examiner Benefit*

Dunham, Phil[199]
1936—Beware of Ladies
1942—Code of the Outlaw

Dunhill, Steve
1951—Buckaroo Sheriff of Texas

Dunn, Eddie[199]
1947—The Flame
1948—Lightnin' in the Forest
Homicide for Three
1950—Lonely Heart Bandits
1951—Buckaroo Sheriff of Texas

Dunn, Emma[199]
1936—The Harvester
1937—Circus Girl
1943—Hoosier Holiday
1944—My Buddy
1946—Night Train to Memphis

Dunn, James[96]
1936—Hearts in Bondage
1939—Pride of the Navy
1946—That Brennan Girl

Dunn, Patricia
1950—Federal Agent at Large*

Dunn, Ralph[199]
1937—The Wrong Road*
1938—King of the Newsboys*
Romance on the Run*
Come on, Leathernecks
Tenth Avenue Kid
Billy the Kid Returns*
Rhythm of the Saddle*
Storm Over Bengal*
1939—The Lone Ranger Rides Again
Smuggled Cargo*
1940—Dark Command*
1945—Love, Honor and Goodbye
An Angel Comes to Brooklyn
1947—The Ghost Goes Wild*
The Fabulous Texan*
1948—King of the Gamblers
Train to Alcatraz
1949—The Fighting Kentuckian*
1950—Singing Guns
Surrender*
Prisoners in Petticoats*
1951—Govt. Agents Vs. Phantom Legion*

Dunne, Stephen[199]
1952—Lady Possessed
The Wac from Walla Walla

Dunsmuir, Danita
1947—Springtime in the Sierras*

DuPrez, June[199]
1946—That Brennan Girl

Duran, Val
1937—Join the Marines

Durand, David[199]
1940—The Tulsa Kid

Durante, Jimmy[96]
1940—Melody Ranch
1941—Variety Reel*

Durbin, Deanna
1941—Variety Reel*

Durfee, Minta
1941—Stars Past and Present*

Durkin, Grace[20]
1936—The Big Show
The Mandarin Mystery
Beware of Ladies*
A Man Betrayed

Duryea, Dan[96]
1944—Man from Frisco
1945—The Great Flamarion

Phil Dunham

Eddie Dunn

Emma Dunn

Ralph Dunn

Dvorak, Ann[76]
1937—Manhattan Merry-Go-Round
1938—Gangs of New York
1945—Flame of Barbary Coast

Dwire, Earl[198]
1935—Westward Ho*
The New Frontier*
Lawless Range
1936—Red River Valley*
King of the Pecos*
Oh, Susanna!*
Cavalry*
The Gun Ranger
1937—The Trusted Outlaw
The Gambling Terror
Two Wise Maids
Git Along Little Dogies*
"Lightnin'" Crandall
Doomed at Sundown
1938—The Purple Vigilantes
The Old Barn Dance
Outlaws of Sonora*
Under Western Stars
Ladies in Distress*
Gold Mine in the Sky*
Man from Music Mountain
1939—Southward, Ho!*
The Arizona Kid
Thou Shalt Not Kill*

Dworshak, Lois
1941—Ice-Capades
1942—Ice-Capades Revue

Pearl Early, Minerva Urecal, Cecil Weston

Dwyer, Jack
1954—Crazylegs

Dwyer, Leslie[199]
1957—Operation Conspiracy

Dwyer, Marlo
1942—South of Santa Fe*
1950—Women from Headquarters
Prisoners in Petticoats
1951—Missing Women

E

Eagles, James
1938—Heroes of the Hills

Earle, Edward[199]
1938—Riders of the Black Hills
A Desperate Adventure*
1939—Woman Doctor*
Man of Conquest*
In Old Monterey*
1940—Dark Command*
1941—Rookies on Parade*
Sleepytime Gal*
1942—Youth on Parade*
1943—King of the Cowboys*
Chatterbox*
Bordertown Gun Fighters
Someone to Remember*
The West Side Kid*
Here Comes Elmer*
California Joe
1944—My Buddy*
Faces in the Fog*
1945—Captain Tugboat Annie*

Early, Pearl[199]
1940—Grand Ole Opry*
1941—Arkansas Judge*
Country Fair*
The Gay Vagabond*
Angels with Broken Wings*
Doctors Don't Tell*
1942—Lady for a Night*
In Old California*
1943—Hoosier Holiday*
Here Comes Elmer*
In Old Oklahoma*
O, My Darling Clementine*
1947—That's My Gal*
1948—Campus Honeymoon*

June DuPrez

David Durand

Leslie Dwyer

Edward Earle

Easton, Bob
1951 – Havana Rose

Eaton, Shirley[179]
1955 – Doctor in the House

Eben, Al
1948 – Lightnin' in the Forest

Eberts, John
1944 – Call of the South Seas

Ebsen, Alix
1951 – Silver City Bonanza

Ebsen, Buddy[97]
1950 – Under Mexicali Stars
1951 – Silver City Bonanza
        Thunder in God's Country
        Rodeo King and the Senorita
        Utah Wagon Train

Eburne, Maude[131]
1936 – The Leavenworth Case
1937 – Paradise Express
1938 – Riders of the Black Hills
1939 – My Wife's Relatives
        Mountain Rhythm
        Sabotage*
        The Covered Trailer
1940 – Colorado
        The Border Legion
1944 – Rosie, the Riveter
        Goodnight Sweetheart
1945 – Hitchhike to Happiness
        Man from Oklahoma
1948 – Slippy McGee
        The Plunderers
1951 – Belle LeGrand*

Eby, Earl
1936 – The Singing Cowboy
        Hearts in Bondage*

Eddy, Helen Jerome[200]
1937 – Jim Hanvey - Detective

Eddy, Nelson[76]
1947 – Northwest Outpost

Eden, Barbara[97]
1957 – The Wayward Girl

Kathleen Eliot

Duke Ellington

Helen Jerome Eddy

Blake Edwards

Bruce Edwards

Cliff Edwards

Elaine Edwards

Sarah Edwards

George Eldredge

Edmunds, William
1940 – Girl from Havana
1943 – Deerslayer

Edwards, Alan
1939 – South of the Border
1941 – Mr. District Attorney
1944 – Thoroughbreds

Edwards, Blake[200]
1944 – Marshal of Reno
        My Buddy*
1945 – Gangs of the Waterfront*

Edwards, Bruce[200]
1947 – The Black Widow
1948 – The Denver Kid
1949 – Federal Agents Vs. Underworld, Inc.
        Powder River Rustlers
1950 – Sands of Iwo Jima*
1951 – Fort Dodge Stampede

Edwards, Cliff "Ukelele Ike"[200]
1939 – Smuggled Cargo
1940 – Friendly Neighbors

Edwards, Elaine[200]
1952 – Old Oklahoma Plains

Edwards, James
1955 – African Manhunt

Edwards, J. C.—and band
1936 – Dancing Feet

Edwards, Joan[77]
1947 – Hit Parade of 1947

Edwards, Lee
1958 – Invisible Avenger

Edwards, Meredith
1955 – A Day to Remember
1957 – Tears for Simon

Edwards, Penny[21]
1950 – Sunset in the West
        North of the Great Divide
        Trail of Robin Hood
1951 – Spoilers of the Plains
        Missing Women
        Heart of the Rockies
        In Old Amarillo
        Million Dollar Pursuit
        Havana Rose*
        Utah Wagon Train
        Street Bandits
        The Wild Blue Yonder
1952 – Woman in the Dark
        Captive of Billy the Kid

Edwards, Ralph
1937 – Manhattan Merry-Go-Round*

Edwards, Sarah[200]
1939 – Man of Conquest*
        Sabotage*
1941 – Mr. District Attorney
        Sunset in Wyoming
1942 – Moonlight Masquerade*
        Sons of the Pioneers*
1944 – Three Little Sisters*
        Storm Over Lisbon
1945 – Girls of the Big House
1946 – Song of Arizona
1948 – The Main Street Kid
        California Firebrand
1951 – Honeychile

Edwards, Thornton
1941 – Down Mexico Way

Eilers, Sally[116]
1938 – Lady, Behave!
1941 – Wampas Baby Stars*
        Stars Past and Present*

Einer, Robert
1951 – Don Daredevil Rides Again

Eitner, Don
1957 – Beginning of the End

Elam, Jack[197]
1954 – Jubilee Trail
1956 – Thunder Over Arizona

Eldredge, George[200]
1938 – Hawk of the Wilderness
1942 – Joan of Ozark*
1945 – The Chicago Kid*
1946 – Passkey to Danger*
1947 – The Fabulous Texan*
1948 – King of the Gamblers*
1949 – The Last Bandit*
1954 – Man with the Steel Whip*

Eldredge, John[131]
1936 – Follow Your Heart
1941 – Mr. District Atty. in the Carter Case
1944 – Song of Nevada
1946 – Passkey to Danger
        The French Key
1950 – Unmasked
        Lonely Heart Bandits
        Rustlers on Horseback
1951 – Insurance Investigator
        Street Bandits

Eliot, Kathleen[200]
1938 – Paroled – to Die

Eliscu, Fernanda
1950 – Harbor of Missing Men

Ellington, Duke[200]**—and band**
1937 – The Hit Parade

Elliot, Robert[200]
1939 – Mickey, the Kid

Elliott, Barbara
1945 – Bells of Rosarita*

Elliott, Bill[150]
        [as Gordon Elliott]
1937 – Michael O'Halloran*
        Boots and Saddles
        [as Bill Elliott]
1941 – Meet Roy Rogers*
1943 – Calling Wild Bill Elliott
        The Man from Thunder River
        Bordertown Gun Fighters
        Wagon Tracks West
        Death Valley Manhunt
        Overland Mail Robbery
1944 – Mojave Firebrand
        Hidden Valley Outlaws
        Tucson Raiders
        Marshal of Reno
        The San Antonio Kid
        Cheyenne Wildcat
        Vigilantes of Dodge City
        Sheriff of Las Vegas
1945 – Great Stagecoach Robbery
        Lone Texas Ranger
        Bells of Rosarita
        Phantom of the Plains
        Marshal of Laredo
        Colorado Pioneers
        Wagon Wheels Westward
1946 – California Gold Rush
        Sheriff of Redwood Valley
        Sun Valley Cyclone
        In Old Sacramento
        Conquest of Cheyenne
        Plainsman and the Lady
1947 – Wyoming
        The Fabulous Texan
1948 – Old Los Angeles
        The Gallant Legion
1949 – The Last Bandit
        Hellfire
1950 – The Savage Horde
        The Showdown

Elliott, Dick[121]
1938 – Under Western Stars
        Riders of the Black Hills
        Man from Music Mountain*
        Tenth Avenue Kid*
1940 – One Man's Law
        Scatterbrain*
        Ride, Tenderfoot, Ride*
        Young Bill Hickok*
        Melody Ranch*
        Behind the News
1941 – A Man Betrayed*
        Mr. District Attorney*
        The Gay Vagabond*
        Mountain Moonlight*
        Sunset in Wyoming
        The Pittsburgh Kid*
        Tuxedo Junction*
1942 – Yokel Boy*
        Affairs of Jimmy Valentine*
1943 – False Faces*
        Nobody's Darling*
        Whispering Footsteps*
1944 – Silent Partner
1945 – Gangs of the Waterfront
        Girls of the Big House*
1946 – Rainbow Over Texas
1947 – That's My Gal*
        Driftwood*
        The Fabulous Texan*
1948 – The Main Street Kid
        Slippy McGee
        Homicide for Three
1949 – Rose of the Yukon
1950 – Belle of Old Mexico*
        Rock Island Trail
        Surrender*
1951 – Belle LeGrand*
        Honeychile
1952 – Gobs and Gals*
        The Wac from Walla Walla*
1955 – Double Jeopardy
        The Twinkle in God's Eye*
1956 – When Gangland Strikes*
1957 – Duel at Apache Wells*

Elliott, Edythe[200]
1938 – The Higgins Family*
1942 – Valley of Hunted Men
1944 – Casanova in Burlesque*
        End of the Road*
1945 – A Sporting Chance*
        Scotland Yard Investigator*
        Girls of the Big House*
1946 – The Madonna's Secret*
        The Undercover Woman
        Santa Fe Uprising
        That Brennan Girl
1947 – Homesteaders of Paradise Valley
        Web of Danger*
        The Fabulous Texan*
1950 – House by the River*
        Hit Parade of 1951*
1951 – Belle LeGrand*
        Missing Women*

Elliott, Gordon
See Bill Elliott.

Elliott, John[200]
1939 – Thou Shalt Not Kill*
1940 – The Tulsa Kid
        Young Bill Hickok*
        Lone Star Raiders
1941 – The Apache Kid
1945 – The Great Flamarion*
1947 – The Pretender*
1950 – The Arizona Cowboy

Elliott, Lorraine
1941 – Wampas Baby Stars*

Elliott, Ross[200]
1948 – Angel on the Amazon
1949 – Streets of San Francisco*
1951 – Desert of Lost Men
1952 – Woman in the Dark
1955 – African Manhunt
        Carolina Cannonball

Elliott, Scott
1946 – King of the Forest Rangers
1949 – Law of the Golden West

Ellis, Edward[77]
1939 – Man of Conquest
        Main Street Lawyer
1941 – A Man Betrayed

Robert Elliot

Edythe Elliott

John Elliott

Ross Elliott

Ellis, Frank[201]
Many films.
1935—Westward Ho*
1936—Comin' 'Round the Mountain*
　　　The Vigilantes Are Coming*
　　　Robinson Crusoe of Clipper Island*
1937—The Riders of the Whistling Skull
　　　The Gambling Terror*
　　　Git Along Little Dogies*
　　　Trail of Vengeance
　　　Guns in the Dark*
　　　Gun Lords of Stirrup Basin
　　　Range Defenders
　　　Boothill Brigade
　　　Public Cowboy No. 1*
　　　S O S Coast Guard*
　　　The Sheik Steps Out*
　　　Springtime in the Rockies*
　　　Zorro Rides Again*
1938—The Purple Vigilantes*
　　　The Lone Ranger*
　　　Call the Mesquiteers*
　　　Durango Valley Raiders*
　　　Storm Over Bengal*
　　　Western Jamboree*
1939—The Lone Ranger Rides Again*
　　　Rough Riders' Round-Up*
　　　Southward, Ho!*
　　　Wyoming Outlaw*
　　　Colorado Sunset*
　　　New Frontier*
　　　In Old Monterey*
　　　Rovin' Tumbleweeds*
　　　Zorro's Fighting Legion*
1940—Drums of Fu Manchu*
　　　Rocky Mountain Rangers*
　　　Young Bill Hickok*
　　　Mysterious Doctor Satan*
1941—Wyoming Wildcat*
　　　The Phantom Cowboy*
　　　Prairie Pioneers*
　　　Back in the Saddle*
　　　Pals of the Pecos*
　　　Sheriff of Tombstone*
1942—Stardust on the Sage*
　　　In Old California*
　　　Sons of the Pioneers*
　　　The Old Homestead*
　　　Sunset Serenade*
1943—Carson City Cyclone*
　　　The Black Hills Express*
　　　Wagon Tracks West*
　　　Man from Music Mountain*
　　　Overland Mail Robbery*
　　　In Old Oklahoma*
1944—Mojave Firebrand*
　　　Cheyenne Wildcat*
　　　Code of the Prairie*
　　　Vigilantes of Dodge City*
　　　Firebrands of Arizona*
1945—Corpus Christi Bandits*
　　　Trail of Kit Carson*
　　　Sunset in El Dorado*
　　　Wagon Wheels Westward*
1946—California Gold Rush*
　　　Santa Fe Uprising*
1947—Son of Zorro*
　　　Under Colorado Skies*
1948—Adv. of Frank and Jesse James*
1949—Ghost of Zorro*
1951—Heart of the Rockies*
　　　In Old Amarillo*
　　　Rodeo King and the Senorita*
　　　Desert of Lost Men*
1952—Wild Horse Ambush*
1953—Woman They Almost Lynched*
　　　A Perilous Journey*

Ellis, Mary[201]
1937—Glamorous Night

Ellis, Patricia[117]
1937—Rhythm in the Clouds
1938—Romance on the Run

Ellis, Paul
1936—The House of a Thousand Candles

Ellison, James[77]
1935—Hitch Hike Lady
1936—The Leathernecks Have Landed
1941—Ice-Capades
　　　Mr. District Atty. in the Carter Case
1946—G. I. War Brides
1947—Calendar Girl
　　　The Ghost Goes Wild

Ellison, Jane
1944—Trocadero

Elton, Edmund
1939—Thou Shalt Not Kill
1941—Back in the Saddle

Emanuel, Elzie
1953—The Sun Shines Bright

Emerson, Hope[201]
1951—Belle LeGrand
1953—The Lady Wants Mink
　　　A Perilous Journey
　　　Champ for a Day

Marla English, Jan Merlin

Emery, Gilbert
1938—Storm Over Bengal
1942—King of the Mounties

Emmett, Fern[131]
1935—Melody Trail
　　　$1000 a Minute
　　　Burning Gold
1936—Oregon Trail*
　　　The Harvester
　　　Ticket to Paradise*
1937—The Riders of the Whistling Skull
　　　Paradise Express
　　　Jim Hanvey - Detective*
　　　Michael O'Halloran*
　　　Come on, Cowboys!
　　　Dangerous Holiday
1938—Overland Stage Raiders*
1939—Saga of Death Valley
1941—Jesse James at Bay*
1942—Yokel Boy*
　　　In Old California*
　　　The Sundown Kid
1943—The West Side Kid*

Emory, Richard
1949—Bandit King of Texas
1950—Code of the Silver Sage
1952—Captive of Billy the Kid
1957—Beginning of the End

Engel, Roy
1952—Zombies of the Stratosphere
1953—Jungle Drums of Africa

England, Sue
1954—Hell's Outpost*

English, Marla[201]
1956—A Strange Adventure

Ennis, Skinnay[201]—and band
1942—Sleepytime Gal

Entwistle, Harold
1935—Two Sinners

Erdman, Richard
1951—The Wild Blue Yonder

Erickson, Leif
1950—The Showdown
1953—A Perilous Journey

Erickson, Louise
1944—Rosie, the Riveter

Ernest, George[77]
1935—Racing Luck
1938—Lady, Behave!
1940—Meet the Missus
1941—Petticoat Politics
　　　Mountain Moonlight
1942—Stardust on the Sage

Erskine, Carl
1954—Roogie's Bump

Erskine, Eileen
1952—Lady Possessed

Erway, Ben
1943—Mountain Rhythm

Erwin, Stu
1941—Variety Reel*
　　　Stars at Play*

Escalante Family, The
1937—Circus Girl

Eslava, Jose—orchestra
1940—Gaucho Serenade

Esmond, Annie
1937—Bulldog Drummond at Bay

Esmond, Carl[173]
1946—The Catman of Paris

Essen, Viola[201]
1946—Specter of the Rose

Estrella, Esther
1941—Prairie Pioneers

Etterre, Estelle[201]
1940—Women in War*
1945—Gangs of the Waterfront*
　　　Sunset in El Dorado*
1946—Gay Blades*
　　　A Guy Could Change*
1947—The Trespasser*
1949—Duke of Chicago*
1951—Insurance Investigator*

Evans, Charles
1947—Twilight on the Rio Grande
　　　Exposed
1952—Desperadoes' Outpost

Evans, Clifford
1943—The Saint Meets the Tiger

Evans, Dale[22]
1943—Swing Your Partner
　　　The West Side Kid
　　　Hoosier Holiday
　　　Here Comes Elmer
　　　In Old Oklahoma
1944—Casanova in Burlesque
　　　Cowboy and the Senorita
　　　The Yellow Rose of Texas
　　　Song of Nevada
　　　San Fernando Valley
　　　Lights of Old Santa Fe
1945—The Big Show-Off
　　　Utah
　　　Bells of Rosarita
　　　Hitchhike to Happiness
　　　Man from Oklahoma
　　　Sunset in El Dorado
　　　Don't Fence Me In
　　　Along the Navajo Trail
1946—Song of Arizona
　　　Rainbow Over Texas
　　　My Pal Trigger
　　　Under Nevada Skies
　　　Roll on Texas Moon
　　　Home in Oklahoma
　　　Out California Way
　　　Heldorado
1947—Apache Rose
　　　Bells of San Angelo
　　　The Trespasser
1948—Slippy McGee
1949—Susanna Pass
　　　Down Dakota Way
　　　The Golden Stallion
1950—Bells of Coronado
　　　Twilight in the Sierras
　　　Trigger, Jr.
1951—South of Caliente
　　　Pals of the Golden West

Frank Ellis

Mary Ellis

Evans, Douglas[201]
1937—Public Cowboy No. 1*
1938—Dick Tracy Returns*
　　　The Higgins Family*
　　　Stand Accused*
1940—Three Faces West*
　　　Oklahoma Renegades*
　　　King of the Royal Mounted*
1941—Sailors on Leave*
　　　Dick Tracy Vs. Crime, Inc.*
1942—Affairs of Jimmy Valentine*
1948—The Main Street Kid
　　　California Firebrand
　　　Secret Service Investigator
1949—Hideout
　　　King of the Rocket Men
　　　The Golden Stallion
　　　Powder River Rustlers
1950—The Arizona Cowboy
　　　Rustlers on Horseback
　　　North of the Great Divide
1951—Cuban Fireball*
1952—The Quiet Man*
　　　South Pacific Trail
1957—Beginning of the End

Evans, Gene[201]
1947—Under Colorado Skies
1952—Thunderbirds
1958—Young and Wild

Evans, Jacqueline
1956—Daniel Boone, Trail Blazer

Evans, Joan[97]
1954—The Outcast
1956—A Strange Adventure

Evans, Joe
1955—The Square Ring

Evans, Madge[97]
1938—Army Girl

Evans, Muriel[201]
1935—The New Frontier
1936—King of the Pecos

Hope Emerson

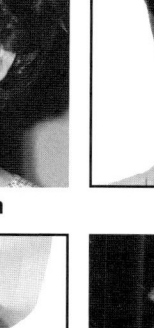

Skinnay Ennis

Viola Essen

Estelle Etterre

Douglas Evans

Gene Evans

Muriel Evans

Evans, Rex
1937 – The Wrong Road

Everest, Barbara[202]
1945 – The Fatal Witness

Evers, Ann[202]
1938 – Riders of the Black Hills
  Hawk of the Wilderness*
1943 – Someone to Remember*

Everton, Paul
1938 – Orphans of the Street

Ewell, Tom[202]
1941 – Desert Bandit

Eyer, Richard
1956 – Come Next Spring

F

Fadden, Tom
1944 – Three Little Sisters
1948 – The Inside Story
1950 – Singing Guns

Fain, Elmer
1937 – Round-Up Time in Texas

Fain, Matty[202]
1936 – Bulldog Edition
1937 – Larceny on the Air
1952 – Hoodlum Empire*

Falken [Falkenburg], Jinx[202]
1939 – The Lone Ranger Rides Again

Falkenberg, Margaret
1945 – Song of Mexico

Falkner Orchestra, The
1942 – Johnny Doughboy

Fallows, Ruth
1937 – Navy Blues

Farber, Jerry
1950 – Macbeth

Fargo, Peter
1939 – The Arizona Kid

Farley, Dot[203]
1938 – The Purple Vigilantes*
1944 – San Fernando Valley

Farley, James
1935 – Westward Ho

Farley, Morgan
1950 – Macbeth

Farmer, Virginia[131]
1941 – Lady from Louisiana*
  Hurricane Smith*
  Gauchos of Eldorado*
1942 – Affairs of Jimmy Valentine*
1945 – The Fatal Witness
1946 – I've Always Loved You*
1950 – Destination Big House*
  Surrender*

Farnum, Franklyn
1940 – Ride, Tenderfoot, Ride*
  Under Texas Skies*
1941 – The Great Train Robbery*
1942 – Stardust on the Sage*
1944 – Cheyenne Wildcat*
1945 – Sunset in El Dorado*
1947 – The Fabulous Texan*
1948 – Old Los Angeles*
1949 – Post Office Investigator*

Farnum, Geraldine[68]
1944 – The Yellow Rose of Texas*
  Lake Placid Serenade*
1945 – Utah*
  Earl Carroll Vanities*
  Bells of Rosarita*
  Trail of Kit Carson*
  The Cheaters*
  Hitchhike to Happiness*
  Man from Oklahoma*
  Tell It to a Star*
  Behind City Lights*
  Love, Honor and Goodbye*
  Sunset in El Dorado*
  The Purple Monster Strikes*
  Don't Fence Me In*
  Girls of the Big House*
  An Angel Comes to Brooklyn*
  Mexicana*
  The Tiger Woman*
  Dakota*
1946 – A Guy Could Change*
  Murder in the Music Hall*

Virginia Gregg, Frank Faylen

Pat Flaherty, Barbara Pepper

Ann Evers

Barbara Everest

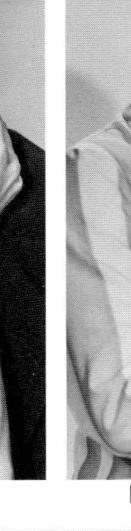

Tom Ewell

Matty Fain

Jinx Falken

William Farnum

Derek Farr

Jane Farrar

Charles Farrell

Jimmy Fawcett

Farnum, William[202]
1936 – Undersea Kingdom
  The Vigilantes Are Coming
1937 – Git Along Little Dogies
  Public Cowboy No. 1
1938 – The Lone Ranger
  Santa Fe Stampede
  Shine on Harvest Moon
1939 – Mexicali Rose
  Should Husbands Work?*
  Colorado Sunset
  Rovin' Tumbleweeds
  South of the Border
1940 – Adventures of Red Ryder
1941 – Gangs of Sonora
  Stars Past and Present*
1950 – Trail of Robin Hood

Farr, Audrey
1949 – Flame of Youth

Farr, Derek[202]
1948 – Code of Scotland Yard
1957 – The Man in the Road

Farr, Patricia[117]
1938 – Lady, Behave!

Farrar, David
1957 – Tears for Simon

Farrar, Jane[202]
1945 – A Song for Miss Julie

Farrell, Charles[202]
1935 – Forbidden Heaven

Farrell, Charles
1942 – Suicide Squadron
1958 – Strange Case of Dr. Manning

Farrell, Marian
1936 – Oregon Trail

Farrington, Betty
1940 – Dark Command*
  In Old Missouri*
  Meet the Missus*
1941 – A Man Betrayed*
  Doctors Don't Tell*
  Mr. District Atty. in the Carter Case*
1942 – Home in Wyomin'*
  Stardust on the Sage
  Shadows on the Sage*
  Ice-Capades Revue*
1943 – Mountain Rhythm*
1947 – Hit Parade of 1947*
  Driftwood*
1952 – The Fabulous Senorita*
1953 – Sweethearts on Parade*

Fauntelle, Dian
1948 – G-Men Never Forget

Faust, Louis R.
1948 – The Plunderers
1949 – The Last Bandit
  Hellfire

Faust, Marty
1941 – Saddlemates

Fawcett, Charles
1951 – Adventures of Captain Fabian

Fawcett, Jimmy[202]
Many films.
1936 – Robinson Crusoe of Clipper Island*
1939 – Three Texas Steers*
  Daredevils of the Red Circle*
  Dick Tracy's G-Men*
  Calling All Marines*
  The Arizona Kid*
  The Covered Trailer*
  Zorro's Fighting Legion*
1940 – Drums of Fu Manchu*
  Adventures of Red Ryder*
  Oklahoma Renegades*
  King of the Royal Mounted*
  Mysterious Doctor Satan*
  Behind the News*
1941 – Adventures of Captain Marvel*
  Country Fair*
  King of the Texas Rangers*
  Dick Tracy Vs. Crime, Inc.*
1942 – Spy Smasher*
  King of the Mounties*
1953 – Can. Mounties Vs. Atomic Invaders*

Fawcett, William
1950 – House by the River*
1951 – Honeychile*
1952 – Oklahoma Annie*
1953 – Nightmare Typhoon
  Can. Mounties Vs. Atomic Invaders*
  Sweethearts on Parade*
1955 – Timberjack*
  Lay that Rifle Down*
1956 – Dakota Incident

Fax, Jesslyn
1958 – The Man Who Died Twice*

Fay, Vivian
1945 – A Song for Miss Julie

Faylen, Frank[202]
1956 – Terror at Midnight

Fazenda, Louise
1941 – Stars Past and Present*

Fears, Tom
1954 – Crazylegs

Feld, Fritz[203]
1942 – Sleepytime Gal
1945 – Captain Tugboat Annie
1946 – The Catman of Paris
  I've Always Loved You
1950 – Belle of Old Mexico
1951 – Missing Women

Feldary, Eric
1948 – I, Jane Doe

Feldmar, Emil
1955 – In Old Vienna

Felix—and Martiniques
1951 – Havana Rose

Feller, Bob
1949 – The Kid from Cleveland

Fellows, Edith[203]
1942 – Heart of the Rio Grande
  Stardust on the Sage

Felton, Felix
1956 – Doctor at Sea

Felton, Verna
1945 – Sunset in El Dorado*
  Girls of the Big House
1957 – Taming Sutton's Gal

Fritz Feld

Edith Fellows

Walter Fenner

Helen Talbot, Maxine Doyle, Dot Farley

Fenner, Walter[203]
1939—My Wife's Relatives*
Mountain Rhythm
Should Husbands Work?*
The Covered Trailer
1940—Dark Command*
The Crooked Road*
1941—The Gay Vagabond*
1942—Flying Tigers*
Youth on Parade*
1943—G-Men Vs. The Black Dragon
Secret Service in Darkest Africa*

Fenton, Frank[203]
1943—A Scream in the Dark
1944—Rosie, the Riveter
1946—The French Key
1947—Hit Parade of 1947
1948—Renegades of Sonora
1949—Ranger of Cherokee Strip
The Golden Stallion
1950—Trigger, Jr.

Fenwick, Jean
1939—Money to Burn

Ference, Ilona
1955—The Divided Heart

Ferguson, Frank[203]
1942—Moonlight Masquerade*
1947—The Fabulous Texan*
1948—The Inside Story
1950—Under Mexicali Stars
1951—Thunder in God's Country
1952—Oklahoma Annie
1953—Woman They Almost Lynched*
1954—Johnny Guitar
The Outcast
The Shanghai Story
1955—The Eternal Sea
City of Shadows
1957—The Lawless Eighties

Ferguson, Helen
1941—Wampas Baby Stars*

Fernandez, Freddy
1956—Daniel Boone, Trail Blazer

Ferniel, Dan
1955—Panther Girl of the Kongo

Ferrari, Mario
1952—The Flying Squadron

Ferro, Michael
1949—King of the Rocket Men

Fetchit, Stepin[203]
1953—The Sun Shines Bright

Fetherston, Eddie[203]
1939—The Mysterious Miss X*
1940—Scatterbrain*
Melody and Moonlight*
Behind the News*
1941—Petticoat Politics*
A Man Betrayed*
Rookies on Parade*
Public Enemies*
1945—Don't Fence Me In*

Fieberling, Hal
See Hal Baylor.

Field, Margaret
1951—The Dakota Kid

Field, Mary[191]
1938—Federal Man-Hunt*
1940—Three Faces West*
The Trail Blazers
1944—Three Little Sisters*
The Port of Forty Thieves
1946—Murder in the Music Hall
Rendezvous with Annie*
1947—The Pilgrim Lady*
Driftwood*
1953—The Lady Wants Mink
Champ for a Day*

Field, Norman
1950—Destination Big House
1951—Street Bandits
1954—Crazylegs

Field, Sylvia
1943—Nobody's Darling

Field, Virginia
1941—Stars at Play*

Fields, Darlene
1956—The Man is Armed

Fields, Eddy[203]
1944—Silent Partner
End of the Road
1946—The Fabulous Suzanne

Fields, Stanley
1936—Ticket to Paradise
1937—The Hit Parade*
The Sheik Steps Out
All Over Town

Fierro, Paul
1953—San Antone
A Perilous Journey

Filmer, Robert
1946—The El Paso Kid

Finlayson, James[203]
1937—All Over Town
1948—Grand Canyon Trail

Finn, Mickey
1958—Girl in the Woods

Firefly
1938—Call of the Yukon

Firehouse Five Plus Two
1950—Hit Parade of 1951

Fisher, Freddie—and his Schnickelfritz Band
1944—Jamboree

Fisher, George "Shug"[132]
1943—Swing Your Partner
Hoosier Holiday
1944—Jamboree
The Yellow Rose of Texas*
Song of Nevada*
San Fernando Valley*
Lights of Old Santa Fe*
1945—Grissly's Millions*
Utah*
Bells of Rosarita*
Man from Oklahoma*
Don't Fence Me In*
Along the Navajo Trail*
1946—Song of Arizona*
Home on the Range*
Rainbow Over Texas*
My Pal Trigger*
Under Nevada Skies*
Roll on Texas Moon*
Heldorado*
1947—Springtime in the Sierras*
On the Old Spanish Trail*
1949—Susanna Pass*
1950—Rio Grande*
1951—Fighting Coast Guard*

Fiske, Robert[203]
1937—Navy Blues*
1938—The Purple Vigilantes
Born to be Wild*
1940—Carolina Moon
Colorado*
Texas Terrors
1941—The Apache Kid
Dick Tracy Vs. Crime, Inc.
1942—A Tragedy at Midnight*
1943—Dead Man's Gulch*

Fitzgerald, Barry[97]
1952—The Quiet Man

Fitzgerald, Johnny Lang
1938—Riders of the Black Hills

Fitzmaurice, Michael
1936—The House of a Thousand Candles

Fitzroy, Emily[203]
1937—The Bold Caballero

FitzSimons, Charles
1952—The Quiet Man

Fix, Paul[132]
1936—Navy Born
1938—The Night Hawk
1939—Wall Street Cowboy*
1940—The Crooked Road
1941—Citadel of Crime
Down Mexico Way
Public Enemies
A Missouri Outlaw
1942—South of Santa Fe
Sleepytime Gal*
Youth on Parade*
1943—In Old Oklahoma
1944—The Fighting Seabees
1945—Grissly's Millions
Flame of Barbary Coast
Dakota
1947—Angel and the Badman*
1948—Angel in Exile
The Plunderers
1949—Wake of the Red Witch
Hellfire
The Fighting Kentuckian
1950—Surrender
California Passage
1951—Bullfighter and the Lady*
1953—Ride the Man Down
Fair Wind to Java
1954—Johnny Guitar
1958—The Notorious Mr. Monks

Flagg, Steve[203]
1950—Hit Parade of 1951
1951—Million Dollar Pursuit

Flaherty, Pat[202]
1938—Hollywood Stadium Mystery!
1952—Hoodlum Empire

Flanagan, Bud
See Dennis O'Keefe.

Flash
1938—Call the Mesquiteers

Flash, Gerry
1953—Savage Frontier

Flateau, Georges
1951—Adventures of Captain Fabian

Flavin, James[203]
1938—Born to be Wild*
1939—Mickey, the Kid
Calling All Marines
1946—Rendezvous with Annie*
1947—Robin Hood of Texas
1948—Secret Service Investigator
The Plunderers
1950—Rock Island Trail*
The Savage Horde
1951—Oh! Susanna
Fighting Coast Guard
1954—The Untamed Heiress*

Frank Fenton

Eddie Fetherston

Frank Ferguson

Eddy Fields

James Finlayson

Stepin Fetchit

Robert Fiske

Emily Fitzroy

Steve Flagg

James Flavin

Fleer, Harry
1957 – The Unearthly

Fleming, Alice[160]
1937 – Dick Tracy*
1943 – The Mantrap
Headin' for God's Country*
Overland Mail Robbery
Mystery Broadcast
1944 – Tucson Raiders
Marshal of Reno
The San Antonio Kid
Cheyenne Wildcat
Storm Over Lisbon
Vigilantes of Dodge City
Sheriff of Las Vegas
1945 – Great Stagecoach Robbery
Lone Texas Ranger
Phantom of the Plains
Marshal of Laredo
Colorado Pioneers
Wagon Wheels Westward
1946 – California Gold Rush
Sheriff of Redwood Valley
Sun Valley Cyclone
Conquest of Cheyenne

Fleming, Ronda [Rhonda][204]
1943 – In Old Oklahoma*

Flint, Kelly
1943 – The Blocked Trail*
Song of Texas*
1944 – Silent Partner*
Man from Frisco*

Flint, Sam[132]
1935 – The New Frontier
1936 – The Lawless Nineties
Red River Valley
The Lonely Trail
Winds of the Wasteland
1937 – Dick Tracy*
Jim Hanvey - Detective*
It Could Happen to You*
Sea Racketeers*
1938 – The Fighting Devil Dogs
1940 – Forgotten Girls*
1941 – The Singing Hill*
Under Fiesta Stars
Tuxedo Junction
1942 – South of Santa Fe
Shepherd of the Ozarks*
Spy Smasher
The Old Homestead*
The Traitor Within*
1943 – Mountain Rhythm
Thundering Trails
Chatterbox*
Swing Your Partner
Someone to Remember*
The Masked Marvel*
Here Comes Elmer*
1944 – Casanova in Burlesque*
The Lady and the Monster*
Goodnight Sweetheart*
Man from Frisco*
Silver City Kid
Lights of Old Santa Fe
1945 – Man from Oklahoma
Captain Tugboat Annie*
Along the Navajo Trail
1946 – My Pal Trigger
The Crimson Ghost
Sioux City Sue*
1947 – Hit Parade of 1947*
The Wild Frontier
The Black Widow
1948 – Old Los Angeles*
Adv. of Frank and Jesse James
1949 – Brimstone*
Alias the Champ*
1950 – Rock Island Trail
1951 – Belle LeGrand*

Rhonda Fleming

Jay C. Flippen

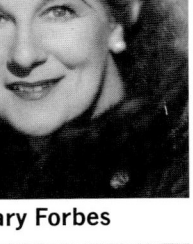
Frank Fontaine

Mary Forbes

Francis Ford

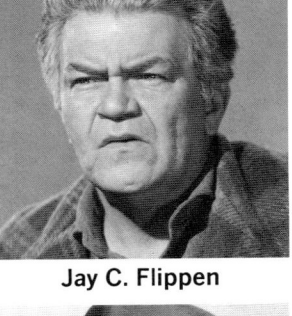
Lee Ford

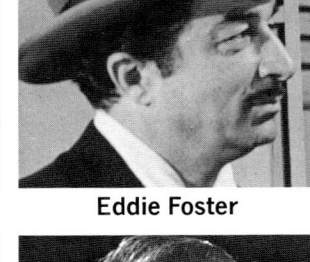
Wallace Ford

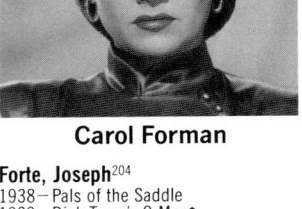
Carol Forman

Flippen, Jay C.[204]
1952 – Woman of the North Country

Flowers, Bess
1947 – That's My Man*

Fluellen, Joel
1953 – Jungle Drums of Africa

Flying "L" Ranch Quartette, The
1946 – Home in Oklahoma

Flynn, Charles
1949 – Flame of Youth

Flynn, Errol[97]
1951 – Adventures of Captain Fabian

Flynn, Joe
1957 – Panama Sal

Fonda, Henry
1941 – Hollywood Visits the Navy*

Fontaine, Frank[204]
[John L. C. Sevony]
1950 – Hit Parade of 1951

Fontaine, Joan[97]
1939 – Man of Conquest

Fontaine, Peter
1958 – Strange Case of Dr. Manning

Forbes, Mary[204]
1938 – Outside of Paradise
1939 – Should Husbands Work?
1945 – Earl Carroll Vanities

Ford, Dorothy[204]
1950 – Sands of Iwo Jima*
1953 – A Perilous Journey

Ford, Francis[204]
1942 – King of the Mounties
Outlaws of Pine Ridge
1944 – The Big Bonanza*
1945 – Love, Honor and Goodbye*
1947 – Driftwood
Bandits of Dark Canyon
1948 – The Timber Trail
Eyes of Texas
The Plunderers
The Far Frontier
1949 – Frontier Investigator
San Antone Ambush
1952 – The Quiet Man
Toughest Man in Arizona
1953 – The Sun Shines Bright

Ford, Glenn
1941 – Variety Reel*

Ford, Lee[204]
1936 – Sitting on the Moon*
Bulldog Edition*
The President's Mystery*
Happy Go Lucky*
1937 – Gunsmoke Ranch*
S O S Coast Guard
1938 – Dick Tracy Returns
1939 – Woman Doctor*
The Zero Hour*

Ford, Patrick M.
1950 – Rio Grande*

Ford, Ross
1950 – Frisco Tornado
1951 – Rough Riders of Durango
Street Bandits

Ford, Ruth
1945 – Woman Who Came Back
1946 – Strange Impersonation

Ford, Wallace[204]
1937 – Exiled to Shanghai
1940 – Scatterbrain
1941 – A Man Betrayed
1946 – A Guy Could Change
Rendezvous with Annie
1956 – The Maverick Queen
Thunder Over Arizona

Ford, Whitey
1941 – Country Fair

Forester, Cay
1944 – San Fernando Valley*
1945 – Dakota*
1946 – Strange Impersonation
That Brennan Girl*
1947 – The Pretender

Forman, Carol[204]
1947 – The Black Widow
1949 – Federal Agents Vs. Underworld, Inc.
1951 – Oh! Susanna*

Forman, Joey
1954 – The Atomic Kid
1955 – The Twinkle in God's Eye

Forrest, John
1945 – Identity Unknown

Forrest, William[132]
1940 – Gangs of Chicago*
1941 – Doctors Don't Tell*
The Pittsburgh Kid*
Mercy Island*
1942 – Pardon My Stripes*
Sleepytime Gal*
Spy Smasher*
Bells of Capistrano*
1943 – G-Men Vs. The Black Dragon*
The Masked Marvel
1944 – The Fighting Seabees
1945 – Gangs of the Waterfront
Road to Alcatraz
Behind City Lights
Love, Honor and Goodbye*
Girls of the Big House
1947 – The Fabulous Texan*
1950 – Hit Parade of 1951*
1951 – Spoilers of the Plains*
Missing Women
Fighting Coast Guard*
Fort Dodge Stampede
The Sea Hornet*

Forsyth, Frank
1957 – Thunder Over Tangier

Forte, Joseph[204]
1938 – Pals of the Saddle
1939 – Dick Tracy's G-Men*
1940 – Dark Command*
The Crooked Road*
Hit Parade of 1941*
1941 – King of the Texas Rangers
1943 – Here Comes Elmer*
1945 – Utah*
Behind City Lights*
Love, Honor and Goodbye*
1946 – The Crimson Ghost
1951 – Rodeo King and the Senorita
1958 – The Man Who Died Twice*

Foster, Eddie[204]
1938 – Dick Tracy Returns
1953 – Nightmare Typhoon
War of the Space Giants
Destroyers of the Sun
Solar Sky Raiders
S. O. S. Ice Age
1957 – Affair in Reno

Foster, Norman
1936 – The Leavenworth Case

Foster, Preston[98]
1938 – Army Girl

Foster, William
1959 – Plunderers of Painted Flats

Joseph Forte

Eddie Foster

Douglas Fowley

Victor Francen

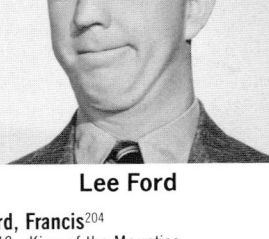
Dorothy Ford, Richard Webb

Fostini, John
1951 — Fugitive Lady

Foulger, Byron[132]
1936 — The President's Mystery*
1937 — Larceny on the Air
    Dick Tracy
    The Duke Comes Back
1938 — Born to be Wild
    King of the Newsboys*
    Tenth Avenue Kid
1939 — Sabotage*
1940 — Heroes of the Saddle
    Three Faces West*
    Behind the News*
1941 — Ridin' on a Rainbow
    Sis Hopkins*
    The Gay Vagabond
1943 — Shantytown*
    Silver Spurs
    In Old Oklahoma
1945 — Grissly's Millions
    The Cheaters*
1946 — The French Key
    Plainsman and the Lady
1948 — Out of the Storm
1950 — Salt Lake Raiders
1951 — The Sea Hornet
1953 — A Perilous Journey*
    Bandits of the West
1956 — Thunder Over Arizona*

Four Step Brothers, The
1947 — That's My Gal

Fowler, Harry
1955 — A Day to Remember

Fowler, Jean
1938 — Under Western Stars
1940 — In Old Missouri*
1941 — Sis Hopkins*

Fowley, Douglas[204]
1936 — Navy Born
1940 — Wagons Westward
1941 — Doctors Don't Tell
    Mr. District Atty. in the Carter Case
1942 — Sunset on the Desert
1943 — Sleepy Lagoon
1945 — Behind City Lights*
    Don't Fence Me In
    Along the Navajo Trail
1946 — The Glass Alibi
1947 — Yankee Fakir
    The Trespasser
1948 — The Denver Kid
1949 — Susanna Pass
1951 — South of Caliente
1953 — Red River Shore
1954 — The Untamed Heiress
1957 — Raiders of Old California

Foy, Jr., Eddie[77]
1940 — Scatterbrain
1941 — Rookies on Parade
    Country Fair
    Puddin' Head
1942 — Yokel Boy
    Moonlight Masquerade
    Joan of Ozark
1951 — Honeychile

Francen, Victor[204]
1951 — Adventures of Captain Fabian

Francia, Maria G.
1952 — The Flying Squadron

Francis, Diana
1958 — Girl in the Woods

Francis, Olin
1938 — Overland Stage Raiders
    Red River Range

Francis, Raymond
1956 — Above Us the Waves

Franco, Abel
1957 — Eighteen and Anxious

Frank, J. L.—Golden West Cowboys
1938 — Gold Mine in the Sky

Frank, Jerry
1937 — Zorro Rides Again
1938 — Heroes of the Hills
1941 — Jungle Girl

Franke, Chris
1936 — Winds of the Wasteland

Franklin, Gloria[205]
1940 — Drums of Fu Manchu
1941 — The Gay Vagabond
1946 — That Brennan Girl*
1947 — Hit Parade of 1947*

Franklin, Gretchen
1957 — Operation Conspiracy

Franklyn, William
1956 — Above Us the Waves
1957 — Time is My Enemy

Frankovich, Mike[205]
1941 — Puddin' Head*
1946 — Rendezvous with Annie*
1947 — Son of Zorro*
1951 — Fugitive Lady*

Franks, Jr., Jerome
1944 — Casanova in Burlesque

Franz, Arthur[205]
1950 — Tarnished
    Sands of Iwo Jima
1954 — Flight Nurse

Franz, Eduard
1949 — Wake of the Red Witch
1955 — The Last Command

Fraser, Elisabeth[205]
1950 — Hills of Oklahoma

Fraser, Phyllis
1936 — The Harvester
    Winds of the Wasteland

Fraser, Richard[117]
1943 — Thumbs Up
1945 — The Fatal Witness
    Scotland Yard Investigator
    The Tiger Woman
1946 — The Undercover Woman
1947 — Blackmail

Frasher, Jimmy
1950 — Redwood Forest Trail

Gloria Franklin

Elisabeth Fraser

Mike Frankovich

William Frawley

Arthur Franz

Robert Frazer

Frawley, William[205]
1941 — Public Enemies
1944 — The Fighting Seabees
    Lake Placid Serenade
1945 — Flame of Barbary Coast
    Hitchhike to Happiness
1946 — Rendezvous with Annie
    The Inner Circle
1947 — Hit Parade of 1947

Frazee, Jane[24]
1940 — Melody and Moonlight
1941 — Angels with Broken Wings
1942 — Moonlight Masquerade
1944 — Rosie, the Riveter
    The Big Bonanza
1945 — Swingin' on a Rainbow
1946 — A Guy Could Change
1947 — Calendar Girl
    Springtime in the Sierras
    On the Old Spanish Trail
1948 — The Gay Ranchero
    Under California Stars
    Grand Canyon Trail

Frazer, Alex
1949 — The Blonde Bandit

Frazer, Robert[205]
1940 — Forgotten Girls*
    The Crooked Road*
    Grand Old Opry*
    One Man's Law
1941 — Pals of the Pecos
    Gangs of Sonora
    Bad Man of Deadwood*
    The Devil Pays Off*
    Dick Tracy Vs. Crime, Inc.
1942 — Code of the Outlaw*
1943 — Dead Man's Gulch*
    Daredevils of the West
    Wagon Tracks West
1944 — Captain America
    The Tiger Woman

Freberg, Stan[205]
1947 — It's a Grand Old Nag*
1954 — Geraldine

Fredericks, Charles
1957 — Hell Canyon Outlaws

Freeman, Helen[205]
1947 — The Pilgrim Lady

Freeman, Howard
1945 — Mexicana

Freeman, Kathleen
1950 — House by the River
    Lonely Heart Bandits
1951 — The Wild Blue Yonder*
1953 — A Perilous Journey
1957 — Pawnee

Freeman, Mona[117]
1946 — That Brennan Girl
1952 — Thunderbirds
1955 — The Road to Denver

French Can-Can Dancers
1952 — Bal Tabarin

French, Richard
1942 — Valley of Hunted Men

Fresco, David
1946 — Crime of the Century

Frey, Arno
1942 — Valley of Hunted Men

Freytag, Robert
1956 — Magic Fire

Friedkin, Joel[205]
1940 — Gaucho Serenade*
    Sing, Dance, Plenty Hot*
    Colorado*
    Who Killed Aunt Maggie?
    The Border Legion*
1941 — Doctors Don't Tell*
    Bad Man of Deadwood*
    Outlaws of Cherokee Trail
1942 — Raiders of the Range*
    Affairs of Jimmy Valentine*
    The Cyclone Kid
    The Sombrero Kid
1944 — Faces in the Fog*
1946 — California Gold Rush
    Night Train to Memphis*
1947 — Saddle Pals*

Friend, Philip[205]
1942 — Suicide Squadron
1957 — Operation Conspiracy

Fries, Ted
1950 — Redwood Forest Trail

Frisco, Joe[205]
1938 — Western Jamboree
1940 — Ride, Tenderfoot, Ride
1944 — Atlantic City
1947 — That's My Man

Frome, Milton
1939 — Dick Tracy's G-Men*
    Calling All Marines*
1954 — The Atomic Kid*

Frost, Don
1950 — Twilight in the Sierras

Frost, Terry[205]
1941 — Gauchos of Eldorado*
    Dick Tracy Vs. Crime, Inc.*
1943 — California Joe
1944 — Captain America*
    The Fighting Seabees
1945 — Sunset in El Dorado*
1947 — Apache Rose
1948 — Oklahoma Badlands
1951 — Heart of the Rockies*
    Govt. Agents Vs. Phantom Legion*
1955 — King of the Carnival
1956 — Thunder Over Arizona*

Frye, Dwight[205]
1935 — The Crime of Doctor Crespi
1936 — Beware of Ladies
1938 — Invisible Enemy
    The Night Hawk
1939 — Mickey, the Kid
1940 — Drums of Fu Manchu
    Gangs of Chicago
1941 — The Devil Pays Off*
1942 — Sleepytime Gal*

Frye, Gilbert
1948 — Sons of Adventure

Frye, Katherine
1936 — Roarin' Lead
1939 — Mexicali Rose

Frye, Theodore
1936 — Roarin' Lead

Stan Freberg

Helen Freeman

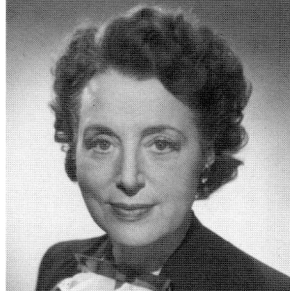
Joel Friedkin

Joe Frisco

Dwight Frye

Philip Friend

Terry Frost

Fuller, Barbra[26]
1949 – The Red Menace
　　　Flame of Youth
　　　Alias the Champ
1950 – Unmasked
　　　Singing Guns*
　　　Tarnished
　　　Harbor of Missing Men
　　　Women from Headquarters
　　　Rock Island Trail
　　　The Savage Horde
　　　Trial Without Jury
　　　Lonely Heart Bandits
　　　Macbeth*

Fulton, Lou
See Oscar and Elmer.

Fulton, Rad
1956 – Come Next Spring

Fung, Paul
1942 – Remember Pearl Harbor!
　　　King of the Mounties

Fung, Willie[206]
1936 – Happy Go Lucky
1937 – Git Along Little Dogies
　　　Come on, Cowboys!
　　　The Trigger Trio
1941 – Public Enemies

Furneaux, Yvonne[117]
1955 – Cross Channel
1956 – Lisbon

Furness, Betty[117]
1936 – The President's Mystery

G

Gagnon, Betty
1948 – The Gay Ranchero

Gagnon, Rene A.
1950 – Sands of Iwo Jima

Gail, Jeanne
1945 – Woman Who Came Back

Gaines, Mel
1958 – Man or Gun

Gale, Gladys
1936 – Dancing Feet*
1937 – Jim Hanvey - Detective*
1938 – Orphans of the Street*
1939 – Jeepers Creepers*
1940 – Village Barn Dance*
1941 – Country Fair*
　　　Doctors Don't Tell*
1942 – Lady for a Night*
1945 – An Angel Comes to Brooklyn*

The Gentle Maniacs

Galindo, Nacho[184]
1947 – Twilight on the Rio Grande
1950 – Belle of Old Mexico
　　　The Showdown
　　　Surrender
1951 – Havana Rose
1953 – Woman They Almost Lynched
1954 – The Outcast
1955 – Headline Hunters
1956 – Jaguar
　　　Thunder Over Arizona

Gallagher, Carole[176]
1947 – Hit Parade of 1947*
1948 – Secret Service Investigator*
　　　The Denver Kid
　　　Homicide for Three*
1950 – Sands of Iwo Jima*
　　　Macbeth*

Gallagher, Gay
1955 – Double Jeopardy*

Gallagher, Skeets
1941 – Citadel of Crime
1949 – Duke of Chicago

Gallant Man
1947 – That's My Man

Gallaudet, John[206]
1938 – Federal Man-Hunt
1939 – Street of Missing Men
1940 – Wagons Westward
1949 – Outcasts of the Trail
1951 – Missing Women
1955 – Double Jeopardy
　　　No Man's Woman
1956 – When Gangland Strikes
　　　Terror at Midnight

Galli, Rosina
1941 – Rags to Riches
　　　Gauchos of Eldorado
1951 – Fugitive Lady

Gallier, Alex
1957 – Thunder Over Tangier
　　　The Fighting Wildcats

Galvani, Dino
1951 – Fugitive Lady

Galvert, Charles
1944 – Trocadero

Gam, Rita[206]
1956 – Magic Fire

Gamboa, Elias
1941 – Under Fiesta Stars

Gambold, Bob
1954 – Crazylegs

Gan, Chester
1940 – The Carson City Kid
1942 – Flying Tigers

Ganzer, Gerry[206]
1949 – Powder River Rustlers

Garabedian, Robert
1952 – Zombies of the Stratosphere

Garber, Jan—and band
1943 – Here Comes Elmer

Garcen, Tony
1955 – The Twinkle in God's Eye

Garden, Irina
1958 – International Counterfeiters

Gardere, Eduardo
1950 – The Avengers

Gardner, Reginald
1941 – Los Angeles Examiner Benefit*

Garey, Peter
1945 – A Song for Miss Julie

Garfield, John
1940 – Chinese Garden Festival*

Gargan, Edward[206]
1936 – Hearts in Bondage
1937 – Jim Hanvey - Detective
1940 – Wolf of New York
　　　Girl from God's Country
　　　Meet the Missus*
　　　Bowery Boy
1941 – Ice-Capades*
1943 – Tahiti Honey
　　　The West Side Kid
　　　In Old Oklahoma*
1944 – San Fernando Valley
1945 – Earl Carroll Vanities
　　　A Sporting Chance
1946 – Gay Blades
　　　The Inner Circle
1947 – The Ghost Goes Wild
　　　That's My Gal
　　　Web of Danger
　　　Saddle Pals
　　　Exposed
1948 – Campus Honeymoon
　　　Daredevils of the Clouds
1950 – Belle of Old Mexico
　　　Hit Parade of 1951
1951 – Cuban Fireball

Gargan, William[98]
1936 – Navy Born
1946 – Strange Impersonation
　　　Murder in the Music Hall

Garland, Judy
1941 – Los Angeles Examiner Benefit*

Garralaga, Martin[132]
1939 – Forged Passport*
1942 – Spy Smasher*
　　　In Old California*
1944 – The Laramie Trail
　　　Man from Frisco*
1945 – Mexicana*
1946 – Plainsman and the Lady*
1947 – Apache Rose*
　　　Twilight on the Rio Grande
1948 – Madonna of the Desert
1949 – Streets of San Francisco
　　　The Last Bandit
　　　Susanna Pass
1951 – Havana Rose
1952 – Woman in the Dark
　　　The Fabulous Senorita
　　　Tropical Heat Wave
1953 – San Antone
1954 – Jubilee Trail
1955 – A Man Alone

Garrick, Gene[206]
1944 – Thoroughbreds
1947 – The Ghost Goes Wild

Garro, Joseph
1948 – Under California Stars
1950 – Twilight in the Sierras

Garson, Greer
1941 – Variety Reel*

Gary, Gene
1949 – Rose of the Yukon

Gastoni, Lisa[206]
1957 – Thunder Over Tangier

Gates, Maxine
1952 – Oklahoma Annie

Gates, Nancy[206]
1954 – Hell's Half Acre
1955 – No Man's Woman

Gateson, Marjorie[207]
1936 – The Gentleman from Louisiana
1939 – My Wife's Relatives
1940 – In Old Missouri
1944 – Casanova in Burlesque

Gauge, Alexander
1955 – The Square Ring

Gay, Gregory[206]
1945 – The Tiger Woman
1946 – Passkey To Danger
1947 – The Trespasser
　　　Blackmail
1950 – Harbor of Missing Men
　　　Flying Disc Man from Mars
1952 – Bal Tabarin
1953 – Enemies of the Universe
　　　Atomic Peril
　　　Cosmic Vengeance
　　　Nightmare Typhoon
　　　War of the Space Giants
　　　Destroyers of the Sun
　　　Robot Monster from Mars
　　　The Hydrogen Hurricane
　　　Solar Sky Raiders
　　　S. O. S. Ice Age
　　　Lost in Outer Space
　　　Captives of the Zero Hour
1955 – King of the Carnival

Gay, Nancy[206]
1943 – The Man from the Rio Grande
　　　Overland Mail Robbery
1944 – Pride of the Plains

Gaynor, Janet
1941 – Wampas Baby Stars*

Gaze, Gwen
1940 – Women in War*

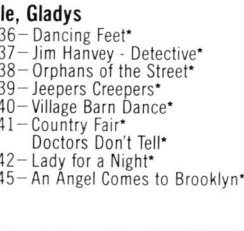

Willie Fung　　**John Gallaudet**　　**Rita Gam**　　**Gerry Ganzer**　　**Edward Gargan**

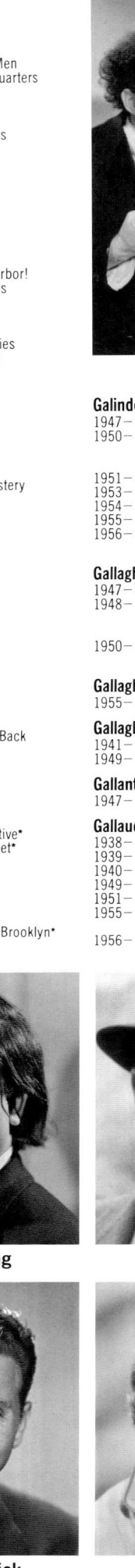

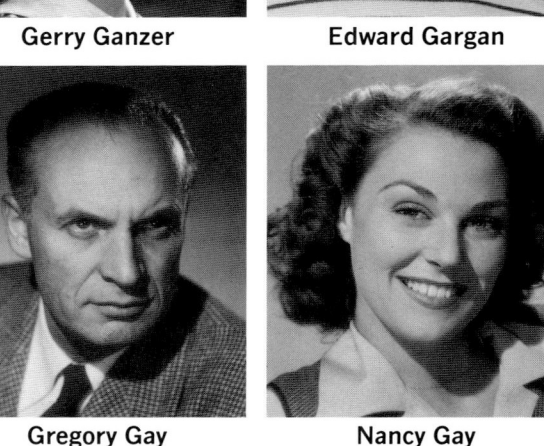

Gene Garrick　　**Lisa Gastoni**　　**Nancy Gates**　　**Gregory Gay**　　**Nancy Gay**

Geary, Bud [Maine][26]
1939—Daredevils of the Red Circle*
 Dick Tracy's G-Men*
 Calling All Marines*
 Jeepers Creepers*
 Zorro's Fighting Legion*
1940—Adventures of Red Ryder*
 Scatterbrain
 King of the Royal Mounted*
 Mysterious Doctor Satan
1941—Adventures of Captain Marvel*
 Jungle Girl
 Gangs of Sonora*
 Outlaws of Cherokee Trail*
 King of the Texas Rangers*
 Gauchos of Eldorado*
 West of Cimarron*
 Dick Tracy Vs. Crime, Inc.*
1942—Cowboy Serenade*
 Raiders of the Range*
 Home in Wyomin'*
 The Phantom Plainsmen*
 The Sombrero Kid*
 The Sundown Kid
1943—G-Men Vs. The Black Dragon*
 Thundering Trails
 The Blocked Trail*
 Carson City Cyclone
 King of the Cowboys*
 Santa Fe Scouts*
 Calling Wild Bill Elliott
 The Man from Thunder River*
 Bordertown Gun Fighters
 Secret Service in Darkest Africa*
 Death Valley Manhunt
 The Man from the Rio Grande*
 The Masked Marvel*
 Overland Mail Robbery
 Canyon City*
 In Old Oklahoma*
 Pistol Packin' Mama*
 Hands Across the Border*
1944—Pride of the Plains
 Captain America*
 Beneath Western Skies
 The Fighting Seabees*
 Mojave Firebrand
 Hidden Valley Outlaws*
 The Laramie Trail
 Outlaws of Santa Fe
 Tucson Raiders
 The Tiger Woman*
 Silent Partner*
 Goodnight Sweetheart*
 Man From Frisco*
 Marshal of Reno
 Call of the Rockies*
 Silver City Kid
 Secrets of Scotland Yard*
 The San Antonio Kid*
 Haunted Harbor
 Stagecoach to Monterey
 Cheyenne Wildcat
 Code of the Prairie
 My Buddy*
 Storm Over Lisbon*
 Lights of Old Santa Fe*
 Sheriff of Sundown
 End of the Road*
 Vigilantes of Dodge City
 Firebrands of Arizona
 The Big Bonanza
 Sheriff of Las Vegas
1945—The Topeka Terror
 Great Stagecoach Robbery
 Lone Texas Ranger
 Three's a Crowd
 Flame of Barbary Coast*
 Santa Fe Saddlemates
 Gangs of the Waterfront*
 Steppin' in Society*
 Trail of Kit Carson
 Oregon Trail
 Phantom of the Plains
 Behind City Lights
 Bandits of the Badlands*
 The Purple Monster Strikes
 Marshal of Laredo
 Colorado Pioneers
 The Cherokee Flash
 Wagon Wheels Westward
1946—California Gold Rush*
 Sheriff of Redwood Valley
 King of the Forest Rangers
 Man from Rainbow Valley

Geldert, Clarence
1936—Go-Get-'Em, Haines

Genardi, Maria
1948—Madonna of the Desert

Gentle Maniacs, The[206]
1937—The Hit Parade

George, Anthony[207]
1958—Gunfire at Indian Gap

George, Carmel
1950—Women from Headquarters*

George, Gladys[207]
1943—Nobody's Darling
1945—Steppin' in Society

Marjorie Gateson, Joe E. Brown, Jack Rice

George, Jac[207]
1937—The Hit Parade*
 Meet the Boy Friend*
1939—Man of Conquest*
1940—In Old Missouri*
 Grand Old Opry*
 Hit Parade of 1941*
 Behind the News*
1941—Puddin' Head*
1942—Lady for a Night*
 Sleepytime Gal*
1944—Secrets of Scotland Yard*
 Storm Over Lisbon*
1945—Federal Operator 99*
1947—That's My Gal*
 The Trespasser*

George, Muriel
1943—Alibi

Geraghty, Carmelita
1941—Wampas Baby Stars*

Gerald, Helen
1946—G. I. War Brides

Gerald, Jim[207]
1937—Bulldog Drummond at Bay
1951—Adventures of Captain Fabian

Gerall, Roscoe
1936—Oh, Susanna!

Geray, Steven[207]
1945—Mexicana
1950—Harbor of Missing Men
1952—Lady Possessed
 Bal Tabarin
1954—Tobor the Great

Germaine, Mary
1955—The Green Buddha

Gerry, Alex
1950—Tarnished
 Covered Wagon Raid
 Prisoners in Petticoats

Gerson, Betty Lou[207]
1949—The Red Menace

Gladys George

Jac George

Jim Gerald

Steven Geray

Betty Lou Gerson

Tamara Geva

Wynne Gibson

James Gillette

Gerstle, Frank
1955—I Cover the Underworld

Geva, Tamara[207]
1937—Manhattan Merry-Go-Round

Gibson, Hoot [Edmund][207]
1937—The Painted Stallion

Gibson, Julie
1958—Street of Darkness

Gibson, Wynne[207]
1937—Michael O'Halloran
1938—Gangs of New York
1940—Forgotten Girls
1943—Mystery Broadcast

Giese, Sugar
1944—Casanova in Burlesque

Gifford, Frances[117]
1941—Jungle Girl

Gilbert, Billy[118]
1936—Bulldog Edition*
1938—Army Girl
1939—Forged Passport
1940—Women in War
 Scatterbrain
 Sing, Dance, Plenty Hot
1941—Angels with Broken Wings
 Meet Roy Rogers*
1942—Sleepytime Gal
1943—Shantytown

Gilbert, Jody[132]
1939—New Frontier*
 Smuggled Cargo*
1940—Grand Ole Opry*
 Hit Parade of 1941*
1949—Hellfire
 Brimstone*
 The Blonde Bandit
1950—House by the River

Gill, Florence
1937—Larceny on the Air

Gillern, Grace
1950—Unmasked

Gillette, James[207]
1941—Desert Bandit

Gillette, Ruth[207]
1935—The Spanish Cape Mystery
1936—The Gentleman from Louisiana*
 Bulldog Edition*
1939—Pride of the Navy*

Anthony George, Vera Ralston

Hoot Gibson, Jack Perrin

Ruth Gillette

Gillie, Jean
1943 – The Saint Meets the Tiger

Gillingwater, Claude
1936 – Ticket to Paradise

Gillis, Anne[208]
1936 – The Singing Cowboy
1943 – Man from Music Mountain
1945 – The Cheaters
1946 – Gay Blades

Gilmore, Virginia[118]
1941 – Mr. District Atty. in the Carter Case

Gilson, Tom[208]
1958 – Young and Wild

Girard, Joe
1936 – Oregon Trail

Givot, George[208]
1937 – The Hit Parade

Gladwin, Frances[69]
1942 – Lady for a Night*
    Sleepytime Gal*
    Youth on Parade*
1944 – Lake Placid Serenade*
1945 – Earl Carroll Vanities*
    Bells of Rosarita*
    The Chicago Kid*
    Road to Alcatraz*
    The Cheaters*
    Hitchhike to Happiness*
    Man from Oklahoma*
    Behind City Lights*
    Love, Honor and Goodbye*
    Sunset in El Dorado*
    Don't Fence Me In*
    Girls of the Big House*
    An Angel Comes to Brooklyn*
    Mexicana*
    Along the Navajo Trail*
    Wagon Wheels Westward*
    Dakota*
1946 – A Guy Could Change*
    California Gold Rush*
    Murder in the Music Hall*

Glass, Ned[208]
1938 – Dick Tracy Returns
    The Night Hawk*
1939 – Woman Doctor*
1954 – Geraldine*

Glassmire, Gus[208]
1939 – Woman Doctor
1940 – Forgotten Girls*
    The Crooked Road*
1941 – Mr. District Attorney*
    Rags to Riches*
1942 – Pardon My Stripes*
1943 – Idaho*
    In Old Oklahoma*
1944 – My Best Gal*

Gleason, James[78]
1937 – Manhattan Merry-Go-Round
1938 – Army Girl
    The Higgins Family
1939 – My Wife's Relatives
    Should Husbands Work?
    The Covered Trailer
    Money to Burn
1940 – Grandpa Goes to Town
    Earl of Puddlestone
1958 – Man or Gun

Gleason, Lucile[78]
1937 – Navy Blues
1938 – The Higgins Family
1939 – My Wife's Relatives
    Should Husbands Work?
    The Covered Trailer
    Money to Burn
1940 – Grandpa Goes to Town
    Earl of Puddlestone
1945 – Don't Fence Me In

Gleason, Pat
1938 – Call the Mesquiteers

Gleason, Russell[78]
1938 – The Higgins Family
1939 – My Wife's Relatives
    Should Husbands Work?
    The Covered Trailer
    Money to Burn
1940 – Grandpa Goes to Town
    Earl of Puddlestone

Gleckler, Robert
1938 – Gangs of New York
    Orphans of the Street

Glendon, Frank
1935 – Sagebrush Troubadour
1936 – King of the Pecos

Glenn, Sr., Roy[208]
1953 – Jungle Drums of Africa
1955 – Panther Girl of the Kongo

Glennon, Gordon
1942 – Suicide Squadron

Goddard, Alf
1943 – The Saint Meets the Tiger

Godfrey, George
1937 – The Riders of the Whistling Skull

Godfrey, Renee
1947 – Winter Wonderland

Godoy, Arturo
1940 – Grandpa Goes to Town

Godoy, Ledda
1940 – Grandpa Goes to Town

Golden Gate Quartette, The
1943 – Hit Parade of 1943

Golden, Michael
1955 – The Square Ring
    Cross Channel
1956 – Track the Man Down

Golden, Miriam[118]
1946 – Specter of the Rose*

Goldi, Erwin
1943 – Secret Service in Darkest Africa

Gombell, Minna[208]
1935 – Two Sinners
1945 – Swingin' on a Rainbow
1947 – Wyoming
1949 – The Last Bandit

Gomez, Antonio
1951 – Bullfighter and the Lady

Gomez, Augie
1939 – Blue Montana Skies
1948 – Old Los Angeles

Gomez, Thomas[98]
1948 – Angel in Exile

Gonzales, Jaime
1956 – A Woman's Devotion

Gonzales, Jose Gonzales
1957 – Panama Sal

Goodall, Grace
1936 – The Singing Vagabond

Goodwin, Bill[208]
1946 – Earl Carroll Sketchbook
1947 – Hit Parade of 1947
1954 – The Atomic Kid

Goodwin, Garry
1952 – Captive of Billy the Kid

Goodwin, Harold[208]
1948 – The Bold Frontiersman
    Carson City Raiders
1949 – Law of the Golden West
    The Wyoming Bandit
    Radar Patrol Vs. Spy King
1950 – The Vanishing Westerner

Gorcey, David
1938 – Prairie Moon
1946 – The French Key

Gorcey, Leo[208]
1937 – Portia on Trial
1941 – Angels with Broken Wings

Bill Goodwin

Harold Goodwin

Leo Gorcey

Bert Gordon

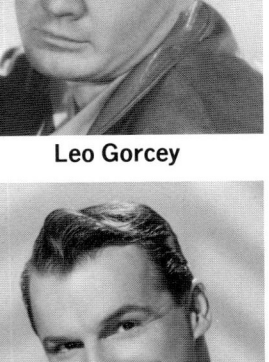

Charles Gordon

Leo Gordon

Gordon, Bert[208]
1938 – Outside of Paradise

Gordon, Charles[208]
1945 – The Vampire's Ghost
    Three's a Crowd
    Road to Alcatraz
    Captain Tugboat Annie

Gordon, C. Henry
1938 – Invisible Enemy
1939 – Man of Conquest

Gordon, Gavin
1936 – The Leavenworth Case

Gordon, Harold
1955 – Yellowneck

Gordon, Huntly
1935 – The Spanish Cape Mystery
1937 – Portia on Trial

Gordon, Joe
1949 – The Kid from Cleveland

Gordon, Leo[208]
1955 – Santa Fe Passage
1958 – The Notorious Mr. Monks

Gordon, Lesley
1942 – Suicide Squadron

Gordon, Mary[209]
1936 – Laughing Irish Eyes
1937 – Meet the Boy Friend
1938 – Lady, Behave!
1939 – She Married a Cop
1943 – Whispering Footsteps
1944 – Secrets of Scotland Yard*
1947 – Exposed

Gordon, Roy[209]
1939 – Sabotage*
1940 – Wolf of New York
1942 – Lady for a Night*
    Secrets of the Underground*
1946 – One Exciting Week*
1949 – The Blonde Bandit*
1950 – The Invisible Monster*
1951 – Insurance Investigator*
1957 – The Unearthly
1959 – Plunderers of Painted Flats*

Gordon, Vera
1937 – Michael O'Halloran

Gorgeous George [Wagner][209]
1949 – Alias the Champ

Gorman, Buddy
1944 – Thoroughbreds

Gorman, Eric
1952 – The Quiet Man

Got, Roland[209]
1938 – The Night Hawk
1943 – G-Men Vs. The Black Dragon

Gotell, Walter
1943 – At Dawn We Die

Gottlieb, Theodore
1947 – The Black Widow

Gould, William[209]
1937 – Wild Horse Rodeo
1938 – The Purple Vigilantes
    Ladies in Distress*
1939 – The Lone Ranger Rides Again
1943 – King of the Cowboys*
1951 – Heart of the Rockies

Grady, Robert
[Jack McLendon]
1945 – Lone Texas Ranger
    Marshal of Laredo
    An Angel Comes to Brooklyn

Graff, Wilton[209]
1945 – Earl Carroll Vanities
    Gangs of the Waterfront
    An Angel Comes to Brooklyn
1946 – Valley of the Zombies
    Traffic in Crime

Graham, Dolores and Don
1947 – That's My Gal

Anne Gillis

George Givot

Gus Glassmire

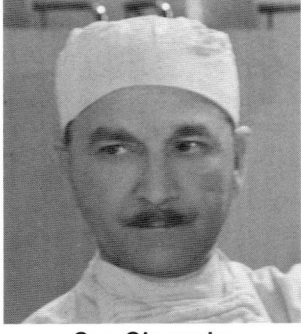

Tom Gilson

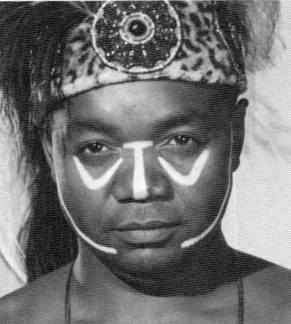

Ned Glass

Roy Glenn, Sr.

Minna Gombell

Graham, Fred[209]
Many films.
1943—The Masked Marvel*
  In Old Oklahoma*
1944—Captain America*
  Mojave Firebrand*
  Outlaws of Santa Fe*
  Tucson Raiders*
  The Tiger Woman*
  Silent Partner*
  The Yellow Rose of Texas*
  Marshal of Reno
  Silver City Kid*
  Song of Nevada*
  Haunted Harbor*
  Stagecoach to Monterey
  Cheyenne Wildcat*
  Firebrands of Arizona*
  Zorro's Black Whip*
  The Big Bonanza*
1945—The Topeka Terror*
  Great Stagecoach Robbery*
  Manhunt of Mystery Island*
  Santa Fe Saddlemates*
  Federal Operator 99*
  Trail of Kit Carson*
  Phantom of the Plains
  Bandits of the Badlands
  Sunset in El Dorado*
  The Purple Monster Strikes*
  Colorado Pioneers*
  The Cherokee Flash
  Wagon Wheels Westward*
  Dakota*
1946—The Phantom Rider*
  Passkey to Danger
  Traffic in Crime*
  My Pal Trigger*
  Red River Renegades*
  Daughter of Don Q
  The Inner Circle
  The Crimson Ghost
  Santa Fe Uprising*
  Out California Way
  Stagecoach to Denver*
1947—Son of Zorro*
  Bells of San Angelo*
  Rustlers of Devil's Canyon*
  The Trespasser
  Wyoming*
  Jesse James Rides Again
  Marshal of Cripple Creek*
  Along the Oregon Trail*
  Exposed*
  On the Old Spanish Trail
1948—Slippy McGee*
  The Bold Frontiersman
  The Timber Trail
  Son of God's Country
  Adv. of Frank and Jesse James*
  Renegades of Sonora*
1949—Wake of the Red Witch*
  The Fighting Kentuckian
1950—Sands of Iwo Jima*
1951—Heart of the Rockies
1952—Colorado Sundown
  Old Oklahoma Plains
  Toughest Man in Arizona*
1953—A Perilous Journey
  Can. Mounties Vs. Atomic Invaders*
  Solar Sky Raiders
1954—Trader Tom of the China Seas
1955—Panther Girl of the Kongo*
  The Road to Denver*
  The Vanishing American*
1956—Thunder Over Arizona*
  Accused of Murder*

Mary Gordon

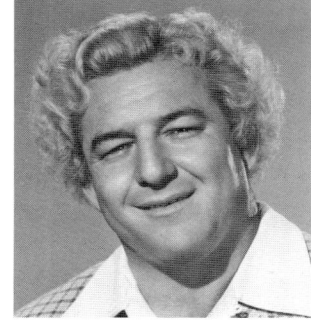
Roy Gordon

Gorgeous George

Roland Got

William Gould

Wilton Graff

Fred Graham

Alexander Granach

Graham, George
1957—Journey to Freedom

Graham, Richard
1943—In Old Oklahoma

Graley, Barbara
1957—Time is My Enemy

Granach, Alexander[209]
1941—A Man Betrayed
1942—Joan of Ozark
1944—My Buddy

Granby, Joseph
1950—Redwood Forest Trail
1951—Belle LeGrand*

Granger, Dorothy[209]
1938—A Desperate Adventure*
1939—Blue Montana Skies
1942—Pardon My Stripes
  In Old California*
  The Old Homestead*
1945—Sunset in El Dorado*
  Marshal of Laredo*
  Girls of the Big House*
1946—That Brennan Girl*
1948—Dangers of the Canadian Mounted
1950—Lonely Heart Bandits

Grant, Frances[209]
1936—Oregon Trail*
  Dancing Feet*
  Red River Valley
  Oh, Susanna!
  Cavalry
1943—Hands Across the Border*
1945—A Sporting Chance*
  Mexicana*

Grant, Harvey
1958—Juvenile Jungle

Grant, Kirby
1938—Red River Range
1944—Rosie, the Riveter*

Grant, Larry
1958—Man or Gun

Grant, Lawrence[209]
1936—The House of a Thousand Candles
1937—S O S Coast Guard
1940—Women in War

Grant, Paul
1957—Beginning of the End

Grant, Stephen
1947—Angel and the Badman

Grapewin, Charley[209]
1939—Sabotage
1944—Atlantic City

Grasso, Giovanni
1952—The Flying Squadron

Graves, Diana
1952—Lady Possessed

Graves, Peter
1957—Beginning of the End

Graves, Ralph
1939—Street of Missing Men
  Three Texas Steers

Gray, Arnold
1935—The Spanish Cape Mystery
  Forced Landing

Gray, Billy
1946—Specter of the Rose
  Rendezvous with Annie*
1947—Driftwood*
  The Fabulous Texan*
1949—The Sponge Diver*
1950—Singing Guns

Gray, Coleen[209]
1955—The Twinkle in God's Eye

Gray, Gary[209]
1949—Streets of San Francisco

Gray, Jenifer
1938—Dick Tracy Returns*
1939—Woman Doctor*
  Frontier Pony Express*
  Wall Street Cowboy*
  The Arizona Kid*
1940—Drums of Fu Manchu*
  The Crooked Road*

Gray, Judy
1943—Alibi

Gray, Lorna
See Adrian Booth.

Gray, Roger
1936—Oh, Susanna!

Gray, Sally[209]
1942—Suicide Squadron

Gray, Vernon
1955—A Day to Remember

Green, Garard
1958—Strange Case of Dr. Manning

Green, Gertrude
1938—Down in "Arkansaw"

Green, Linda
1947—Wyoming

Sally Gray, Anton Walbrook

Dorothy Granger

Frances Grant

Lawrence Grant

Charley Grapewin

Coleen Gray

Gary Gray

Green, Duke [William][210]
Many films.
1938 — The Lone Ranger*
    The Fighting Devil Dogs*
    Dick Tracy Returns*
1939 — Man of Conquest*
1940 — Drums of Fu Manchu*
    Adventures of Red Ryder*
    King of the Royal Mounted*
    Mysterious Doctor Satan*
1941 — Saddlemates*
    Jungle Girl*
    King of the Texas Rangers*
1942 — Spy Smasher*
    Perils of Nyoka*
    King of the Mounties*
    Outlaws of Pine Ridge*
1943 — Daredevils of the West*
    Days of Old Cheyenne*
    Secret Service in Darkest Africa*
    The Masked Marvel
1944 — Captain America*
    Tucson Raiders*
    The Tiger Woman
    Haunted Harbor
    Zorro's Black Whip
1945 — Great Stagecoach Robbery*
    Manhunt of Mystery Island
    Bells of Rosarita*
    Federal Operator 99*
1947 — Robin Hood of Texas*
    The Black Widow*
1948 — G-Men Never Forget*
    Adv. of Frank and Jesse James*
1949 — The James Brothers of Missouri*
1950 — Bells of Coronado*
1953 — The Sun Shines Bright*
1958 — Juvenile Jungle*

Duke Green

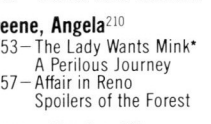

Angela Greene

Jaclynne Greene

Mary Murphy, Ron Hagerthy

"MAKE HASTE TO LIVE"

Greenaway, Mavis
1957 — Operation Conspiracy

Greenberg, Hank
1949 — The Kid from Cleveland

Greene, Angela[210]
1953 — The Lady Wants Mink*
    A Perilous Journey
1957 — Affair in Reno
    Spoilers of the Forest

Greene, Harrison[132]
1935 — Hitch Hike Lady*
1936 — Dancing Feet*
    Darkest Africa*
    The Singing Cowboy
    Guns and Guitars
    Hearts in Bondage*
    The Gentleman from Louisiana
    Down to the Sea*
    Country Gentlemen*
    The Old Corral*
1937 — Larceny on the Air*
    Dick Tracy
    Dangerous Holiday*
    It Could Happen to You*
    Range Defenders
1938 — Born to be Wild*
    Dick Tracy Returns*
1939 — Fighting Thoroughbreds*
    Woman Doctor*
    Street of Missing Men*
    S. O. S. Tidal Wave*
    New Frontier
    Dick Tracy's G-Men
    Days of Jesse James*
1940 — Heroes of the Saddle*
    Forgotten Girls*
    Wagons Westward*
    Scatterbrain*
    Melody and Moonlight*
    The Trail Blazers*
1941 — Arkansas Judge
    The Pittsburgh Kid*
    Bad Man of Deadwood*
    Tuxedo Junction*
    Mr. District Atty. in the Carter Case*
1942 — The Old Homestead*
    Ice-Capades Revue*
    The Traitor Within*
1943 — King of the Cowboys*
    Headin' for God's Country*
    Here Comes Elmer*
1944 — Man from Frisco*
    Atlantic City*
    Faces in the Fog*
    Thoroughbreds*

Phillip Pine, Reed Hadley, William Tannen

Greene, Jaclynne[210]
1955 — I Cover the Underworld

Greene, Joseph J.[210]
1945 — Behind City Lights

Greenleaf, Raymond[210]
1955 — Headline Hunters
1956 — When Gangland Strikes
1957 — Spoilers of the Forest*

Greenwood, Charlotte[78]
1947 — Driftwood

Greenwood, Eva
See Louisiana Lou.

Greer, Dabbs
1950 — Trial Without Jury*
    California Passage*
1957 — Pawnee

Gregg, Alan
1937 — S O S Coast Guard*
1938 — Hollywood Stadium Mystery!*
    The Fighting Devil Dogs
    Dick Tracy Returns
    Rhythm of the Saddle*
1939 — Dick Tracy's G-Men*
    Zorro's Fighting Legion*
1940 — Drums of Fu Manchu*
    King of the Royal Mounted*
    Mysterious Doctor Satan*
1941 — King of the Texas Rangers*

Gregg, Everley
1957 — Tears for Simon

Gregg, Hubert
1956 — Doctor at Sea

Gregg, Virginia[202]
1956 — Terror at Midnight

Gregory, Stephen
1949 — Radar Patrol Vs. Spy King

Gregson, John
1956 — Above Us the Waves

Greig, Robert[210]
1937 — Michael O'Halloran
1938 — Lady, Behave!
1945 — Earl Carroll Vanities
    The Cheaters
    Love, Honor and Goodbye

Grey, Corinne
1957 — Operation Conspiracy

Grey, Madeline[210]
1939 — The Covered Trailer*
1943 — Hit Parade of 1943*
    Thumbs Up*
    Someone to Remember
    Whispering Footsteps*
1944 — Casanova in Burlesque*
    That's My Baby
1945 — An Angel Comes to Brooklyn*

Grey, Virginia[118]
1938 — Ladies in Distress
1942 — Bells of Capistrano
    Secrets of the Underground
1943 — Idaho
1944 — Strangers in the Night
1945 — Grissly's Millions
    Flame of Barbary Coast
1947 — Wyoming
1951 — Bullfighter and the Lady
1953 — A Perilous Journey
1955 — The Eternal Sea
    The Last Command
1956 — Accused of Murder

Gribbon, Eddie[210]
1941 — Stars Past and Present*
1943 — Canyon City

Griffin, Robert E.
1957 — Pawnee
1958 — No Place to Land

Raymond Greenleaf

Joseph J. Greene

Robert Greig

Madeline Grey

Eddie Gribbon

Griffith, Edith M.
1946 — Affairs of Geraldine

Griffith, Helen
1947 — Jesse James Rides Again*
1949 — The James Brothers of Missouri*

Griffith, James[170]
1954 — The Shanghai Story
1955 — I Cover the Underworld

Griffith, Julia
1935 — Lawless Range
    Forced Landing

Griffith, Kay
1940 — Covered Wagon Days

Griffith, William H.
1937 — Larceny on the Air

Griffiths, Kenneth
1948 — Code of Scotland Yard
1955 — The Green Buddha
1956 — Track the Man Down

Grimes, Karolyn
1950 — Rio Grande
1951 — Honeychile

Gromek, Steve
1949 — The Kid from Cleveland

Grosskurth, Kurt
1956 — Magic Fire

Grueneberg, William
1950 — Trial Without Jury

Grundei, Fred
1955 — In Old Vienna

Grunning, Ilka
1946 — Murder in the Music Hall

Guadalajara Trio, The
1947 — That's My Gal

Guard, Kit
1937 — Dick Tracy*
    The Hit Parade*
    S O S Coast Guard*
1938 — Heroes of the Hills
1940 — Wagons Westward*
    The Carson City Kid*
    Bowery Boy*
1941 — A Man Betrayed*
    Doctors Don't Tell*
    The Pittsburgh Kid*
    Jesse James at Bay*
1944 — Haunted Harbor*
    My Buddy*
1945 — Girls of the Big House*

Gudrun, Ann
1954 — Trouble in the Glen
1955 — Doctor in the House

Guebhard, Mark
1955 — The Divided Heart

Guhl, George
1938 — Gold Mine in the Sky

Guilfoyle, Paul[211]
1935 — The Crime of Doctor Crespi
1939 — Sabotage
    Thou Shalt Not Kill

Guizar, Tito[78]
1944 — Brazil
1945 — Mexicana
1947 — On the Old Spanish Trail
1948 — The Gay Ranchero

Gulliver, Dorothy
1942 — A Tragedy at Midnight*
    The Traitor Within*

Gumley, Leonard
1950 — Sands of Iwo Jima

Gunnels, Chester[211]
1938 — Down in "Arkansaw"
    Come on, Rangers
    Shine on Harvest Moon
1940 — Village Barn Dance*
    In Old Missouri*
    Friendly Neighbors*
1941 — Arkansas Judge*

Paul Guilfoyle

Chester Gunnels

Sigrid Gurie

Anne Gwynne

Gurie, Sigrid[211]
1940 — Three Faces West

Guta, Raymond
1957 — The Unearthly

Guy, Eula
1946 — The Glass Alibi
1947 — Yankee Fakir
        The Pretender

Gwynne, Anne[211]
1946 — The Glass Alibi
1947 — The Ghost Goes Wild

Gynt, Greta
1943 — At Dawn We Die
1958 — Strange Case of Dr. Manning

Haade, William[113]
1937 — Exiled to Shanghai*
1938 — Hollywood Stadium Mystery!
1939 — Sabotage*
1940 — Who Killed Aunt Maggie?
1941 — Robin Hood of the Pecos
        In Old Cheyenne
        Desert Bandit
        Kansas Cyclone
        Citadel of Crime
        Sailors on Leave
1942 — Man from Cheyenne
        Heart of the Rio Grande
        Shepherd of the Ozarks
        Heart of the Golden West
1943 — Daredevils of the West
        Days of Old Cheyenne
        Song of Texas
        A Scream in the Dark
1944 — The Yellow Rose of Texas
        Man from Frisco*
        Sheriff of Las Vegas
1945 — Phantom of the Plains
        Dakota*
1946 — A Guy Could Change
        Valley of the Zombies
        In Old Sacramento*
        My Pal Trigger
        Affairs of Geraldine
1947 — The Pilgrim Lady*
        The Magnificent Rogue*
        Exposed
        Under Colorado Skies
1948 — The Inside Story
1949 — The Wyoming Bandit
1950 — Rock Island Trail*
        Trial Without Jury
        The Old Frontier
1951 — Oh! Susanna
        Buckaroo Sheriff of Texas
        The Sea Hornet
1953 — San Antone*
        Red River Shore
1954 — The Untamed Heiress
        Jubilee Trail*
1955 — The Road to Denver*
1957 — Spoilers of the Forest*

Haas, Hugo[211]
1945 — Jealousy
        Dakota
1947 — Northwest Outpost
1949 — The Fighting Kentuckian

Hackett, Hal[211]
1948 — Campus Honeymoon

Hackett, Karl[211]
1936 — Down to the Sea
        Cavalry
        Happy Go Lucky
        Border Phantom
1937 — Trail of Vengeance
        Gun Lords of Stirrup Basin
        Rootin' Tootin' Rhythm*
        The Red Rope
        The Arizona Gunfighter
        The Colorado Kid
1938 — Paroled-to Die
        The Feud Maker
        Durango Valley Raiders
        Down in "Arkansaw"
1940 — Colorado*
        The Border Legion*
1941 — Lady from Louisiana*
        Bad Man of Deadwood*
        Outlaws of Cherokee Trail*
        Death Valley Outlaws
        Jesse James at Bay*
        A Missouri Outlaw*
1942 — Jesse James, Jr.
        In Old California*
        Sons of the Pioneers*
        Sunset Serenade*
1943 — Thundering Trails
        Idaho*
        Fugitive from Sonora*
        Bordertown Gun Fighters
        California Joe
1944 — Mojave Firebrand
        Tucson Raiders
        Code of the Prairie*
1947 — The Fabulous Texan*

Haddon, Harriette[69]
1944 — Lake Placid Serenade*
1945 — Earl Carroll Vanities*
        Bells of Rosarita*
        Federal Operator 99*
        The Cheaters*
        Hitchhike to Happiness*
        Man from Oklahoma*
        Tell It to a Star*
        Behind City Lights*
        Love, Honor and Goodbye*
        Sunset in El Dorado*
        The Purple Monster Strikes*
        Don't Fence Me In*
        Rough Riders of Cheyenne
        Girls of the Big House*
        An Angel Comes to Brooklyn*
        Mexicana*
        The Tiger Woman*
        Dakota*
1946 — A Guy Could Change*

Haddon, Pauline
1937 — Escape by Night*
1939 — My Wife's Relatives*
        Man of Conquest*

Hadley, Reed[210]
1938 — Hollywood Stadium Mystery!
        Orphans of the Street
1939 — Zorro's Fighting Legion
1941 — Adventures of Captain Marvel
1942 — Arizona Terrors
1947 — The Fabulous Texan
1951 — Insurance Investigator
        The Wild Blue Yonder*
1953 — Woman They Almost Lynched

Hagerthy, Ron[210]
1953 — City that Never Sleeps
1954 — Make Haste to Live
1957 — Eighteen and Anxious

Haggerty, Don[211]
1948 — Train to Alcatraz
        Angel in Exile*
1949 — King of the Rocket Men
        South of Rio
1950 — Sands of Iwo Jima*
        The Vanishing Westerner
        Vigilante Hideout
        Lonely Heart Bandits*
1951 — Spoilers of the Plains
        Fighting Coast Guard*
1952 — Hoodlum Empire*
1954 — Phantom Stallion
        Jubilee Trail*
        The Atomic Kid*
1955 — The Eternal Sea*
        I Cover the Underworld*
1957 — Spoilers of the Forest*
        The Crooked Circle
1958 — The Man Who Died Twice

Hagney, Frank
1936 — Ghost-Town Gold
        A Man Betrayed*
1937 — Escape by Night*
1938 — Army Girl*
        Dick Tracy Returns*
1940 — Dark Command*
        Melody Ranch*
1941 — Mr. District Attorney*
1942 — In Old California*
1943 — Calling Wild Bill Elliott*
1945 — Flame of Barbary Coast*
        Scotland Yard Investigator*
1953 — A Perilous Journey*
1955 — Timberjack*
        The Last Command*
        A Man Alone*

Hale, Jr., Alan[211]
1951 — Honeychile
1955 — A Man Alone
1957 — Affair in Reno

Hale, Jonathan[211]
1936 — Happy Go Lucky
1937 — Exiled to Shanghai
1938 — Gangs of New York
1939 — In Old Monterey
1940 — Melody and Moonlight
1941 — The Pittsburgh Kid
1943 — Nobody's Darling
1944 — My Buddy
        End of the Road
1945 — The Phantom Speaks
        Dakota
1946 — Gay Blades
1947 — The Ghost Goes Wild
1948 — King of the Gamblers
1949 — Rose of the Yukon
1950 — Federal Agent at Large
1951 — Insurance Investigator
        Rodeo King and the Senorita
1956 — Jaguar

Hale, Monte[152]
1944 — The Big Bonanza
1945 — The Topeka Terror*
        Steppin' in Society*
        Oregon Trail*
        Bandits of the Badlands
        The Purple Monster Strikes
        Rough Riders of Cheyenne
        Colorado Pioneers
1946 — The Phantom Rider
        California Gold Rush
        Home on the Range
        Sun Valley Cyclone
        Man from Rainbow Valley
        Out California Way
1947 — Last Frontier Uprising
        Along the Oregon Trail
        Under Colorado Skies
1948 — California Firebrand
        The Timber Trail
        Son of God's Country
        Sundown in Santa Fe*
1949 — Prince of the Plains
        Law of the Golden West
        Outcasts of the Trail
        South of Rio
        San Antone Ambush
        Ranger of Cherokee Strip
        Pioneer Marshal
1950 — The Vanishing Westerner
        The Old Frontier
        The Missourians
        Trail of Robin Hood

Hale, Richard
1953 — San Antone
1954 — Sea of Lost Ships

Hall, Archie
1938 — Overland Stage Raiders
        Rhythm of the Saddle
1941 — Two Gun Sheriff

Hall, Ben
1935 — Racing Luck
1938 — Riders of the Black Hills

Hall, Eddie
1944 — Thoroughbreds
1945 — Gangs of the Waterfront

Hall, Ellen[211]
1944 — Call of the Rockies

Hall, Fern[211]
1955 — City of Shadows
        Double Jeopardy
        No Man's Woman

Hall, Genee
1938 — Santa Fe Stampede

Hall, Henry
1936 — The Lawless Nineties*
        The Vigilantes Are Coming*
1937 — Rootin' Tootin' Rhythm*
        Yodelin' Kid from Pine Ridge
        The Trigger Trio*
1938 — Under Western Stars*
1940 — Wagons Westward*
1941 — Robin Hood of the Pecos
        The Great Train Robbery*
        King of the Texas Rangers*
1942 — The Old Homestead*
1943 — Riders of the Rio Grande*
1945 — Phantom of the Plains*

Hall, Jon[98]
        [as Charles Locher]
1936 — Winds of the Wasteland
        [as Jon Hall]
1958 — Hell Ship Mutiny

Hugo Haas

Hal Hackett

Karl Hackett

Don Haggerty

Alan Hale, Jr.

Jonathan Hale

Ellen Hall

Fern Hall

Lois Hall

Thurston Hall

John Halloran

Hall, Lois[212]
1949 — Daughter of the Jungle
  Duke of Chicago
1951 — Cuban Fireball*
  Secrets of Monte Carlo

Hall, Michael[174]
1952 — The Last Musketeer
  Black Hills Ambush

Hall, Porter
1940 — Dark Command
1941 — Variety Reel*

Hall, Thurston[212]
1939 — Jeepers Creepers
  Money to Burn
1940 — In Old Missouri
  Friendly Neighbors
1941 — Tuxedo Junction
1942 — Sleepytime Gal
  Shepherd of the Ozarks
  Call of the Canyon
1943 — Hoosier Holiday
  Here Comes Elmer
1944 — Goodnight Sweetheart
  Song of Nevada
1948 — King of the Gamblers
1950 — Belle of Old Mexico
  Federal Agent at Large
1951 — Belle LeGrand
1952 — Woman of the North Country*
  The Wac from Walla Walla
1957 — Affair in Reno

Hall, Virginia
1953 — Old Overland Trail

Hall, William[118]
1937 — Escape by Night
1939 — In Old Monterey
1947 — Web of Danger

Halligan, William
1940 — Earl of Puddlestone
1943 — The Black Hills Express

Halloran, John[212]
1947 — Angel and the Badman
1952 — Hoodlum Empire*
  Woman of the North Country*

Halls, Ethel May
1938 — I Stand Accused*
1939 — Man of Conquest*
  Mickey, the Kid*
  Thou Shalt Not Kill
1940 — Heroes of the Saddle
  Forgotten Girls*
1941 — Outlaws of Cherokee Trail*
1943 — A Scream in the Dark*
1944 — Three Little Sisters*
1947 — The Fabulous Texan*
1948 — Old Los Angeles*

Halton, Charles[212]
1938 — Federal Man-Hunt
1940 — Gangs of Chicago
  Behind the News
1941 — Mr. District Attorney
1942 — In Old California
1943 — Whispering Footsteps
1947 — The Ghost Goes Wild
1949 — Hideout

Hamblen, Stuart[78]
1939 — In Old Monterey
  The Arizona Kid
1942 — The Sombrero Kid
1943 — Carson City Cyclone
  King of the Cowboys*
1945 — Flame of Barbary Coast*
1946 — King of the Forest Rangers
  Plainsman and the Lady
1950 — The Savage Horde

Hambling, Arthur
1943 — The Saint Meets the Tiger

Hamilton, Charles
1946 — Valley of the Zombies

Hamilton, Donna
1950 — Gunmen of Abilene

Hamilton, Fred[26]
1936 — Beware of Ladies*
1937 — Dick Tracy

Hamilton, Jane
1940 — Chinese Garden Festival*

Hamilton, J. Frank
1943 — Shantytown
  Headin' for God's Country

Hamilton, John[113]
1936 — A Man Betrayed
1937 — Two Wise Maids
  It Could Happen to You
1938 — I Stand Accused
1939 — Forged Passport
1940 — Meet the Missus*
1943 — G-Men Vs. The Black Dragon*
  Daredevils of the West
1944 — Captain America
  Goodnight Sweetheart*
  Man from Frisco*
  The Girl Who Dared
  The Port of Forty Thieves
  Zorro's Black Whip
  Lake Placid Serenade*
  Sheriff of Las Vegas
1945 — The Great Flamarion*
1946 — The Phantom Rider
  The Madonna's Secret
  Home on the Range
  One Exciting Week*
1947 — That's My Gal
  The Fabulous Texan*
  Bandits of Dark Canyon
1948 — The Gallant Legion*
  Desperadoes of Dodge City
1949 — Sheriff of Wichita
  Law of the Golden West
  The Wyoming Bandit
  Bandit King of Texas
  The James Brothers of Missouri
  Alias the Champ
  Pioneer Marshal
1950 — Bells of Coronado
  The Invisible Monster*
  The Missourians
1951 — Belle LeGrand*
  Night Riders of Montana*
  Million Dollar Pursuit
1953 — Marshal of Cedar Rock
  Iron Mountain Trail
  El Paso Stampede*
1958 — Outcasts of the City

Hamilton, Margaret[98]
1939 — Main Street Lawyer
1941 — The Gay Vagabond
1947 — Driftwood
1949 — The Red Pony

Hamilton, Neil[78]
1937 — Portia on Trial
1938 — Lady, Behave!
  Hollywood Stadium Mystery!
  Army Girl
1941 — King of the Texas Rangers
1942 — X Marks the Spot
  Secrets of the Underground

Charles Halton

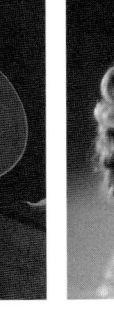

Ralf Harolde

Hamlin, Walter
1958 — Street of Darkness

Hammer, Alvin
1946 — The Fabulous Suzanne
1947 — Winter Wonderland

Hammond, Reid
1956 — Scandal Incorporated

Hampton, Louise
1943 — The Saint Meets the Tiger

Handl, Irene
1948 — Code of Scotland Yard

Hanlon, Bert
1946 — Specter of the Rose

Hanna, Mark
1952 — Border Saddlemates

Harbord, Carl
1943 — London Blackout Murders

Harden, Jack
1952 — Zombies of the Stratosphere

Hardie, Russell[212]
1936 — The Harvester
  Down to the Sea

Harding, John
1958 — Outcasts of the City

Hardy, Oliver[98]
1949 — The Fighting Kentuckian

Hare, Lumsden
1943 — London Blackout Murders

Hare, Marilyn[27]
1941 — Angels with Broken Wings
  Ice-Capades*
1942 — Lady for a Night
  Pardon My Stripes*
  A Tragedy at Midnight*
  Yokel Boy
  Shepherd of the Ozarks
  Hi, Neighbor
  Youth on Parade*
  Ice-Capades Revue
1957 — Eighteen and Anxious*

Russell Hardie

Otis Harlan

John Harmon

Arlene Harris

Harell, Marte
1957 — The Congress Dances

Harlan, Kenneth[212]
1935 — Cappy Ricks Returns
1937 — Gunsmoke Ranch
1938 — Under Western Stars
1939 — Dick Tracy's G-Men
1940 — Mysterious Doctor Satan*
1941 — Dick Tracy Vs. Crime, Inc.
1942 — Sleepytime Gal*
  The Sundown Kid*
1943 — G-Men Vs. The Black Dragon*
  Daredevils of the West
  The Masked Marvel

Harlan, Otis[212]
1935 — Hitch Hike Lady
1938 — Outlaws of Sonora

Harmer, Lillian
1936 — Dancing Feet

Harmon, John[212]
1939 — I Was a Convict
1940 — Gangs of Chicago
  Bowery Boy*
1941 — The Pittsburgh Kid
1942 — Call of the Canyon
1944 — Silent Partner
1949 — Streets of San Francisco
  Alias the Champ
1950 — Destination Big House

Harmon, Marie[212]
1946 — The El Paso Kid
  The Last Crooked Mile*
1948 — Night Time in Nevada

Harolde, Ralf[212]
1935 — Forced Landing
1936 — A Man Betrayed
1941 — Ridin' on a Rainbow
  Rags to Riches
  Bad Man of Deadwood
1943 — Secret Service in Darkest Africa
1944 — Captain America*
1945 — The Phantom Speaks

Harrigan, William
1937 — Exiled to Shanghai
1954 — Roogie's Bump

Kenneth Harlan

Marie Harmon

John Hartley

Harrington, James
1949 — The Red Menace

Harris, Arlene[212]
1943 — Here Comes Elmer
1945 — Hitchhike to Happiness
1946 — One Exciting Week
1948 — The Main Street Kid

Harris, Edna
1942 — X Marks the Spot

Harris, Phil[98]
1951 — The Wild Blue Yonder

Harris, Sibyl
1938 — Federal Man-Hunt

Harris, Winifred
1939 — Money to Burn

Harrison, Dorothy
1940 — Barnyard Follies

Harrison, Kathleen
1948 — Code of Scotland Yard

Hart, Eddie
1938 — Call the Mesquiteers
  Rhythm of the Saddle

Hart, Gordon
1938 — Overland Stage Raiders
1939 — Home on the Prairie
  Rovin' Tumbleweeds

Hart, John
1950 — Hit Parade of 1951*
1951 — Belle LeGrand*
  The Wild Blue Yonder*

Hart, Mary
See Lynne Roberts.

Hartley, John[212]
1940 — Grand Ole Opry
  Friendly Neighbors

Hartmann, Georg
1955 — In Old Vienna

Hartnell, William
1958 — Scotland Yard Dragnet

Harvey, Don
1950 — Gunmen of Abilene
1951 — Night Riders of Montana
1957 — Beginning of the End

Harvey, Forrester
1940 — Earl of Puddlestone
1941 — Mercy Island
1944 — Secrets of Scotland Yard
1945 — Scotland Yard Investigator

Harvey, Jr., Harry
1938 — Billy the Kid Returns*
1939 — Pride of the Navy*
1941 — Angels with Broken Wings*
1955 — The Eternal Sea*

Harvey, Sr., Harry[133]
1936 — Oregon Trail
    Ticket to Paradise*
    The Gentleman from Louisiana*
    The President's Mystery*
    Ghost-Town Gold*
    Country Gentlemen
1938 — Born to be Wild*
    Prison Nurse*
    Man from Music Mountain*
1939 — Street of Missing Men*
1941 — Bad Man of Deadwood
1948 — Train to Alcatraz
1949 — Death Valley Gunfighter
1950 — Unmasked
1951 — Silver City Bonanza
    Rodeo King and the Senorita
    Arizona Manhunt
1952 — Colorado Sundown*
    Thunderbirds*
1953 — Old Overland Trail
    Bandits of the West
1954 — Man with the Steel Whip*
1955 — The Twinkle in God's Eye*

Harvey, Jean
1951 — Insurance Investigator*
1955 — King of the Carnival*

Harvey, Paul[133]
1938 — The Higgins Family
1940 — Behind the News
1941 — Puddin' Head
    Mr. District Atty. in the Carter Case
1942 — A Tragedy at Midnight
    Moonlight Masquerade
    Heart of the Golden West
1943 — Man from Music Mountain
    Mystery Broadcast
1944 — Jamboree
    Thoroughbreds
1945 — The Chicago Kid
    Swingin' on a Rainbow
    Don't Fence Me In
1946 — Gay Blades
    Heldorado
    That Brennan Girl*
1947 — Wyoming
1948 — Lightnin' in the Forest
1949 — Duke of Chicago
1950 — Unmasked
1951 — Thunder in God's Country

Hasse, O. E.
1956 — Above Us the Waves

Hasson, Jamiel
1937 — The Sheik Steps Out

Hatton, Raymond[79]
1936 — Laughing Irish Eyes
    Undersea Kingdom
    The Vigilantes Are Coming
1938 — Come on, Rangers
1939 — Rough Riders' Round-Up
    Frontier Pony Express
    Wyoming Outlaw
    New Frontier
    Wall Street Cowboy
    The Kansas Terrors
    Cowboys from Texas
1940 — Heroes of the Saddle
    Pioneers of the West
    Hi-Yo-Silver*
    Covered Wagon Days
    Rocky Mountain Rangers
    Oklahoma Renegades
1942 — The Girl from Alaska
1955 — The Twinkle in God's Eye
1957 — Pawnee

Hatton, Rondo[213]
1942 — The Cyclone Kid*
1943 — Sleepy Lagoon*

Hauser, Gilgi
1955 — The Divided Heart

Hauser, Philo
1955 — The Divided Heart

Havoc, June[98]
1944 — Casanova in Burlesque
1952 — Lady Possessed

Hawkins, Jimmy
1949 — The Red Menace
1953 — Savage Frontier

Hawkins, Patricia
1950 — Women from Headquarters*

Hawks, Michael[213]
1946 — The Madonna's Secret

Hay, George Dewey
1940 — Grand Ole Opry
1943 — Hoosier Holiday

Hayden, Barbara
1953 — A Perilous Journey

Hayden, Harry
1939 — Flight at Midnight
1941 — A Man Betrayed
    Mountain Moonlight
1942 — Joan of Ozark
1948 — Out of the Storm
1951 — Street Bandits

Hayden, Russ[213]
1948 — Sons of Adventure

Hayden, Sterling[79]
1954 — Johnny Guitar
1955 — Timberjack
    The Eternal Sea
    The Last Command

Hayes, Allison[213]
1955 — Double Jeopardy
1957 — The Unearthly

Hayes, Bernadene[213]
1938 — Prison Nurse
1941 — The Gay Vagabond

Hayes, George "Gabby"[79]
1935 — Tumbling Tumbleweeds
    $1000 a Minute
    Hitch Hike Lady
1936 — The Lawless Nineties
    Hearts in Bondage
1939 — Fighting Thoroughbreds
    Man of Conquest
    Southward, Ho!
    In Old Caliente
    In Old Monterey
    Wall Street Cowboy
    The Arizona Kid
    Saga of Death Valley
    Days of Jesse James
1940 — Young Buffalo Bill
    Dark Command
    Wagons Westward
    The Carson City Kid
    The Ranger and the Lady
    Colorado
    Young Bill Hickok
    Melody Ranch
    The Border Legion
1941 — Robin Hood of the Pecos
    Variety Reel*
    In Old Cheyenne
    Sheriff of Tombstone
    Nevada City
    Meet Roy Rogers*
    Stars Past and Present*
    Bad Man of Deadwood
    Jesse James at Bay
    Red River Valley
1942 — Man from Cheyenne
    South of Santa Fe
    Sunset on the Desert
    Romance on the Range
    Sons of the Pioneers
    Sunset Serenade
    Heart of the Golden West
    Ridin' Down the Canyon
1943 — Calling Wild Bill Elliott
    The Man from Thunder River
    Bordertown Gun Fighters
    Wagon Tracks West
    Death Valley Manhunt
    Overland Mail Robbery
    In Old Oklahoma
1944 — Mojave Firebrand
    Hidden Valley Outlaws
    Tucson Raiders
    Marshal of Reno
    Lights of Old Santa Fe
    The Big Bonanza
1945 — Utah
    Bells of Rosarita
    Man from Oklahoma
    Sunset in El Dorado
    Don't Fence Me In
    Along the Navajo Trail
1946 — Song of Arizona
    Rainbow Over Texas
    My Pal Trigger
    Under Nevada Skies
    Roll on Texas Moon
    Home in Oklahoma
    Heldorado
1947 — Wyoming

Hayes, Ira H.
1950 — Sands of Iwo Jima

Hayes, Lind
1938 — Outside of Paradise

Rondo Hatton

Michael Hawks

Allison Hayes

Bernadene Hayes

Linda Hayes

Hayes, Linda[213]
1941 — Citadel of Crime
1942 — South of Santa Fe
    Romance on the Range
    Ridin' Down the Canyon

Hayes, Lorraine[213]
1937 — Doomed at Sundown

Hayes, Maggie
1958 — Girl in the Woods

Haynes, Patricia
1957 — Operation Conspiracy

Haynes, Roberta
1958 — Hell Ship Mutiny

Hays, Barry
1938 — Heroes of the Hills

Hayter, James
1955 — A Day to Remember

Hayter, John
1957 — Operation Conspiracy

Hayward, Chuck
Many films.
1950 — Desperadoes of the West*
1954 — Man with the Steel Whip*

Hayward, Louis[99]
1950 — House by the River

Hayward, Susan[118]
1941 — Sis Hopkins
1943 — Hit Parade of 1943
1944 — The Fighting Seabees

Haywood, Billie
1945 — An Angel Comes to Brooklyn

Hayworth, Rita[93]
    [as Rita Cansino]
1937 — Hit the Saddle
    [as Rita Hayworth]
1940 — Chinese Garden Festival*
1941 — Stars at Play*

Hazard, Jayne[213]
1941 — Wampas Baby Stars*
1942 — A Tragedy at Midnight*
    Shepherd of the Ozarks*
    Westward Ho*
1946 — Gay Blades*
    Affairs of Geraldine*
1948 — Daredevils of the Clouds

Healey, Myron[213]
1946 — That Brennan Girl*
1948 — I, Jane Doe*
1949 — Wake of the Red Witch*
    The Wyoming Bandit*
    South of Rio
    Pioneer Marshal
1950 — Salt Lake Raiders
1951 — Night Riders of Montana
    The Wild Blue Yonder*
1952 — Desperadoes' Outpost
1955 — Panther Girl of the Kongo
    African Manhunt
1957 — Hell's Crossroads
    The Unearthly

Healy, Bill[213]
1943 — The Masked Marvel

Healy, Eunice
1936 — Follow Your Heart

Healy, Mary
1940 — Chinese Garden Festival*

Heard, Charles
1956 — Hidden Guns

Hearn, Edward[213]
1935 — Tumbling Tumbleweeds
1936 — The Lawless Nineties*
    The Leathernecks Have Landed*
    Red River Valley
    King of the Pecos
    Navy Born*
    The Big Show*
1937 — Springtime in the Rockies
1938 — I Stand Accused*
1939 — I Was a Convict*
    Man of Conquest*
    Dick Tracy's G-Men*
    Cowboys from Texas*
1940 — Wolf of New York*
    Dark Command*
    Covered Wagon Days*
    Gangs of Chicago*
    Adventures of Red Ryder*
1941 — Mr. District Attorney*
    Tuxedo Junction*
    Dick Tracy Vs. Crime, Inc.*

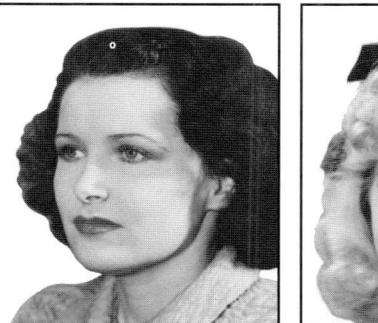
Lorraine Hayes

Jayne Hazard

Myron Healey

Bill Healy

Edward Hearn

Hearn, Lou
1946 — Specter of the Rose

Hearn, Reginald
1957 — Thunder Over Tangier

Heath, Ariel[214]
1943 — The Black Hills Express

Heathcote, Thomas
1956 — Doctor at Sea
     Above Us the Waves

Hecht, Ted[214]
1944 — End of the Road
1945 — Three's a Crowd
1947 — Spoilers of the North

Hecker, Norbert
1954 — Crazylegs

Hedloe, John
1951 — Missing Women

Hegan, Jim
1949 — The Kid from Cleveland

Heigh, Helene
1946 — The Undercover Woman

Heller, John G.
1957 — Operation Conspiracy

Helm, Fay
1946 — That Brennan Girl

Helton, Percy[214]
1950 — Harbor of Missing Men
     Under Mexicali Stars
1952 — I Dream of Jeanie
1953 — Down Laredo Way
1954 — Geraldine*
1955 — No Man's Woman
1956 — Terror at Midnight

Henderson, A. C.
1937 — The Arizona Gunfighter

Henderson, Dell
1935 — Hitch Hike Lady

Henderson, Douglas
1958 — No Place to Land

Henderson, Marcia[214]
1957 — The Wayward Girl

Hendricks, Jr., Ben
1938 — Born to be Wild

Hendricks, Sr., Ben
1936 — Oregon Trail

Hendriks, Jan
1956 — Magic Fire

Hendrix, Wanda[214]
1954 — Sea of Lost Ships

Henning, Pat
1938 — Shine on Harvest Moon

Henreid, Paul[99]
1956 — A Woman's Devotion

Henry, Charlotte[79]
1935 — Forbidden Heaven
1936 — The Return of Jimmy Valentine
     Hearts in Bondage
     The Gentleman from Louisiana
     The Mandarin Mystery

Henry, Dee "Buzzy"[214]
1942 — Ridin' Down the Canyon
1943 — Calling Wild Bill Elliott
     Chatterbox*
1948 — Moonrise*
1951 — Heart of the Rockies
1954 — Jubilee Trail*
     The Outcast
     Hell's Outpost*
1955 — The Road to Denver
     The Last Command*
1956 — Dakota Incident*
1957 — Duel at Apache Wells*
     The Lawless Eighties

Henry, Louise[214]
1937 — The Hit Parade

Henry, Thomas Browne[214]
1949 — Flaming Fury*
     Post Office Investigator
1951 — Belle LeGrand*
1952 — Hoodlum Empire*
1953 — The Lady Wants Mink
1954 — Flight Nurse*
1955 — A Man Alone
1956 — A Strange Adventure
1957 — Beginning of the End

Henry, William[27]
1938 — Mama Runs Wild
1942 — Pardon My Stripes
     Stardust on the Sage
1943 — False Faces
1944 — The Lady and the Monster
     Silent Partner
     Call of the South Seas
1946 — G. I. War Brides
     The Invisible Informer
     The Mysterious Mr. Valentine
     The Fabulous Suzanne
1947 — Trail to San Antone
1948 — King of the Gamblers
     The Denver Kid
1949 — Death Valley Gunfighter
     Streets of San Francisco
1950 — The Old Frontier
1952 — Thundering Caravans
1953 — Marshal of Cedar Rock
     Savage Frontier
     War of the Space Giants
     Can. Mounties Vs. Atomic Invaders
     S. O. S. Ice Age
1956 — Accused of Murder*

Henville, Sandra
1942 — Johnny Doughboy

Hepburn, Barton
1945 — A Song for Miss Julie

Heppner, Cynthia
1942 — Suicide Squadron

Herbert, Dorothy
1940 — Mysterious Doctor Satan

Herbert, Harry
1955 — The Square Ring

Herbert, Holmes
1936 — The Gentleman from Louisiana
1945 — Swingin' on a Rainbow*
1947 — The Ghost Goes Wild
1949 — Post Office Investigator

Herbert, Hugh[214]
1940 — Hit Parade of 1941
1951 — Havana Rose

Herbert, Tom
1945 — Steppin' in Society

Herman, Al
1940 — Oklahoma Renegades

Herman, Gil
1950 — Women from Headquarters
1953 — Old Overland Trail

Herman, Woody[215]**—and orchestra**
1945 — Earl Carroll Vanities
1947 — Hit Parade of 1947

Herman's Mountaineers
1937 — Heart of the Rockies

Hern, Pepe
1951 — Heart of the Rockies
1952 — Thunderbirds
1954 — Make Haste to Live
1956 — Jaguar

Hernandez, Joe
1947 — That's My Man

Herrera Sisters, The
1941 — Down Mexico Way

Herrick, F. Herrick
1936 — Ghost-Town Gold

Herbert Heyes, Fred Kohler, Jr., Cliff Parkinson

Thomas Browne Henry

Hugh Herbert

Herrick, Virginia
1950 — Vigilante Hideout

Hertner, Walter
1943 — At Dawn We Die

Hervey, Irene[215]
1940 — The Crooked Road

Heugly, Archie
1950 — Macbeth

Hewlett, Bentley
1938 — Born to be Wild
     Western Jamboree

Heyburn, Weldon[215]
1937 — Git Along Little Dogies
     Jim Hanvey - Detective*
     Sea Racketeers
1940 — The Trail Blazers
1942 — Code of the Outlaw
1943 — Death Valley Manhunt
     Overland Mail Robbery
1944 — My Best Gal*
     The Yellow Rose of Texas
     Man from Frisco*
     Bordertown Trail
     Code of the Prairie

Heydt, Louis Jean[215]
1944 — Army 102 — Trench Foot*
1946 — That Brennan Girl*
1947 — Spoilers of the North
1949 — The Kid from Cleveland
1955 — The Eternal Sea
     No Man's Woman
1956 — Stranger at My Door
1957 — Raiders of Old California
1958 — The Man Who Died Twice

Heyes, Herbert[214]
1943 — The Purple V*
     King of the Cowboys*
     Calling Wild Bill Elliott
     Chatterbox*
     Death Valley Manhunt
     Here Comes Elmer*
1944 — The Fighting Seabees*
     Outlaws of Santa Fe

Heywood, Herbert
1936 — King of the Pecos

Hickman, Cordell
1941 — West of Cimarron
1944 — The Big Bonanza

Hickman, Darryl
1954 — Sea of Lost Ships

Hickman, Howard[133]
1936 — Happy Go Lucky
1937 — Join the Marines
     Jim Hanvey - Detective
1938 — King of the Newsboys*
     Come on, Leathernecks
     I Stand Accused
1939 — The Kansas Terrors
1940 — Dark Command*
     Gangs of Chicago
     Bowery Boy
1941 — Robin Hood of the Pecos*
     Lady from Louisiana*
     Angels with Broken Wings*
     Hurricane Smith
     Ice-Capades*
     Doctors Don't Tell
     Tuxedo Junction
     Dick Tracy Vs. Crime, Inc.
1942 — Lady for a Night*
     Bells of Capistrano*
1943 — The Masked Marvel
1944 — Captain America*
     Casanova in Burlesque*

Hicks, Chuck
1958 — Gunfire at Indian Gap

Hicks, Russell[133]
1935 — $1000 a Minute
1936 — Laughing Irish Eyes
     Ticket to Paradise
     Hearts in Bondage
1939 — I Was a Convict
     Man of Conquest*
1941 — Arkansas Judge
     A Man Betrayed
     Doctors Don't Tell
     The Pittsburgh Kid*
     Public Enemies
1942 — King of the Mounties
1943 — King of the Cowboys
     Someone to Remember
1944 — Captain America
     The Port of Forty Thieves
1945 — Flame of Barbary Coast
1946 — Gay Blades
     G. I. War Brides
     Earl Carroll Sketchbook*
     Plainsman and the Lady
1947 — The Pilgrim Lady
     Web of Danger
     Exposed
     The Fabulous Texan*
1948 — The Gallant Legion
     The Plunderers
1950 — Unmasked
1951 — Belle LeGrand*
1952 — Old Oklahoma Plains

Hickson, Joan
1955 — Doctor in the House
1956 — Doctor at Sea

Ariel Heath

Ted Hecht

Percy Helton

Marcia Henderson

Wanda Hendrix

Dee "Buzzy" Henry

Louise Henry

Phillips Holmes, Mae Clarke

Woody Herman

Hiess, Henriette
1955 — In Old Vienna

Hiestand, John
1942 — King of the Mounties

Higgins family — series
1938 — The Higgins Family
1939 — My Wife's Relatives
 Should Husbands Work?
 The Covered Trailer
 Money to Burn
1940 — Grandpa Goes to Town
 Earl of Puddlestone
 Meet the Missus
1941 — Petticoat Politics

Hildebrand, Rodney
1936 — The Lonely Trail

Hill, Arthur
1955 — A Day to Remember

Hill, Carmen
1957 — Operation Conspiracy

Hill, Ramsey
1954 — Trader Tom of the China Seas
1955 — Panther Girl of the Kongo

Hill, Riley
1945 — Sheriff of Cimarron
1953 — Captives of the Zero Hour

Hillard, Ruth
1944 — Trocadero

Hilliard, Ernest
1935 — Racing Luck
1936 — Go-Get-'Em, Haines

Hillias, Peg
1957 — The Wayward Girl

Hillman, June
1945 — A Song for Miss Julie

Hines, Alf
1955 — The Square Ring

Hinton, Ed
1952 — Leadville Gunslinger

Hird, Thora
1955 — A Day to Remember
1957 — Tears for Simon

Hirsch, Elroy "Crazylegs"
1954 — Crazylegs

Hirsch, Win
1954 — Crazylegs

Hit Parade — series
1937 — The Hit Parade
1940 — Hit Parade of 1941
1943 — Hit Parade of 1943
1947 — Hit Parade of 1947
1950 — Hit Parade of 1951

Hitchcock, Keith
1940 — Earl of Puddlestone*
1943 — London Blackout Murders
1944 — Secrets of Scotland Yard*
1945 — The Fatal Witness*
1951 — Belle LeGrand*

Hobart, Rose[215]
1940 — Wolf of New York
 Chinese Garden Festival*

Hobbes, Halliwell[215]
1938 — Storm Over Bengal

Hodgins, Earle[133]
1936 — The Singing Cowboy
 Guns and Guitars
 Ticket to Paradise*
 The Gentlemen from Louisiana*
 Oh, Susanna!
 Ghost-Town Gold*
1937 — Round-Up Time in Texas
 Trail of Vengeance
 A Lawman is Born
 Range Defenders
 All Over Town
1938 — The Purple Vigilantes
 The Old Barn Dance
 Call the Mesquiteers
 Under Western Stars*
1939 — Home on the Prairie
 Daredevils of the Red Circle*
1940 — Under Texas Skies
 Friendly Neighbors*
1941 — Sunset in Wyoming*
 Sailors on Leave*
 Sierra Sue
1942 — Call of the Canyon*
1943 — Idaho*
 The Blocked Trail*
 King of the Cowboys*
 Chatterbox*
 Thumbs Up*
 The Man from the Rio Grande*
 Here Comes Elmer*
1944 — Hidden Valley Outlaws
 Sing Neighbor Sing*
 The San Antonio Kid
 Firebrands of Arizona
1945 — The Topeka Terror
 Bells of Rosarita*
 Oregon Trail
 Phantom of the Plains*
 Behind City Lights*
 Love, Honor and Goodbye*
1946 — Crime of the Century
 Valley of the Zombies
 Traffic in Crime*
 My Pal Trigger*
 The Last Crooked Mile*
 That Brennan Girl*
1947 — Calendar Girl*
 Vigilantes of Boomtown
 Oregon Trail Scouts
1948 — The Main Street Kid
 Oklahoma Badlands
 Old Los Angeles
1949 — Sheriff of Wichita
1950 — The Savage Horde

Hodgson, Leland
1936 — The Girl from Mandalay*
1940 — Gangs of Chicago*
1941 — Adventures of Captain Marvel
1946 — Under Nevada Skies

Hoey, Dennis[215]
1946 — Roll on Texas Moon
1949 — Wake of the Red Witch

Hoff, Carl[215] — and the
Hit Parade Orchestra
1937 — The Hit Parade

Hoffman, Gertrude
1936 — The Gentleman from Louisiana

Hoffman, Jr., Max
1936 — The President's Mystery*
 The Old Corral*
1937 — Rootin' Tootin' Rhythm
1938 — The Night Hawk*
1939 — She Married a Cop*

Hoffman, Otto
1937 — All Over Town

Hogan, Brenda
1957 — Time is My Enemy

Hogan, Dick[118]
1940 — Rancho Grande

Hogan, Pat
1954 — Man with the Steel Whip

Hogg, Charles
1938 — Orphans of the Street*
 Shine on Harvest Moon*

Hohl, Arthur
1943 — Idaho

Hokanson, Mary Alan
1951 — Belle LeGrand*
 Missing Women

Holden, James[215]
1950 — Sands of Iwo Jima
1954 — Flight Nurse

Holden, William
1941 — Variety Reel*

Holderness, Fay
1937 — Dangerous Holiday*
 Youth on Parole*

Rose Hobart

Dennis Hoey

James Holden

Irene Hervey

Holdren, Judd[215]
1950 — Lonely Heart Bandits*
 Frisco Tornado*
1952 — Zombies of the Stratosphere
1953 — Enemies of the Universe
 Atomic Peril
 Cosmic Vengeance
 Nightmare Typhoon
 War of the Space Giants
 Destroyers of the Sun
 Robot Monster from Mars
 The Hydrogen Hurricane
 Solar Sky Raiders
 S. O. S. Ice Age
 Lost in Outer Space
 Captives of the Zero Hour
1957 — Spoilers of the Forest*

Hole, William
1937 — Springtime in the Rockies

Holland, John[28]
1937 — Join the Marines
 Dick Tracy*
 Paradise Express
 Circus Girl
1941 — Pals of the Pecos
1942 — Yokel Boy*
 Call of the Canyon
1948 — King of the Gamblers
 Sons of Adventure
1949 — Law of the Golden West
1950 — Rock Island Trail
1951 — Belle LeGrand*
1954 — Jubilee Trail*

Halliwell Hobbes

Carl Hoff

Judd Holdren

Weldon Heyburn

Louis Jean Heydt

Holand, Zeke
1947 — Driftwood
 The Fabulous Texan*

Holles, Anthony
1937 — Glamorous Night
1943 — At Dawn We Die

Holloway, Stanley
1955 — A Day to Remember

Holloway, Sterling[79]
1935 — $1000 a Minute
1937 — Join the Marines
1940 — Hit Parade of 1941
1946 — Sioux City Sue
1947 — Trail to San Antone
 Twilight on the Rio Grande
 Saddle Pals
 Robin Hood of Texas

Hollywood, Jimmy
1938 — The Purple Vigilantes*
 The Lone Ranger*
1943 — O, My Darling Clementine*

Holman, Harry
1938 — Western Jamboree
1939 — I Was a Convict
1942 — Shadows on the Sage

Holmes, Maynard
1936 — The Leathernecks Have Landed
1942 — Remember Pearl Harbor!

Holmes, Phillips[215]
1936 — The House of a Thousand Candles

Holmes, Ralph
1936 — Undersea Kingdom

Holmes, Taylor[215]
1948 — The Plunderers
1952 — Hoodlum Empire
 Woman of the North Country
1953 — Ride the Man Down
1954 — The Untamed Heiress
 The Outcast
 Tobor the Great
 Hell's Outpost
1955 — The Fighting Chance
1956 — The Maverick Queen

Taylor Holmes

Holmes, Wendell
1958 — Young and Wild

Holmes, William
1951 — In Old Amarillo
Utah Wagon Train

Holt, David[216]
1945 — The Cheaters
1946 — Affairs of Geraldine

Holt, Jack[216]
1941 — Stars at Play*
1946 — My Pal Trigger
1947 — The Wild Frontier
1948 — The Gallant Legion
1949 — The Last Bandit
Brimstone
1950 — Trail of Robin Hood

Holt, Jennifer[216]
1943 — Raiders of Sunset Pass

Holt, Tim
1941 — Stars at Play*

Homans, Robert[133]
1936 — Laughing Irish Eyes
Ride Ranger Ride
The President's Mystery
A Man Betrayed*
1937 — Jim Hanvey - Detective
Exiled to Shanghai*
1938 — Outside of Paradise*
Hollywood Stadium Mystery!
Gold Mine in the Sky
The Night Hawk
1939 — Smuggled Cargo
Thou Shalt Not Kill*
1940 — Forgotten Girls*
Barnyard Follies
Behind the News*
Bowery Boy*
1941 — A Man Betrayed*
Puddin' Head*
Hurricane Smith*
Sierra Sue
Red River Valley
1942 — Yokel Boy*
In Old California*
The Sombrero Kid
X Marks the Spot
1943 — G-Men Vs. The Black Dragon
Shantytown
Nobody's Darling*
The Man from the Rio Grande*
1944 — Haunted Harbor
1945 — The Phantom Speaks*
1946 — Earl Carroll Sketchbook

Homeier, Skip[216]
1955 — The Road to Denver
1956 — Stranger at My Door
Dakota Incident
Thunder Over Arizona
1959 — Plunderers of Painted Flats

Homolka, Oscar[216]
1948 — Code of Scotland Yard

Hoosier Hot Shots
1939 — In Old Monterey
1943 — Hoosier Holiday

Hopper, DeWolfe[28]
1936 — Beware of Ladies*
1937 — Larceny on the Air
Join the Marines*

Hopper, Hedda[99]
1937 — Dangerous Holiday

Hopton, Russell
1935 — Frisco Waterfront
1936 — Beware of Ladies

Horne, Victoria
1945 — Love, Honor and Goodbye
1946 — In Old Sacramento
1951 — Cuban Fireball

Horsley, John
1956 — Above Us the Waves

Horton, Edward Everett[99]
1944 — Brazil
1945 — Steppin' in Society
1946 — Earl Carroll Sketchbook
1947 — The Ghost Goes Wild

Horton, Robert[216]
1956 — The Man is Armed

Horvath, Charles
1956 — Dakota Incident
1957 — Pawnee

Hot Shots, The
1943 — Thumbs Up

Houcke, Gilbert
1956 — Circus Girl

Hould, Ra[216]
1937 — Dangerous Holiday
Boots and Saddles

Houston, Donald
1955 — Doctor in the House

Houston, Renee
1956 — Jaguar

Hoven, Adrian
1956 — Circus Girl

Howard, Boothe
1936 — Red River Valley
Undersea Kingdom
Oh, Susanna!

Howard, Eddie
1955 — The Twinkle in God's Eye

Howard, Esther
1937 — Rhythm in the Clouds
1945 — The Great Flamarion
1949 — Hellfire

Howard, Frederick[217]
1944 — Cheyenne Wildcat*
Code of the Prairie*
1945 — Great Stagecoach Robbery*
Manhunt of Mystery Island*
Lone Texas Ranger*
The Vampire's Ghost*
A Sporting Chance*
Federal Operator 99*
Hitchhike to Happiness*
Sunset in El Dorado*
The Purple Monster Strikes
1946 — Crime of the Century
Passkey to Danger*
Daughter of Don Q*
The Last Crooked Mile*

Howard, Gordon
1958 — International Counterfeiters

Howard, Joan
1939 — Woman Doctor

Howard, John[217]
1942 — A Tragedy at Midnight
1948 — I, Jane Doe
1949 — The Fighting Kentuckian
1954 — Make Haste to Live

Howard, Lewis
1946 — I've Always Loved You

Howard, Mary[216]
1937 — All Over Town
1940 — Chinese Garden Festival*

Howard, Shemp[217]
1946 — One Exciting Week

Howe, Wally
1935 — Lawless Range

Robert Horton

Howell, Jean[217]
1957 — Hell's Crossroads

Howell, Ken
1951 — In Old Amarillo

Howells, Ursula
1956 — Track the Man Down
1957 — The Fighting Wildcats

Howes, Reed[217]
1937 — Zorro Rides Again
1938 — The Lone Ranger*
Born to be Wild*
The Fighting Devil Dogs
Dick Tracy Returns
Come on, Rangers*
1939 — Daredevils of the Red Circle*
Dick Tracy's G-Men*
Calling All Marines*
South of the Border*
Zorro's Fighting Legion*
1940 — Heroes of the Saddle
Covered Wagon Days
Adventures of Red Ryder*
Texas Terrors
Lone Star Raiders*
Bowery Boy*
1941 — Back in the Saddle*
Kansas Cyclone*
Sunset in Wyoming*
Death Valley Outlaws*
Down Mexico Way*
1943 — Thundering Trails
Carson City Cyclone*
King of the Cowboys*
Santa Fe Scouts*
Secret Service in Darkest Africa*
The Black Hills Express*
1950 — The Savage Horde*

Howland, Olin
See Olin Howlin.

Ra Hould

Howlin, Olin[134]
[as Olin Howland]
1936 — Country Gentlemen
1939 — Days of Jesse James
[as Olin Howlin]
1942 — Home in Wyomin'
Joan of Ozark*
Secrets of the Underground
Ridin' Down the Canyon
1944 — Goodnight Sweetheart
Man from Frisco
Sing Neighbor Sing
1945 — Grissly's Millions*
Sheriff of Cimarron
Santa Fe Saddlemates
Dakota
1947 — Angel and the Badman
Apache Rose
Wyoming*
The Fabulous Texan*
1949 — Hellfire*
1950 — Rock Island Trail
1951 — Fighting Coast Guard
1952 — The Fabulous Senorita
Gobs and Gals

Howlitt, Jeanne
1941 — Stars at Play*

Hoyos, Jr., Rodolfo
1955 — The Fighting Chance

Hoyt, Arthur[196]
1935 — $1000 a Minute
1937 — Join the Marines
Paradise Express
The Wrong Road
1939 — Should Husbands Work?

Hruba, Vera
See Vera Ralston.

Hubbard, John[79]
1940 — Who Killed Aunt Maggie?
1942 — Youth on Parade
Secrets of the Underground
1943 — Chatterbox
Whispering Footsteps
1944 — Cowboy and the Senorita
1951 — Bullfighter and the Lady

Hubbard, Tom[217]
1956 — Hidden Guns
1957 — Hell Canyon Outlaws
Raiders of Old California

Huber, Harold[217]
1938 — Gangs of New York
1939 — Main Street Lawyer
1941 — A Man Betrayed
Country Fair
Down Mexico Way
1942 — Pardon My Stripes
Sleepytime Gal
Ice-Capades Revue

Hudman, Wesley
1951 — Fort Dodge Stampede
1952 — Leadville Gunslinger
Black Hills Ambush

Hudson, Bill
1949 — The Red Menace*
1950 — Sands of Iwo Jima*
1954 — Trader Tom of the China Seas*
1955 — The Eternal Sea*

Hudson, John[217]
1954 — Sea of Lost Ships
1956 — When Gangland Strikes

Hudson, Rochelle[217]
1938 — Storm Over Bengal
1939 — Pride of the Navy
Smuggled Cargo

Hughes, Anthony
1938 — Ladies in Distress

Hughes, Carol[119]
1937 — Meet the Boy Friend
1938 — Under Western Stars
Gold Mine in the Sky
Man from Music Mountain
1940 — The Border Legion
1941 — Under Fiesta Stars
1946 — Home in Oklahoma

Mary Howard, Harry Stockwell

Eddie Dew, Jennifer Holt

David Holt

Jack Holt

Skip Homeier

Oscar Homolka

 Frederick Howard
 John Howard
 Shemp Howard
 Jean Howell
 Reed Howes

 Tom Hubbard
 Harold Huber 
 John Hudson
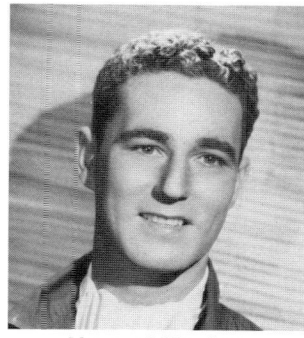 Rochelle Hudson
 Howard Hughes

Hughes, Howard[217]
1941 — Angels with Broken Wings*
Mountain Moonlight*
Sailors on Leave*
King of the Texas Rangers*
1942 — Pardon My Stripes*
Spy Smasher*

Hughes, Jackie
1941 — Stars at Play*

Hughes, Kay[28]
1936 — The Vigilantes Are Coming
The Three Mesquiteers
Ride Ranger Ride
Ghost-Town Gold
The Big Show
The Mandarin Mystery
A Man Betrayed
1937 — Dick Tracy

Hughes, Lloyd[217]
1936 — A Man Betrayed

Hughes, Mary Beth[79]
1939 — The Covered Trailer
1940 — Chinese Garden Festival*
1941 — Los Angeles Examiner Benefit*
1945 — The Great Flamarion

Hughes, Michael
1947 — The Ghost Goes Wild

Hughes, Robin
1951 — Secrets of Monte Carlo

Hughes, Whitey
1958 — No Place to Land

Hugo, Mauritz[217]
1943 — Santa Fe Scouts*
1944 — End of the Road*
1945 — Jealousy*
1947 — Homesteaders of Paradise Valley
1948 — Renegades of Sonora
1949 — Death Valley Gunfighter
Susanna Pass*
The Golden Stallion*
1950 — Women from Headquarters*
Desperadoes of the West*
Frisco Tornado
1951 — The Dakota Kid
Govt. Agents Vs. Phantom Legion
1952 — Captive of Billy the Kid
1953 — Lost in Outer Space
Captives of the Zero Hour
1954 — Man with the Steel Whip
1955 — King of the Carnival
1956 — Scandal Incorporated*

Hulett, Otto
1953 — City that Never Sleeps

Hull, Henry[99]
1943 — The West Side Kid
1944 — Goodnight Sweetheart

Hull Twins, The
1940 — Wagons Westward

Hull, Warren[99]
1937 — Michael O'Halloran
Rhythm in the Clouds
1940 — Ride, Tenderfoot, Ride

Humphrey, Harry
1939 — Dick Tracy's G-Men

Hunnicutt, Arthur[99]
1955 — The Last Command

Hunt, Eleanor[217]
1936 — Go-Get-'Em, Haines

Hunt, Jane
1937 — Springtime in the Rockies

Hunt, Jimmy
1950 — Rock Island Trail

Hunt, Marsha[100]
1938 — Come on, Leathernecks
1948 — The Inside Story

Hunter, Alistair
1957 — Time is My Enemy

Hunter, Ann
1940 — Chinese Garden Festival*

Huntley, Jr., G. P.
1937 — Michael O'Halloran

Huntley, Raymond
1956 — Doctor at Sea

Hurst, Paul[134]
1940 — Bowery Boy
1941 — Petticoat Politics
1942 — Pardon My Stripes
1945 — The Big Show-Off
Steppin' in Society
Dakota
1946 — Murder in the Music Hall
In Old Sacramento
Plainsman and the Lady
1947 — Angel and the Badman
Under Colorado Skies
1948 — Madonna of the Desert
California Firebrand
Heart of Virginia
Son of God's Country
1949 — Prince of the Plains
Law of the Golden West
Outcasts of the Trail
South of Rio
San Antone Ambush
Ranger of Cherokee Strip
Pioneer Marshal
1950 — The Vanishing Westerner
The Old Frontier
The Missourians
1951 — Million Dollar Pursuit
1952 — Toughest Man in Arizona
1953 — The Sun Shines Bright

Hussey, Ruth[100]
1948 — I, Jane Doe
1952 — Woman of the North Country
1953 — The Lady Wants Mink

Huston, Virginia[217]
1950 — Women from Headquarters

Hutchison, Charles
1940 — Adventures of Red Ryder

Hutton, Robert[217]
1952 — Gobs and Gals
Tropical Heat Wave
1956 — Scandal Incorporated
1957 — Thunder Over Tangier
1958 — Outcasts of the City

Hyams, John
1936 — Hearts in Bondage

Hyams, Leila[217]
1935 — $1000 a Minute

Hyatt, Bobby
1945 — Stagecoach to Denver
1952 — Toughest Man in Arizona

Hyde, Eva
1943 — The Purple V

Hyde-White, Wilfrid
1941 — Poison Pen*

Hyer, Martha[217]
1950 — Salt Lake Raiders
Frisco Tornado

Hylton, Jane
1955 — Secret Venture

Hymer, Warren[217]
1935 — Hitch Hike Lady
1936 — The Leavenworth Case
Laughing Irish Eyes
1937 — Join the Marines
Navy Blues
Meet the Boy Friend
Sea Racketeers
1938 — Lady, Behave!
Arson Gang Busters
1939 — Calling All Marines

Hytten, Olaf[217]
1935 — Two Sinners
The Spanish Cape Mystery
1936 — The House of a Thousand Candles
1937 — Dangerous Holiday
1939 — Man of Conquest*
1940 — Drums of Fu Manchu
Gaucho Serenade*
1942 — Affairs of Jimmy Valentine*
1943 — London Blackout Murders*
Hit Parade of 1943*
1945 — Scotland Yard Investigator*
1947 — The Ghost Goes Wild*
Bells of San Angelo

 Lloyd Hughes
 Mauritz Hugo
 Eleanor Hunt
 Virginia Huston

 Robert Hutton
 Leila Hyams
 Martha Hyer
 Warren Hymer 
 Olaf Hytten

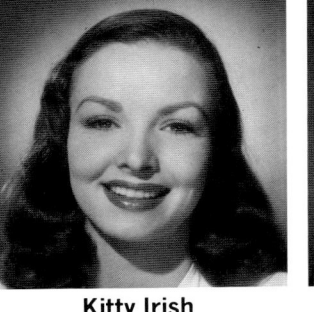

Kitty Irish

George Irving

Richard Irving

Perry Ivins

I

Ice-Capades[80]**—series**
1941—Ice-Capades
1942—Ice-Capades Revue

Imhof, Roger
1944—Casanova in Burlesque

Ince, John
1936—Comin' 'Round the Mountain*
    The Three Mesquiteers*
1939—Flight at Midnight*
    Main Street Lawyer*
1940—Wolf of New York*
1942—Code of the Outlaw
1945—Don't Fence Me In*
    Girls of the Big House*
1946—Roll on Texas Moon*
1947—Last Frontier Uprising
    Hit Parade of 1947*
    That's My Gal*

Inescort, Frieda[80]
1937—Portia on Trial
1939—Woman Doctor
    The Zero Hour
1955—Flame of the Islands

Infuhr, Teddy
1946—Gay Blades*
    Song of Arizona*
    Affairs of Geraldine*
1947—Driftwood
1948—Campus Honeymoon
1949—Brimstone*
1950—California Passage*

Ingraham, Lloyd[134]
1935—Westward Ho*
    Burning Gold
1936—The Lawless Nineties*
    Red River Valley*
    The Lonely Trail
    Go-Get-'Em, Haines
    Hearts in Bondage*
    The Vigilantes Are Coming
    Under Cover Man
1937—The Gambling Terror
    "Lightnin'" Crandall
    Gun Lords of Stirrup Basin*
1938—The Feud Maker
    Man from Music Mountain
    Billy the Kid Returns*
    Shine on Harvest Moon*
1939—I Was a Convict*
    Street of Missing Men*
    The Zero Hour*
    S. O. S. Tidal Wave*
    Should Husbands Work?*
    Dick Tracy's G-Men*
1940—Forgotten Girls*
    Dark Command*
    Adventures of Red Ryder
    The Ranger and the Lady*
    Earl of Puddlestone*
    Colorado
    Melody Ranch*
1941—A Man Betrayed*
    Mountain Moonlight*
    Bad Man of Deadwood*
    Outlaws of Cherokee Trail*
    Jesse James at Bay*
1942—The Phantom Plainsmen*
1945—The Cheaters*
1950—The Savage Horde

Ingram, Jack[134]
1936—The Lonely Trail*
    Undersea Kingdom*
    Winds of the Wasteland*
    The Gentleman from Louisiana*
    The Vigilantes Are Coming*
    Country Gentlemen*
    The Old Corral*
1937—Dick Tracy*
    Gunsmoke Ranch*
    Doomed at Sundown*
    Yodelin' Kid from Pine Ridge*
    Public Cowboy No. 1*
    S O S Coast Guard*
    The Trigger Trio*
    Zorro Rides Again
    Wild Horse Rodeo
1938—The Lone Ranger*
    Call the Mesquiteers*
    Outlaws of Sonora
    Under Western Stars*
    The Fighting Devil Dogs*
    Desert Patrol
    Riders of the Black Hills
    Dick Tracy Returns
    Durango Valley Raiders
    Western Jamboree*
    Shine on Harvest Moon*
1939—Home on the Prairie
    Mexicali Rose*
    The Night Riders
    Frontier Pony Express*
    Blue Montana Skies
    Man of Conquest*
    Southward, Ho!*
    Mountain Rhythm
    Wyoming Outlaw
    Colorado Sunset
    New Frontier
    Dick Tracy's G-Men*
    Wall Street Cowboy
    The Arizona Kid*
    Rovin' Tumbleweeds
    Saga of Death Valley
    Days of Jesse James*
1940—Rancho Grande*
    Ghost Valley Raiders
    One Man's Law*
    The Carson City Kid*
    Under Texas Skies
    Young Bill Hickok
    Melody Ranch*
1941—Robin Hood of the Pecos*
    Prairie Pioneers
    The Great Train Robbery*
    Sheriff of Tombstone
    Nevada City
    King of the Texas Rangers
1942—Man from Cheyenne
    Code of the Outlaw*
    South of Santa Fe*
    Raiders of the Range*
    Sunset Serenade*
    The Sundown Kid*
1943—Idaho*
    King of the Cowboys*
    Santa Fe Scouts
    Riders of the Rio Grande
    The Man from Thunder River
    Wagon Tracks West*
    Raiders of Sunset Pass*
1944—Beneath Western Skies*
    Mojave Firebrand
    My Buddy*
1945—Sheriff of Cimarron
    Manhunt of Mystery Island
    The Phantom Speaks*
    Federal Operator 99
    Bandits of the Badlands
1947—The Fabulous Texan*
1948—The Gallant Legion*
1950—Unmasked*
    Trigger, Jr.*
    Desperadoes of the West*
1951—Heart of the Rockies*
    Don Daredevil Rides Again*
    Fort Dodge Stampede

Ingram, Joan
1955—Trouble in Store

Ingram, Rex
1948—Moonrise

Ingrams, Michael
1955—The Square Ring

Ireland, John[100]
1951—This is Korea!*
1958—No Place to Land

Irish, Kitty[218]
1947—That's My Man

Irving, George[218]
1936—Navy Born
    The Mandarin Mystery
1942—King of the Mounties

Irving, Margaret
1936—Follow Your Heart

Irving, Richard[218]
1948—Train to Alcatraz
    Sons of Adventure
1949—The Blonde Bandit
1950—Flying Disc Man from Mars
1952—Woman in the Dark

Irwin, Boyd
1948—Campus Honeymoon

Irwin, Charles
1943—Thumbs Up
1944—Sing Neighbor Sing

Isabelita
1947—That's My Gal

Isabell, Henry
1937—Wild Horse Rodeo

Isley, Phylis[100]
[Jennifer Jones]
1939—New Frontier
    Dick Tracy's G-Men

Ivan, Rosalind
1946—That Brennan Girl

Ivins, Perry[218]
1938—The Fighting Devil Dogs
    Red River Range
1939—Dick Tracy's G-Men*
1950—The Missourians
1951—Belle LeGrand*

Ivo, Tommy[218]
1945—Earl Carroll Vanities
1946—Song of Arizona
1948—Secret Service Investigator
    Moonrise*
1949—Outcasts of the Trail

J

Jackson and Lynam
1941—Ice-Capades
1942—Ice-Capades Revue

Jackson, Eugene[218]
1935—Tumbling Tumbleweeds
1936—Red River Valley
    The Lonely Trail
    Guns and Guitars
1938—Outside of Paradise*
    King of the Newsboys*
1940—Melody and Moonlight*

Jackson, Harry
1957—Panama Sal

Jackson, Jackie
1949—The Red Pony

Jackson, Jr., Joe
1942—Ice-Capades Revue

Jackson, Peggy
1945—The Fatal Witness

Jackson, Thomas[218]
1936—Beware of Ladies
    A Man Betrayed
1937—Dangerous Holiday
1938—I Stand Accused
1940—Girl from God's Country
1946—Valley of the Zombies
    The Mysterious Mr. Valentine

Jackson, Warren
1938—Call the Mesquiteers

Jacques, Ted
1949—Powder River Rustlers

Jaeckel, Richard[170]
1950—Sands of Iwo Jima
1951—Fighting Coast Guard
    The Sea Hornet
1952—Hoodlum Empire
1954—Sea of Lost Ships
    The Shanghai Story

Jaffe, Carl
1955—Cross Channel

Jaggberg, Kurt
1955—In Old Vienna

Jagger, Dean[100]
1937—Escape by Night
    Exiled to Shanghai
1947—Driftwood
1955—The Eternal Sea

James, Gardner
1940—Adventures of Red Ryder

James, Ida
1944—Trocadero

James, Jesse—films
1939—Days of Jesse James
1941—Jesse James at Bay
1942—Jesse James, Jr.
1947—Jesse James Rides Again
1948—Adventures of Frank and Jesse James
1949—The James Brothers of Missouri
1957—Hell's Crossroads

Jackson, Selmer[134]
1936—Robinson Crusoe of Clipper Island
1937—Two Wise Maids
    Meet the Boy Friend
    The Wrong Road
    Manhattan Merry-Go-Round*
    The Duke Comes Back
1938—Prison Nurse
    Arson Gang Busters
    Down in "Arkansaw"
1939—Calling All Marines
    South of the Border
1940—Wagons Westward
    Bowery Boy
1941—The Devil Pays Off*
    Dick Tracy Vs. Crime, Inc.*
1942—Romance on the Range*
1943—Someone to Remember*
1944—Sheriff of Las Vegas
1945—A Sporting Chance
    Along the Navajo Trail*
    Dakota
1946—The Glass Alibi
    The French Key
1947—The Pretender
    The Fabulous Texan*
1948—King of the Gamblers
1950—Gunmen of Abilene
    The Mardi Gras*
1951—Buckaroo Sheriff of Texas
1954—Crazylegs
1955—The Eternal Sea*

Jackson, Sherry
1950—Covered Wagon Raid
1956—Come Next Spring

Tommy Ivo

Eugene Jackson

Thomas Jackson

John James

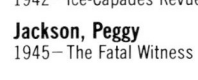

Lois January

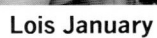

Claude Jarman, Jr.

James, John[218]
1941 — Outlaws of Cherokee Trail*
King of the Texas Rangers*
West of Cimarron*
Dick Tracy Vs. Crime, Inc.*
1942 — Spy Smasher
Westward Ho
Remember Pearl Harbor!*
The Cyclone Kid
The Sombrero Kid
Flying Tigers
1943 — G-Men Vs. The Black Dragon*
Thundering Trails
Santa Fe Scouts
Riders of the Rio Grande*
The Man from Thunder River
1944 — Beneath Western Skies*
The Fighting Seabees
Hidden Valley Outlaws
The Laramie Trail
Bordertown Trail
1945 — Great Stagecoach Robbery
1947 — Homesteaders of Paradise Valley
The Wild Frontier

James, Joni
1956 — The Maverick Queen

James, Rosemonde[69]
1944 — Lake Placid Serenade*
1945 — Utah*
Earl Carroll Vanities*
Bells of Rosarita*
The Cheaters*
Hitchhike to Happiness*
Man from Oklahoma*
Tell It to a Star*
Love, Honor and Goodbye*
Sunset in El Dorado*
The Purple Monster Strikes
Don't Fence Me In*
Girls of the Big House*
An Angel Comes to Brooklyn*
Mexicana*
The Tiger Woman*
Along the Navajo Trail*
Dakota*
1946 — A Guy Could Change*
Murder in the Music Hall*
Earl Carroll Sketchbook*

James, Roy
1938 — Overland Stage Raiders

James, Sidney
1955 — The Square Ring

James, Walter
1936 — Oh, Susanna!

Jamieson, Harold
1956 — Lisbon

Janis, Elsie[100]
1940 — Women in War

Janney, William
1936 — Sitting on the Moon

Janssen, Eileen[157]
1947 — Driftwood*
1951 — Buckaroo Sheriff of Texas
The Dakota Kid
Arizona Manhunt
1952 — Wild Horse Ambush
1957 — Beginning of the End

Janssen, Elsa
1937 — It Could Happen to You

January, Lois[218]
1937 — Bar-Z Bad Men
The Trusted Outlaw
"Lightnin'" Crandall
The Red Rope

Jaquet, Frank[134]
1938 — Shine on Harvest Moon
1940 — Behind the News*
1941 — Lady from Louisiana*
Hurricane Smith*
Mr. District Atty. in the Carter Case*
1942 — Raiders of the Range
In Old California*
Call of the Canyon*
Ice-Capades Revue*
1943 — Someone to Remember*
1944 — Beneath Western Skies*
Call of the South Seas
Call of the Rockies
Silver City Kid
1945 — Grissly's Millions
The Topeka Terror
The Vampire's Ghost
Flame of Barbary Coast*
Santa Fe Saddlemates
Federal Operator 99
Oregon Trail
Colorado Pioneers
The Cherokee Flash
1949 — Prince of the Plains*
1950 — House by the River*
Rock Island Trail*
Lonely Heart Bandits*
1952 — The Wac from Walla Walla*
1955 — Timberjack*

Frank Jenks

Chubby Johnson

Jara, Maurice
1951 — Pals of the Golden West

Jarman, Jr., Claude[218]
1950 — Rio Grande
1953 — Fair Wind to Java

Jarmyn, Jil[80]
1955 — The Eternal Sea*
Lay that Rifle Down
The Twinkle in God's Eye
No Man's Woman
1958 — Man or Gun

Jason, Sybil
1939 — Woman Doctor

Jayawardena, Sujata
1956 — Circus Girl

Jeayes, Allan
1943 — At Dawn We Die

Jeffrey, Michael
1937 — Dangerous Holiday

Jeffreys, Anne[29]
1942 — Yokel Boy*
Moonlight Masquerade*
Joan of Ozark
The Old Homestead
Flying Tigers*
X Marks the Spot
1943 — Calling Wild Bill Elliott
Chatterbox
The Man from Thunder River
Bordertown Gun Fighters
Wagon Tracks West
Death Valley Manhunt
Overland Mail Robbery
Raiders of Sunset Pass*
1944 — Mojave Firebrand
Hidden Valley Outlaws

Jeffries, Jim
1940 — Barnyard Follies

Jenkins, Allen
1948 — The Inside Story
1952 — Oklahoma Annie
The Wac from Walla Walla

Jenkins, Meg
1955 — Trouble in Store

Si "Rawhide" Jenks

Linda Johnson

Jenkins, Polly — and Plowboys
1938 — Man from Music Mountain

Jenks, Frank[219]
1939 — S. O. S. Tidal Wave
1940 — Melody and Moonlight
1943 — Shantytown
1944 — Rosie, the Riveter
Three Little Sisters
1945 — Steppin' in Society
1946 — That Brennan Girl
1947 — That's My Gal
1951 — Silver City Bonanza
Utah Wagon Train

Jenks, Si "Rawhide"[219]
1936 — Follow Your Heart
The President's Mystery
1940 — Three Faces West*
Girl from God's Country
The Ranger and the Lady
Ride, Tenderfoot, Ride
The Trail Blazers
1941 — The Great Train Robbery
Mountain Moonlight*
Gauchos of Eldorado*
Mr. District Atty. in the Carter Case*
1942 — Cowboy Serenade*
Ice-Capades Revue
1944 — The Yellow Rose of Texas*
Song of Nevada*
Zorro's Black Whip
1945 — Manhunt of Mystery Island*
Flame of Barbary Coast*
Road to Alcatraz*
Oregon Trail
Man from Oklahoma*
Bandits of the Badlands
1947 — Son of Zorro
1952 — Oklahoma Annie

Jennings, Maxine
1946 — G. I. War Brides

Jerky Journeys — series
1949 — Beyond Civilization to Texas
The 3 Minnies: Sota, Tonka & Ha Ha!
Romantic Rumbolia
Bungle in the Jungle

Jerome, Elmer
1943 — Swing Your Partner
1947 — That's My Gal

Jerome, Jerry
1948 — Lightnin' in the Forest

Isabel Jewell

Jewell, Isabel[219]
1936 — Dancing Feet
The Leathernecks Have Landed
1940 — Scatterbrain
1945 — Steppin' in Society

Jimenez, Edwardo
1951 — Pals of the Golden West

Jiminez, Soledad
1937 — The Bold Caballero

Jimmy
1936 — The Leavenworth Case

Jimmy's Saddle Pals
1937 — Springtime in the Rockies

Johnson, Ben[119]
1943 — Riders of the Rio Grande*
Bordertown Gun Fighters*
1945 — Santa Fe Saddlemates*
1946 — California Gold Rush*
Out California Way*
1947 — Angel and the Badman*
Wyoming*
The Fabulous Texan*
1948 — The Gallant Legion*
1950 — Rio Grande

Johnson, Bob
1953 — Jungle Drums of Africa

Johnson, Brad
1953 — The Lady Wants Mink

Johnson, Casey
1941 — Hurricane Smith

Johnson, Chic [Harold][83]
1936 — Country Gentlemen
1937 — All Over Town

Johnson, Chubby[219]
1951 — Night Riders of Montana
Wells Fargo Gunmaster
Fort Dodge Stampede
1955 — Headline Hunters
1958 — Gunfire at Indian Gap

Johnson, Eddie
1942 — The Traitor Within

Johnson, Erskine
1944 — Trocadero

Johnson, Fred
1957 — The Weapon

Johnson, Hall — choir
1936 — Follow Your Heart
1940 — In Old Missouri
1942 — Lady for a Night
Heart of the Golden West

Johnson, June[30]
1936 — The Big Show
The Mandarin Mystery
Beware of Ladies*
1937 — Jim Hanvey - Detective*
The Hit Parade*
Gunsmoke Ranch*
1940 — Lone Star Raiders
1941 — Pals of the Pecos
Gangs of Sonora

Johnson, Linda[219]
[as Melinda Leighton]
1942 — Cowboy Serenade
Code of the Outlaw
[as Linda Johnson]
The Sundown Kid
1946 — That Brennan Girl*
1947 — Bandits of Dark Canyon

Johnson, Noble[219]
1938 — Hawk of the Wilderness
1939 — Frontier Pony Express
1940 — The Ranger and the Lady
1946 — Plainsman and the Lady
1947 — Along the Oregon Trail*
1948 — The Gallant Legion*
1950 — Rock Island Trail*
North of the Great Divide

Johnson, Tor
1949 — Alias the Champ*
1957 — Journey to Freedom
The Unearthly

Joiner, Patricia
1951 — Missing Women

Jolley, I. Stanford[219]
1936 — The Gentleman from Louisiana*
Ghost-Town Gold*
The Big Show*
1937 — Dick Tracy*
1939 — Street of Missing Men*
S. O. S. Tidal Wave*
1942 — The Sombrero Kid*
1943 — Man from Music Mountain*
1946 — Daughter of Don Q
The Crimson Ghost
1947 — The Black Widow
1948 — Dangers of the Canadian Mounted
Adv. of Frank and Jesse James
1949 — Ghost of Zorro
King of the Rocket Men
Bandit King of Texas
1950 — Sands of Iwo Jima*
Rock Island Trail*
Trigger, Jr.
Desperadoes of the West
California Passage*
1951 — Don Daredevil Rides Again
1952 — Leadville Gunslinger
1953 — Cosmic Vengeance
1954 — Man with the Steel Whip

Joliffe, John
1946 — Murder in the Music Hall

Jores Boys
1936 — The Big Show

Jones, Buck [Charles][100]
1940 — Wagons Westward

Jones, Carolyn
1954 — Geraldine
Make Haste to Live

Jones, Dickie[219]
1935 — Westward Ho
1939 — Woman Doctor
1940 — Hi-Yo-Silver*
1943 — Mountain Rhythm
1948 — Angel on the Amazon*
1950 — Sands of Iwo Jima*
Redwood Forest Trail

Jones, Gordon[219]
1938 — I Stand Accused
1939 — Pride of the Navy
1940 — Girl from Havana
1942 — Flying Tigers
1948 — Sons of Adventure
1950 — Belle of Old Mexico
The Arizona Cowboy
Trigger, Jr.
Sunset in the West
North of the Great Divide
Trail of Robin Hood
1951 — Spoilers of the Plains
Heart of the Rockies
1952 — Gobs and Gals
1953 — Woman They Almost Lynched

Noble Johnson

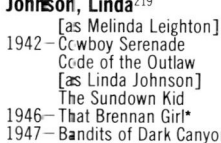
I. Stanford Jolley

Dickie Jones

Gordon Jones

Jones, Griffith
1959 — Hidden Homicide

Jones, Jennifer
See Phylis Isley.

Jones, Marcia Mae[220]
1937 — Two Wise Maids
1938 — Lady, Behave!
1943 — Nobody's Darling

Jones, Peter
1955 — A Day to Remember

Jones, Stan[220]
1950 — Rio Grande
1952 — The Last Musketeer

Jones, Thomas
1953 — City that Never Sleeps

Jones, Trefor
1937 — Glamorous Night

Jons, Beverly[220]
1948 — Carson City Raiders

Jordan, Bob
1956 — The Man is Armed

Jordan, Charles
1945 — Identity Unknown

Jordan, Dorothy
1953 — The Sun Shines Bright

Jordan, Joanne[220]
1953 — Captives of the Zero Hour
1955 — I Cover the Underworld

Jordan, Patrick
1957 — Operation Conspiracy

Jory, Victor[101]
1937 — Bulldog Drummond at Bay
       Glamorous Night
1939 — Man of Conquest
1940 — Girl from Havana
1952 — Toughest Man in Arizona
1957 — Last Stagecoach West

Joslyn, Allyn[101]
1948 — Moonrise

Journet, Marcel
1949 — Post Office Investigator
1951 — Adventures of Captain Fabian

Joyce, Brenda[119]
1941 — Variety Reel*
       Stars Past and Present*
1943 — Thumbs Up

Joyce, Jean[220]
1936 — Follow Your Heart*
1938 — Invisible Enemy*
       Outlaws of Sonora
       Romance on the Run
       The Night Hawk*
1939 — Sabotage*

Judels, Charles[220]
1936 — The Big Show
1937 — Rhythm in the Clouds
1943 — Swing Your Partner
1946 — In Old Sacramento
       Plainsman and the Lady

Judge, Arline[220]
1943 — Song of Texas

Jung, Allen
1942 — King of the Mounties
1943 — G-Men Vs. The Black Dragon

Jurado, Katy[101]
1951 — Bullfighter and the Lady
1953 — San Antone

Justice, James Robertson
1955 — Doctor in the House
1956 — Doctor at Sea
       Above Us the Waves

K

Kaaren, Suzanne[220]
1936 — Under Cover Man
1937 — Rhythm in the Clouds
1939 — Pride of the Navy*
       Mexicali Rose*
1941 — Rags to Riches

Kacher, Bunny
1953 — City that Never Sleeps

Kahanamoku, Duke
1949 — Wake of the Red Witch

Marcia Mae Jones

Stan Jones

Beverly Jons

Joanne Jordan

Jean Joyce

Charles Judels

Arline Judge

Suzanne Kaaren

Kallman, Dick[220]
1957 — Hell Canyon Outlaws

Kane, Eddie[134]
1937 — The Hit Parade*
       All Over Town
       Manhattan Merry-Go-Round*
1938 — The Higgins Family*
1939 — Fighting Thoroughbreds*
       Rovin' Tumbleweeds
1940 — Carolina Moon*
1941 — Mr. District Atty. in the Carter Case*
1942 — Moonlight Masquerade*
       Secrets of the Underground*
1943 — Idaho*
       Tahiti Honey*
1944 — Lake Placid Serenade*
1945 — Bells of Rosarita*
       Man from Oklahoma
       Tell It to a Star*
       Swingin' on a Rainbow*
       Along the Navajo Trail*
1946 — Song of Arizona*
       Heldorado*
1947 — Hit Parade of 1947*

Kane, Louise
1947 — Wyoming
1951 — Oh! Susanna

Kane, Marjorie "Babe"
1940 — Scatterbrain*
       Earl of Puddlestone*
       Melody and Moonlight*
       Hit Parade of 1941*
1941 — The Gay Vagabond*
       Sailors on Leave*
       Dick Tracy Vs. Crime, Inc.*
1942 — Sunset on the Desert*
1944 — Goodnight Sweetheart*
       Man from Frisco*
1945 — Behind City Lights*
       Girls of the Big House*

Kann, Lilly
1955 — A Day to Remember

Kaplan, Marvin
1952 — The Fabulous Senorita

Karlan, Richard[220]
1956 — Accused of Murder
1957 — The Crooked Circle
1958 — The Man Who Died Twice

Karnes, Robert
1950 — Hills of Oklahoma
1951 — Fighting Coast Guard*
       Utah Wagon Train
       The Wild Blue Yonder*
1957 — Spoilers of the Forest*

Karns, Roscoe[80]
1940 — Meet the Missus
1941 — Petticoat Politics
       The Gay Vagabond
       Stars at Play*
1942 — A Tragedy at Midnight
       Yokel Boy
1947 — Vigilantes of Boomtown
       That's My Man
1948 — The Inside Story

Kasznar, Kurt[220]
1955 — Flame of the Islands

Katch, Kurt[220]
1943 — The Purple V
       Secret Service in Darkest Africa

Katchenaro, Pete
1942 — King of the Mounties*

Kauffman, Tamara Lynn
1936 — Roarin' Lead

Kaufmann, Maurice
1955 — Secret Venture

Kay, Geraldine
1935 — The Crime of Doctor Crespi

Kay, Mary Ellen[30]
1951 — Silver City Bonanza
       Thunder in God's Country
       Wells Fargo Gunmaster
       Govt. Agents Vs. Phantom Legion
       Rodeo King and the Senorita
       Fort Dodge Stampede
       Utah Wagon Train*
       The Sea Hornet*
       Desert of Lost Men
1952 — Colorado Sundown
       The Last Musketeer
       Border Saddlemates

Kay, Patricia
1944 — Trocadero

Kaye, Lucie[30]
1937 — Jim Hanvey - Detective
       Portia on Trial*

Kean, Betty[30]
1942 — Yokel Boy*
       Moonlight Masquerade

Kean, Jane[30]
1941 — Sailors on Leave

Keane, Edward[220]
1939 — My Wife's Relatives
       Frontier Pony Express
1942 — The Old Homestead*
       Ice-Capades Revue*
       The Traitor Within
1943 — G-Men Vs. The Black Dragon*
       Someone to Remember*
       Death Valley Manhunt*
       California Joe*
1944 — Captain America
       The Lady and the Monster*
       Goodnight Sweetheart*
       Haunted Harbor
1946 — Roll on Texas Moon
       Out California Way
1947 — Trail to San Antone
       Calendar Girl*
       Saddle Pals*
       On the Old Spanish Trail*
1949 — Hellfire*
1950 — Twilight in the Sierras
       The Invisible Monster*
1951 — Belle LeGrand*

Keane, Robert Emmett[220]
1936 — The President's Mystery*
       Beware of Ladies
1937 — Jim Hanvey - Detective
1938 — Born to be Wild
       Billy the Kid Returns
1940 — The Border Legion
1942 — Remember Pearl Harbor!
1946 — Rainbow Over Texas
1948 — The Timber Trail
       Out of the Storm
1949 — Susanna Pass
       Frontier Investigator
       Navajo Trail Raiders
1950 — Hills of Oklahoma
1954 — The Atomic Kid
1956 — When Gangland Strikes

Kearney, Carolyn[221]
1958 — Young and Wild

Dick Kallman

Richard Karlan

Kurt Kasznar

Kurt Katch

Edward Keane

Robert Emmett Keane

Keckley, Jane[221]
1936 — Roarin' Lead
1937 — Dick Tracy*
 Git Along Little Dogies
 Gunsmoke Ranch
 Dangerous Holiday*
1938 — The Lone Ranger*
 Under Western Stars*
1939 — The Night Riders*
 Man of Conquest*
 Southward, Ho!*
 Colorado Sunset*
 Sabotage*
 Rovin' Tumbleweeds*
1940 — Pioneers of the West*
 Three Faces West*
 Melody Ranch*
1941 — Mountain Moonlight*
1942 — South of Santa Fe*

Keefe, Cornelius
1936 — The Old Corral
1937 — The Trigger Trio
1941 — Saddlemates

Keefer, Phil
1935 — The New Frontier

Keen, Geoffrey
1955 — Doctor in the House
 The Divided Heart
1956 — Doctor at Sea

Keene, Richard
1939 — She Married a Cop

Keiley, Virginia
1958 — Strange Case of Dr. Manning

Keir, David
1943 — At Dawn We Die

Keith, Alan
1942 — Suicide Squadron

Keith, Brian
1957 — Hell Canyon Outlaws

Keith, Ian[221]
1942 — Remember Pearl Harbor!
 The Sundown Kid
1943 — The Man from Thunder River
 Bordertown Gun Fighters
1944 — Casanova in Burlesque
1945 — Identity Unknown
 Phantom of the Plains
1946 — Valley of the Zombies

Keith, Rosalind[221]
1938 — Arson Gang Busters

Kellard, Robert[221]
1940 — Drums of Fu Manchu
 King of the Royal Mounted
1941 — Prairie Pioneers

Keller, Martin
1955 — The Divided Heart

Kelley, Alice[221]
1951 — Buckaroo Sheriff of Texas

Carolyn Kearney

Jane Keckley

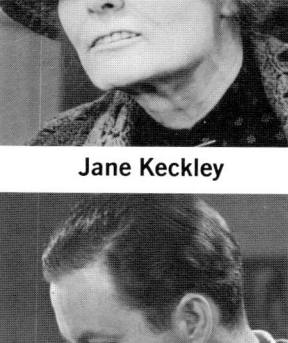
Ian Keith

Rosalind Keith

Alice Kelley, Hugh O'Brian

Kelley, Barry[170]
1950 — Singing Guns
1952 — Woman of the North Country
1953 — Champ for a Day
1954 — The Shanghai Story
1956 — Accused of Murder
1958 — Gunfire at Indian Gap

Kelley, Bob
1954 — Crazylegs

Kelley, DeForest[221]
1949 — Duke of Chicago

Kellino [Mason], Pamela[221]
1952 — Lady Possessed

Kellogg, Bruce[221]
1943 — Deerslayer

Kellogg, Gayle
1952 — Zombies of the Stratosphere
1953 — Can. Mounties Vs. Atomic Invaders

Kellogg, John
1947 — Robin Hood of Texas
1948 — Secret Service Investigator
1955 — African Manhunt

Kelly, Carol
1956 — Daniel Boone, Trail Blazer

Kelly, Claire
1956 — Scandal Incorporated

Kelly, Craig[221]
1952 — Zombies of the Stratosphere
1953 — Enemies of the Universe
 Atomic Peril
 Cosmic Vengeance
 Nightmare Typhoon
 War of the Space Giants
 Destroyers of the Sun
 Robot Monster from Mars
 The Hydrogen Hurricane
 Solar Sky Raiders
 S. O. S. Ice Age
 Lost in Outer Space
 Captives of the Zero Hour

Kelly, Don[221]
1957 — The Crooked Circle
1958 — The Notorious Mr. Monks

Kelly, Jack[221]
1951 — The Wild Blue Yonder
1955 — Double Jeopardy
1957 — Taming Sutton's Gal

Kelly, Jeanne
1935 — The Crime of Doctor Crespi

Kelly, Jimmie
1950 — Harbor of Missing Men

Kelly, John
1937 — Portia on Trial
1940 — Bowery Boy
1941 — The Pittsburgh Kid
1945 — The Tiger Woman

Kelly, Judy
1943 — At Dawn We Die

Kelly, Lew[221]
1936 — Winds of the Wasteland
1937 — Paradise Express
 All Over Town
1938 — Man from Music Mountain
1939 — Three Texas Steers
 Saga of Death Valley
1941 — The Great Train Robbery

Kelly, Nancy[101]
1945 — Woman Who Came Back
1946 — Murder in the Music Hall

Kelly, Patrick
1938 — Hawk of the Wilderness

Kelly, Patsy[221]
1940 — Hit Parade of 1941
1942 — In Old California

Kelly, Paul[101]
1937 — Join the Marines
1939 — Forged Passport
1942 — Flying Tigers
1943 — Man from Music Mountain
1944 — Faces in the Fog
1945 — Grissly's Millions
1946 — The Glass Alibi
1947 — Spoilers of the North

Kelly, P. J.
1944 — That's My Baby

Kelly, Walter C.
1936 — Laughing Irish Eyes

Kelsall, Moultrie
1954 — Trouble in the Glen

Kelsey, Fred[221]
1935 — Sagebrush Troubadour
1937 — All Over Town
1942 — X Marks the Spot
1951 — Havana Rose*
1952 — Tropical Heat Wave*

Kelso, Vernon
1955 — The Square Ring

Keltner, Ken
1949 — The Kid from Cleveland

Kelton, Pert[221]
1936 — Sitting on the Moon
1937 — The Hit Parade
 Meet the Boy Friend
1938 — Rhythm of the Saddle

Pamela Kellino

Bruce Kellogg

Craig Kelly

Don Kelly

Jack Kelly

Lew Kelly

Patsy Kelly

Fred Kelsey

Pert Kelton

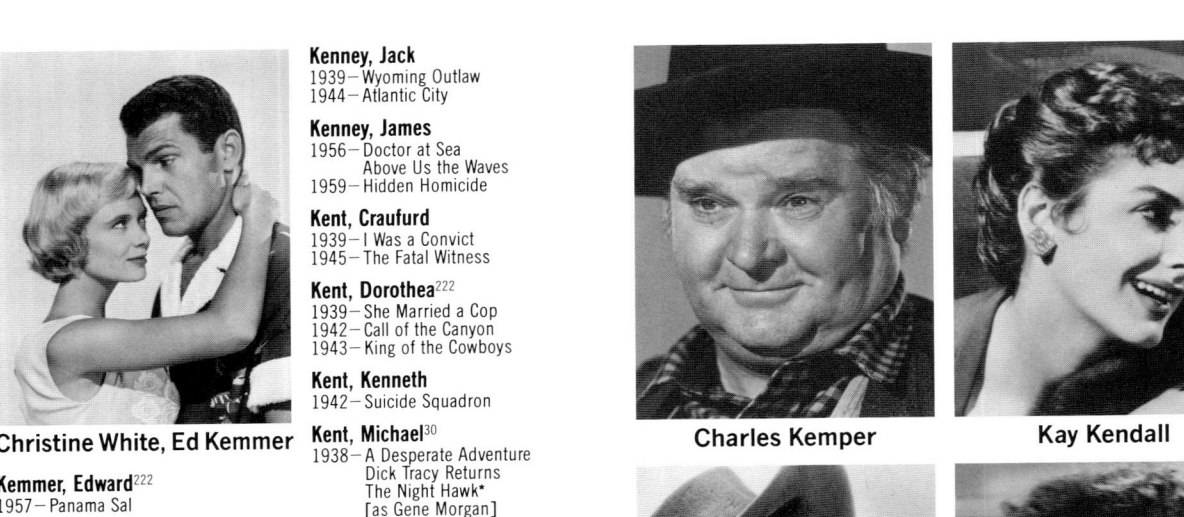

Christine White, Ed Kemmer

Kemmer, Edward[222]
1957—Panama Sal

Kemper, Charles[222]
1945—An Angel Comes to Brooklyn
1950—California Passage

Kendall, Cy[134]
1935—Hitch Hike Lady*
1936—Dancing Feet
    King of the Pecos
    The Lonely Trail
    Bulldog Edition
1937—It Could Happen to You*
    Meet the Boy Friend
1938—The Night Hawk
1939—Man of Conquest*
    Mickey, the Kid*
    Calling All Marines
1941—Robin Hood of the Pecos
1943—A Gentle Gangster
    Whispering Footsteps
1945—The Tiger Woman
1946—The Glass Alibi
    The Invisible Informer

Kendall, Kay[222]
1955—The Square Ring
    Doctor in the House

Kennedy, Bill[222]
1946—That Brennan Girl
1947—Web of Danger
1951—Silver City Bonanza

Kennedy, Bob
1949—The Kid from Cleveland

Kennedy, Douglas[223]
1949—South of Rio
    Ranger of Cherokee Strip
1951—Oh! Susanna
1952—Hoodlum Empire*
1953—Ride the Man Down
    San Antone
1954—Sea of Lost Ships
1955—The Eternal Sea
1957—Hell's Crossroads

Kennedy, Edgar[222]
1935—$1000 a Minute
1936—The Return of Jimmy Valentine
1940—Who Killed Aunt Maggie?
1941—Stars Past and Present*
    Public Enemies
1942—Pardon My Stripes
    In Old California
1945—Captain Tugboat Annie

Kennedy, Fred
1950—Rio Grande

Kennedy, Jack
1936—Red River Valley

Kennedy, King
1940—Chinese Garden Festival*

Kennedy, Madge
1959—Plunderers of Painted Flats

Kennedy, Phyllis
1941—Sailors on Leave*
1950—The Missourians*
1951—Spoilers of the Plains*
    Fighting Coast Guard*
1952—The Wac from Walla Walla*

Kennedy, Ron
1956—Hidden Guns

Kennedy, Tom[222]
1939—The Covered Trailer
1941—Angels with Broken Wings
    Sailors on Leave
1942—Pardon My Stripes
1943—Hit Parade of 1943
    Here Comes Elmer
    O, My Darling Clementine
1944—Rosie, the Riveter
1947—The Pretender
1951—Havana Rose

Kenney, Jack
1939—Wyoming Outlaw
1944—Atlantic City

Kenney, James
1956—Doctor at Sea
    Above Us the Waves
1959—Hidden Homicide

Kent, Craufurd
1939—I Was a Convict
1945—The Fatal Witness

Kent, Dorothea[222]
1939—She Married a Cop
1942—Call of the Canyon
1943—King of the Cowboys

Kent, Kenneth
1942—Suicide Squadron

Kent, Michael[30]
1938—A Desperate Adventure
    Dick Tracy Returns
    The Night Hawk*
    [as Gene Morgan]
    Federal Man-Hunt
1940—Gaucho Serenade*
    Girl from God's Country

Kent, Robert[222]
1939—Calling All Marines
1941—Sunset in Wyoming
1942—Stagecoach Express
1946—The Phantom Rider
1950—Federal Agent at Large
1951—Missing Women*
    The Wild Blue Yonder*

Kenworthy, Katherine
1939—Wyoming Outlaw
    Colorado Sunset*

Kenyon, Mary[30]
1939—Should Husbands Work?*
1940—Carolina Moon*
    Earl of Puddlestone
1943—Chatterbox*
    Swing Your Partner*
    The West Side Kid*
    Here Comes Elmer*
1944—Song of Nevada*
    Sing Neighbor Sing*
    San Fernando Valley*
    Code of the Prairie*
    Lights of Old Santa Fe*
    Brazil*
1945—Mexicana*

Kerima
1954—The She Wolf

Kerman, David
1938—Outside of Paradise

Kerr, Donald
1935—The Spanish Cape Mystery
1937—Circus Girl
1944—Atlantic City
1951—Pride of Maryland

Kerrigan, J. M.[222]
1936—Laughing Irish Eyes
    Hearts in Bondage
1939—The Zero Hour
    Sabotage
1944—The Fighting Seabees
    The Big Bonanza

Kerrigan, Marian[69]
1944—Brazil*
    Lake Placid Serenade*
1945—Utah*
    Earl Carroll Vanities*
    Bells of Rosarita*
    Federal Operator 99*
    The Cheaters*
    Hitchhike to Happiness*
    Man from Oklahoma*
    Tell It to a Star*
    Behind City Lights*
    Sunset in El Dorado*
    The Purple Monster Strikes*
    Don't Fence Me In*
    Girls of the Big House*
    An Angel Comes to Brooklyn*
    Colorado Pioneers*
    Mexicana*
    The Tiger Woman*
    The Cherokee Flash*
    Along the Navajo Trail*
    Dakota*
1946—A Guy Could Change*
    California Gold Rush*
    Murder in the Music Hall*
1947—That's My Gal*

Kerwin, David
1939—The Arizona Kid

Kevin, James
1958—Young and Wild

Keyes, Evelyn[101]
1954—Hell's Half Acre

Charles Kemper

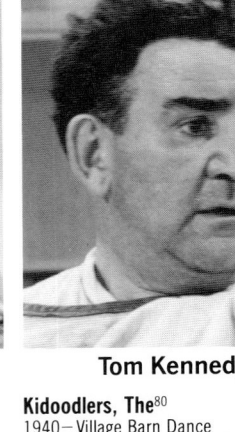

Kay Kendall

Bill Kennedy

Edgar Kennedy

Tom Kennedy

Dorothea Kent

Keymas, George[222]
1955—Santa Fe Passage
    The Vanishing American
1956—The Maverick Queen
    Thunder Over Arizona
1958—Gunfire at Indian Gap

Keys, Robert
1958—Street of Darkness

Keystone Cops
1941—Stars Past and Present*

Kibbee, Guy[101]
1937—Jim Hanvey - Detective
1941—Variety Reel*

Kibbee, Milton[223]
1938—A Desperate Adventure*
    Overland Stage Raiders*
    I Stand Accused*
1939—Fighting Thoroughbreds*
    Woman Doctor*
    Street of Missing Men*
    Jeepers Creepers*
1940—Wolf of New York*
    Village Barn Dance*
    Behind the News*
1941—Petticoat Politics*
    Two Gun Sheriff
    The Gay Vagabond*
    Kansas Cyclone
    Hurricane Smith*
    Citadel of Crime*
    Sailors on Leave*
1942—Heart of the Rio Grande*
    Westward Ho*
    In Old California
1943—Hit Parade of 1943*
    The Black Hills Express*
1944—Three Little Sisters
    My Buddy*
1946—One Exciting Week*
    Conquest of Cheyenne
1947—Homesteaders of Paradise Valley
    Springtime in the Sierras*
1951—Pride of Maryland*
    Fighting Coast Guard*

Kidoodlers, The[80]
1940—Village Barn Dance
    Melody and Moonlight
    Barnyard Follies

Kiffe, Karl
1942—Johnny Doughboy

Kikume, Al[223]
1937—Join the Marines*
1940—Meet the Missus*
1941—Adventures of Captain Marvel*
    Jungle Girl
1942—Remember Pearl Harbor!*
    Perils of Nyoka*
1949—Daughter of the Jungle
    Wake of the Red Witch*
1953—Fair Wind to Java*

Kilburn, Martin
1951—The Wild Blue Yonder

Kilburn, Terry[223]
1941—Mercy Island

Kilian, Victor[223]
1938—Orphans of the Street
1939—Fighting Thoroughbreds
1940—Barnyard Follies
1945—Behind City Lights
1946—Specter of the Rose*
1949—The Wyoming Bandit
1950—The Old Frontier
    The Showdown

Killick, Robert
1955—In Old Vienna

Kimbley, Billy
1951—Silver City Bonanza

Kimmell, Leslie
1950—House by the River

Dorothea Kent

King, Charles[223]
1935—Tumbling Tumbleweeds*
    Burning Gold*
1936—The Singing Vagabond*
    The Lawless Nineties
    Red River Valley
    The Lonely Trail*
    Guns and Guitars
    Hearts in Bondage*
1937—The Trusted Outlaw
    The Gambling Terror
    "Lightnin'" Crandall
    Rootin' Tootin' Rhythm
    The Painted Stallion
    Doomed at Sundown*
    A Lawman is Born
    The Red Rope
    Ridin' the Lone Trail
1938—The Lone Ranger*
    Thunder in the Desert
    Gold Mine in the Sky*
    Santa Fe Stampede*
1939—Frontier Pony Express*
    Cowboys from Texas*
    South of the Border*
    Zorro's Fighting Legion
1940—One Man's Law*
    Under Texas Skies*
1941—Desert Bandit*
    The Apache Kid*
1942—Stagecoach Express*
1943—King of the Cowboys*
    Calling Wild Bill Elliott*
    Riders of the Rio Grande
    The Man from Thunder River
    Bordertown Gun Fighters*
    California Joe
1944—Marshal of Reno*
    Code of the Prairie*
    The Big Bonanza*
1947—Son of Zorro*
    Wyoming*
    Jesse James Rides Again*
1949—Ghost of Zorro*

King, Claude
1935—$1000 a Minute
1936—The Leathernecks Have Landed
    Happy Go Lucky

Robert Kent

J.M. Kerrigan

George Keymas

Jack Kirk [30]

1935 — Westward Ho*
  The New Frontier*
  Lawless Range*
1936 — The Lawless Nineties*
  King of the Pecos*
  The Singing Cowboy*
  The Lonely Trail*
  Guns and Guitars
  Oh, Susanna!*
  The Vigilantes Are Coming*
  The Gun Ranger*
  Roarin' Lead*
1937 — The Riders of the Whistling Skull*
  The Bold Caballero*
  Round-Up Time in Texas*
  Paradise Express*
  Hit the Saddle
  Git Along Little Dogies*
  Trail of Vengeance*
  Gunsmoke Ranch
  Gun Lords of Stirrup Basin*
  Come on, Cowboys!*
  Doomed at Sundown*
  Yodelin' Kid from Pine Ridge*
  Range Defenders*
  Heart of the Rockies*
  The Arizona Gunfighter*
  Ridin' the Lone Trail*
  Springtime in the Rockies*
  Zorro Rides Again*
  Wild Horse Rodeo*
1938 — The Purple Vigilantes*
  The Lone Ranger*
  Call the Mesquiteers*
  Outlaws of Sonora*
  Under Western Stars*
  Gold Mine in the Sky*
  Heroes of the Hills*
  Man from Music Mountain*
  Pals of the Saddle
  Billy the Kid Returns*
  Overland Stage Raiders*
  Prairie Moon*
  Rhythm of the Saddle*
  Come on, Rangers*
  Shine on Harvest Moon*
1939 — Home on the Prairie*
  The Lone Ranger Rides Again*
  Rough Riders' Round-Up*
  Mexicali Rose*
  The Night Riders*
  Frontier Pony Express*
  Blue Montana Skies*
  Three Texas Steers*
  Mountain Rhythm*
  Wyoming Outlaw*
  Colorado Sunset*
  In Old Monterey*
  The Arizona Kid*
  Rovin' Tumbleweeds*
  Cowboys from Texas*
  South of the Border*
1940 — Pioneers of the West*
  Rancho Grande*
  Young Buffalo Bill*
  Covered Wagon Days*
  Gaucho Serenade*
  Rocky Mountain Rangers
  Adventures of Red Ryder*
  One Man's Law*
  The Carson City Kid*
  Carolina Moon*
  The Ranger and the Lady*
  The Tulsa Kid
  Ride, Tenderfoot, Ride*
  Colorado*
  Under Texas Skies*
  Young Bill Hickok*
  The Trail Blazers*
  Melody Ranch*
  Texas Terrors*
  The Border Legion*
  Lone Star Raiders*
1941 — Robin Hood of the Pecos*
  Prairie Pioneers*
  In Old Cheyenne
  Pals of the Pecos*
  The Singing Hill
  Sheriff of Tombstone*
  Saddlemates*
  Nevada City
  Kansas Cyclone
  Gangs of Sonora*
  Under Fiesta Stars
  Bad Man of Deadwood
  Death Valley Outlaws*
  Jesse James at Bay
  Sierra Sue
  Red River Valley*
1942 — Arizona Terrors*
  Man from Cheyenne*
  Code of the Outlaw*
  South of Santa Fe
  Jesse James, Jr.
  Home in Wyomin'*
  Westward Ho
  Romance on the Range*
  In Old California*
  The Phantom Plainsmen
  Sunset Serenade
  Valley of Hunted Men*
  Ridin' Down the Canyon*
1943 — Mountain Rhythm*
  Idaho*
  Carson City Cyclone
  King of the Cowboys*
  Santa Fe Scouts*
  Silver Spurs*
  Beyond the Last Frontier*
  Death Valley Manhunt
  The Man from the Rio Grande
  Overland Mail Robbery*
  Canyon City*
  In Old Oklahoma*
  Raiders of Sunset Pass
  Hands Across the Border*
1944 — Pride of the Plains
  Captain America*
  Beneath Western Skies
  Mojave Firebrand
  Hidden Valley Outlaws*
  Outlaws of Santa Fe*
  Rosie, the Riveter*
  Cowboy and the Senorita
  Tucson Raiders*
  Silent Partner*
  Man from Frisco*
  Marshal of Reno
  Call of the Rockies
  Silver City Kid
  Bordertown Trail
  The San Antonio Kid
  Stagecoach to Monterey
  Cheyenne Wildcat
  Code of the Prairie
  Storm Over Lisbon*
  Lights of Old Santa Fe*
  Sheriff of Sundown
  Firebrands of Arizona
  Zorro's Black Whip
  Thoroughbreds*
  Sheriff of Las Vegas
1945 — The Topeka Terror
  Sheriff of Cimarron
  Corpus Christi Bandits
  Lone Texas Ranger
  Federal Operator 99*
  Trail of Kit Carson
  Phantom of the Plains
  Bandits of the Badlands*
  Sunset in El Dorado*
  Marshal of Laredo*
  Colorado Pioneers*
  Wagon Wheels Westward*
1946 — The Phantom Rider
  California Gold Rush
  Sheriff of Redwood Valley*
  Alias Billy the Kid*
  Home on the Range
  King of the Forest Rangers
  Sun Valley Cyclone*
  Night Train to Memphis*
  Conquest of Cheyenne
  Out California Way*
1947 — Son of Zorro
  Angel and the Badman*
  Homesteaders of Paradise Valley*
  Oregon Trail Scouts
1948 — Oklahoma Badlands
  The Bold Frontiersman
  Dangers of the Canadian Mounted*
  The Gallant Legion*
  Adv. of Frank and Jesse James

Milton Kibbee

Al Kikume

Terry Kilburn

Victor Kilian

Charles King

Leonid Kinskey

King Cole Trio, The
1943 — Here Comes Elmer
  Pistol Packin' Mama

King, Eugene
1937 — Bill Cracks Down

King, Manuel
1936 — Darkest Africa

King, Patty
1949 — The Red Pony

King, Rex
1936 — The Big Show

King, Stanley
1937 — It Could Happen to You

King of the Royal Mounted — series
1940 — King of the Royal Mounted
1942 — King of the Mounties

Kingsford, Guy
1936 — Happy Go Lucky
1939 — Sabotage*
1942 — Stagecoach Express
1946 — G. I. War Brides*

Kingsford, Walter
1937 — It Could Happen to You
1944 — Secrets of Scotland Yard

Kinkead, Randal
1955 — The Divided Heart

Kinskey, Leonid [223]
1937 — Meet the Boy Friend
  The Sheik Steps Out
1938 — Outside of Paradise
1942 — Lady for a Night
1944 — The Fighting Seabees
  That's My Baby
1951 — Honeychile
1952 — Gobs and Gals

Kippen, Manart
1945 — Flame of Barbary Coast

Kirby, George
1936 — The Girl from Mandalay

Kirby, Jay [223]
1944 — Marshal of Reno
  Zorro's Black Whip
  Sheriff of Las Vegas
1945 — Wagon Wheels Westward
1946 — Days of Buffalo Bill
  King of the Forest Rangers*
  Conquest of Cheyenne
1948 — Oklahoma Badlands
  Son of God's Country

Kirk, Joseph
1942 — X Marks the Spot
1943 — Pistol Packin' Mama

Kirke, Donald [223]
1936 — Oh, Susanna!
  Country Gentlemen
1937 — Paradise Express
  Range Defenders*
1942 — Outlaws of Pine Ridge
1943 — G-Men Vs. The Black Dragon
1956 — Scandal Incorporated

Kirkwood, James
1947 — Driftwood
1952 — I Dream of Jeanie
1953 — The Sun Shines Bright

Kirov, Ivan [223]
1946 — Specter of the Rose

Klekas, Harry
1958 — Man or Gun

Kline, Bob
1959 — Plunderers of Painted Flats

Klingenberg, Heinz
1956 — Magic Fire

Knaggs, Skelton [223]
1943 — Thumbs Up*
  Headin' for God's Country

Knapp, Evalyn [223]
1936 — Bulldog Edition
1941 — Wampas Baby Stars*

Alice Talton, Douglas Kennedy

Jay Kirby

Donald Kirke

Ivan Kirov

Skelton Knaggs

Evalyn Knapp

Knapp, Robert
1956—Scandal Incorporated

Knight, Charles
1938—Pals of the Saddle

Knight, David[224]
1957—Tears for Simon

Knight, Fuzzy [John][224]
1944—Cowboy and the Senorita
1950—Hills of Oklahoma
1951—Honeychile
1952—Oklahoma Annie
1954—Geraldine*
1958—The Notorious Mr. Monks

Knight, Patricia[224]
1947—The Fabulous Texan

Knowles, Patric[102]
1938—Storm Over Bengal
1940—Women in War
1955—No Man's Woman

Knox, Alexander
1955—The Divided Heart

Knox, Elyse[224]
1941—Sheriff of Tombstone

Knox, Mickey
1950—Destination Big House

Knox, Mona
1952—Thundering Caravans

Knox, Patricia[189]
1941—A Man Betrayed*
       Sailors on Leave*
1942—Lady for a Night
       A Tragedy at Midnight*
       Heart of the Golden West*
1943—O, My Darling Clementine
1944—Casanova in Burlesque
       Silent Partner
       Man from Frisco*
       The Port of Forty Thieves
1945—Flame of Barbary Coast*
1947—Exposed
1948—Homicide for Three*
1949—The James Brothers of Missouri
       Post Office Investigator
1951—Insurance Investigator

Koenig, Mabelle
1949—The Fighting Kentuckian

Kohler, Jr., Fred[214]
1938—Prison Nurse
1939—Man of Conquest*
1941—Two Gun Sheriff
       Nevada City
       Dick Tracy Vs. Crime, Inc.*
1942—Raiders of the Range
1943—Calling Wild Bill Elliott
1944—The Big Bonanza
1948—The Gallant Legion*
1949—Hellfire*
1950—Twilight in the Sierras
       Desperadoes of the West*
1951—Spoilers of the Plains
1952—Hoodlum Empire*
1956—Daniel Boone, Trail Blazer
1957—Journey to Freedom

Kohler, Sr., Fred[224]
1936—The Vigilantes Are Coming
1938—Gangs of New York
       Billy the Kid Returns

Koko
Horse. Credited on-screen in last 13
Rex Allen westerns during 1951-54
as "The Miracle Horse of the Movies."

Kolb, Clarence[224]
1937—Portia on Trial
1939—I Was a Convict
1945—Road to Alcatraz
1947—The Pilgrim Lady

Kolker, Henry
1935—Frisco Waterfront
1936—Sitting on the Moon
1939—Should Husbands Work?
       Main Street Lawyer
1940—Grand Ole Opry

Komai, Tetsu
1941—Adventures of Captain Marvel

Kornman, Mary
1937—Youth on Parole
1938—King of the Newsboys

Kortman, Bob[224]
1935—Lawless Range*
1936—The Lonely Trail
       Winds of the Wasteland
       The Vigilantes Are Coming
       Ghost-Town Gold
       Robinson Crusoe of Clipper Island
1937—Zorro Rides Again
1938—The Lone Ranger*
       The Fighting Devil Dogs*
       Come on, Rangers*
1940—Adventures of Red Ryder
1941—Lady from Louisiana*
       Death Valley Outlaws*
1942—Jesse James, Jr.*
       The Sundown Kid
1943—Days of Old Cheyenne
       Riders of the Rio Grande*
       The Black Hills Express
       Man from Music Mountain*
       California Joe
1944—Beneath Western Skies*
       Outlaws of Santa Fe
       Call of the Rockies

Kortner, Fritz[224]
1943—The Purple V

Kosleck, Martin[224]
1941—The Devil Pays Off
1944—Secrets of Scotland Yard
1945—Gangs of the Waterfront
1946—Crime of the Century

Koumani, Maya
1957—The Fighting Wildcats

Krah, Marc
1948—Train to Alcatraz

Kramer, Marc[30]
1936—The Mandarin Mystery*
       Beware of Ladies*

David Knight

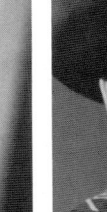
Fuzzy Knight

Patricia Knight

Elyse Knox

Fred Kohler, Sr.

Clarence Kolb

Kreig, Frank
1950—Lonely Heart Bandits

Kreuger, Kurt[224]
1943—The Purple V
       Secret Service in Darkest Africa

Kroeger, Berry
1955—Yellowneck

Krueger, Lorraine
1941—Los Angeles Examiner Benefit*
1946—One Exciting Week

Kruger, Alma[224]
1941—Puddin' Head

Kruger, Otto[224]
1935—Two Sinners
1937—Glamorous Night
1939—The Zero Hour
1941—Mercy Island
1944—Storm Over Lisbon
1945—Earl Carroll Vanities
       The Chicago Kid
       Woman Who Came Back
1946—The Fabulous Suzanne
1955—The Last Command

Kruschen, Jack[172]
1950—Women from Headquarters
1951—Cuban Fireball
1952—Tropical Heat Wave
1954—The Untamed Heiress
1955—Carolina Cannonball

Kuhn, Mickey
1939—S. O. S. Tidal Wave

Kulky, Henry
See Bomber Kulkovich.

Kuter, Kay
1955—City of Shadows

Kuznetzoff, Adia
1944—That's My Baby

Kydd, Sam
1953—Trent's Last Case

L

Lackteen, Frank[224]
1936—Comin' 'Round the Mountain*
1939—The Kansas Terrors
       South of the Border*
1940—Girl from Havana
1941—Jungle Girl
1942—The Girl from Alaska
1943—Headin' for God's Country*
1947—Oregon Trail Scouts
       The Black Widow*
1949—Daughter of the Jungle
1950—North of the Great Divide
1955—The Twinkle in God's Eye*
1956—Jaguar*

Ladd, Alan[102]
1937—All Over Town*
1938—Come on, Leathernecks*
1939—The Mysterious Miss X*
1940—In Old Missouri
       Meet the Missus
1941—Petticoat Politics

Laffan, Patricia
1959—Hidden Homicide

Laidlaw, Ethan[225]
1937—All Over Town*
       Escape by Night*
1938—Born to be Wild*
       Call the Mesquiteers*
       Rhythm of the Saddle
1939—Home on the Prairie
       The Night Riders
       Blue Montana Skies*
       Three Texas Steers
       Man of Conquest*
       Colorado Sunset*
       Dick Tracy's G-Men*
       Cowboys from Texas
1940—Dark Command*
       The Tulsa Kid
1941—Wyoming Wildcat*
       Lady from Louisiana*
1942—Cowboy Serenade*
       Stagecoach Express
1943—Fugitive from Sonora
1947—Spoilers of the North*
       The Fabulous Texan*

Laird, Effie[225]
1944—Beneath Western Skies
       Man from Frisco*
1950—House by the River
       California Passage*
1953—Sweethearts on Parade*
1955—The Road to Denver*

Lake, Arthur[225]
1937—Exiled to Shanghai
1941—Los Angeles Examiner Benefit*
1945—The Big Show-Off

Lake, Fred
1957—Thunder Over Tangier

Lally, William J.
1949—The Red Menace

LaMal, Isabel
1943—The Black Hills Express*
       Man from Music Mountain*
       Raiders of Sunset Pass*
1944—Casanova in Burlesque*
       The Yellow Rose of Texas*
1945—Identity Unknown*

Lamas, Fernando[102]
1950—The Avengers

Lamb, Gil[225]
1947—Hit Parade of 1947

Lambert, Jack[225]
1946—Plainsman and the Lady
1949—Brimstone
1950—North of the Great Divide

Lambert, Jack
1955—Cross Channel
1956—Track the Man Down

Lamble, Lloyd
1955—The Green Buddha
1956—Track the Man Down

Lamont, Duncan
1957—Time is My Enemy

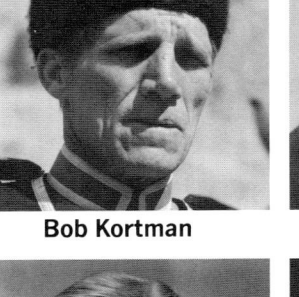
Bob Kortman

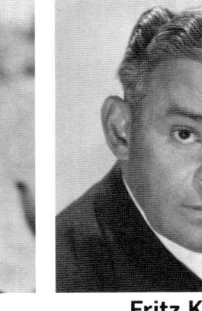
Fritz Kortner

Martin Kosleck

Kurt Kreuger

Alma Kruger

Otto Kruger

Frank Lackteen

Lamont, Marten[30]
1937—All Over Town*
1940—Melody and Moonlight
  Mysterious Doctor Satan*
1941—Adventures of Captain Marvel*
1945—Federal Operator 99
1950—Redwood Forest Trail

Lamont, Molly
1943—A Gentle Gangster
  Thumbs Up

Lamour, Dorothy
1940—Chinese Garden Festival*

Lanchester, Elsa[225]
1943—Thumbs Up
1947—Northwest Outpost
1954—Hell's Half Acre

Land of Opportunity—series
1949—The American Rodeo
  The Sponge Diver
1950—Tillers of the Soil
  The Mardi Gras

Landis, Carole[102]
1939—Three Texas Steers
  Daredevils of the Red Circle
  Cowboys from Texas
1941—Hollywood Visits the Navy*

Landon, Hal[225]
1947—Springtime in the Sierras
  The Black Widow*
1948—Carson City Raiders
  The Gallant Legion
1949—Navajo Trail Raiders
1951—Oh! Susanna*

Lane, Allan[154]
1937—The Duke Comes Back
1940—Grand Ole Opry
  King of the Royal Mounted
1942—King of the Mounties
1943—Daredevils of the West
1944—The Tiger Woman
  Call of the South Seas
  Silver City Kid
  Stagecoach to Monterey
  Sheriff of Sundown
1945—The Topeka Terror
  Corpus Christi Bandits
  Bells of Rosarita
  Trail of Kit Carson
  Don't Fence Me In*
1946—Gay Blades
  A Guy Could Change
  Night Train to Memphis
  Santa Fe Uprising
  Out California Way
  Stagecoach to Denver
1947—Vigilantes of Boomtown
  Homesteaders of Paradise Valley
  Oregon Trail Scouts
  Rustlers of Devil's Canyon
  Marshal of Cripple Creek
  The Wild Frontier
  Bandits of Dark Canyon
1948—Oklahoma Badlands
  The Bold Frontiersman
  Carson City Raiders
  Marshal of Amarillo
  Desperadoes of Dodge City
  The Denver Kid
  Sundown in Santa Fe
  Renegades of Sonora
1949—Sheriff of Wichita
  Death Valley Gunfighter
  Frontier Investigator
  The Wyoming Bandit
  Bandit King of Texas
  Navajo Trail Raiders
  The American Rodeo
  Powder River Rustlers
1950—Gunmen of Abilene
  Code of the Silver Sage
  Salt Lake Raiders
  Covered Wagon Raid
  Vigilante Hideout
  Frisco Tornado
  Rustlers on Horseback
  Trail of Robin Hood
1951—Rough Riders of Durango
  Night Riders of Montana
  Wells Fargo Gunmaster
  Fort Dodge Stampede
  Desert of Lost Men
1952—Captive of Billy the Kid
  Leadville Gunslinger
  Black Hills Ambush
  Thundering Caravans
  Desperadoes' Outpost
1953—Marshal of Cedar Rock
  Savage Frontier
  Bandits of the West
  El Paso Stampede

Lane, Arthur
1955—Secret Venture
1956—Track the Man Down

Ethan Laidlaw

Effie Laird

Arthur Lake

Gil Lamb

Jack Lambert

Elsa Lanchester

Hal Landon

Lenita Lane

Lola Lane

Nora Lane

Richard Lane

Rosemary Lane

Lane, Charles
1936—Ticket to Paradise*
1940—The Crooked Road
1941—Sis Hopkins*
1942—Yokel Boy*
  Home in Wyomin'
  Flying Tigers*
1946—The Invisible Informer
1948—Out of the Storm
  Moonrise*

Lane, Dick
1954—Crazylegs

Lane, Lenita[225]
1936—Federal Agent

Lane, Lola[225]
1937—The Sheik Steps Out
1940—Gangs of Chicago
1945—Identity Unknown
  Steppin' in Society

Lane, Mike
1957—Hell Canyon Outlaws

Lane, Morgan
1957—Journey to Freedom

Lane, Nora[225]
1941—The Gay Vagabond*
  Angels with Broken Wings*
  Puddin' Head
  Mountain Moonlight*
  The Pittsburgh Kid*
  Dick Tracy Vs. Crime, Inc.*
1942—Lady for a Night*
  A Tragedy at Midnight*
  Heart of the Rio Grande*
  Joan of Ozark*
  Secrets of the Underground*
1943—Chatterbox*
  The Masked Marvel*
1944—The Fighting Seabees*
  Atlantic City*
  Lake Placid Serenade*

Lane, Richard[225]
1939—Main Street Lawyer
1943—Swing Your Partner
1944—Brazil
1946—Sioux City Sue
1947—Hit Parade of 1947

Lane, Rosemary[225]
1943—Chatterbox
1944—Trocadero

Lang, June[225]
1939—Forged Passport

Lang, Kathryn
1949—Flame of Youth

Langdon, Harry[225]
1945—Swingin' on a Rainbow

Lange, Elaine[225]
1945—Federal Operator 99
  Man from Oklahoma
  The Fatal Witness*
  Girls of the Big House*
1946—The Undercover Woman
  The Catman of Paris
  In Old Sacramento*

Langford, Frances[80]
1937—The Hit Parade
1940—Hit Parade of 1941

Langley, Bruce[31]
1942—Youth on Parade
1946—Red River Renegades
  G.I. War Brides*

Langton, Paul
1958—Girl in the Woods

Lannes, Georges
1959—O.S.S. 117 is Not Dead

Lansing, Joi
1956—Terror at Midnight*

LaPlanche, Rosemary[225]
1943—Swing Your Partner
1949—Federal Agents Vs. Underworld, Inc.

Largay, Raymond
1948—Slippy McGee

Larkin, Jerry
1936—The Big Show

June Lang

Harry Langdon

Elaine Lange

Rosemary LaPlanche

LaRocque, Rod[226]
1935 — Frisco Waterfront

LaRoy, Rita[226]
1936 — The Mandarin Mystery
1937 — The Hit Parade*

Larsen, Peter
1955 — In Old Vienna

Larson, Bobby
1942 — Affairs of Jimmy Valentine
1950 — Redwood Forest Trail

Larson, Christine
1950 — Trail Without Jury

Larson, Jack
1950 — Redwood Forest Trail

Rod LaRocque

Rita LaRoy

Lyle Latell

Harry Lauter

LaRue, Frank[227]
1935 — Forced Landing*
1936 — The Singing Vagabond
        Red River Valley
1937 — Bar-Z Bad Men
        "Lightnin'" Crandall
        Trail of Vengeance
        Gun Lords of Stirrup Basin
        Dangerous Holiday*
        A Lawman is Born
        Boothill Brigade
        Public Cowboy No. 1
        The Colorado Kid
1938 — Outlaws of Sonora
        Dick Tracy Returns*
        Overland Stage Raiders
        Come on, Rangers*
1941 — A Missouri Outlaw
1942 — Stardust on the Sage*
        The Cyclone Kid
        The Old Homestead*

LaRue, Jack[135]
1935 — The Spanish Cape Mystery
1937 — Dangerous Holiday
1938 — Arson Gang Busters
1939 — In Old Caliente
1940 — Forgotten Girls
1942 — X Marks the Spot
1943 — A Gentle Gangster
        Secret Service in Darkest Africa*
        A Scream in the Dark
        Pistol Packin' Mama
1945 — Steppin' in Society
        Dakota
1946 — Murder in the Music Hall
        In Old Sacramento
        Santa Fe Uprising
1953 — Ride the Man Down

Lasky, Art
1937 — The Duke Comes Back

Latell, Lyle[226]
1944 — That's My Baby
1945 — The Chicago Kid*
1946 — The Mysterious Mr. Valentine
        That Brennan Girl*
1955 — I Cover the Underworld*
1957 — Affair in Reno*

LaTorre, Charles
1950 — Harbor of Missing Men
        Sunset in the West
1951 — Secrets of Monte Carlo

Laughlan, Agnes
1957 — Time is My Enemy

Laurence, Charles
1955 — Cross Channel

Laurencic, Dora
1955 — The Divided Heart

Laurenz, John
1947 — Apache Rose

Laurie, John
1942 — Suicide Squadron

Lauter, Harry[226]
1947 — The Magnificent Rogue*
        Hit Parade of 1947*
1948 — Moonrise*
1949 — Prince of the Plains
        Frontier Investigator
        Bandit King of Texas
1950 — Flying Disc Man from Mars
1951 — Silver City Bonanza
        Thunder in God's Country
1953 — Can. Mounties Vs. Atomic Invaders
1954 — Trader Tom of the China Seas
        Flight Nurse*
1955 — The Eternal Sea*
        King of the Carnival
1957 — The Lawless Eighties*
        Raiders of Old California

Lawford, Peter[102]
1943 — London Blackout Murders*
        The Purple V
        Someone to Remember*
        The West Side Kid

Marc Lawrence

Priscilla Lawson

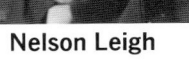

Tracy Layne

Anna Lee

Ruta Lee

Lawless, Kevin
1952 — The Quiet Man

Lawrence, Edna
1938 — The Lone Ranger*
        Born to be Wild*
1940 — Rancho Grande*

Lawrence, Hugh
1958 — Juvenile Jungle

Lawrence, Jack
1940 — Oklahoma Renegades*
        Frontier Vengeance
1941 — Gangs of Sonora*

Lawrence, Mady
1942 — A Tragedy at Midnight*
        Sleepytime Gal*
        Heart of the Rio Grande*
        Yokel Boy*

Dorothy Lee

Nelson Leigh

Lawrence, Marc[226]
1939 — S.O.S. Tidal Wave
1941 — Public Enemies
1942 — Yokel Boy
        Call of the Canyon
1945 — Flame of Barbary Coast
        Don't Fence Me In
1947 — Yankee Fakir
1948 — Out of the Storm

Lawrence, Muriel[31]
1951 — Belle LeGrand
1952 — Woman in the Dark*
        Bal Tabarin
        I Dream of Jeanie

Lawrence, Sheldon
1957 — The Fighting Wildcats

Lawrence, Tedd
1954 — Roogie's Bump

Lawrence-Brown, Stan
1950 — Jungle Stampede

Lawson, Kate
1940 — Girl from God's Country
1950 — Rock Island Trail

Lawson, Priscilla[226]
1938 — Heroes of the Hills

Lay, Eugene
1946 — G.I. War Brides

Layne, Tracy[226]
1935 — Tumbling Tumbleweeds*
        Melody Trail
1936 — The Lawless Nineties
        King of the Pecos*
        Comin' 'Round the Mountain
        The Singing Cowboy
        The Lonely Trail*
        Undersea Kingdom*
        Guns and Guitars
        Winds of the Wasteland
        The Vigilantes are Coming
        The Three Mesquiteers*
        Robinson Crusoe of Clipper Island
        The Big Show*
1937 — The Riders of the Whistling Skull*
        Git Along Little Dogies*

Rex Lease

Francis Lederer

Lila Lee

Queenie Leonard

Layton, Howard
1957 — Time is My Enemy

Leary, Nolan[135]
1943 — The Blocked Trail*
        Carson City Cyclone*
        Days of Old Cheyenne
        Riders of the Rio Grande*
        The West Side Kid*
        Sleepy Lagoon*
        The Masked Marvel*
1944 — My Best Gal*
        Outlaws of Santa Fe
        The Tiger Woman
        Man from Frisco*
        Call of the Rockies*
        Atlantic City*
        Code of the Prairie*
        My Buddy*
        Sheriff of Sundown*
        Faces in the Fog*
        Zorro's Black Whip*
        Thoroughbreds*
1945 — The Phantom Speaks*
        Lone Texas Ranger*
        Santa Fe Saddlemates*
        Federal Operator 99*
        Hitchhike to Happiness*
        Love, Honor and Goodbye*
1946 — California Gold Rush*
        Murder in the Music Hall*
        Out California Way
1947 — That's My Gal*
        That's My Man*
        Web of Danger*
        Saddle Pals*
        Driftwood*
        The Fabulous Texan*
1948 — I, Jane Doe*
1949 — The Wyoming Bandit*
        The James Brothers of Missouri
1953 — Red River Shore

Monte Montague, Don "Red" Barry, Frank LaRue

Ann Rutherford, Fritz Leiber

Lease, Rex[226]
1937—S O S Coast Guard*
1938—Desert Patrol
1939—The Lone Ranger Rides Again
    S.O.S. Tidal Wave*
    In Old Monterey*
    Calling All Marines*
    South of the Border
1940—Rancho Grande
    One Man's Law
    Under Texas Skies
    The Trail Blazers
    Lone Star Raiders
1941—The Phantom Cowboy
    Saddlemates*
    Nevada City*
    Citadel of Crime*
    Bad Man of Deadwood*
    Outlaws of Cherokee Trail
    Death Valley Outlaws
    Jesse James at Bay*
    Sierra Sue
    Mr. District Atty. in the Carter Case*
1942—Arizona Terrors
    Home in Wyomin'*
    Stardust in the Sage*
    In Old California*
    The Cyclone Kid
    Sunset Serenade*
    Shadows on the Sage*
1943—Dead Man's Gulch
    Idaho*
    King of the Cowboys*
    Santa Fe Scouts*
    Daredevils of the West
    Riders of the Rio Grande*
1944—Cowboy and the Senorita*
    The Tiger Woman*
    Silent Partner*
    The Yellow Rose of Texas*
    Man from Frisco*
    Call of the Rockies*
    Bordertown Trail
    Cheyenne Wildcat*
    Code of the Prairie*
    Sheriff of Sundown*
    Firebrands of Arizona
1945—Earl Carroll Vanities*
    Lone Texas Ranger
    Three's a Crowd*
    Flame of Barbary Coast
    Santa Fe Saddlemates
    Bells of Rosarita*
    The Chicago Kid*
    Federal Operator 99*
    Oregon Trail*
    Swingin' on a Rainbow*
    Rough Riders of Cheyenne*
    Dakota*
1946—The Phantom Rider
    Days of Buffalo Bill
    King of the Forest Rangers*
    Sun Valley Cyclone
    The Crimson Ghost
    Plainsman and the Lady*
    Heldorado
1947—Angel and the Badman*
    Wyoming*
1948—The Gallant Legion*
    Out of the Storm
    Night Time in Nevada*
    The Plunderers*
1949—Rose of the Yukon*
    Hideout*
    The Last Bandit*
1950—Bells of Coronado
    Singing Guns
    Code of the Silver Sage
    Hills of Oklahoma
    Covered Wagon Raid
    Frisco Tornado
1951—Spoilers of the Plains*
    Pals of the Golden West*
1952—Colorado Sundown*
    Toughest Man in Arizona*
1953—Shadows of Tombstone*

Leaver, Philip
1943—Alibi

LeBaron, Bert
Many films.
1939—Daredevils of the Red Circle*
    Dick Tracy's G-Men*
1940—Drums of Fu Manchu*
    Mysterious Doctor Satan*
1941—King of the Texas Rangers*
    Dick Tracy Vs. Crime, Inc.*
1942—Spy Smasher*
1944—Captain America*
    The Tiger Woman*
1947—Jesse James Rides Again*
1949—Federal Agents Vs. Underworld, Inc.*
    King of the Rocket Men*
    The James Brothers of Missouri*
    Radar Patrol Vs. Spy King
1950—The Invisible Monster*
    Desperadoes of the West*
    Don Daredevil Rides Again*
1954—Trader Tom of the China Seas*
1955—King of the Carnival*

LeBaron, Eddie—and orchestra
1944—Trocadero

Lederer, Francis[226]
1941—Puddin' Head
1946—The Madonna's Secret
1950—Surrender
1956—Lisbon

Lee, Anna[226]
1942—Flying Tigers
1946—G.I. War Brides

Lee, Billy
1939—In Old Monterey
    Jeepers Creepers
1941—Nevada City

Lee, Canada
1942—Henry Browne, Farmer

Lee, Dorothy[226]
1939—S.O.S. Tidal Wave

Lee, Earl
1952—Tropical Heat Wave
1954—Geraldine

Lee, Eddie
1943—The Man from Thunder River
    Headin' for God's Country
1950—Bells of Coronado

Lee, Lila[226]
1936—Country Gentlemen
1937—Two Wise Maids

Lee, Mary[32]
1939—South of the Border
1940—Rancho Grande
    Gaucho Serenade
    Carolina Moon
    Sing, Dance, Plenty Hot
    Ride, Tenderfoot, Ride
    Melody and Moonlight
    Melody Ranch
    Barnyard Follies
1941—Ridin' on a Rainbow
    Back in the Saddle
    Hollywood Visits the Navy*
    The Singing Hill
    Angels with Broken Wings
    Meet Roy Rogers*
    Stars Past and Present*
1943—Shantytown
    Nobody's Darling
1944—Cowboy and the Senorita
    Three Little Sisters
    Song of Nevada

Lee, Pinky[32]
1945—Earl Carroll Vanities
1946—One Exciting Week
1947—That's My Gal
1951—In Old Amarillo
    South of Caliente
    Pals of the Golden West

Lee, Robin
1942—Ice-Capades Revue

Lee, Ruta[226]
1955—The Twinkle in God's Eye

Lee, Ruth
1944—Tucson Raiders
1945—Corpus Christi Bandits
    Swingin' on a Rainbow
1947—The Magnificent Rogue
1951—Insurance Investigator
1954—Hell's Outpost
1956—Terror at Midnight*

Lee, Scott
1952—Wild Horse Ambush

Leeds, Andrea[119]
1937—It Could Happen to You
1941—Stars at Play*

Leeds, Lila
1948—Moonrise

Leeds, Peter
1954—The Atomic Kid

Lefton, Abe
1935—Melody Trail
1936—The Old Corral

LeGall, Andre
1959—O. S. S. 117 is Not Dead

Leiber, Fritz[227]
1936—Hearts in Bondage
    Down to the Sea
1947—Bells of San Angelo

Leigh, Frank
1935—The Spanish Cape Mystery

Leigh, George
1945—The Fatal Witness

Leigh, Nelson[226]
1945—Identity Unknown

Leigh, Patrick Dennis
1958—No Place to Land

Leighton, Melinda
See Linda Johnson.

Lemon, Bob
1949—The Kid from Cleveland

Lemus, Conchita
1947—Apache Rose

Lenhart, Billy
See Butch and Buddy.

Lennon, Jim
1949—Alias the Champ

Lenoir, Leon
1944—Brazil

Leon, Connie
1946—That Brennan Girl

Leonard, Queenie[226]
1943—Thumbs Up

Leonard, Sheldon[227]
1944—Trocadero
1946—Rainbow Over Texas
    The Last Crooked Mile
1948—Madonna of the Desert
1949—Daughter of the Jungle

Leong, James B.
1942—Remember Pearl Harbor!
1943—Headin' for God's Country

Leontovitsch, Maria
1955—The Divided Heart

Leopold, Ethelrita[227]
1945—Earl Carroll Vanities*
    Three's a Crowd*
1947—That's My Man*

Lescoulie, Jack
1940—Oklahoma Renegades
1941—A Man Betrayed*

Leslie, Eddie
1955—Trouble in Store

Leslie, Joan[80]
1941—Wampas Baby Stars*
1952—Toughest Man in Arizona
1953—Woman They Almost Lynched
1954—Flight Nurse
    Jubilee Trail
    Hell's Outpost

Leslie, Kay
1941—Wampas Baby Stars*

Leslie, Maxine
1942—Pardon My Stripes

Leslie, Nan[227]
1949—Pioneer Marshal
1953—Iron Mountain Trail

Lessey, George
1943—Pistol Packin' Mama

Lester, Bruce
1951—Secrets of Monte Carlo

Lester, Jerry
1942—Sleepytime Gal

Lester, Vicki
1942—Sleepytime Gal*

Lester, William
1950—Twilight in the Sierras

Letz, George
See George Montgomery.

Levey, Gerry
1957—Operation Conspiracy

Lewis, Dorothy[81]
1941—Ice-Capades

Lewis, George J.[135]
1936—Ride Ranger Ride
1941—Kansas Cyclone*
    Death Valley Outlaws*
1942—Spy Smasher*
    Perils of Nyoka
    Outlaws of Pine Ridge
1943—G-Men Vs. The Black Dragon
    The Blocked Trail
    Daredevils of the West
    Secret Service in Darkest Africa*
    The Black Hills Express
    The Masked Marvel*
1944—Captain America
    The Laramie Trail
    The Tiger Woman
    Haunted Harbor
    Brazil*
    Zorro's Black Whip
1945—Federal Operator 99
    Mexicana*
    Wagon Wheels Westward
    Song of Mexico
1946—The Phantom Rider
    Rainbow Over Texas
    Passkey to Danger
    Under Nevada Skies
1947—Twilight on the Rio Grande
    Web of Danger*
    Blackmail
1948—Adv. of Frank and Jesse James
    Renegades of Sonora
1949—Ghost of Zorro
    Radar Patrol Vs. Spy King
1951—South of Caliente*

Lewis, Harry
1956—The Man is Armed

Lewis, Jarma
1952—The Wac from Walla Walla*

Lewis, Jean Ann
1957—Journey to Freedom

Lewis, Jimmie—and Texas Cowboys
1940—Carolina Moon

Lewis, Kay
1942—Suicide Squadron

Lewis, Mitchell[227]
1953—The Sun Shines Bright

Lewis, Ronald
1955—The Square Ring

Lewis, Ted—and orchestra
1937—Manhattan Merry-Go-Round

Lewis, Woodley
1954—Crazylegs

Lezard, Cecile
1950—The Avengers

Lie, Henry
1946—Murder in the Music Hall

Light Crust Doughboys
1936—Oh, Susanna!
    The Big Show

Lightning
1937—Escape by Night
1938—Call of the Yukon

Sheldon Leonard

Ethelrita Leopold

Nan Leslie

Mitchell Lewis

James Lilburn

Lilburn, James[228]
1952 — The Quiet Man
1953 — San Antone

Liliane and Mario
1945 — Earl Carroll Vanities

Linaker, Kay[228]
1936 — The Girl from Mandalay

Lincoln, Elmo
1939 — Blue Montana Skies*
Mountain Rhythm*
Wyoming Outlaw
Colorado Sunset
1940 — Gangs of Chicago*

Linder, Leslie
1955 — The Green Buddha

Lindley, Virginia
1947 — The Black Widow

Lindo, Olga
1943 — Alibi

Lindsay, Margaret[228]
1942 — A Tragedy at Midnight

Lindsey, Marilyn
1953 — Woman They Almost Lynched

Linn, James
1945 — The Cherokee Flash
1946 — Alias Billy the Kid

Lister, Moira
1955 — Trouble in Store

Litel, John[228]
1944 — My Buddy
Faces in the Fog
Lake Placid Serenade
1946 — The Madonna's Secret
1948 — I, Jane Doe
1951 — Cuban Fireball
1955 — Double Jeopardy

Little Brown Jug
See Don Reynolds.

Littlefield, Lucien[228]
1935 — Cappy Ricks Returns
1938 — Hollywood Stadium Mystery!
The Night Hawk
1939 — Sabotage
Jeepers Creepers
Money to Burn
1942 — Bells of Capistrano
1944 — Casanova in Burlesque
Cowboy and the Senorita
Goodnight Sweetheart
Lights of Old Santa Fe
Zorro's Black Whip
1946 — In Old Sacramento*
Rendezvous with Annie
That Brennan Girl
1948 — Lightnin' in the Forest
1949 — Susanna Pass
1952 — Woman of the North Country*

Little Vagabonds
1941 — Tuxedo Junction

Livermore, Paul
1951 — The Wild Blue Yonder*
1952 — Hoodlum Empire*
Thunderbirds
1953 — Woman They Almost Lynched*
Nightmare Typhoon
Captives of the Zero Hour
1954 — Flight Nurse*

Livingston, Mary
1941 — Variety Reel*

Livingston, Robert[33]
1936 — The Vigilantes Are Coming
The Three Mesquiteers
Ghost-Town Gold
Roarin' Lead
1937 — The Riders of the Whistling Skull
Larceny on the Air
The Bold Caballero
Circus Girl
Hit the Saddle
Gunsmoke Ranch
Come on, Cowboys!
Range Defenders
Heart of the Rockies
Wild Horse Rodeo
1938 — The Purple Vigilantes
Call the Mesquiteers
Arson Gang Busters
Outlaws of Sonora
Ladies in Distress
Riders of the Black Hills
Heroes of the Hills
The Night Hawk
Orphans of the Street
Federal Man-Hunt
1939 — The Lone Ranger Rides Again
The Kansas Terrors
Cowboys from Texas
1940 — Heroes of the Saddle
Pioneers of the West
Covered Wagon Days
Rocky Mountain Rangers
Oklahoma Renegades
Under Texas Skies
The Trail Blazers
Lone Star Raiders
1941 — Prairie Pioneers
Pals of the Pecos
Saddlemates
Gangs of Sonora
1943 — Pistol Packin' Mama
1944 — Pride of the Plains
Beneath Western Skies
The Laramie Trail
Goodnight Sweetheart
Storm Over Lisbon
Brazil
Lake Placid Serenade
The Big Bonanza
1945 — Bells of Rosarita
Steppin' in Society
The Cheaters
Tell It to a Star
Don't Fence Me In
Dakota
1946 — The Undercover Woman
Valley of the Zombies
That's My Gal*
1948 — King of the Gamblers*
Daredevils of the Clouds
Grand Canyon Trail

Lloyd, Doris[228]
1945 — Scotland Yard Investigator
1946 — G. I. War Brides

Lloyd, George[135]
1936 — The Return of Jimmy Valentine*
Bulldog Edition*
1937 — Exiled to Shanghai*
1938 — Arson Gang Busters*
1940 — Gaucho Serenade*
1941 — In Old Cheyenne*
Lady from Louisiana*
Bad Man of Deadwood*
1942 — In Old California*
The Traitor Within*
1944 — Man from Frisco*
My Buddy*
1946 — A Guy Could Change*
Home in Oklahoma*
1947 — Vigilantes of Boomtown
The Fabulous Texan*
1948 — Under California Stars
The Denver Kid
1949 — Death Valley Gunfighter
Susanna Pass*
Frontier Investigator
Outcasts of the Trail
South of Rio*
Bandit King of Texas
San Antone Ambush*
1950 — The Arizona Cowboy
Rustlers on Horseback*
1951 — Heart of the Rockies*
Don Daredevil Rides Again*
Govt. Agents Vs. Phantom Legion
1953 — Iron Mountain Trail

Lloyd-Pack, Charles
1956 — Track the Man Down

Locher, Charles
See Jon Hall.

Locher, Felix
1958 — Hell Ship Mutiny

Locke, Harry
1955 — Doctor in the House

Locke, Philip
1957 — Operation Conspiracy

Kay Linaker

Margaret Lindsay

John Litel

Lucien Littlefield

Lockhart, Gene[228]
1937 — The Sheik Steps Out
1944 — Man from Frisco
1948 — The Inside Story
I, Jane Doe
1952 — Hoodlum Empire
1953 — The Lady Wants Mink
1955 — The Vanishing American

Lockhart, Kathleen
1939 — Man of Conquest

Lockwood, Alexander
1957 — Hell Canyon Outlaws

Lockwood, Margaret[228]
1943 — Alibi
1953 — Trent's Last Case
1954 — Laughing Anne
Trouble in the Glen

Loder, John
1945 — Jealousy
Woman Who Came Back

Lodge, John[228]
1937 — Bulldog Drummond at Bay

Loes, Billy
1954 — Roogie's Bump

Margaret Lockwood

John Lodge

Loft, Arthur[135]
1937 — Paradise Express
Public Cowboy No. 1
1938 — Down in "Arkansaw"
Rhythm of the Saddle
1939 — Southward, Ho!
Smuggled Cargo
Days of Jesse James
1940 — Dark Command*
Covered Wagon Days*
The Crooked Road
The Carson City Kid
Colorado
Texas Terrors
1941 — Back in the Saddle
Down Mexico Way
1942 — South of Santa Fe
1943 — Silver Spurs*
A Scream in the Dark
In Old Oklahoma*
1944 — My Best Gal*
Rosie, the Riveter
My Buddy*
Lights of Old Santa Fe
1945 — Man from Oklahoma
1946 — Sheriff of Redwood Valley
One Exciting Week
Traffic in Crime

Doris Lloyd

Gene Lockhart

Loftin, Carey[228]
1939 — S. O. S. Tidal Wave*
Dick Tracy's G-Men*
The Covered Trailer*
1941 — A Man Betrayed*
The Great Train Robbery*
Public Enemies*
1942 — Spy Smasher*
Perils of Nyoka*
1943 — King of the Cowboys*
Shantytown*
Secret Service in Darkest Africa*
The Masked Marvel*
1944 — The Lady and the Monster*
The Tiger Woman*
Haunted Harbor*
Zorro's Black Whip*
Army 101 — Equip. Maintenance*
1945 — The Purple Monster Strikes*
1946 — King of the Forest Rangers*
The Crimson Ghost*
1947 — Jesse James Rides Again*
The Black Widow*
1948 — G-Men Never Forget*
Dangers of the Canadian Mounted*
Adv. of Frank and Jesse James*
1949 — Federal Agents Vs. Underworld, Inc.*
King of the Rocket Men*
Radar Patrol Vs. Spy King*
1950 — The Invisible Monster*
Flying Disc Man from Mars*
1951 — Don Daredevil Rides Again*
1952 — Radar Men from the Moon*
1953 — Can. Mounties Vs. Atomic Invaders*

Logan, James
1955 — Panther Girl of the Kongo

Logan, Stanley
1940 — Women in War
1951 — Pride of Maryland

Lom, Herbert
1943 — At Dawn We Die

Lombard, Linda
1947 — Twilight on the Rio Grande*
1948 — Moonrise*

London, Julie[228]
1955 — The Fighting Chance

Lone Ranger — series
1938 — The Lone Ranger
1939 — The Lone Ranger Rides Again

Long, Audrey[229]
1948 — Homicide for Three
1949 — Duke of Chicago
Post Office Investigator
Alias the Champ
1950 — Trial Without Jury
1951 — Insurance Investigator

Long, Lotus
1949 — Rose of the Yukon

Long, Robert
1951 — Street Bandits

Long, Walter[229]
1937 — The Bold Caballero

Carey Loftin

Julie London

Tom London[30]

1935 — Tumbling Tumbleweeds
 Cappy Ricks Returns*
 Sagebrush Troubadour*
1936 — The Lawless Nineties
 Guns and Guitars
 Bulldog Edition*
1937 — Bar-Z Bad Men
 Springtime in the Rockies
 Zorro Rides Again
1938 — The Lone Ranger
 Outlaws of Sonora
 Gangs of New York*
 The Fighting Devil Dogs
 Riders of the Black Hills
 Prairie Moon
 Rhythm of the Saddle*
 Santa Fe Stampede
1939 — Mexicali Rose*
 The Night Riders
 Blue Montana Skies*
 Southward, Ho!
 Mountain Rhythm
1940 — Ghost Valley Raiders
 Dark Command*
 Covered Wagon Days
 Gaucho Serenade*
 The Ranger and the Lady*
 Melody Ranch*
 Lone Star Raiders
1941 — Ridin' on a Rainbow*
 Pals of the Pecos
 Sheriff of Tombstone*
 Bad Man of Deadwood*
1942 — Arizona Terrors
 Cowboy Serenade*
 Spy Smasher
 Stardust on the Sage
 Sons of the Pioneers*
 Shadows on the Sage
 Ridin' Down the Canyon*
1943 — Idaho*
 Carson City Cyclone*
 Santa Fe Scouts
 Daredevils of the West*
 Song of Texas*
 Silver Spurs*
 The Black Hills Express*
 Wagon Tracks West
 The Man from the Rio Grande*
 The Masked Marvel*
 Here Comes Elmer*
 Overland Mail Robbery
 Canyon City*
 In Old Oklahoma*
 California Joe*

1944 — Captain America*
 Beneath Western Skies
 The Fighting Seabees*
 Mojave Firebrand*
 Hidden Valley Outlaws
 Rosie, the Riveter*
 The Lady and the Monster*
 Tucson Raiders*
 The Tiger Woman*
 Silent Partner*
 The Yellow Rose of Texas
 Man from Frisco*
 Marshal of Reno
 Call of the Rockies
 Silver City Kid
 Three Little Sisters
 The Girl Who Dared*
 Bordertown Trail*
 The San Antonio Kid
 Stagecoach to Monterey
 Cheyenne Wildcat
 Code of the Prairie
 My Buddy*
 Sheriff of Sundown
 Vigilantes of Dodge City
 Faces in the Fog
 Firebrands of Arizona
 Zorro's Black Whip
 Thoroughbreds
1945 — Grissly's Millions
 The Topeka Terror
 Great Stagecoach Robbery*
 Sheriff of Cimarron
 Earl Carroll Vanities
 Corpus Christi Bandits
 Three's a Crowd
 Flame of Barbary Coast*
 A Sporting Chance*
 Bells of Rosarita*
 Federal Operator 99
 Steppin' in Society*
 Road to Alcatraz*
 Trail of Kit Carson
 Oregon Trail
 Man from Oklahoma*
 Phantom of the Plains*
 Behind City Lights
 Sunset in El Dorado
 Marshal of Laredo
 Don't Fence Me In
 Rough Riders of Cheyenne
 Girls of the Big House*
 Colorado Pioneers
 The Cherokee Flash
 Wagon Wheels Westward
 Dakota*

1946 — The Phantom Rider
 California Gold Rush
 Days of Buffalo Bill
 Crime of the Century
 Sheriff of Redwood Valley
 Murder in the Music Hall
 The Undercover Woman
 Alias Billy the Kid
 King of the Forest Rangers
 Sun Valley Cyclone
 Passkey to Danger
 The El Paso Kid*
 In Old Sacramento*
 Man from Rainbow Valley
 My Pal Trigger*
 Night Train to Memphis*
 Conquest of Cheyenne
 Red River Renegades
 G. I. War Brides*
 The Invisible Informer
 Rio Grande Raiders
 Roll on Texas Moon
 Plainsman and the Lady*
 Santa Fe Uprising
 Affairs of Geraldine*
 Out California Way
 Stagecoach to Denver*
1947 — Son of Zorro*
 Last Frontier Uprising
 Apache Rose*
 Homesteaders of Paradise Valley
 Twilight on the Rio Grande*
 That's My Man*
 Saddle Pals
 Rustlers of Devil's Canyon
 Blackmail*
 Wyoming
 Jesse James Rides Again
 Marshal of Cripple Creek
 Along the Oregon Trail
 Driftwood*
 The Wild Frontier
 Under Colorado Skies
1948 — Marshal of Amarillo
 The Far Frontier*
1949 — Frontier Investigator
 South of Rio
 San Antone Ambush
1950 — The Old Frontier
1951 — Rough Riders of Durango

Loo, Richard[229]
1942 — Remember Pearl Harbor!*
 Flying Tigers*
1947 — Web of Danger
1954 — The Shanghai Story

Lorch, Theodore
1935 — The New Frontier
1937 — Dick Tracy

Lord, Marjorie[119]
1943 — Shantytown
1953 — Down Laredo Way

Lorimer, Louise[229]
1940 — Forgotten Girls*
 Grand Ole Opry*
1954 — Crazylegs

Loring, Teala[229]
1950 — The Arizona Cowboy

Lorraine, Guido
1956 — Above Us the Waves

Lorre, Peter[102]
1941 — Mr. District Attorney
1958 — Hell Ship Mutiny

Los Angeles Rams
1954 — Crazylegs

Loser, Hanni
1955 — In Old Vienna

Louden, Thomas
1943 — The Masked Marvel

Loughery, Jackie
1957 — Eighteen and Anxious

Louise, Anita[229]
1939 — Main Street Lawyer
1940 — Wagons Westward
1941 — Wampas Baby Stars*

Louisiana Lou
[Eva Greenwood]
1939 — Wall Street Cowboy

Love, Montagu[229]
1938 — The Fighting Devil Dogs
1942 — Lady for a Night

Love, Ula
1937 — Meet the Boy Friend*
 Youth on Parole
 The Trigger Trio*
 Portia on Trial*
 Springtime in the Rockies

Lovelady, Ann
1950 — Prisoners in Petticoats*

Lovell, Raymond
1943 — Alibi

Lovett, Dorothy
1943 — The Mantrap

Lovewell, Cupie
1943 — Shantytown*
 Nobody's Darling*

Lovsky, Celia[229]
1949 — Flaming Fury
1953 — Champ for a Day*

Low, Jack
1939 — Bowery Boy*
1951 — Belle LeGrand*

Lowe, Edmund[229]
1940 — Wolf of New York
 The Crooked Road
1941 — Stars at Play*
1959 — Plunderers of Painted Flats

Lowe, Ellen[229]
1940 — Rancho Grande
 Grand Ole Opry*
1941 — Saddlemates
 Tuxedo Junction*
1943 — Idaho*
 The Blocked Trail*
 Sleepy Lagoon
 Here Comes Elmer*
1944 — Rosie, the Riveter
 Goodnight Sweetheart
 Bordertown Trail
 The Port of Forty Thieves
1945 — Gangs of the Waterfront*
 Swingin' on a Rainbow*
1950 — Hit Parade of 1951*

Lowe, K. Elmo[229]
1949 — The Kid from Cleveland
1950 — Women from Headquarters
 Trial Without Jury

Lowell, Helen
1937 — Michael O'Halloran

Lowery, Robert[229]
1943 — A Scream in the Dark
1945 — Road to Alcatraz
1948 — Heart of Virginia
1955 — Lay that Rifle Down

Loy, Myrna[102]
1949 — The Red Pony

Loyd, Beverly[34]
1943 — Pistol Packin' Mama*
1944 — The Fighting Seabees*
 My Best Gal*
 The Lady and the Monster*
 Jamboree
 Silent Partner
 Sing Neighbor Sing
1945 — Utah
 Earl Carroll Vanities
 An Angel Comes to Brooklyn*
 The Tiger Woman

Lubin, Lou
1952 — Tropical Heat Wave

Luden, Jack B.
1944 — Bordertown Trail

Luff, Beverly
1936 — Roarin' Lead

Audrey Long

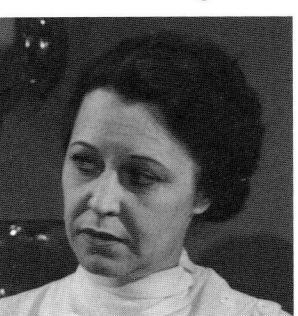
Walter Long

Richard Loo

Anita Louise

Louise Lorimer

Teala Loring

Montagu Love

Celia Lovsky

Edmund Lowe

Ellen Lowe

K. Elmo Lowe

Robert Lowery

Bela Lugosi

Lugosi, Bela[230]
1937—S O S Coast Guard

Luke, Keye[230]
1942—A Tragedy at Midnight
1953—Fair Wind to Java*
1954—Hell's Half Acre

Lulu Belle and Scotty[81]
[Myrtle and Scott Wiseman]
1938—Shine on Harvest Moon
1940—Village Barn Dance
1941—Country Fair
1942—Hi, Neighbor
1943—Swing Your Partner
1944—Sing Neighbor Sing

Lund, John[103]
1953—Woman They Almost Lynched
1956—Dakota Incident
1957—Affair in Reno

Lundigan, William[119]
1941—Sailors on Leave
1943—Headin' for God's Country
1948—The Inside Story

Lundy, Kenneth[230]
1941—Public Enemies*
       Tuxedo Junction
1946—Sioux City Sue

Lung, Charlie
1943—Headin' for God's Country
1951—Secrets of Monte Carlo

Lupton, John
1957—Taming Sutton's Gal

Lurie, Allan
1959—Plunderers of Painted Flats

Luther, Lester[230]
1949—The Red Menace

Lyden, Pierce[230]
1940—Forgotten Girls*
       Grand Ole Opry*
1943—Dead Man's Gulch
       The Blocked Trail
       Chatterbox*
       Daredevils of the West*
       Fugitive from Sonora
       The Black Hills Express
       Death Valley Manhunt
       Canyon City
       California Joe
1944—Outlaws of Santa Fe*
       San Fernando Valley*
       Firebrands of Arizona*
1945—The Cherokee Flash
1946—Alias Billy the Kid
       Rainbow Over Texas
       Roll on Texas Moon
1947—Son of Zorro*
       Rustlers of Devil's Canyon
       The Fabulous Texan*
1950—Twilight in the Sierras
       Covered Wagon Raid
       Hit Parade of 1951*
1951—Govt. Agents Vs. Phantom Legion

Lydon, James[81]
1940—Bowery Boy
1944—My Best Gal
1946—Affairs of Geraldine
1948—Out of the Storm
1950—Tarnished
       Destination Big House
1951—Oh! Susanna

Lynch, Ken
1958—Young and Wild
       Man or Gun

Lynd, Helen
1939—Flight at Midnight

Lynn, Emmett "Pappy"[230]
1940—Grandpa Goes to Town
       Scatterbrain
1941—Puddin' Head*
1942—Stagecoach Express
       Shepherd of the Ozarks*
       Westward Ho
       In Old California
       Joan of Ozark*
       Outlaws of Pine Ridge
       The Sundown Kid
1943—Mountain Rhythm*
       Dead Man's Gulch
       Carson City Cyclone
       Days of Old Cheyenne
1944—The Laramie Trail
       Outlaws of Santa Fe
       Goodnight Sweetheart
1945—The Big Show-Off*
       Wagon Wheels Westward
1946—Man from Rainbow Valley
       Conquest of Cheyenne
       Santa Fe Uprising
       Stagecoach to Denver
1947—Oregon Trail Scouts
       Rustlers of Devil's Canyon
       Jesse James Rides Again*
1948—Grand Canyon Trail
       The Far Frontier*
1949—The Last Bandit*
       Brimstone*
1950—Rock Island Trail*
1952—Oklahoma Annie
       Woman of the North Country*
1954—Jubilee Trail*
1955—The Twinkle in God's Eye*

Lynn, George[230]
1937—The Duke Comes Back
1941—Adventures of Captain Marvel
       Saddlemates
       Rags to Riches*
1943—G-Men Vs. The Black Dragon*
1946—Under Nevada Skies
1948—Homicide for Three
1951—Insurance Investigator*
1958—Girl in the Woods

Lynn, Leni[35]
1941—Angels with Broken Wings

Lynn, Peggy
1941—Outlaws of Cherokee Trail

Lynn, Rita
1957—The Wayward Girl

Cactus Mack

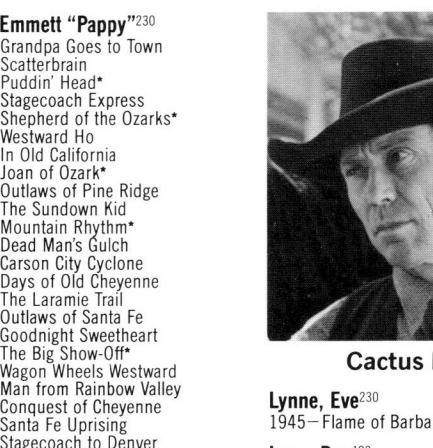

Helen Mack

Lynne, Eve[230]
1945—Flame of Barbary Coast

Lyon, Ben[103]
1935—Frisco Waterfront
1936—Dancing Feet
       Down to the Sea

Lyon, Therese
1945—Love, Honor and Goodbye

Lyons, Cliff[231]
1935—Tumbling Tumbleweeds*
1936—The Lawless Nineties
       The Three Mesquiteers*
       The Big Show*
1938—Army Girl*
1939—Three Texas Steers*
       Man of Conquest*
       Dark Command*
       Rocky Mountain Rangers*
       Under Texas Skies*
1941—Outlaws of Cherokee Trail*
1943—Calling Wild Bill Elliott*
       The Man from Thunder River*
       Silver Spurs*
       Wagon Tracks West
       Death Valley Manhunt*
       Man from Music Mountain*
       Overland Mail Robbery*
       In Old Oklahoma*
       Hands Across the Border*
1944—The Tiger Woman
       Stagecoach to Monterey*
       Zorro's Black Whip*
       Army 101—Equip. Maintenance*
1945—The Purple Monster Strikes*
       Dakota*
1946—The Phantom Rider*
       Red River Renegades*
1947—Angel and the Badman*
       Vigilantes of Boomtown*
1948—Oklahoma Badlands*
1949—The Fighting Kentuckian*
1950—Rio Grande*
1953—The Sun Shines Bright*

Lyons, Collette
1939—Three Texas Steers

Lytton, Herbert
1953—Marshal of Cedar Rock

M

MacBride, Donald[81]
1940—Hit Parade of 1941
1951—Cuban Fireball
1952—Gobs and Gals

MacDonald, Edmund[230]
1942—Call of the Canyon
       Flying Tigers
       Heart of the Golden West
1943—The Mantrap

MacDonald, Ian
1949—Streets of San Francisco
1951—Thunder in God's Country
1952—Toughest Man in Arizona
1953—A Perilous Journey
1954—Johnny Guitar
1955—Timberjack
1956—Accused of Murder
1957—Duel at Apache Wells

MacDonald, J. Farrell[135]
1935—Hitch Hike Lady
1937—The Hit Parade
1938—Come on, Rangers
1939—The Lone Ranger Rides Again
       Mickey, the Kid
1940—Dark Command
       Friendly Neighbors
1941—In Old Cheyenne
1945—Woman Who Came Back
1947—Web of Danger
1949—Streets of San Francisco

MacDonald, Kenneth[230]
1939—Smuggled Cargo*
1940—Frontier Vengeance
1941—Prairie Pioneers
1944—Pride of the Plains
1947—The Fabulous Texan*
1948—Train to Alcatraz
       The Plunderers*
1949—Hellfire*
1950—Federal Agent at Large
       Salt Lake Raiders
1951—Fighting Coast Guard*
       Desert of Lost Men
1952—Leadville Gunslinger
1953—Marshal of Cedar Rock
       Savage Frontier
       Destroyers of the Sun
       Robot Monster from Mars
       The Hydrogen Hurricane
       Bandits of the West*

MacFarlane, Bruce[35]
1938—Come on, Leathernecks
       A Desperate Adventure*
       Dick Tracy Returns*
       Billy the Kid Returns*
       The Night Hawk*
       Come on, Rangers
       Orphans of the Street*
       Federal Man-Hunt*
1939—The Mysterious Miss X*
       Forged Passport
       Smuggled Cargo*

MacGregor, Lee
1952—Toughest Man in Arizona

Mack, Cactus[230]
[Taylor McPeters]
Many films, mostly westerns.
1941—The Singing Hill
1951—Don Daredevil Rides Again

Mack, Helen[230]
1937—The Wrong Road
1938—King of the Newsboys
       I Stand Accused
1939—The Night Riders*
       Calling All Marines

Mack, Jack
1935—Frisco Waterfront

Keye Luke

Kenneth Lundy

Lester Luther

Pierce Lyden

Emmett "Pappy" Lynn

George Lynn

Dorothy Mackaill

Eve Lynne

Edmund MacDonald

Kenneth MacDonald

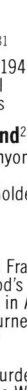

Helen MacKellar

230

Mack, Willard
1937 — Larceny on the Air

Mackaill, Dorothy[230]
1937 — Bulldog Drummond at Bay

MacKar, Mitzi
1938 — King of the Newsboys*

Mackay, Barry
1937 — Glamorous Night
1939 — Smuggled Cargo

MacKellar, Helen[230]
1940 — Dark Command
　　　Three Faces West
1941 — The Great Train Robbery
　　　Gangs of Sonora
　　　Down Mexico Way*
1942 — The Sundown Kid
1943 — Silver Spurs*

Mackenzie, Mary[231]
1954 — Trouble in the Glen
1956 — Track the Man Down
1957 — Operation Conspiracy

Macklin, James
1958 — No Place to Land

MacLane, Barton[231]
1939 — I Was a Convict
1940 — Gangs of Chicago
　　　Melody Ranch
1943 — A Gentle Gangster
　　　Song of Texas
1946 — Santa Fe Uprising
1948 — Angel in Exile
1952 — Thunderbirds
1954 — Sea of Lost Ships
　　　Jubilee Trail
　　　Hell's Outpost
1956 — Jaguar
　　　The Man is Armed
1957 — Hell's Crossroads
1958 — Girl in the Woods

MacLaren, Ian
1937 — Portia on Trial
1938 — Invisible Enemy

MacLaren, Mary[135]
1935 — Westward Ho
　　　The New Frontier
1936 — The Return of Jimmy Valentine*
　　　King of the Pecos
1937 — Michael O'Halloran*
　　　A Lawman is Born
1939 — Man of Conquest*
1940 — Ghost Valley Raiders*
　　　Rocky Mountain Rangers*
1941 — Prairie Pioneers
　　　Sunset in Wyoming*
　　　The Apache Kid*
1942 — Shepherd of the Ozarks*
　　　The Cyclone Kid*
　　　Sunset Serenade*

MacLeod, Gavin
1958 — Young and Wild*

Barton MacLane, Beverly Roberts, Horace MacMahon

MacMahon, Horace[231]
1937 — Navy Blues
　　　The Wrong Road
1938 — King of the Newsboys
　　　Ladies in Distress
　　　Tenth Avenue Kid
　　　Federal Man-Hunt
1939 — Pride of the Navy
　　　I Was a Convict
　　　She Married a Cop
　　　Sabotage
1940 — Gangs of Chicago
　　　Melody Ranch
1941 — Rookies on Parade
1953 — Champ for a Day

MacMurray, Fred[103]
1953 — Fair Wind to Java

MacNamara, Major James H.
1941 — Lady from Louisiana

Macollum, Barry
1941 — Arkansas Judge

Macon, Uncle Dave—and son Dorris
1940 — Grand Ole Opry

MacQuarrie, Murdock
1935 — The New Frontier

MacRae, Gordon
1955 — The Last Command

Macready, George[231]
1956 — Thunder Over Arizona
1958 — Gunfire at Indian Gap
1959 — Plunderers of Painted Flats

Madden, Jeanne[231]
1937 — Sea Racketeers

Madeira, Humberto
1956 — Lisbon

Madison, Julian
1937 — Guns in the Dark
1938 — Desert Patrol
1939 — Dick Tracy's G-Men

Madison, Noel
1943 — Shantytown

Magill, James
1950 — Trail of Robin Hood

Magrill, George
1948 — G-Men Never Forget

Main, Marjorie
1937 — The Wrong Road
1938 — King of the Newsboys*
1940 — Dark Command

Makeham, Eliot
1955 — Doctor in the House

Mala, Ray[231]
1936 — Robinson Crusoe of Clipper Island
1938 — Call of the Yukon
　　　Hawk of the Wilderness
1940 — Girl from God's Country
1942 — The Girl from Alaska

Malatesta, Fred
1935 — $1000 a Minute

Malleson, Miles
1953 — Trent's Last Case

Mary Mackenzie

George Macready

Mallinson, Rory[231]
1948 — The Denver Kid
1949 — Wake of the Red Witch*
　　　Prince of the Plains
　　　South of Rio
1950 — Salt Lake Raiders
　　　California Passage*
1951 — Oh! Susanna*
　　　Rodeo King and the Senorita
　　　Fort Dodge Stampede
1957 — Spoilers of the Forest*
1958 — The Notorious Mr. Monks*

Malneck, Matty—and orchestra
1940 — Scatterbrain
1943 — Shantytown
1944 — Trocadero

Maloney, James
1957 — Hell Canyon Outlaws

Malyon, Eily[231]
1941 — Arkansas Judge
1945 — Grissly's Millions

Mamakos, Peter
1955 — The Twinkle in God's Eye*
　　　I Cover the Underworld
1956 — When Gangland Strikes*
1957 — The Crooked Circle
1958 — The Man Who Died Twice*

Mander, Miles[231]
1937 — Youth on Parole
1939 — Daredevils of the Red Circle
1942 — A Tragedy at Midnight
　　　Secrets of the Underground

Man Mountain Dean
1935 — Cappy Ricks Returns

Frank M. Thomas, Eily Malyon

Jeanne Madden

Mann, Margaret
1938 — Federal Man-Hunt

Manners, David
1936 — Hearts in Bondage

Manners, Marjorie[231]
1944 — Trocadero
　　　That's My Baby
1945 — The Big Show-Off
　　　Identity Unknown
　　　Woman Who Came Back*
1946 — The French Key

Manni, Ettore
1954 — The She Wolf

Manning, Hope[35]
1936 — The Old Corral
1937 — Two Wise Maids
　　　Michael O'Halloran

Ray Mala

Rory Mallinson

Miles Mander

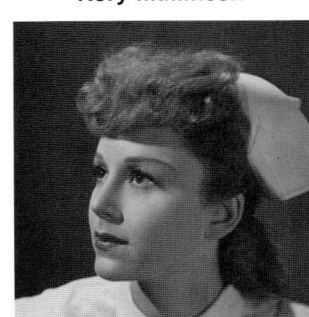

Marjorie Manners

Earle Hodgins, Bill Yrigoyen, Duke Taylor, Peggy Stewart, Bud Wolfe, Tom Steele, Cliff Lyons

Knox Manning

Manning, Knox[232]
1939—Sabotage*
1942—Remember Pearl Harbor!*
1947—Hit Parade of 1947

Mannone, Wingy
1944—Trocadero

Mannors, Sheila[232]
1935—Westward Ho
　　　Lawless Range

Manogoff, Bobby
1949—Alias the Champ

Manson, Helena
1951—Adventures of Captain Fabian

Many Treaties
1943—Deerslayer

Mapes, Ted[195]
1938—Hawk of the Wilderness*
1939—The Lone Ranger Rides Again
　　　Blue Montana Skies*
　　　Three Texas Steers*
　　　Daredevils of the Red Circle*
　　　In Old Caliente*
　　　In Old Monterey*
　　　Dick Tracy's G-Men
　　　Wall Street Cowboy*
　　　Calling All Marines*
　　　The Arizona Kid*
　　　Zorro's Fighting Legion*
1940—The Carson City Kid*
　　　The Ranger and the Lady
　　　King of the Royal Mounted*
　　　Under Texas Skies*
　　　Friendly Neighbors*
　　　The Border Legion*
1941—Robin Hood of the Pecos*
　　　In Old Cheyenne*
　　　Adventures of Captain Marvel*
　　　Lady from Louisiana*
　　　Gauchos of Eldorado*
　　　Red River Valley*
1942—Home in Wyomin'
1943—Calling Wild Bill Elliott*
1946—The Phantom Rider*
　　　My Pal Trigger*
　　　Conquest of Cheyenne*
　　　Daughter of Don Q*
1947—Son of Zorro*
　　　Jesse James Rides Again*
　　　The Wild Frontier
　　　The Black Widow*
　　　The Fabulous Texan*
1948—Dangers of the Canadian Mounted*
　　　Desperadoes of Dodge City
1949—Outcasts of the Trail
　　　Brimstone*
1950—Rock Island Trail*
1951—Silver City Bonanza*

Maple, Christine[35]
1936—The Big Show
　　　Roarin' Lead
　　　Beware of Ladies*
　　　A Man Betrayed

Maple City Four
1937—Git Along Little Dogies
1938—The Old Barn Dance
　　　Under Western Stars

Mara, Adele[36]
1944—The Fighting Seabees*
　　　Call of the South Seas
　　　Atlantic City
　　　San Fernando Valley*
　　　Faces in the Fog
　　　Thoroughbreds
1945—Grissly's Millions
　　　Earl Carroll Vanities*
　　　The Vampire's Ghost
　　　Flame of Barbary Coast*
　　　Bells of Rosarita
　　　Girls of the Big House
　　　The Tiger Woman
　　　Song of Mexico
1946—A Guy Could Change
　　　The Catman of Paris
　　　Passkey to Danger
　　　Traffic in Crime
　　　Night Train to Memphis
　　　The Inner Circle
　　　The Last Crooked Mile
　　　The Invisible Informer
　　　I've Always Loved You
　　　That Brennan Girl*
1947—The Magnificent Rogue
　　　Twilight on the Rio Grande
　　　Web of Danger
　　　The Trespasser
　　　Robin Hood of Texas
　　　Blackmail
　　　Exposed
　　　The Black Widow*
1948—The Main Street Kid
　　　Campus Honeymoon
　　　I, Jane Doe
　　　The Gallant Legion
　　　Night Time in Nevada
　　　Angel in Exile
1949—Wake of the Red Witch
1950—Sands of Iwo Jima
　　　Rock Island Trail
　　　The Avengers
　　　California Passage
1951—The Sea Hornet

Maran, Francisco
1936—Down to the Sea

March, Eve[232]
1943—Calling Wild Bill Elliott
　　　Song of Texas
1949—Streets of San Francisco
1950—Rio Grande*
1953—The Sun Shines Bright

March, Hal
1954—The Atomic Kid

March, Sally[232]
1939—The Arizona Kid

Marchetti, Guilio
1951—Fugitive Lady

Marcus, James
1936—The Lonely Trail

Marden, Adrienne
1951—Utah Wagon Train*

Margetson, Arthur
1943—Thumbs Up

Sheila Mannors

Mona Maris

Margot, Herta
1940—Chinese Garden Festival*

Maricle, Leona
1943—Someone to Remember

Marin, Pablo
1945—Song of Mexico

Marion, Paul[232]
1939—In Old Caliente
　　　Zorro's Fighting Legion
1940—Drums of Fu Manchu*
　　　Covered Wagon Days
　　　Mysterious Doctor Satan
1943—Secret Service in Darkest Africa*
1944—Captain America*
1946—The Catman of Paris
1949—Flaming Fury
1950—Harbor of Missing Men
　　　Lonely Heart Bandits*

Marion, Sid
1950—Women from Headquarters
　　　Trial Without Jury

Maris, Mona[232]
1950—The Avengers

Mark, Michael
1945—The Great Flamarion
1947—The Pretender

Markey, Gene
1941—Variety Reel*

Markey, Melinda
1941—Variety Reel*

Markham, Pigmeat
1944—That's My Baby

Markova, Alicia
1945—A Song for Miss Julie

Marks, Joe E.
1938—Outside of Paradise

Marle, Arnold
1955—The Green Buddha
　　　Cross Channel

Marlowe, Don
1957—Journey to Freedom

Marlowe, Faye[120]
1946—Rendezvous with Annie

Marlowe, Frank[232]
1945—Identity Unknown

Marlowe, Jo Ann
1946—Man from Rainbow Valley

Marlowe, Scott[232]
1958—Young and Wild

Marly, Florence[232]
1952—Gobs and Gals

Marmont, Percy
1956—Lisbon

Eve March

Frank Marlowe

Maron, Alfred
1957—The Man in the Road

Marr, Eddie
1945—Tell It to a Star

Marriot, Bobby
1954—Roogie's Bump

Marsh, Anthony[233]
1937—Portia on Trial
1938—Overland Stage Raiders

Marsh, Charles
1944—Atlantic City

Marsh, Garry
1948—Code of Scotland Yard

Marsh, Joan[232]
1936—Dancing Feet
1943—Secret Service in Darkest Africa

Marsh, Mae[120]
1949—The Fighting Kentuckian
1952—The Quiet Man*
1953—The Sun Shines Bright

Marsh, Marian[81]
1937—Youth on Parole
1938—Prison Nurse
　　　A Desperate Adventure

Paul Marion

Scott Marlowe

Marsh, Myra
1939—The Kansas Terrors

Marshal, Alan[232]
1938—Invisible Enemy

Marshall, Brenda[232]
1946—Strange Impersonation

Marshall, Charles "Red"
1946—Specter of the Rose

Marshall, George
1955—Timberjack

Marshall, Gregory
1947—That's My Man
　　　Bandits of Dark Canyon

Marshall, Herbert[233]
1957—The Weapon

Marshall, Tully
1939—Blue Montana Skies

Marshall, William[38]
1943—The Mantrap*
1946—Murder in the Music Hall
　　　Earl Carroll Sketchbook
　　　That Brennan Girl
1947—Calendar Girl
　　　Blackmail
　　　Wyoming*

Florence Marly

Joan Marsh

Sally March, Roy Rogers

Alan Marshall

Brenda Marshall

Marshe, Vera
1948 — King of the Gamblers*
1949 — The Last Bandit*
Post Office Investigator
1957 — Affair in Reno*

Marston, Joel
1952 — Old Oklahoma Plains
1954 — Crazylegs

Martel, June[233]
1936 — Sitting on the Moon
1937 — Wild Horse Rodeo
1938 — Santa Fe Stampede

Martel, William
1949 — The Red Menace

Martell, Alphonse
1946 — The Catman of Paris

Martell, Gregg
1949 — The Red Menace

Martell, Karl
1956 — Circus Girl

Martin, Chris-Pin[233]
1937 — The Bold Caballero
Boots and Saddles
Zorro Rides Again*
1938 — Born to be Wild*
Billy the Kid Returns*
1939 — Rough Riders' Round-Up*
Frontier Pony Express*
Man of Conquest*
1948 — Old Los Angeles*
1950 — The Arizona Cowboy
1953 — Ride the Man Down
San Antone*

Martin, Freddy—and orchestra
1943 — Hit Parade of 1943

Martin, Janet[39]
1943 — Hands Across the Border
1944 — The Lady and the Monster
The Yellow Rose of Texas
Call of the South Seas
Lake Placid Serenade*
1945 — A Sporting Chance
Bells of Rosarita
1947 — Calendar Girl
Saddle Pals*
Northwest Outpost*
The Trespasser
1948 — The Main Street Kid
Heart of Virginia
King of the Gamblers*
I, Jane Doe*
Train to Alcatraz

Martin, Jill[40]
1938 — Dick Tracy Returns*
The Night Hawk*
Hawk of the Wilderness
1939 — Woman Doctor*

Martin, Lewis
1957 — Last Stagecoach West

Herbert Marshall

June Martel

Martin, Marian[135]
1940 — Women in War*
Scatterbrain*
1945 — The Phantom Speaks
Gangs of the Waterfront
Girls of the Big House
1946 — Gay Blades*
That Brennan Girl
1947 — That's My Gal
1952 — Oklahoma Annie*

Martin, Mary
1940 — Chinese Garden Festival*
1941 — Los Angeles Examiner Benefit*
Stars Past and Present*

Martin, Tony
1941 — Stars at Play*

Marvey, Gene
1936 — The Three Mesquiteers

Marvin, Frankie[233]
Many films, mostly westerns.
1935 — Tumbling Tumbleweeds
Melody Trail*
Sagebrush Troubadour*
1936 — The Singing Vagabond*
Red River Valley
Comin' 'Round the Mountain*
The Singing Cowboy*
Undersea Kingdom
Guns and Guitars
Oh, Susanna!
The Vigilantes Are Coming*
Ride Ranger Ride*
The Big Show*
The Old Corral
1937 — Round-Up Time in Texas
Git Along Little Dogies*
Rootin' Tootin' Rhythm
The Painted Stallion
Yodelin' Kid from Pine Ridge
Public Cowboy No. 1
S O S Coast Guard*
Heart of the Rockies*
Boots and Saddles
Manhattan Merry-Go-Round*
Springtime in the Rockies
Zorro Rides Again*
1938 — The Purple Vigilantes*
The Old Barn Dance
The Lone Ranger*
Under Western Stars
Gold Mine in the Sky
Man from Music Mountain
Prairie Moon*
Rhythm of the Saddle*
Western Jamboree*
1939 — Home on the Prairie*
Mexicali Rose*
Frontier Pony Express*
Blue Montana Skies*
Mountain Rhythm
Colorado Sunset*
New Frontier*
In Old Monterey*
Rovin' Tumbleweeds*
Saga of Death Valley*
South of the Border*
1940 — Pioneers of the West*
Rancho Grande*
Gaucho Serenade*
Rocky Mountain Rangers*
Adventures of Red Ryder*
Carolina Moon*
Oklahoma Renegades*
Ride, Tenderfoot, Ride*
Melody Ranch*
1941 — Ridin' on a Rainbow*
Back in the Saddle*
The Singing Hill*
Sunset in Wyoming*
Under Fiesta Stars*
Down Mexico Way*
Sierra Sue*
1942 — Cowboy Serenade*
Heart of the Rio Grande*
Home in Wyomin'*
Stardust on the Sage*
Call of the Canyon*
The Old Homestead*
Bells of Capistrano*
The Traitor Within*
1945 — Flame of Barbary Coast*
1946 — Sioux City Sue*
1947 — Trail to San Antone*
Twilight on the Rio Grande*
Saddle Pals*
Robin Hood of Texas*

Marx, Neyle
1941 — The Phantom Cowboy

Mason, Bill
1955 — Yellowneck

Mason, James[103]
1943 — Alibi
1952 — Lady Possessed

Mason, LeRoy[40]
1936 — Comin' 'Round the Mountain
Go-Get-'Em, Haines
Ghost-Town Gold
1937 — Round-Up Time in Texas
The Painted Stallion
Yodelin' Kid from Pine Ridge
1938 — Gold Mine in the Sky
Heroes of the Hills
Rhythm of the Saddle
Santa Fe Stampede
1939 — Mexicali Rose
Wyoming Outlaw
New Frontier
1940 — Ghost Valley Raiders
Rocky Mountain Rangers
The Ranger and the Lady
1941 — The Apache Kid
1943 — The Black Hills Express*
The Man from the Rio Grande*
Overland Mail Robbery*
Canyon City
In Old Oklahoma*
Raiders of Sunset Pass
California Joe
Hands Across the Border
1944 — Captain America*
Beneath Western Skies
The Fighting Seabees*
Mojave Firebrand
Hidden Valley Outlaws
Outlaws of Santa Fe
Rosie, the Riveter*
The Lady and the Monster
Tucson Raiders
The Tiger Woman
The Yellow Rose of Texas*
Marshal of Reno
Song of Nevada
The San Antonio Kid
Atlantic City*
San Fernando Valley
Stagecoach to Monterey
Cheyenne Wildcat*
Code of the Prairie*
My Buddy*
Vigilantes of Dodge City
Firebrands of Arizona
Zorro's Black Whip*
The Big Bonanza*
Navy MN 3387 — Your Weapons*
1945 — Sheriff of Cimarron*
Utah*
Lone Texas Ranger*
Three's a Crowd*
Gangs of the Waterfront*
Federal Operator 99
Sunset in El Dorado*
Dakota*
1946 — Gay Blades*
The Phantom Rider
Strange Impersonation*
Sheriff of Redwood Valley*
Murder in the Music Hall
Home on the Range
King of the Forest Rangers
Sun Valley Cyclone*
Valley of the Zombies
In Old Sacramento*
One Exciting Week*
My Pal Trigger
Night Train to Memphis
Conquest of Cheyenne*
Red River Renegades
Daughter of Don Q
G. I. War Brides*
Earl Carroll Sketchbook*
Under Nevada Skies
Rio Grande Raiders*
Roll on Texas Moon*
Plainsman and the Lady*
Sioux City Sue*
Heldorado
Stagecoach to Denver*
That Brennan Girl*
1947 — Angel and the Badman*
Apache Rose
Vigilantes of Boomtown*
Homesteaders of Paradise Valley*
Twilight on the Rio Grande*
Oregon Trail Scouts*
That's My Gal*
Saddle Pals*
Robin Hood of Texas*
Jesse James Rides Again
Along the Oregon Trail
The Wild Frontier*
The Fabulous Texan*
The Black Widow
Bandits of Dark Canyon
Under Colorado Skies
1948 — The Gay Ranchero
California Firebrand
[died while filming 10-13-47]

Mason, Louis
1945 — Grissly's Millions

Mason, Pamela
See Pamela Kellino.

Mason, Sydney
1953 — Robot Monster from Mars
S. O. S. Ice Age

Frieda Inescort, Anthony Marsh

Chris-Pin Martin

Frankie Marvin

Osa Massen

Lester Matthews

Massen, Osa[233]
1941 — The Devil Pays Off
1958 — Outcasts of the City

Massey, Ilona[81]
1941 — Variety Reel*
Stars Past and Present*
1947 — Northwest Outpost*
1948 — The Plunderers

Massis, Louis
1959 — O. S. S. 117 is Not Dead

Mather, Aubrey
1940 — Earl of Puddlestone

Mathews, Allan
1938 — The Fighting Devil Dogs

Mathews, Carl
1943 — The Blocked Trail

Mathews, Carol
1942 — Pardon My Stripes*

Matthews, Lester[233]
1940 — Gaucho Serenade*
Women in War
Sing, Dance, Plenty Hot
1943 — London Blackout Murders
1955 — Flame of the Islands

Johanna Matz

Matz, Johanna[233]
1957 — The Congress Dances

Maude, Beatrice[233]
1941 — Arkansas Judge

Beatrice Maude, Ruth Robinson, June Weaver

Nicole Maurey

Maurey, Nicole[234]
1957 — The Weapon

Mauu, Charles
1958 — Hell Ship Mutiny

Max, Edwin
1952 — Tropical Heat Wave

Maxey, Paul[234]
1951 — Belle LeGrand*
1955 — City of Shadows

Maxted, Stanley
1957 — The Weapon

Maxwell, Edwin
1936 — A Man Betrayed
1938 — Romance on the Run
1948 — Campus Honeymoon

Maxwell, Jane
1955 — Mystery of the Black Jungle

Maxwell, John
1942 — Arizona Terrors
1943 — False Faces
1953 — Champ for a Day*
1955 — The Eternal Sea
      I Cover the Underworld*
      City of Shadows*
1956 — Terror at Midnight
      A Strange Adventure
1957 — The Wayward Girl
1958 — The Man Who Died Twice

Mayer, Ray
1938 — Prison Nurse

Maynard, Kermit[234]
1938 — Western Jamboree
1939 — The Night Riders
      Wyoming Outlaw*
      Colorado Sunset
      Rovin' Tumbleweeds*
1940 — Heroes of the Saddle*
1941 — Wyoming Wildcat*
      King of the Texas Rangers
      Sierra Sue
      A Missouri Outlaw*
1942 — Arizona Terrors*
      Jesse James, Jr.*
      Home in Wyomin'*
      Valley of Hunted Men*
1943 — The Blocked Trail
      Santa Fe Scouts
      Silver Spurs*
      Beyond the Last Frontier
1947 — Along the Oregon Trail*
1948 — The Gallant Legion*
1950 — The Savage Horde*
      Trail of Robin Hood
1951 — In Old Amarillo*
      Fort Dodge Stampede

Mayne, Ferdy
1955 — The Divided Heart

Mayo, Frank
1935 — Burning Gold

Mazurki, Mike[234]
1942 — Flying Tigers*
1945 — Dakota
1946 — The French Key
1958 — Hell Ship Mutiny
      The Man Who Died Twice

McArt, Don
1957 — Journey to Freedom

McCallum, John
1953 — Trent's Last Case
1954 — Trouble in the Glen

McCambridge, Mercedes[103]
1954 — Johnny Guitar

McCann, Doreen
1945 — The Phantom Speaks

McCardle, Mary
1945 — Earl Carroll Vanities*

McCarroll, Frank[234]
Many films, mostly westerns.
1943 — Fugitive from Sonora
1944 — Outlaws of Santa Fe
1946 — Sheriff of Redwood Valley
      Conquest of Cheyenne
1952 — Captive of Billy the Kid

McCarthy, Lin
1955 — Yellowneck

McCarthy, Red
1941 — Ice-Capades
1942 — Ice-Capades Revue
1946 — Murder in the Music Hall

McCarty, Mary[234]
1941 — Stars at Play*
1942 — Ice-Capades Revue*
      The Traitor Within*
1945 — Bells of Rosarita*
      Tell It to a Star
      Girls of the Big House*
1946 — Gay Blades*
1947 — Hit Parade of 1947*

McClory, Sean[234]
1952 — The Quiet Man
1955 — I Cover the Underworld

McClung, Bob
1937 — Two Wise Maids
      Paradise Express

McClure, Greg
1949 — The Golden Stallion

McClure, M'liss
1951 — Insurance Investigator

McConnell, Keith
1952 — Border Saddlemates

McCormick, Merrill[198]
Many films, mostly westerns.
1936 — Winds of the Wasteland
      The Old Corral
1937 — Guns in the Dark*
      Come on, Cowboys!
      Range Defenders*
      Boots and Saddles*
      Zorro Rides Again*
1938 — The Purple Vigilantes*
      Outlaws of Sonora
      Prairie Moon*
1939 — Rough Riders' Round-Up*
      Mexicali Rose*
      Man of Conquest*
      In Old Caliente
      Dick Tracy's G-Men*
      The Kansas Terrors*
1940 — Drums of Fu Manchu*
      Adventures of Red Ryder*
      The Trail Blazers*
      Melody Ranch*
1941 — In Old Cheyenne*
      Desert Bandit*
1942 — South of Santa Fe*
      Stardust on the Sage*
      In Old California*
      The Sombrero Kid*
1948 — The Gallant Legion*
1950 — Desperadoes of the West*
1951 — Oh! Susanna*

McCourt, Margaret
1954 — Trouble in the Glen

McCowen, Alec
1955 — The Divided Heart

McCrea, Ann
1953 — Sweethearts on Parade

McCrindle, Alex
1954 — Trouble in the Glen

McDaniel, Etta[234]
1936 — The Lawless Nineties
      The Lonely Trail
      Hearts in Bondage
1940 — Carolina Moon
1941 — The Pittsburgh Kid
1942 — Johnny Doughboy
1943 — False Faces

McDaniel, Hattie[103]
1947 — The Flame

McDaniel, Sam "Deacon"
1942 — The Traitor Within
1944 — Three Little Sisters
1948 — Heart of Virginia
      Secret Service Investigator

McDermott, Hugh
1953 — Trent's Last Case

Paul Maxey

Mike Mazurki

Kermit Maynard

Frank McCarroll

McDonald, Francis[234]
1940 — The Carson City Kid
1942 — The Girl from Alaska
1944 — Bordertown Trail
      Cheyenne Wildcat
      Zorro's Black Whip
1945 — Great Stagecoach Robbery
      Corpus Christi Bandits
1946 — The Catman of Paris
      My Pal Trigger
      Night Train to Memphis
      The Invisible Informer
      Roll on Texas Moon
1947 — Spoilers of the North
      That's My Man*
      Saddle Pals
1948 — The Bold Frontiersman
      Son of God's Country
1949 — Rose of the Yukon
      Daughter of the Jungle
      Powder River Rustlers
1950 — California Passage
1951 — Oh! Susanna*
1953 — Ride the Man Down*
      San Antone*
1955 — The Road to Denver*
      The Vanishing American*
1956 — Thunder Over Arizona
1957 — Duel at Apache Wells
      Last Stagecoach West
      Pawnee

McDonald, Jack "Sockeye"
1949 — Alias the Champ

McDonald, Marie[120]
1943 — A Scream in the Dark
1950 — Hit Parade of 1951

McDonald, Ray
1949 — Flame of Youth

McDowall, Roddy[103]
1950 — Macbeth

McDowell, Candy
1949 — Flame of Youth*
1950 — House by the River*
      Hit Parade of 1951*

McDowell, Nelson
1945 — Lone Texas Ranger

McFarland, Frank
1950 — Federal Agent at Large

McFarland, Spanky [George][234]
1942 — Johnny Doughboy
1944 — Cowboy and the Senorita*

McGinnis, Joel
1944 — Faces in the Fog

McGlynn, Jr., Frank
1935 — Westward Ho
      Lawless Range

McGlynn, Sr., Frank
1936 — Hearts in Bondage
1938 — The Lone Ranger

McGowan and Mack
1944 — Lake Placid Serenade

McGowan, J. P.
1936 — Guns and Guitars
      The Three Mesquiteers
1937 — Hit the Saddle
      Heart of the Rockies

McGowran, Jack
1952 — The Quiet Man

McGrail, Walter[234]
1939 — Calling All Marines
1940 — Mysterious Doctor Satan
1941 — Stars Past and Present*
      Dick Tracy Vs. Crime, Inc.*

McGraw, Charles
1947 — On the Old Spanish Trail

McGregor, Malcolm
1936 — Undersea Kingdom

McGuinn, Joe[235]
1939 — Street of Missing Men*
      The Zero Hour*
      Daredevils of the Red Circle*
      She Married a Cop*
      Dick Tracy's G-Men
      Calling All Marines*
      Jeepers Creepers*
      Rovin' Tumbleweeds*
      Zorro's Fighting Legion*
1940 — Wolf of New York*
      Village Barn Dance*
      Pioneers of the West
      Dark Command*
      Wagons Westward*
      Ride, Tenderfoot, Ride
      Colorado*
      Mysterious Doctor Satan
1941 — Back in the Saddle
      Jungle Girl
1942 — South of Santa Fe*
      In Old California*
      The Cyclone Kid
      The Old Homestead*
      Bells of Capistrano*
      The Sundown Kid*
1944 — Navy MN 3387 — Your Weapons*
1945 — Sunset in El Dorado*
      The Cherokee Flash
1950 — The Missourians*
1952 — Colorado Sundown*
      Old Oklahoma Plains*
      South Pacific Trail

Mary McCarty

Sean McCory

Etta McDaniel

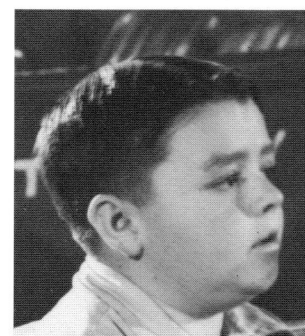

Francis McDonald

Spanky McFarland

Walter McGrail

Joe McGuinn

Kitty McHugh

Matt McHugh

Doreen McKay

Wanda McKay

Robert McKenzie

Harry McKim

McGuire, Dorothy[104]
1954 – Make Haste to Live

McGuire, John
1947 – Bells of San Angelo
1950 – Sands of Iwo Jima
Federal Agent at Large

McGuire, Paul
1952 – Radar Men from the Moon

McHugh, Kitty[235]
1937 – Youth on Parole*
1938 – Orphans of the Street*
1943 – Sleepy Lagoon
A Scream in the Dark

McHugh, Matt[235]
1936 – The Gentleman from Louisiana
1938 – Federal Man-Hunt
1943 – The West Side Kid
Whispering Footsteps
1944 – My Buddy
1949 – Duke of Chicago

McKay, Doreen[235]
1938 – Pals of the Saddle
The Higgins Family
1939 – The Night Riders
1940 – Bowery Boy*

McKay, George
1942 – Pardon My Stripes

McKay, Wanda[235]
1941 – Stars Past and Present*
1943 – Deerslayer

McKenzie, Fay[40]
1939 – Man of Conquest*
1941 – Down Mexico Way
Sierra Sue
1942 – Lady for a Night*
Cowboy Serenade
Heart of the Rio Grande
Home in Wyomin'
Remember Pearl Harbor!
1946 – Murder in the Music Hall

McKenzie, Robert[235]
1935 – Hitch Hike Lady*
1936 – Comin' 'Round the Mountain
1937 – Gunsmoke Ranch*
1938 – Billy the Kid Returns*
Red River Range*
1939 – Frontier Pony Express*
1940 – Village Barn Dance*
In Old Missouri*
Barnyard Follies*
1941 – Citadel of Crime
Death Valley Outlaws
Sierra Sue*
A Missouri Outlaw*
1942 – In Old California
Hi, Neighbor*
The Sombrero Kid
1945 – Wagon Wheels Westward*

McKim, David
1939 – The Night Riders*
1941 – Tuxedo Junction*
1942 – A Tragedy at Midnight*

McKim, Harry[235]
1939 – Cowboys from Texas*
1942 – In Old California*
Johnny Doughboy*
1943 – Shantytown*
Days of Old Cheyenne
Song of Texas*
1944 – Mojave Firebrand
1954 – Sea of Lost Ships*
Flight Nurse*
Geraldine*

McKim, Peggy
1937 – Gunsmoke Ranch*
1938 – Mama Runs Wild*

McKim, Sammy[40]
1936 – Country Gentlemen
1937 – Hit the Saddle
Gunsmoke Ranch
The Painted Stallion
Heart of the Rockies
The Trigger Trio
1938 – Mama Runs Wild
The Old Barn Dance
The Lone Ranger
Call the Mesquiteers
Red River Range
1939 – The Night Riders
Man of Conquest*
New Frontier
Dick Tracy's G-Men*
Rovin' Tumbleweeds
1940 – Rocky Mountain Rangers
Texas Terrors
1941 – Public Enemies*
1948 – I, Jane Doe*
1950 – Tillers of the Soil*
Destination Big House*
Lonely Heart Bandits
1952 – Thunderbirds
1954 – Flight Nurse*

McKinley, Ray – and orchestra
1943 – Hit Parade of 1943

McKinney, Florine
1935 – Cappy Ricks Returns
1940 – Oklahoma Renegades

McKinney, Mira[235]
1936 – The President's Mystery*
1938 – Arson Gang Busters*
Prairie Moon*
1939 – Woman Doctor*
1940 – Forgotten Girls*
1945 – Rough Riders of Cheyenne
1946 – I've Always Loved You*
1950 – Destination Big House*
Prisoners in Petticoats*
1951 – Heart of the Rockies

McKinney, Nina Mae
1946 – Night Train to Memphis

McLaglen, Victor[81]
1945 – Love, Honor and Goodbye
1947 – Calendar Girl
1950 – Rio Grande
1952 – The Quiet Man
1953 – Fair Wind to Java
1954 – Trouble in the Glen
1955 – City of Shadows

McLaughlin, Gibb
1943 – At Dawn We Die

McLaughlin, Leon
1954 – Crazylegs

McLeay, Janet
1939 – Calling All Marines

McLendon, Jack
See Robert Grady.

McLeod, Catherine[41]
1946 – I've Always Loved You
1947 – That's My Man
The Fabulous Texan
1948 – Old Los Angeles
1954 – The Outcast

McLeod, Gordon
1943 – The Saint Meets the Tiger

McLeod, Mary[120]
1943 – London Blackout Murders
The Purple V
1946 – G. I. War Brides

McNally, Stephen[104]
1954 – Make Haste to Live
1957 – Hell's Crossroads

McNamara, James H.
1940 – One Man's Law

McNaughton, Jack
1953 – Trent's Last Case

McNear, Howard[235]
1957 – Affair in Reno

McNeil, Ron
1958 – Man or Gun

McNulty, Dorothy
See Penny Singleton.

McPeters, Taylor
See Cactus Mack.

McQueen, Butterfly[104]
1945 – Flame of Barbary Coast

McTaggart, Malcolm "Bud"
See James Taggart.

McVey, Paul
1938 – The Night Hawk
1940 – King of the Royal Mounted

McWade, Edward
1936 – Darkest Africa

McWade, Robert
1935 – Cappy Ricks Returns

McWilliams, Paul
1957 – The Unearthly

Meade, Claire
1946 – Daughter of Don Q
1950 – Belle of Old Mexico*

Meader, George
1941 – Petticoat Politics

Meadows, Denny
See Dennis Moore.

Medina, Patricia[104]
1956 – Stranger at My Door

Medwin, Michael
1956 – Doctor at Sea
Above Us the Waves

Mira McKinney

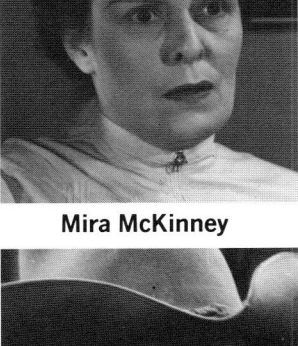
Howard McNear

Meehan, Lew[235]
1936 – The Lawless Nineties*
Oh, Susanna!
The Gun Ranger*
1937 – "Lightnin'" Crandall
Trail of Vengeance
Guns in the Dark*
Gun Lords of Stirrup Basin
Doomed at Sundown*
Yodelin' Kid from Pine Ridge*
A Lawman is Born*
The Red Rope
Boothill Brigade*
The Arizona Gunfighter
Ridin' the Lone Trail
Springtime in the Rockies*
1938 – Thunder in the Desert
The Feud Maker
Prairie Moon*
1939 – The Lone Ranger Rides Again*
Southward, Ho!
Cowboys from Texas*

Meek, Donald[235]
1946 – Affairs of Geraldine

Meeker, George[136]
1936 – Beware of Ladies
1937 – Escape by Night
1938 – The Higgins Family*
1939 – Rough Riders' Round-Up
1941 – The Singing Hill
Mountain Moonlight
Hurricane Smith*
1944 – Silent Partner
Song of Nevada
The Port of Forty Thieves
1945 – The Big Show-Off
1946 – Home in Oklahoma
1947 – Apache Rose
1948 – The Gay Ranchero
King of the Gamblers
The Denver Kid
1949 – Ranger of Cherokee Strip
1950 – Twilight in the Sierras
The Invisible Monster
1951 – Spoilers of the Plains
Wells Fargo Gunmaster
Govt. Agents Vs. Phantom Legion
Honeychile*

Meeker, Ralph[104]
1956 – A Woman's Devotion

Meet the Stars – series
1940 – Chinese Garden Festival
1941 – Wampas Baby Stars
Variety Reel
Los Angeles Examiner Benefit
Hollywood Visits the Navy
Stars at Play
Meet Roy Rogers
Stars Past and Present

Megin Kiddies, The
1936 – Roarin' Lead

Megowan, Don
1957 – Hell Canyon Outlaws
1958 – The Man Who Died Twice

Mehra, Lal Chand
1936 – The Leathernecks Have Landed
The House of a Thousand Candles*
1938 – Storm Over Bengal*
1940 – Drums of Fu Manchu

Meinrad, Josef
1957 – The Congress Dances

Meins, Douglas
1939 – Money to Burn
1940 – Grandpa Goes to Town

Meisel, Kurt
1958 – International Counterfeiters

Melton, Frank[235]
1936 – The Return of Jimmy Valentine
1937 – Affairs of Cappy Ricks
1938 – Riders of the Black Hills
1948 – Daredevils of the Clouds

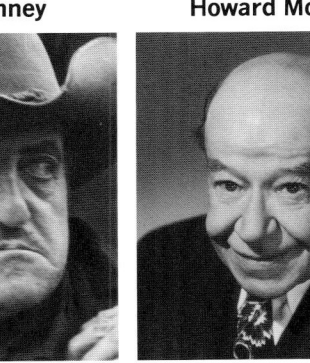
Donald Meek

Frank Melton

Menacker, Sammy
1949—Alias the Champ

Menjou, Adolphe[104]
1955—Timberjack

Menken, Shepard
1949—The Red Menace

Mercedes, Maria
1957—Operation Conspiracy

Mercer, Beryl
1935—Forbidden Heaven
　　　　Hitch Hike Lady

Mercer, Freddie
1942—Shadows on the Sage

Meremblum, Peter—Junior Orchestra
1945—Mexicana

Meredith, Charles
1949—Streets of San Francisco

Meredith, Frank
1951—Govt. Agents Vs. Phantom Legion

Meredith, Iris[236]
1936—Ticket to Paradise*
　　　　The Gentleman from Louisiana*
　　　　Bulldog Edition*
1937—The Gambling Terror
　　　　Trail of Vengeance
　　　　A Lawman is Born

Merivale, Philip
1942—Lady for a Night

Merlin, Jan[201]
1956—A Strange Adventure

Merrall, Mary
1955—The Green Buddha

Merrick, Doris[236]
1947—The Pilgrim Lady

Merrick, Lynn[42]
1941—Two Gun Sheriff
　　　　Sis Hopkins
　　　　The Gay Vagabond
　　　　Desert Bandit
　　　　Kansas Cyclone
　　　　Hurricane Smith*
　　　　Ice-Capades*
　　　　The Apache Kid
　　　　Death Valley Outlaws
　　　　A Missouri Outlaw
1942—Arizona Terrors
　　　　Stagecoach Express
　　　　Jesse James, Jr.
　　　　The Cyclone Kid
　　　　The Sombrero Kid
　　　　Youth on Parade
　　　　Outlaws of Pine Ridge
1943—Mountain Rhythm
　　　　Dead Man's Gulch
　　　　Carson City Cyclone
　　　　Days of Old Cheyenne
　　　　Fugitive from Sonora

Merrick, Marilyn
1941—Wampas Baby Stars*

Merritt, George
1943—Alibi

Merry Meisters, The
1944—Lake Placid Serenade

Mersen, Anne-Marie
1959—O.S.S. 117 is Not Dead

Merton, John[236]
1936—Undersea Kingdom
　　　　The Vigilantes Are Coming
　　　　The Three Mesquiteers
　　　　The Gun Ranger
1937—The Bold Caballero*
　　　　Gunsmoke Ranch*
　　　　Range Defenders
　　　　The Arizona Gunfighter
　　　　The Colorado Kid
1938—The Lone Ranger
　　　　The Fighting Devil Dogs*
　　　　Riders of the Black Hills*
　　　　Dick Tracy Returns
1939—Rough Riders' Round-Up*
　　　　Three Texas Steers*
　　　　Daredevils of the Red Circle*
　　　　Zorro's Fighting Legion
1940—Drums of Fu Manchu
　　　　Dark Command*
　　　　Covered Wagon Days
　　　　The Trail Blazers
　　　　Melody Ranch*
　　　　Lone Star Raiders
1941—Two Gun Sheriff*
　　　　Under Fiesta Stars
　　　　Gauchos of Eldorado*
　　　　A Missouri Outlaw
　　　　Dick Tracy Vs. Crime, Inc.*
1942—Arizona Terrors*
1944—Zorro's Black Whip
1945—Oregon Trail
　　　　Bandits of the Badlands
　　　　The Cherokee Flash
1949—Radar Patrol Vs. Spy King

Messinger, Gertrude
1935—Melody Trail

Metaxa, George
1943—The West Side Kid
1945—Scotland Yard Investigator

Metcalfe, Bradley
1935—Westward Ho
1936—King of the Pecos

Meyer, Emile
1956—The Maverick Queen

Meyer, Greta[236]
1937—Bill Cracks Down

Meyer, Russ
1954—Roogie's Bump

Meyers, Charles
1937—Rootin' Tootin' Rhythm

Michael, Gertrude[236]
1944—Faces in the Fog
1945—Three's a Crowd

Johnny Mack Brown, Iris Meredith

Michael, Peter
1943—Overland Mail Robbery
1947—Yankee Fakir
　　　　The Pretender

Michaels, Johnny
1943—Deerslayer

Michaels, Pat
1946—Santa Fe Uprising

Middlemass, Robert[236]
1937—Meet the Boy Friend
1938—I Stand Accused
1939—The Arizona Kid
1945—A Sporting Chance

Middleton, Charles[136]
1937—Yodelin' Kid from Pine Ridge
1938—Dick Tracy Returns
1939—Daredevils of the Red Circle
　　　　Wyoming Outlaw
　　　　Cowboys from Texas
　　　　Thou Shalt Not Kill
1942—Perils of Nyoka
1947—Wyoming*
　　　　The Pretender
1949—The Last Bandit

Middleton, Guy
1942—Suicide Squadron

Middleton, Ray[42]
1940—Gangs of Chicago
1941—Lady from Louisiana
　　　　Hurricane Smith
　　　　Mercy Island
1942—Lady for a Night
　　　　The Girl from Alaska
1952—I Dream of Jeanie
1953—Sweethearts on Parade
1954—Jubilee Trail
1955—I Cover the Underworld
　　　　The Road to Denver

Middleton, Robert[104]
1958—No Place to Land

Mikhelson, Andre
1955—The Divided Heart

Milan, Frank
1938—Pals of the Saddle

Miles, Betty
1943—The Masked Marvel*

Miles, John
1947—The Fabulous Texan

Miles, Peter[120]
1949—The Red Pony
1950—Trigger, Jr.
　　　　California Passage

Miljan, John[236]
1936—The Gentleman from Louisiana
1940—Young Bill Hickok
1946—The Last Crooked Mile
1947—That's My Man
　　　　The Flame

Millan, Victor
1952—Thunderbirds

Milland, Ray[82]
1955—A Man Alone
1956—Lisbon

Millar, Marjie[236]
1956—When Gangland Strikes

Miller, Ann[105]
1940—Hit Parade of 1941
　　　　Melody Ranch
1941—Variety Reel*
　　　　Stars Past and Present*

Miller, Charles[236]
1942—South of Santa Fe
　　　　Raiders of the Range
　　　　The Phantom Plainsmen
1943—Thundering Trails
　　　　The Blocked Trail
　　　　Daredevils of the West
　　　　Days of Old Cheyenne
　　　　The Black Hills Express
　　　　Wagon Tracks West
　　　　Beyond the Last Frontier
　　　　Raiders of Sunset Pass
1944—Pride of the Plains
　　　　Beneath Western Skies
　　　　Hidden Valley Outlaws

Miller, Hugh
1937—Bulldog Drummond at Bay

Miller, Ivan[236]
1936—Bulldog Edition
　　　　Country Gentlemen
1938—The Old Barn Dance
　　　　Call of the Yukon
　　　　Man from Music Mountain
　　　　Down in "Arkansaw"
1939—Forged Passport
　　　　Wall Street Cowboy
　　　　Sabotage*
　　　　Cowboys from Texas
1940—Young Buffalo Bill*
　　　　In Old Missouri*
　　　　Frontier Vengeance
1941—Rags to Riches*
　　　　Under Fiesta Stars
　　　　Jesse James at Bay
　　　　The Devil Pays Off
1942—Lady for a Night
　　　　Man from Cheyenne*
　　　　Youth on Parade*
1943—G-Men Vs. The Black Dragon

Miller, Kristine[236]
1952—Tropical Heat Wave
1954—Flight Nurse
　　　　Geraldine
　　　　Hell's Outpost
1956—Thunder Over Arizona

Miller, Lorraine[237]
1943—Riders of the Rio Grande
　　　　Beyond the Last Frontier

Miller, Marvin
1954—The Sanghai Story

Miller, Peter
1956—A Strange Adventure

Miller, Ray
1939—Daredevils of the Red Circle

Miller, Walter[237]
1937—Wild Horse Rodeo
1938—Come on, Leathernecks
　　　　Down in "Arkansaw"
1939—Home on the Prairie
　　　　Dick Tracy's G-Men
1940—Grandpa Goes to Town
　　　　Gaucho Serenade*
1941—Dick Tracy Vs. Crime, Inc.*

Milletaire, Carl
1952—Bal Tabarin
1955—The Fighting Chance

Millett, Arthur
1936—Winds of the Wasteland

Doris Merrick

John Merton

Greta Meyer

Gertrude Michael

Robert Middlemass

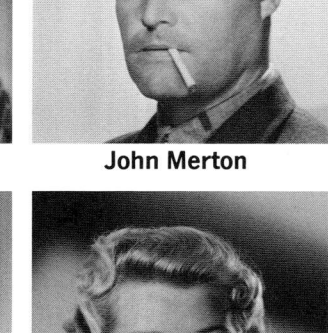

John Miljan

Marjie Millar

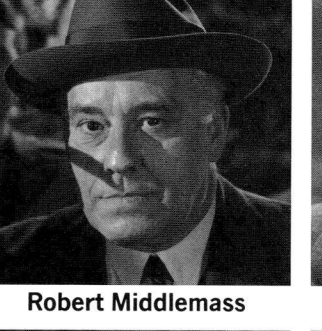

Charles Miller

Ivan Miller

Kristine Miller

Millican, James[237]
1946—Rendezvous with Annie
1947—Spoilers of the North
1951—Missing Women
1954—Jubilee Trail
   The Outcast
1955—The Vanishing American

Millot, Charles
1959—O.S.S. 117 is Not Dead

Mills Brothers, The
1943—Chatterbox

Mills, Gordon
1956—Daniel Boone, Trail Blazer

Mills, John
1956—Above Us the Waves

Milner, Martin[237]
1950—Sands of Iwo Jima
1951—Fighting Coast Guard

Milo Twins, The
1944—Sing Neighbor Sing

Milton, Gerald
1958—The Man Who Died Twice

Minevitch, Borrah—and his Harmonica Rascals
1940—Hit Parade of 1941

Miranda, Aurora[237]
1944—Brazil
1945—Tell It to a Star

Miranda, Carmen
1941—Hollywood Visits the Navy*

Mitchel, Helen
1939—Zorro's Fighting Legion

Mitchell, Barry[237]
[Brad Dexter]
1946—Heldorado

Mitchell, Belle
1936—The Leavenworth Case

Mitchell, Beverlee
1946—Earl Carroll Sketchbook*
1947—The Pilgrim Lady*

Mitchell, Bruce
1937—Paradise Express

Mitchell, Chris
1955—King of the Carnival

Mitchell, Dale
1949—The Kid from Cleveland

Mitchell, Frank
1944—That's My Baby

Mitchell, Grant
1938—Lady, Behave!

Mitchell, Howard
1950—The Invisible Monster

Mitchell, Norval
1951—Govt. Agents Vs. Phantom Legion

Lorraine Miller

Aurora Miranda

Mitchell, Robert—Boy Choir
1943—Idaho
1945—Bells of Rosarita
1946—Song of Arizona

Mitchell, Shirley[237]
1944—Jamboree

Mitchell, Steve
1953—Jungle Drums of Africa

Mitchell, Stuart
1957—Operation Conspiracy

Mitchell, Yvonne
1955—The Divided Heart

Mitchum, John
1956—The Man is Armed

Mitchum, Robert[121]
1943—Beyond the Last Frontier
1949—The Red Pony

Mitrovich, Marta
1948—I, Jane Doe
1950—Prisoners in Petticoats

Patsy Montana

Clayton Moore

Walter Miller

Barry Mitchell

Moehring, Kansas
1943—The Man from the Rio Grande

Mohr, Gerald[237]
1941—Adventures of Captain Marvel*
   Jungle Girl
1943—King of the Cowboys
1946—A Guy Could Change
   The Catman of Paris
   Passkey to Danger
   The Invisible Informer
1947—The Magnificent Rogue
1949—The Blonde Bandit
1957—Raiders of Old California*

Molasses and January
1937—The Hit Parade

Molieri, Lillian
1951—South of Caliente

Molina, Carlos—and orchestra
1950—Belle of Old Mexico

Molina, Carmen
1945—Song of Mexico

Molina, Joe
1939—Zorro's Fighting Legion

Molinas, Richard
1955—The Divided Heart

Monaghan, John P.
1952—Lady Possessed

Monroe, Tom
1949—Powder River Rustlers
1950—Rustlers on Horseback
1953—El Paso Stampede

Monroe, Vaughn[105]
1950—Singing Guns
1952—Toughest Man in Arizona

Goodee Montgomery

Dennie Moore

James Millican

Shirley Mitchell

Montague, Monte[227]
1938—Riders of the Black Hills
1940—Young Bill Hickok
1941—The Apache Kid
   King of the Texas Rangers
1942—The Cyclone Kid
   The Phantom Plainsmen
1952—The Last Musketeer

Montana, Montie
1949—Down Dakota Way

Montana, Patsy[237]
1939—Colorado Sunset

Monteros, Rosenda
1956—A Woman's Devotion

Montes, Lola
1944—The Lady and the Monster

Montgomery, George[105]
   [as George Letz]
1936—The Singing Vagabond*
1937—Springtime in the Rockies*
1938—The Old Barn Dance*
   The Lone Ranger
   Under Western Stars*
   Gold Mine in the Sky*
   Army Girl*
   Pals of the Saddle*
   Billy the Kid Returns*
   Santa Fe Stampede*
   Come on, Rangers*
   Hawk of the Wilderness*
   Shine on Harvest Moon*
1939—The Mysterious Miss X*
   I Was a Convict*
   Rough Riders' Round-Up*
   The Night Riders*
   [as George Montgomery]
   Frontier Pony Express*
   Man of Conquest*
   Southward, Ho!*
   S. O. S. Tidal Wave*
   In Old Caliente*
   Wyoming Outlaw*
   New Frontier*
   In Old Monterey*
   Wall Street Cowboy*
   The Arizona Kid*
   Saga of Death Valley*
   South of the Border*
1957—Pawnee

Montgomery, Goodee[237]
1936—Beware of Ladies

Montgomery, Jack
1935—The New Frontier

Montgomery, Martha
1946—The Inner Circle

Dennis Moore

Martin Milner

Gerald Mohr

Montgomery, Ray
1953—Bandits of the West

Montoya, Alex
1949—Daughter of the Jungle
   Ghost of Zorro
1952—Wild Horse Ambush

Moody, Ralph
1957—Pawnee

Moore, Charles
1939—Southward, Ho!
1941—Petticoat Politics
   Desert Bandit
   Kansas Cyclone

Moore, Clayton[237]
1941—Tuxedo Junction
1942—Perils of Nyoka
   Outlaws of Pine Ridge
1946—The Crimson Ghost
   Heldorado*
1947—Jesse James Rides Again
   Along the Oregon Trail
1948—G-Men Never Forget
   Marshal of Amarillo
   Adv. of Frank and Jesse James
   The Plunderers*
   The Far Frontier
1949—Sheriff of Wichita
   Ghost of Zorro
   Frontier Investigator
1950—Flying Disc Man from Mars*
1952—Radar Men from the Moon
   Captive of Billy the Kid
1953—Jungle Drums of Africa
   Down Laredo Way

Moore, Constance[43]
1941—Los Angeles Examiner Benefit*
   Stars at Play*
1944—Atlantic City
1945—Earl Carroll Vanities
   Mexicana
1946—In Old Sacramento
   Earl Carroll Sketchbook*
1947—Hit Parade of 1947

Moore, Dennie[237]
1940—Women in War

Moore, Dennis[237]
   [as Denny Meadows]
1935—Sagebrush Troubadour
1936—The Lonely Trail
   [as Dennis Moore]
1940—Rocky Mountain Rangers
1941—Pals of the Pecos
1942—Raiders of the Range
1945—The Purple Monster Strikes
1948—The Gay Ranchero
1949—Navajo Trail Raiders
1950—Singing Guns*
   Desperadoes of the West*
1957—Beginning of the End*

Moore, Eva
1945—Scotland Yard Investigator

Ida Moore

Moore, Ida[238]
1945 — Girls of the Big House
1951 — Honeychile

Moore, Jacqueline
1945 — Love, Honor and Goodbye

Moore, Mary[238]
1945 — The Purple Monster Strikes

Moore, Pauline[238]
1939 — Days of Jesse James
1940 — Young Buffalo Bill
        The Carson City Kid
        Colorado
        The Trail Blazers
1941 — Arkansas Judge
        King of the Texas Rangers
1957 — Spoilers of the Forest*

Moorehead, Agnes[105]
1951 — Adventures of Captain Fabian

Moorehead, Dick
1936 — Under Cover Man

Moorhouse, Bert[238]
1938 — King of the Newsboys*
1941 — Mountain Moonlight*
1943 — Mountain Rhythm*
1944 — Lake Placid Serenade*
1945 — Utah*
        A Sporting Chance*
        Hitchhike to Happiness*
        Behind City Lights*
        Sunset in El Dorado*
        Along the Navajo Trail*
1946 — Gay Blades*
        One Exciting Week*
        That Brennan Girl*
1947 — Angel and the Badman*
        That's My Man*

Moran, Betty[238]
1940 — Frontier Vengeance

Moran, Jackie[121]
1937 — Michael O'Halloran
1938 — Arson Gang Busters
1943 — Nobody's Darling
1944 — Three Little Sisters

Moran, Jim
1946 — Specter of the Rose

Moran, Patsy
1948 — Homicide for Three

Moran, Peggy[238]
1938 — Rhythm of the Saddle
1943 — King of the Cowboys

Moran, Polly[82]
1937 — Two Wise Maids
1938 — Ladies in Distress
        Red River Range
1940 — Meet the Missus
1941 — Petticoat Politics

Morante, Milburn[238]
1936 — Ghost-Town Gold
        The Old Corral
1937 — Bar-Z Bad Men
        Dick Tracy*
        Gun Lords of Stirrup Basin*
        Come on, Cowboys!*
        Range Defenders*
        Public Cowboy No. 1
1938 — Under Western Stars*
        Riders of the Black Hills*
        Gold Mine in the Sky
        Pals of the Saddle*
1942 — South of Santa Fe*

Mordant, Edwin
1938 — Outlaws of Sonora

More, Kenneth
1955 — Doctor in the House

Morel, Rose Marie[69]
1944 — Lake Placid Serenade*
1945 — Utah*
        Earl Carroll Vanities*
        Corpus Christi Bandits*
        The Phantom Speaks*
        Bells of Rosarita*
        Hitchhike to Happiness*
        Tell It to a Star*
        Swingin' on a Rainbow*
        Behind City Lights*
        Scotland Yard Investigator*
        Marshal of Laredo*
        Girls of the Big House*
        An Angel Comes to Brooklyn*

Moreland, Mantan[238]
1940 — Bowery Boy*
1945 — Captain Tugboat Annie

Moreno, Rita[105]
1952 — The Fabulous Senorita

Moreno, Rosita
1936 — The House of a Thousand Candles

Morgan, Boyd "Red"[238]
1951 — Desert of Lost Men
1952 — The Last Musketeer
        Thundering Caravans

Morgan, Eula
1945 — An Angel Comes to Brooklyn

Morgan, Gene
See Michael Kent.

Mary Moore

Betty Moran

Morgan, Helen[238]
1936 — Frankie and Johnnie

Morgan, Henry [Harry][238]
1948 — Moonrise
1950 — The Showdown
1951 — Belle LeGrand
1952 — Toughest Man in Arizona
1953 — Champ for a Day

Morgan, Lee[238]
1948 — Dangers of the Canadian Mounted
1956 — Daniel Boone, Trail Blazer

Morgan, Ralph[238]
1938 — Army Girl
        Orphans of the Street
1939 — Man of Conquest
        Smuggled Cargo
1941 — Dick Tracy Vs. Crime, Inc.
1942 — The Traitor Within
1944 — Trocadero
1951 — Heart of the Rockies

Morgan, Raymond L.
1956 — Hidden Guns

Morin, Alberto
1950 — Rio Grande
        Under Mexicali Stars

Pauline Moore

Peggy Moran

Morison, Patricia
1940 — Chinese Garden Festival*
1941 — Stars at Play*
        Stars Past and Present*

Morita, Miki
1936 — Border Phantom

Morley, Karen[238]
1945 — Jealousy

Morley, Kay
1948 — Campus Honeymoon

Morrell Trio, The
1944 — San Fernando Valley

Morris, Adrian
1939 — Wall Street Cowboy

Morris, Chester[105]
1936 — Frankie and Johnnie
1940 — Wagons Westward
        Girl from God's Country

Morris, Corbet
1939 — Daredevils of the Red Circle

Morris, Dorothy[121]
1943 — Someone to Remember

Morris, Frances
1946 — Crime of the Century

Bert Moorhouse

Milburn Morante

Morris, Lana
1955 — Trouble in Store

Morris, Michael
1941 — Rags to Riches

Morris, Wayne
1955 — The Green Buddha
        Cross Channel

Morrison, Barbara
1952 — Lady Possessed*

Morrison, Chuck[238]
1941 — Dick Tracy Vs. Crime, Inc.
1942 — Code of the Outlaw

Morrow, Brad
1951 — Honeychile

Morrow, Katherine
1935 — The Spanish Cape Mystery

Morrow, Neyle
1947 — Spoilers of the North
1949 — Ranger of Cherokee Strip
1950 — Harbor of Missing Men

Morrow, Susan[239]
1953 — Can. Mounties Vs. Atomic Invaders

Morton, Charles
1944 — Outlaws of Santa Fe
        Firebrands of Arizona

Morton, Danny[239]
1945 — An Angel Comes to Brooklyn*
1948 — Eyes of Texas
        [as Tony Cannon]
1949 — Post Office Investigator
        [as Dann Morton]
1950 — Destination Big House
1951 — The Dakota Kid

Morton, James C.[239]
1937 — Two Wise Maids
        Rhythm in the Clouds
        Public Cowboy No. 1
1938 — Mama Runs Wild
1940 — Earl of Puddlestone
1941 — Lady from Louisiana
1942 — Yokel Boy

Moser, Hans
1957 — The Congress Dances

Mosier, Enid
1952 — Lady Possessed

Moss, Jimmie
1952 — Border Saddlemates

Mothershed, Daisy Lee[239]
1940 — Who Killed Aunt Maggie?
1941 — Sis Hopkins*
        Rags to Riches
1944 — Atlantic City

Moultrie, Freddie
1952 — I Dream of Jeanie

Movita
1950 — The Avengers*
1952 — Wild Horse Ambush

Mantan Moreland

Boyd "Red" Morgan

Helen Morgan

Henry Morgan

Lee Morgan

Ralph Morgan

Karen Morley

Chuck Morrison

Susan Morrow

Danny Morton

James C. Morton

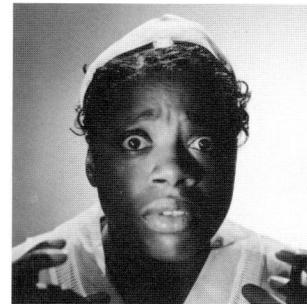

Daisy Lee Mothershed

Mowbray, Alan[239]
1940 — Scatterbrain
1941 — Ice-Capades
1942 — Yokel Boy
1945 — Earl Carroll Vanities
Tell It to a Star
1947 — The Pilgrim Lady
1948 — The Main Street Kid

Mowbray, Henry
1936 — The Leathernecks Have Landed

Mr. District Attorney—series
1941 — Mr. District Attorney
Mr. District Att. in the Carter Case
1942 — Secrets of the Underground

Muir, Esther
1935 — Racing Luck
1938 — Western Jamboree
1942 — X Marks the Spot

Mulhall, Jack[239]
1936 — Undersea Kingdom
1937 — Dangerous Holiday
1938 — Outlaws of Sonora
1939 — Home on the Prairie
1940 — Grandpa Goes to Town*
Mysterious Doctor Satan
1941 — Adventures of Captain Marvel
Stars Past and Present*
Dick Tracy Vs. Crime, Inc.
1943 — Idaho*
1944 — My Buddy*
1945 — Flame of Barbary Coast*

Muller, Paul
1955 — Mystery of the Black Jungle

Mullin, Dan
1958 — Invisible Avenger

Mumby, Diana[239]
1945 — Earl Carroll Vanities*
An Angel Comes to Brooklyn*
1946 — Earl Carroll Sketchbook*
Out California Way*
1947 — Winter Wonderland

Mundin, Herbert
1938 — Invisible Enemy

Munier, Ferdinand
1935 — Two Sinners
1937 — The Bold Caballero

Munson, Ona[82]
1940 — Wagons Westward
Chinese Garden Festival*
1941 — Lady from Louisiana
1943 — Idaho
1945 — The Cheaters
Dakota

Murdock, Perry
1936 — Border Phantom

Murphy, Al[121]
1945 — Flame of Barbary Coast
1947 — Angel and the Badman*
1948 — The Bold Frontiersman
1950 — Surrender*
Hit Parade of 1951

Murphy, Bob
1937 — Portia on Trial

Murphy, George
1941 — Hollywood Visits the Navy*

Murphy, Horace[239]
1936 — Under Cover Man
The President's Mystery*
Ghost-Town Gold*
The Gun Ranger
Lawless Land
Border Phantom
1937 — Bar-Z Bad Men*
The Trusted Outlaw*
The Gambling Terror
Paradise Express*
"Lightnin'" Crandall
Trail of Vengeance*
Gun Lords of Stirrup Basin*
Come on, Cowboys!
Doomed at Sundown*
The Red Rope
Boothill Brigade
Ridin' the Lone Trail*
The Colorado Kid
1938 — Paroled—to Die
Thunder in the Desert
Durango Valley Raiders
Billy the Kid Returns
The Night Hawk*
1939 — Fighting Thoroughbreds*
The Night Riders*
Man of Conquest*
Rovin' Tumbleweeds*
Saga of Death Valley*
Cowboys from Texas*
Days of Jesse James*
1940 — Ghost Valley Raiders
Carolina Moon*
Melody Ranch*
1941 — The Great Train Robbery*
Bad Man of Deadwood
1943 — Song of Texas*
1946 — Traffic in Crime*

Murphy, Mary[82]
1954 — Make Haste to Live
1955 — A Man Alone
1956 — The Maverick Queen

Murphy, Maurice[239]
1936 — Down to the Sea
1939 — Forged Passport
The Covered Trailer
1940 — Wolf of New York

Murphy, William
1950 — Sands of Iwo Jima
1951 — Fighting Coast Guard
1952 — Hoodlum Empire
1953 — Fair Wind to Java

Murray, Jr., Charlie
1943 — Death Valley Manhunt

Mary Beth Hughes, Maurice Murphy

Murray, Sr., Charlie[239]
1937 — Circus Girl
1941 — Stars Past and Present*

Murray, Forbes[239]
1936 — Country Gentlemen*
Roarin' Lead*
1937 — Dick Tracy*
Navy Blues*
The Wrong Road*
The Trigger Trio*
1938 — The Lone Ranger*
The Night Hawk*
1939 — S. O. S. Tidal Wave*
Flight at Midnight*
The Arizona Kid*
Sabotage*
Cowboys from Texas*
1940 — Wolf of New York*
In Old Missouri
Ride, Tenderfoot, Ride
Hit Parade of 1941*
Friendly Neighbors*
1941 — Sis Hopkins*
Saddlemates
Mountain Moonlight*
The Apache Kid
Tuxedo Junction*
1942 — Lady for a Night*
Cowboy Serenade*
Jesse James, Jr.*
Perils of Nyoka
Hi, Neighbor*
The Traitor Within*
1943 — Mountain Rhythm*
G-Men Vs. The Black Dragon
Thundering Trails
Tahiti Honey*
Calling Wild Bill Elliott*
Swing Your Partner
The Masked Marvel*
Canyon City
1944 — The Fighting Seabees*
Hidden Valley Outlaws*
Man from Frisco
1945 — Manhunt of Mystery Island
Santa Fe Saddlemates
Bells of Rosarita*
Love, Honor and Goodbye*
1946 — I've Always Loved You*
1947 — That's My Gal*
1949 — Radar Patrol Vs. Spy King
1952 — Gobs and Gals*
1954 — Sea of Lost Ships*

Alan Mowbray

Murray, Ken
1948 — Bill and Coo

Murray, Zon[239]
1946 — The El Paso Kid
1948 — Grand Canyon Trail*
1951 — Night Riders of Montana
1952 — Border Saddlemates
Desperadoes' Outpost
1953 — Old Overland Trail
Enemies of the Universe
Cosmic Vengeance
Down Laredo Way
1954 — Phantom Stallion
1957 — Beginning of the End*

Muse, Clarence[239]
1936 — Laughing Irish Eyes
Follow Your Heart*
1946 — Affairs of Geraldine*
1948 — King of the Gamblers*
1953 — The Sun Shines Bright

Music Maids, The
1943 — Hit Parade of 1943
Hoosier Holiday
1944 — Jamboree

Myers, Carmel
1942 — Lady for a Night

Myrtil, Odette[239]
1949 — The Fighting Kentuckian
1952 — Lady Possessed

Jack Mulhall

Diana Mumby

Horace Murphy

Charlie Murray, Sr.

Forbes Murray

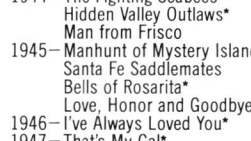

Zon Murray

Clarence Muse

Odette Myrtil

239

N

Naba
1939 – Three Texas Steers

Nader, George[240]
1950 – Rustlers on Horseback

Naefe, Jester
1957 – The Congress Dances

Nagel, Anne[121]
1937 – Escape by Night
1941 – Hollywood Visits the Navy*
1946 – Murder in the Music Hall
Traffic in Crime

Nagel, Conrad[121]
1936 – The Girl from Mandalay

Nagy, Bill
1957 – Operation Conspiracy

Nahera, Alex—Dancers
1943 – Song of Texas

Naish, J. Carrol[105]
1936 – The Return of Jimmy Valentine
The Leathernecks Have Landed
1937 – Sea Racketeers
1941 – Stars at Play*
1950 – Rio Grande
1952 – Woman of the North Country
1953 – Ride the Man Down
1955 – The Last Command

Naismith, Laurence
1957 – The Weapon

Nalder, Reggie
1951 – Adventures of Captain Fabian

Napier, Alan[240]
1947 – Driftwood
1950 – Macbeth

Napier, Russell
1957 – The Man in the Road

Narciso, Grazia
1948 – Madonna of the Desert

Nash, Mary
1944 – The Lady and the Monster

Nash, Robert
1957 – Pawnee

Natheaux, Louis
1936 – Go-Get-'Em, Haines

Natwick, Mildred
1952 – The Quiet Man

Nazarro, Cliff[240]
1938 – Outside of Paradise
A Desperate Adventure
1939 – Forged Passport
1940 – Grandpa Goes to Town*
The Crooked Road*
Scatterbrain*
Sing, Dance, Plenty Hot*
Chinese Garden Festival*
1941 – Rookies on Parade
Sailors on Leave
1942 – Pardon My Stripes
Call of the Canyon
1943 – Shantytown
1944 – Trocadero

Neal, Ella[122]
1940 – Mysterious Doctor Satan

Neal, Tom[240]
1941 – Jungle Girl
1942 – Flying Tigers
1944 – Thoroughbreds

Needham, Gordon
1958 – Scotland Yard Dragnet

Negley, Howard J.[240]
1947 – Twilight on the Rio Grande
1948 – King of the Gamblers
1950 – Lonely Heart Bandits
The Missourians
California Passage*
1951 – Belle LeGrand*
1953 – The Lady Wants Mink*
1955 – The Eternal Sea*
Santa Fe Passage*
A Man Alone

Neher, Jeanne
1958 – Invisible Avenger

Neil, Robert
1950 – The Missourians
1952 – I Dream of Jeanie
Thunderbirds

Neill, Noel[240]
1948 – Adv. of Frank and Jesse James
1949 – The James Brothers of Missouri

Neilson, Nigel
1957 – Time is My Enemy

Neise, George
1942 – Valley of Hunted Men
1958 – Outcasts of the City

Nelson, Billy
1943 – False Faces

Nelson, Bob
1955 – Double Jeopardy

Nelson, Bobby
1937 – The Gambling Terror
The Red Rope
Boothill Brigade

Nelson, Edwin
1958 – Street of Darkness

Nelson, Felix
1953 – Jungle Drums of Africa

Nelson, Frank
1949 – The 3 Minnies: Sota, Tonka & Ha Ha!
Romantic Rumbola
Bungle in the Jungle

Nesbitt, Norman
1942 – King of the Mounties
1944 – Captain America

Nestell, William
1939 – The Night Riders

Neubert, Carl
1946 – The Catman of Paris

Newcombe, Jessica
1942 – The Traitor Within

Newell, William[44]
1936 – Navy Born
Sitting on the Moon
Bulldog Edition
Robinson Crusoe of Clipper Island
The Big Show
The Mandarin Mystery
Happy Go Lucky
Beware of Ladies
A Man Betrayed
1937 – Larceny on the Air
Bill Cracks Down
The Hit Parade*
Dangerous Holiday
Rhythm in the Clouds
1938 – Orphans of the Street*
1940 – Girl from Havana*
Melody and Moonlight*
Mysterious Doctor Satan
1941 – The Gay Vagabond*
Puddin' Head*
Ice-Capades*
Sailors on Leave*
The Devil Pays Off*
1942 – Pardon My Stripes*
A Tragedy at Midnight
Moonlight Masquerade*
The Old Homestead*
Ice-Capades Revue*
1943 – Nobody's Darling*
1947 – Angel and the Badman*
The Magnificent Rogue*
That's My Gal*
1955 – The Eternal Sea*

Newlan, Paul
1941 – The Gay Vagabond

Newland, John
1948 – Sons of Adventure
Homicide for Three

Newley, Anthony
1956 – Above Us the Waves

Newton, Mary
1944 – My Best Gal
1945 – Girls of the Big House

Newton, Robert
1941 – Poison Pen

Nibert, Terry
1940 – Carolina Moon

Nichols, C. H.
1955 – The Square Ring

Nichols, Dandy
1957 – Time is My Enemy

Nicodemus
See Nicodemus Stewart.

Nicol, Alex[106]
1953 – Champ for a Day

Nielsen, Hans
1958 – International Counterfeiters

George Nader

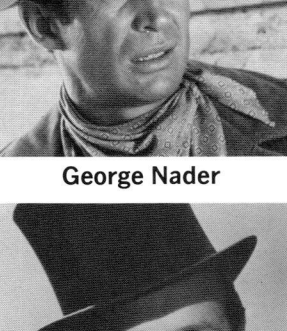

Cliff Nazarro

Niesen, Gertrude
1940 – Chinese Garden Festival*
1941 – Rookies on Parade
1943 – Thumbs Up

Niles, Ken
1946 – The Inner Circle

Niles, Wendell[240]
1940 – Gaucho Serenade
Three Faces West
1941 – Puddin' Head
1942 – A Tragedy at Midnight
1943 – The Masked Marvel
Here Comes Elmer
1945 – Swingin' on a Rainbow

Nilsson, Anna Q.
1943 – Headin' for God's Country

Nimoy, Leonard[240]
1952 – Zombies of the Stratosphere
1953 – Old Overland Trail

Nissen, Greta[44]
No films.

Noble, Peter
1958 – Strange Case of Dr. Manning

Noble, Ray—and orchestra
1944 – Lake Placid Serenade

Noel, Hattie
1942 – Lady for a Night

Tom Neal

Noel, Magali
1959 – O. S. S. 117 is Not Dead

Nokes, George
1948 – Slippy McGee

Nolan, Bob
See Sons of the Pioneers.

Nolan, Danni[240]
1949 – Bandit King of Texas
Flame of Youth
1950 – Prisoners in Petticoats

Nolan, Jeanette[240]
1950 – Macbeth

Nolan, Jim
1948 – Sons of Adventure*
Night Time in Nevada
Son of God's Country
1949 – Daughter of the Jungle
Wake of the Red Witch*
Death Valley Gunfighter
Bandit King of Texas
Flame of Youth*
Alias the Champ

Nolan, Lloyd[106]
1940 – Gangs of Chicago
Behind the News
1954 – Crazylegs

Noriega, Eduardo
1956 – Daniel Boone, Trail Blazer

Norman, B. G.
1948 – Sundown in Santa Fe

Norman, Jack[241]
[as Norman Willis]
1938 – Prison Nurse
1940 – Girl from God's Country*
King of the Royal Mounted
1941 – Gauchos of Eldorado
1943 – G-Men Vs. The Black Dragon*
King of the Cowboys
[as Jack Norman]
1946 – G. I. War Brides*
Plainsman and the Lady*
1947 – Angel and the Badman*
Bandits of Dark Canyon
1952 – Zombies of the Stratosphere*
1957 – Thunder Over Tangier*

Norman, Lucille[82]
1953 – Sweethearts on Parade

Norris, Edward[82]
1941 – Back in the Saddle
Angels with Broken Wings
Doctors Don't Tell
1944 – End of the Road
1946 – Murder in the Music Hall
1950 – Surrender

Norris, Jay[241]
1944 – The Fighting Seabees

North, Sherle
1945 – An Angel Comes to Brooklyn

Norton, Barry
1939 – Should Husbands Work?

Norton, Edgar
1937 – Bill Cracks Down

Norton, Jack[241]
1945 – Flame of Barbary Coast
Captain Tugboat Annie

Nova, Lou
1947 – Calendar Girl

Novak, Eve [Eva][241]
1945 – The Topeka Terror
Corpus Christi Bandits*
Three's a Crowd*
Steppin' in Society*
The Fatal Witness*
1946 – That Brennan Girl*
1947 – Robin Hood of Texas*
Blackmail
1948 – I, Jane Doe*
Train to Alcatraz*
1949 – Hellfire*
The Blonde Bandit*
1950 – Women from Headquarters*
The Savage Horde*
Sunset in the West*
1951 – Havana Rose*
1953 – A Perilous Journey*
1956 – Dakota Incident*
1957 – Duel at Apache Wells*

Alan Napier

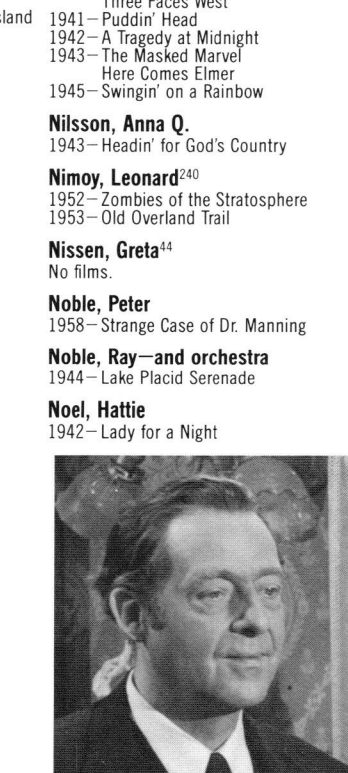

Howard J. Negley

Leonard Nimoy

Noel Neill

Danni Nolan

Wendell Niles

Jeanette Nolan

Novarro, Ramon[83]
1937—The Sheik Steps Out
1938—A Desperate Adventure

Novello, Jay[136]
1938—Tenth Avenue Kid
1939—Calling All Marines
1940—Forgotten Girls*
 Girl from Havana
 Colorado*
 The Border Legion
1941—Robin Hood of the Pecos
 The Great Train Robbery
 Two Gun Sheriff
 Sheriff of Tombstone
 Citadel of Crime
 Bad Man of Deadwood
1942—Sleepytime Gal
 Bells of Capistrano*
 King of the Mounties
1943—Sleepy Lagoon*
 Man from Music Mountain
1944—Captain America
1945—The Chicago Kid
 Federal Operator 99
 Behind City Lights*
1956—Jaguar
 Lisbon

Nowell, Wedgewood
1936—The Big Show
1937—Dick Tracy

Nugent, Carol
1950—Trail of Robin Hood

Nugent, Eddie[83]
1935—Forced Landing
1936—Dancing Feet
 The Harvester
 A Man Betrayed

Nugent, Judy
1953—Down Laredo Way

Nusser, James
1957—Hell Canyon Outlaws

Nye, Carroll
1940—The Trail Blazers

Nyoka—series
1941—Jungle Girl
1942—Perils of Nyoka

Oakland, Dagmar
1936—The Leavenworth Case*
1937—The Hit Parade*
 Michael O'Halloran*
1938—A Desperate Adventure*
1940—In Old Missouri*

Oakland, Vivien
1942—A Tragedy at Midnight*
1944—The Girl Who Dared
1945—Utah*
1947—That's My Gal*

Oakman, Wheeler
1936—Darkest Africa
1939—The Lone Ranger Rides Again*
1941—Stars Past and Present*

O'Brian, Hugh[241]
1951—Buckaroo Sheriff of Texas
 Fighting Coast Guard
1955—The Twinkle in God's Eye

O'Brien, Dave[241]
1936—Oregon Trail*
 Dancing Feet
1937—"Lightnin'" Crandall
 Youth on Parole*
1939—Wyoming Outlaw*
 New Frontier
 The Arizona Kid*
 Main Street Lawyer*

O'Brien, Edmond[106]
1954—The Shanghai Story

O'Brien, George
1941—Hollywood Visits the Navy*

O'Brien, Pat[106]
1954—Jubilee Trail

O'Brien-Moore, Erin
1936—The Leavenworth Case
1954—Sea of Lost Ships

O'Casey, Ronan
1955—Trouble in Store

O'Connell, Hugh
1941—Puddin' Head

O'Connor, Frank[136]
Many films.
1935—$1000 a Minute*
1936—The President's Mystery*
 The Mandarin Mystery*
 A Man Betrayed*
1938—The Purple Vigilantes*
 Born to be Wild*
 Riders of the Black Hills
 Dick Tracy Returns*
 Billy the Kid Returns*
1939—The Mysterious Miss X*
 I Was a Convict*
 Mexicali Rose*
 The Night Riders*
 Wyoming Outlaw*
 Dick Tracy's G-Men*
1940—The Crooked Road*
 The Tulsa Kid*
 Ride, Tenderfoot, Ride*
 Barnyard Follies*
1941—Wyoming Wildcat*
 A Man Betrayed*
 Two Gun Sheriff*
 Nevada City*
 Bad Man of Deadwood*
1942—Pardon My Stripes*
 Stagecoach Express*
 Shepherd of the Ozarks*
 Sunset on the Desert*
 Stardust on the Sage*
 X Marks the Spot*
 The Traitor Within*
1943—Swing Your Partner*
 Hoosier Holiday*
 Beyond the Last Frontier*
 The Masked Marvel*
 Here Comes Elmer*
 O, My Darling Clementine*
1944—Captain America*
 Hidden Valley Outlaws*
 Rosie, the Riveter*
 Silver City Kid*
 The Big Bonanza*
1945—Utah*
 Lone Texas Ranger*
 Three's a Crowd*
 Gangs of the Waterfront*
 Sunset in El Dorado*
 Rough Riders of Cheyenne*
 Colorado Pioneers*
 Woman Who Came Back*
1946—Days of Buffalo Bill
 Strange Impersonation*
 Home on the Range*
 Sun Valley Cyclone*
 Affairs of Geraldine*
 Out California Way*
 Stagecoach to Denver*
1947—Son of Zorro*
 Last Frontier Uprising
 Homesteaders of Paradise Valley*
 Saddle Pals*
 Rustlers of Devil's Canyon*
 Marshal of Cripple Creek*
 Along the Oregon Trail*
 The Black Widow*
 Under Colorado Skies*
1948—G-Men Never Forget
 Dangers of the Canadian Mounted
 Heart of Virginia*
 I, Jane Doe*
 Night Time in Nevada*
 Adv. of Frank and Jesse James*
 Sundown in Santa Fe*
 Renegades of Sonora*
1949—Ghost of Zorro
 King of the Rocket Men
 The Wyoming Bandit*
 Bandit King of Texas*
 The James Brothers of Missouri
 The Fighting Kentuckian*
 Navajo Trail Raiders*
 Radar Patrol Vs. Spy King
1950—Singing Guns*
 Tarnished*
 Sands of Iwo Jima*
 The Invisible Monster
 Desperadoes of the West*
1951—In Old Amarillo*
 Govt. Agents Vs. Phantom Legion*
 Fort Dodge Stampede*
 Honeychile*
1952—Leadville Gunslinger*
 Gobs and Gals*
1953—Woman They Almost Lynched*
 Savage Frontier*
 El Paso Stampede*
1956—When Gangland Strikes*

O'Day, Nell[241]
1943—Thundering Trails

O'Dea, Joseph
1952—The Quiet Man

O'Dell, Doye[44]
1946—Man from Rainbow Valley
 Heldorado
1947—Last Frontier Uprising
 Hit Parade of 1947*
1948—The Gay Ranchero*
 Under California Stars*

Jack Norman

Jay Norris

O'Donnell, Paddy
1952—The Quiet Man

O'Dowd, Don
1957—Journey to Freedom

O'Driscoll, Martha[122]
1942—Youth on Parade

O'Farrell, Bernadette
1955—The Square Ring

O'Farrell, Broderick
1938—Come on, Rangers*
1939—The Mysterious Miss X*
 Daredevils of the Red Circle*
1942—Call of the Canyon*
 Ice-Capades Revue*
1943—Mountain Rhythm*
 Someone to Remember*
1946—Under Nevada Skies*
1947—That's My Gal*

Offerman, Jr., George
1940—Frontier Vengeance

O'Flynn, Damian[241]
1942—X Marks the Spot
1947—Web of Danger
 Saddle Pals
1949—Pioneer Marshal
1951—Fighting Coast Guard
1952—Hoodlum Empire
1956—Hidden Guns
 Daniel Boone, Trail Blazer
1957—Eighteen and Anxious

O'Gatty, Jimmy
1950—Flying Disc Man from Mars

Ogg, Jimmy
1950—Redwood Forest Trail
1951—Pride of Maryland*
 Belle LeGrand*

O'Hara, Barry
1957—Journey to Freedom

O'Hara, Brian[241]
1943—California Joe

O'Hara, Maureen[122]
1950—Rio Grande
1952—The Quiet Man
1956—Lisbon

Eve Novak

Hugh O'Brian

O'Herlihy, Dan[241]
1950—Macbeth

O'Keefe, Dennis[83]
 [as Bud Flanagan]
1935—Burning Gold*
 [as Dennis O'Keefe]
1940—Girl from Havana
 Bowery Boy
1941—Mr. District Attorney
1942—Affairs of Jimmy Valentine
 Moonlight Masquerade
1943—Tahiti Honey
1944—The Fighting Seabees
1945—Earl Carroll Vanities
1953—The Lady Wants Mink

O'Kelly, Dorothy
1942—Flying Tigers*
 Johnny Doughboy*

Olaguivel, Juan
1950—The Avengers

Oliver, Anthony
1957—Tears for Simon

Oliver, Gordon[122]
1937—Youth on Parole
1939—Pride of the Navy
 Sabotage

Dave O'Brien

Olsen and Johnson—series
 [Ole Olsen and Chic Johnson]
1936—Country Gentlemen
1937—All Over Town

Olsen, Larry[83]
1945—Lone Texas Ranger

Olsen, Moroni[241]
1937—Manhattan Merry-Go-Round*
1945—Behind City Lights*
 Don't Fence Me In

Olsen, Olaf
1943—At Dawn We Die

Olsen, Ole [John][83]
1936—Country Gentlemen
1937—All Over Town

O'Malley, John
1945—A Sporting Chance

O'Malley, Pat
1940—Rocky Mountain Rangers
1941—Pals of the Pecos
1943—Thumbs Up

O'Moore, Pat
1946—G.I. War Brides

Nell O'Day

Damian O'Flynn

Brian O'Hara

Dan O'Herlihy

Moroni Olsen

Anne O'Neal

O'Neal, Anne[242]
1939—Woman Doctor*
1940—Girl from Havana*
1941—Mr. District Attorney*
        Sis Hopkins*
        Rookies on Parade*
        Ice-Capades*
1942—In Old California
        The Sombrero Kid
1943—Here Comes Elmer*
        In Old Oklahoma
1944—Strangers in the Night
1945—Three's a Crowd
        Girls of the Big House*
1946—Earl Carroll Sketchbook*
1950—Belle of Old Mexico
1951—Wells Fargo Gunmaster

O'Neil, Barbara[242]
1955—Flame of the Islands

O'Neill, Henry[242]
1953—The Sun Shines Bright

O'Neill, Maire
1937—Bulldog Drummond at Bay
        Glamorous Night

Orlando, Don
1938—Pals of the Saddle

Orloff, Orest
1955—The Divided Heart

O'Rorke, Brefni
1943—At Dawn We Die

Orr, William T.
1941—Variety Reel*
        Stars Past and Present*

Orth, Frank
1944—Storm Over Lisbon
1945—Tell It to a Star
1946—Murder in the Music Hall

Ortiz, Peter
1950—Rio Grande
1953—The Hydrogen Hurricane

Osborn, Judy
1952—Lady Possessed

Osborne, Bud [Len][242]
1936—The Lawless Nineties*
        The Vigilantes are Coming
        Ghost-Town Gold*
        Robinson Crusoe of Clipper Island*
1937—Yodelin' Kid from Pine Ridge*
        Boots and Saddles
1938—The Lone Ranger*
        The Fighting Devil Dogs*
        Riders of the Black Hills*
        Overland Stage Raiders*
        Prairie Moon
        Santa Fe Stampede*
1939—Rough Riders' Round-Up*
        The Night Riders*
        Frontier Pony Express*
        New Frontier
        Rovin' Tumbleweeds*
        Cowboys from Texas*
        Days of Jesse James*
1940—Rancho Grande*
        Ghost Valley Raiders*
        Rocky Mountain Rangers*
        One Man's Law*
        The Trail Blazers*
        Lone Star Raiders
1941—The Phantom Cowboy
        Pals of the Pecos*
        Two Gun Sheriff*
        Gangs of Sonora*
        Outlaws of Cherokee Trail*
        The Apache Kid*
1942—Arizona Terrors*
        Code of the Outlaw*
        Westward Ho*
        In Old California*
1943—The Blocked Trail*
        Carson City Cyclone
        King of the Cowboys*
        Riders of the Rio Grande*
        Silver Spurs*
        Canyon City*
1944—Pride of the Plains*
        Mojave Firebrand*
        The Laramie Trail
        Cheyenne Wildcat*
1945—Flame of Barbary Coast*
        Oregon Trail*
        Sunset in El Dorado*
        The Cherokee Flash
1946—California Gold Rush*
        Rainbow Over Texas*
1947—Twilight on the Rio Grande*
        Yankee Fakir*
1948—The Gallant Legion*
        Adv. of Frank and Jesse James*
        The Plunderers*
1950—The Savage Horde*
        Covered Wagon Raid*
        Desperadoes of the West
        The Missourians*
1951—Night Riders of Montana*
        Don Daredevil Rides Again*
1952—Colorado Sundown*
        Border Saddlemates*

Osborne, Lucille[242]
1937—Circus Girl

Osborne, Vivienne[242]
1936—Follow Your Heart

Oscar and Elmer[44]
[Ed Platt and Lou Fulton]
1936—The Old Corral
1937—Dick Tracy
        The Hit Parade
        Gunsmoke Ranch
        The Painted Stallion
        Meet the Boy Friend

Osceola, Roy
1955—Yellowneck

O'Shea, Jack[136]
Many films, mostly westerns.
1936—The Big Show
1944—The San Antonio Kid
1945—Sheriff of Cimarron
        Gangs of the Waterfront
        Rough Riders of Cheyenne
1946—Rio Grande Raiders
1947—Son of Zorro
        Wyoming
1948—G-Men Never Forget
1949—Sheriff of Wichita
        Federal Agents Vs. Underworld, Inc.
        Ghost of Zorro

O'Shea, Michael[122]
1944—Man From Frisco

O'Shea, Oscar
1938—King of the Newsboys
1939—S.O.S. Tidal Wave
        She Married a Cop
1944—Haunted Harbor

Osterloh, Robert
1950—Harbor of Missing Men

Otho, Henry
1938—The Fighting Devil Dogs
        Overland Stage Raiders
1939—The Lone Ranger Rides Again
        Mexicali Rose

Oulton, Brian
1955—Doctor in the House

Ouspenskaya, Mme. Maria[106]
1940—Chinese Garden Festival*
1946—I've Always Loved You
1947—Wyoming

Overman, Jack
1948—Secret Service Investigator

Owen, Bill
1955—The Square Ring
        A Day to Remember

Owen, Michael
1941—Outlaws of Cherokee Trail*
        Death Valley Outlaws
        King of the Texas Rangers*
        Dick Tracy Vs. Crime, Inc.
1943—Someone to Remember*
1944—Three Little Sisters*
        Thoroughbreds*
        Navy MN 3387—Your Weapons*

Barbara O'Neil

Henry O'Neill

Bud Osborne

Lucille Osborne

Owens, Garry[242]
1938—Call of the Yukon
1940—Grandpa Goes to Town
1941—Sailors on Leave
1945—The Phantom Speaks
        The Tiger Woman
1946—Crime of the Century
1947—The Flame

Owens, Harry—and Royal Hawaiians
1944—Lake Placid Serenade

Owsley, Monroe[242]
1937—The Hit Parade

P

Pacemakers, The
1940—Ride, Tenderfoot, Ride

Padden, Sarah[242]
1937—Youth on Parole
        Exiled to Shanghai
1939—Man of Conquest*
        The Zero Hour
1940—Forgotten Girls
        Lone Star Raiders
1941—Outlaws of Cherokee Trail*
1942—Heart of the Rio Grande
1945—Identity Unknown
        Marshal of Laredo
        Dakota
1946—Earl Carroll Sketchbook*
        That Brennan Girl
1950—House by the River
        The Missourians
1951—Oh! Susanna*
        Utah Wagon Train

Padjan, Jack
1937—Gunsmoke Ranch

Padilla, Ruben
1951—Bullfighter and the Lady

Padula, Vincente
1950—The Avengers
1957—Hell Canyon Outlaws

Pagan, William
1939—Daredevils of the Red Circle

Page, Bradley[242]
1935—Cappy Ricks Returns
        Forced Landing
1940—Girl from Havana
1941—Mr. District Atty. in the Carter Case
1942—Sons of the Pioneers
        King of the Mounties
        The Traitor Within

Page, Dorothy[44]
1938—Mama Runs Wild

Page, Joy[242]
1951—Bullfighter and the Lady

Page, Sam
1958—Invisible Avenger

Paige, Anne
1957—Tears for Simon

Paige, Janis[243]
1951—Fugitive Lady

Paige, Mabel[122]
1943—Someone to Remember

Paige, Robert[243]
        [as David Carlyle]
1936—Hearts in Bondage*
1937—Rhythm in the Clouds
        Meet the Boy Friend
        [as Robert Paige]
1938—I Stand Accused
1947—The Flame

Paige, Satchell
1949—The Kid from Cleveland

Paiva, Nestor[243]
1942—The Girl from Alaska
        Flying Tigers*
        King of the Mounties
1945—Along the Navajo Trail
1946—The Last Crooked Mile
1952—The Fabulous Senorita
        South Pacific Trail
1956—Scandal Incorporated
1958—Outcasts of the City

Palacios, Angel M. Gordordo
1950—The Avengers

Palange, Ines
1937—Portia on Trial
1941—Under Fiesta Stars

Pall, Gloria
1953—Nightmare Typhoon
        War of the Space Giants
        Destroyers of the Sun
        Robot Monster from Mars
        The Hydrogen Hurricane
        Solar Sky Raiders
        S.O.S. Ice Age
        Lost in Outer Space
1955—City of Shadows

Pallette, Eugene[83]
1944—Lake Placid Serenade
1945—The Cheaters
1946—In Old Sacramento

Palmer, Conway
1942—Suicide Squadron

Palmer, Maria[243]
1950—Surrender
1954—Flight Nurse
1958—Outcasts of the City

Pals of the Golden West
1939—Rovin' Tumbleweeds
1940—Rancho Grande

Vivienne Osborne

Garry Owens

Monroe Owsley

Sarah Padden

Bradley Page

Joy Page

Janis Paige

Robert Paige

Pampanini, Silvana
1955—Don Juan's Night of Love

Panalle, Juan
1946—Specter of the Rose

Pangborn, Franklin[136]
1935—$1000 a Minute
1936—The Mandarin Mystery
1937—Dangerous Holiday
All Over Town
1940—Hit Parade of 1941
1941—Mr. District Atty. in the Carter Case
1942—Moonlight Masquerade
1944—My Best Gal
1945—Tell It to a Star
1947—Calendar Girl

Pape, Lionel
1938—Outside of Paradise

Paris, Jonni
1952—Gobs and Gals*

Paris, Manuel
1951—Havana Rose

Park, Post[243]
Many films, mostly westerns.
1938—The Lone Ranger*
1939—The Lone Ranger Rides Again*
1940—Adventures of Red Ryder*
The Trail Blazers*
Melody Ranch*
The Border Legion*
1941—The Apache Kid*
1943—Song of Texas*
Fugitive from Sonora*
Bordertown Gun Fighters*
Silver Spurs*
Beyond the Last Frontier*
The Man from the Rio Grande*
In Old Oklahoma*
California Joe*
1944—Captain America*
Song of Nevada*
Vigilantes of Dodge City*
Firebrands of Arizona*
Zorro's Black Whip*
1945—Bandits of the Badlands*
1946—The Phantom Rider*
The El Paso Kid
Plainsman and the Lady*
1947—Son of Zorro*
Marshal of Cripple Creek*
1948—Under California Stars*
Grand Canyon Trail*
1949—Federal Agents Vs. Underworld, Inc.*
Ghost of Zorro*
The Wyoming Bandit*
The James Brothers of Missouri*
1950—Bells of Coronado*
Rio Grande*
1952—Border Saddlemates*
Old Oklahoma Plains*
1953—Woman They Almost Lynched*
Iron Mountain Trail*
Shadows of Tombstone*
1954—The Outcast*
1955—Santa Fe Passage*
The Last Command*

Parker, Barnett
1936—The President's Mystery
1939—She Married a Cop
1940—Hit Parade of 1941
1941—A Man Betrayed

Parker, Cecil
1942—Suicide Squadron

Parker, Eddie[243]
1935—Westward Ho*
The New Frontier*
1936—Darkest Africa*
Undersea Kingdom*
Ticket to Paradise*
1937—Git Along Little Dogies*
Come on, Cowboys!*
Rhythm in the Clouds
It Could Happen to You*
1938—The Fighting Devil Dogs*
Dick Tracy Returns*
Down in "Arkansaw"*
1939—The Lone Ranger Rides Again
Mexicali Rose*
Street of Missing Men*
Daredevils of the Red Circle*
Smuggled Cargo*
Dick Tracy's G-Men*
1940—Rancho Grande*
Mysterious Doctor Satan*
1941—Wyoming Wildcat*
A Man Betrayed*
Dick Tracy Vs. Crime, Inc.*
1942—Raiders of the Range*
1943—G-Men Vs. The Black Dragon*
Thundering Trails*
Daredevils of the West*
Days of Old Cheyenne*
Secret Service in Darkest Africa*
The Masked Marvel
In Old Oklahoma*
Pistol Packin' Mama
1944—The Tiger Woman
Haunted Harbor*
1945—Manhunt of Mystery Island*
Corpus Christi Bandits*
The Phantom Speaks*
Flame of Barbary Coast*
1946—The Phantom Rider*
Days of Buffalo Bill
King of the Forest Rangers
My Pal Trigger*
Daughter of Don Q
The Inner Circle
The Last Crooked Mile*
Under Nevada Skies*
The Crimson Ghost*
1947—Son of Zorro
Angel and the Badman*
Vigilantes of Boomtown*
Bells of San Angelo*
Jesse James Rides Again
1948—Dangers of the Canadian Mounted
Adv. of Frank and Jesse James*
1949—Ghost of Zorro*
Death Valley Gunfighter*
King of the Rocket Men
Radar Patrol Vs. Spy King
Powder River Rustlers*
1950—The Invisible Monster
Desperadoes of the West*
Under Mexicali Stars*
1951—Govt. Agents Vs. Phantom Legion*
Rodeo King and the Senorita*
1955—King of the Carnival*

Parker, Eleanor
1944—Atlantic City*

Parker, Franklin
1938—The Higgins Family

Parker, Jean[106]
1939—She Married a Cop
Flight at Midnight
1941—The Pittsburgh Kid
1942—The Girl from Alaska
Hi, Neighbor
The Traitor Within
1943—Deerslayer
1952—Toughest Man in Arizona

Parker, Willard
1939—The Zero Hour

Parkes, Gay
1941—Wampas Baby Stars*
1945—Behind City Lights*

Parkinson, Cliff[214]
1944—Bordertown Trail
The San Antonio Kid

Parks, Eddie
1943—O, My Darling Clementine

Parks, Larry
1943—Deerslayer

Parkyakarkus[243]
1945—Earl Carroll Vanities

Parnell, Emory[136]
1938—Arson Gang Busters
Call of the Yukon*
1940—Hit Parade of 1941*
1943—London Blackout Murders*
1947—Calendar Girl
1949—Rose of the Yukon
Hideout
Hellfire
1950—Unmasked
Rock Island Trail
Trail of Robin Hood
1951—Belle LeGrand*
Honeychile
1952—Oklahoma Annie
The Fabulous Senorita
Gobs and Gals
1953—Sweethearts on Parade
Shadows of Tombstone
1955—The Road to Denver*
1958—The Notorious Mr. Monks

Parrish, Helen[243]
1942—In Old California
Sunset Serenade
X Marks the Spot

Parry, Harvey
1949—Duke of Chicago

Parsons, Louella
1941—Variety Reel*

Parsons, Milton[243]
1940—Who Killed Aunt Maggie?
Behind the News
1942—The Girl from Alaska
1948—Secret Service Investigator
1949—Outcasts of the Trail

Parsons, Patsy Lee[243]
1940—Heroes of the Saddle
1942—Affairs of Jimmy Valentine*

Parsons, Percy
1942—Suicide Squadron

Passante, Mario
1954—The She Wolf*

Patisson, Danik
1959—O. S. S. 117 is Not Dead

Paton, Tony
1940—King of the Royal Mounted

Patrick, Dorothy[44]
1949—The Blonde Bandit
1950—Tarnished
Belle of Old Mexico
Federal Agent at Large
House by the River
Destination Big House
Lonely Heart Bandits
Under Mexicali Stars
1953—Savage Frontier

Patrick, Gail[123]
1939—Man of Conquest
1941—Variety Reel*
Stars at Play*
1943—Hit Parade of 1943
1946—The Madonna's Secret
Rendezvous with Annie
Plainsman and the Lady
1947—Calendar Girl
1948—The Inside Story

Patrick, Lee[243]
1943—Nobody's Darling
1944—Faces in the Fog

Patterson, Elizabeth[243]
1940—Who Killed Aunt Maggie?
1946—I've Always Loved You

Patterson, Hank[243]
1939—The Arizona Kid*
Sabotage*
The Covered Trailer*
1940—Three Faces West*
1946—The El Paso Kid
Santa Fe Uprising
1947—Bells of San Angelo*
Robin Hood of Texas*
Springtime in the Sierras
Under Colorado Skies*
1948—Oklahoma Badlands
Night Time in Nevada
The Denver Kid
The Plunderers*
1949—Outcasts of the Trail*
The James Brothers of Missouri
1950—Code of the Silver Sage
Desperadoes of the West
1951—Silver City Bonanza
Don Daredevil Rides Again
1953—Woman They Almost Lynched*
Can. Mounties Vs. Atomic Invaders
1957—Beginning of the End

Patterson, Lee
1956—Above Us the Waves

Paul, Don
1954—Crazylegs

Pavelec, Ted
1951—Million Dollar Pursuit

Pavlow, Muriel
1948—Code of Scotland Yard
1955—Doctor in the House

Nestor Paiva

Maria Palmer

Post Park

Eddie Parker

Parkyakarkus

Helen Parrish

Milton Parsons

Patsy Lee Parsons

Lee Patrick

Elizabeth Patterson

Hank Patterson

Pawley, Anthony
1936 — Robinson Crusoe of Clipper Island
1937 — Paradise Express

Pawley, Edward
1942 — Romance on the Range

Pawley, William
1938 — Prairie Moon
1939 — Rough Riders' Round-Up

Payne, John[106]
1955 — Santa Fe Passage
       The Road to Denver

Payne, Sally[83]
1936 — The Big Show
1937 — Exiled to Shanghai
1938 — Man from Music Mountain
       The Higgins Family
1939 — My Wife's Relatives
1940 — Young Bill Hickok
1941 — Robin Hood of the Pecos
       In Old Cheyenne
       Sheriff of Tombstone
       Nevada City
       Bad Man of Deadwood
       Jesse James at Bay
       Tuxedo Junction
       Red River Valley
1942 — Man from Cheyenne
       Romance on the Range
1943 — Mountain Rhythm

Payson, Blanche
1937 — All Over Town

Payton, Lew
1942 — Lady for a Night

Pearce, Adele
See Pamela Blake.

Pearce, Al[83]
1937 — The Hit Parade
1943 — Here Comes Elmer
1945 — Hitchhike to Happiness
1946 — One Exciting Week
1948 — The Main Street Kid

Pearson, Ted
1939 — Dick Tracy's G-Men

Peary, Harold
1941 — Country Fair

Pedersen, Eric
1951 — Fighting Coast Guard

Pegg, Vester
1939 — Frontier Pony Express*
1940 — The Ranger and the Lady*
       Colorado
       Under Texas Skies*
1941 — Sheriff of Tombstone*

Peil, Sr., Edward
1936 — Oh, Susanna!
1937 — Come on, Cowboys!
1939 — The Night Riders
1940 — One Man's Law
1943 — Canyon City

Peluffo, Stelita[244]
1938 — Born to be Wild*
       Outlaws of Sonora

Pembroke, George[244]
1939 — Smuggled Cargo*
       Calling All Marines*
1940 — Drums of Fu Manchu
1941 — Adventures of Captain Marvel
1942 — Perils of Nyoka
1943 — Daredevils of the West*
       The Masked Marvel*
1947 — That's My Man*
1957 — Hell Canyon Outlaws

Stelita Peluffo

Gil Perkins

Pendleton, Ann
1937 — Rootin' Tootin' Rhythm

Pendleton, Gaylord
See Steve Pendleton.

Pendleton, Steve
       [as Gaylord Pendleton]
1940 — Young Buffalo Bill
1946 — That Brennan Girl*
1950 — Sunset in the West
       [as Steve Pendleton]
       Rio Grande
1951 — Buckaroo Sheriff of Texas
       Desert of Lost Men

Penn, Leonard[123]
1938 — Ladies in Distress
1950 — Women from Headquarters
       Lonely Heart Bandits
1951 — South of Caliente

Pennick, Jack[244]
1935 — Cappy Ricks Returns*
       Hitch Hike Lady*
1938 — King of the Newsboys
1939 — Mountain Rhythm
1941 — Lady from Louisiana
1949 — The Fighting Kentuckian
1950 — Rock Island Trail*
       Rio Grande*
1951 — Fighting Coast Guard
       The Sea Hornet
1952 — Hoodlum Empire*
1953 — The Sun Shines Bright*

Pennington, Ann
1940 — Texas Terrors

Pepito
1938 — Army Girl

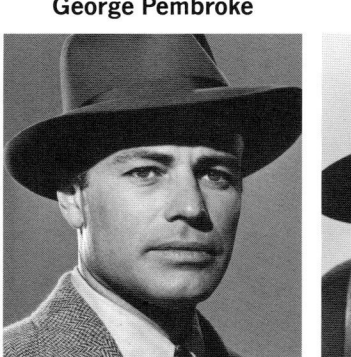
George Pembroke

Pepper, Barbara[45]
1935 — Forced Landing
       Sagebrush Troubadour
       Frisco Waterfront
1936 — The Singing Vagabond
1937 — Portia on Trial
1938 — Hollywood Stadium Mystery!
       Army Girl
1939 — Colorado Sunset
       Flight at Midnight
1940 — Forgotten Girls
       Women in War
1950 — Unmasked
1952 — Thunderbirds

Pepper, Buddy
1941 — Los Angeles Examiner Benefit*
       Stars at Play*

Peppy & Peanuts
1943 — Swing Your Partner

Perez, Ismael
1951 — Bullfighter and the Lady

Perkins, Gil[244]
1938 — Storm Over Lisbon*
1942 — Spy Smasher*
1943 — G-Men Vs. The Black Dragon*
1944 — Captain America*
1945 — Bells of Rosarita*
       The Fatal Witness*
1946 — The Mysterious Mr. Valentine*
1947 — Son of Zorro*
       Twilight on the Rio Grande*
       Jesse James Rides Again*
       The Black Widow*
1948 — G-Men Never Forget*
1952 — Gobs and Gals*

Perkins, Peter
1948 — Marshal of Amarillo

Perkins, Valentine[45]
1950 — Rock Island Trail
       Prisoners in Petticoats
1951 — Cuban Fireball*

Perreau, Janine
1954 — The Shanghai Story

Perrin, Jack[207]
1937 — The Painted Stallion
       The Wrong Road*
       The Trigger Trio*
1938 — The Purple Vigilantes
       The Lone Ranger*
       Western Jamboree*
1939 — The Arizona Kid*
1940 — Ride, Tenderfoot, Ride*
1945 — The Phantom Speaks*
       The Chicago Kid*
1948 — I, Jane Doe*

Perrins, Leslie
1937 — Bulldog Drummond at Bay

Perry, Barbara
1945 — An Angel Comes to Brooklyn

Perry, Pascale
1947 — Springtime in the Sierras
1948 — Eyes of Texas

Jack Pennick

Howard Petrie

Peters, Jr., House[244]
1937 — Public Cowboy No. 1
1939 — Frontier Pony Express*
1948 — Oklahoma Badlands
       Dangers of the Canadian Mounted*
       Under California Stars
       Desperadoes of Dodge City
       Adv. of Frank and Jesse James
       Renegades of Sonora
       The Plunderers*
1949 — Rose of the Yukon*
       Sheriff of Wichita
       King of the Rocket Men
1950 — Twilight in the Sierras
1951 — Spoilers of the Plains
       The Dakota Kid
1952 — Oklahoma Annie

Peters, John
1936 — Border Phantom

Peters, Ralph
1938 — Outlaws of Sonora
1939 — Rovin' Tumbleweeds
1940 — Ghost Valley Raiders
1947 — Trail to San Antone

Peterson, Dorothy[244]
1939 — Sabotage
1940 — Women in War
1944 — Faces in the Fog

Petrie, Howard[244]
1952 — Woman of the North Country
1953 — Fair Wind to Java
1955 — Timberjack
1956 — The Maverick Queen

Petroff, Gloria
1957 — The Unearthly

Petruzzi, Julian
1938 — Tenth Avenue Kid

Phelps, Lee[244]
1935 — $1000 a Minute
1950 — Hills of Oklahoma
       Desperadoes of the West
1951 — Don Daredevil Rides Again

Philipp, Gunther
1957 — The Congress Dances

Philippe, Michele
1955 — Don Juan's Night of Love

Phillippi, Patti
1946 — Murder in the Music Hall

Phillips, Eddie
1943 — Death Valley Manhunt

Phillips, Howard
1938 — Gangs of New York

Phillips, John
1946 — Heldorado
1951 — Govt. Agents Vs. Phantom Legion

Phipps, Nicholas
1955 — Doctor in the House

Phipps, William[244]
1948 — Train to Alcatraz
       Desperadoes of Dodge City
1950 — The Vanishing Westerner
1953 — Savage Frontier
       Red River Shore
1955 — The Eternal Sea*

Picerni, Paul[245]
1950 — Prisoners in Petticoats*
1954 — The Shanghai Story
1958 — The Man Who Died Twice

Pichel, Irving[245]
1936 — The House of a Thousand Candles
       Hearts in Bondage
       Down to the Sea
1937 — Join the Marines
1939 — Dick Tracy's G-Men

Pick and Pat
1937 — The Hit Parade

Pickard, John[245]
1949 — Wake of the Red Witch*
1950 — Twilight in the Sierras*
       Prisoners in Petticoats*
       California Passage*
1951 — Oh! Susanna
       Govt. Agents Vs. Phantom Legion
1952 — Hoodlum Empire*
1955 — Flame of the Islands*
1956 — A Strange Adventure*

Pickard, Obed "Dad"
1940 — Frontier Vengeance

Pickens, Slim[45]
1952 — Colorado Sundown
       The Last Musketeer
       Border Saddlemates
       Old Oklahoma Plains
       South Pacific Trail
       Thunderbirds
1953 — Old Overland Trail
       The Sun Shines Bright
       Iron Mountain Trail
       Down Laredo Way
       Shadows of Tombstone
       Red River Shore
1954 — Phantom Stallion
       The Outcast
1955 — Santa Fe Passage
       The Last Command
1956 — When Gangland Strikes
       Stranger at My Door

Pickford, Mary
1940 — Chinese Garden Festival*

Picorri, John[245]
1936 — Down to the Sea*
       Robinson Crusoe of Clipper Island
1937 — Dick Tracy
       S O S Coast Guard
1938 — The Fighting Devil Dogs
1940 — Drums of Fu Manchu*

Pidgeon, Walter[123]
1940 — Dark Command
       Chinese Garden Festival*
1941 — Variety Reel*

Lee Phelps

William Phipps

Johnny Russell, Dorothy Peterson

Pierce, Jim
1939 — Zorro's Fighting Legion

Pierlot, Francis[137]
1941 — Public Enemies*
1943 — Mystery Broadcast
1945 — Grissly's Millions
1946 — The Catman of Paris
G. I. War Brides
1947 — The Trespasser
1948 — I, Jane Doe
1952 — Hoodlum Empire*

Pierreux, Jacqueline
1959 — O. S. S. 117 is Not Dead

Piltz, George
1949 — Daughter of the Jungle

Pine, Phillip[210]
1951 — Insurance Investigator
The Wild Blue Yonder
1952 — Hoodlum Empire*

Piper, Frederick
1956 — Doctor at Sea
1957 — The Man in the Road

Pipitone, Nino
1943 — G-Men Vs. The Black Dragon

Pitts, Zasu[245]
1939 — Mickey, the Kid

Platt, Ed
See Oscar and Elmer.

Platt, Louise
1940 — Forgotten Girls

Plues, George[183]
1937 — Hit the Saddle
Come on, Cowboys!

Pollard, Snub
1936 — The Gentleman from Louisiana

Pollina, Ferdinand
1946 — Specter of the Rose

Pollock, Ellen
1958 — Scotland Yard Dragnet

Pom Pom
1941 — Petticoat Politics

Pomeroy, Allen
Many films.
1938 — Dick Tracy Returns*
1939 — Dick Tracy's G-Men*
1943 — Daredevils of the West*
The Masked Marvel*
1944 — Captain America*

Pope, Bud
1936 — The Vigilantes Are Coming

Pops and Louie
1943 — Hit Parade of 1943

Porcasi, Paul[245]
1936 — The Leathernecks Have Landed
Down to the Sea
1940 — The Border Legion
1941 — Rags to Riches
Doctors Don't Tell

Pork Chop & Kidney Stew
1958 — Street of Darkness

Porter, Jean[123]
1942 — Heart of the Rio Grande
1944 — San Fernando Valley

Posten, Patti[69]
1944 — Lake Placid Serenade*
1945 — Utah*
Earl Carroll Vanities*
The Phantom Speaks*
Bells of Rosarita*
Steppin' in Society*
Road to Alcatraz*
Hitchhike to Happiness*
Tell It to a Star*
Behind City Lights*

Poston, Thomas
1953 — City that Never Sleeps

Potel, Vic[245]
1936 — Down to the Sea
1939 — Rovin' Tumbleweeds
1940 — Three Faces West*
Girl from God's Country
1941 — Puddin' Head*
1945 — Flame of Barbary Coast*
Captain Tugboat Annie*
1946 — The Glass Alibi
Heldorado*
1947 — Calendar Girl*
Yankee Fakir*

Potter, Peter
1938 — Prairie Moon

Powell, Lee[245]
1938 — The Lone Ranger
The Fighting Devil Dogs
Come on, Rangers

Powell, Russ
1937 — The Wrong Road

Power, Hartley
1943 — Alibi

Power, Paul
1948 — Under California Stars

Powers, Jimmy
1951 — Robinson Vs. Turpin

Powers, Mala[123]
1953 — City that Never Sleeps
1954 — Geraldine

Powers, Richard[245]
1944 — Goodnight Sweetheart*
The Port of Forty Thieves
Lights of Old Santa Fe
1945 — Girls of the Big House
1950 — Desperadoes of the West
[as Tom Keene]
Trail of Robin Hood

Paul Picerni

Powers, Tom[245]
1945 — The Phantom Speaks
The Chicago Kid
1946 — The Last Crooked Mile
1947 — Angel and the Badman
1948 — Angel in Exile
1951 — Fighting Coast Guard
1952 — The Fabulous Senorita
Bal Tabarin
The Wac from Walla Walla*
1954 — Sea of Lost Ships
1955 — The Eternal Sea*
Double Jeopardy

Prack, Rudolf
1957 — The Congress Dances

Prather, Lee
1935 — The Spanish Cape Mystery

Pratt, Purnell[123]
1935 — $1000 a Minute
Frisco Waterfront
1936 — Dancing Feet
1937 — Join the Marines
1938 — Come on, Rangers
1939 — My Wife's Relatives
Colorado Sunset
1940 — Grand Ole Opry
1941 — Doctors Don't Tell*

Prelle, Micheline[107]
1951 — Adventures of Captain Fabian

Prescott, Elsie[245]
1939 — Thou Shalt Not Kill

Prescott, Guy
1957 — The Unearthly

Presson, Jay
1945 — An Angel Comes to Brooklyn
1946 — Gay Blades*

Previn, Andre
1946 — I've Always Loved You*

Price, Alonzo
1937 — Navy Blues

Price, Dennis
1957 — Time is My Enemy

Irving Pichel

John Picorri

Price, Hal[137]
1935 — $1000 a Minute*
1936 — Navy Born*
Cavalry
1937 — The Trusted Outlaw
Dick Tracy*
Public Cowboy No. 1*
The Arizona Gunfighter*
Youth on Parole*
Ridin' the Lone Trail
1938 — Call the Mesquiteers
Gangs of New York*
Man from Music Mountain*
Prairie Moon*
Federal Man-Hunt*
1939 — Home on the Prairie
I Was a Convict*
The Night Riders*
New Frontier
In Old Monterey*
South of the Border*
1940 — Village Barn Dance*
The Crooked Road*
The Carson City Kid*
Ride, Tenderfoot, Ride*
Frontier Vengeance*
Mysterious Doctor Satan*
Lone Star Raiders
1941 — Ridin' on a Rainbow*
Sis Hopkins*
The Singing Hill*
Gangs of Sonora
The Apache Kid*
Sierra Sue*
1942 — Cowboy Serenade*
Raiders of the Range
Home in Wyomin'*
In Old California*
The Cyclone Kid*
Valley of Hunted Men*
Ice-Capades Revue*
1943 — The Blocked Trail
Riders of the Rio Grande*
Wagon Tracks West*
Someone to Remember*
1944 — Mojave Firebrand
Man from Frisco*
Marshal of Reno*
Silver City Kid*
Faces in the Fog*
1945 — Sheriff of Cimarron*
Utah*
Corpus Christi Bandits*
Lone Texas Ranger*
The Chicago Kid*
Behind City Lights*
1946 — The Phantom Rider*
Sun Valley Cyclone*
1950 — Singing Guns*
Tarnished
Frisco Tornado
1951 — Belle LeGrand*
Rough Riders of Durango
1952 — Colorado Sundown*
Oklahoma Annie*

Price, Peter
1954 — Phantom Stallion

John Pickard

Zasu Pitts

Paul Porcasi

Price, Stanley[245]
1938 — Romance on the Run*
The Fighting Devil Dogs*
1939 — Daredevils of the Red Circle*
Dick Tracy's G-Men*
1940 — One Man's Law*
1941 — Adventures of Captain Marvel
Dick Tracy Vs. Crime, Inc.*
1942 — King of the Mounties*
Outlaws of Pine Ridge
1943 — G-Men Vs. The Black Dragon*
The Masked Marvel*
1944 — Captain America*
The Tiger Woman
Zorro's Black Whip
1945 — Earl Carroll Vanities*
Gangs of the Waterfront*
Federal Operator 99*
Sunset in El Dorado*
1946 — Alias Billy the Kid
Red River Renegades*
The Crimson Ghost
Stagecoach to Denver*
1947 — Son of Zorro
Angel and the Badman*
The Black Widow*
1948 — G-Men Never Forget*
1949 — Sheriff of Wichita*
King of the Rocket Men
Hellfire*
1950 — The Invisible Monster

Price, Vincent[107]
1951 — Adventures of Captain Fabian

Priest, Bobby
1945 — Flame of Barbary Coast*
Mexicana*

Prima, Louis — and band
1937 — Manhattan Merry-Go-Round

Prince
1936 — Country Gentlemen

Prival, Lucien
1936 — Darkest Africa
1940 — King of the Royal Mounted
1941 — King of the Texas Rangers
1944 — Storm Over Lisbon*

Richard Powers

Vic Potel

Lee Powell

Stanley Price

Elsie Prescott

Tom Powers

Hugh Prosser

Prosser, Hugh[246]
1938—Come on, Leathernecks*
1939—The Night Riders*
1941—Mr. District Attorney*
　　　Sis Hopkins*
　　　Lady from Louisiana*
　　　The Devil Pays Off*
　　　Sierra Sue*
　　　West of Cimarron
　　　Dick Tracy Vs. Crime, Inc.*
1942—Spy Smasher*
1944—The Fighting Seabees*
1945—Flame of Barbary Coast*
1946—The Phantom Rider
　　　The French Key*
1948—Daredevils of the Clouds
　　　The Plunderers*

Prouse, Peter
1950—Destination Big House

Prouty, Jed[246]
1936—Happy Go Lucky
1937—Dangerous Holiday
1940—Barnyard Follies
1942—Affairs of Jimmy Valentine*
　　　Moonlight Masquerade
　　　The Old Homestead

Pryor, Maureen
1955—Doctor in the House

Pryor, Roger[84]
1935—$1000 a Minute
1936—The Return of Jimmy Valentine
　　　Ticket to Paradise
　　　Sitting on the Moon
1940—Bowery Boy
1941—Hollywood Visits the Navy*
1944—Thoroughbreds
1945—Identity Unknown
　　　Man from Oklahoma

Puailoa, Satini
1944—Call of the South Seas

Puente, Laurita
1936—Comin' 'Round the Mountain

Puglia, Frank[246]
1936—Bulldog Edition*
1938—Invisible Enemy*
1939—Forged Passport
　　　In Old Caliente
1940—Girl from Havana*
　　　Behind the News*
1944—Brazil
1950—Federal Agent at Large
1954—Jubilee Trail*
　　　The Shanghai Story
1956—Accused of Murder
1957—Duel at Apache Wells

Puig, Eva
1946—Plainsman and the Lady

Pulido, Jose[45]
1945—Mexicana*
　　　Song of Mexico
1946—Days of Buffalo Bill*

Pullen, William
1957—Hell Canyon Outlaws

Purcell, Bob
1949—Flaming Fury
　　　The Red Menace

Purcell, Dick[123]
1937—Navy Blues
1941—The Pittsburgh Kid
1942—In Old California
　　　The Old Homestead
　　　X Marks the Spot
1943—Idaho
1944—Captain America
　　　Trocadero

Purcell, Noel
1956—Doctor at Sea

Putnam, Duane
1954—Crazylegs

Pyle, Denver[246]
1948—Train to Alcatraz
　　　Marshal of Amarillo
1949—Streets of San Francisco
　　　Hellfire
　　　Flame of Youth
1950—Singing Guns*
　　　Federal Agent at Large
　　　The Old Frontier
1951—Rough Riders of Durango
　　　Million Dollar Pursuit
1952—Oklahoma Annie
1953—A Perilous Journey*
　　　The Hydrogen Hurricane
1954—Johnny Guitar*

Q

Qualen, John[246]
1939—Mickey, the Kid
1951—Belle LeGrand

Quartaro, Nena
1936—The Three Mesquiteers

Queant, Gilles
1951—Adventures of Captain Fabian

Queen, Ellery—series
1935—The Spanish Cape Mystery
1936—The Mandarin Mystery

Quest, Hans
1956—Magic Fire

Quigley, Charles[246]
1939—Daredevils of the Red Circle
1942—Yokel Boy*
1946—The Crimson Ghost
　　　Affairs of Geraldine
　　　That Brennan Girl*
1950—Unmasked

Quigley, Juanita
1941—Variety Reel*
1943—Whispering Footsteps
1944—The Lady and the Monster

Quigley, Rita[246]
1941—Variety Reel*
1943—Whispering Footsteps

Quillan, Eddie[107]
1936—The Gentleman from Louisiana
　　　The Mandarin Mystery
1941—Stars Past and Present*
1946—A Guy Could Change

Quillan, Marie
1935—Melody Trail

Quinlan, Volney
1954—Crazylegs

Quinn, Tom[246]
1943—Chatterbox*
1944—My Best Gal*
1945—Love, Honor and Goodbye*
1946—Gay Blades*
　　　Song of Arizona
　　　Daughter of Don Q
　　　Under Nevada Skies
　　　Out California Way*
1947—Apache Rose*
　　　Hit Parade of 1947*

Quinn, Tony
1943—The Saint Meets the Tiger

R

Rachel [Veach][246]
1940—Grand Ole Opry
1944—Sing Neighbor Sing

Radio Rogues, The
1943—O, My Darling Clementine
1944—Trocadero

Rafferty, Frances[170]
1954—The Shanghai Story

Raft, George
1941—Stars at Play*

Ragan, Mike[246]
　　　[as Holly Bane]
1947—Jesse James Rides Again
1948—Dangers of the Canadian Mounted*
　　　Carson City Raiders
　　　Night Time in Nevada
　　　Renegades of Sonora
　　　The Far Frontier
1949—Ghost of Zorro
　　　Prince of the Plains*
1950—Desperadoes of the West*
　　　North of the Great Divide
　　　[as Michael Ragan]
1951—Don Daredevil Rides Again
　　　The Dakota Kid
　　　[as Mike Ragan]
1953—Can. Mounties Vs. Atomic Invaders
1955—Panther Girl of the Kongo
　　　Headline Hunters*
1956—The Man is Armed*

Raglan, Robert
1957—Thunder Over Tangier
1958—Strange Case of Dr. Manning

Raine, Patricia
1955—A Day to Remember

Raines, Ella[84]
1950—Singing Guns
1951—Fighting Coast Guard
1953—Ride the Man Down
1957—The Man in the Road

Raines, Steve
1947—Along the Oregon Trail*
　　　Under Colorado Skies
1948—Oklahoma Badlands*
　　　Desperadoes of Dodge City*
　　　Sundown in Santa Fe*
1949—Sheriff of Wichita
1958—Street of Darkness*

Rains, Claude[107]
1956—Lisbon

Raisch, Bill
1946—Specter of the Rose*

Ralph, Jessie[246]
1939—Mickey, the Kid

Ralston, Esther[247]
1935—Forced Landing
1936—The Girl from Mandalay

Ralston, Jobyna
1941—Wampas Baby Stars*

Ralston, Vera[46]
　　　[as Vera Hruba]
1941—Ice-Capades
1942—Ice-Capades Revue
　　　[as Vera Hruba Ralston]
1944—The Lady and the Monster
　　　Storm Over Lisbon
　　　Lake Placid Serenade
1945—Dakota
1946—Murder in the Music Hall
　　　[as Vera Ralston]
　　　Plainsman and the Lady
1947—Wyoming
　　　The Flame
1948—I, Jane Doe
　　　Angel on the Amazon
1949—The Fighting Kentuckian
1950—Surrender
1951—Belle LeGrand
　　　The Wild Blue Yonder
1952—Hoodlum Empire
1953—A Perilous Journey
　　　Fair Wind to Java
1954—Jubilee Trail
1955—Timberjack
1956—Accused of Murder
1957—Spoilers of the Forest
1958—Gunfire at Indian Gap
　　　The Notorious Mr. Monks
　　　The Man Who Died Twice

Rama, Rudy
1950—Prisoners in Petticoats

Rambeau, Marjorie[107]
1943—In Old Oklahoma

Rameau, Emil
1945—Scotland Yard Investigator
1947—The Ghost Goes Wild
1948—The Main Street Kid

Ramirez, Dario
1951—Bullfighter and the Lady

Ramos, Bobby—and Rumba Band
1950—Hit Parade of 1951

Jed Prouty

Frank Puglia

Ranch Boys, The
1939—In Old Monterey

Rand, Edwin
1946—Rendezvous with Annie
1951—Utah Wagon Train

Rand, Sally
1936—The Big Show*

Rand, Torchy
1946—That Brennan Girl*
1947—That's My Man*
1948—Slippy McGee*

Randall, Addison [Jack][247]
1936—Navy Born

Randall, Rebel[247]
1943—In Old Oklahoma*
1944—Atlantic City*
1947—That's My Gal*

Randall, Stuart[247]
1950—Bells of Coronado
　　　Rustlers on Horseback
1951—Rough Riders of Durango
　　　Wells Fargo Gunmaster
　　　Arizona Manhunt
1953—Champ for a Day*
1954—Man with the Steel Whip
1955—Headline Hunters

Denver Pyle

John Qualen

Charles Quigley

Rita Quigley

Tom Quinn

Rachel

Mike Ragan

Jessie Ralph

 Esther Ralston
 Addison Randall
 Rebel Randall
 Stuart Randall
 Isabel Randolph

 Jane Randolph
 Lillian Randolph
 Paula Raymond
 Robin Raymond
 Marshall Reed

Randell, Pamela
1940 — Women in War

Randell, Ron
1958 — Strange Case of Dr. Manning

Randle, Karen
1944 — Storm Over Lisbon*

Randolph, Isabel[247]
1940 — Ride, Tenderfoot, Ride
Barnyard Follies
1943 — Hoosier Holiday
O, My Darling Clementine
1944 — Jamboree
1945 — Tell It to a Star
1951 — Belle LeGrand*
Oh! Susanna*
Secrets of Monte Carlo
1952 — I Dream of Jeanie*
Thundering Caravans
1953 — The Lady Wants Mink
1954 — The Shanghai Story

Randolph, Jane[247]
1945 — A Sporting Chance
Jealousy

Randolph, Lillian[247]
1940 — Barnyard Follies*
1942 — Hi, Neighbor
1943 — Hoosier Holiday
1944 — Three Little Sisters
1945 — A Song for Miss Julie

Randolph, Marion
1951 — Oh! Susanna

Ranevsky, Boris
1957 — Operation Conspiracy

Ranson, Lois[48]
1939 — Money to Burn
1940 — Grandpa Goes to Town
The Crooked Road*
Grand Ole Opry
Earl of Puddlestone
Under Texas Skies
Friendly Neighbors
Meet the Missus
1941 — Wampas Baby Stars*
Petticoat Politics
Angels with Broken Wings

Raquello, Edward
1938 — Western Jamboree

Rasp, Fritz
1956 — Magic Fire

Rasumny, Mikhail[124]
1942 — Yokel Boy
1950 — Hit Parade of 1951

Ratib, Gamil
1959 — O. S. S. 117 is Not Dead

Raven, Karen
1944 — Brazil*
1945 — Mexicana*
1946 — Earl Carroll Sketchbook*

Rawlinson, Herbert[137]
1936 — Dancing Feet
Ticket to Paradise
Robinson Crusoe of Clipper Island
1937 — S O S Coast Guard
1938 — Orphans of the Street
1939 — Days of Jesse James*
Money to Burn
1940 — King of the Royal Mounted
1941 — Sheriff of Tombstone*
Bad Man of Deadwood
King of the Texas Rangers
1942 — Perils of Nyoka*
Sons of the Pioneers*
1943 — King of the Cowboys*
Daredevils of the West*
Days of Old Cheyenne
The Masked Marvel*
1944 — Marshal of Reno
Sheriff of Sundown
1948 — The Gallant Legion
1949 — Brimstone

Ray, Charles
1941 — Stars Past and Present*

Ray, Jimmy
1936 — Sitting on the Moon

Ray, Michel
1955 — The Divided Heart

Ray, Roland
1936 — Oregon Trail

Ray, Vivian
1950 — The Avengers

Ray, Wade
1949 — The James Brothers of Missouri

Raybould, Harry
1958 — Girl in the Woods

Raymond, Dean
1935 — The Crime of Doctor Crespi

Raymond, Jack
1943 — Sleepy Lagoon

Raymond, Paula[247]
1953 — City that Never Sleeps

Raymond, Robin[247]
1942 — Secrets of the Underground

Raymond, Royal
1949 — The Red Menace

Raynor Lehr Circus
1950 — Trigger, Jr.

Redmond, Liam
1955 — The Divided Heart

Redwing, Rodd
1956 — Jaguar

Reed, Alan
1954 — Geraldine

Reed, Donald
1936 — Darkest Africa

Reed, Marshall[247]
1943 — Bordertown Gun Fighters*
The Black Hills Express*
Wagon Tracks West*
Death Valley Manhunt*
1944 — Beneath Western Skies*
Mojave Firebrand
The Laramie Trail*
Tucson Raiders
The Tiger Woman*
Marshal of Reno*
Song of Nevada*
Haunted Harbor
My Buddy*
Zorro's Black Whip*
Navy MN 3387 — Your Weapons*
1945 — The Chicago Kid*
Bandits of the Badlands*
1946 — In Old Sacramento*
1947 — Angel and the Badman
Homesteaders of Paradise Valley*
Yankee Fakir*
Spoilers of the North*
That's My Man*
Web of Danger*
Wyoming*
On the Old Spanish Trail
1948 — Lightnin' in the Forest*
The Bold Frontiersman
Dangers of the Canadian Mounted*
The Gallant Legion
The Denver Kid*
Renegades of Sonora
1949 — Federal Agents Vs. Underworld, Inc.
Ghost of Zorro
Frontier Investigator
The James Brothers of Missouri
Navajo Trail Raiders
Pioneer Marshal*
1950 — The Invisible Monster
Rock Island Trail*
The Savage Horde
Covered Wagon Raid*
Rustlers on Horseback*
California Passage*
1951 — Silver City Bonanza*
Oh! Susanna
1952 — Thundering Caravans*
1953 — Ride the Man Down*
San Antone*
Old Overland Trail*
Destroyers of the Sun*
The Hydrogen Hurricane*
1954 — Jubilee Trail*

Reed, Maxwell
1955 — The Square Ring

Reed, Phillip
1946 — Rendezvous with Annie

Reed, Walter[247]
1948 — Angel on the Amazon
1950 — Flying Disc Man from Mars
1951 — Wells Fargo Gunmaster
Govt. Agents Vs. Phantom Legion
1952 — Thunderbirds
1955 — The Eternal Sea*
The Last Command*
1957 — The Lawless Eighties

Reedy, Beverly[69]
1944 — Lake Placid Serenade*
1945 — The Topeka Terror*
Utah*
Earl Carroll Vanities*
The Phantom Speaks*
Three's a Crowd*
Flame of Barbary Coast*
Bells of Rosarita*
Federal Operator 99*
Steppin' in Society*
Road to Alcatraz*
The Cheaters*
Hitchhike to Happiness*
Man from Oklahoma*
Tell It to a Star*
Swingin' on a Rainbow*
Behind City Lights*
Love, Honor and Goodbye*
Sunset in El Dorado*
The Purple Monster Strikes*
Don't Fence Me In*
Rough Riders of Cheyenne*
Girls of the Big House*
An Angel Comes to Brooklyn*
Mexicana*
The Tiger Woman*
Dakota*
Song of Mexico*
1946 — California Gold Rush*

 Walter Reed

 Richard Reeves

 Frank Reicher

Rees, Lanny
1946 — Home in Oklahoma
1948 — California Firebrand

Reeves, Richard[247]
1952 — Hoodlum Empire*
Gobs and Gals*
Thunderbirds*
1954 — Trader Tom of the China Seas
1955 — City of Shadows
1956 — The Man is Armed

Regan, Charles
1950 — The Invisible Monster

Regan, Phil[84]
1936 — Laughing Irish Eyes
Happy Go Lucky
1937 — The Hit Parade
Manhattan Merry-Go-Round
1938 — Outside of Paradise
1939 — She Married a Cop
Flight at Midnight

Regas, George
1936 — The Girl from Mandalay

Regnier, Charles
1956 — Magic Fire

Reicher, Frank[247]
1938 — Prison Nurse
1939 — Woman Doctor
Sabotage*
South of the Border
1944 — Captain America
The Big Bonanza
1945 — The Tiger Woman
1945 — A Guy Could Change*
Song of Arizona*
My Pal Trigger*
Home in Oklahoma
1947 — Yankee Fakir
1948 — Carson City Raiders
I, Jane Doe*
1950 — The Arizona Cowboy

Reicher, Hedwiga
1936—The House of a Thousand Candles

Reichow, Otto
1941—King of the Texas Rangers*
1942—Joan of Ozark

Reid, Carl Benton
1957—Spoilers of the Forest

Reid, Margaret
1943—Sleepy Lagoon

Reihl, Kay
1949—The Red Menace

Remley, Ralph
1938—Outside of Paradise

Renaldo, Duncan[48]
1937—The Painted Stallion
　　　Zorro Rides Again
1939—The Lone Ranger Rides Again
　　　Rough Riders' Round-Up*
　　　The Kansas Terrors
　　　Cowboys from Texas
　　　South of the Border
1940—Heroes of the Saddle
　　　Pioneers of the West
　　　Covered Wagon Days
　　　Gaucho Serenade
　　　Rocky Mountain Rangers
　　　Oklahoma Renegades
1941—King of the Texas Rangers
　　　Down Mexico Way
　　　Gauchos of Eldorado
1942—King of the Mounties
1943—Secret Service in Darkest Africa
　　　Hands Across the Border
1944—The Fighting Seabees
　　　The Tiger Woman
　　　Call of the South Seas
　　　The San Antonio Kid
　　　Sheriff of Sundown

Renaldo, Tito
1948—Old Los Angeles
1952—The Fabulous Senorita

Renavent, George
1937—The Sheik Steps Out
1942—Spy Smasher
　　　Perils of Nyoka
1943—Secret Service in Darkest Africa
1944—The Tiger Woman*
　　　Storm Over Lisbon*
1945—Scotland Yard Investigator*
1946—The Catman of Paris
1947—The Trespasser*
1951—Secrets of Monte Carlo

Rennie, Michael
1942—Suicide Squadron

Rentschler, Mickey
1936—Follow Your Heart
1941—West of Cimarron

Republic Rhythm Riders, The[49]
1952—Colorado Sundown
　　　The Last Musketeer
　　　Border Saddlemates
　　　Old Oklahoma Plains
　　　The Wac from Walla Walla
　　　South Pacific Trail
1953—Old Overland Trail
　　　Sweethearts on Parade*

Rettig, Tommy[107]
1952—Gobs and Gals
1953—The Lady Wants Mink

Revere, Anne[107]
1943—Shantytown

Revere, John Paul—series
1943—Beyond the Last Frontier
　　　Raiders of Sunset Pass
1944—Pride of the Plains
　　　Beneath Western Skies

Revier, Dorothy
1935—Frisco Waterfront

Rex
1936—Robinson Crusoe of Clipper Island
1939—Woman Doctor

Rex, Jack
1955—Mystery of the Black Jungle

Reynolds, Craig
1938—Romance on the Run
　　　Gold Mine in the Sky
1939—Wall Street Cowboy

Reynolds, Don
[Little Brown Jug]
1944—The Yellow Rose of Texas*
1946—Song of Arizona*
1949—The Red Pony

Reynolds, Harrington
1935—Two Sinners

Reynolds, Marjorie[248]
1941—Robin Hood of the Pecos

Rhodes, Betty Jane[248]
1941—Mountain Moonlight

Rhodes, Grandon
1943—Hit Parade of 1943*
1950—Women from Headquarters
1955—The Eternal Sea*
　　　Headline Hunters*
　　　A Man Alone
1957—The Wayward Girl
1958—The Notorious Mr. Monks

Rhodes, Marjorie
1957—Tears for Simon

Riano, Renie[248]
1938—Outside of Paradise
1941—Ice-Capades*
1943—Man from Music Mountain
1945—A Song for Miss Julie
1947—Winter Wonderland

Rice, Florence[248]
1941—Mr. District Attorney
　　　Doctors Don't Tell

Rice, Frank
1936—Oregon Trail

Rice, Jack[207]
1938—Arson Gang Busters
1939—Money to Burn

Rice, Joan
1955—A Day to Remember

Rice, Marie
1936—The Leavenworth Case

Rich, Dick[248]
1938—Prison Nurse*
1940—Dark Command*
1942—Secrets of the Underground
1943—King of the Cowboys*
　　　Shantytown*
　　　In Old Oklahoma*
1952—Radar Men from the Moon*
1955—A Man Alone*

Rich, Gloria[49]
1937—The Hit Parade*
　　　Manhattan Merry-Go-Round*
　　　Exiled to Shanghai*
1938—The Old Barn Dance
　　　Outside of Paradise*
　　　King of the Newsboys
　　　Outlaws of Sonora
　　　Riders of the Black Hills*
　　　Heroes of the Hills*
　　　A Desperate Adventure
　　　Dick Tracy Returns*
　　　Down in "Arkansaw"

Rich, Irene[248]
1947—Calendar Girl
　　　Angel and the Badman

Richards, Addison[137]
1938—Prison Nurse
1939—I Was a Convict*
1940—Gangs of Chicago
　　　Girl from Havana
1941—Back in the Saddle
　　　Sheriff of Tombstone
1942—Cowboy Serenade
　　　Flying Tigers
　　　Ridin' Down the Canyon
1943—Hit Parade of 1943*
　　　Headin' for God's Country
　　　Deerslayer
　　　Mystery Broadcast
1944—The Fighting Seabees
　　　Three Little Sisters
　　　Bordertown Trail
1945—Grissly's Millions
　　　Bells of Rosarita
　　　The Chicago Kid
　　　The Tiger Woman
1956—When Gangland Strikes

Richards, Jr., Danny
1958—Hell Ship Mutiny

Richards, Frank
1951—South of Caliente

June Lang, Dewey Robinson

Richards, Keith[248]
1946—Heldorado*
　　　That Brennan Girl*
1947—Calendar Girl*
　　　Hit Parade of 1947*
　　　Twilight on the Rio Grande*
　　　Jesse James Rides Again*
　　　The Black Widow
1948—The Gay Ranchero
　　　Sons of Adventure
　　　The Far Frontier*
1949—Duke of Chicago
　　　Flaming Fury*
　　　The James Brothers of Missouri
　　　The Blonde Bandit*
1950—The Invisible Monster
　　　North of the Great Divide
1951—Spoilers of the Plains
1953—War of the Space Giants
　　　The Hydrogen Hurricane
1955—King of the Carnival

Richards, Paul
1956—Scandal Incorporated

Richardson, Duncan
1950—Gunmen of Abilene
1951—Pride of Maryland

Richman, Charles
1938—Lady, Behave!

Richmond, Kane[248]
1935—Forced Landing
1941—Mountain Moonlight
1942—Spy Smasher
　　　Army 156—Horsemanship*
1944—Haunted Harbor
1945—The Tiger Woman
1946—Passkey to Danger
　　　Traffic in Crime

Richmond, Leo C.
1949—Daughter of the Jungle

Richmond, Warner[198]
1935—The New Frontier
1936—The Singing Vagabond
　　　Hearts in Bondage*
1937—Trail of Vengeance
　　　Doomed at Sundown
　　　A Lawman is Born
1938—Prairie Moon

Ricks, Cappy—series
1935—Cappy Ricks Returns
1937—Affairs of Cappy Ricks

Rico, Mona
1937—Zorro Rides Again

Riders of the Purple Sage, The[84]
1946—Out California Way
1947—Last Frontier Uprising
　　　Along the Oregon Trail
　　　Under Colorado Skies
1948—California Firebrand
　　　The Timber Trail
　　　Grand Canyon Trail
　　　The Far Frontier
1949—Susanna Pass
　　　Down Dakota Way
　　　The Golden Stallion
1950—Bells of Coronado
　　　Twilight in the Sierras
　　　Trigger, Jr.
　　　Sunset in the West
　　　North of the Great Divide
　　　Trail of Robin Hood
1951—Spoilers of the Plains
　　　Heart of the Rockies

Ridgely, John
1947—That's My Man
1951—Thunder in God's Country

Ridges, Stanley[249]
1941—Mr. District Attorney
1943—False Faces
1945—The Phantom Speaks

Riebe, Loren[249]
1936—Robinson Crusoe of Clipper Island*
1937—Dick Tracy*
　　　Gunsmoke Ranch
　　　Come on, Cowboys!
　　　The Painted Stallion
　　　S O S Coast Guard*
　　　Zorro Rides Again*
1938—The Lone Ranger*
　　　Call the Mesquiteers*
　　　Dick Tracy Returns*
　　　Hawk of the Wilderness*
1939—Daredevils of the Red Circle*
　　　The Covered Trailer*
1940—King of the Royal Mounted*
1941—Adventures of Captain Marvel*
　　　King of the Texas Rangers*
1942—Spy Smasher*
　　　Perils of Nyoka*
1946—The Crimson Ghost*
1947—Angel and the Badman*
　　　Jesse James Rides Again*
1949—Federal Agents Vs. Underworld, Inc.*
1950—Bells of Coronado*
　　　Sands of Iwo Jima*
　　　Hit Parade of 1951*

Riedmann, Gerhard
1956—Magic Fire

Rigby, Edward
1941—Poison Pen

Riley, Elaine
1952—Leadville Gunslinger

Riley, Mike—and orchestra
1943—Sleepy Lagoon

Rilla, Walter
1955—The Green Buddha
1956—Track the Man Down

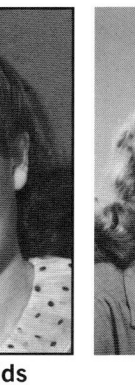

Marjorie Reynolds

Betty Jane Rhodes

Renie Riano

Florence Rice

Dick Rich

Irene Rich

Keith Richards

Kane Richmond

Ring, Cyril[249]
- 1938 – King of the Newsboys*
- 1941 – Ice-Capades*
- Public Enemies*
- 1942 – Sleepytime Gal*
- Yokel Boy*
- Home in Wyomin'*
- Joan of Ozark*
- Ice-Capades Revue*
- The Traitor Within*
- 1944 – My Best Gal*
- Silent Partner*
- 1945 – Identity Unknown*
- The Cheaters*
- Swingin' on a Rainbow*
- 1947 – The Flame*

Ripper, Michael
- 1955 – Secret Venture

Riquelme, Carlos
- 1956 – A Woman's Devotion

Risdon, Elisabeth[249]
- 1940 – Sing, Dance, Plenty Hot
- 1945 – Grissly's Millions
- A Song for Miss Julie
- 1946 – Roll on Texas Moon
- 1949 – Down Dakota Way
- 1950 – Hills of Oklahoma
- 1951 – In Old Amarillo

Ritter, Fred
- 1940 – Carolina Moon

Ritz Brothers
- 1941 – Stars at Play*

Rivas, Carlos
- 1957 – Panama Sal

Rivero, Julian[249]
- 1935 – Sagebrush Troubadour
- 1936 – Lawless Land
- 1937 – Ridin' the Lone Trail
- 1939 – South of the Border*
- 1940 – Young Buffalo Bill
- Gaucho Serenade*
- 1941 – Down Mexico Way
- 1942 – Bells of Capistrano*
- 1943 – Hands Across the Border*
- 1944 – Cowboy and the Senorita*
- 1945 – Mexicana*
- 1948 – Old Los Angeles
- 1950 – Belle of Old Mexico*
- 1951 – Cuban Fireball*
- 1952 – Wild Horse Ambush
- 1953 – Shadows of Tombstone
- 1954 – Make Haste to Live*
- 1955 – A Man Alone*
- The Vanishing American
- 1956 – Thunder Over Arizona

Roach, Bert
- 1936 – The Mandarin Mystery
- 1938 – Romance on the Run
- 1946 – Man from Rainbow Valley

Roadman, Betty
- 1938 – Billy the Kid Returns*
- 1939 – The Lone Ranger Rides Again*
- 1940 – Forgotten Girls*
- Rocky Mountain Rangers*

Roan, Vinegar
- 1937 – Gunsmoke Ranch
- The Painted Stallion

Robards, Sr., Jason
- 1948 – Son of God's Country
- 1949 – Post Office Investigator

Robbins, Archie
- 1936 – The Leavenworth Case

Robbins, Gale[249]
- 1955 – Double Jeopardy

Robbins, Marty
- 1957 – Raiders of Old California

Roberson, Chuck[249]
- 1946 – Plainsman and the Lady*
- 1947 – Calendar Girl*
- Wyoming*
- Jesse James Rides Again*
- The Fabulous Texan*
- The Flame*
- 1949 – The James Brothers of Missouri*
- The Fighting Kentuckian*
- 1950 – Hills of Oklahoma*
- Rio Grande*
- 1951 – Fort Dodge Stampede
- 1955 – Timberjack*
- 1956 – Dakota Incident*

Robertos, The
- 1945 – A Song for Miss Julie

Roberts, Allene
- 1952 – Thunderbirds

Roberts, Arlyn[49]
- 1944 – Storm Over Lisbon*
- Lights of Old Santa Fe*
- Lake Placid Serenade*
- 1945 – Utah*
- Earl Carroll Vanities*
- The Phantom Speaks*
- The Vampire's Ghost*
- Three's a Crowd*
- Flame of Barbary Coast*
- A Sporting Chance*
- Bells of Rosarita*
- The Chicago Kid*
- Gangs of the Waterfront*
- Steppin' in Society*
- Hitchhike to Happiness*
- Tell It to a Star*
- Swingin' on a Rainbow*
- The Fatal Witness*

Roberts, Beatrice[84]
- 1937 – Bill Cracks Down
- 1940 – Pioneers of the West

Roberts, Beverly[107]
- 1938 – Call of the Yukon
- Tenth Avenue Kid
- 1939 – I Was a Convict
- Main Street Lawyer

Roberts, Don
- 1936 – Ghost-Town Gold

Roberts, Jack
- 1938 – Dick Tracy Returns

Stanley Ridges

Loren Riebe

Cyril Ring

Elisabeth Risdon

Julian Rivero

Leona Roberts

Roberts, J. H.
- 1942 – Suicide Squadron

Roberts, Lee
- 1949 – The James Brothers of Missouri
- 1950 – Covered Wagon Raid
- Desperadoes of the West
- 1951 – Wells Fargo Gunmaster
- 1952 – Desperadoes' Outpost
- 1953 – Lost in Outer Space
- Captives of the Zero Hour
- 1955 – King of the Carnival

Roberts, Leona[249]
- 1938 – I Stand Accused
- 1939 – Thou Shalt Not Kill
- 1940 – Gangs of Chicago
- 1941 – A Man Betrayed*
- 1946 – The Madonna's Secret

Roberts, Lynne[50]
[as Lynn Roberts]
- 1936 – Bulldog Edition*
- 1937 – Circus Girl*
- Dangerous Holiday
- Heart of the Rockies
- 1938 – Mama Runs Wild
- The Lone Ranger
- Hollywood Stadium Mystery!
- Call the Mesquiteers
- Dick Tracy Returns
- The Higgins Family
[as Mary Hart]
- Billy the Kid Returns
- Come on, Rangers
- Shine on Harvest Moon
- 1939 – The Mysterious Miss X
- Rough Riders' Round-Up
- My Wife's Relatives
- Frontier Pony Express
- Southward, Ho!
- In Old Caliente
- Should Husbands Work?
[as Lynn Roberts]
- 1944 – The Port of Forty Thieves
[as Lynne Roberts]
- My Buddy
- The Big Bonanza
- 1945 – The Phantom Speaks
- The Chicago Kid
- Behind City Lights
- Girls of the Big House
- 1946 – Sioux City Sue
- 1947 – The Pilgrim Lady
- The Magnificent Rogue
- That's My Gal
- Winter Wonderland
- Saddle Pals
- Robin Hood of Texas
- 1948 – Madonna of the Desert
- Lightnin' in the Forest
- Secret Service Investigator
- The Timber Trail
- Eyes of Texas
- Sons of Adventure

Roberts, Paul
- 1955 – In Old Vienna

Gale Robbins

Roy Roberts

Roberts, Roy[249]
- 1949 – Flaming Fury
- 1951 – Fighting Coast Guard
- 1952 – Hoodlum Empire
- 1953 – San Antone
- 1954 – Sea of Lost Ships
- 1955 – The Eternal Sea*
- I Cover the Underworld
- The Last Command

Roberts, Tracey
- 1957 – The Wayward Girl

Robertson, Dale[108]
- 1956 – Dakota Incident
- 1957 – Hell Canyon Outlaws

Robertson, Willard
- 1935 – Forced Landing
- 1937 – Larceny on the Air
- 1938 – Gangs of New York
- 1939 – Main Street Lawyer

Robie, Earl
- 1953 – The Lady Wants Mink

Robinson, Bartlett
- 1958 – Girl in the Woods

Robinson, Dewey[248]
- 1936 – The Return of Jimmy Valentine
- 1938 – Mama Runs Wild
- Army Girl
- 1939 – Forged Passport
- 1944 – Trocadero
- 1949 – Hellfire

Robinson, Edward G.[249]
- 1942 – Moscow Strikes Back

Robinson, Ralph
- 1937 – Wild Horse Rodeo

Robinson, Ruth[233]
- 1939 – The Arizona Kid*
- The Kansas Terrors
- 1940 – In Old Missouri*
- Covered Wagon Days
- Texas Terrors*
- 1941 – Arkansas Judge*
- Sis Hopkins*
- Down Mexico Way
- 1942 – In Old California*
- 1943 – Shantytown*
- Chatterbox*
- 1946 – That Brennan Girl*
- 1951 – Belle LeGrand*

Robson, Flora
- 1941 – Poison Pen

Roc, Patricia
- 1958 – Scotland Yard Dragnet

Rochelle, Ben
- 1944 – Cowboy and the Senorita

Rochelle, Claire[249]
- 1937 – Guns in the Dark
- Affairs of Cappy Ricks*
- Boothill Brigade
- Ridin' the Lone Trail
- 1939 – Woman Doctor*

Rochester
See Eddie Anderson.

Chuck Roberson

Edward G. Robinson

Claire Rochelle

Rockwell, Jack[250]
- 1935 – Tumbling Tumbleweeds
- 1936 – The Lawless Nineties
- The Singing Cowboy
- Guns and Guitars
- Winds of the Wasteland
- The Big Show*
- 1937 – Bar-Z Bad Men
- Range Defenders*
- The Red Rope
- Springtime in the Rockies*
- 1938 – The Old Barn Dance*
- The Lone Ranger*
- Born to be Wild*
- Under Western Stars*
- Prairie Moon
- Shine on Harvest Moon
- 1939 – Rough Riders' Round-Up*
- Wyoming Outlaw*
- Days of Jesse James
- 1940 – Dark Command*
- Wagons Westward*
- Adventures of Red Ryder*
- The Carson City Kid*
- Colorado*
- Frontier Vengeance*
- Young Bill Hickok*
- 1941 – Wyoming Wildcat*
- The Singing Hill*
- Sheriff of Tombstone*
- Bad Man of Deadwood*
- Jesse James at Bay*
- Red River Valley*
- 1942 – Man from Cheyenne*
- The Cyclone Kid*
- Sunset Serenade*
- Shadows on the Sage*
- The Sundown Kid*
- 1943 – Dead Man's Gulch*
- Daredevils of the West
- The Man from Thunder River
- The Black Hills Express
- Wagon Tracks West
- Beyond the Last Frontier*
- Overland Mail Robbery*
- In Old Oklahoma*
- Raiders of Sunset Pass*
- 1944 – My Buddy
- The Big Bonanza
- 1945 – Phantom of the Plains
- Rough Riders of Cheyenne
- Colorado Pioneers*
- 1946 – Alias Billy the Kid*
- Sun Valley Cyclone*
- Conquest of Cheyenne*
- Red River Renegades*

Rockwell, Robert[49]
1949 — The Red Menace
  Alias the Champ
  The Sponge Diver
  The Blonde Bandit
1950 — Unmasked
  Singing Guns*
  Belle of Old Mexico
  Federal Agent at Large
  The Vanishing Westerner*
  Women from Headquarters
  Destination Big House
  Trial Without Jury
  Lonely Heart Bandits
  Prisoners in Petticoats

Rodman, Nancy
1956 — Daniel Boone, Trail Blazer

Rodoliers, The
1939 — Home on the Prairie

Rodriguez, Estelita[52]
1945 — Mexicana
  Along the Navajo Trail
1947 — On the Old Spanish Trail
1948 — The Gay Ranchero
  Old Los Angeles
1949 — Susanna Pass
  The Golden Stallion
1950 — Belle of Old Mexico
  Federal Agent at Large
  Twilight in the Sierras
  Sunset in the West
  Hit Parade of 1951
  California Passage
1951 — Cuban Fireball
  In Old Amarillo
  Havana Rose
  Pals of the Golden West
1952 — The Fabulous Senorita
  Tropical Heat Wave
  South Pacific Trail
1953 — Sweethearts on Parade

Roebuck, Tiny
1936 — Robinson Crusoe of Clipper Island

Roehn, Franz
1954 — Tobor the Great

Jack Roper

Roettinger, Heinz
1955 — In Old Vienna

Rogers, Charles "Buddy"
1940 — Chinese Garden Festival*

Rogers, Gene
1944 — That's My Baby

Rogers, Jean[250]
1946 — Gay Blades

Rogers, John
1936 — The Girl from Mandalay

Rogers, Roy[158]
  [as Leonard Slye]
1936 — The Big Show*
  The Old Corral*
  [as Dick Weston]
1937 — Wild Horse Rodeo
1938 — The Old Barn Dance
  [as Roy Rogers]
  Under Western Stars
  Billy the Kid Returns
  Come on, Rangers
  Shine on Harvest Moon
1939 — Rough Riders' Round-Up
  Frontier Pony Express
  Man of Conquest*
  Southward, Ho!
  In Old Caliente
  Wall Street Cowboy
  The Arizona Kid
  Jeepers Creepers
  Saga of Death Valley
  Days of Jesse James
1940 — Young Buffalo Bill
  Dark Command
  The Carson City Kid
  The Ranger and the Lady
  Colorado
  Young Bill Hickok
  The Border Legion
1941 — Robin Hood of the Pecos
  Arkansas Judge
  In Old Cheyenne
  Sheriff of Tombstone
  Nevada City
  Meet Roy Rogers*
  Bad Man of Deadwood
  Jesse James at Bay
  Red River Valley
1942 — Man from Cheyenne
  South of Santa Fe
  Sunset on the Desert
  Romance on the Range
  Sons of the Pioneers
  Sunset Serenade
  Heart of the Golden West
  Ridin' Down the Canyon
1943 — Idaho
  King of the Cowboys
  Song of Texas
  Silver Spurs
  Man from Music Mountain
  Hands Across the Border
1944 — Cowboy and the Senorita
  The Yellow Rose of Texas
  Song of Nevada
  San Fernando Valley
  Lights of Old Santa Fe
  Brazil
  Lake Placid Serenade
1945 — Utah
  Bells of Rosarita
  Man from Oklahoma
  Sunset in El Dorado
  Don't Fence Me In
  Along the Navajo Trail
1946 — Song of Arizona
  Rainbow Over Texas
  My Pal Trigger
  Under Nevada Skies
  Roll on Texas Moon
  Home in Oklahoma
  Out California Way
  Heldorado
  Schine Circuit Trailer
1947 — Apache Rose
  Hit Parade of 1947
  Bells of San Angelo
  Springtime in the Sierras
  On the Old Spanish Trail
1948 — The Gay Ranchero
  Under California Stars
  Eyes of Texas
  Night Time in Nevada
  Grand Canyon Trail
  The Far Frontier
1949 — Susanna Pass
  Down Dakota Way
  The Golden Stallion
1950 — Bells of Coronado
  Twilight in the Sierras
  Trigger, Jr.
  Sunset in the West
  North of the Great Divide
  Trail of Robin Hood
1951 — Spoilers of the Plains
  Heart of the Rockies
  In Old Amarillo
  South of Caliente
  Pals of the Golden West

Rogers, Roy—Riders[85]
1951 — In Old Amarillo
  South of Caliente
  Pals of the Golden West

Rogers, Ruth[250]
1939 — The Night Riders

Roginsky, Miguel
1950 — Jungle Stampede

Roland, Gilbert[108]
1941 — Angels with Broken Wings
1951 — Bullfighter and the Lady

Rollins, June
1939 — The Zero Hour*

Roman, Ric[250]
1951 — South of Caliente
1952 — Hoodlum Empire*
1953 — Shadows of Tombstone
1955 — Timberjack*
  The Road to Denver*
1956 — Terror at Midnight
1957 — Duel at Apache Wells
  The Wayward Girl

Roman, Ruth[108]
1944 — Song of Nevada*
  Storm Over Lisbon*
1954 — The Shanghai Story

Romer, Jeanne
1945 — Hitchhike to Happiness

Romer, Lynn
1945 — Hitchhike to Happiness

Romero, Cesar
1940 — Chinese Garden Festival*
1941 — Stars at Play*
  Stars Past and Present*

Romney, Edana
1943 — Alibi

Rondell, Ronnie
1938 — King of the Newsboys*
1941 — Sis Hopkins*
1944 — Song of Nevada*

Gene Roth

Henry Rowland

Rooney, Mickey[108]
1941 — Los Angeles Examiner Benefit*
1954 — The Atomic Kid
1955 — The Twinkle in God's Eye

Roope, Fay[250]
1954 — The Atomic Kid

Roosevelt, Buddy[250]
1936 — Robinson Crusoe of Clipper Island*
  The Old Corral
1937 — Dick Tracy
  S O S Coast Guard*
1938 — The Fighting Devil Dogs*
1939 — The Lone Ranger Rides Again*
  Man of Conquest*
1941 — Wyoming Wildcat*
  Kansas Cyclone*
  Gangs of Sonora*
  The Apache Kid*
  King of the Texas Rangers*
  Dick Tracy Vs. Crime, Inc.*
1942 — Spy Smasher*
1943 — G-Men Vs. The Black Dragon*
  Secret Service in Darkest Africa*
1946 — King of the Forest Rangers*
  Daughter of Don Q
1949 — King of the Rocket Men*
1955 — The Last Command*

Roper, Jack[250]
1939 — Wall Street Cowboy
1940 — Heroes of the Saddle
  Drums of Fu Manchu*
1941 — A Man Betrayed*
  The Pittsburgh Kid
1952 — The Quiet Man*

Roquemore, Henry
1935 — Racing Luck
1936 — The Singing Vagabond
1940 — Grandpa Goes to Town*
1941 — In Old Cheyenne*
1942 — Moonlight Masquerade*

Rorke, Hayden
1955 — The Eternal Sea

Rory, Rossana[250]
1957 — Hell Canyon Outlaws

Rosas, Raymond
1956 — Jaguar

Lionel Royce

Selena Royle

William Royle

Christian Rub

Rose, George
1955 — The Square Ring
1956 — Track the Man Down

Rose, Harry
1945 — An Angel Comes to Brooklyn

Rose, Polly
1946 — Specter of the Rose

Rose, Robert
1948 — The Gay Ranchero

Rosenbloom, Maxie
1937 — Two Wise Maids
Ridin' the Lone Trail*
1938 — Gangs of New York
1940 — Grandpa Goes to Town

Rosener, George
1940 — The Carson City Kid
1941 — Arkansas Judge
In Old Cheyenne

Rosett, Rose
1950 — Hit Parade of 1951

Rosing, Bodil
1936 — Hearts in Bondage
1937 — Michael O'Halloran

Ross, Bob
1941 — Variety Reel*

Ross, Earl
1936 — Cavalry
1937 — The Riders of the Whistling Skull

Ross, George
1957 — Hell Canyon Outlaws

Ross, Shirley[250]
1941 — Variety Reel*
Sailors on Leave
1945 — A Song for Miss Julie

Ross, Stanley
1947 — The Pretender

Roth, Gene[250]
[as Gene Stutenroth]
1947 — Homesteaders of Paradise Valley
Jesse James Rides Again
Marshal of Cripple Creek
The Black Widow
1948 — Oklahoma Badlands
The Gallant Legion*
Adv. of Frank and Jesse James
[as Gene Roth]
1949 — Sheriff of Wichita
Ghost of Zorro
The Last Bandit
The James Brothers of Missouri
1950 — Redwood Forest Trail*
1951 — Oh! Susanna*
Don Daredevil Rides Again*
1955 — Panther Girl of the Kongo*

Roubert, Matty
1938 — Shine on Harvest Moon
1940 — Frontier Vengeance

Rough-Ridin' Kids — series
1951 — Buckaroo Sheriff of Texas
The Dakota Kid
Arizona Manhunt
1952 — Wild Horse Ambush

Rouverol, Jean
1936 — The Leavenworth Case
1938 — Western Jamboree

Roux, Tony
1941 — Gauchos of Eldorado

Rowan, Don
1937 — Sea Racketeers

Rowland, Henry[250]
1942 — The Phantom Plainsmen
1950 — Bells of Coronado*
The Showdown
1952 — Zombies of the Stratosphere*
1953 — Jungle Drums of Africa
1958 — Street of Darkness

Rowles, Polly[251]
1937 — Springtime in the Rockies

Roy, Billy
1943 — Mountain Rhythm

Roy, Bob
1946 — Rendezvous with Annie

Royce, John
See John Crawford.

Royce, Lionel[250]
1943 — Secret Service in Darkest Africa

Royle, Selena[250]
1948 — Moonrise

Royle, William[251]
1938 — Hawk of the Wilderness
Red River Range
1939 — Mexicali Rose
Frontier Pony Express
Man of Conquest*
1940 — Heroes of the Saddle
Drums of Fu Manchu

Royse, Frosty
1940 — Oklahoma Renegades

Rub, Christian[251]
1935 — Hitch Hike Lady
1936 — The Leathernecks Have Landed
1937 — It Could Happen to You
1939 — Forged Passport

Rubini, Jan
1952 — Bal Tabarin

Ruby, Mike
1949 — Alias the Champ

Ruby, Wade
1956 — Come Next Spring

Ruetting, Barbara
1958 — International Counterfeiters

Ruggles, Wesley
1941 — Stars Past and Present*

Ruhl, William[251]
1937 — Navy Blues*
1939 — Sabotage*
1940 — Gaucho Serenade
Oklahoma Renegades
Texas Terrors
1941 — Gauchos of Eldorado
1943 — Days of Old Cheyenne
1950 — Unmasked*
Code of the Silver Sage
California Passage*
1951 — Pals of the Golden West*

Ruick, Mel
1936 — The President's Mystery
1937 — Navy Blues

Ruiz, Albert[124]
1947 — Hit Parade of 1947

Rule, Janice[108]
1956 — A Woman's Devotion

Ruman, Sig[172]
1937 — The Bold Caballero
1942 — Remember Pearl Harbor!
1955 — Carolina Cannonball

Rumistrzewicz, Krystyna
1955 — The Divided Heart

Rush, Dick
1938 — Santa Fe Stampede

Ruskin, Shimen
1941 — Lady from Louisiana

Russell, Elizabeth
1943 — A Scream in the Dark

Russell, Gail[124]
1947 — Angel and the Badman
1948 — Moonrise
1949 — Wake of the Red Witch
1958 — No Place to Land

Russell, Harriet
1935 — The Crime of Doctor Crespi

Russell, Jane
1941 — Stars Past and Present*

Russell, John[85]
1951 — Fighting Coast Guard
1952 — Oklahoma Annie
Hoodlum Empire
1953 — Fair Wind to Java
The Sun Shines Bright
1954 — Jubilee Trail
Hell's Outpost
1955 — The Last Command

Russell, Johnny[244]
1937 — The Duke Comes Back
1939 — Sabotage

Russell, Mary[54]
1936 — The Big Show
The Mandarin Mystery
Roarin' Lead
Beware of Ladies*
1937 — The Riders of the Whistling Skull

Russell, Rosalind
1940 — Chinese Garden Festival*

Russell, William
1956 — Above Us the Waves

Rutherford, Ann[54]
1935 — Melody Trail
1936 — The Singing Vagabond
Oregon Trail
The Lawless Nineties
Comin' 'Round the Mountain
The Harvester
The Lonely Trail
Down to the Sea
1937 — Public Cowboy No. 1
1941 — Variety Reel*
1946 — The Madonna's Secret
Murder in the Music Hall

Rutherford, Jack
1936 — Oregon Trail
1945 — Utah

Rutherford, Margaret
1955 — Trouble in Store

Rutherford, Tom
1938 — A Desperate Adventure
1940 — Chinese Garden Festival*

Ruysdael, Basil
1954 — The Shanghai Story

Ryan, Irene[251]
1943 — O, My Darling Clementine
1952 — The Wac from Walla Walla

Gene Autry, Polly Rowles

William Ruhl

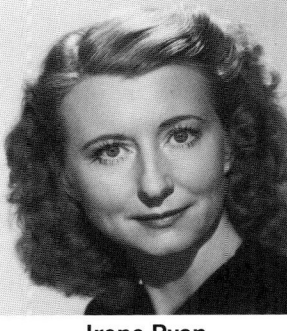
Irene Ryan

Ryan, Peggy
1939 — She Married a Cop

Ryan, Sheila[124]
1941 — Wampas Baby Stars*
1942 — Pardon My Stripes
1943 — Song of Texas
1949 — Hideout
1958 — Street of Darkness

Ryan, Tim
1941 — A Man Betrayed
Sis Hopkins*
Angels with Broken Wings*
Hurricane Smith*
Citadel of Crime*
Ice-Capades
Public Enemies
The Devil Pays Off*
1942 — Pardon My Stripes*
A Tragedy at Midnight*
Yokel Boy*
1943 — Hit Parade of 1943
1945 — Swingin' on a Rainbow
1951 — Cuban Fireball

Ryan, Tommy[55]
1938 — Tenth Avenue Kid
Prairie Moon
Orphans of the Street
1939 — My Wife's Relatives
Street of Missing Men
Mickey, the Kid
Should Husbands Work?
The Covered Trailer
Money to Burn
1940 — Grandpa Goes to Town
Earl of Puddlestone
1946 — That Brennan Girl*
1947 — Son of Zorro*
Calendar Girl*
The Magnificent Rogue*
Hit Parade of 1947*

Ryder, Red — series
[Elliott-Blake-Fleming]
1944 — Tucson Raiders
Marshal of Reno
The San Antonio Kid
Cheyenne Wildcat
Vigilantes of Dodge City
Sheriff of Las Vegas
1945 — Great Stagecoach Robbery
Lone Texas Ranger
Phantom of the Plains
Marshal of Laredo
Colorado Pioneers
Wagon Wheels Westward
1946 — California Gold Rush
Sheriff of Redwood Valley
Sun Valley Cyclone
Conquest of Cheyenne
[Lane-Blake-Wentworth]
Santa Fe Uprising
Stagecoach to Denver
1947 — Vigilantes of Boomtown
Homesteaders of Paradise Valley
Oregon Trail Scouts
Rustlers of Devil's Canyon
Marshal of Cripple Creek

Sabu[108]
1956 — Jaguar

Sachs, Leonard
1957 — Thunder Over Tangier

Saenz, Bob
1940 — Dark Command*
1941 — A Man Betrayed*
Lady from Louisiana
Angels with Broken Wings*
1942 — Lady for a Night*
In Old California*

Sagebrush Serenaders
1945 — Man from Rainbow Valley

Sais, Marin[251]
1933 — I Stand Accused*
Santa Fe Stampede*
1940 — One Man's Law*
Bowery Boy*
1941 — Two Gun Sheriff
The Gay Vagabond*
Saddlemates
Sierra Sue*
1942 — A Tragedy at Midnight*
South of Santa Fe*
1945 — Bells of Rosarita*
Love, Honor and Goodbye*
Girls of the Big House*
Along the Navajo Trail*
1945 — King of the Forest Rangers*
Stagecoach to Denver*

Sale, Charles "Chic"
1935 — The Gentleman from Louisiana

Sale, Richard
1946 — Rendezvous with Annie

Sale, Virginia[251]
1937 — Dangerous Holiday
1939 — Should Husbands Work?*
1941 — Arkansas Judge
The Great Train Robbery*

Salew, John
1943 — At Dawn We Die
The Saint Meets the Tiger

Sally
1958 — Hell Ship Mutiny

Samuels, Maurice
1951 — Insurance Investigator

Marin Sais

Virginia Sale

Walter Sande

Sande, Walter[252]
1938 – Arson Gang Busters
 Ladies in Distress
 Gold Mine in the Sky*
 Army Girl*
 Tenth Avenue Kid
1939 – The Mysterious Miss X*
1943 – The Purple V
1956 – The Maverick Queen

Sanders, George
1958 – Outcasts of the City

Sanders, Hugh
1954 – The Untamed Heiress
1955 – I Cover the Underworld
 The Last Command

Sanders, Sandy
1950 – Desperadoes of the West
 Flying Disc Man from Mars
1951 – Don Daredevil Rides Again
1953 – Robot Monster from Mars

Sands, Johnny[124]
1946 – Affairs of Geraldine
1947 – The Fabulous Texan

Sanford, Erskine[252]
1945 – Girls of the Big House
1949 – Wake of the Red Witch
1950 – Macbeth

Sanford, Ralph[252]
1937 – Sea Racketeers
 Escape by Night*
1939 – Jeepers Creepers*
1940 – In Old Missouri*
 Gaucho Serenade*
 Carolina Moon
1941 – Arkansas Judge*
 Mr. District Attorney*
 Country Fair*
1942 – The Old Homestead*
1946 – My Pal Trigger
 Sioux City Sue
 That Brennan Girl*
1947 – Hit Parade of 1947
 Web of Danger
1951 – Missing Women*
 Fighting Coast Guard*
1955 – The Road to Denver*
1957 – Beginning of the End*

Sarfati, Maurice
1959 – O.S.S. 117 is Not Dead

Sarie and Sally
1939 – In Old Monterey

Saris, Marilyn[193]
1957 – The Lawless Eighties

Sarracino, Ernest[252]
1939 – South of the Border*
 Zorro's Fighting Legion*
1940 – Drums of Fu Manchu*
 Adventures of Red Ryder*
 Mysterious Doctor Satan*
1941 – Adventures of Captain Marvel
 Under Fiesta Stars*
 Outlaws of Cherokee Trail*
 King of the Texas Rangers*

Sassoli, Dina
1952 – The Flying Squadron

Saunders, Nikki
1945 – Earl Carroll Vanities*

Savage, Ann[252]
1946 – The Last Crooked Mile
1953 – Woman They Almost Lynched

Savage, Archie
1955 – Panther Girl of the Kongo

Savage, Babs
1941 – Ice-Capades*
1942 – Ice-Capades Revue

Savage, Carol
1946 – G.I. War Brides

Savitt, Jan—and Top Hatters
1947 – That's My Gal

Sawyer, Joseph[252]
1936 – The Leathernecks Have Landed
1937 – Navy Blues
1939 – Sabotage
1940 – Dark Command
 Melody Ranch
 The Border Legion
1941 – Down Mexico Way
1943 – Sleepy Lagoon
1946 – G.I. War Brides
1951 – Pride of Maryland

Sayles, Francis
1938 – The Purple Vigilantes
1941 – Rags to Riches

Saylor, Syd[85]
1936 – The Three Mesquiteers
1937 – Guns in the Dark
 Meet the Boy Friend
 Sea Racketeers
 The Wrong Road
 Exiled to Shanghai
1941 – Wyoming Wildcat
 Nevada City*
 Sunset in Wyoming*
 Sierra Sue*
1943 – Nobody's Darling*
1945 – Bells of Rosarita*

Scannell, Frank[252]
1945 – Utah*
 Behind City Lights
 Love, Honor and Goodbye*
 An Angel Comes to Brooklyn
1947 – Hit Parade of 1947
 That's My Man*
1949 – Alias the Champ
1951 – The Sea Hornet*

Scar, Sam
1952 – Hoodlum Empire*
1955 – The Fighting Chance

Scardon, Paul
1941 – Lady from Louisiana
1943 – The Man from the Rio Grande

Schallert, William
1950 – Lonely Heart Bandits
1951 – Belle LeGrand*
1952 – Hoodlum Empire*
1953 – Enemies of the Universe
 Atomic Peril
 Cosmic Vengeance
1954 – Tobor the Great*
1958 – Juvenile Jungle*

Scheerer, Bob
1945 – An Angel Comes to Brooklyn

Schild, Marlyn
1942 – Youth on Parade

Schildkraut, Joseph[85]
1938 – Lady, Behave!
1945 – Flame of Barbary Coast
 The Cheaters
1946 – Plainsman and the Lady
1947 – Northwest Outpost
1948 – Old Los Angeles
 The Gallant Legion

Schiller, Fanny
1956 – A Woman's Devotion

Schiller, Norbert
1958 – Outcasts of the City

Schilling, Gus[55]
1941 – Ice-Capades
1943 – Chatterbox
1947 – Calendar Girl
1948 – Angel on the Amazon
1950 – Hit Parade of 1951
 Macbeth
1951 – Honeychile

Schlesinger, John
1955 – The Divided Heart

Schofield, Johnnie
1948 – Code of Scotland Yard

Schomberg, Hermann
1956 – Circus Girl

Schonauer, Marianne
1955 – In Old Vienna

Schonbock, Karl
1957 – The Congress Dances

Schopp, Herman
1950 – Jungle Stampede

Schrier, Capt. Harold G.
1950 – Sands of Iwo Jima

Schumann, Eric
1956 – Magic Fire

Schumm, Hans
1940 – Women in War*
1942 – Spy Smasher

Schunzel, Reinhold
1946 – Plainsman and the Lady

Schuster, Hugo
1955 – Secret Venture

Scott, Dick
1945 – Identity Unknown
1946 – Strange Impersonation
 The Glass Alibi

Scott, Dorothy
1947 – The Pretender

Scott, Hampton J.
1947 – That's My Man

Scott, Jacques
1957 – Journey to Freedom

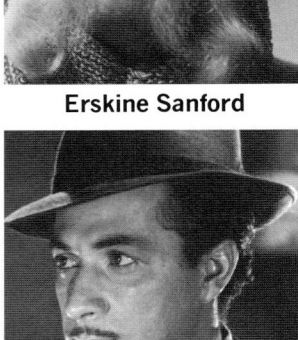

Erskine Sanford

Ralph Sanford

Ernest Sarracino

Ann Savage

Scott, John
1957 – Operation Conspiracy

Scott, Lizabeth[108]
1957 – The Weapon

Scott, Martha[109]
1941 – Variety Reel*
1943 – In Old Oklahoma
1957 – Eighteen and Anxious

Scott, Morton
1942 – Moonlight Masquerade*

Scott, Randolph
1941 – Stars at Play*

Scott, Robert[252]
1947 – Exposed

Scott, Zachary[109]
1955 – Flame of the Islands

Scotti, Vito
1952 – The Fabulous Senorita

Seabrook, Gay[252]
1938 – The Higgins Family

Searl, Jackie
1937 – Two Wise Maids

Sears, Allan
1936 – The Singing Vagabond

Seay, James[182]
1940 – Oklahoma Renegades
1942 – Man from Cheyenne
 Home in Wyomin'
 Ridin' Down the Canyon
1948 – Slippy McGee
1954 – Sea of Lost Ships*
1957 – Beginning of the End
1958 – Street of Darkness

Sebastian, Dorothy
1939 – Rough Riders' Round-Up
 The Arizona Kid
1941 – Kansas Cyclone

Sedan, Rolfe[252]
1935 – $1000 a Minute*
1937 – Bill Cracks Down*
 Rhythm in the Clouds*
1938 – A Desperate Adventure
1939 – She Married a Cop*
1941 – Angels with Broken Wings*

Seddon, Margaret
1935 – Two Sinners
1940 – Friendly Neighbors
1950 – House by the River

Joseph Sawyer

Frank Scannell

Robert Scott

Gay Seabrook

Rolfe Sedan

Tom Seidel

Maxine Semon

Massimo Serato

Dan Seymour

Harry Shannon

Seese, Dorothy Ann
1940 — Meet the Missus

Seidel, Tom[252]
1938 — Dick Tracy Returns
1942 — A Tragedy at Midnight*
Sunset on the Desert*
Westward Ho
Flying Tigers*
1943 — G-Men Vs. The Black Dragon*
Tahiti Honey
Someone to Remember

Seidner, Irene
1943 — The Purple V

Self, William
1947 — Marshal of Cripple Creek
1950 — Sands of Iwo Jima

Selk, George
1954 — Trader Tom of the China Seas

Semon, Maxine[252]
1945 — A Sporting Chance
1948 — Campus Honeymoon

Sennett, Mack
1941 — Stars Past and Present*

Sen Yung, Victor[170]
1946 — G. I. War Brides*
1947 — Web of Danger
The Flame
1951 — Secrets of Monte Carlo*
1954 — Trader Tom of the China Seas
Jubilee Trail*
The Shanghai Story
1956 — Accused of Murder*

Sepulveda, Carl
1943 — Bordertown Gun Fighters
1944 — Stagecoach to Monterey

Serato, Massimo[252]
1951 — Fugitive Lady
1952 — The Flying Squadron

Serberoli, Alex
1951 — Fugitive Lady

Sessions, Almira
1945 — Woman Who Came Back
1950 — Tarnished*
The Old Frontier
1951 — Oh! Susanna*
1952 — Oklahoma Annie
1953 — The Sun Shines Bright*
Sweethearts on Parade*
1954 — Hell's Outpost*

Seton, Bruce
1957 — The Fighting Wildcats
1958 — Strange Case of Dr. Manning
1959 — Hidden Homicide

Severn, Jr., Clifford
1940 — Gaucho Serenade

Sevony, John L. C.
See Frank Fontaine.

Seymour, Al
Many films.
1936 — Undersea Kingdom*
1940 — Mysterious Doctor Satan*
1941 — Dick Tracy Vs. Crime, Inc.*
1942 — Spy Smasher*

Seymour, Dan[253]
1943 — Tahiti Honey
1955 — I Cover the Underworld*

Shackelford, Floyd
1936 — The Lonely Trail

Shadow — film
1958 — Invisible Avenger

Shannon, Frank
1937 — Affairs of Cappy Ricks

Shannon, Harry[253]
1942 — Affairs of Jimmy Valentine*
In Old California
1943 — Idaho
Song of Texas
Someone to Remember
Headin' for God's Country
In Old Oklahoma*
1944 — The Yellow Rose of Texas
1946 — The Last Crooked Mile
1947 — Exposed
1950 — Singing Guns
Tarnished
1951 — Pride of Maryland
1954 — Phantom Stallion
1955 — The Road to Denver*
1956 — Come Next Spring
1957 — Duel at Apache Wells
Hell's Crossroads
1958 — Man or Gun

Shannon, Peggy[253]
1937 — Youth on Parole

Sharbutt, Del
1947 — Hit Parade of 1947

Sharpe, David[253]
1937 — Doomed at Sundown
1938 — Riders of the Black Hills*
Dick Tracy Returns
Shine on Harvest Moon*
1939 — The Lone Ranger Rides Again*
The Night Riders*
Street of Missing Men*
Three Texas Steers
Daredevils of the Red Circle
Wyoming Outlaw
The Kansas Terrors*
Rovin' Tumbleweeds*
Cowboys from Texas*
1940 — Drums of Fu Manchu*
Covered Wagon Days*
Adventures of Red Ryder*
King of the Royal Mounted*
Mysterious Doctor Satan*
1941 — Adventures of Captain Marvel*
Country Fair*
Jungle Girl*
Gangs of Sonora*
King of the Texas Rangers*
Dick Tracy Vs. Crime, Inc.*
1942 — Raiders of the Range*
Spy Smasher*
The Phantom Plainsmen*
Perils of Nyoka*
King of the Mounties*
1946 — Crime of the Century*
King of the Forest Rangers*
The Last Crooked Mile*
1947 — Homesteaders of Paradise Valley*
Bells of San Angelo
The Trespasser*
Marshal of Cripple Creek*
1948 — The Gay Ranchero*
G-Men Never Forget*
California Firebrand*
Dangers of the Canadian Mounted*
Under California Stars*
Train to Alcatraz*
Grand Canyon Trail*
Adv. of Frank and Jesse James*
The Far Frontier*
1949 — Federal Agents Vs. Underworld, Inc.*
Susanna Pass
King of the Rocket Men
The James Brothers of Missouri*
The Fighting Kentuckian*
Radar Patrol Vs. Spy King*
1950 — The Invisible Monster*
Lonely Heart Bandits*
Flying Disc Man from Mars*
Trail of Robin Hood*
1951 — Don Daredevil Rides Again*
Govt. Agents Vs. Phantom Legion*
Honeychile*
The Wild Blue Yonder*
1952 — Oklahoma Annie*
1953 — Can. Mounties Vs. Atomic Invaders*
1956 — Dakota Incident*

Sharpe, Lester[253]
1938 — Riders of the Black Hills*
1942 — Pardon My Stripes*
1943 — The Purple V*
1944 — Storm Over Lisbon*
1948 — The Gallant Legion*
1950 — Unmasked

Shaw, Betty[253]
1945 — Dakota*
1946 — A Guy Could Change
Crime of the Century

Shaw, C. Montague[253]
1935 — Two Sinners
1936 — The Leathernecks Have Landed*
Undersea Kingdom
1937 — The Riders of the Whistling Skull
The Sheik Steps Out
1938 — I Stand Accused*
1939 — Daredevils of the Red Circle
Zorro's Fighting Legion
1940 — Mysterious Doctor Satan
1941 — Puddin' Head*
Dick Tracy Vs. Crime, Inc.*
1943 — G-Men Vs. The Black Dragon
1944 — Faces in the Fog*
1945 — An Angel Comes to Brooklyn

Shaw, Denis
1957 — The Weapon

Shaw, Hazel[253]
1951 — Arizona Manhunt

Shaw, Janet[253]
1943 — False Faces

Shaw, Richard
1957 — Thunder Over Tangier
The Fighting Wildcats

Shaw, Susan
1957 — Time is My Enemy

Shay, Mildred
1940 — In Old Missouri
Ride, Tenderfoot, Ride

Shayne, Konstantin
1948 — Angel on the Amazon

Shayne, Robert[253]
1948 — The Inside Story
1951 — Missing Women
The Dakota Kid
1953 — Marshal of Cedar Rock
The Lady Wants Mink*
1954 — Trader Tom of the China Seas
Sea of Lost Ships*
Flight Nurse*
Tobor the Great*
1955 — The Eternal Sea*
Double Jeopardy*
King of the Carnival
1956 — Accused of Murder*

Shayne, Tamara[253]
1947 — Northwest Outpost

Shdanoff, George
1946 — Specter of the Rose

Shea, Jack
1951 — Million Dollar Pursuit
1952 — Zombies of the Stratosphere

Shean, Al
1937 — It Could Happen to You
1940 — Friendly Neighbors
1944 — Atlantic City

Sheehan, John[253]
1936 — Laughing Irish Eyes
1937 — Join the Marines
All Over Town
1938 — Mama Runs Wild
1941 — Mr. District Atty. in the Carter Case

Sheldon, Kathryn
1937 — Circus Girl

Shelton, Marla
1942 — Bells of Capistrano
Secrets of the Underground

Shepard, Elaine
1936 — The Singing Vagabond*
Darkest Africa

Shepard, Miles
1957 — Journey to Freedom

Shepley, Michael
1956 — Doctor at Sea

Sheridan, Ann[109]
1956 — Come Next Spring

Sheridan, Daniel M.[253]
1948 — California Firebrand

Sheridan, Frank
1935 — The Spanish Cape Mystery
1936 — The Leavenworth Case
Country Gentlemen

Peggy Shannon

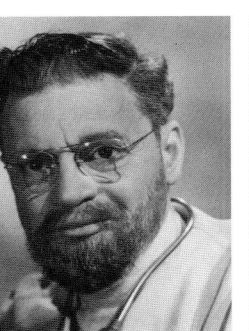

Lester Sharpe

Betty Shaw

C. Montague Shaw

Hazel Shaw

Janet Shaw

Robert Shayne

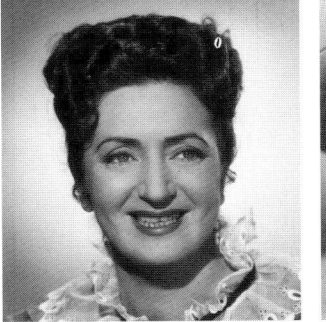

Tamara Shayne

John Sheehan

Daniel M. Sheridan

Sheridan, Tommy
1949—The Red Pony

Sherman, Annyse
1944—Storm Over Lisbon*
1945—Earl Carroll Vanities*

Sherman, Fred
1942—Shepherd of the Ozarks
Hi, Neighbor

Sherman, Ransom[254]
1943—Swing Your Partner
1947—Yankee Fakir
1949—Flaming Fury

Sherwood, George
1938—Overland Stage Raiders
1941—Wyoming Wildcat
1945—Man from Oklahoma
1946—Conquest of Cheyenne
1950—Flying Disc Man from Mars

Shield, Robert
1954—Hell's Half Acre

Shields, Arthur
1952—The Quiet Man

Shields, Frank[124]
1937—Affairs of Cappy Ricks

Shiner, Ronald
1954—Laughing Anne

Shirley, Anne[109]
1944—Man from Frisco

Shirley, Bill[55]
1941—Rookies on Parade
Ice-Capades*
Doctors Don't Tell
Sailors on Leave
Mercy Island*
1942—Lady for a Night*
A Tragedy at Midnight*
In Old California*
Hi, Neighbor
Flying Tigers
Ice-Capades Revue
1944—Three Little Sisters
1952—I Dream of Jeanie
1953—A Perilous Journey*
Sweethearts on Parade
1954—Sea of Lost Ships*

Shoemaker, Ann
1944—Man from Frisco
1950—House by the River

Short, Antrim
1936—The Big Show

Shoup, Col. D. M.
1950—Sands of Iwo Jima

Shrum, Cal—Gang
1940—Scatterbrain

Shrum, Walter—and his Colorado Hillbillies
1938—The Old Barn Dance
1939—Blue Montana Skies

Shumway, Lee[254]
1935—Frisco Waterfront
1936—Go-Get-'Em, Haines
1941—Prairie Pioneers
Two Gun Sheriff
1942—Arizona Terrors
Jesse James, Jr.
1943—Dead Man's Gulch
1945—Oregon Trail
1946—Roll on Texas Moon

Sigaloff, Eugene
1949—Rose of the Yukon

Silvani, Aldo
1951—Stormbound

Silver Chief
1938—The Lone Ranger
1939—The Lone Ranger Rides Again

Silverheels, Jay
[as Harry Smith]
1941—Jungle Girl*
1942—Perils of Nyoka*
1943—Daredevils of the West*
1944—The Tiger Woman*
Haunted Harbor*
[as Jay Silverheels]
1947—Northwest Outpost*
1951—The Wild Blue Yonder*
1955—The Vanishing American

Silvers, Phil[125]
1940—Hit Parade of 1941
1941—Ice-Capades

Silvestre, Armando
1952—Thunderbirds

Sima, Oskar
1957—The Congress Dances

Simmons, Georgia
1937—Heart of the Rockies
1938—Romance on the Run

Simmons, Richard[254]
1940—King of the Royal Mounted*
1941—King of the Texas Rangers*
1952—I Dream of Jeanie
Thunderbirds
1953—Woman They Almost Lynched
1954—Flight Nurse
Man with the Steel Whip

Simmons, Sada
1937—It Could Happen to You*
1942—Affairs of Jimmy Valentine*

Simms, Eddie Lou
1947—Vigilantes of Boomtown

Simon, Simone[254]
1943—Tahiti Honey

Simon, Bob
1954—Roogie's Bump

Simon, Jr., William H.
1948—Campus Honeymoon

Simp Phonies, The
1941—Country Fair

Simpson, Ivan
1938—Invisible Enemy
1942—Youth on Parade

Simpson, Mickey
1949—The Fighting Kentuckian
1950—Surrender
1952—Leadville Gunslinger

Simpson, Napoleon
1949—The Red Menace

Simpson, Russell[254]
1936—The Harvester
1937—Yodelin' Kid from Pine Ridge
1940—Three Faces West
1941—Citadel of Crime
1944—Man from Frisco
The Big Bonanza
1946—California Gold Rush
1947—The Fabulous Texan
1948—Sundown in Santa Fe
1953—The Sun Shines Bright
1955—The Last Command

Sims, Joan
1955—Trouble in Store
The Square Ring
Doctor in the House
1956—Doctor at Sea

Sinclair, Eric[254]
1944—Faces in the Fog
1950—Lonely Heart Bandits

Martha Sleeper

Elizabeth Slifer

Gerald Oliver Smith

John Smith

Sinclair, Hugh
1943—At Dawn We Die
Alibi
The Saint Meets the Tiger

Sinclair, Peter
1954—Trouble in the Glen
1955—Cross Channel

Sinden, Donald
1955—Doctor in the House
A Day to Remember
1956—Above Us the Waves

Singing Riders, The
1935—Westward Ho

Singleton, Doris[254]
1956—Terror at Midnight*
1957—Affair in Reno

Singleton, Penny[254]
[as Dorothy McNulty]
1937—Sea Racketeers
[As Penny Singleton]
1938—Outside of Paradise

Singuineau, Frank
1957—Thunder Over Tangier

Sitka, Emil
1951—The Sea Hornet

Six Hits and a Miss
1940—Hit Parade of 1941

Skippy
1937—Sea Racketeers

Skipworth, Alison[55]
1935—Hitch Hike Lady
1937—Two Wise Maids
1938—King of the Newsboys
Ladies in Distress

Slater, Barbara
1942—Youth on Parade*
1944—Atlantic City*

Slater, John
1943—The Saint Meets the Tiger

Slaughter, Anna May
1950—The Mardi Gras*

Slavin, Slick
1957—Eighteen and Anxious

Sleeper, Martha[254]
1935—Two Sinners

Slifer, Elizabeth[254]
1952—The Fabulous Senorita*
Gobs and Gals*
The Wac from Walla Walla
1953—The Sun Shines Bright*
1954—Hell's Outpost*
1956—The Man is Armed*

Sloane, Michael
1945—Rough Riders of Cheyenne
1946—Days of Buffalo Bill

Sloane, Olive
1957—The Man in the Road

Slocum, Cy
Many films.
1939—Daredevils of the Red Circle*
Dick Tracy's G-Men*
1940—King of the Royal Mounted*
Mysterious Doctor Satan*
1941—King of the Texas Rangers*
1942—Spy Smasher*
Perils of Nyoka*

Slye, Leonard
See Roy Rogers.

Smith, Adele
1941—Sis Hopkins*
Country Fair*
1942—Code of the Outlaw*

Smith, Alexis[109]
1955—The Eternal Sea

Smith, Art
1948—Angel in Exile

Smith, Charles[125]
1940—Scatterbrain*
Behind the News*
1942—Youth on Parade
1944—San Fernando Valley
1948—Campus Honeymoon

Smith, Drake
1952—Wild Horse Ambush

Smith, Ernie
1936—Undersea Kingdom

Smith, Gerald Oliver[254]
1938—Invisible Enemy
1941—The Singing Hill
Puddin' Head
1946—Rainbow Over Texas
1950—Belle of Old Mexico*

Smith, Hal
1957—Eighteen and Anxious

Smith, Harry
See Jay Silverheels.

Smith, Jack C.
1937—A Lawman is Born
1938—Paroled—to Die
The Feud Maker

Smith, John[254]
1957—The Lawless Eighties
The Crooked Circle

Smith, Paul
1956—A Strange Adventure

Smith, Queenie
1950—Prisoners in Petticoats
1951—Belle LeGrand*

Smith, Robert
1937—Hit the Saddle

Ransom Sherman

Lee Shumway

Richard Simmons

Simone Simon

Russell Simpson

Eric Sinclair

Doris Singleton

Penny Singleton

254

Snowflake

Walter Soderling

Kristina Soederbaum

Hugh Sothern

Olan Soule

Arthur Space

Fay Spain

Smith, Roberta
1943 — Nobody's Darling

Smith, Sir C. Aubrey[109]
1944 — Secrets of Scotland Yard
1945 — Scotland Yard Investigator
1946 — Rendezvous with Annie

Snowflake[255]
[Fred Toones]
1936 — The Lawless Nineties
　　　The Singing Cowboy*
　　　The Lonely Trail
　　　Oh, Susanna!
　　　Bulldog Edition*
1937 — Gunsmoke Ranch*
　　　Yodelin' Kid from Pine Ridge
　　　Range Defenders
　　　Youth on Parole*
　　　The Duke Comes Back
　　　Wild Horse Rodeo
1938 — Riders of the Black Hills
　　　Gold Mine in the Sky*
　　　Hawk of the Wilderness
　　　Red River Range*
1939 — Mexicali Rose*
　　　Daredevils of the Red Circle
　　　Rovin' Tumbleweeds*
　　　Days of Jesse James*
1940 — Gaucho Serenade*
　　　One Man's Law
　　　The Tulsa Kid
　　　Ride, Tenderfoot, Ride*
　　　Frontier Vengeance
　　　Texas Terrors
1941 — Ridin' on a Rainbow*
　　　Back in the Saddle*
　　　Two Gun Sheriff
　　　The Gay Vagabond*
　　　The Apache Kid
　　　Death Valley Outlaws
　　　A Missouri Outlaw
1942 — Arizona Terrors*
1944 — Hidden Valley Outlaws
　　　The Yellow Rose of Texas*
　　　Firebrands of Arizona*
1946 — G.I. War Brides*
1947 — Bells of San Angelo

Socher, Hylton
1957 — Beginning of the End

Sochor, Judy[176]
1950 — Sands of Iwo Jima*
　　　House by the River*
　　　Hit Parade of 1951*

Soderling, Walter[255]
1943 — The Blocked Trail
1944 — Outlaws of Santa Fe
1946 — The Glass Alibi
　　　King of the Forest Rangers
　　　The French Key
1947 — Yankee Fakir

Soederbaum, Kristina[255]
1956 — The Circus Girl

Sokou, Ekali
1956 — Doctor at Sea

Soldani, Charles
1945 — Man from Oklahoma
1949 — Daughter of the Jungle

Somers, Esther
1950 — Tarnished

Sons of the Pioneers[85]
1936 — The Big Show
　　　The Old Corral
1941 — Red River Valley
1942 — Man from Cheyenne
　　　South of Santa Fe
　　　Sunset on the Desert
　　　Romance on the Range
　　　Sons of the Pioneers
　　　Call of the Canyon
　　　Sunset Serenade
　　　Heart of the Golden West
　　　Ridin' Down the Canyon
1943 — Idaho
　　　King of the Cowboys
　　　Song of Texas
　　　Silver Spurs
　　　Man from Music Mountain
　　　Hands Across the Border
1944 — Cowboy and the Senorita
　　　The Yellow Rose of Texas
　　　Song of Nevada
　　　San Fernando Valley
　　　Lights of Old Santa Fe
1945 — Utah
　　　Bells of Rosarita
　　　Man from Oklahoma
　　　Sunset in El Dorado
　　　Don't Fence Me In
　　　Along the Navajo Trail
1946 — Song of Arizona
　　　Home on the Range
　　　Rainbow Over Texas
　　　My Pal Trigger
　　　Under Nevada Skies
　　　Roll on Texas Moon
　　　Home in Oklahoma
　　　Heldorado
1947 — Apache Rose
　　　Hit Parade of 1947
　　　Bells of San Angelo
　　　Springtime in the Sierras
　　　On the Old Spanish Trail
1948 — The Gay Ranchero
　　　Under California Stars
　　　Eyes of Texas
　　　Night Time in Nevada
1950 — Rio Grande
1951 — Fighting Coast Guard

Soo Hoo, Hayward
1944 — The Big Bonanza

Sorel, George
1937 — The Sheik Steps Out
1947 — Northwest Outpost

Sorel, Jacqueline
1957 — Eighteen and Anxious

Sothern, Hugh[255]
1938 — The Fighting Devil Dogs
1940 — Young Buffalo Bill
1943 — King of the Cowboys*
1944 — Captain America

Soule, Olan[255]
1950 — Destination Big House
1951 — Cuban Fireball*
1958 — The Notorious Mr. Monks*

Space, Arthur[255]
1946 — The Mysterious Mr. Valentine
　　　Home in Oklahoma
　　　That Brennan Girl*
1947 — Rustlers of Devil's Canyon
1950 — The Vanishing Westerner
1951 — Night Riders of Montana
　　　Govt. Agents Vs. Phantom Legion
　　　Utah Wagon Train
1953 — Can. Mounties Vs. Atomic Invaders
1955 — Panther Girl of the Kongo
　　　The Eternal Sea*
　　　A Man Alone

Spadaro, Umberto
1952 — The Flying Squadron

Spain, Fay[255]
1957 — The Crooked Circle

Spalding, Kim
1955 — A Man Alone

Sparks, Jack[255]
1945 — Colorado Pioneers*
　　　Wagon Wheels Westward*
1946 — Sun Valley Cyclone*
　　　The El Paso Kid*
　　　Conquest of Cheyenne*
　　　Heldorado
1947 — Homesteaders of Paradise Valley*
　　　Oregon Trail Scouts*
　　　Marshal of Cripple Creek*
　　　The Wild Frontier*
1948 — The Gallant Legion*
1949 — The Golden Stallion
1950 — The Showdown
1953 — San Antone*

Speaker, Tris
1949 — The Kid from Cleveland

Spellman, Martin
1938 — Santa Fe Stampede

Spence, Sandra[255]
1951 — Fighting Coast Guard

Spencer, Douglas
1955 — A Man Alone

Spencer, Johnny
1953 — Jungle Drums of Africa

Spencer, Marion
1942 — Suicide Squadron

Spencer, Sarah
1952 — The Wac from Walla Walla

Sportsmen, The
1941 — Puddin' Head
1943 — Here Comes Elmer

Spottswood, James
1938 — Hollywood Stadium Mystery!

St. Angelo, Robert
1949 — Federal Agents Vs. Underworld, Inc.

St. Clair and Vilova
1947 — That's My Gal

St. John, Al "Fuzzy"[255]
1937 — A Lawman is Born
1938 — Call of the Yukon
1940 — Friendly Neighbors
　　　Texas Terrors
1941 — The Apache Kid
　　　A Missouri Outlaw
1942 — Arizona Terrors
　　　Stagecoach Express
　　　Jesse James, Jr.

St. Luke's Choristers
1945 — The Cheaters
　　　Mexicana
1946 — Out California Way

St. Polis, John
1940 — Rocky Mountain Rangers

Stack, Robert[109]
1941 — Variety Reel*
1951 — Bullfighter and the Lady

Stader, Paul
1950 — Surrender*
1952 — Zombies of the Stratosphere
1954 — Jubilee Trail*
　　　Hell's Outpost*
1955 — Timberjack*
1957 — Spoilers of the Forest

Staff, Ivan
1955 — The Square Ring

Stafford, Bess
1936 — The Leavenworth Case

Stafford Sisters
1938 — The Old Barn Dance
　　　Gold Mine in the Sky

Stahl, William
1939 — Dick Tracy's G-Men

Stamp-Taylor, Enid
1943 — Alibi

Stander, Lionel[255]
1940 — Hit Parade of 1941*
1943 — Tahiti Honey
1945 — The Big Show-Off
1946 — In Old Sacramento
　　　Specter of the Rose

Standing, Joan
1940 — Grand Ole Opry*
　　　Colorado*

Stanhope, Ted
1946 — The Glass Alibi

Stanley, Barbara
1950 — Harbor of Missing Men

Stanley, Edwin[137]
1936 — The Mandarin Mystery
1937 — Dick Tracy
1938 — Born to be Wild
　　　The Fighting Devil Dogs*
　　　Billy the Kid Returns
1939 — I Was a Convict
　　　Sabotage*
1940 — The Crooked Road*
　　　Mysterious Doctor Satan
　　　Behind the News*
1941 — Arkansas Judge
　　　A Man Betrayed
　　　Mr. District Attorney*
　　　Rookies on Parade*
　　　Mountain Moonlight
　　　Hurricane Smith*
　　　Citadel of Crime*
　　　Ice-Capades*
1942 — Pardon My Stripes
　　　Ice-Capades Revue*
1943 — O, My Darling Clementine
1944 — Jamboree
　　　Faces in the Fog*

Starley, Helene[255]
1949 — Bandit King of Texas

Jack Sparks

Sandra Spence

Al "Fuzzy" St. John

Lionel Stander

Helene Stanley

Louise Stanley

Stanley, Louise[256]
1936 — Lawless Land
1937 — Gun Lords of Stirrup Basin
1938 — Thunder in the Desert
　　　 Durango Valley Raiders

Stanton, Ernie
1941 — Desert Bandit

Stanton, Paul[256]
1937 — It Could Happen to You
　　　 Youth on Parole
　　　 Portia on Trial
1938 — Army Girl
1946 — Crime of the Century
1947 — That's My Gal

Stanton, Will
1936 — The Gentleman from Louisiana

Stanwyck, Barbara[109]
1956 — The Maverick Queen

Stapp, Marjorie
1956 — Scandal Incorporated

Stardusters, The
1944 — Trocadero

Paul Stanton

Henry Stephenson

Starling, Pat
1943 — Hit Parade of 1943*
　　　 Shantytown*
　　　 Chatterbox*
1944 — San Fernando Valley*

Starr, Jimmy
1940 — Scatterbrain
1946 — Out California Way

Stebbins, Bob
1944 — Faces in the Fog

Steele, Bob[85]
1936 — Cavalry
　　　 The Gun Ranger
　　　 Border Phantom
1937 — The Trusted Outlaw
　　　 "Lightnin'" Crandall
　　　 Gun Lords of Stirrup Basin
　　　 Doomed at Sundown
　　　 The Red Rope
　　　 The Arizona Gunfighter
　　　 Ridin' the Lone Trail
　　　 The Colorado Kid
1938 — Paroled — to Die
　　　 Thunder in the Desert
　　　 The Feud Maker
　　　 Desert Patrol
　　　 Durango Valley Raiders
1940 — The Carson City Kid
　　　 Under Texas Skies
　　　 The Trail Blazers
　　　 Lone Star Raiders
1941 — Prairie Pioneers
　　　 The Great Train Robbery
　　　 Pals of the Pecos
　　　 Saddlemates
　　　 Gangs of Sonora
　　　 Outlaws of Cherokee Trail
　　　 Gauchos of Eldorado
　　　 West of Cimarron
1942 — Code of the Outlaw
　　　 Raiders of the Range
　　　 Westward Ho
　　　 The Phantom Plainsmen
　　　 Shadows on the Sage
　　　 Valley of Hunted Men
1943 — Thundering Trails
　　　 The Blocked Trail
　　　 Santa Fe Scouts
　　　 Riders of the Rio Grande
1946 — Sheriff of Redwood Valley
　　　 Rio Grande Raiders
1947 — Twilight on the Rio Grande
　　　 Exposed
　　　 Bandits of Dark Canyon
1950 — The Savage Horde
1953 — San Antone
　　　 Savage Frontier
1954 — The Outcast
1955 — The Fighting Chance
1957 — Duel at Apache Wells

Steele, Freddie
1941 — The Pittsburgh Kid

Steele, William[184]
1950 — The Showdown

Tom Steele[55]

Many films.
1936 — Undersea Kingdom*
1937 — The Riders of the Whistling Skull*
　　　 Two Wise Maids*
　　　 Paradise Express*
　　　 Bill Cracks Down*
1938 — Call the Mesquiteers*
　　　 The Fighting Devil Dogs*
　　　 Dick Tracy Returns*
1939 — In Old Monterey*
　　　 Dick Tracy's G-Men*
1940 — Girl from Havana*
　　　 Under Texas Skies*
　　　 Mysterious Doctor Satan*
1941 — A Man Betrayed*
　　　 Country Fair*
　　　 Jungle Girl*
　　　 King of the Texas Rangers*
　　　 Public Enemies*
1942 — Raiders of the Range*
　　　 Spy Smasher*
　　　 Perils of Nyoka*
　　　 King of the Mounties*
　　　 Outlaws of Pine Ridge*
1943 — G-Men Vs. The Black Dragon*
　　　 Carson City Cyclone*
　　　 Daredevils of the West*
　　　 Secret Service in Darkest Africa*
　　　 Wagon Tracks West*
　　　 Beyond the Last Frontier*
　　　 The Masked Marvel*
　　　 Overland Mail Robbery*
　　　 Canyon City*
　　　 In Old Oklahoma*
　　　 California Joe*
1944 — Pride of the Plains*
　　　 Captain America*
　　　 Beneath Western Skies*
　　　 The Fighting Seabees*
　　　 Mojave Firebrand*
　　　 Hidden Valley Outlaws*
　　　 The Laramie Trail*
　　　 Outlaws of Santa Fe*
　　　 The Lady and the Monster*
　　　 Tucson Raiders
　　　 The Tiger Woman*
　　　 Marshal of Reno
　　　 Silver City Kid
　　　 Song of Nevada*
　　　 The San Antonio Kid*
　　　 Haunted Harbor
　　　 Stagecoach to Monterey*
　　　 Cheyenne Wildcat*
　　　 Code of the Prairie
　　　 End of the Road*
　　　 Firebrands of Arizona*
　　　 Zorro's Black Whip*
　　　 Sheriff of Las Vegas*

1945 — The Topeka Terror*
　　　 Great Stagecoach Robbery*
　　　 Manhunt of Mystery Island*
　　　 Utah*
　　　 Corpus Christi Bandits*
　　　 Lone Texas Ranger*
　　　 The Vampire's Ghost*
　　　 Federal Operator 99*
　　　 Trail of Kit Carson*
　　　 Oregon Trail*
　　　 The Purple Monster Strikes*
　　　 Don't Fence Me In*
　　　 The Cherokee Flash*
　　　 Wagon Wheels Westward*
1946 — The Phantom Rider*
　　　 Sheriff of Redwood Valley*
　　　 Alias Billy the Kid*
　　　 King of the Forest Rangers*
　　　 Sun Valley Cyclone*
　　　 One Exciting Week*
　　　 Daughter of Don Q
　　　 The Crimson Ghost
　　　 Santa Fe Uprising*
　　　 Out California Way*
　　　 Stagecoach to Denver*
1947 — Son of Zorro
　　　 Apache Rose*
　　　 Vigilantes of Boomtown*
　　　 Hit Parade of 1947*
　　　 Homesteaders of Paradise Valley*
　　　 Spoilers of the North*
　　　 Web of Danger*
　　　 Jesse James Rides Again
　　　 Marshal of Cripple Creek*
　　　 The Black Widow
　　　 Bandits of Dark Canyon*
1948 — G-Men Never Forget
　　　 Oklahoma Badlands*
　　　 The Bold Frontiersman*
　　　 Dangers of the Canadian Mounted
　　　 Carson City Raiders*
　　　 Marshal of Amarillo*
　　　 The Denver Kid
　　　 Adv. of Frank and Jesse James
　　　 Renegades of Sonora*
1949 — Federal Agents Vs. Underworld, Inc.
　　　 Ghost of Zorro
　　　 Frontier Investigator*
　　　 Outcasts of the Trail*
　　　 King of the Rocket Men
　　　 The Wyoming Bandit*
　　　 Bandit King of Texas*
　　　 The James Brothers of Missouri
　　　 Ranger of Cherokee Strip*
　　　 Radar Patrol Vs. Spy King
　　　 Powder River Rustlers*

1950 — Gunmen of Abilene*
　　　 Code of the Silver Sage*
　　　 Salt Lake Raiders*
　　　 The Invisible Monster
　　　 Trigger, Jr.*
　　　 The Old Frontier*
　　　 Desperadoes of the West*
　　　 Vigilante Hideout*
　　　 Lonely Heart Bandits*
　　　 Rustlers on Horseback*
　　　 Flying Disc Man from Mars
1951 — Rough Riders of Durango*
　　　 Night Riders of Montana*
　　　 Silver City Bonanza*
　　　 Don Daredevil Rides Again
　　　 Buckaroo Sheriff of Texas*
　　　 In Old Amarillo*
　　　 Wells Fargo Gunmaster*
　　　 Secrets of Monte Carlo*
　　　 Govt. Agents Vs. Phantom Legion*
　　　 Fort Dodge Stampede*
　　　 Desert of Lost Men*
1952 — Radar Men from the Moon*
　　　 Captive of Billy the Kid*
　　　 Leadville Gunslinger*
　　　 Black Hills Ambush*
　　　 Zombies of the Stratosphere*
　　　 Thundering Caravans*
　　　 Desperadoes' Outpost*
　　　 The Wac from Walla Walla*
　　　 South Pacific Trail*
1953 — Jungle Drums of Africa*
　　　 Marshal of Cedar Rock*
　　　 Old Overland Trail*
　　　 Enemies of the Universe*
　　　 Atomic Peril*
　　　 Cosmic Vengeance*
　　　 Savage Frontier*
　　　 City that Never Sleeps*
　　　 Destroyers of the Sun*
　　　 Can. Mounties Vs. Atomic Invaders
　　　 Captives of the Zero Hour*
　　　 Bandits of the West*
　　　 El Paso Stampede*
1954 — Trader Tom of the China Seas
　　　 Phantom Stallion*
　　　 Hell's Half Acre*
　　　 Man with the Steel Whip*
　　　 Hell's Outpost*
1955 — Panther Girl of the Kongo*
　　　 Santa Fe Passage*
　　　 King of the Carnival

Stein, Sammy
1942 — Remember Pearl Harbor!
1946 — The French Key

Stelita
See Stelita Peluffo.

Stepanek, Herbert
1955 — In Old Vienna

Stepanek, Karel
1943 — At Dawn We Die
1955 — Secret Venture
1957 — The Man in the Road
　　　 The Fighting Wildcats

Stephens, Marvin
1939 — Fighting Thoroughbreds

Stephenson, Henry[256]
1941 — Lady from Louisiana
1943 — The Mantrap
1944 — Secrets of Scotland Yard

Stephenson, James[125]
1940 — Wolf of New York

Sterling, Lynne
1936 — Happy Go Lucky*
1940 — Melody and Moonlight*
1941 — Mr. District Atty. in the Carter Case*
1943 — Hit Parade of 1943*
　　　 Nobody's Darling*
1944 — My Best Gal*
　　　 San Fernando Valley*
1945 — Mexicana*
1950 — Hit Parade of 1951*

Stevens, Bill
1945 — Federal Operator 99

Stevens, Charles[184]
1937 — The Bold Caballero
1939 — Man of Conquest*
1940 — Wagons Westward
　　　 Behind the News*
1945 — Bandits of the Badlands*
1950 — The Savage Horde
　　　 The Showdown
　　　 California Passage
1951 — Oh! Susanna
1953 — San Antone*
1954 — Jubilee Trail
　　　 Man with the Steel Whip*
1955 — The Last Command*
　　　 The Vanishing American
1956 — Jaguar*
1957 — Duel at Apache Wells*

Stevens, Connie
1957 — Eighteen and Anxious

Stevens, Dorothy[69]
1942 — Lady for a Night*
1944 — Lake Placid Serenade*
　　　 The Big Bonanza*
1945 — Great Stagecoach Robbery*
　　　 Utah*
　　　 Earl Carroll Vanities*
　　　 Bells of Rosarita*
　　　 Hitchhike to Happiness*
　　　 Man from Oklahoma*
　　　 Tell It to a Star*
　　　 Behind City Lights*
　　　 The Fatal Witness*
　　　 Love, Honor and Goodbye*
　　　 Sunset in El Dorado*
　　　 The Purple Monster Strikes*
　　　 Don't Fence Me In*
　　　 An Angel Comes to Brooklyn*
　　　 Mexicana*
　　　 Along the Navajo Trail*
　　　 Dakota*
　　　 Song of Mexico*
1946 — A Guy Could Change*
　　　 California Gold Rush*
　　　 Murder in the Music Hall*

Stevens, Jean[256]
1945 — Mexicana
1946 — That Brennan Girl

Stevens, Kathryn
1941 — Variety Reel*

Stevens, Landers[256]
1937 — Join the Marines
　　　 Bill Cracks Down
　　　 Navy Blues*
　　　 Meet the Boy Friend*
1938 — I Stand Accused*
1939 — Fighting Thoroughbreds*
　　　 My Wife's Relatives*
　　　 The Zero Hour
　　　 S.O.S. Tidal Wave*
1940 — Wolf of New York*

Stevens, Martin
1955 — The Divided Heart

Jean Stevens

Landers Stevens

Onslow Stevens

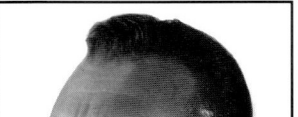

Warren Stevens

Anna Marie Stewart

Eleanor Stewart

Carl Stockdale

George E. Stone

Robert Strange

Milburn Stone

Clarence Straight

Harry Strang

Robert Strong

Glenn Strange

Gloria Stuart

Stevens, Onslow[256]
1935 — Forced Landing
1940 — Who Killed Aunt Maggie?
1942 — Sunset Serenade
1943 — Idaho
Hands Across the Border

Stevens, Ruthelma
1950 — Trial Without Jury

Stevens, Warren[256]
1956 — Accused of Murder
1958 — Man or Gun

Stevenson, Bob
1952 — Radar Men from the Moon

Stevenson, Houseley
1945 — Dakota*
1946 — Rendezvous with Annie*
1948 — Moonrise
1952 — Oklahoma Annie

Stevenson, Kent
1942 — Suicide Squadron

Stevenson, Robert
1942 — Valley of Hunted Men

Stevenson, Tom
1943 — London Blackout Murders
The Mantrap

Stewart, Anna Marie[256]
1942 — Valley of Hunted Men

Stewart, Eleanor[257]
1936 — The Gun Ranger
1937 — Range Defenders
1938 — The Fighting Devil Dogs

Stewart, Larry[55]
1943 — Silver Spurs*
Sleepy Lagoon*
A Scream in the Dark*
Mystery Broadcast*
In Old Oklahoma*
Raiders of Sunset Pass*
Hands Across the Border*
1944 — The Fighting Seabees*
Rosie, the Riveter*

Stewart, Nick
1955 — Flame of the Islands

Stewart, Nicodemus
1943 — False Faces
Hoosier Holiday
1945 — Dakota
1946 — Night Train to Memphis

Stewart, Peggy[56]
1944 — Tucson Raiders
Silver City Kid
Stagecoach to Monterey
Cheyenne Wildcat
Code of the Prairie
End of the Road*
Firebrands of Arizona
Sheriff of Las Vegas
1945 — Utah
The Vampire's Ghost
Oregon Trail
Bandits of the Badlands
Marshal of Laredo
Rough Riders of Cheyenne
The Tiger Woman
1946 — Gay Blades*
The Phantom Rider
California Gold Rush
Days of Buffalo Bill
Sheriff of Redwood Valley
Alias Billy the Kid
Passkey to Danger*
The El Paso Kid*
Conquest of Cheyenne
Red River Renegades
The Invisible Informer
Affairs of Geraldine*
Stagecoach to Denver
1947 — Son of Zorro
Trail to San Antone
Vigilantes of Boomtown
The Ghost Goes Wild*
Rustlers of Devil's Canyon
1951 — Pride of Maryland

Stirling, Linda[58]
1944 — The Tiger Woman
The San Antonio Kid
Strangers in the Night*
Sheriff of Sundown
Vigilantes of Dodge City
Zorro's Black Whip
1945 — The Topeka Terror
Sheriff of Cimarron
Manhunt of Mystery Island
Santa Fe Saddlemates
The Purple Monster Strikes
The Cherokee Flash
Wagon Wheels Westward
Dakota*
1946 — The Madonna's Secret
Passkey to Danger*
The Invisible Informer
The Mysterious Mr. Valentine
Rio Grande Raiders
The Crimson Ghost
That Brennan Girl*
1947 — The Magnificent Rogue*
Jesse James Rides Again
The Pretender

Stirling, Pamela
1955 — The Divided Heart

Stockdale, Carl[257]
1936 — The Leavenworth Case
Oh, Susanna!
1937 — Paradise Express*
Youth on Parole*
1938 — The Lone Ranger*
1939 — Frontier Pony Express*
Main Street Lawyer*

Stockwell, Harry[216]
1937 — All Over Town

Stoloff, Jackie
1952 — Bal Tabarin*

Stone, Bob
1948 — Train to Alcatraz

Stone, George E.[257]
1942 — Affairs of Jimmy Valentine
1944 — My Buddy

Stone, Marianne
1957 — Operation Conspiracy
Thunder Over Tangier

Stone, Milburn[257]
1936 — The Three Mesquiteers
1937 — Youth on Parole
1940 — Colorado
1941 — The Phantom Cowboy
The Great Train Robbery
Death Valley Outlaws
1948 — Train to Alcatraz
1953 — The Sun Shines Bright

Stooge
1938 — Born to be Wild

Storey, June[60]
1938 — Down in "Arkansaw"
Orphans of the Street
1939 — Home on the Prairie
Blue Montana Skies
Mountain Rhythm
Mickey, the Kid
Colorado Sunset
In Old Monterey
South of the Border
1940 — Rancho Grande
In Old Missouri
Gaucho Serenade
Carolina Moon
Ride, Tenderfoot, Ride
Barnyard Follies
1944 — End of the Road
1945 — Road to Alcatraz
1948 — Secret Service Investigator
Train to Alcatraz

Storm, Gale[110]
1941 — Saddlemates
Jesse James at Bay
Red River Valley
1942 — Man from Cheyenne
1952 — Woman of the North Country

Storm, Rafael
1936 — The House of a Thousand Candles

Stossel, Ludwig
1944 — Lake Placid Serenade
1953 — The Sun Shines Bright
1954 — Geraldine

Straight, Clarence[257]
1944 — The Fighting Seabees*
My Best Gal*
1946 — G. I. War Brides*
1947 — Apache Rose*
Hit Parade of 1947*
1948 — The Far Frontier
1949 — The Golden Stallion
Powder River Rustlers
Pioneer Marshal
1950 — Trail of Robin Hood*
1952 — Colorado Sundown
1953 — Shadows of Tombstone*

Strang, Harry[257]
Many films.
1936 — Hearts in Bondage*
Robinson Crusoe of Clipper Island*
Happy Go Lucky*
1937 — Dick Tracy*
Paradise Express*
The Hit Parade*
S O S Coast Guard*
Zorro Rides Again
1938 — The Purple Vigilantes
The Fighting Devil Dogs*
Army Girl*
Come on, Leathernecks
1939 — The Mysterious Miss X*
Pride of the Navy*
Frontier Pony Express*
Street of Missing Men*
Man of Conquest*
Southward, Ho!*
Daredevils of the Red Circle*
Main Street Lawyer*
Cowboys from Texas*
1940 — Heroes of the Saddle*
Drums of Fu Manchu*
Dark Command*
Gaucho Serenade*
Oklahoma Renegades*
The Trail Blazers*
Mysterious Doctor Satan*
1941 — Ridin' on a Rainbow*
A Man Betrayed*
Rags to Riches*
Doctors Don't Tell*
Death Valley Outlaws*
1944 — Captain America*
My Buddy*
1945 — Manhunt of Mystery Island
Federal Operator 99*
1946 — The Madonna's Secret*
King of the Forest Rangers
Rendezvous with Annie*
Roll on Texas Moon
1948 — I, Jane Doe*
1950 — Twilight in the Sierras*

Strange, Glenn[257]
1935 — Westward Ho
The New Frontier
Lawless Range*
1936 — The Lonely Trail*
1939 — The Lone Ranger Rides Again
Rough Riders' Round-Up*
The Night Riders*
Blue Montana Skies
Days of Jesse James
1940 — Dark Command*
1941 — Saddlemates
1942 — Sunset on the Desert
Romance on the Range
1944 — Silver City Kid
The San Antonio Kid
1947 — Northwest Outpost*
Wyoming*
The Fabulous Texan*
1948 — California Firebrand*
The Gallant Legion*
1950 — Surrender*
1952 — I Dream of Jeanie*
1954 — Jubilee Trail*
1955 — The Road to Denver
The Vanishing American
1957 — Last Stagecoach West
1958 — Gunfire at Indian Gap

Strange, Robert[257]
1936 — The Leathernecks Have Landed*
Beware of Ladies
1938 — I Stand Accused
1940 — King of the Royal Mounted
1941 — Robin Hood of the Pecos
Mr. District Attorney*
Adventures of Captain Marvel
Desert Bandit
1942 — South of Santa Fe*
Perils of Nyoka
1943 — G-Men Vs. The Black Dragon*
1944 — Captain America*
Rosie, the Riveter*
Thoroughbreds*
Navy MN 3387 — Your Weapons*
1945 — Gangs of the Waterfront*
1948 — The Far Frontier
1952 — Zombies of the Stratosphere*

Stratford, Peggy
1936 — The Leavenworth Case

Straubinger, Frank
1936 — Guns and Guitars

Strauch, Jr., Joe[86]
1941 — Under Fiesta Stars
1942 — Heart of the Rio Grande
Home in Wyomin'
Call of the Canyon
Bells of Capistrano
1944 — Beneath Western Skies

Strauss, Robert
1954 — The Atomic Kid

Street, David
1945 — An Angel Comes to Brooklyn
1948 — Moonrise

Strong, Leonard
1954 — Hell's Half Acre

Strong, Robert[257]
1937 — Paradise Express*
1945 — The Chicago Kid*
Hitchhike to Happiness*
Man from Oklahoma*
Tell It to a Star*
The Tiger Woman*

Strudwick, Sheppard[110]
1949 — The Red Pony

Stuart, Gloria[257]
1943 — Here Comes Elmer

Stuart, Nicholas
1955 — The Divided Heart

Stuart, Sheila[61]
1943 — O, My Darling Clementine*
1944 — Faces in the Fog*
Lake Placid Serenade
1945 — Three's a Crowd*
Gangs of the Waterfront*
Oregon Trail*
Hitchhike to Happiness*
Swingin' on a Rainbow*
Girls of the Big House*
An Angel Comes to Brooklyn*

Stubbs, Harry
1935 — The Spanish Cape Mystery
1936 — The Girl from Mandalay
1938 — I Stand Accused
1941 — The Singing Hill

Stutenroth, Gene
See Gene Roth

Sujata
1953 — Fair Wind to Java

Sullivan, Barry[110]
1956 — The Maverick Queen

Sullivan, Charles[137]
1936—The Old Corral
1938—Prison Nurse*
Ladies in Distress*
Army Girl*
Dick Tracy Returns*
Federal Man-Hunt*
1939—Dick Tracy's G-Men*
1940—Gangs of Chicago*
Scatterbrain*
Earl of Puddlestone*
Frontier Vengeance*
Bowery Boy*
1941—A Man Betrayed*
Citadel of Crime*
The Pittsburgh Kid*
Sailors on Leave*
A Missouri Outlaw*
1942—Pardon My Stripes*
The Old Homestead*
The Traitor Within*
1943—Dead Man's Gulch*
King of the Cowboys*
The Mantrap*
Riders of the Rio Grande*
Fugitive from Sonora*
Bordertown Gun Fighters*
The West Side Kid*
Nobody's Darling*
Death Valley Manhunt*
Canyon City*
In Old Oklahoma*
1944—The Fighting Seabees*
Tucson Raiders*
The Yellow Rose of Texas*
Man from Frisco*
Marshal of Reno*
Strangers in the Night*
My Buddy*
Thoroughbreds
1945—Earl Carroll Vanities*
The Phantom Speaks*
The Vampire's Ghost*
Flame of Barbary Coast*
A Sporting Chance*
Bells of Rosarita*
The Chicago Kid*
Bandits of the Badlands*
Girls of the Big House*
1946—Gay Blades*
King of the Forest Rangers*
Rainbow Over Texas*
The El Paso Kid*
Traffic in Crime
Daughter of Don Q*
The Last Crooked Mile*
G. I. War Brides*
The Mysterious Mr. Valentine*
That Brennan Girl*
1947—Bells of San Angelo*
The Wild Frontier*
The Black Widow*
1948—G-Men Never Forget*
Heart of Virginia*
Secret Service Investigator*
Daredevils of the Clouds*
Out of the Storm
Homicide for Three*
1949—Duke of Chicago*
Flaming Fury*
1950—Unmasked*
The Invisible Monster
Hit Parade of 1951*
1952—Woman in the Dark
The Fabulous Senorita*
Tropical Heat Wave*
1953—Woman They Almost Lynched*
Fair Wind to Java*
Champ for a Day*
1954—Trader Tom of the China Seas*
Make Haste to Live*
Man with the Steel Whip*
The Shanghai Story*
1955—Panther Girl of the Kongo*
I Cover the Underworld*
1956—Stranger at My Door*
The Man is Armed*
1957—Hell's Crossroads*
The Crooked Circle*

Sullivan, Elliott
1938—Gangs of New York
1943—A Gentle Gangster

Sully, Frank
1941—Mountain Moonlight
1942—Sleepytime Gal

Summerfield, Eleanor
1957—Tears for Simon

Summers, Brian
1958—Strange Case of Dr. Manning

Summerville, Slim [George][258]
1941—Puddin' Head

Sundberg, Clinton
1953—Sweethearts on Parade

Super Swedish Angel
1949—Alias the Champ

Surette, Al
1941—Ice-Capades

Slim Summerville

James Taggart

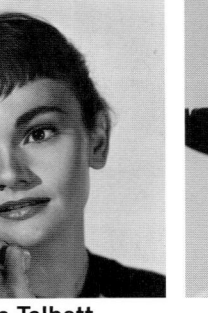
Gloria Talbott

Kay Sutton

Lyle Talbot

Hal Taliaferro

Suss, Bernard
1939—Mountain Rhythm

Sutherland, Eddie
1941—Stars Past and Present*

Sutton, Grady[137]
1937—Dangerous Holiday
1940—Bowery Boy*
1941—Mr. District Attorney*
Doctors Don't Tell
1945—Grissly's Millions
Three's a Crowd
1946—Plainsman and the Lady*
The Fabulous Suzanne
1947—The Magnificent Rogue

Sutton, John
1936—The House of a Thousand Candles*

Sutton, Kay[258]
1939—S.O.S. Tidal Wave

Sutton, Paul
1942—In Old California

Suzanne, George
Many films.
1940—Drums of Fu Manchu*
1941—Adventures of Captain Marvel*
1942—Perils of Nyoka*
1943—The Masked Marvel*

Swan, Bob
1956—Thunder Over Arizona
1957—The Lawless Eighties
The Crooked Circle

Switzer, Carl "Alfalfa"[258]
1940—Barnyard Follies
1942—Johnny Doughboy
1943—Shantytown
1944—Rosie, the Riveter
1947—Driftwood*
1949—Alias the Champ*
1950—House by the River*
Redwood Forest Trail
1951—Belle LeGrand*
1952—I Dream of Jeanie
The Wac from Walla Walla*
1954—Flight Nurse*

Sydney, Derek
1957—Thunder Over Tangier

T

Tafler, Sydney
1955—The Square Ring

Taggart, Ben
1937—Youth on Parole*
1938—King of the Newsboys*
1939—S.O.S. Tidal Wave*
Daredevils of the Red Circle
1941—Mr. District Atty. in the Carter Case*
1942—A Tragedy at Midnight*
Secrets of the Underground*
1943—Chatterbox*
1944—Captain America*
The Fighting Seabees*
Man from Frisco*
Atlantic City*
1951—Govt. Agents Vs. Phantom Legion*

Taggart, James[258]
[as Ward "Bud" McTaggart]
1937—Rhythm in the Clouds*
1939—Wyoming Outlaw*
1940—Behind the News*
1941—Gangs of Sonora*
[As Malcolm "Bud" McTaggart]
1942—Flying Tigers
1943—Dead Man's Gulch*
[As James Taggart]
1946—Earl Carroll Sketchbook*
Heldorado
1947—Last Frontier Uprising

Talbot, Helen[62]
1943—Canyon City
Pistol Packin' Mama
California Joe
1944—Outlaws of Santa Fe
The Lady and the Monster*
San Fernando Valley*
Faces in the Fog
1945—Corpus Christi Bandits
Lone Texas Ranger
Bells of Rosarita*
Federal Operator 99
Trail of Kit Carson
Swingin' on a Rainbow
Don't Fence Me In*
Song of Mexico*
1946—Gay Blades*
King of the Forest Rangers
The Last Crooked Mile*
Affairs of Geraldine*
I've Always Loved You*

Talbot, Lyle[258]
1937—Affairs of Cappy Ricks
1938—Call of the Yukon
I Stand Accused
1939—Forged Passport
1946—Song of Arizona
Strange Impersonation
1952—Desperadoes' Outpost
1953—Nightmare Typhoon
War of the Space Giants
Destroyers of the Sun
Robot Monster from Mars
The Hydrogen Hurricane
Solar Sky Raiders
S.O.S. Ice Age
1954—Trader Tom of the China Seas
Tobor the Great*
1958—The Notorious Mr. Monks

Talbott, Gloria[258]
1957—Taming Sutton's Gal

Taliaferro, Hal[258]
1936—The Gun Ranger*
1937—Rootin' Tootin' Rhythm
The Painted Stallion
Heart of the Rockies
The Trigger Trio
1938—The Lone Ranger
1939—Man of Conquest*
Saga of Death Valley
1940—Pioneers of the West
Dark Command*
Adventures of Red Ryder
The Carson City Kid
Colorado
Young Bill Hickok
Texas Terrors*
The Border Legion
1941—The Great Train Robbery
In Old Cheyenne
Sheriff of Tombstone
Under Fiesta Stars*
Bad Man of Deadwood
Jesse James at Bay
Red River Valley
1942—Romance on the Range
Sons of the Pioneers
King of the Mounties*
Heart of the Golden West*
Ridin' Down the Canyon
1943—Idaho
Song of Texas
Silver Spurs
Man from Music Mountain
1944—The Fighting Seabees*
Cowboy and the Senorita
The Yellow Rose of Texas
Haunted Harbor
Atlantic City*
Vigilantes of Dodge City
Zorro's Black Whip
1945—Utah
Federal Operator 99
The Cheaters*
1946—The Phantom Rider
In Old Sacramento*
Plainsman and the Lady
1948—The Gallant Legion
1949—Brimstone
1950—The Savage Horde
California Passage*
1951—The Sea Hornet

Talley, Marion[86]
1936—Follow Your Heart

Tallichet, Margaret[125]
1938—A Desperate Adventure
1940—Chinese Garden Festival*
1941—The Devil Pays Off

Talman, William[125]
1953—City that Never Sleeps
1956—The Man is Armed

Talton, Alice[223]
1949—Ranger of Cherokee Strip

Tamblyn, Rusty[259]
1949—The Kid from Cleveland

Tamez, Al
1955—Yellowneck

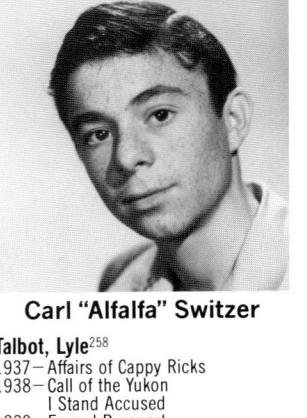
Carl "Alfalfa" Switzer

Tannen, Julius
1938—Mama Runs Wild

Tannen, William[210]
1950—Sunset in the West
1951—Insurance Investigator
1953—El Paso Stampede

Tansey, Emma
1937—The Gambling Terror

Tansey, Sherry
1938—Paroled—to Die

Tapley, Colin[259]
1938—Storm Over Bengal
1940—Women in War

Tashman, Lilyan
1936—Frankie and Johnnie*

Tate, Reginald
1941—Poison Pen

Taylor, Al[259]
1936—The Lawless Nineties
Comin' 'Round the Mountain*
Guns and Guitars
The Vigilantes are Coming*
Robinson Crusoe of Clipper Island*
The Old Corral*
1937—Round-Up Time in Texas*
Dick Tracy*
Paradise Express*
Git Along Little Dogies*
Come on, Cowboys!
Yodelin' Kid from Pine Ridge*
Range Defenders*
The Sheik Steps Out*
Zorro Rides Again*
1938—The Lone Ranger*
Call the Mesquiteers*
The Fighting Devil Dogs*
Gold Mine in the Sky*
Man from Music Mountain
Dick Tracy Returns*
Billy the Kid Returns*
Prairie Moon*
Rhythm of the Saddle*
Come on, Rangers*
Red River Range*
Shine on Harvest Moon*
1939—The Lone Ranger Rides Again
Mexicali Rose*
Frontier Pony Express*
Mountain Rhythm*
Daredevils of the Red Circle*
In Old Caliente*
Wyoming Outlaw*
Colorado Sunset*
Dick Tracy's G-Men*
Wall Street Cowboy*
Zorro's Fighting Legion
1940—Heroes of the Saddle
Drums of Fu Manchu*
Ghost Valley Raiders*
Dark Command*
Covered Wagon Days*
Adventures of Red Ryder*
The Carson City Kid*
The Ranger and the Lady*
King of the Royal Mounted*
Mysterious Doctor Satan
1941—Robin Hood of the Pecos*
Adventures of Captain Marvel*
Jungle Girl
Gangs of Sonora*
Bad Man of Deadwood*
Outlaws of Cherokee Trail*
King of the Texas Rangers*
Jesse James at Bay*
Dick Tracy Vs. Crime, Inc.*
1942—Man from Cheyenne*
Code of the Outlaw*
Raiders of the Range*
Westward Ho*
The Cyclone Kid*
The Phantom Plainsmen*
Call of the Canyon*
Outlaws of Pine Ridge*
1943—Thundering Trails*
Dead Man's Gulch*
The Blocked Trail*
Santa Fe Scouts*
Calling Wild Bill Elliott*
Daredevils of the West*
The Man from Thunder River*
The Black Hills Express
Beyond the Last Frontier*
Death Valley Manhunt
Overland Mail Robbery*
Raiders of Sunset Pass*
1944—Marshal of Reno*
1946—Rio Grande Raiders*
1948—Dangers of the Canadian Mounted*
1950—Desperadoes of the West*

Taylor, Brad[64]
1944—Sing Neighbor Sing
Atlantic City
Lake Placid Serenade*
1945—Hitchhike to Happiness
Swingin' on a Rainbow

Taylor, Dub "Cannonball"
1940 — One Man's Law
1952 — Woman of the North Country*
1958 — Street of Darkness

Taylor, Duke [Fenton][231]
1937 — Bill Cracks Down*
Gunsmoke Ranch*
Come on, Cowboys!*
The Painted Stallion
S O S Coast Guard*
Heart of the Rockies*
Boots and Saddles*
The Trigger Trio*
Zorro Rides Again*
1938 — The Lone Ranger*
Call the Mesquiteers*
Outlaws of Sonora*
Under Western Stars*
Riders of the Black Hills*
The Night Hawk*
Prairie Moon*
Rhythm of the Saddle*
Come on, Rangers*
Shine on Harvest Moon*
1939 — The Lone Ranger Rides Again*
Man of Conquest*
Daredevils of the Red Circle*
In Old Caliente*
1940 — Pioneers of the West*
Drums of Fu Manchu*
Covered Wagon Days*
King of the Royal Mounted*
Under Texas Skies*
Mysterious Doctor Satan*
Lone Star Raiders*
1941 — Wyoming Wildcat*
Adventures of Captain Marvel*
Country Fair*
Jungle Girl*
King of the Texas Rangers*
Dick Tracy Vs. Crime, Inc.*
1942 — Spy Smasher*
The Phantom Plainsmen*
Perils of Nyoka*
King of the Mounties*
Outlaws of Pine Ridge*
1943 — G-Men Vs. The Black Dragon*
1944 — Zorro's Black Whip*
1945 — Sheriff of Cimarron*
Manhunt of Mystery Island*
Santa Fe Saddlemates*
Don't Fence Me In*
1946 — The Phantom Rider*
Roll on Texas Moon*
The Crimson Ghost*
1947 — Son of Zorro*
Vigilantes of Boomtown*
Jesse James Rides Again*
1948 — Adv. of Frank and Jesse James*
1949 — Rose of the Yukon*
Federal Agents Vs. Underworld, Inc.*
The James Brothers of Missouri*
Radar Patrol Vs. Spy King*
Pioneer Marshal*
1950 — Harbor of Missing Men*
The Invisible Monster*
Covered Wagon Raid*
Desperadoes of the West*
Under Mexicali Stars*
1951 — Govt. Agents Vs. Phantom Legion*
Rodeo King and the Senorita*
Utah Wagon Train*
Pals of the Golden West*
1953 — Can. Mounties Vs. Atomic Invaders*
1955 — King of the Carnival*

Taylor, Ferris[137]
1937 — The Wrong Road*
1938 — King of the Newsboys*
Santa Fe Stampede
Federal Man-Hunt*
1939 — Man of Conquest
The Zero Hour
S.O.S. Tidal Wave
Mountain Rhythm
Flight at Midnight*
Main Street Lawyer
1940 — Rancho Grande
Dark Command*
Grand Ole Opry
1941 — Ridin' on a Rainbow
A Man Betrayed
Country Fair
The Gay Vagabond*
1943 — Hoosier Holiday
1944 — End of the Road
1946 — Man from Rainbow Valley
1947 — That's My Gal*
1948 — The Gallant Legion*
1953 — Sweethearts on Parade*

Taylor, Forrest[138]
1937 — The Red Rope
1938 — King of the Newsboys*
The Feud Maker
The Fighting Devil Dogs
Desert Patrol
Heroes of the Hills
Dick Tracy Returns
Durango Valley Raiders
1939 — The Lone Ranger Rides Again*
Street of Missing Men*
S.O.S. Tidal Wave
Dick Tracy's G-Men
Rovin' Tumbleweeds
1940 — Under Texas Skies*
Friendly Neighbors*
The Trail Blazers*
1941 — Ridin' on a Rainbow
Pals of the Pecos*
The Singing Hill*
Kansas Cyclone
Hurricane Smith*
King of the Texas Rangers*
Dick Tracy Vs. Crime, Inc.*
1942 — Cowboy Serenade*
Code of the Outlaw*
Sunset on the Desert
Home in Wyomin'
In Old California*
Perils of Nyoka*
Sons of the Pioneers
King of the Mounties*
Outlaws of Pine Ridge
Ridin' Down the Canyon
1943 — Thundering Trails
Idaho*
King of the Cowboys*
Song of Texas*
Silver Spurs
Sleepy Lagoon
1944 — Beneath Western Skies*
Mojave Firebrand
Outlaws of Santa Fe*
Three Little Sisters
Song of Nevada
Haunted Harbor
Cheyenne Wildcat*
Zorro's Black Whip*
1945 — Manhunt of Mystery Island
Identity Unknown
Federal Operator 99
Steppin' in Society*
Bandits of the Badlands
1946 — Strange Impersonation*
The Glass Alibi
The Crimson Ghost
Santa Fe Uprising
Stagecoach to Denver
1947 — Yankee Fakir
Rustlers of Devil's Canyon
The Pretender
Along the Oregon Trail
The Black Widow
1948 — The Plunderers*
1949 — Death Valley Gunfighter
Navajo Trail Raiders
1950 — Code of the Silver Sage
The Arizona Cowboy*
Rustlers on Horseback
1951 — Don Daredevil Rides Again*
Wells Fargo Gunmaster
Utah Wagon Train*
1952 — Border Saddlemates
South Pacific Trail
1953 — Iron Mountain Trail

Taylor, George
1951 — Buckaroo Sheriff of Texas

Taylor, Kent[259]
1950 — Federal Agent at Large
Trial Without Jury
1955 — Secret Venture
1956 — Track the Man Down

Taylor, Larry
1957 — Operation Conspiracy

Taylor, Megan[259]
1941 — Ice-Capades
1942 — Ice-Capades Revue

Taylor, Norma[259]
1935 — Tumbling Tumbleweeds

Taylor, Phil
1941 — Ice-Capades
1942 — Ice-Capades Revue

Taylor, William
1942 — Suicide Squadron

Taylor Smith, Jean
1955 — Doctor in the House

Teague, Guy[184]
1950 — Desperadoes of the West
Vigilante Hideout
The Showdown
1951 — Don Daredevil Rides Again
1954 — Man with the Steel Whip

Teal, Ray[259]
1937 — Zorro Rides Again*
1938 — Western Jamboree
1940 — Adventures of Red Ryder
The Trail Blazers*
Melody Ranch*
1943 — A Gentle Gangster
1945 — Don't Fence Me In*
1947 — Northwest Outpost*
Driftwood
The Fabulous Texan*
1948 — Daredevils of the Clouds
1950 — Harbor of Missing Men
1951 — Oh! Susanna*
1957 — The Wayward Girl

Tearle, Godfrey
1943 — At Dawn We Die

Tedrow, Irene
1943 — Nobody's Darling*
1955 — Santa Fe Passage

Teen-Agers, The
1946 — One Exciting Week

Telaak, William
1939 — Calling All Marines*
1941 — Kansas Cyclone*
The Pittsburgh Kid*
Death Valley Outlaws*
1942 — The Sombrero Kid*
Bells of Capistrano*

Tellegan, Mike
1936 — Down to the Sea

Temple, George
1949 — Alias the Champ

Ray Teal, Rosella Towne

Tempo, Nino
1949 — The Red Pony

Tenbrook, Henry
1937 — Hit the Saddle

Tennessee Ramblers, The
1936 — Ride Ranger Ride
1937 — Yodelin' Kid from Pine Ridge
1943 — Swing Your Partner
O, My Darling Clementine

Terhune, Max[64]
1936 — Ride Ranger Ride
Ghost-Town Gold
The Big Show
Roarin' Lead
1937 — The Riders of the Whistling Skull
Hit the Saddle
The Hit Parade
Gunsmoke Ranch
Come on, Cowboys!
Range Defenders
Heart of the Rockies
Boots and Saddles*
The Trigger Trio
Manhattan Merry-Go-Round
Wild Horse Rodeo
1938 — Mama Runs Wild
The Purple Vigilantes
Call the Mesquiteers
Outlaws of Sonora
Ladies in Distress
Riders of the Black Hills
Heroes of the Hills
Pals of the Saddle
Overland Stage Raiders
Santa Fe Stampede
Red River Range
1939 — The Night Riders
Three Texas Steers
Man of Conquest
1944 — Sheriff of Sundown
1947 — Along the Oregon Trail

Terrell, Ken[260]
1939 — Daredevils of the Red Circle*
Dick Tracy's G-Men
Zorro's Fighting Legion*
1940 — Drums of Fu Manchu*
Covered Wagon Days*
Adventures of Red Ryder*
Oklahoma Renegades*
Girl from Havana*
King of the Royal Mounted*
Under Texas Skies*
Mysterious Doctor Satan
1941 — Adventures of Captain Marvel*
Country Fair*
Saddlemates*
Jungle Girl
Sailors on Leave*
King of the Texas Rangers*
Dick Tracy Vs. Crime, Inc.*
1942 — Cowboy Serenade*
Raiders of the Range*
Spy Smasher*
Perils of Nyoka
King of the Mounties*
Outlaws of Pine Ridge*
1943 — G-Men Vs. The Black Dragon*
Daredevils of the West*
Days of Old Cheyenne*
Bordertown Gun Fighters*
Secret Service in Darkest Africa*
The Man from the Rio Grande*
The Masked Marvel*
1944 — Captain America*
The Tiger Woman
Marshal of Reno*
Haunted Harbor*
Code of the Prairie*
Zorro's Black Whip*
1945 — Federal Operator 99*
Trail of Kit Carson*
The Purple Monster Strikes
Marshal of Laredo*
1946 — The Catman of Paris*
King of the Forest Rangers*
Rainbow Over Texas*
Daughter of Don Q*
The Crimson Ghost*
1947 — Son of Zorro*
Vigilantes of Boomtown*
Robin Hood of Texas*
Jesse James Rides Again*
The Black Widow*
1948 — The Gay Ranchero*
G-Men Never Forget
The Bold Frontiersman
Dangers of the Canadian Mounted*
The Timber Trail*
Grand Canyon Trail
Adv. of Frank and Jesse James*
The Plunderers*
1949 — Federal Agents Vs. Underworld, Inc.*
Ghost of Zorro*
The James Brothers of Missouri*
Radar Patrol Vs. Spy King*
1950 — Bells of Coronado*
The Invisible Monster*
Flying Disc Man from Mars*
Trail of Robin Hood*
1951 — Secrets of Monte Carlo*
Pals of the Golden West*
1952 — Radar Men from the Moon*
Zombies of the Stratosphere*
1953 — Old Overland Trail*
Iron Mountain Trail*
Red River Shore*
1954 — Trader Tom of the China Seas*
1955 — The Last Command*
1956 — A Strange Adventure*

Rusty Tamblyn

Colin Tapley

Al Taylor

Kent Taylor

Megan Taylor

Norma Taylor

Terry, Albert
1938—Man from Music Mountain

Terry, Gordon
1956—Hidden Guns

Terry, Phillip[125]
1941—Public Enemies

Terry, Robert
1938—Dick Tracy Returns

Terry, Ruth[64]
1940—Sing, Dance, Plenty Hot
1941—Rookies on Parade
1942—Sleepytime Gal
    Affairs of Jimmy Valentine
    Call of the Canyon
    Youth on Parade
    Heart of the Golden West
1943—Man from Music Mountain
    Mystery Broadcast
    Pistol Packin' Mama
    Hands Across the Border
1944—Jamboree
    Goodnight Sweetheart
    Three Little Sisters
    Sing Neighbor Sing
    My Buddy
    Brazil*
    Lake Placid Serenade
1945—Steppin' in Society
    The Cheaters
    Tell It to a Star

Terry, Sheila[180]
1936—Go-Get-'Em, Haines

Terry, Tex[260]
1945—Bandits of the Badlands
    Rough Riders of Cheyenne
1946—Alias Billy the Kid
    The El Paso Kid
    Rio Grande Raiders
1947—Apache Rose
    Twilight on the Rio Grande
1948—The Gallant Legion
1953—Sweethearts on Parade
1955—Timberjack
    The Road to Denver

Terry, William[260]
1944—Three Little Sisters
    Strangers in the Night
1945—Behind City Lights

Tetley, Walter
1938—Prairie Moon
1940—Under Texas Skies
1943—Mystery Broadcast*

Texas Wanderers, The
1940—Village Barn Dance

Thane, Dirk
1941—Two Gun Sheriff

Thatcher, Heather
1940—Chinese Garden Festival*

Thayer, Julia
See Jean Carmen.

Theodores, The
1936—Sitting on the Moon

Thimig, Helene
1944—Strangers in the Night

This World of Ours—series
1950—Norway
    Denmark
    Glacier National Park
    Sweden
    France
    Holland
1951—London
    Portugal
    Spain
    England
    Hawaii
    Greece
    Belgium
    Switzerland
    Italy
    Egypt
1952—Puerto Rico
    Chile
    Israel
    India
    The Philippines
1953—Ceylon
    City of Destiny
    Singapore
    Germany
    Japan
1954—Hong Kong
    Formosa
    Ireland
    Thailand
    Bali
1955—Venezuela
    Caribbean Sky Cruise
    Turkey

Ken Terrell

Tex Terry

William Terry

Helene Thimig

Thomas, Charles Bob
1941—Two Gun Sheriff

Thomas, Dagmar
1955—In Old Vienna

Thomas, Frank M.[231]
1939—The Mysterious Miss X
    Saga of Death Valley
1941—Wyoming Wildcat
    Arkansas Judge
    Sierra Sue
1942—Sunset on the Desert
    Sunset Serenade
1943—Mountain Rhythm

Thomas, Lyn[260]
1950—Covered Wagon Raid
    The Missourians
1953—Red River Shore

Thomas, Madoline
1955—The Square Ring

Thomas, Robert C.
1936—Ghost-Town Gold

Thomas, William "Buckwheat"
1945—Colorado Pioneers

Thompson, Carl
1952—Woman in the Dark

Thompson, Carlos
1956—Magic Fire

Thompson, Kay—and ensemble
1937—Manhattan Merry-Go-Round

Thompson, Larry
1936—Robinson Crusoe of Clipper Island*
1945—Dakota*
1946—King of the Forest Rangers

Thompson, Mort
1951—Night Riders of Montana

Thompson, Nick
1941—The Phantom Cowboy

Thomson, Kenneth
1937—Jim Hanvey - Detective

Thorgersen, Ed
1937—The Hit Parade

Thornton, Cyril
1946—The Glass Alibi

Thornton, Frank
1957—Operation Conspiracy

Thorpe, Jim
1939—Man of Conquest*
1944—Outlaws of Santa Fe*
1945—The Vampire's Ghost*

Thorpe, Ted
1952—Radar Men from the Moon

Three Cheers, The
1943—Hit Parade of 1943

Lyn Thomas

Three Chocolateers, The
1942—Moonlight Masquerade

Three Mesquiteers—series
    [Livingston-Corrigan-Saylor]
1936—The Three Mesquiteers
    [Livingston-Corrigan-Terhune]
    Ghost-Town Gold
    Roarin' Lead
1937—The Riders of the Whistling Skull
    Hit the Saddle
    Gunsmoke Ranch
    Come on, Cowboys!
    Range Defenders
    Heart of the Rockies
    [Byrd-Corrigan-Terhune]
    The Trigger Trio
    [Livingston-Corrigan-Terhune]
    Wild Horse Rodeo
1938—The Purple Vigilantes
    Call the Mesquiteers
    Outlaws of Sonora
    Riders of the Black Hills
    Heroes of the Hills
    [Wayne-Corrigan-Terhune]
    Pals of the Saddle
    Overland Stage Raiders
    Santa Fe Stampede
    Red River Range
1939—The Night Riders
    Three Texas Steers
    [Wayne-Corrigan-Hatton]
    Wyoming Outlaw
    New Frontier
    [Livingston-Renaldo-Hatton]
    The Kansas Terrors
    Cowboys from Texas
1940—Heroes of the Saddle
    Pioneers of the West
    Covered Wagon Days
    Rocky Mountain Rangers
    Oklahoma Renegades
    [Livingston-Steele-Davis]
    Under Texas Skies
    The Trail Blazers
    Lone Star Raiders
1941—Prairie Pioneers
    Pals of the Pecos
    Saddlemates
    Gangs of Sonora
    [Tyler-Steele-Davis]
    Outlaws of Cherokee Trail
    Gauchos of Eldorado
    West of Cimarron
1942—Code of the Outlaw
    Raiders of the Range
    Westward Ho
    The Phantom Plainsmen
    [Tyler-Steele-Dodd]
    Shadows on the Sage
    Valley of Hunted Men
1943—Thundering Trails
    The Blocked Trail
    Santa Fe Scouts
    Riders of the Rio Grande

Thunder
1946—Sun Valley Cyclone

Chief Thunder Cloud

Thunder Cloud, Chief[260]
1936—The Singing Vagabond*
    Ride Ranger Ride
1937—The Riders of the Whistling Skull
    The Bold Caballero*
1938—The Lone Ranger
1939—The Lone Ranger Rides Again
    Man of Conquest*
1940—Young Buffalo Bill
1943—Daredevils of the West
1944—The Fighting Seabees*
1946—The Phantom Rider

Thurston, Helen
1940—Mysterious Doctor Satan*
1941—The Great Train Robbery*
    Jungle Girl*
1942—Perils of Nyoka*
1943—Sleepy Lagoon*
1944—Captain America*
    Army 101—Equip. Maintenance*
1949—Radar Patrol Vs. Spy King*

Thyssen, Greta[260]
1956—Accused of Murder

Tic Toc Girls[86]
1937—The Hit Parade

Tiger Men
1936—Darkest Africa

Tilbury, Zeffie
1937—Rhythm in the Clouds
1941—Sheriff of Tombstone

Timblin, Charles
1937—Larceny on the Air

Tipica Orchestra
1945—Song of Mexico

Tobey, Dan
1938—Hollywood Stadium Mystery!
1941—The Pittsburgh Kid
1949—Duke of Chicago

Tobey, Ruth
1941—Variety Reel*

Tobin, Genevieve[260]
1937—The Duke Comes Back

Todd, Ann[260]
1939—The Zero Hour
1941—Variety Reel*
1947—Homesteaders of Paradise Valley

Todd, Ann
1941—Poison Pen

Todd, Mabel
1939—The Mysterious Miss X
    Street of Missing Men

Todd, Sally
1957—The Unearthly

Tomack, Sid
1948—Homicide for Three

Tombes, Andrew[138]
1936—Ticket to Paradise
1937—Meet the Boy Friend
1938—Romance on the Run
    A Desperate Adventure
1939—Money to Burn
1940—Wolf of New York
    Village Barn Dance
    In Old Missouri
    Melody and Moonlight*
1941—Sis Hopkins*
    Mountain Moonlight
    Down Mexico Way
1944—San Fernando Valley
    Lake Placid Serenade
1945—Don't Fence Me In
1951—Belle LeGrand*
1952—Oklahoma Annie
    I Dream of Jeanie

Greta Thyssen

Genevieve Tobin

Ann Todd

Mabel Todd

Tomlin, Pinky[261]
1938 — Down in "Arkansaw"
1943 — Here Comes Elmer

Tony, Jim
1936 — The Lonely Trail

Toomey, Regis[261]
1936 — Bulldog Edition
1939 — The Mysterious Miss X
Street of Missing Men
1956 — Dakota Incident

Toone, Geoffrey
1941 — Poison Pen

Toones, Fred
See Snowflake.

Topper, Burt
1958 — No Place to Land
1959 — Plunderers of Painted Flats

Tor, Michael
1951 — Fugitive Lady

Tor, Sigurd[261]
1943 — The Purple V*
Secret Service in Darkest Africa

Torvay, Jose
1956 — A Woman's Devotion

Tosi, Luigi
1955 — Mystery of the Black Jungle

Totter, Audrey[126]
1953 — Woman They Almost Lynched
Champ for a Day
1955 — The Vanishing American
1958 — Man or Gun

Toughie and Roughie
1938 — Call of the Yukon

Tours, Joan
1940 — Barnyard Follies*
1941 — Sis Hopkins*
Ice-Capades*

Tovar, Lupita
1939 — South of the Border
1941 — Two Gun Sheriff

Towb, Harry
1956 — Above Us the Waves

Towler, Dan
1954 — Crazylegs

Towne, Aline[261]
1950 — Harbor of Missing Men
The Vanishing Westerner
The Invisible Monster
1951 — Rough Riders of Durango
Don Daredevil Rides Again
1952 — Radar Men from the Moon
Zombies of the Stratosphere
1953 — Enemies of the Universe
Atomic Peril
Cosmic Vengeance
Nightmare Typhoon
War of the Space Giants
Destroyers of the Sun
Robot Monster from Mars
The Hydrogen Hurricane
Solar Sky Raiders
S. O. S. Ice Age
Lost in Outer Space
Captives of the Zero Hour
1954 — Trader Tom of the China Seas

Towne, Rosella[259]
1940 — Rocky Mountain Rangers
1943 — A Gentle Gangster

Townley, Toke
1956 — Doctor at Sea

Toxton, Candy
1948 — Moonrise*

Tracy, Dick—series
1937 — Dick Tracy
1938 — Dick Tracy Returns
1939 — Dick Tracy's G-Men
1941 — Dick Tracy Vs. Crime, Inc.

Training films
1941 — Army 146—60mm Mortar
Army 147—60mm Mortar
Army 148—60mm Mortar
1942 — Army 156—Horsemanship
Army 220—Cavalry Rifle Platoon
Army 681—Keep It Clean
Army 682—Cracking Tanks
1943 — Army 220A—Cavalry Rifle Platoon
Army 828—First Aid
1944 — Army 7167—Frequency Modulation
Army 9652—Car Sharing
Army 150—National Labor
Army 101—Equip. Maintenance
Army 102—Trench Foot
Navy MN 3387—Your Weapons
1945 — Army—Maintenance for LVT's

Pinky Tomlin

Sigurd Tor

Regis Toomey

Henry Travers

Aline Towne

Travers, Bill
1955 — The Square Ring

Travers, Henry[261]
1947 — The Flame

Travis, June[126]
1937 — Join the Marines
Circus Girl
Exiled to Shanghai
1938 — The Night Hawk
Federal Man-Hunt

Travis, Richard[261]
1948 — Out of the Storm
1950 — Lonely Heart Bandits
1955 — City of Shadows

Treacher, Arthur[261]
1935 — Hitch Hike Lady

Treadway, Charlotte
1937 — The Sheik Steps Out

Tree, Dorothy[261]
1936 — Navy Born
1938 — Storm Over Bengal*
1939 — The Mysterious Miss X

Treen, Mary[138]
1939 — Pride of the Navy*
1943 — Hit Parade of 1943
Mystery Broadcast
Hands Across the Border
1946 — A Guy Could Change
Strange Impersonation
One Exciting Week
1955 — The Eternal Sea*
1956 — When Gangland Strikes

Trenk, Willy
1945 — Hitchhike to Happiness

Trent, Philip
1941 — Outlaws of Cherokee Trail

Trevor, Claire[110]
1940 — Dark Command
1952 — Hoodlum Empire

Triana, Antonio
1944 — The Lady and the Monster

Trigger
Horse. Credited on-screen in last 45 Roy Rogers westerns during 1943-51 as "The Smartest Horse in the Movies."

Richard Travis

Arthur Treacher

Jerry Tucker

Trowbridge, Charles[138]
1937 — Sea Racketeers
Exiled to Shanghai
1938 — Gangs of New York
1939 — Pride of the Navy
1940 — Mysterious Doctor Satan
1941 — Hurricane Smith
Rags to Riches
King of the Texas Rangers
1944 — Captain America
The Fighting Seabees*
Faces in the Fog
1946 — Valley of the Zombies
1950 — Unmasked
1952 — Hoodlum Empire*

Troy, Helen
1940 — Village Barn Dance

Truex, Ernest
1938 — Mama Runs Wild
1941 — The Gay Vagabond
1943 — Sleepy Lagoon

Tubb, Ernest—and his Texas Troubadors
1944 — Jamboree

Dorothy Tree

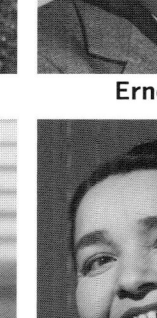

Ernest Truex

Richard Tucker

Tucker, Forrest[86]
1948 — The Plunderers
1949 — The Last Bandit
Hellfire
Brimstone
1950 — Sands of Iwo Jima
Rock Island Trail
California Passage
1951 — Oh! Susanna
Fighting Coast Guard
The Wild Blue Yonder
1952 — Hoodlum Empire
1953 — Ride the Man Down
San Antone
1954 — Flight Nurse
Laughing Anne
Jubilee Trail
Trouble in the Glen
1955 — The Vanishing American
1958 — Girl in the Woods

Tucker, Harland
1947 — Hit Parade of 1947

Tucker, Jerry[261]
1938 — Dick Tracy Returns
Federal Man-Hunt
1955 — Flame of the Islands*

Tucker, Richard[261]
1938 — The Higgins Family
1939 — The Covered Trailer

Rosa Turich

Tuffie
1938 — Hawk of the Wilderness
1939 — Daredevils of the Red Circle

Tufts, Sonny [Bowen][110]
1956 — Come Next Spring

Tully, Tom
1954 — Sea of Lost Ships

Tumiati, Gualtiero
1955 — Don Juan's Night of Love

Turich, Rosa[261]
1937 — Zorro Rides Again*
1939 — Man of Conquest*
The Kansas Terrors*
1941 — Prairie Pioneers*
1948 — Old Los Angeles*
Adv. of Frank and Jesse James*
1950 — Belle of Old Mexico*
1951 — Cuban Fireball
Havana Rose
1954 — Phantom Stallion
Make Haste to Live*
1957 — Duel at Apache Wells*

Turnbull, Glenn
1952 — I Dream of Jeanie

Turner, Anna
1957 — Tears for Simon

Turner, Col. Roscoe[86]
1939 — Flight at Midnight

George Turner

Turner, George[262]
1939—S. O. S. Tidal Wave*
    Daredevils of the Red Circle*
1946—Rendezvous with Annie*
1947—Son of Zorro
    Vigilantes of Boomtown

Turner, Lana
1941—Stars at Play*

Turner, Ray
1936—Darkest Africa
1937—Two Wise Maids*
1940—In Old Missouri*
    Grandpa Goes to Town
1947—Bells of San Angelo*

Tuttle, Lurene[262]
1950—Macbeth

Twelvetrees, Helen[110]
1935—The Spanish Cape Mystery
    Frisco Waterfront

20 Minus Club
1942—Johnny Doughboy

Twitchell, Archie[138]
See Michael Branden.

Tyler, Harry[138]
1937—Jim Hanvey - Detective
    Youth on Parole
1938—Federal Man-Hunt*
1940—Gangs of Chicago*
    Meet the Missus
    Behind the News
1941—Sis Hopkins*
    Mr. District Atty. in the Carter Case*
1942—In Old California*
1944—Casanova in Burlesque
    Atlantic City
1945—Identity Unknown
    Woman Who Came Back
1946—The Fabulous Suzanne
1947—Winter Wonderland
1949—Streets of San Francisco*
    Hellfire
1951—Cuban Fireball*
1952—The Quiet Man*
1953—A Perilous Journey*
1955—I Cover the Underworld*
    The Twinkle in God's Eye*

Tyler, Leon
1945—Great Stagecoach Robbery
1953—Sweethearts on Parade
1955—Lay that Rifle Down
1958—Outcasts of the City
    Juvenile Jungle

Tyler, Tom[66]
1939—The Night Riders
1941—Adventures of Captain Marvel
    Outlaws of Cherokee Trail
    Gauchos of Eldorado
    West of Cimarron
1942—Code of the Outlaw
    Raiders of the Range
    Westward Ho
    The Phantom Plainsmen
    Shadows on the Sage
    Valley of Hunted Men
1943—Thundering Trails
    The Blocked Trail
    Santa Fe Scouts
    Riders of the Rio Grande
    Wagon Tracks West
1950—Trail of Robin Hood

Tyne, George
1950—Sands of Iwo Jima

Tyrrell, Alice[262]
1945—An Angel Comes to Brooklyn
1948—California Firebrand

U

Ukonu—and Afro-Calypsonians
1957—Panama Sal

Ulric, Lenore[262]
1947—Northwest Outpost

Urecal, Minerva[138]
1936—Bulldog Edition*
1937—Portia on Trial*
    Exiled to Shanghai
1938—Prison Nurse
1939—S. O. S. Tidal Wave*
    She Married a Cop*
    Should Husbands Work?*
    Sabotage*
1941—Arkansas Judge
    A Man Betrayed*
    Sailors on Leave*
1942—Lady for a Night*
    A Tragedy at Midnight*
    In Old California*
    Sons of the Pioneers
1943—Wagon Tracks West*
    Here Comes Elmer*
1944—Man from Frisco*
1946—Rainbow Over Texas
    Sioux City Sue*
1947—Apache Rose
    Saddle Pals*
1948—Secret Service Investigator
    Marshal of Amarillo
    Sundown in Santa Fe
1949—Outcasts of the Trail
1950—The Arizona Cowboy
1952—Oklahoma Annie
    Gobs and Gals
1953—Woman They Almost Lynched
1955—Double Jeopardy
    A Man Alone*

Lurene Tuttle

Alice Tyrrell

Lenore Ulric

Guy Usher

Helen Valkis

Rudy Vallee

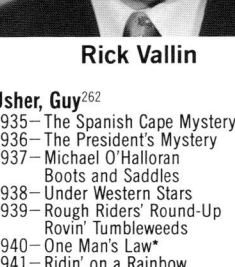
Rick Vallin

Lee Van Cleef

Dale Van Sickel

Usher, Guy[262]
1935—The Spanish Cape Mystery
1936—The President's Mystery
1937—Michael O'Halloran
    Boots and Saddles
1938—Under Western Stars
1939—Rough Riders' Round-Up
    Rovin' Tumbleweeds
1940—One Man's Law*
1941—Ridin' on a Rainbow
    The Great Train Robbery
    The Gay Vagabond*
    Kansas Cyclone*
    Rags to Riches*
    Public Enemies*
    West of Cimarron
1942—Lady for a Night
    Man from Cheyenne*
    Affairs of Jimmy Valentine*
    Shepherd of the Ozarks
    In Old California*
    The Old Homestead*
    Bells of Capistrano*

V

Vague, Vera[86]
[Barbara Jo Allen]
1938—Down in "Arkansaw"*
1940—Village Barn Dance
    Sing, Dance, Plenty Hot
    Melody and Moonlight
    Melody Ranch
    Chinese Garden Festival*
1941—Ice-Capades
1942—Hi, Neighbor
    Ice-Capades Revue
1943—Swing Your Partner
1944—Rosie, the Riveter
    Lake Placid Serenade
1946—Earl Carroll Sketchbook

Valentine, Barbara
1944—My Best Gal*
    Cowboy and the Senorita*

Valentine, Elizabeth
1939—S.O.S Tidal Wave*
1943—Santa Fe Scouts
    Whispering Footsteps*

Valentine, Jimmy—films
1936—The Return of Jimmy Valentine
1942—Affairs of Jimmy Valentine

Valk, Frederick
1942—Suicide Squadron
1955—Secret Venture
1956—Magic Fire

Valkis, Helen[262]
1938—The Old Barn Dance

Vallee, Rudy[262]
1946—The Fabulous Suzanne

Valli, Vicki
1945—Earl Carroll Vanities*

Vallin, Rick[262]
1942—Pardon My Stripes*
    Sleepytime Gal*
    Youth on Parade*
1943—Riders of the Rio Grande
    Wagon Tracks West
1947—Northwest Outpost
1951—Fighting Coast Guard*
1952—Woman in the Dark
1953—War of the Space Giants
    S. O. S. Ice Age
1955—King of the Carnival
1956—Terror at Midnight*

Vallon, Michael
1950—Tarnished

Vallon, Nenette
1945—Three's a Crowd

Vallon, Ric
1957—Raiders of Old California

Vallone, Raf
1955—Don Juan's Night of Love

Valmy, Andre
1959—O. S. S. 117 is Not Dead

Van, Frankie
1949—Duke of Chicago

Van, Gus
1944—Atlantic City

Van, Jean
1947—Saddle Pals

Van Atta, Lee
1936—Undersea Kingdom
    Beware of Ladies*
1937—Dick Tracy
    Dangerous Holiday*

Van Brocklin, Norman
1954—Crazylegs

Van Cleef, Lee[262]
1955—I Cover the Underworld
    The Road to Denver
    A Man Alone
    The Vanishing American
1956—Accused of Murder
1957—Last Stagecoach West
    Raiders of Old California

Van Cleve, Patricia
1941—Wampas Baby Stars*

Van Horn, Emil
1942—Perils of Nyoka*
    Ice-Capades Revue*
1943—Sleepy Lagoon*

Van Hulsen, Joop
1951—Fugitive Lady

Van Loewen, Jan
1948—Code of Scotland Yard

Van Pelt, John
1936—The Singing Cowboy
1937—The Riders of the Whistling Skull

Van Sickel, Bill
1948—Dangers of the Canadian Mounted

Veloz and Yolanda

Van Sickel, Dale[262]
Many films.
1938 – King of the Newsboys*
1940 – King of the Royal Mounted*
1943 – G-Men Vs. The Black Dragon*
The Purple V*
The Masked Marvel
1944 – Captain America*
The Tiger Woman*
Silent Partner*
Silver City Kid*
Haunted Harbor
Vigilantes of Dodge City*
Firebrands of Arizona*
Zorro's Black Whip
Army 101 – Equip. Maintenance*
1945 – Manhunt of Mystery Island
Lone Texas Ranger*
A Sporting Chance*
Bells of Rosarita*
Federal Operator 99*
Trail of Kit Carson*
Hitchhike to Happiness*
The Purple Monster Strikes*
Don't Fence Me In*
1946 – The Phantom Rider*
King of the Forest Rangers
Daughter of Don Q
The Crimson Ghost
1947 – Son of Zorro
Vigilantes of Boomtown*
Spoilers of the North*
Bells of San Angelo*
Web of Danger*
The Trespasser
Jesse James Rides Again
The Black Widow
Bandits of Dark Canyon*
1948 – G-Men Never Forget
Oklahoma Badlands
Lightnin' in the Forest
Dangers of the Canadian Mounted
Carson City Raiders
The Timber Trail*
Night Time in Nevada*
Desperadoes of Dodge City*
Adv. of Frank and Jesse James
Renegades of Sonora
1949 – Sheriff of Wichita*
Federal Agents Vs. Underworld, Inc.
Duke of Chicago
Ghost of Zorro
Frontier Investigator*
King of the Rocket Men
The James Brothers of Missouri
Ranger of Cherokee Strip*
The Golden Stallion
Radar Patrol Vs. Spy King
Powder River Rustlers*
1950 – Unmasked*
Tarnished*
Belle of Old Mexico*
Federal Agent at Large*
Code of the Silver Sage*
Harbor of Missing Men*
The Vanishing Westerner*
Salt Lake Raiders*
The Invisible Monster
Destination Big House*
Trigger, Jr.*
Desperadoes of the West
Lonely Heart Bandits*
Prisoners in Petticoats*
Rustlers on Horseback*
Flying Disc Man from Mars
1951 – Rough Riders of Durango
Night Riders of Montana*
Don Daredevil Rides Again*
Wells Fargo Gunmaster*
Govt. Agents Vs. Phantom Legion
1952 – Radar Men from the Moon
Woman in the Dark*
Leadville Gunslinger*
Wild Horse Ambush*
Black Hills Ambush*
Zombies of the Stratosphere
Thundering Caravans*
Desperadoes' Outpost*
The Wac from Walla Walla*
1953 – Marshal of Cedar Rock*
Enemies of the Universe*
Atomic Peril*
Cosmic Vengeance*
Savage Frontier*
Nightmare Typhoon
City that Never Sleeps*
War of the Space Giants
Destroyers of the Sun
Robot Monster from Mars
Can. Mounties Vs. Atomic Invaders
The Hydrogen Hurricane
Solar Sky Raiders
S. O. S. Ice Age
Lost in Outer Space
Down Laredo Way*
Captives of the Zero Hour
Bandits of the West*
El Paso Stampede*
Shadows of Tombstone
1954 – Trader Tom of the China Seas
Man with the Steel Whip

Edward Van Sloan

Philip Van Zandt

Norma Varden

Nina Varela

Dorothy Vaughan

William Vaughn

Van Sloan, Edward[263]
1938 – Storm Over Bengal
1942 – Valley of Hunted Men
1943 – Riders of the Rio Grande
The Masked Marvel
1944 – Captain America*
End of the Road

Van Zandt, Philip[263]
1943 – Hit Parade of 1943*
Deerslayer
1947 – Last Frontier Uprising
1949 – The Blonde Bandit*
1951 – Missing Women*
1953 – A Perilous Journey*
Champ for a Day*
1955 – I Cover the Underworld
1957 – The Crooked Circle

Vandegrift, Monte
1936 – The Mandarin Mystery

Varconi, Victor
1938 – King of the Newsboys
1945 – Scotland Yard Investigator

Varden, Norma[263]
1940 – Hit Parade of 1941*
1941 – Mr. District Attorney*
1942 – Johnny Doughboy
1945 – The Cheaters*
Girls of the Big House

Varela, Nina[263]
1953 – Woman They Almost Lynched
1954 – Jubilee Trail

Varga, Billy
1949 – Alias the Champ

Varno, Roland
1940 – Three Faces West*
1941 – The Devil Pays Off
1942 – Valley of Hunted Men
1945 – Three's a Crowd

Vass Family, The
1941 – Country Fair

Vaughan, Dorothy[263]
1937 – Michael O'Halloran
1938 – Billy the Kid Returns*
1939 – Pride of the Navy*
1940 – Village Barn Dance*
1946 – Earl Carroll Sketchbook*
That Brennan Girl
1947 – Trail to San Antone
Robin Hood of Texas

Vaughn, Robert[110]
1957 – Hell's Crossroads

Vaughn, William[263]
[as William Von Brincken]
1938 – Invisible Enemy*
[as William Vaughn]
1942 – Joan of Ozark*
King of the Mounties
1943 – The Purple V
Secret Service in Darkest Africa

Veach, Rachel
See Rachel.

Veeck, Bill
1949 – The Kid from Cleveland

Velascos, The
1940 – Gaucho Serenade

Veloz and Yolanda[262]
1944 – Brazil

Venable, Evelyn[86]
1936 – Happy Go Lucky
1938 – Hollywood Stadium Mystery!

Veness, Amy
1943 – The Saint Meets the Tiger

Venuta, Benay[263]
1948 – I, Jane Doe

Venuti, Joe
1950 – Belle of Old Mexico

Verdi, Joe
1935 – The Crime of Doctor Crespi

Verdon, Gwyneth
1941 – Sis Hopkins*
1943 – Sleepy Lagoon*
Hoosier Holiday*

Verdugo, Elena[263]
1957 – Panama Sal

Verebes, Erno[86]
1938 – A Desperate Adventure
1942 – Moonlight Masquerade
1947 – Northwest Outpost

Vernon and Draper
1944 – San Fernando Valley

Vernon, Glen
1948 – Heart of Virginia
1951 – Belle LeGrand

Vernon, Howard
1951 – Adventures of Captain Fabian

Benay Venuta

Herb Vigran

Vernon, Mickey
1949 – The Kid from Cleveland

Vernon, Wally[66]
1943 – Hit Parade of 1943*
Tahiti Honey
Fugitive from Sonora
Thumbs Up*
The Black Hills Express
The Man from the Rio Grande
A Scream in the Dark
Here Comes Elmer
Canyon City
Pistol Packin' Mama
California Joe
1944 – Outlaws of Santa Fe
Silent Partner
Call of the South Seas
Silver City Kid
Stagecoach to Monterey
1948 – King of the Gamblers

Versois, Odile
1955 – A Day to Remember

Victor, Charles
1943 – The Saint Meets the Tiger

Vigran, Herb[263]
1940 – Grandpa Goes to Town*
Scatterbrain*
Behind the News*
1941 – Country Fair*
Rags to Riches*
1942 – Secrets of the Underground*
1943 – Nobody's Darling*
Sleepy Lagoon*
1952 – Oklahoma Annie*
1957 – The Wayward Girl*
1958 – The Notorious Mr. Monks*
1959 – Plunderers of Painted Flats*

Elena Verdugo

June Vincent

Villiers, Mavis
1957 – Time is My Enemy

Villoldo, Jorge
1950 – The Avengers

Vincent, Allen
1938 – Ladies in Distress
Army Girl

Vincent, Billy
1957 – Affair in Reno

Vincent, June[263]
1951 – Secrets of Monte Carlo
1952 – Colorado Sundown
The Wac from Walla Walla
1955 – City of Shadows

Vincent, Russ
1945 – Manhunt of Mystery Island
1947 – Apache Rose
1950 – Twilight in the Sierras
1951 – Cuban Fireball

Vincent, Yves
1959 – C. S. S. 117 is Not Dead

Vinson, Helen[264]
1940 – Bowery Boy
1944 – The Lady and the Monster

Vitarelli, Arthur J.
1942 – Ice-Capades Revue*

Vogan, Emmett[138]
1936 – Ticket to Paradise*
1937 – Navy Blues*
The Hit Parade*
1938 – King of the Newsboys*
Rhythm of the Saddle*
1939 – My Wife's Relatives*
Smuggled Cargo*
Calling All Marines*
Main Street Lawyer*
Thou Shalt Not Kill
1940 – Grandpa Goes to Town*
Scatterbrain*
Behind the News*
1941 – Petticoat Politics
Mr. District Attorney*
Sis Hopkins*
Hurricane Smith
Citadel of Crime*
Doctors Don't Tell*
Sailors on Leave*
Tuxedo Junction*
Mr. District Atty. in the Carter Case*
1942 – Pardon My Stripes*
Yokel Boy*
Affairs of Jimmy Valentine*
Stardust on the Sage
The Old Homestead*
The Traitor Within
1943 – King of the Cowboys*
Chatterbox
Mystery Broadcast
Canyon City
In Old Oklahoma*
O, My Darling Clementine
1944 – Trocadero
The Yellow Rose of Texas*
Song of Nevada
My Buddy*
End of the Road
Faces in the Fog
1945 – Utah
Corpus Christi Bandits
The Vampire's Ghost
Flame of Barbary Coast*
Behind City Lights
Love, Honor and Goodbye*
The Purple Monster Strikes*
Colorado Pioneers
Woman Who Came Back
Along the Navajo Trail
1946 – Gay Blades
Crime of the Century*
The French Key
Earl Carroll Sketchbook*
The Crimson Ghost
Heldorado*
1947 – Homesteaders of Paradise Valley
That's My Gal*
1948 – Train to Alcatraz*
The Gallant Legion*
The Denver Kid
1949 – South of Rio
Post Office Investigator
Down Dakota Way
Alias the Champ
1951 – Pride of Maryland
Street Bandits
Pals of the Golden West
1953 – City that Never Sleeps*
Red River Shore
1954 – Tobor the Great*

Vogeding, Fredrik
1936—The House of a Thousand Candles

Vohs, Joan[264]
1954—Crazylegs
1956—Terror at Midnight

Voice of Experience, The
1937—The Hit Parade

Von Brincken, William
See William Vaughn.

Von Eltz, Theodor[264]
1936—Ticket to Paradise
      A Man Betrayed
1937—Jim Hanvey - Detective
      Youth on Parole
1942—A Tragedy at Midnight*
1950—Trial Without Jury

Von Morhart, Hans
1937—It Could Happen to You*
1942—Spy Smasher
1943—Secret Service in Darkest Africa

Von Nauckhoff, Rolf
1956—Circus Girl

Von Stroheim, Erich[110]
1935—The Crime of Doctor Crespi
1944—The Lady and the Monster
      Storm Over Lisbon
1945—The Great Flamarion
      Scotland Yard Investigator

Von Twardowski, H. H.
1942—Joan of Ozark

Vosper, John[191]
1943—Dead Man's Gulch
1952—Black Hills Ambush

Vye, Murvyn
1958—Girl in the Woods

W

Wade, John
1938—Riders of the Black Hills
      Heroes of the Hills

Wade, Mary Ruth
1948—The Plunderers

Wadsworth, Henry
1936—Sitting on the Moon

Wagenheim, Charles
1951—Street Bandits

Wager, Anthony
1956—Above Us the Waves

Waggner, Shy
1949—The Fighting Kentuckian
1950—Prisoners in Petticoats*

Wagner, George
See Gorgeous George.

Wainwright, Godfrey
1951—Pride of Maryland*
1952—Oklahoma Annie*
1954—Johnny Guitar*
1955—King of the Carnival*
1956—Jaguar*

Waite, Eric
1942—Ice-Capades Revue

Waizman, Max[264]
1939—Fighting Thoroughbreds*
      Street of Missing Men*
      Man of Conquest*
1940—Wagons Westward*
      Adventures of Red Ryder*
1941—Gangs of Sonora*
      Citadel of Crime*
      Bad Man of Deadwood*
      The Apache Kid*
      King of the Texas Rangers*
      Dick Tracy Vs. Crime, Inc.*
1942—Code of the Outlaw
      Raiders of the Range
      Spy Smasher*
      In Old California*
      Outlaws of Pine Ridge*

Wakely, Jimmy
1939—Saga of Death Valley*
1940—The Tulsa Kid
      Texas Terrors
1942—Heart of the Rio Grande

Walbrook, Anton[209]
1942—Suicide Squadron

Walburn, Raymond[264]
1940—Dark Command
1941—Puddin' Head
1945—The Cheaters
1946—Rendezvous with Annie
      Plainsman and the Lady
      Affairs of Geraldine

Walcott, George
1936—The Mandarin Mystery
1938—Western Jamboree

Walcott, Gregory
1956—Thunder Over Arizona

Wald, John
1948—Under California Stars
1949—Alias the Champ

Waldis, Otto
1950—Women from Headquarters
1951—Secrets of Monte Carlo

Waldo, Elizabeth
1945—Song of Mexico

Waldo, Janet[264]
1940—One Man's Law

Waldrige, Harold
1935—Hitch Hike Lady

Waldron, Charles
1937—Escape by Night
1939—Thou Shalt Not Kill
1940—Three Faces West

Wales, Ethel[264]
1939—Frontier Pony Express
      In Old Caliente
      Days of Jesse James
1940—Dark Command*
      Young Bill Hickok
1946—In Old Sacramento*
1950—Tarnished

Walker, Bill
1953—Jungle Drums of Africa
1954—The Outcast

Walker, Bob
1937—Gunsmoke Ranch

Walker, Cheryl[264]
1942—Shadows on the Sage
1944—Three Little Sisters
1945—A Song for Miss Julie
      Identity Unknown

Walker, Cindy
1940—Ride, Tenderfoot, Ride
      Frontier Vengeance

Walker, Helen[111]
1946—Murder in the Music Hall

Walker, Nellie[264]
1937—The Bold Caballero*
      Springtime in the Rockies*
1938—Born to be Wild*
      Under Western Stars*
      Gold Mine in the Sky*
      Pals of the Saddle*
      Down in "Arkansaw"*
      Come on, Rangers*
1939—Rough Riders' Round-Up*
      My Wife's Relatives*
      The Night Riders*
      Southward, Ho!*
      Mountain Rhythm*
      In Old Caliente*
      The Arizona Kid*
      The Covered Trailer*
      Cowboys from Texas*
1940—In Old Missouri*
      Wagons Westward*
      The Ranger and the Lady*
      Colorado*
      Young Bill Hickok*
1941—Wyoming Wildcat*
      Robin Hood of the Pecos*
      Sheriff of Tombstone*
      Saddlemates*
      Nevada City*
      Citadel of Crime*
      Sailors on Leave*
1942—South of Santa Fe*
      The Girl from Alaska*
      Romance on the Range*
      Sons of the Pioneers*
      Sunset Serenade*
1943—Mountain Rhythm*
      Idaho*
      Man from Music Mountain*
      In Old Oklahoma*
1947—Jesse James Rides Again*
1948—Madonna of the Desert*
      Sons of Adventure*
      Grand Canyon Trail*
1949—Daughter of the Jungle*
      Prince of the Plains*
      Streets of San Francisco*

Walker, Pax
1946—G. I. War Brides

Walker, Peter
1957—The Wayward Girl

Walker, Ray[139]
1935—Cappy Ricks Returns
1936—Laughing Irish Eyes
      Bulldog Edition
1944—Silent Partner
      Man from Frisco
      My Buddy
1946—Gay Blades
      Crime of the Century
      Earl Carroll Sketchbook*
1947—The Pilgrim Lady
      That's My Gal
      That's My Man*
      Robin Hood of Texas
1949—Pioneer Marshal
1950—Under Mexicali Stars
1954—The Atomic Kid*

Wall, Geraldine
1945—Girls of the Big House
1946—The Madonna's Secret

Walla, Marianne
1955—The Divided Heart

Wallace, Beryl[264]
1942—Sunset on the Desert

Helen Vinson

Joan Vohs

Theodor Von Eltz

Max Waizman

Wallace, George[264]
1952—Radar Men from the Moon

Wallace, Helen
1946—Sioux City Sue
1947—Marshal of Cripple Creek
1948—Out of the Storm
1951—Street Bandits

Wallace, Morgan[264]
1935—$1000 a Minute
1938—Billy the Kid Returns

Waller, Eddy[87]
1938—Call the Mesquiteers
1939—Rough Riders' Round-Up*
      New Frontier
1940—Carolina Moon
      Texas Terrors
1941—Public Enemies*
1942—Call of the Canyon*
1943—Silver Spurs*
      Headin' for God's Country
1944—Man from Frisco*
1945—Steppin' in Society*
      Rough Riders of Cheyenne
      Dakota
1946—Sun Valley Cyclone
      In Old Sacramento*
      Rendezvous with Annie*
      Plainsman and the Lady*
1947—Wyoming*
      The Wild Frontier
      Bandits of Dark Canyon
1948—Oklahoma Badlands
      The Bold Frontiersman
      Carson City Raiders
      Marshal of Amarillo
      Desperadoes of Dodge City
      The Denver Kid
      Sundown in Santa Fe
      Renegades of Sonora
1949—Sheriff of Wichita
      Death Valley Gunfighter
      Frontier Investigator
      The Wyoming Bandit
      Bandit King of Texas
      Navajo Trail Raiders
      Powder River Rustlers
1950—Gunmen of Abilene
      Code of the Silver Sage
      Salt Lake Raiders
      Covered Wagon Raid
      Vigilante Hideout
      Frisco Tornado
      Rustlers on Horseback
      California Passage
1952—Leadville Gunslinger
      Black Hills Ambush
      Thundering Caravans
      Desperadoes' Outpost
1953—Marshal of Cedar Rock
      Savage Frontier
      Bandits of the West
      Champ for a Day
      El Paso Stampede
1954—Make Haste to Live

Wallington, Jimmy
1938—Hollywood Stadium Mystery!

Raymond Walburn

Janet Waldo

Ethel Wales

Cheryl Walker

Nellie Walker

Beryl Wallace

George Wallace

Morgan Wallace

Douglas Walton

Fred Walton

Walsh, Arthur
1949—Flame of Youth
Ranger of Cherokee Strip
1950—Gunmen of Abilene
1951—Street Bandits

Walters, Don
1952—Radar Men from the Moon

Walters, Elizabeth
1948—Bill and Coo

Walters, Luana[126]
1937—Youth on Parole*
1939—Mexicali Rose
1940—Drums of Fu Manchu
The Tulsa Kid
1947—Bells of San Angelo*

Walthall, Henry B.
1936—Hearts in Bondage

Walton, Douglas[265]
1935—Hitch Hike Lady
1938—Storm Over Bengal
1942—Jesse James, Jr.

Walton, Fred[265]
1935—Two Sinners
Forbidden Heaven
1936—The House of a Thousand Candles

Robert Warwick

Minor Watson

Warburton, John
1955—Headline Hunters

Ward, Alan
1945—Bandits of the Badlands
1946—The French Key

Ward, Amelita[265]
1945—Swingin' on a Rainbow

Ward, Bill
1956—Hidden Guns
1958—No Place to Land

Ward, John[265]
1936—Robinson Crusoe of Clipper Island
1937—The Riders of the Whistling Skull
Dick Tracy*
Boots and Saddles
1940—Drums of Fu Manchu*

Ward, Lucille
1936—The Leavenworth Case
The Harvester

Ward, Michael
1955—Trouble in Store

Ward, Owen
1941—Stars Past and Present*

Warde, Anthony[265]
1937—Escape by Night
1938—Hollywood Stadium Mystery!*
King of the Newsboys*
Come on, Leathernecks
1941—Ridin' on a Rainbow
Dick Tracy Vs. Crime, Inc.
1942—King of the Mounties
1943—Shantytown*
A Gentle Gangster
Secret Service in Darkest Africa*
The Masked Marvel
1945—The Purple Monster Strikes
Captain Tugboat Annie
1946—King of the Forest Rangers
1947—The Black Widow
1948—Dangers of the Canadian Mounted
1949—Radar Patrol Vs. Spy King

Warde, Harlan
1948—Sons of Adventure*
1949—Wake of the Red Witch*

Ware, Irene
1936—Federal Agent

Warner, H. B.[265]
1938—Army Girl
1944—Faces in the Fog
1945—Captain Tugboat Annie
1946—Strange Impersonation
1947—Driftwood
1949—Hellfire

Warner, Jack
1955—The Square Ring

Warner, Ronnie
1941—Variety Reel*

Warner, Wes
1936—The Singing Cowboy
Guns and Guitars
1937—Gunsmoke Ranch

Bryant Washburn

Stanley Waxman

Warren, Janet[265]
1946—Rendezvous with Annie*
Earl Carroll Sketchbook*
That Brennan Girl*
1947—Hit Parade of 1947*
Winter Wonderland

Warren, Phil
1948—Dangers of the Canadian Mounted

Warren, Steve
1957—Beginning of the End
1958—Gunfire at Indian Gap

Warrick, Ruth[111]
1947—Driftwood
1954—Roogie's Bump

Warwick, Robert[265]
1936—The Return of Jimmy Valentine
The Vigilantes Are Coming
Bulldog Edition
1937—The Bold Caballero
The Trigger Trio
1938—Army Girl
Come on, Leathernecks
1939—Fighting Thoroughbreds*
In Old Monterey
1943—Deerslayer
In Old Oklahoma*
1944—Man from Frisco

Washburn, Bryant[265]
1937—Sea Racketeers
1939—I Was a Convict*
1940—King of the Royal Mounted
1941—Adventures of Captain Marvel
Mountain Moonlight*
1942—Shadows on the Sage
1943—Carson City Cyclone
Wagon Tracks West*

Washington, Bill
1953—Jungle Drums of Africa

Waterfield, Bob
1954—Crazylegs

Waterman, Willard
1949—Flaming Fury*
Flame of Youth
1950—Hit Parade of 1951*

Watkin, Pierre[139]
1936—The Gentleman from Louisiana
Sitting on the Moon
Country Gentlemen
1937—Larceny on the Air
Bill Cracks Down
The Hit Parade
Michael O'Halloran
1939—The Mysterious Miss X
Wall Street Cowboy
The Covered Trailer
1940—Gangs of Chicago*
1941—Petticoat Politics
A Man Betrayed
Nevada City
Jesse James at Bay
1942—Lady for a Night*
Heart of the Rio Grande
Yokel Boy
Ice-Capades Revue
Secrets of the Underground*
1944—My Best Gal*
Three Little Sisters*
Atlantic City
End of the Road
1945—The Phantom Speaks
Three's a Crowd
Captain Tugboat Annie
Dakota
1946—The Madonna's Secret
G. I. War Brides
Earl Carroll Sketchbook*
Plainsman and the Lady*
Sioux City Sue
1947—The Ghost Goes Wild*
The Wild Frontier
The Fabulous Texan*
1948—Daredevils of the Clouds
1950—Rock Island Trail
Redwood Forest Trail
Sunset in the West
1951—Belle LeGrand*
In Old Amarillo
1952—Thundering Caravans
1953—Can. Mounties Vs. Atomic Invaders
1955—The Eternal Sea*
Lay that Rifle Down*
1956—The Maverick Queen
Thunder Over Arizona*

Watling, Jack
1954—Trouble in the Glen

Watson, John
1958—Strange Case of Dr. Manning

Watson, Minor[265]
1941—Mr. District Attorney
1944—That's My Baby

Watson, Wylie
1943—The Saint Meets the Tiger

Amelita Ward

Watts, George
1941—Mr. District Attorney

Watts, Twinkle[66]
1943—The Man from the Rio Grande
Canyon City
California Joe
1944—Outlaws of Santa Fe
Silver City Kid
Stagecoach to Monterey
Sheriff of Sundown
Lake Placid Serenade
1945—The Topeka Terror
Corpus Christi Bandits
Trail of Kit Carson
Woman Who Came Back*
1946—A Guy Could Change

Wave, Virginia
1945—A Sporting Chance*
Dakota

Waxman, Stanley[265]
1950—Trial Without Jury
1952—Hoodlum Empire*
Zombies of the Stratosphere
1953—Atomic Peril

Wayne, Billy
1938—Ladies in Distress
1949—Flaming Fury

Wayne, Frank
Many films.
1937—S O S Coast Guard*
1938—Dick Tracy Returns*
1939—Daredevils of the Red Circle*
1940—Drums of Fu Manchu*
King of the Royal Mounted*
1941—Adventures of Captain Marvel*
1942—King of the Mounties*

Wayne, Fredd
1956—The Man is Armed

Wayne, John[166]
1935—Westward Ho
The New Frontier
Lawless Range
1936—Oregon Trail
The Lawless Nineties
King of the Pecos
The Lonely Trail
Winds of the Wasteland
1938—Pals of the Saddle
Overland Stage Raiders
Santa Fe Stampede
Red River Range
1939—The Night Riders
Three Texas Steers
Wyoming Outlaw
New Frontier
1940—Dark Command
Three Faces West
1941—A Man Betrayed
Lady from Louisiana
Stars Past and Present*
1942—Lady for a Night
In Old California
Flying Tigers
1943—In Old Oklahoma
1944—The Fighting Seabees
1945—Flame of Barbary Coast
Dakota
1947—Angel and the Badman
1949—Wake of the Red Witch
The Fighting Kentuckian
1950—Sands of Iwo Jima
Rio Grande
1952—The Quiet Man

Wayne, Melinda
1952—The Quiet Man*

Wayne, Michael
1941—Variety Reel*
1952—The Quiet Man*

Wayne, Patrick
1950—Rio Grande*
1952—The Quiet Man*
1953—The Sun Shines Bright*

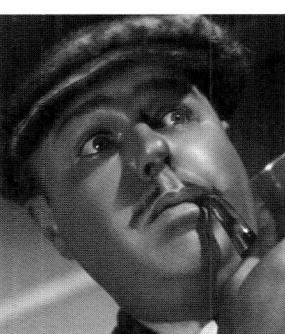
John Ward

Anthony Warde

H. B. Warner

Janet Warren

Wayne, Robert
1939—Dick Tracy's G-Men

Wayne, Steve
1956—A Strange Adventure

Wayne, Toni
1941—Variety Reel*
1952—The Quiet Man*

Wear, Clarie—Embassy Orchestra
1943—Alibi

Weaver Brothers and Elviry[87]
[Leon, Frank, and June Weaver]
1938—Down in "Arkansaw"
1939—Jeepers Creepers
1940—In Old Missouri
Grand Ole Opry
Friendly Neighbors
1941—Arkansas Judge
Mountain Moonlight
Tuxedo Junction
1942—Shepherd of the Ozarks
The Old Homestead
1943—Mountain Rhythm

Weaver, Doodles
1939 – Flight at Midnight*
1944 – San Fernando Valley*
    Thoroughbreds

Weaver, Leon
1938 – Romance on the Run

Weaver, Loretta[266]
1939 – Jeepers Creepers
1940 – Heroes of the Saddle
    In Old Missouri
    Grand Ole Opry
    Friendly Neighbors
1941 – Arkansas Judge
    Mountain Moonlight

Webb, Richard[111]
1940 – Rancho Grande*
1950 – Sands of Iwo Jima
    The Invisible Monster
1954 – Jubilee Trail

Webber, Peggy[266]
1950 – Macbeth
1951 – Fighting Coast Guard*

Weber, Dave
1938 – Pals of the Saddle

Weber, Herbert
1936 – Robinson Crusoe of Clipper Island
1937 – Dick Tracy

Webster, Mary
1957 – Eighteen and Anxious

Weeks, Anson—and orchestra
1945 – The Big Show-Off

Weeks, Jane
1943 – The Mantrap
    Chatterbox*

Weeks, Ranny[66]
1937 – Bill Cracks Down
    The Hit Parade*
    Rhythm in the Clouds*
    S O S Coast Guard
    Heart of the Rockies
    Youth on Parole

Weidenaar, Clair
1954 – Hell's Half Acre

Welch, Elisabeth
1943 – Alibi

Welch, John
1957 – The Man in the Road

Welch, Niles
1936 – The Singing Vagabond

Welden, Ben[266]
1937 – The Duke Comes Back
1938 – Prison Nurse
    Tenth Avenue Kid
    The Night Hawk
    Federal Man-Hunt
1939 – I Was a Convict
1940 – Wolf of New York
1941 – Mr. District Attorney*
1942 – Secrets of the Underground
1943 – Here Comes Elmer
1944 – The Fighting Seabees
1946 – The Last Crooked Mile
1947 – Hit Parade of 1947*
    Blackmail*
    The Pretender
1952 – Tropical Heat Wave*
1956 – Hidden Guns
1957 – The Crooked Circle*

Weldon, Marion[266]
1937 – The Colorado Kid
1938 – The Feud Maker
    Desert Patrol

Welles, Christopher
1950 – Macbeth

Welles, Dorit
1955 – The Divided Heart

Welles, Mel
1955 – The Fighting Chance

Welles, Orson[111]
1950 – Macbeth
1953 – Trent's Last Case
1954 – Trouble in the Glen

Welles, Rebecca[266]
1958 – Juvenile Jungle

Wells, Alan
1954 – Man with the Steel Whip

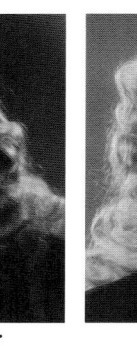

Loretta Weaver   Peggy Webber

Ben Welden   Marion Weldon

Rebecca Welles   Dick Wessel

Wells, Jacqueline[126]
See Julie Bishop.

Wells, Ted
Many films.
1938 – Dick Tracy Returns*
1939 – The Lone Ranger Rides Again*
1940 – Drums of Fu Manchu*

Welsh, John
1955 – The Divided Heart

Welsh, William
1936 – Cavalry

Wendell, Howard
1955 – The Fighting Chance

Wendhausen, F. R.
1943 – At Dawn We Die

Wengraf, John
1951 – Belle LeGrand*

Wentworth, Martha[161]
1940 – Who Killed Aunt Maggie?*
1946 – Santa Fe Uprising
    Stagecoach to Denver
1947 – Vigilantes of Boomtown
    Homesteaders of Paradise Valley
    Oregon Trail Scouts
    Rustlers of Devil's Canyon
    Marshal of Cripple Creek

Wescoatt, Rusty
1950 – Sunset in the West*

Wescott, Helen
1958 – Invisible Avenger

Wessel, Dick[266]
1937 – Round-Up Time in Texas
1938 – Arson Gang Busters
    Hawk of the Wilderness
1939 – Main Street Lawyer*
1940 – The Border Legion
1941 – The Great Train Robbery
    Desert Bandit
    Red River Valley*
1942 – Romance on the Range*
    Sunset Serenade*
    Bells of Capistrano*
    X Marks the Spot
    The Traitor Within
1943 – King of the Cowboys*
    A Gentle Gangster
    False Faces
    Silver Spurs
1945 – Dakota*
1946 – In Old Sacramento
1950 – Sands of Iwo Jima*
1951 – Honeychile
1952 – Hoodlum Empire*
    The Wac from Walla Walla
1953 – Champ for a Day
1954 – Flight Nurse*
    The Untamed Heiress*
1955 – The Eternal Sea*

West, Stan
1954 – Crazylegs

Westbrook, Joline
1942 – Johnny Doughboy

Westermeier, Paul
1957 – The Congress Dances

Westley, Helen
1941 – Lady from Louisiana

Weston, Cecil[199]
1937 – Youth on Parole*
1938 – Hollywood Stadium Mystery!*
1939 – Days of Jesse James*
1940 – Pioneers of the West*
    Dark Command*
    Grand Ole Opry*
    Ride, Tenderfoot, Ride*
    Barnyard Follies*
    Behind the News*
1941 – Arkansas Judge*
    Mountain Moonlight*
1942 – A Tragedy at Midnight*
    Yokel Boy*
    In Old California*
    Johnny Doughboy*
1943 – Carson City Cyclone*
    Mystery Broadcast*
    O, My Darling Clementine*
1946 – Affairs of Geraldine*
1947 – That's My Gal*
1951 – Honeychile*
1955 – A Man Alone*

Weston, Dick
See Roy Rogers.

Weston, Doris[266]
1938 – Born to be Wild

Weston, Leslie
1956 – Above Us the Waves

Doris Weston

Slim Whitaker

Whalen, Michael[266]
1939 – The Mysterious Miss X
1943 – Tahiti Honey

Wheatcroft, Stanhope
1938 – King of the Newsboys*

Whelan, Arleen[126]
1939 – Sabotage
1953 – San Antone
    The Sun Shines Bright
1957 – Raiders of Old California

Whiley, Manning
1948 – Code of Scotland Yard

Whipper, Leigh
1941 – Robin Hood of the Pecos
1942 – Lady for a Night*
    Heart of the Golden West

Whitaker, Slim [Charles][266]
1935 – Tumbling Tumbleweeds*
    Lawless Range*
1936 – The Big Show*
1937 – The Bold Caballero*
    The Trusted Outlaw*
    Round-Up Time in Texas*
    Guns in the Dark*
    The Sheik Steps Out*
    Heart of the Rockies*
1938 – The Lone Ranger*
    Under Western Stars
    Overland Stage Raiders*
    Shine on Harvest Moon*
1939 – The Lone Ranger Rides Again*
    Man of Conquest*
    Mountain Rhythm*
    Colorado Sunset*
    New Frontier
    South of the Border*
1940 – Rancho Grande*
    Ride, Tenderfoot, Ride*
    Young Bill Hickok*
    Melody Ranch*
1941 – Ridin' on a Rainbow*
    Saddlemates*
    King of the Texas Rangers*
1942 – In Old California*
1943 – Fugitive from Sonora*
    Silver Spurs*
    Man from Music Mountain*
    In Old Oklahoma*
1944 – The Laramie Trail

White, Alice
1938 – King of the Newsboys

White, Christine[222]
1957 – Panama Sal

White, Crystal
1949 – The Fighting Kentuckian

White, Daniel
1955 – The Road to Denver
1958 – Gunfire at Indian Gap

White, Dorothy Ann
1950 – Sunset in the West

White, Jesse[266]
1953 – Champ for a Day
1954 – Hell's Half Acre

Michael Whalen

Jesse White

White, Jette
1938 – Outside of Paradise*
    Outlaws of Sonora*
    Riders of the Black Hills*
    Heroes of the Hills*

White, Lee "Lasses"
1939 – Rovin' Tumbleweeds
1940 – Grandpa Goes to Town
    Oklahoma Renegades

White, Paul
1940 – Carolina Moon

White, Sammy
1937 – The Hit Parade

White, Will J.
1957 – The Lawless Eighties

Whiteford, Blackie[266]
1937 – Heart of the Rockies*
    The Wrong Road*
1938 – The Lone Ranger*
1941 – A Man Betrayed*
    Lady from Louisiana*
1953 – Fair Wind to Java*

Whitehead, Joe
1938 – Gold Mine in the Sky*
    Red River Range*
    Shine on Harvest Moon
1943 – Shantytown*
1945 – The Purple Monster Strikes

Whiteley, Jon
1957 – The Weapon

Whiteman, Paul—and orchestra
1944 – Atlantic City

Whiteman, Russ[267]
1944 – Song of Nevada*
    My Buddy*
1946 – The Madonna's Secret*
    Alias Billy the Kid
    One Exciting Week*
1948 – G-Men Never Forget*
    Desperadoes of Dodge City*
1949 – San Antone Ambush*
1951 – Rough Riders of Durango

Blackie Whiteford

Russ Whiteman

Anne Whitfield

Whitfield, Anne[267]
1958—Juvenile Jungle

Whitfield, Smoki
1948—Out of the Storm
1949—Hideout

Whitley, Crane[139]
1938—Prison Nurse*
 The Night Hawk*
1939—S. O. S. Tidal Wave*
1942—Spy Smasher
1943—G-Men Vs. The Black Dragon*
 Daredevils of the West*
 A Gentle Gangster
 The Masked Marvel*
1944—Captain America
 The Fighting Seabees*
 The Tiger Woman
1947—Angel and the Badman*
 The Fabulous Texan*
1948—Train to Alcatraz*
1949—Hellfire*
1950—The Savage Horde
 California Passage*
1951—Oh! Susanna*
 Insurance Investigator

Whitling, Townsend
1943—At Dawn We Die

The Wilde Twins

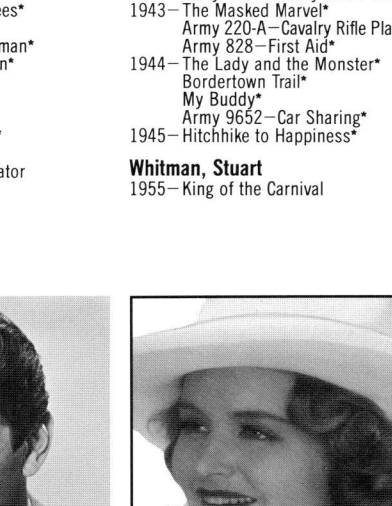

Robert Wilcox

Jan Wiley

Whitlock, Lloyd[267]
1936—Undersea Kingdom
 Ride Ranger Ride
 Robinson Crusoe of Clipper Island
1938—Arson Gang Busters

Whitman, Ernest
1941—The Pittsburgh Kid
1953—The Sun Shines Bright

Whitman, Gayne[267]
1936—The Return of Jimmy Valentine
1940—In Old Missouri*
 The Crooked Road*
 Adventures of Red Ryder
1941—Tuxedo Junction*
1942—Army 220—Cavalry Rifle Platoon*
1943—The Masked Marvel*
 Army 220-A—Cavalry Rifle Platoon*
 Army 828—First Aid*
1944—The Lady and the Monster
 Bordertown Trail*
 My Buddy*
 Army 9652—Car Sharing*
1945—Hitchhike to Happiness*

Whitman, Stuart
1955—King of the Carnival

Lois Wilde

Martin Wilkins

Whitney, Claire[267]
1937—The Wrong Road*
1943—False Faces*
1948—Oklahoma Badlands
 California Firebrand*
1949—Frontier Investigator

Whitney, Eve
1949—Radar Patrol Vs. Spy King
 The Blonde Bandit

Whitney, John
1944—Tucson Raiders
1950—Trial Without Jury

Whitney, Peter
1947—Northwest Outpost

Whittell, Josephine[267]
1936—Follow Your Heart
 Beware of Ladies
1937—Larceny on the Air
1946—Rendezvous with Annie*
 Affairs of Geraldine
 That Brennan Girl*
1948—Train to Alcatraz*

Whynemah, Princess
1943—Deerslayer

Widrin, Tanya
1941—Wampas Baby Stars*

Wiere Brothers
1943—Hands Across the Border

Wilcox, Frank[267]
1952—Thunderbirds*
1955—Carolina Cannonball
1956—A Strange Adventure
1957—Hell's Crossroads
 Beginning of the End

Wilcox, Robert[267]
1940—Mysterious Doctor Satan

Wilcoxon, Henry[87]
1936—The President's Mystery
1938—Prison Nurse
1939—Woman Doctor
1940—The Crooked Road
1942—Johnny Doughboy

Wilde, Adele[66]
1937—Exiled to Shanghai*

Wilde, Lee[267]
1948—Campus Honeymoon

Wilde, Lois[267]
1936—The Singing Cowboy
 Undersea Kingdom

Wilde, Lyn[267]
1948—Campus Honeymoon
1949—Sheriff of Wichita

Wilding, Michael
1953—Trent's Last Case

Wiley, Jan[267]
1941—Dick Tracy Vs. Crime, Inc.

Wilke, Bob[139]
1937—S O S Coast Guard*
1938—The Fighting Devil Dogs*
 Heroes of the Hills*
 Prairie Moon*
 Down in "Arkansaw"*
 Come on, Rangers*
1939—Woman Doctor*
 I Was a Convict*
 Street of Missing Men*
 Man of Conquest*
 S. O. S. Tidal Wave*
 Daredevils of the Red Circle*
 In Old Monterey*
 Jeepers Creepers*
1940—In Old Missouri*
 The Crooked Road*
 Grand Ole Opry*
 Adventures of Red Ryder*
 Girl from Havana*
 Hit Parade of 1941*
1941—Arkansas Judge*
 Country Fair*
 Tuxedo Junction*
 Dick Tracy Vs. Crime, Inc.*
1942—Shepherd of the Ozarks*
 Spy Smasher*
 The Old Homestead*
 Johnny Doughboy
1943—Mountain Rhythm*
 The Masked Marvel*
 Overland Mail Robbery*
 Pistol Packin' Mama*
 California Joe*
1944—Captain America*
 Beneath Western Skies*
 The Fighting Seabees*
 Hidden Valley Outlaws*
 Cowboy and the Senorita*
 The Tiger Woman*
 The Yellow Rose of Texas*
 Marshal of Reno*
 Call of the Rockies*
 Bordertown Trail*
 The San Antonio Kid
 Haunted Harbor*
 Cheyenne Wildcat*
 Code of the Prairie*
 Sheriff of Sundown
 Vigilantes of Dodge City
 Faces in the Fog*
 Firebrands of Arizona*
 Zorro's Black Whip*
 Thoroughbreds*
 The Big Bonanza*
 Sheriff of Las Vegas*
 Navy MN 3387—Your Weapons*
1945—The Topeka Terror
 Great Stagecoach Robbery*
 Sheriff of Cimarron
 Earl Carroll Vanities*
 Corpus Christi Bandits
 Lone Texas Ranger*
 Santa Fe Saddlemates
 Bells of Rosarita*
 The Chicago Kid*
 Trail of Kit Carson
 Hitchhike to Happiness*
 Man from Oklahoma*
 Bandits of the Badlands
 Sunset in El Dorado
 The Purple Monster Strikes*
 Rough Riders of Cheyenne
 The Tiger Woman*
1946—The Phantom Rider*
 The Catman of Paris*
 King of the Forest Rangers*
 Passkey to Danger*
 The El Paso Kid*
 Traffic in Crime
 Rendezvous with Annie*
 Daughter of Don Q*
 The Inner Circle
 The Crimson Ghost*
 Out California Way*
1947—The Pilgrim Lady*
 The Ghost Goes Wild*
 Twilight on the Rio Grande*
 Web of Danger*
 The Black Widow*
1948—G-Men Never Forget*
 Dangers of the Canadian Mounted*
 Carson City Raiders
 Daredevils of the Clouds
 Out of the Storm*
 Desperadoes of Dodge City*
 Sundown in Santa Fe*
 Homicide for Three*
1949—Federal Agents Vs. Underworld, Inc.
 Ghost of Zorro*
 Death Valley Gunfighter*
 The Wyoming Bandit
 Flaming Fury*
 The James Brothers of Missouri*
 Post Office Investigator*
 San Antone Ambush*
 The Blonde Bandit*
1950—Twilight in the Sierras*

Wilkerson, Billy
1950—Rock Island Trail

Lloyd Whitlock

Gayne Whitman

Claire Whitney

Josephine Whittell

Frank Wilcox

Wilkerson, Guy
1937—Paradise Express
 Yodelin' Kid from Pine Ridge
 Heart of the Rockies
1945—Captain Tugboat Annie*

Wilkins, Martin[267]
1945—The Vampire's Ghost

Wilkus, Bill
Mary films.
1939—Daredevils of the Red Circle*
 Dick Tracy's G-Men*
1940—Drums of Fu Manchu*
 Adventures of Red Ryder*
 King of the Royal Mounted*
 Mysterious Doctor Satan*
1941—King of the Texas Rangers*
 Dick Tracy Vs. Crime, Inc.*
1942—Spy Smasher*
1946—The Crimson Ghost*
1950—Flying Disc Man from Mars*

Willes, Jean
1952 – Gobs and Gals*

Willey, Leonard
1938 – Invisible Enemy

Williams, Ben
1943 – The Saint Meets the Tiger
1955 – The Square Ring

Williams, Bill[111]
1950 – California Passage
1951 – Havana Rose
1957 – Pawnee

Williams, Bob—and Red Dust
1941 – Los Angeles Examiner Benefit*

Williams, Bransby
1943 – At Dawn We Die

Williams, Buddy
1937 – Round-Up Time in Texas

Williams, Charles[139]
1936 – The President's Mystery*
1937 – Jim Hanvey - Detective
1938 – The Lone Ranger*
    Born to be Wild
    Hollywood Stadium Mystery!
1939 – My Wife's Relatives*
    Sabotage*
    Days of Jesse James*
1940 – Grand Ole Opry*
1941 – Mr. District Attorney*
    Sis Hopkins*
    Angels with Broken Wings*
1942 – Affairs of Jimmy Valentine*
    Joan of Ozark*
    Call of the Canyon*
    Ice-Capades Revue*
    Secrets of the Underground*
1943 – Chatterbox*
    The West Side Kid*
    Nobody's Darling*
    Whispering Footsteps*
1944 – Rosie, the Riveter*
    Silent Partner*
    Goodnight Sweetheart*
    Call of the Rockies
    Atlantic City
    End of the Road
    Lake Placid Serenade*
1945 – Identity Unknown
    Hitchhike to Happiness*
    Love, Honor and Goodbye*
1946 – A Guy Could Change*
    Rainbow Over Texas*
    Passkey to Danger
    Red River Renegades*
    Heldorado
1947 – Yankee Fakir*
    Saddle Pals
    The Trespasser*
1948 – Marshal of Amarillo
1950 – The Missourians
1955 – The Twinkle in God's Eye*

Williams, David
1949 – Brimstone

Williams, D. J.
1943 – At Dawn We Die

Williams, Duke
1949 – The Red Menace

Williams, Guinn "Big Boy"[268]
1936 – The Vigilantes Are Coming
1937 – Dangerous Holiday
1938 – Army Girl
    Down in "Arkansaw"
1939 – Street of Missing Men
1940 – Wagons Westward
1941 – Country Fair
1943 – Hands Across the Border
1944 – Cowboy and the Senorita
1949 – Brimstone
1956 – Hidden Guns

Williams, Jack
1943 – Hit Parade of 1943

Williams, Ken
1953 – The Sun Shines Bright

Williams, Mack
1950 – Destination Big House
1954 – Crazylegs

Williams, Maston[268]
1936 – Roarin' Lead*
1937 – The Painted Stallion
    Public Cowboy No. 1
    Heart of the Rockies
1938 – The Lone Ranger*
    Born to be Wild*
    Call the Mesquiteers
    Arson Gang Busters*
    Riders of the Black Hills*
    Heroes of the Hills
    Dick Tracy Returns*

Guinn "Big Boy" Williams

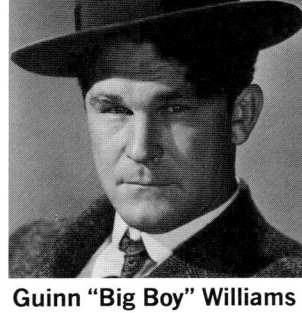

Rex Williams

Henry Wills

Williams, Rex[268]
1943 – The Purple V
    False Faces

Williams, Rhys[184]
1942 – Remember Pearl Harbor!
1950 – The Showdown
    California Passage
1951 – Million Dollar Pursuit
1954 – Johnny Guitar

Williams, Robert
1949 – Pioneer Marshal

Williams, Roger[268]
1937 – The Riders of the Whistling Skull
    Bill Cracks Down
    Guns in the Dark
    Come on, Cowboys!
    Zorro Rides Again
1938 – Call the Mesquiteers
    The Feud Maker
    Heroes of the Hills
    Red River Range
1939 – Mountain Rhythm

**Williams, "Sleepy"—and his
Three Shades of Rhythm**
1943 – Hoosier Holiday

Willing, Foy
See the Riders of the Purple Sage.

Willis, Norman
See Jack Norman.

Willock, Dave
1950 – Belle of Old Mexico

Wills, Chill[87]
1950 – Rock Island Trail
    Rio Grande
1951 – Oh! Susanna
    The Sea Hornet
1953 – Ride the Man Down
    City that Never Sleeps
1954 – Hell's Outpost
1955 – Timberjack

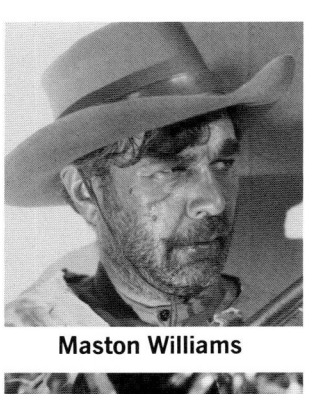

Maston Williams

Roger Williams

Walter Wills

Wills, Henry[268]
1938 – Come on, Rangers*
    Hawk of the Wilderness*
1939 – Mexicali Rose*
    In Old Caliente*
    The Kansas Terrors*
    Zorro's Fighting Legion*
1940 – Pioneers of the West*
    Drums of Fu Manchu*
    The Ranger and the Lady*
    Under Texas Skies*
    Young Bill Hickok*
1941 – Adventures of Captain Marvel*
    Saddlemates*
    Nevada City*
    Outlaws of Cherokee Trail*
1942 – South of Santa Fe*
    Sunset on the Desert
    Romance on the Range*
    Perils of Nyoka*
    Ridin' Down the Canyon*
1943 – Silver Spurs*
    Beyond the Last Frontier*
1944 – Song of Nevada*
    Bordertown Trail
    The San Antonio Kid*
    Stagecoach to Monterey*
    Code of the Prairie*
    The Big Bonanza*
1945 – Great Stagecoach Robbery*
    Sheriff of Cimarron*
    Corpus Christi Bandits*
    Santa Fe Saddlemates
    Trail of Kit Carson*
    Oregon Trail*
    Phantom of the Plains*
    Bandits of the Badlands*
    The Purple Monster Strikes*
    Rough Riders of Cheyenne*
1946 – The Phantom Rider*
    California Gold Rush*
    Plainsman and the Lady*
1947 – Angel and the Badman*
1950 – Salt Lake Raiders*

Wills, Walter[268]
1938 – Ladies in Distress*
    Dick Tracy Returns*
    Santa Fe Stampede
1939 – The Lone Ranger Rides Again*
    The Night Riders
    Sabotage*
    Cowboys from Texas
1940 – Wolf of New York*

Wilson, Charles[268]
1935 – Hitch Hike Lady
1936 – The Return of Jimmy Valentine
    Ticket to Paradise*
    The Gentleman from Louisiana
1938 – Tenth Avenue Kid
    The Night Hawk
1939 – Fighting Thoroughbreds
    I Was a Convict*
1940 – Gangs of Chicago*
1943 – Silver Spurs
    A Scream in the Dark*
1944 – Man from Frisco*
    My Buddy*
1946 – Crime of the Century
    Passkey to Danger

Wilson, Clarence
1937 – Two Wise Maids
1940 – Friendly Neighbors
    Melody Ranch

Wilson, Don[268]
1940 – Village Barn Dance
1942 – Hi, Neighbor
1944 – Jamboree

Wilson, Ernest
1941 – The Phantom Cowboy

Wilson, James
1958 – Outcasts of the City

Wilson, Lois
1935 – Cappy Ricks Returns
1936 – The Return of Jimmy Valentine
1941 – Wampas Baby Stars*

Wilson, Marie[127]
1939 – Should Husbands Work?
1941 – Rookies on Parade

Wilton, Eric
1935 – Forbidden Heaven
1936 – Beware of Ladies

Wimpy
1938 – Call of the Yukon

Windsor, Claire
1941 – Wampas Baby Stars*

Windsor, Joy[176]
1950 – Sands of Iwo Jima*

Windsor, Marie[269]
1943 – Chatterbox*
1949 – Hellfire
    The Fighting Kentuckian
1950 – The Showdown
1953 – City that Never Sleeps
1954 – Hell's Half Acre
1955 – No Man's Woman

Wing, Toby[269]
1935 – Forced Landing

Winkler, Jim
1954 – Crazylegs

Winkler, Robert
1939 – Blue Montana Skies
    Daredevils of the Red Circle
1941 – Pals of the Pecos

Winninger, Charles[111]
1948 – The Inside Story
1953 – A Perilous Journey
    The Sun Shines Bright
    Champ for a Day

Winslow, Dick
1942 – A Tragedy at Midnight*
1954 – The Atomic Kid*
1955 – The Twinkle in God's Eye*
1956 – Jaguar*

Winston, Steve
1945 – Oregon Trail

Winters, Gloria
1954 – Geraldine*

Winters, Val
1958 – Street of Darkness

Wisdom, Norman
1955 – Trouble in Store

Wise, Vic
1955 – The Square Ring

Wiseman, Joseph[269]
1953 – Champ for a Day

Wiseman, Myrtle
See Lulu Belle and Scotty.

Wiseman, Scott
See Lulu Belle and Scotty.

Withers, Grant[67]
1937 – Paradise Express
    Bill Cracks Down
1943 – In Old Oklahoma
1944 – The Fighting Seabees
    Silent Partner
    Goodnight Sweetheart
    The Yellow Rose of Texas
    The Girl Who Dared
1945 – Utah
    The Vampire's Ghost
    Bells of Rosarita
    Road to Alcatraz
    Dakota
1946 – In Old Sacramento
    Affairs of Geraldine
1947 – The Ghost Goes Wild
    The Trespasser
    Blackmail
    Wyoming
1948 – Old Los Angeles
    The Gallant Legion
    Daredevils of the Clouds
    Sons of Adventure
    Night Time in Nevada
    Angel in Exile
    The Plunderers
    Homicide for Three
1949 – Wake of the Red Witch
    Duke of Chicago
    The Last Bandit
    Hellfire
    The Fighting Kentuckian
1950 – Bells of Coronado
    Singing Guns*
    Rock Island Trail
    The Savage Horde
    Trigger, Jr.
    Hit Parade of 1951
    Rio Grande
1951 – Belle LeGrand
    Spoilers of the Plains
    Buckaroo Sheriff of Texas*
    Million Dollar Pursuit
    Utah Wagon Train
    The Sea Hornet
    The Wild Blue Yonder*
1952 – Captive of Billy the Kid
    Leadville Gunslinger
    Oklahoma Annie
    Hoodlum Empire
    Bal Tabarin*
    Woman of the North Country
    Tropical Heat Wave
1953 – A Perilous Journey*
    Fair Wind to Java
    The Sun Shines Bright
    Iron Mountain Trail
    Destroyers of the Sun*
    Sweethearts on Parade*
    Champ for a Day
1954 – Jubilee Trail*
1957 – Hell's Crossroads
    Last Stagecoach West

Withers, Isabel[269]
1945 – A Sporting Chance
1946 – The Undercover Woman

Charles Wilson

Don Wilson

Withers, Jane[87]
1940 — Chinese Garden Festival*
1941 — Stars at Play*
1942 — Johnny Doughboy
1944 — My Best Gal
  Faces in the Fog
1946 — Affairs of Geraldine

Witherspoon, Cora
1936 — Frankie and Johnnie*
1939 — Woman Doctor
1946 — I've Always Loved You

Witney, William
1951 — The Wild Blue Yonder

Wolfe, Bud [Marion][231]
1938 — Dick Tracy Returns*
  Storm Over Bengal*
  Federal Man-Hunt*
1939 — The Lone Ranger Rides Again*
  Blue Montana Skies*
  Daredevils of the Red Circle*
  Dick Tracy's G-Men*
1940 — Girl from Havana*
  Mysterious Doctor Satan*
  Behind the News*
1941 — A Man Betrayed*
  King of the Texas Rangers*
  Dick Tracy Vs. Crime, Inc.*
1942 — Cowboy Serenade*
  Spy Smasher*
  Perils of Nyoka*
1943 — G-Men Vs. The Black Dragon*
1944 — The Tiger Woman*
  Silver City Kid*
  Haunted Harbor*
  Army 101 — Equip. Maintenance*
1946 — The Catman of Paris*
  King of the Forest Rangers*
  Daughter of Don Q*
  The Crimson Ghost
1947 — Son of Zorro*
  Vigilantes of Boomtown*
  Blackmail
  Jesse James Rides Again*
  The Black Widow*
  Bandits of Dark Canyon*
1948 — G-Men Never Forget*
  Lightnin' in the Forest
  California Firebrand*
  Dangers of the Canadian Mounted*
  Heart of Virginia*
  Sons of Adventure*
  Adv. of Frank and Jesse James*
1949 — Federal Agents Vs. Underworld, Inc.*
  Law of the Golden West*
  King of the Rocket Men*
  South of Rio*
  The James Brothers of Missouri*
  Radar Patrol Vs. Spy King*
1950 — The Invisible Monster
  Lonely Heart Bandits*
1951 — Pride of Maryland*
1954 — Jubilee Trail*

Wolfe, David[269]
1949 — Flaming Fury
1950 — Prisoners in Petticoats

Marie Windsor

Toby Wing

Joseph Wiseman

Isabel Withers

David Wolfe

Ian Wolfe

Wilson Wood

Joan Woodbury

Wolfe, Ian[269]
1935 — $1000 a Minute
1936 — The Leavenworth Case
1937 — The Bold Caballero
1938 — Orphans of the Street
1948 — Angel in Exile

Wolfit, Donald
1957 — The Man in the Road

Wong, Anna May
1940 — Chinese Garden Festival*

Wood, Douglas
1936 — Navy Born
  Hearts in Bondage
1955 — No Man's Woman

Wood, Harley
1936 — Border Phantom

Wood, Marjorie
1953 — Sweethearts on Parade

Wood, Mary Laura
1956 — Doctor at Sea

Wood, Natalie[127]
1947 — Driftwood

Wood, Robert W.
1950 — Redwood Forest Trail

Wood, Wilson[269]
1948 — Campus Honeymoon
1951 — Insurance Investigator
  Thunder in God's Country
1952 — Radar Men from the Moon
  Zombies of the Stratosphere

Woodbridge, George
1955 — The Green Buddha

Woodbury, Joan[269]
1940 — Barnyard Follies
1941 — In Old Cheyenne
1942 — Sunset Serenade
1947 — Yankee Fakir
1956 — Come Next Spring

Wooddell, Barbara
1946 — The Mysterious Mr. Valentine

Woods, Craig
1947 — Angel and the Badman

Woods, Donald[269]
1938 — Romance on the Run
1940 — Forgotten Girls

Woods, Edward
1937 — Navy Blues

Woods, Harry[139]
1936 — The Lawless Nineties
  Ticket to Paradise*
1937 — Range Defenders
1938 — Come on, Rangers
1939 — Blue Montana Skies*
  In Old Caliente
  Days of Jesse James
1940 — Dark Command*
  The Ranger and the Lady
  Meet the Missus
1941 — Petticoat Politics
  Sheriff of Tombstone
1942 — Sunset on the Desert*
  Romance on the Range
1943 — Bordertown Gun Fighters
  Beyond the Last Frontier
  The Masked Marvel*
  In Old Oklahoma*
1944 — Call of the Rockies
  Silver City Kid
1947 — Wyoming
  The Fabulous Texan*
1948 — The Gallant Legion
1949 — Hellfire
1953 — Ride the Man Down*
1954 — Hell's Outpost*
1955 — The Last Command*

Woods, Ira "Buck"
1942 — Lady for a Night*
  Heart of the Rio Grande*
  Moonlight Masquerade*
1944 — Man from Frisco*
1945 — Man from Oklahoma*

Woodward, Bob
1939 — Home on the Prairie

Wooley, Sheb
1952 — Toughest Man in Arizona*
1954 — Johnny Guitar*

Wootton, Stephen
1956 — Stranger at My Door

Worden, Hank[139]
1936 — Ghost-Town Gold*
1939 — The Night Riders*
1940 — Rancho Grande*
  Gaucho Serenade*
  Ride, Tenderfoot, Ride*
1942 — Cowboy Serenade*
  Code of the Outlaw*
1943 — Canyon City*
1947 — Angel and the Badman*
1948 — Slippy McGee*
  Lightnin' in the Forest
1949 — Hellfire*
  The Fighting Kentuckian*
1952 — Woman of the North Country
1954 — The Outcast*
1955 — The Road to Denver*
  The Vanishing American*
1956 — Thunder Over Arizona*
  Accused of Murder*
1957 — Spoilers of the Forest
1958 — The Notorious Mr. Monks

Worlock, Frederic[269]
1943 — London Blackout Murders
  The Mantrap
  Thumbs Up*
  Secret Service in Darkest Africa
1944 — Secrets of Scotland Yard
1945 — The Fatal Witness
  Scotland Yard Investigator

Worth, Barbara
1935 — Racing Luck

Worth, Constance[127]
1943 — G-Men Vs. The Black Dragon

Worth, Harry [Michael][269]
1936 — The Big Show
1939 — Days of Jesse James
1940 — Adventures of Red Ryder
1941 — Adventures of Captain Marvel
  Kansas Cyclone
1943 — Riders of the Rio Grande

Worth, Nancy
1943 — Raiders of Sunset Pass

Wray, Fay
1941 — Wampas Baby Stars*
  Stars at Play*

Wray, John[269]
1936 — The President's Mystery
  A Man Betrayed
1937 — Circus Girl
1938 — Gangs of New York
  Tenth Avenue Kid
1939 — Smuggled Cargo

Wright, Jr., Cobina
1941 — Variety Reel*

Wright, Howard
1955 — Headline Hunters
1956 — Stranger at My Door

Wright, Jean
1953 — Can. Mounties Vs. Atomic Invaders

Wright, John Wayne
1946 — Sheriff of Redwood Valley

Wright, Patricia
1956 — Scandal Incorporated

Wright, Wen
1946 — California Gold Rush

Wright, Will[134]
1943 — Sleepy Lagoon
  Here Comes Elmer
  In Old Oklahoma*
1945 — Grissly's Millions
1946 — The Madonna's Secret
  One Exciting Week
  Rendezvous with Annie
  The Inner Circle
1947 — Along the Oregon Trail
1948 — The Inside Story
1949 — Brimstone
1950 — Tillers of the Soil*
  House by the River
  The Savage Horde
  Sunset in the West
1954 — Johnny Guitar*

Wright, William[127]
194. — Rookies on Parade
  The Devil Pays Off
1948 — King of the Gamblers
1949 — Rose of the Yukon
  Daughter of the Jungle

Wrixon, Maris[127]
1939 — Jeepers Creepers
1941 — Sunset in Wyoming
1942 — Sons of the Pioneers
  The Old Homestead
1946 — The Glass Alibi

Wyatt, Charlene[127]
1937 — Michael O'Halloran

Wyatt, Jane[111]
1940 — Girl from God's Country
1941 — Hurricane Smith
1950 — House by the River

Wyenn, Than
1957 — Beginning of the End

Wynn, Gordon
1953 — Scandal Incorporated

Wynn, May[269]
1955 — The Man is Armed
1957 — Taming Sutton's Gal

Donald Woods

Frederic Worlock

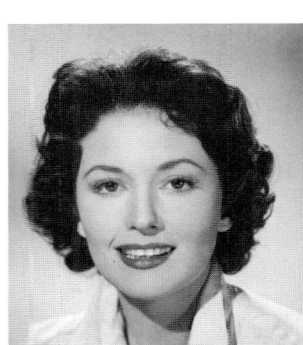
May Wynn

Harry Worth | John Wray

Wynne, Peggy
1947 – The Pretender
        The Black Widow*
1948 – The Main Street Kid*
        Desperadoes of Dodge City
        The Denver Kid

Wynters, Charlotte[270]
1939 – Pride of the Navy
1945 – The Phantom Speaks
1957 – Eighteen and Anxious

Y

Yaconelli, Frank[270]
1936 – Down to the Sea
        The Three Mesquiteers
1937 – It Could Happen to You
1940 – Sing, Dance, Plenty Hot*
1948 – Madonna of the Desert
1949 – Alias the Champ

Yarborough, Barton
1945 – Captain Tugboat Annie

Yarde, Margaret
1943 – At Dawn We Die

Yetter, William
1943 – Secret Service in Darkest Africa

York, Carl
1958 – Man or Gun

York, Duke
1936 – The Three Mesquiteers
1941 – Public Enemies
1948 – California Firebrand
1950 – Hit Parade of 1951

York, Jeff
1950 – Surrender

Young, Billy
1938 – Outside of Paradise

Young, Carleton[67]
1936 – Happy Go Lucky
        A Man Betrayed
1937 – Larceny on the Air*
        Join the Marines
        Round-Up Time in Texas*
        Dick Tracy
        Circus Girl*
        Git Along Little Dogies
        Navy Blues
        The Hit Parade*
        Michael O'Halloran*
        Come on, Cowboys!*
        Dangerous Holiday
        It Could Happen to You*
        S O S Coast Guard
        All Over Town*
1938 – The Old Barn Dance
        Gangs of New York
        The Fighting Devil Dogs
        Heroes of the Hills
1939 – The Lone Ranger Rides Again
        Zorro's Fighting Legion
1940 – Adventures of Red Ryder
        One Man's Law*
1941 – Prairie Pioneers*
        Adventures of Captain Marvel
        Two Gun Sheriff*
        A Missouri Outlaw
1942 – Code of the Outlaw
        South of Santa Fe*
        Spy Smasher*
        King of the Mounties*
1952 – Toughest Man in Arizona*
        Thunderbirds*

Young, Clara Kimball
1936 – Oh, Susanna!

Young, Clifton
1950 – Bells of Coronado
        Salt Lake Raiders
        Trail of Robin Hood

Charlotte Wynters

Young, Faron[270]
1956 – Hidden Guns
        Daniel Boone, Trail Blazer
1957 – Raiders of Old California

Young, Gig[127]
1949 – Wake of the Red Witch
1953 – City that Never Sleeps

Young, Nedrick
1946 – Gay Blades

Younger, Paul
1954 – Crazylegs

Yrigoyen, Bill[231]
Many films, mostly westerns.
1936 – Undersea Kingdom*
        The Gentleman from Louisiana*
        The Big Show*
1938 – The Lone Ranger*
        Army Girl*
        Pals of the Saddle*
        Rhythm of the Saddle*
1939 – The Lone Ranger Rides Again*
        Man of Conquest*
        Southward, Ho!*
        Colorado Sunset*
        In Old Monterey*
        Dick Tracy's G-Men*
        Wall Street Cowboy*
        The Arizona Kid*
        The Kansas Terrors*
        Saga of Death Valley*
        Cowboys from Texas*
        Zorro's Fighting Legion*
        Days of Jesse James*
1940 – Pioneers of the West*
        Drums of Fu Manchu*
        Rancho Grande*
        Ghost Valley Raiders*
        Dark Command*
        Adventures of Red Ryder*
        One Man's Law*
        The Tulsa Kid*
        Under Texas Skies*
        Frontier Vengeance*
        The Trail Blazers*
        Texas Terrors*
        The Border Legion*
        Barnyard Follies*
        Mysterious Doctor Satan*
        Lone Star Raiders*
1941 – Wyoming Wildcat*
        Ridin' on a Rainbow*
        The Phantom Cowboy*
        Prairie Pioneers*
        The Great Train Robbery*
        Two Gun Sheriff*
        Country Fair*
        Desert Bandit*
        Nevada City*
        Kansas Cyclone*
        Citadel of Crime*
        Rags to Riches*
        Outlaws of Cherokee Trail*
        The Apache Kid*
        Death Valley Outlaws*
        A Missouri Outlaw*
1942 – Arizona Terrors*
        Stagecoach Express*
        Jesse James, Jr.*
        The Cyclone Kid*
        The Sombrero Kid*
        Outlaws of Pine Ridge*
        Heart of the Golden West*
        The Sundown Kid*
1943 – Dead Man's Gulch*
        King of the Cowboys*
        Chatterbox*
        Daredevils of the West*
        Days of Old Cheyenne*
        Swing Your Partner*
        Song of Texas*
        Fugitive from Sonora*
        Bordertown Gun Fighters*
        The Black Hills Express*
        Sleepy Lagoon*
        Death Valley Manhunt*
        The Man from the Rio Grande*
        Man from Music Mountain*
        Canyon City*
        In Old Oklahoma*
        California Joe*
1944 – Outlaws of Santa Fe*
        Song of Nevada*
        Faces in the Fog*
        Zorro's Black Whip*
        Army 101 – Equip. Maintenance*
1945 – The Topeka Terror*
1946 – The Phantom Rider
        California Gold Rush*
        The Crimson Ghost*
1947 – Vigilantes of Boomtown*

Yu, Chin
1957 – Operation Conspiracy

Yurka, Blanche[270]
1942 – Lady for a Night
1947 – The Flame

Joe Yrigoyen[270]

Many films, mostly westerns.
1935 – Tumbling Tumbleweeds*
1936 – Winds of the Wasteland*
        The Big Show*
        The Old Corral*
1937 – The Bold Caballero*
        Round-Up Time in Texas*
        The Painted Stallion*
1938 – The Lone Ranger*
        Under Western Stars*
        The Fighting Devil Dogs*
        Gold Mine in the Sky*
        Army Girl*
        Man from Music Mountain*
        Pals of the Saddle*
        Billy the Kid Returns*
        Rhythm of the Saddle*
        Come on, Rangers*
        Shine on Harvest Moon*
1939 – The Lone Ranger Rides Again*
        Rough Riders' Round-Up*
        Frontier Pony Express*
        Three Texas Steers*
        Man of Conquest*
        Southward, Ho!*
        Daredevils of the Red Circle*
        In Old Caliente*
        Should Husbands Work?*
        Colorado Sunset*
        In Old Monterey*
        Dick Tracy's G-Men*
        Wall Street Cowboy*
        The Arizona Kid*
        Rovin' Tumbleweeds*
        Saga of Death Valley*
        South of the Border*
        Zorro's Fighting Legion*
        Days of Jesse James*

Z

Zarco, Estelita
1940 – Young Buffalo Bill

Zaremba, John
1958 – Young and Wild

Zelaya, Don
1940 – Girl from God's Country

Zepeda, Elsa Lorraine
1948 – Angel in Exile

Zilzer, Wolfgang
1942 – Joan of Ozark

Zorro—films
1937 – The Bold Caballero
        Zorro Rides Again
1939 – Zorro's Fighting Legion
1944 – Zorro's Black Whip
1947 – Son of Zorro
1949 – Ghost of Zorro
        [pseudo-Zorro]
1951 – Don Daredevil Rides Again
1954 – Man with the Steel Whip

Zucco, George[270]
1948 – Secret Service Investigator
1950 – Harbor of Missing Men

Zynda, Henry
1939 – Calling All Marines*
1942 – Spy Smasher

1940 – Heroes of the Saddle*
        Pioneers of the West*
        Drums of Fu Manchu*
        Rancho Grande*
        Young Buffalo Bill*
        Dark Command*
        Gaucho Serenade*
        Wagons Westward*
        Adventures of Red Ryder*
        Carolina Moon*
        The Ranger and the Lady*
        Ride, Tenderfoot, Ride*
        Colorado*
        Under Texas Skies*
        Young Bill Hickok*
        Melody Ranch*
        The Border Legion*
1941 – Robin Hood of the Pecos*
        Ridin' on a Rainbow*
        Prairie Pioneers*
        The Great Train Robbery*
        Back in the Saddle*
        In Old Cheyenne*
        The Singing Hill*
        Country Fair*
        Sheriff of Tombstone*
        Saddlemates*
        Nevada City*
        Sunset in Wyoming*
        Citadel of Crime*
        Rags to Riches*
        Ice-Capades*
        Under Fiesta Stars*
        Bad Man of Deadwood*
        Outlaws of Cherokee Trail*
        King of the Texas Rangers*
        Down Mexico Way*
        Jesse James at Bay*
        Sierra Sue*
        Red River Valley*
1942 – Man from Cheyenne*
        Cowboy Serenade*
        South of Santa Fe*
        Heart of the Rio Grande*
        Sunset on the Desert*
        Home in Wyomin'*
        Romance on the Range*
        Stardust on the Sage*
        Sons of the Pioneers*
        Call of the Canyon*
        Sunset Serenade*
        Bells of Capistrano*
        Outlaws of Pine Ridge*
        Heart of the Golden West*
        The Sundown Kid*
1943 – Idaho*
        King of the Cowboys*
        Chatterbox*
        Daredevils of the West*
        Swing Your Partner*
        Song of Texas*
        Secret Service in Darkest Africa*
        Silver Spurs*
        Man from Music Mountain*
        The Masked Marvel*
        In Old Oklahoma*
        Hands Across the Border*
1944 – Captain America*
        The Laramie Trail*
        Cowboy and the Senorita*
        Tucson Raiders*
        The Yellow Rose of Texas*
        Song of Nevada*
        San Fernando Valley*
        Lights of Old Santa Fe*
        Sheriff of Sundown*
        Firebrands of Arizona*

1945 – Utah*
        Bells of Rosarita*
        Man from Oklahoma*
        Sunset in El Dorado*
        Don't Fence Me In*
        Along the Navajo Trail*
1946 – The Phantom Rider*
        California Gold Rush*
        Song of Arizona*
        King of the Forest Rangers*
        Rainbow Over Texas*
        My Pal Trigger*
        Daughter of Don Q*
        Under Nevada Skies*
        Rio Grande Raiders*
        Roll on Texas Moon*
        The Crimson Ghost*
        Home in Oklahoma*
        Heldorado*
1947 – Angel and the Badman*
        Apache Rose*
        Bells of San Angelo*
        Saddle Pals*
        Robin Hood of Texas*
        Springtime in the Sierras*
        On the Old Spanish Trail*
        Under Colorado Skies*
1948 – The Gay Ranchero*
        Under California Stars*
        Eyes of Texas*
        Night Time in Nevada*
        Grand Canyon Trail*
        Adv. of Frank and Jesse James*
        The Far Frontier*
1949 – Federal Agents Vs. Underworld, Inc.*
        Ghost of Zorro*
        Susanna Pass*
        Down Dakota Way*
        The Golden Stallion*
1950 – Bells of Coronado*
        Twilight in the Sierras*
        Trigger, Jr.*
        Sunset in the West*
        North of the Great Divide*
        Trail of Robin Hood*
1951 – Spoilers of the Plains*
        Heart of the Rockies*
        In Old Amarillo*
        South of Caliente*
        Pals of the Golden West*
1952 – Colorado Sundown*
        Border Saddlemates*
        The Wac from Walla Walla*
1953 – Jungle Drums of Africa*
        Marshal of Cedar Rock*
        Old Overland Trail*
        Woman They Almost Lynched*
        Can. Mounties Vs. Atomic Invaders*
        Down Laredo Way*
        Shadows of Tombstone*
        Red River Shore*
1955 – Santa Fe Passage*
        The Road to Denver*
        The Last Command*
        Headline Hunters*
        The Twinkle in God's Eye*
        The Vanishing American*
1956 – Stranger at My Door*
        Terror at Midnight*
        Dakota Incident*
1958 – Gunfire at Indian Gap*

Frank Yaconelli   **Faron Young**

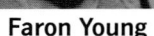
Blanche Yurka   **George Zucco**